A Passionate
Apprentice

A Passionate Apprentice

The Early Journals
1897–1909

Virginia Woolf

EDITED BY
MITCHELL A. LEASKA

A Harvest/HBJ Book
Harcourt Brace Jovanovich, Publishers
SAN DIEGO   NEW YORK   LONDON

Published in 1990 by Hogarth Press,
an imprint of Chatto & Windus

Library of Congress Cataloging-in-Publication Data
Woolf, Virginia, 1882–1941.
A passionate apprentice: the early journals, 1897–1909/Virginia
Woolf: edited by Mitchell A. Leaska.
p.   cm.
Includes bibliographical references and index.
ISBN 0-15-171287-5
ISBN 0-15-671160-5
1. Woolf, Virginia, 1882–1941—Diaries.   2. Novelists,
English—20th century—Diaries.   I. Leaska, Mitchell Alexander.
II. Title.
PR6045.O72Z473   1990
828′.91203—dc20
[B]   90-42126

Printed in the United States of America

First Harvest/HBJ edition 1992

A B C D E

Contents

Editor's Preface

THESE early journals, intermittently spanning the years 1897 to 1909, and printed in their entirety, are contained within seven holograph notebooks, the first six of which are located in the Henry W. and Albert A. Berg Collection of English and American Literature in The New York Public Library, Astor, Lenox and Tilden Foundations; the seventh is in the British Library.

The 1897 journal is more in the nature of a diary than any of the others, crowded as it is with the daily record of people, places and events; and its abbreviated style can be attributed partly to the limitations of space for each entry. The 1899 journal that follows consists largely of exercises in essay writing, as does the 1903 with its thirty essays written during the summer and autumn of that year. The fourth journal resumes the diary format and was kept from Christmas 1904 to 31 May 1905; Virginia began writing professionally at the end of 1904, and at the back of this notebook she kept an account of the books she was reading for review as well as some reading notes. The fifth journal was written in Cornwall, St Ives, where the Stephen children spent their summer holiday from 11 August to mid-September 1905, and the sketches are mainly of people and places she remembered from childhood. The sixth notebook is a travel journal Virginia kept from April 1906 to mid-August 1908, in which she wrote brief descriptions of the short trips she made to Yorkshire, Norfolk, the New Forest, Sussex, Somerset and Wales. The seventh and last journal (with her biographical sketch of Clive Bell) contains the travel essays she wrote during her holiday in Greece in the autumn of 1906 and during her two separate trips to Italy – one in 1908, the other in 1909 – with autograph itineraries in the front and itemised travel expenditures at the back. In order to preserve the journals' chronology, I have removed the Greek journal from the seventh notebook and inserted it between the 1906 visits to Blo' Norton, Norfolk, in August and to the New Forest in December. A description of the notebooks is in Appendix A.

Leonard Woolf left a typescript of all these journals, which is now kept in the University of Sussex Library. I was unaware of its existence until after making a complete transcription of the first six journals. (A typescript of the seventh was already in the Berg Collection, the original being housed in the British Library.) Virginia's handwriting at this time was small, irregular and hard to decipher, particularly in the 1897 and 1899 notebooks. Yet, despite this difficulty, on only a few occasions has it been necessary to admit defeat with the insertion of an [*illegible*] or to add a question mark in square brackets – [?] – indicating editorial doubt. In terms of autographic clarity, the remaining five were fairly accessible. Essentially, then, the seven journals have undergone two separate and distinct transcriptions, and I have had the advantage of being able to check one against the other.

There are a number of breaks in calendar sequence, some of considerable duration. In order to furnish the reader with a sense of continuity as well as with a clear temporal point of reference, brief connecting narratives have been inserted. For a fuller account of the people and events in Virginia's life during these hiatuses, one can turn to Quentin Bell's *Virginia Woolf: A Biography* and to *The Letters of Virginia Woolf*.

The annotations explain some of the more obscure allusions and identify the cast of characters who appear in these pages. The task of identifying them required much search and patience. Virginia came from a very large family who knew many other very large families from all walks of life. The prominent figures in the world of art, literature, politics, law and education who daily crossed her path were reasonably easy to trace, but those not so well known – women especially – presented problems. Standard directories at the turn of the century were weighted towards the man's world; and, though it is regrettable, it is also true that a good many husbands, fathers and brothers often blandly wrote their memoirs or autobiographies without ever mentioning the wives, the daughters or the sisters who played so central a role in their lives. Post Office Directories, moreover, listed a woman as 'Miss' or 'Mrs', with no Christian name to identify her. So that when Virginia referred to someone simply as 'Mrs Jones' or 'Miss Malone' and gave nothing further, with no electoral or similar register to turn to, it was necessary to abandon Miss Malone and Mrs Jones to the spoils of oblivion.

Notes identifying characters are provided not necessarily when they first appear, but rather on their first significant appearance. Cross-references to earlier or later notes have not been furnished except in cases of special relevance. Finally, because this edition is published in both Great Britain and America, I have included some notes that might seem gratuitous to a British reader but which are essential to an American. Such redundancy was unavoidable. In a number of instances some small item has been left unexplained for the simple reason that I myself have been unable to find an explanation. Each of these has been indicated, however. In the few notes where Virginia Woolf's fiction has been cited, the texts refer to the Uniform Edition published in London by the Hogarth Press and to the editions published in New York by Harcourt Brace Jovanovich.

The journals for 1897 and for Christmas 1904 to May 1905 are the only two that were dated regularly. The other five sometimes had a date attached at the beginning of the notebook, and sometimes a date was written into the body of the text. In these, dates have been supplied in square brackets whenever they could be inferred with a high degree of certainty either from internal evidence or from external sources. And although the aim has been to reproduce as faithfully as possible the original holograph, the dates in these journals have been standardised and set to conform to conventional dating practice.

Although Virginia wrote a precise and grammatical English, several matters of autography need a word of explanation. The first journal, for instance, begins with the use of 'ands' only, but about midway the 'ands' begin to mix with ampersands, and towards the last quarter ampersands alone gain ascendancy (with the exception of sentences which begin with 'And') and are used almost without variation throughout the next six journals. There is also the matter of abbreviations. Throughout all of the journals, family Christian names are indicated for the most part with the first initial only: thus Thoby is contracted to 'T.', Adrian to 'A.', Vanessa to 'N.' (Nessa) and so on. Virginia also abbreviated the names of those who appeared on a fairly regular basis. If there is any doubt whether 'G.' stands for 'George' or 'Gerald' then the name has been expanded to 'G[eorge].' or 'G[erald].' Similarly, when non-family names first appear they too have been expanded by means of brackets – 'M[argaret]. M[assingberd].', for example. When the context makes clear who the person is, however, then the initials alone remain. Other abbreviations such as 'wh.' (which) or 'fr' (from) have been retained when they are clear in context.

On the whole Virginia was an accurate speller, and the few inadvertencies that do appear ('dafodils' 'dissapear' and 'parrafin' come immediately to mind) have been allowed to remain, followed by [*sic*]. Most of the time she spelled 'grey' with an 'e', but occasionally it appears as 'gray'. Place-names are sometimes written with alternative spellings: 'Bosphorus' in one line, for example, and 'Bosporus' in another. The same is true for surnames, as with 'Pascoe'/'Pasco', and for nicknames – 'Marnie'/'Marney' and 'Kittie'/'Kitty'. The verb 'eat' is always the same, whether past tense or present – 'At about eleven Thoby arrived . . . He eat an enormous breakfast . . . ' – a habit probably picked up from her father. Words inadvertently omitted but plain from context have been supplied (without a footnote) and placed within square brackets.

It is in matters of punctuation, however, that Virginia was most random. Commas in a series, for instance, are frequently omitted, and apostrophes in contracted forms or in the possessive case are often ignored; capitalisation is sometimes observed and sometimes not. Occasionally there is a closing quotation mark with no opening, and vice versa; these have been supplied when the sense might be lost without it. Paragraphing too has needed some attention; exactly where paragraphs began and ended was not always clear. Very often, however, a new paragraph was indicated when a line of script stopped midway across the page and the first word of the next line was capitalised and began flush at the left margin. In these cases, I have resorted to the more traditional use of indentation.

Although the immediacy one feels in reading the original drafts of these pages is lost in the fixative of cold print, all of the autographic peculiarities have been retained – to the extent that readability and type-setting skill permit – in order to remind the reader, as Virginia more than once reminded herself, of the unpremeditated nature of the writing. These journals were very private books, written quickly, spontaneously, in a kind of 'shorthand', as she called it, to propitiate her own eye. These are the pages of an apprentice learning her craft, and writing at a speed that often sacrificed standard conventions of form. Consequently they are remarkably free of correction and revision. The few alterations Virginia did make, when they were judged substantive, have been indicated in the text by [ ] and are preserved in Appendix D. Biographical sketches of the principals have been provided in Appendix B.

Acknowledgements

FIRST I want to extend my thanks to the Adminstrators of Virginia Woolf's literary estate, Quentin Bell and Angelica Garnett, for the opportunity to edit this text. The preparation of these journals for publication, interrupted several times for various other professional commitments, has been rather a long, drawn-out affair, and so my acknowledgements reach back to the early 1980s. In the early stage of the work, a preliminary transcription of the 1897 journal and of some of the 1906 pieces was made by Louise DeSalvo. Quentin and Anne Olivier Bell furnished me with a holograph transcription of the Warboys journal of 1899, and provided me as well with much valuable information which only they could supply.

The work of transcribing the journals was conducted in the Berg Collection, whose Curator, the late Dr Lola L. Szladits, presided over that enterprise with equanimity, high expectation and complete confidence. For that alone, my thanks remain inadequate. I am also grateful to her staff, Brian McInerney and Patrick Lawlor, for daily hauling out the increasingly fragile notebooks as I checked and rechecked their pages. Thanks also go to the staff of the British Library for making available a photocopy of the seventh holograph journal. A large part of the annotation research was done at the Elmer Holmes Bobst Library at New York University, and I want to thank George Thompson, Reference Librarian, and his two assistants, Ricki Twersky and Mark Swartz, for all their careful and time-saving efforts. Timothy Saxon, of Luton, Bedfordshire, was my transatlantic collaborator for over a year, and did much to earn my deep and abiding appreciation.

Dr Elmer E. Baker Jr and Dean W. Gabriel Carras of New York University twice considered my requests for a sabbatical leave when extra working time was sorely needed, and twice those requests were granted. I therefore formally register here my indebtedness to them both.

By the time I came to these journals and during their preparation, several people had already done or were in the process of doing work on Virginia Woolf that was helpful in my editing of the present volume, and I should like to acknowledge them individually: Quentin Bell, *Virginia Woolf: A Biography* (2 vols); Anne Olivier Bell, ed., *The Diary of Virginia Woolf* (5 vols); B.J. Kirkpatrick, *A Bibliography of Virginia Woolf*, 3rd ed.; Nigel Nicolson and Joanne Trautmann, eds, *The Letters of Virginia Woolf* (6 vols); Andrew McNeillie, ed., *The Essays of Virginia Woolf* (Vols I-III); Jeanne Schulkind, ed., Virginia Woolf's *Moments of Being*; and Brenda Silver, *Virginia Woolf's Reading Notebooks*.

I want also to thank the following for furnishing me with information in matters both large and small: K. Akerman, Roy Allen, Professor Seth Benardete, Professor John W. Bicknell, R.J.E. Bush, the Rev. D.H.G. Clark, C.R. Davey, Professor Charles Dunmore, Suzanne M. Eward, Ronald E. Farthing, Dorothy Hawkins, Christopher Millis, Annabel Osborne, Dr Nis Adolph Petersen, (Mrs) G.K. Quarm, the Rev. G.D. Rhodes, John Richardson, D.A. Ruddom, Sister Marguerita Smith, Charles Spooler, Cécile Wajsbrot, (Mrs) Leslie Webster, and Dr P.N.R. Zutshi.

This volume began to take shape in 1986 under the editorial guidance of Christine Carswell of Chatto & Windus and The Hogarth Press. Her move to the United States in September 1988 cut short the beginning of a productive working partnership. Alison Samuel, her successor, from late 1988 has generously given me the benefit of her wide experience, helped me through an intricate maze of details, and seen the book through press with expert and knowledgeable efficiency. It would be difficult to exaggerate my gratitude to her. And to Robert Lacey, under whose surveillance the text gained substantially in editorial uniformity, I also tender my thanks.

To John Ferrone of Harcourt Brace Jovanovich, Virginia Woolf's American publisher, I mark here my continuing appreciation for his generous counsel over the years.

Anne Olivier Bell set a very high editorial standard in *The Diary of Virginia Woolf*, and I have felt extremely privileged in being the beneficiary of her meticulous help throughout the preparation of these journals. She read through the entire text and notes in typescript and saved me from more than one error of fact and form; she further helped to identify a number of people who might otherwise have been left to founder in obscurity. For that considerable labour and for her unfailing goodwill, I can think of nothing that will acknowledge adequately my very large debt to her.

Final acknowledgement is reserved for Catherine Coughlin, who joined me in the work in October 1986 and remained, undaunted, my scholar-companion and friend. Not once in all that time did she refuse a challenge, and never did she hesitate to pursue some fresh path of enquiry when all resources seemed exhausted and our hope dwindling. For the energy, I salute her. For the care, I thank her.

MITCHELL A. LEASKA
New York University
8 September 1989

Introduction

I

THESE journals begin in early January 1897, when Virginia was almost fifteen, and span twelve years – seven of them the most turbulent of her life. The pages open at a time when she was slowly recovering from a period of madness following her mother's death in May 1895. Between this January and the autumn of 1904, she would suffer through the deaths of her half-sister and of her father, and survive a summer of madness and suicidal depression.

Behind the loss and confusion, however, always near the surface, there was a constructive force at work, a powerful impulse towards health. It was an urge, through writing, to bring order and continuity out of chaos. Putting things into words and giving them deliberate expression had the effect of restoring reality to much that might otherwise have remained insubstantial. Words, she had discovered in childhood, were her most potent medium. So this opening chronicle represents the beginning of the future Virginia Woolf's apprenticeship as a novelist; only now it was Adeline Virginia Stephen teaching herself to write, preparing herself for the profession of letters.

These pages thus represent that rare instance when a writer of great importance leaves behind not only the actual documents of an apprenticeship, but also a biographical record of that momentous period as well. For, as Virginia wrote at the end of the first journal, 'Here is a volume of fairly acute life (the first really *lived* year of my life) . . .'[1] And so it was.

The first notebook, much in the character of a diary, is the longest. Virginia kept this journal regularly for the first seven months of 1897 and sporadically for the remainder of the year, ending it on the first day of 1898. Against a crowded canvas of the many people recorded in these pages and the events she deemed worthy of noting – visits to art galleries and museums, theatrical performances, Queen Victoria's Diamond Jubilee, preparations for the wedding of her half-sister, Stella – Virginia, in the role of family historian, provides a vivid record of daily life at 22

Hyde Park Gate: what happened during the morning hours; who came to lunch, to tea, to dinner; how the afternoons were passed, and the evening hours. Often we get a sense of the compulsive nature of the entries – 'This is written just before father calls for me to go out, and I can think of no sentence to fill the blank.'

Many of the days of the 1897 journal are just different enough from one another to make the sketch of a 'typical' day impossible without some distortion. Yet, in late February and early March, a kind of 'specimen day' does emerge which can be generally described. In the morning, after breakfast, George Duckworth, her older half-brother, went off to his job as unpaid secretary to Charles Booth, and Gerald, his younger brother, set off for Dent's, the publisher, where he worked; on Mondays, Wednesdays and Fridays, her sister, Vanessa, went to art classes at Arthur Cope's school; on weekdays, Adrian their younger brother, leaving behind half his belongings, departed for Westminster School; sometimes the morning post brought a letter from her older brother, Thoby, who was now at Clifton College in Bristol. Her half-sister, Stella Duckworth, now in her mother's role as mistress of the house, descended to the basement to arrange the day's meals with the cook, Sophia Farrell; and Virginia, with her father, began the daily exercise, prescribed by Dr Seton, in Kensington Gardens for an hour or so, after which Leslie Stephen retired to his study at the top of the house and Virginia to the back room or to the day nursery to translate German or Latin, or to read history.

After lunch there was more exercise. (Dr Seton had ordered four hours a day, out of doors.) This time, perhaps with Stella, she went to shop or to pay calls or to visit Dr Seton; Stella, who had been ill since her 'gastric chill' at Christmas 1896, also consulted Elizabeth Garrett Anderson from time to time. In the afternoon there was another walk through the Gardens, now with Vanessa, back from her art classes. Then tea, with any number of Stephen or Fisher relations, followed by more reading. And finally dinner, with usually a guest or two, after which there might be a theatre party or an evening at home with Leslie reading aloud from a novel or from a volume of poetry.

Apart from the medical regimen set down for Virginia, however, the family routine was not noticeably rigid, for the house seemed always swarming with visitors – the Milmans, the Stillmans, the Fishers, the Stephens, Cousin Mia, Aunt Minna, Aunt Anny, Kitty Maxse, Margery Snowden, Susan Lushington. It was a busy and congested household. Sometimes Virginia seemed amused by the Victorian upper middle class trooping through the drawing-room. Sometimes, however, everything was cause for nervous irritability and apprehension. Even the neighbouring streets for her were alive with danger and casualty: runaway horses, overturned carts, injured bicyclists, and so on. It was almost as if she were caught in a battle zone whenever she ventured out into the streets of London. And there were days when her illness, never made explicit, caused these pages to crackle with rage and frustration.

In February, visiting the Stillmans, for instance, 'poor Miss Jan [Virginia herself] utterly lost her wits, dropped her umbrella, answered at random, talked nonsense, and grew as red as a turkey cock.' In April, 'To bed very furious and tantrumical –' Later, 'I regret to say that various circumstances conspiring to irritate me, I broke my umbrella in half –' And, as in her later years, so too during this period, books became in part a refuge – 'the greatest help and comfort.'

The number of books the fifteen-year-old Virginia read during this interval is extraordinary: volume after volume of history and biography, of diary and essay; as well as many volumes of fiction and poetry. Leslie Stephen, from Virginia's earliest years, had hoped she would become his literary successor and intellectual heir, and tutored her accordingly.[2] But even he at times found that his 'Ginia was 'devouring books, almost faster than I like.'[3] But Virginia knew that the more she read the more favoured she was by her father, and more than anything in the world she wanted his affection and his approval.

Reading was, of course, a crucial part of a writer's apprenticeship, but it also had a narcotic effect; and she sometimes read as though she were trying to escape from something troubling: 'Read Mr [Henry] James to quiet me, and my beloved Macaulay.' 'Finished the 5th and last v. of my beloved Macaulay!' 'Finished the 3rd and last vol. of Cromwell.' 'Finished 1st vol of Arnold's Rome.'

These entries were written after Stella had returned from her honeymoon, again with the 'gastric chill' which time would prove far deadlier. From late April to mid-July the illness lingered unpredictably, with Stella alternately improving and worsening. During its course, Virginia began to show a curious change in mood. At the end of April, for instance, at the onset of Stella's illness: 'I slept with Nessa, as I was unhappy. News that she is better at about 11 o'clock – What shall I write tomorrow?' The next day: 'Slept with Nessa again.' On 4 May, Stella rallied briefly and to Virginia this was 'most satisfactory – but I am unreasonable enough to be irritated –'. Five days later: '. . . I was examined by Dr. Seton. No lessons – milk and some medicine which I forget.' On 21 May Aunt Minna's morning gossip with Stella 'made me so angry that I turned my back, & made myself generally unpleasant!'

The significance of Stella's illness appears to have been more complicated than the simple concern for the well-being of a family member. For some reason, Virginia maintained a certain critical attitude towards Stella that put considerable distance between them. For example, there was her odd reaction to Stella's rallying for a second time on 9 May: 'Now that old cow is most ridiculously well & cheerful – hopping about out of bed etc: Thank goodness, nevertheless – ' that 'nevertheless', as Quentin Bell points out, 'certainly gives one cause for speculation. Without attempting to probe . . . we can, at least, note that between a good, kind, not very clever woman standing in a position of vague authority – half elder sister, half surrogate mother – and a very nervous, irritable, intelligent girl of fifteen, there can be plenty of causes for friction and some kind of friction there surely was. During that summer of 1897 Virginia's health and Stella's were in some way connected; they were bound, not only by feelings of affection on both sides, but on Virginia's, by a sentiment of guilt.'[4]

The surest index that a profound disturbance was welling to the surface can be found in the dwindling of Virginia's journal after Stella's death on 17 July. Although there was an occasional attempt to revive it, either the words would not come or there was insufficient energy to urge them on to paper; and without the armamentarium of words to protect her from a world that seemed 'strange and hopeless,' she felt defenceless once more, and surrounded by nameless danger. Her room became once more her 'refuge and hiding place.' The remaining months of 1897, so far as journal writing went, were, with a few exceptions, shrouded in silence.

Apart from Virginia's lessons in Greek and Latin, no record survives of 1898 or of 1899 until August, when the Stephen family went for their holiday to Warboys in Huntingdonshire. Whatever transpired during those nineteen months, however, seems to have had a salutary effect on Virginia, and the journal she kept after this time is markedly different from that of 1897. With the impulse to health once more ascendant, the writing became more determined, less personal, the voice calmer and more confident. The abbreviated telegraphic diary form of 1897 gave way to a more sustained prose line as Virginia articulated on paper something new to her, and technically different.

She was now practising the art of the essay and, perhaps for the first time, was becoming conscious of the reader, that unknown entity who would be responding to the effects she was trying to achieve: '(I suppose a reader sometimes for the sake of variety when I write; it makes me put on my dress clothes such as they are) . . .' Some of the essays are witty and analytical – and evidently more difficult to write, for as she says at the end of one of them, about 'a somewhat grim day of pleasure' (a picnic with her Stephen aunt and cousins): 'This has taken me considerably longer to write than the whole day itself: such a relation of details is extraordinarily difficult, dull & unprofitable to read. However there is no end to writing, & each time I hope that I may make better stuff of it.'

The remarkable feature of these essays is that their author, aged seventeen, was already showing signs of developing those stylistic features – understatement and contrastive imagery, most notably – that would characterise the elegant voice of her later years.

A day at 22 Hyde Park Gate at the turn of the century started each morning with Virginia's translating Greek (she had begun private lessons with Janet Case in 1902), while Vanessa, in the Royal Academy Schools since 1901, drew or painted. Their afternoons and evenings were given up to occupations 'which the men of the family thought suitable: looking after the house, presiding at the teatable, making conversation, being agreeable to George and Gerald and to *their* friends . . .'[5] But it was the social events of the evening which became the focus of the London essays of 1903, with the gaiety and glitter of dances and nights spent 'drinking champagne & devouring quails'. Virginia confessed after one of these to deriving greater pleasure in imaginatively reconstructing a dance she herself had not attended. Her shyness made this often the case in her round of London society: 'I could have been well content to take my evening's pleasure in observation merely.'

And it becomes evident in the writing of this period that Virginia was learning to observe in the way a writer observes. For, as she wrote at the end of her last London essay: ' . . . the only use of this book is that it shall serve for a sketch book; as an artist fills his pages with scraps & fragments, studies of drapery – legs, arms & noses . . . so I take up my pen & trace here whatever shapes I happen to have in my head. It is an exercise – training for eye & hand – '

On the family's return from their summer holiday in Salisbury in the autumn of 1903, Virginia wrote a piece called 'The Serpentine', an account of a drowned woman. Halfway through the essay, while considering the woman's isolation, she slips inadvertently from 'she' and 'her' to 'I' and 'my': 'Without husband or children, I yet had parents. If they were alive now I should not be alone. Whatever my sin my father & mother would have given me protection & comfort.' This unconscious identification with the drowned woman is significant, because in 1902 Sir Leslie (he had been knighted during the June Coronation Honours) was told he had cancer. One year later, then, when 'The Serpentine' was written, he was slowly dying. The essay, without conscious design, thus became Virginia's first small requiem for her father.

Sir Leslie died on 22 February 1904. Eleven weeks later, Virginia, for a second time, descended into madness and remained desperately ill throughout the summer, hearing voices, birds singing in Greek and Edward VII's foul language from behind bushes. Her suicidal despair at this time parallels that of Septimus in *Mrs Dalloway*, a novel written from the source memory of those convalescent months spent with Violet Dickinson in Burnham Wood, Welwyn.

When she was well enough again to read and write, she began her 1904-5 journal, which, in its outward aspect of diary format, is like that of 1897. It was as though an obstinate record of life from day to day provided her once more with a grasp of reality she could find nowhere else. But the resemblance is only superficial, for in substance and tone the entries are on the whole decidedly more optimistic than the earlier ones – and with good reason.

At least four events took place in the autumn of 1904 and winter of 1904-5 that dramatically changed the character and quality of Virginia's life. First, during her convalescence with Violet and later with her aunt, Caroline Emelia Stephen, in Cambridge, the other Stephens moved to 46 Gordon Square, Bloomsbury, leaving behind them 22 Hyde Park Gate, a house filled, for Virginia especially, with unhappy memories. Second, Frederic Maitland, engaged now in writing the authorised life of Sir Leslie Stephen, asked for Virginia's assistance. The request went far beyond making her feel useful, which doubtless had a therapeutic effect; it helped her, more importantly, to feel that she was engaged in the labour of resurrecting her father for posterity, making of him and for him a permanent monument in words. Third, on 14 January 1905, she was pronounced normal again and able to accept a weekly teaching post at Morley College, an evening institute for working men and women. Last, and most significant of all, in December of 1904, Virginia had three pieces published in the Anglo-Catholic newspaper *The Guardian* – two book reviews and an essay – then, in 1905, an essay in the *National Review*; and in February an invitation to review books for *The Times Literary Supplement*. She was at last a professional writer.

Her years of apprenticeship were beginning to bear fruit. She had entered the professional ranks and was, finally, like her father, earning money by her pen. In a modest way, she had taken the right steps towards becoming his literary successor. Whatever grumbles she may have had in early January about London's 'interminable roar & rattle & confusion of wheels & voices' now ceased altogether. On her breakfast plate on 10 January lay her first instalment of wages – '£2.7.6 for Guardian articles, which gave me great pleasure'.

In entering this new phase of her life, Virginia now had a new perception of herself. Soon she would become acquainted with other matters to trouble the artistic vanity; in the meantime, however, she would know the pleasure of watching the way a commissioned essay 'expands under my hands'. There might be anger at an editor's tampering with her words, especially if those words were signed 'Virginia Stephen', but she would also feel the relief and pleasure that an editor was 'delighted to accept my article – which is a load off my mind – ' By late February, the 1904-5 journal becomes in part the personal record of a young professional woman.

Time was now a saleable commodity, and a strict working schedule was essential. When there was no essay in progress or a book to review, there was always some Greek or Latin to translate. Even the Sunday Afternoon Concerts at Queen's Hall became regularly scheduled entertainments, as in March were Thoby's Thursday Evenings 'at home' – those early gatherings whose members would one day become known as the Bloomsbury Group.

By March, with her writing, reviewing and teaching, Virginia was feeling not just recognised and valued, but free and independent as well. It is true that a review was returned for cutting and that *The Times Literary Supplement* rejected her *Catherine de Medici* piece. But she took all this in her stride, as well she might, for now 'I earn money anyhow.' Certainly her holiday with Adrian on the Iberian peninsula was a sign of her new status, and the freedom that went with it.

The journey to Cornwall in the August of 1905 was a journey in time 'to another world, almost into another age'. Here once again in St Ives was Talland House, where Virginia had spent twelve summers, and here was the escalonia hedge, and there the Love Corner, and over there the stone urns. This cherished 'little corner of England', on the evening of their arrival, had lost none of its enchantment. In substance and detail it had remained unchanged, and here Virginia found her 'past preserved'.

The sketches in the Cornwall journal seem an attempt to infuse that past once more with the life-blood of the present: the old woman in the church recalling Julia Stephen's kindness; the garrulous Mrs Pascoe chiefly memorable for 'some trouble in the "pipes"', the vigorous morning of pilchard fishing – all of them, though quickly drawn, are vibrant with life. 'These are rough notes to serve as landmarks', wrote Virginia. But, rough as they are, her evocations measure the height to which she had grown as a writer. One essay, 'A Walk by Night',[6] published the following December, would result from this journey. Not until twenty years passed, however, would the visit to St Ives fuse with earlier memories in an image of the Ramsay family in *To the Lighthouse*, the novel which would establish her fame and remain for many readers her crowning achievement.

Virginia began teaching at Morley College in 1905 and remained in London during term time. It was not until April 1906, during her Easter break, that she returned to Giggleswick in Yorkshire to see Madge and Will Vaughan, with whom she had stayed in November 1904. This time too she went alone, with Gurth on his leash. The Vaughans lived within easy reach of Virginia's lodgings if she wanted companionship, but it was solitude that she sought.

The sketches written here reflect the melancholy of her unhurried wanderings through the barren wilds of Yorkshire, at peace in the bleak grandeur of the moors. When she rose, when she dined, where she walked, what she read – these were for her alone to decide. She was free. 'I settle precisely according to my own taste & then the door is shut on me, . . .' In mood, the words are only one short revision from the 'solitary traveller' of Peter Walsh's reverie in *Mrs Dalloway*.[7] The solitary Virginia, however, had travelled a long distance to be alone in this little northern town, 'swept clean & simplified, out of all pettiness & vulgarity by the nobility of the country in which it lies'.

In June she ventured into fiction and wrote a short story called 'Phyllis and Rosamond' and also, at about this time, another called 'The Mysterious Case of Miss V.'[8] In August, now with Vanessa as companion, she went to Blo' Norton. Here we have a record of Virginia Stephen, the emerging professional, reflecting for the first time on how her mind worked as a writer: 'It is one of the wilful habits of the brain, let me generalise for the sake of comfort, that it will only work at its own terms. You bring it directly opposite an object, & bid it discourse; it merely shuts its eye, & turns away. But in one month, or three or seven, suddenly without any bidding, it pours out the whole picture, gratuitously.'[9]

Although Vanessa's illness required some alterations in the itinerary of their expedition to Greece in the autumn of 1906, Virginia flourished in the classical world. She was soothed by its order and symmetry, and began to pause longer over what she saw, catching the smallest details of people, places, manners and morals. Something new was finding its way into the style in which she conveyed her impressions: whether she was describing a site rich in ancient history or creating a portrait of some fellow guest at the hotel, her writing was becoming more suggestive, and more resonant.

In Greece, as later in Constantinople, Virginia was beginning to model her meaning in a way not evident in her earlier journals. She seemed engaged now in transforming simple visual impressions into verbal images capable of bringing to life something residual in the reader, amplifying and heightening odd angles and relations which went beyond the object of contemplation and verged increasingly on the metaphoric. Something of this new mode of evocation she herself tried to express when, at Mycenae, she wrote: 'There was never a sight, I think, less manageable; it travels through all the chambers of the brain, wakes odd memories & imaginations; forecasts a remote future; retells a remote past. And all the while it is – let me write it down – but a great congeries of ruined houses, on a hill side.'

This was a new prismatic quality in its earliest stages of cultivation and it found expression not only in Greece but in Constantinople too, whether she was describing the devotions in St Sophia or haggling over a scrap of silk in the Grand Bazaar. It is an element of style not precisely identifiable yet undeniably perceptible. It was a movement away from rational meaning and a step towards those nether regions of sensation and ambiguity.

When the party sailed for Constantinople on 21 October, Thoby left them and returned to London, but the visit in Turkey was cut short by Vanessa's illness, so that, with Violet Dickinson in charge, the remaining Stephens returned to England by the Orient Express, arriving in London on 1 November. From this expedition came only one story, recently published under the title 'A Dialogue Upon Mount Pentelicus.'[10] But this visit to Greece would linger on in Virginia's memory and emerge once more in *Jacob's Room*. For, just as Jacob Flanders died after his tour of Greece, so too would his life model, Thoby Stephen.

Thoby's sudden death on 20 November left him a mystery to Virginia. There were so many things she did not know about this private and melancholy brother who mattered so much to her. A quarter of a century later, she would seek to recover him in all his youth and splendour through Percival in *The Waves*. But at present there was only grief and bewilderment.

She had lost her brother and she would soon be losing her sister, who, two days after Thoby's death, had accepted Clive Bell's proposal of marriage. The wedding took place on 7 February 1907. In March, Virginia and Adrian left 46 Gordon Square to the Bells and moved to 29 Fitzroy Square, an address just close enough to Vanessa to diminish somewhat the sense of dereliction Virginia now felt. Apart from her odd flirtation with the eccentric Hellenist Walter Headlam, sixteen years her senior, Virginia's marital prospects did not look promising. Nor was it easy for her to accept Clive Bell as a brother-in-law. Whether or not she consciously admitted to herself her sense of desertion, it is clear that she thought of Clive as a kind of interloper, and as a result she harboured grave reservations about his worthiness as Vanessa's husband.

Virginia and Adrian spent part of the 1907 summer holiday in Playden, with the Bells, who had taken a nearby cottage in Rye. Here in Sussex, feeling perhaps a little aimless, Virginia began once more to write her journal: descriptions of the land, the sea, the salt marshes. In its pages she also began to speculate on how one goes about creating a scene in fiction: 'I should have to begin by saying . . .' And it was presumably during this holiday that she started to write the life of Vanessa,[11] who was going to have a baby. The future Julian Bell would one day have these reminiscences to help him understand something about his Stephen grandparents, life at 22 Hyde Park Gate, the story of Stella and Jack Hills, and a little about George and Gerald Duckworth. Four chapters were completed that summer, but there is no evidence that Virginia ever returned to it.

During the autumn months Virginia and Adrian revived the Thursday Evening 'at homes' begun by Thoby in March 1905, and, at the end of the year, she stopped teaching at Morley College. In February 1908, Julian Heward Bell was born. The small noisy presence would soon put Virginia's relation to Clive on a different footing, but the really 'great event', as Quentin Bell called it, took place at the end of 1907 – it was the birth of *Melymbrosia*, which approximately eight years later would be published as *The Voyage Out*. When precisely the idea for this novel came to her, no one knows, but it might have been as early as her first visit to Manorbier in Wales in March 1904.[12] At any rate, by the time she left Manorbier, where she went for a second time in August 1908, she had completed a hundred pages of her novel, and in October she sent them not to Violet Dickinson, who had begun to recede into the background, but to Clive Bell, now her literary confidant. It is clear from the few sketches contained in the Wells and Manorbier journals that the young novelist's energies were being siphoned off in fiction.

On 3 September Virginia set off with Clive and Vanessa for Italy, visiting chiefly Siena and Perugia. A few of her journal pages are devoted to the cathedral and the Feast Day, but her mind was on literature: 'I should like to write not only with the eye, but with the mind; & discover real things beneath the show;' and, while pondering a fresco by Perugino, she articulated for the first time the primary aesthetic principle which would guide her in the years ahead: she would achieve beauty and symmetry 'by means of infinite discords, showing all the traces of the minds passage through the world; & achieve in the end, some kind of whole made of shivering fragments; . . .'

Throughout this period Virginia continued to write her novel, submitting chapters to Clive Bell for his comment. 'My intention now', she wrote in February 1909, 'is to write straight on, & finish the book; & then, if that day ever comes, to catch the first imagination & go over the beginning again with broad touches, keeping much of the original draft, & trying to deepen the atmosphere. . . . Ah, how you encourage me! It makes all the difference.'[13]

In April 1909, Virginia made a journey to Florence, again with Clive and Vanessa. The entries in the journal at this time are brief, but the miniature character sketches she made are both sharp and penetrating. They are the cameos of a novelist determined to ferret out the 'essence' – the 'personal myth' it has sometimes been called – the buried core of a person, out of which everything else in the personality radiates. Despite their roughness, they are still remarkable, for Virginia was now evoking character by means of 'suggestion', and leaving the reader to infer the rest. Of Contessa Rasponi, for example, she writes: 'Look at the conflict of lines on the brow – She is much like a peasant woman; & is a woman of cultivation & race at the same time. Her talk is bold & free, also tentative.' Of Janet Ross: 'Mrs Ross lives in a great villa, is the daughter of distinguished parents; the friend of writers, & the character of the country side. She sells things off her walls. She is emphatic, forcible, fixes you with her straight grey eye as though it were an honour to occupy, even for a moment, its attention.' Of Alice Meynell: 'Among the guests was a lean, attenuated woman, who had a face like that of a transfixed hare – the lower part was drawn out in anguish – while the eyes appealed piteously . . . She clasped the arm of a chair, & seemed uncomfortably out of place.'

But what has happened to the morbidly shy Virginia of old, we wonder, as she sits beside these old ladies, some of them rather formidable, asking questions, drawing them out, sometimes 'pressing to the verge of impertinence'? Has Florence suddenly caused her to shed her inhibitions, and turned her into an aggressive journalist? No, it is something deeper than that. The Virginia we see here in these final pages is now a novelist, surveying her cast of characters, probing their depths, gauging their perceptions, searching out their deepest secrets. Tomorrow, on the pale unlined page, all of these observations will be cast in the integument of words and made permanent. And, because of that promise of tomorrow, her shyness is covered, so that the writer, observant as she must be (and in quest of 'copy'), is capable of sallying into territories that Virginia, the young woman of twenty-six or twenty-seven, would have trembled at even in anticipation. It appears then that, somewhere in these years between 1907 and 1909, Virginia the apprentice began fading into the background, and Virginia the untried novelist came into being.[14]

II

To 'discover real things beneath the show', to 'achieve a symmetry by means of infinite discords' and in the end 'some kind of whole made of shivering fragments . . .' Here, in the Italian journal of 1908, was Virginia Stephen articulating her artistic credo. Between the surface shimmer of reality and its submerged side – so the statement implies – was always some inconsistency, some dissonance; and it was out of these infinite discords that her art would spring, whole and harmonious. Three decades later, she would bring these incongruities to their finest arrangement in her posthumously published *Between the Acts*. For it was in this novel that she most daringly dramatised the fusion of opposites.

But what was behind this declaration of artistic aim? What inconsistencies so obstinately held the foreground of her mind? What conflicting impressions did she perceive? To find the answer we must look ahead some thirty years to her own analysis of this dual vision, which remained with her throughout her life. As it happened, sometime between 18 April and 2 May 1939, when Virginia began writing the notes for her memoir, 'A Sketch of the Past',[15] she turned to these early journals for echoes of the past. We know this from the number of references made in the 'Sketch' which coincide with those people named in the following pages, a coincidence that cannot be attributed to chance alone. On 15 May, from her 'little platform of present time',[16] to use her own words, she began looking back with some concentration to the years before and immediately following May 1895; that is, to the years covered in these journals. The journals provided her not only with a means of reviving long-forgotten memories, but also with the chance to refine and interpret, now from a mature point of view, her earlier conceptions of justice and equality and family love and personal loss. (It was in fact the same memory source she drew upon to write *The Voyage Out*.[17])

As she turned the clock back to those earlier years, she saw the reasons for her gathering despair: her mother's death in 1895, Stella's in 1897, her father's in 1904, Thoby's in 1906, and in 1907 her loss of Vanessa in marriage, which left Virginia feeling more alone and more an orphan than ever before. As she rummaged through the dusty pages of private history, she arrived inevitably at her 'life' of Vanessa[18] written at Playden in 1907, whose first chapter contains a description of the married life of Leslie and Julia Stephen. If we turn to those 'Reminiscences', we see much that sheds light on her memoir of 1939-40. But the most astonishing discovery is that, as far back as 1907, Virginia had concluded that whatever harmony there was in the domestic life of her mother and father was reached only 'by rich, rapid scales of discord, and incongruity';[19] for both were 'much tried and by no means easy-going people . . .'

First there was Leslie Stephen, the distinguished man of letters, author of the *History of English Thought in the Eighteenth Century*, *The Science of Ethics* and *Social Rights and Duties*, respected by the intellectual world and loved by his fellows. This was the 'show'. The 'real things beneath the show' were Leslie Stephen in the privacy of 22 Hyde Park Gate. There he was 'the tyrant of inconceivable selfishness',[20] whose nature it was to express what he felt openly, heedlessly, regardless of others; whose second widowhood sent him into an orgy of emotion, with 'lamentations that passed the normal limits of sorrow'.[21] And, indulging himself in the cruel story of his loneliness and remorse, he turned his wife into an 'unlovable phantom'.[22] Was this the same man who wrote on ethics and social rights? Was this Leslie once the small sickly, evangelical boy who, so the story goes, in a fit of rage threw a flowerpot at his adoring mother?

In the 'Sketch of the Past', written some thirty-two years later, Virginia Woolf saw with even greater discrimination the two separate, incongruous fathers under whose tyranny she so often raged and suffered. He was aware of his competent 'second class mind'[23] yet was 'childishly greedy for compliments'. Surrounded by his bevy of women at home he was ferocious, egotistical, devouring; yet to the patriarchal world in which he stood high, he was all simplicity, integrity and lovable eccentricity. To his daughter, however, he was the 'tyrant father – the exacting, the violent, the histrionic, the demonstrative, the self-centred, the self-pitying, the deaf, the appealing, the alternately loved and hated father – that dominated me then [i.e. 1897-1904]. It was like being shut in the same cage with a wild beast.'[24] Yet it was precisely because she loved him – he 'made me feel we were in league together'[25] – that Virginia could feel this appalling inconsistency.

Then there was the beautiful, sad, enigmatic mother, Julia Stephen, commemorated in *To the Lighthouse* by her daughter and eulogised in the *Mausoleum Book* by her husband, neither of whom fully understood her. As in her life, so too after her death, some inevitable mystery eddied around her memory. Like Leslie, she was full of contradictions. For Julia's complex nature, wrote Virginia, was the result of a character 'sharpened by the mixture of simplicity and scepticism. She was sociable yet severe; very amusing; but very serious; extremely practical but with a depth in her . . .'[26] She was, above all, to her young daughter unpredictable, 'dispersed', a 'general presence'[27] rather than a specific mother to a child of seven or eight: 'Can I remember ever being alone with her for more than a few minutes?' Significantly, one of those 'few minutes' is associated with pain: 'My first memory is of her lap; the scratch of some beads on her dress comes back to me as I pressed my cheek against it.'[28] She was also to the child Virginia a woman obsessed with dispensing charity, visiting workhouses, carrying on her increasingly frail shoulders a heavy mantle, scented with illness and death; a woman so extended in every direction that she had neither the time nor the strength 'to concentrate . . . upon me, or anyone else –'.[29]

The spectrum of inconsistency Julia represented to her infant daughter must have been bewildering, for how could a mother love her children, or a wife her husband, and yet disregard them so heedlessly while she nursed the sick – her 'victims'[30] Virginia called them – wasting herself so wantonly, in 'alleys in St Ives, London slums, and many other more prosperous but no less exacting quarters . . .'?[31] Wasn't her gallantry futile? How, moreover, could a woman of such deep sympathy be so severe with her own children? And how did one reconcile the gallantry with the futility of that profoundly depressed woman who believed so completely in life's sorrow, who saw living as an endless procession 'towards death'?[32] How had she made so crowded a world of 'natural life and gaiety'[33] and kept it spinning throughout Virginia's childhood?

Then there were her two husbands, both considerably her senior: Herbert Duckworth (b. 1833) by thirteen years, and Leslie Stephen (b. 1832) by fourteen. How was it possible for the same woman to marry two such entirely different men: one (the 'pink of propriety') for love, the other ('the pink of intellectuality')[34] with a measure of pity mixed in? Each was opposite the other; they were 'two incongruous choices'.[35] Her death left her children unprotected from their father's rapacity.[36] No, there was no way to sum up Julia Stephen: her contradictions were bewildering.

Then there was Stella, who, in assuming her mother's role as mistress of 22 Hyde Park Gate, became Leslie Stephen's next 'nearest support'.[37] From the age of fifteen, she had taken over many of Julia's duties, and from her eighteenth year had undertaken the task of nursing Leslie himself. Like her mother, she was overly careful of her step-father's health, and like her mother she was very beautiful. Was it not natural that Virginia in 1897, when she was sufficiently recovered, should note the delicacy of Stella's ministrations and see the danger of her father's position? Was it not also natural that Virginia should perceive, however dimly, Stella – her over-anxious surrogate mother – as an intruder, trespassing upon territory to which she had no claim? For, as a widower, Leslie took for granted his step-daughter's servile observances and automatically assumed towards her an attitude of total dependency and ownership. It is unlikely that Stella, who thought herself second-rate, was alert enough to realise that she needed above all to protect herself from becoming her step-father's surrogate wife.

For in manhood, as in childhood, Leslie Stephen depended upon the coddling of a sympathetic woman, and would not have seen Stella's concern for his countless aches and sniffles as being anything out of the ordinary. And certainly he was too puritanical by temperament and training to see how his behaviour towards her might be construed as anything but normal, and not sufficiently imaginative to see how others might interpret his relations with Stella as being perhaps just a little too intimate. Yet we need only read a few select lines of the letter he wrote to her on the day of her wedding to Jack Hills, 10 April 1897, to see the authentic cast of his feeling:

> . . . I know that we love each other & shall continue to love each other. I know that you will do all you can for me . . . I said to her [Julia] that I not only loved but reverenced her . . . Now one cannot exactly reverence a daughter but I have the feeling which corresponds to it – you may find a name for it – but I mean that my love of you is something more than mere affection: it includes complete confidence & trust . . . Love me still & tell me sometimes that you love me.[38]

There is no question that Leslie was blind to his emotions, but to his perceptive fifteen-year-old daughter, that intimacy, or whatever we wish to call it, must have appeared incredibly misplaced.

Stella had become a second mother to Virginia in 1895. Now she had turned traitor, or so it must have seemed, to the memory of the woman both had so recently lost. It is not hard to imagine, then, the ambivalence Virginia felt, and the confusion, when Stella herself died, in July 1897. Leslie Stephen's reaction to her death added to the turmoil. The distinguished old man, it is true, was jealous of the youthful Jack Hills, and grew increasingly tyrannical during the unnecessarily long months of the engagement. But as long as Stella served and soothed him, he accepted her offering as his due. When she died, however, he appeared, at least to his younger daughter, strangely unaffected. 'We remembered how he had tasked Stella's strength, embittered her few months of joy, and now when he should be penitent, he showed less grief than anyone.'[39]

Stella's death had cheated Virginia once more out of the normal life that might have followed had she lived. The most poignant note of all, however, is sounded in those passages where Virginia recalled Jack and Stella's engagement. It was 'my first vision . . . of love between man and woman . . . It gave me a conception of love . . . a sense that nothing in the whole world is so lyrical, so musical, as a young man and a young woman in their first love for each other.'[40] So the shock of Stella's death in a sense robbed that love of its authenticity, making it, like so much else during those early years, a chimera, something not to be trusted. Love and marriage must have appeared as something on the same level as all the other catastrophes so scrupulously preserved in the pages of the earliest journal.

The world was no easy place to live in. Louring always just beyond the horizon was the promise of injury or annihilation. Even the social arrangement was a ruthless machine where 'a girl had no chance against its fangs.'[41] Whether this perception was genuine or exaggerated or even imagined is beside the point; what mattered was that Virginia believed this, and that belief made it true. But there was something else, just barely perceptible in Virginia's record of these years, far deeper, more private, a subject she could only talk about to herself in whispers. And that was the truth of her madness, about which there is, strangely, nothing explicit in the 1897 journal. She had collapsed into that nightmare world once and might do so again, at any time, without warning.

Looking back in later years at 1897, Virginia described herself as half mad 'with shyness and nervousness', and from other hints in the 1939-40 memoir we know that there were difficulties pre-dating 1895 – her 'early fears' she called them. During the winter months, as a child, for instance, she often slipped into the nursery at night before the others to 'see that the fire was low, because it frightened me if it burnt after we went to bed. I dreaded that little flickering flame on the walls . . .'[42] Then there was the morbid fear that came over her when her mother was out late doing 'good work': she waited 'in agony peeping surreptitiously behind the blind for her to come down the street . . . (Once my father found me peeping; questioned me; and said rather anxiously but re-provingly, "You shouldn't be so nervous, Jinny.")'[43]

There were other telling childhood memories: 'Two I always remember. There was the moment of the puddle in the path; when for no reason I could discover, everything suddenly became unreal; I was suspended; I could not step across the puddle; I tried to touch something . . .'[44] This episode was residual enough to find its way many years later into a scene in *The Waves*: 'I came to a puddle. I could not cross it. Identity failed me,' reflects the suicidal Rhoda.[45] The second memory is of the 'idiot boy' who 'sprang up with his hand outstretched mewing, slit-eyed, red-rimmed; and without saying a word, with a sense of the horror in me, I poured into his hand a bag of Russian toffee. But it was not over, for that night in the bath the dumb horror came over me. Again I had that hopeless sadness; that collapse that I have described before . . .'[46]

Then there was Virginia's mad cousin, James Kenneth Stephen, in love with Stella and a favourite of Julia's, who once dashed 'in at breakfast. "[Dr] Savage has just told me I'm in danger of dying or going mad", he laughed. And soon he ran naked through Cambridge; was taken to an asylum; and died.'[47]

Even her beloved Thoby had had a brush with insanity in March 1894, and had attempted suicide by jumping from a window of his preparatory school. He had been in bed with influenza when the incident occurred. The master, Mr G.T. Worsley, wrote to Julia that Thoby was suddenly

> attacked with delirium and before the nurse could get to him he was half through the window which he had smashed to shivers! Luckily I was within call and I soon quieted him and got him into bed again and barricaded the window.

There was another attack in April, when Thoby was at Hyde Park Gate being looked after by Julia.[48]

Closest to home, however, and a daily reminder, was Virginia's half-sister, Laura Makepeace Stephen, daughter of Leslie's first marriage, to Minny Thackeray. Born in December 1870 and about eleven years old at the time of Virginia's birth, Laura was the 'vacant-eyed girl whose idiocy was becoming daily more obvious, who could hardly read, who would throw the scissors into the fire, who was tongue-tied and stammered and yet had to appear at table with the rest of us.'[49] Although Virginia and Vanessa saw Laura as something of an oddity, perhaps even a joke, there can be little doubt that Virginia felt moments of silent terror about her own state of mind after her first nervous collapse in 1895.

The idea of a 'hereditary taint' in the family preoccupied Sir Leslie and in the *Mausoleum Book* he did not conceal his blasted hopes for Laura: 'I will never forget the shock to me, when we were in Brighton . . . We had sent Laura to a "kindergarten" and the Mistress told me she would never learn to read.'[50] Then, in April 1897, he turned to his convalescing daughter: ''Ginia is devouring books, almost faster than I like.'[51] It was almost as if Virginia were showing her father that she would never be compared with Laura. She knew that it gave her father pleasure to find her reading a book that no child of her age could understand: 'I was a snob no doubt, and read partly to make him think me a very clever little brat.'[52]

The letters between Leslie and Julia, which Virginia read in 1904 for Maitland's *Life and Letters of Leslie Stephen* while she was convalescing in Cambridge, revealed to her the full impact of Laura's deficiency. Most of all, the letters made clear that Leslie simply did not understand Laura's predicament. Some of them are full of his pain and bafflement and shame. Others show his frustration and anger: she was 'mulish' and 'perverse'.[53] In all of them was a father trying to deal rationally with a situation where reason had yet no scientifically valid ground.

What passed through Virginia's mind, one wonders, as she recorded in her journal one of her own 'tantrumical' episodes? What fear descended when she considered her own madness? Did her father think her also 'perverse' and 'mulish'? However little she spoke of her illness, it could not have been often very far from her thoughts. Her horror of madness is fully expressed in a diary entry of 9 January 1915. She had been out for a walk with Leonard:

> On the tow path we met & had to pass a long line of imbeciles. The first was a very tall young man, just queer enough to look twice at, but no more; the second shuffled, and looked aside; and then one realised that every one in that long line was a miserable ineffective shuffling idiotic creature with no forehead, or no chin, & an imbecile grin, or a wild suspicious stare. It was perfectly horrible. They should certainly be killed.[54]

In *Mrs Dalloway*, too, we see again that horror in a scene where Septimus Warren Smith remembers once having observed 'a maimed file of lunatics being exercised or displayed for the diversion of the populace (who laughed aloud), ambled and nodded and grinned past him, in the Tottenham Court Road . . .'[55] And in 1904, when she threw herself from a window, in suicidal madness, Virginia must have felt much the same as Septimus did when he plunged, also from a window, to his death, convinced 'that human beings have neither kindness, nor faith, nor charity . . . They desert the fallen.'[56] With the threat of madness hanging over her from 1895 to 1941, it is understandable that Virginia thought someone with mental illness 'should certainly be killed'.

III

One of the effects of the deaths of Julia and Stella was suddenly to transform what had previously only been Virginia's sense of powerlessness into a stark and irreversible fact. Even the most cursory sketch of her life tells us that she grew up in an atmosphere congested with tension and conflicting emotions. Despite all that was good and beautiful in the distinguished Julia and Leslie Stephen, and however much she loved them, it was impossible for her not to register a certain disturbing irregularity and inconsistency in the dispensation of their care and attention. The most crucial set of links in Virginia's opening years was her sense of the connection between her own helplessness, her parents' protection and her survival; and those links had to have been very weak, for there is no other way to account for her childhood terrors.

This statement needs some qualification, however, for we cannot ignore the alleged sexual interference of the Duckworth half-brothers. Some extraordinary claims have been made about those unverified transgressions that give undue weight to their effect on Virginia's life and work.

As long ago as 1972, Quentin Bell wrote that Virginia felt 'that George had spoilt her life before it had fairly begun.'[57] This conclusion, like other more recent ones, is based primarily on her allegations in 'A Sketch of the Past', where she spoke openly and often harshly of her half-brothers' sexual behaviour towards her.[58] What Virginia wrote in 1897, however, does not convincingly support claims of sexual inter- ference. There are too many references to George Duckworth in the 1897 journal which cast him in a different, almost benign, light. For example, she 'bicycled with Georgie' on 3 January, and accompanied him on a tour of the General Post Office on the next day. She notes that 'Georgie [is] away at Canterbury' on 6 January, and records his depar- ture for Paris on 7 January. On 23 February, together with Stella, she goes to Charles Booth's offices, where 'Georgie was correcting proofs –' On three separate occasions in March, Virginia has lunch with George: once at Romano's Restaurant and twice at the Old Grasshop- per opposite Talbot Court. On 15 May, George treats Virginia and Vanessa to 'the most gorgeous strawberry ices' at Gunter's after a cricket match. On 30 May, Vanessa's birthday, Virginia notes his lavish- ness: 'Behold! Georgie presents Nessa with a wonderful *opal necklace* . . . This is my envy & my delight.' Such entries continue throughout 1897; and there are as many for Gerald.

Of course, the fact that the entries do not sound like those of a sex- ually abused victim writing about her abuser – even in a private diary kept under lock and key – is inconclusive evidence of her feelings for her half-brothers or of their attitudes to her.

Her later behaviour towards them, however, does raise more questions. The fact that as an *adult* she entrusted her first two novels to Gerald for publication with apparently no real misgivings, the fact that she sent *Night and Day* to Duckworth & Co. even after the Hogarth Press had been established, is hard to understand if the effects of his abuse were as destructive and traumatic to her as has been claimed.

This is not to question Virginia's integrity; nor, certainly, is it meant to prove her half-brothers' innocence. It is simply to suggest that her perception of the Duckworth brothers in 1939, when she began writing her memoir, does not seem to coincide with her record of them in this earliest of her journals, written when the molestations were alleged to have occurred, or with some of her later actions.

The most eloquent scenes of childhood sexuality Virginia ever wrote can be found in her most troublesome novel, *The Years*. They focus on the ten-year-old Rose Pargiter. The leap from fiction to biography is always a hazardous and rarely verifiable business; but, even so, in the 1880 section of *The Years*, young Rose's trauma appears to have resulted not from her confrontation with 'street sex' as such – Virginia called it 'street love, common love' in *The Pargiters*[59] – but rather from what that sexual encounter represented. Several times in the text, Virginia insinuates the strong attachment Rose Pargiter has for her father; it was the beginning of the little girl's feeling of desire for the opposite sex.[60] And the street encounter transformed Rose's vaguely perceived and profoundly forbidden fantasy of erotic desire for her father into a psychological reality, and in that transformation lay the havoc and confusion and guilt.

It is not only possible but highly probable that a similar transformation took hold in Virginia's *adult* imagination. The Duckworth brothers, guilty as they might have been of sexual interference, very probably became the despised objects on to which she could attach the deeply disturbing fantasies she herself harboured for her father. It was so much easier to lay the full weight of these unmentionable crimes on the shoulders of her half-brothers than to acknowledge fully the shame generated by her equally unmentionable incestuous fantasies.[61]

This, of course, is pure speculation. But, whatever the truth was, there is no verifiable evidence that the molesting went beyond fondling, distressing though this may have been to someone of Virginia's sensitive nature. Since the publication of Quentin Bell's biography in 1972, when this part of her past was made public, some readers have tended to see her life as fairly tragic in some respects and triumphant in others. And a number of feminist critics have unintentionally belittled Virginia by turning her into a pitiful, maimed figure.

In childhood, however, her sense of susceptibility was exacerbated by deep divisions. For instance, in order to keep her father and herself 'in league together', she had to be robust enough to keep up with his strenuous walks; but to get her mother's fleeting attention, she must be 'ill or in some child's crisis'[62] or in some other way dependent. For Julia was not particularly drawn to people whose good health made her irrelevant. Thus Virginia had to act separate roles for each parent if she was to get any attention at all – robust in the morning, sick in the afternoon, and studious ill or well. How could a child make so divided a world cohere?

But there were still further divisions. After her mother's death, there was no longer anything to buffer the intellectual world of her father from the social world of her conventional Duckworth half-brothers, a world into which she was carelessly and sometimes painfully forced to enter. So, with Stella's death, these colliding worlds left her at fifteen years old ever more 'unprotected, unformed, unshielded, apprehensive, receptive, anticipatory'.[63] She lived now with the intensity and vulnerability of a moth, 'filmy eyed as I was, with my wings still creased, sitting there on the edge of my broken chrysalis'.[64]

The division further weakened her hold on reality as she began to see that what the world 'was' and what it 'could be' were very different things. This realisation was profoundly linked to her determination to become a writer. For during those early years she discovered that through words she could bridge the chasm separating those constantly conflicting worlds, and through imagination bring them under her control. To Virginia, that meant power.

In the 'Sketch of the Past', she lingered over the significance writing had for her, and reinforced the 1908 statement – 'to discover real things beneath the show' – by her almost verbatim phrasing of her need to discover 'some real thing behind appearances', written now in 1939. 'Moments of being' she described as blows of 'sledge-hammer force': they were 'dominant', Virginia 'passive'. 'This suggests', she goes on to say,

> that as one gets older one has a greater power through reason to provide an explanation; and that this explanation blunts the sledge-hammer force of the blow. I think this is true, because though I still have the peculiarity that I receive these sudden shocks, they are now always welcome . . . And I go on to suppose that the shock-receiving capacity is what makes me a writer. I hazard the explanation that a shock is at once in my case followed by the desire to explain it. I feel that I have had a blow; but it is not, as I thought as a child, simply a blow from an enemy hidden behind the cotton-wool of daily life; it is or will become a revelation of some order; it is a token of some real

thing behind appearances; and I make it real by putting it into words. It is only by putting it into words that I make it whole; this wholeness means that it has lost its power to hurt me; it gives me, perhaps because by doing so I take away the pain, a great delight to put the severed parts together. Perhaps this is the strongest pleasure known to me.[65]

With words, Virginia could, and temporarily did, transform life's 'orts, scraps, and fragments'[66] into wholeness and harmony. It was thus that she gained power over the 'shocks' that had earlier made her the helpless pawn of misfortune. It was with words that she learned to bring coherence to an existence that was otherwise contradictory and hopelessly fragmented. And she was just beginning to discover, in the early years of the century, that any sorrow could be borne so long as she could write about it later.

Virginia read these journals in 1939 and was reminded again of her unhappiness: 'I shrink from the years 1897-1904, the seven unhappy years.'[67] But why was 1906 not included – the year of Thoby's death? Surely his loss was as pointless and brutal as the earlier deaths in this chiaroscuro of memory. We need only review her private history, however, to realise that Virginia, the writer, emerged at the end of 1904; that from 1905, as a journalist, she had achieved an acknowledged self – a verifiable 'I' – and this new status accounts for her choice of years. From 1905 she saw herself no longer a defenceless and faceless child in a capricious and recalcitrant world. The publication of her three pieces at the end of 1904 was symbolic: they stood for the freedom and autonomy she had never known before. Thoby's death did not devastate her in 1906. Grief-stricken she was, but no longer powerless. When the time came, she would resurrect his memory and give him a more permanent reality in *Jacob's Room* and in *The Waves*. It was this new life-giving force she had discovered in writing that she was referring to when she said, 'I make it real by putting it into words.'

'I cannot remember a time', wrote Vanessa some years after her sister's death, 'when Virginia did not mean to be a writer . . . She was very sensitive to criticism and the opinion of the grown-ups. I remember putting the paper [*Hyde Park Gate News*, the family newspaper produced between 1891 and 1895] on the table by my mother's sofa while they were at dinner.' As they waited in hiding for their parents' verdict, Virginia trembled 'with excitement'. Eventually Julia looked at it and pronounced it ' "Rather clever," . . . But it was enough to thrill her daughter; she had had approval and had been called clever . . .'[68]

This extraordinary excitement tells us the degree to which, even as a young child, Virginia identified herself with her invention. If what she had written was 'clever', then she herself must be clever as well. The need for recognition found its way into the nursery at bedtime each night. At Vanessa's bidding, Virginia told the nursery inmates stories until 'one by one we dropped off to sleep . . .'[69] To entertain her sister and brothers nightly made them her friends: she could hold them in her thrall, absorb their affection, feel a little more secure in their approval – and all of this from her powers of invention. Her stories had a valuable function. And, like all story-tellers, she needed a listener. Years later, Bernard, Virginia's spokesman in *The Waves*, would confess that 'Soliloquies in back streets soon pall. I need an audience . . . I need the illumination of other people's eyes.'[70]

Her need for outside acceptance remained crucial throughout her life: the story-teller needed the audience's endorsement. For it was here that the feeling of power came to life. Nowhere is this made more explicit than in an early typescript of *Pointz Hall*, which was to become *Between the Acts*. Miss La Trobe, after the performance of her play, confesses that 'She was happy; triumphant. She had given the world her gift – with a village pageant. Take it from me, she said, addressing the world humbly, yet confidently. The world had taken it.'[71] Her audience had seen and believed what she meant them to see. She had imposed her will, and it had been accepted.

As with Miss La Trobe, so too with Virginia: no triumph was possible without an audience. When it accepted the work of art, it accepted the artist as well. Overtly, this, or something like it, was what the gift of fiction meant. Her triumph in the nursery, therefore, could not have been a small one. Further, it was this preoccupation with pleasing others that made Virginia expert in identifying herself with her audience. Carried over into her ordinary life, it made her overly sensitive to what other people were feeling, made her quick to sense what might disturb. Many of her 'shocks' were probably due to this extraordinary responsiveness to others.

To get at the deeper significance her writing had for her, we need to remain a little longer in the childhood years preceding these journals. For it is there that we best see the generative force of those 'infinite discords' that created havoc in her daily life – chiefly Leslie's irrational behaviour and Julia's sleight-of-hand disappearances, which made them seem untrustworthy and erratic in the extreme to the precocious child of six or seven. But more fundamentally, these represented an inexplicable fracture between fact and feeling. That is to say, in the child's mind, feeling – 'I need my mother' – was in constant collision with fact – 'But your mother is gone.' One of the consequences of this split was perhaps an almost endless sense of frustration: *fact* and *feeling* were forever out of synchrony and often discordant.

With so much frustration and so few opportunities for satisfaction, it was natural that a certain amount of fear should eventually infiltrate the business of daily life for the young Virginia; and it follows that the more persistent the fear, the greater would be her tendency to avoid it by retreating to the domain of imagination where *fantasy* and *feeling* could be brought into perfect alignment and made stable. Discontentment, in a sense, mobilised her creative imagination and brought her a certain measure of peace. That was an advantage in story-telling to be remembered.

There were other advantages, too, as Virginia was soon to discover. Because story-telling was a solitary occupation, it meant being in an atmosphere free of dependency and expectation and disappointment – free of the feeling of hopeless passivity she knew so well. For, after all, the realm of fantasy was entirely of her own making. In the fictional universe, Virginia was mistress. Whatever she bid her imaginary people to say or do, they said and did. Omniscience and power were hers for the taking. Here no one could meddle, frustrate or hurt.

There was, however, an even subtler benefit to writing that Virginia discovered when she went into London society with George Duckworth. The evenings out, the dances, the social rounds George insisted upon – these were ordeals that were forced upon her; but no matter how much she 'squirmed', she obeyed, feeling always the 'outsider'. Yet through all this Virginia had one 'good friend', she wrote in 1940, and that 'good friend, who is still with me, upheld me; that sense of the spectacle; the dispassionate separate sense that I am seeing what will be useful later; I could even find the words for the scene as I stood there.'[72] So long as there were pen and ink handy in the privacy of her room, she would survive the squirming, the terror and the humiliation. For Virginia remained always observant, taking mental notes that next day would be recast into the steadier and more permanent stuff of fiction. Words thus became her shield, her protection, against whatever caused pain.

These aesthetic transformations, reaching back at least to 1907, appear to have become her deepest and most persistent motive for writing. Indeed, if one looks at the whole of her work against her fifty-nine years, one discovers that those periods of greatest stress were also periods of greatest productivity. The stronger the pain, the higher she soared into those airy spaces of imagination. What she said in *To the Lighthouse* of Lily Briscoe's art she might have said of her own: that the pen was 'the one dependable thing in a world of strife, ruin, chaos . . .',[73] and the godlike power she felt as a writer is perfectly embodied in a passage from that novel. On the beach one of the Ramsay children is crouched over a little puddle of water: 'Brooding, she changed the pool into the sea, and made the minnows into sharks and whales, and cast vast clouds over this tiny world by holding her hand against the sun, and so brought darkness and desolation, like God himself . . .'[74]

Pitted against this image, however, was the darker equally persistent one of futility and helplessness. She carried it with her through life. It is found in one of the 'poems' for *Pointz Hall*:

> Am I not burdened? The last little donkey in the long caravanserai crossing the desert? Burdened with bales roughly bound with thongs? my memories, my possessions. What the past laid on my back; saying little donkey, kneel down. Fill your paniers. Then rise up, little donkey, and go on your way, burdened, with litter, possessions, dust and jewels, till the heels blister and the hoofs crack . . . Such was the burden laid on me in the cradle . . .[75]

Everything Virginia Woolf wrote would contain this contrastive scheme, this polarisation between 'God himself' and some equivalent to the helpless 'little donkey'. It reflected her perception of the world as incongruous and conflictive; a world that was 'quick to pounce on you if you gave it a chance.'[76] It was the divided, contrary world inhabited by Leslie and Julia Stephen at 22 Hyde Park Gate that as a child she could not make cohere. In every novel, too, she would try to bring together the 'infinite discords' she had discovered in coming to know that world.

In May of 1925, when the idea of her autobiographical novel, *To the Lighthouse*, first came to her, she saw the book centre around her father, 'sitting in a boat, reciting We perished, each alone, while he crushes a dying mackerel.'[77] But that was not what got written. The finished work became instead a lyrical record of images recalled from childhood – had she not discovered at Blo' Norton in 1906 that 'the images of childhood . . . stay bright'? Did she not find preserved at Cornwall in 1905 her childhood, almost intact? By casting into that poetic mould those prosaic angers and fears of earlier years, she succeeded in bridging the gap between fact and feeling, and came to know the solipsistic power of the artist, recreating *on her own terms* that childhood world of powerlessness and passivity.

The Years, too, is a chronicle of the Stephen family. But here Virginia adopted a different method. The characters are seen with an adult's perceptions, and registered from the adult's point of view. In shifting away from the child's vision in *To the Lighthouse* to the presumably more 'objective' perspective, Virginia discovered that she was giving biographical rather than aesthetic facts,[78] that she was documenting rather than 'explaining'; and, in that documentation, lyrical fluency gave way to factual truculence. Reality had become too strong. The 'real thing behind appearances', from the adult point of view, loomed up before her an unalterable and ugly fact. From the adult perspective, her 'explanation' did nothing to blunt the 'sledge-hammer force of the blow'. Above all, she was seeing too much of herself in the sacrificial character of Eleanor Pargiter, who

> must have been young, almost a girl; and that girl was dead; had vanished . . . and the pigeons were crooning a requiem, for her past; for one of the selves that had been her; for one of the many million human beings who had walked, who had suffered, who had thought so intensely.[79]

For the adult perspective made clear that Eleanor Pargiter's father, in sacrificing her to his own needs, had committed an unforgivable crime – just as biographically Virginia, now in her mature years, must have seen that Leslie Stephen had also sacrificed her and was equally in error, equally unforgiven. An intolerable realisation it must have been.

The 'truth', as Virginia was woefully to discover, was that biographical fact and aesthetic fact would not mix. If by writing she got at truth – the 'real thing behind appearances' – she did so only by her own words and on her own terms; the wholeness she achieved was consequently hers alone. Here finally was the crux of the difficulty that probably began during the writing of these journals, and would persist, varying only in intensity, for the remainder of her life.

'Nothing is real unless I write it down,' said Virginia in 1937, twelve days after Julian Bell's death. 'I know by this time what an odd effect Time has: it does not destroy people . . . I still think, perhaps more fully than I did . . . of Thoby: but it brushes away the actual personal presence.' On 8 March 1941, in the penultimate diary entry, she wrote:

'Haddock & sausage meat. I think it is true that one gains a certain hold on sausage & haddock by writing them down.'[80]

Was it possible now, twenty days before her death, to tell the writer from the written? They seemed to have become indistinguishable. The only real world appeared now to be the world of her own making. For some curious reason her state of mind in these last days of her life came very close to that of her 'seven unhappy years'. And we need only look at the last page of her 1903 journal to discover some lines that today seem uncannily reminiscent of a passage she was to write almost forty years later. Here are the lines of 1903:

> October begins work & pleasure lifts the curtain on that particular act of our drama which is played in London. Actors may change – their parts may be different but the sameness of scene gives a certain continuity to the whole, & does in fact influence our lives to no little extent.

The following lines were written in 1940. They are from the last page of *Pointz Hall*.

> It was the first act of a new play. But who had written the play? What was the meaning of the play? And who made them act their parts?[81]

The earlier proposition has turned into an unanswered question. But what it means or where it leads we have no way of knowing. A curtain of inscrutability has been drawn. The rest is speculation. All we know is that the apprenticeship of Virginia Stephen began in 1897, and part of it came to an end in the last days of 1904. The money she earned as a journalist from 1905 and would later earn as a novelist provided her with the freedom and independence she sought. Writing gave her the identity and power she needed. And these early journals mark the beginning.

NOTES

1. Quotations from these early journals have not been annotated.
2. Katherine C. Hill. 'Virginia Woolf and Leslie Stephen: History and Literary Revolution,' *PMLA*, 96, no. 3, May 1981, p. 351.
3. *Sir Leslie Stephen's Mausoleum Book*, ed. Alan Bell (Oxford, 1977), p. 103.
4. *Virginia Woolf: A Biography*, Quentin Bell, Vol. I (London and New York, 1972), p. 56.
5. *Ibid.*, p. 70.
6. In *The Essays of Virginia Woolf*, ed. Andrew McNeillie, Vol. I (London and New York, 1986).
7. London, pp. 63-5; New York, pp. 85-8.

8. In *The Complete Shorter Fiction of Virginia Woolf*, ed. Susan Dick (London and New York, 1985).

9. Thirty-four years later, as Virginia Woolf, she would enlarge upon this germinal idea: 'Unconsciousness, which means presumably that the under-mind drowses, is a state we all know. We all have experience of the work done by unconsciousness in our daily lives. You have had a crowded day, let us suppose, sightseeing in London. Could you say what you had seen and done when you came back? Was it not all a blur, a confusion? But after what seemed a rest, a chance to turn aside and look at something different, the sights and sounds and sayings that had been of most interest to you swam to the surface, apparently of their own accord; and remained in memory; what was unimportant sank into forgetfulness. So it is with a writer. After a hard day's work, trudging round, seeing all he can see, feeling all he can, taking in the book of his mind innumerable notes, the writer becomes – if he can – unconscious. In fact, his under-mind works at top speed while his upper-mind drowses. Then, after a pause, the veil lifts; and there is the thing – the thing he wants to write about – simplified, composed.' From 'The Leaning Tower' in *The Moment and Other Essays* (London, 1952, pp. 109-10; New York,, 1974, p. 134).

10. In *The Complete Shorter Fiction of Virginia Woolf*, ed. Susan Dick, revised ed. (London, 1989).

11. 'Reminiscences' in *Moments of Being*, ed. Jeanne Schulkind, 2nd ed. (London and New York, 1985).

12. Q. Bell, I. p. 125.

13. *The Letters of Virginia Woolf*, Vol. 1, eds Nigel Nicolson and Joanne Trautmann (London and New York, 1975) No. 471.

14. Although it is difficult to pin-point precisely these years of apprenticeship, it is probably accurate to see them as broadly divided into two stages: 1897-1904 marking Virginia's apprenticeship in journalism, and 1905-9 as her preparation for the writing of fiction.

15. In *Moments of Being*.

16. *Ibid.*, p. 85.

17. Mitchell A. Leaska, *The Novels of Virginia Woolf: From Beginning to End* (London and New York, 1977), pp. 12-38.

18. *Moments of Being*, pp. 28-59.

19. *Ibid.*, p. 37.

20. *Ibid.*, p. 56.

21. *Ibid.*, p. 40.

22. *Ibid.*, p. 45.

23. *Ibid.*, p. 110.

24. *Ibid.*, p. 116.

25. *Ibid.*, p. 111.

26. *Ibid.*, p. 90.

27. *Ibid.*, pp. 83-4.

28. *Ibid.*, p. 81.

29. *Ibid.*, p. 83.

30. Mrs Ramsay's 'beneficiaries' in *To the Lighthouse* (London, p. 157; New York, p. 153).

31. *Moments of Being*, p. 38.

32. *Ibid.*, p. 36.

33. *Ibid.*, p. 94.
34. *Ibid.*, p. 85.
35. *Ibid.*, p. 90.
36. *Ibid.*, p. 137.
37. Q. Bell, I, p. 41.
38. *Mausoleum Book*, pp. xxvi-xxvii.
39. *Moments of Being*, pp. 55-6.
40. *Ibid.*, p. 105.
41. *Ibid.*, p. 157.
42. *Ibid.*, p. 78.
43. *Ibid.*, p. 84.
44. *Ibid.*, p. 78.
45. London, p. 46; New York, p. 64. See also 30 Sept. 1926, in *The Diary of Virginia Woolf*, Vol. III, ed. Anne Olivier Bell (London and New York, 1980).
46. *Moments of Being*, p. 78.
47. *Ibid.*, p. 99.
48. Martine Stemerick, 'Virginia Woolf and Julia Stephen: The Distaff Side of History' in *Virginia Woolf: Centennial Essays*, eds. E.K. Ginsberg and L.M. Gottlieb (Troy, New York, 1983), p. 60.
49. *Moments of Being*, p. 182.
50. *Mausoleum Book*, p. 92.
51. *Ibid.*, p. 103.
52. *Moments of Being*, pp. 111-12.
53. Leslie Stephen to Julia Stephen: 9 April and 29 Sept. 1882 and 29 April 1881 (Berg Collection, The New York Public Library).
54. *Diary*, I, p. 13.
55. London, p. 100; New York, p. 136.
56. London, p. 99; New York, p. 135.
57. Q. Bell, Vol. I, p. 44.
58. *Moments of Being*, pp. 67-9.
59. *The Pargiters*, ed. Mitchell A. Leaska, London and New York, 1977, p. 50.
60. *Ibid.*, p. 51: 'At ten years old, tomboy though she was, she was beginning to feel desire, which was much more highly developed in her sisters, for the approval of the other sex. When her father had said "grubby little monster" and pointed to the stain on her pinafore, she at once covered it with her hand; although when Milly noticed it, she did not care in the least, and said what was a lie . . .'
61. See M.A. Leaska, *The Novels of Virginia Woolf*, pp. 198-9. In the holograph version of *The Years*, Vol. VII, dated 5 August 1934, Virginia wrote a scene in which one of the young Pargiter women sees her father across a crowded room and thinks: '. . . love of father & daughter. Spontaneous. Rather suspect all the same. Of mixed origin. Do I love my father sexually? . . .' Nowhere in the Woolf canon is the suggestion of father-daughter incest made more explicit.
62. *Moments of Being*, p. 83.
63. *Ibid.*, p. 124.
64. *Ibid.*, p. 124.
65. *Ibid.*, pp. 72-3.

66. *Between the Acts*, London, pp. 219-20; New York, p. 188. See also Shakespeare, *Troilus and Cressida*, V, iii, 158-9.

67. *Moments of Being*, p. 136.

68. *Notes on Virginia's Childhood*, ed. Richard J. Schaubeck, Jr (New York, 1974), pp. 10-11.

69. V. Bell, p. 6.

70. London, p. 83; New York, p. 115.

71. *Pointz Hall: The Earlier and Later Typescripts of Between the Acts*, ed. Mitchell A. Leaska (New York, 1983), pp. 175-6.

72. *Moments of Being*, pp. 155-6. In *The Waves* Virginia gives us, through Rhoda, a sharper sense of what those ordeals felt like: 'But here the door opens and people come . . . Throwing faint smiles to mask their cruelty, their indifference . . . I must take his hand; I must answer. But what answer shall I give? I am thrust back to stand burning in this clumsy, this ill-fitting body . . . A million arrows pierce me. Scorn and ridicule pierce me . . . Hide me, I cry, protect me, for I am the youngest, the most naked of you all.' (London, p. 76; New York, pp. 105-6).

73. London, p. 232; New York, p. 224.

74. London, p. 119; New York, p. 114.

75. *Pointz Hall*, p. 557.

76. *To the Lighthouse* (London, p. 96; New York, p. 92).

77. *Diary*, III, 14 May 1925.

78. See *The Common Reader: First Series* (London, 1962, p. 181; New York, 1955, p. 148).

79. *The Years*, Holograph, Vol. VIII (unpaginated) (Berg Collection, The New York Public Library).

80. *Diary*, V, 8 March 1941.

81. *Pointz Hall*, p. 188.

Abbreviations

AVS	Adeline Virginia Stephen. The initials are used in the notes and 'Virginia' in the narrative sections. ('VW' or 'Virginia Woolf' is used when referring to texts published after 10 August 1912.)
Kp	B.J. Kirkpatrick, *A Bibliography of Virginia Woolf*, 3rd ed., Oxford University Press, Oxford, 1980.
MoB	Virginia Woolf, *Moments of Being*, ed. Jeanne Schulkind, 2nd ed., Hogarth Press, London, and Harcourt Brace Jovanovich, New York, 1985
QB,I	Quentin Bell, *Virginia Woolf: A Biography, Volume I, Virginia Stephen, 1882-1912*, Hogarth Press, London, and Harcourt Brace Jovanovich, New York, 1972.
TLS	*The Times Literary Supplement.*
VW Diary	*The Diary of Virginia Woolf*, ed. Anne Olivier Bell, 5 vols, Hogarth Press, London, and Harcourt Brace Jovanovich, New York, 1977-84.
VW Essays	*The Essays of Virginia Woolf*, ed. Andrew McNeillie, 6 vols. Hogarth Press, London, and Harcourt Brace Jovanovich, New York, 1986-95.
VW Letters	*The Letters of Virginia Woolf*, ed. Nigel Nicolson and Joanne Trautmann, 6 vols, Hogarth Press, London, and Harcourt Brace Jovanovich, New York, 1975-80.

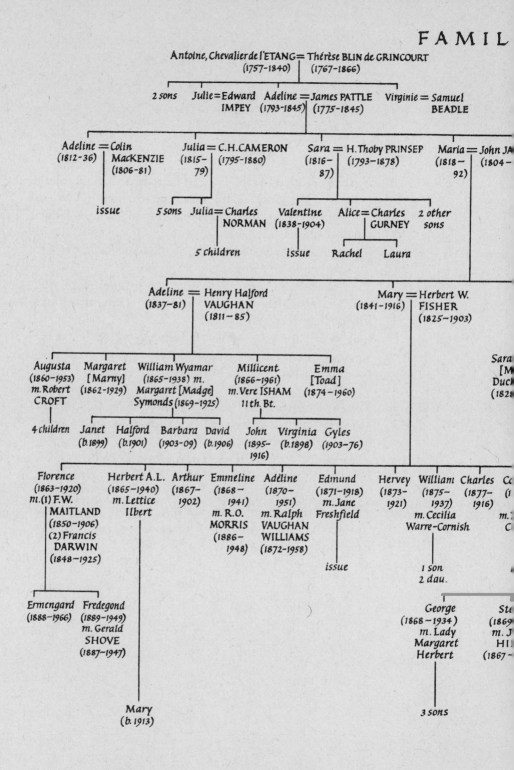

Antoine, Chevalier de l'ETANG = Thérèse BLIN de GRINCOURT
(1757-1840) (1767-1866)

2 sons   Julie = Edward   Adeline = James PATTLE   Virginie = Samuel
                    IMPEY   (1793-1845) (1775-1845)   BEADLE

Adeline = Colin   Julia = C.H.CAMERON   Sara = H.Thoby PRINSEP   Maria = John JA
(1812-36) MacKENZIE   (1815- (1795-1880)   (1816- (1793-1878)   (1818- (1804-
           (1806-81)   79)   87)   92)

issue   5 sons   Julia = Charles   Valentine   Alice = Charles   2 other
                         NORMAN   (1838-1904)   GURNEY   sons

5 children   issue   Rachel   Laura

Adeline = Henry Halford   Mary = Herbert W.
(1837-81) VAUGHAN   (1841-1916) FISHER
           (1811-85)   (1825-1903)

Augusta   Margaret   William Wyamar   Millicent   Emma   Sara
(1860-1953) [Marny]   (1865-1938) m.   (1866-1961)   [Toad]   [M
m.Robert   (1862-1929)   Margaret [Madge]   m.Vere ISHAM   (1874-1960)   Duc
CROFT   Symonds (1869-1925)   11th. Bt.   (182

4 children   Janet   Halford   Barbara   David   John   Virginia   Gyles
             (b.1899) (b.1901) (1903-09) (b.1906) (1895- (b.1898) (1903-76)
                                                      1916)

Florence   Herbert A.L.   Arthur   Emmeline   Adeline   Edmund   Hervey   William   Charles   C
(1863-1920) (1865-1940) (1867-   (1868-   (1870-   (1871-1918) (1873-   (1875-   (1877-   (1
m.(1) F.W.   m. Lettice   1902)   1941)   1951)   m. Jane   1921)   1937)   1916)   m.
MAITLAND   Ilbert   m. R.O.   m. Ralph   Freshfield   m. Cecilia   C
(1850-1906)   MORRIS   VAUGHAN   Warre-Cornish
(2) Francis   (1886-   WILLIAMS
DARWIN   1948)   (1872-1958)
(1848-1925)   issue   1 son
                                                      2 dau.

Ermengard   Fredegond   George   Ste
(1888-1966) (1889-1949) (1868-1934) (1869
             m. Gerald   m. Lady   m. J
             SHOVE   Margaret   HI
             (1887-1947)   Herbert   (1867-

Mary   3 sons
(b.1913)

TREE

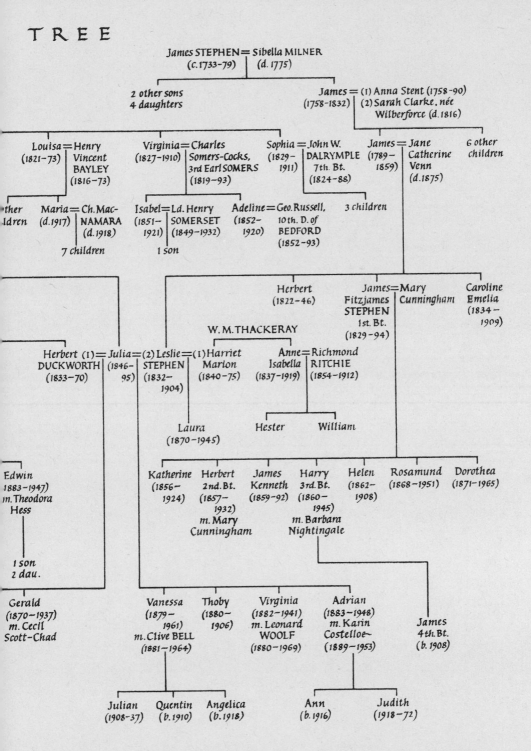

James STEPHEN = Sibella MILNER
(c.1733-79)   (d.1775)

2 other sons
4 daughters

James = (1) Anna Stent (1758-90)
(1758-1832) (2) Sarah Clarke, née
              Wilberforce (d.1816)

Louisa = Henry   Virginia = Charles   Sophia = John W.   James = Jane   6 other
(1821-73) Vincent   (1827-1910) Somers-Cocks, (1829- DALRYMPLE   (1789- Catherine children
           BAYLEY   3rd Earl SOMERS 1911)   7th. Bt.   1859)   Venn
           (1816-73)   (1819-93)   (1824-88)   (d.1875)

·ther   Maria = Ch.Mac-   Isabel = Ld.Henry   Adeline = Geo.Russell,   3 children
·ldren   (d.1917) NAMARA   (1851-   SOMERSET   (1852-   10th.D.of
                   (d.1918) 1921)   (1849-1932) 1920)   BEDFORD
                                                          (1852-93)
         7 children   1 son

                              Herbert   James = Mary   Caroline
                              (1822-46)   Fitzjames Cunningham Emelia
                                                     STEPHEN   (1834-
                              W. M. THACKERAY   1st. Bt.   1909)
                                                     (1829-94)

Herbert (1) = Julia = (2) Leslie = (1)Harriet   Anne = Richmond
DUCKWORTH   (1846-   STEPHEN   Marion   Isabella RITCHIE
(1833-70)   95)   (1832-   (1840-75)   (1837-1919) (1854-1912)
                      1904)

                      Laura   Hester   William
                      (1870-1945)

Edwin   Katherine Herbert   James   Harry   Helen   Rosamund   Dorothea
1883-1947)   (1856-   2nd.Bt.   Kenneth 3rd.Bt. (1862-   (1868-1951) (1871-1965)
m.Theodora   1924)   (1857-   (1859-92) (1860- 1908)
Hess   1932)   1945)
                                 m.Mary   m.Barbara
                                 Cunningham   Nightingale
1 son
2 dau.

Gerald   Vanessa   Thoby   Virginia   Adrian
(1870-1937)   (1879-   (1880-   (1882-1941) (1883-1948) James
m.Cecil   1961)   1906)   m.Leonard   m.Karin   4th.Bt.
Scott-Chad   m.Clive BELL   WOOLF   Costelloe   (b.1908)
                      (1881-1964)   (1880-1969) (1889-1953)

         Julian   Quentin   Angelica   Ann   Judith
         (1908-37) (b.1910) (b.1918)   (b.1916)   (1918-72)

A Passionate
Apprentice

The Early Journals

When I read this book, which I do sometimes on a hot Sunday evening in London, I am struck by the wildness of its statements – the carelessness of its descriptions – the repetition of its adjectives – & in short I pronounce it a very hasty work, but excuse myself by remembering in what circumstances it was written. After a days outing, or when half an hour is vacant, or as a relief from some Greek tragedy – at different times, & in different moods it is written, & I am certain that if I imposed any other conditions upon myself it would never be written at all. Did I not take it to Cornwall at Easter, & determine to note something serviceable – & did I even write my address?

So once more I return to the old method; & protesting merely, that I am conscious of its faults – the protest of vanity.

VIRGINIA STEPHEN
August 1908

1897

Soon after her mother's death in May 1895, Virginia suffered her first mental breakdown. Very little is known about this period. It was, as Quentin Bell has written, 'a great interval of nothingness, a kind of positive death which cannot be described and of which Virginia herself probably knew little . . .' On 3 January 1897, when this journal opens, Virginia, now almost fifteen, was slowly recovering from her illness, and the pages that follow provide us with a richly detailed account of this momentous year of her life.

Sunday 3 January

We have all started to keep a record of the new year – Nessa,[1] Adrian and I. Bicycled with Georgie to Mr Studds[2] but found he was away, and so went on to Battersea Park –

There was a great crowd of bikers and lookers on – Miss Jan [Virginia][3] rode her new bicycle, whose seat unfortunately, is rather uncomfortable – Thoby[4] was on Geralds, and Adrian on Jacks, which was given him (A.) on Christmas. In the afternoon we did nothing –

After tea Thoby read the Ent[omological]. Soc,[5] a paper upon the History of the Club. Also a retrospect of 1896 – It was agreed to send

---

1 For Vanessa (Nessa) Stephen, Adrian Stephen and George (Georgie) Duckworth, see Appendix B.

2 Arthur (Peter) Studd (1863-1919), painter, educated at Eton and King's College, Cambridge. He trained at the Académie Julian in Paris and at the Slade School of Art, and lived at 97 Cheyne Walk, Chelsea. He had a particular passion for the work of Whistler (see Feb. 1905, n.28), which he collected.

3 It has been suggested that 'Miss Jan' derives from January, AVS's month of birth.

4 For Thoby Stephen, Gerald Duckworth and John (Jack) Waller Hills, see Appendix B.

5 Encouraged by their parents, and in particular by Jack Hills, the Stephen children had for many years been enthusiastic lepidopterists – or 'bug-hunters' as they termed it. At the end of the 1897 journal is a reference to their Society; see p. 134.

S[tella]. D[uckworth].[6] and J[ohn]. W[aller]. H[ills]. a letter of congratulations – also that the lectures of the Pres. etc.[7] should not be entered in the book.

Monday 4 January

Met Georgie at the General Post Office[8] at 12, and went with him to Mr Higgs. We were shown round the telegraph place, where all the people (two thousand) were working. But they made such a noise that I could not hear the guide explaining what was happening; so it is impossible to describe any of it to you, my dear diary.

We lunched at Pimms[9] with Mr Higgs. Mr Ives was to have come but did not – After lunch we four bussed back home – A[drian]. and I lay down to rest for the evening. Theodore Davies[10] came to dinner which was at 6.30, and went with us to Drury Lane – The Pantomime was Aladdin[11] and very good Miss Jan thought, more suited to her comprehension than a grown up play. Got home at 11.30 being defrauded of one penny.

O [12]

Tuesday 5 January

Got up at half past 10, and stayed in and read the whole morning. After

---

6 For Stella Duckworth, see Appendix B. Engaged in August 1896, Stella and Jack were married in April 1897.

7 No longer survive.

8 The Telegraph Department of the General Post Office, St Martin's le Grand, in its large galleries, contained 500 instruments with their attendants, and four 50 h.p. steam engines which transmitted messages through pneumatic tubes to other offices. The galleries could be visited at the request of a banker or other well-known citizen. H. C. Higgs was employed in the General Post Office Secretary's Office and C. F. Ives in the Accountant General's Department.

9 Probably at 3-5 Poultry Street, EC.

10 Theodore Llewelyn Davies (1870-1905), youngest of the six sons of the Rev. John Llewelyn Davies, who had coached Leslie Stephen and whose family and his remained friends; the only sister was Margaret (1861-1944), General Secretary of the Women's Co-operative Guild, 1889-1921.

11 Arranged by Oscar Barrett.

12 The ciphers at the bottom of some of the pages of the 1897 journal are a mystery. However, as AVS was still under Dr Seton's care since her 1895 breakdown, it is possible that they were a private code she used for keeping an account of her moods, especially her bad days; but this is pure conjecture.

luncheon Nessa and Thoby went to the Royal Academy to see Lord Leightons[13] pictures. Adrian Stella and I bussed to Piccadilly circus. Stella left us there and went on to Oxford Street to pay calls. Adrian and I bussed to Sloane St, and there dismounted – A insisted upon buying a luggage carrier for his bicycle for 3/9 – which was a piece of great extravagance, Miss Jan thought. We walked back home.

After tea we gave a most striking representation of the tragedy "Clementinas Lovers" by J. T[hoby] S[tephen] in which *everyone* is killed. The servants – Pauline (who thought we were acting Aladdin) Elizabeth and Florrie, pronounced it most excellent. Finished vol 1 of Three Generations of English Women, and began vol 2.[14]

0

Wednesday 6 January
Will[15] came in the morning and talked to Stella a great deal, so that we did not get out till late – We went for a short walk in the gardens – Jerry lost his muzzle[16] somehow, and had to be carried home muffled up in Nessas cloak. Luncheon was at 1. Aunt Anny[17] came for lunch, and was most amusing – As soon as she was out of the door after lunch, she said to father in a loud voice – "Oh Leslie what a noble boy Thoby is!" Adrian, Thoby and Father[18] went to Highgate.[19] Aunt Anny and Stella on some private business of their own, and Nessa and I to the National Gallery. We saw *everything* – old Italians, Dutches, English and a great room full of Turner water colours. Stella and Jack and Gerald went to

---

13 Frederic Leighton (1830-96), later (1896) 1st Baron Leighton of Stretton, painter of classical themes. He was President of the Royal Academy, 1878-96.

14 Janet Ross, *Three Generations of English Women*, 1888.

15 AVS's first cousin, William (Will) Wyamar Vaughan (1865-1938), son of her mother's sister Adeline (1837-81) and Henry Halford Vaughan (1811-85), historian.

16 The Muzzling of Dogs Act (1871) was enforced from 1897-1900 in an effort to eliminate rabies in Great Britain.

17 Anne Isabella Ritchie (1837-1919), novelist, the elder daughter of W. M. Thackeray and sister of Harriet Marian (Minny), Leslie Stephen's first wife. In 1877 she married her second cousin, Richmond Ritchie (1854-1912). See AVS's 'The Enchanted Organ: Anne Thackeray' in *The Moment and Other Essays*, 1947 (Kp A29) and reprinted in *VW Essays*, III.

18 For Leslie Stephen, see Appendix B.

19 The cemetery where Julia Stephen was buried. See Appendix B for Julia Stephen.

dine at the Stanleys,[20] to see French plays,[21] and danced afterwards. Georgie away at Canterbury – Pauline found the key of this book so that I am fast[?] locked[?] up.

O

Thursday 7 January

Yesterday morning we went to Mrs Simpson[22] in Cornwall Gdns with a parcel, and then straight back home, as we thought Georgie was coming – Stella went with Jo[23] to see the place where Jo is to build her [Stella's] cottages.[24] He stayed for lunch. In the afternoon he took us four to Covent Garden. We walked to Sloane St, and explored the Brompton Oratory. We went to the animal man in Covent Garden, and saw two baby crocodiles – most delightful critturs – Afterwards Jo plunged us down a little back street and so to his office, which is one small room, with a hideous green paper, with yellow peacocks and lions, and with a window looking on to the river. Georgie came home about 5. He started for Paris[25] at a quarter to nine, where he will be for 6 weeks. Finished Three Generations of English Women, and began Froudes Life of Carlyle.[26]

O

20 Mary Katharine, *née* Bell (1848-1929), and Edward Lyulph Stanley (1839-1926), 4th Baron Stanley of Alderly and 4th Baron Sheffield, lawyer, active in the organisation and administration of public education.

21 Possibly *A Pierrot's Life, A Play Without Words*, by F. Bessier with music by M.Costa, at the Prince of Wales's Theatre.

22 Probably Mary C. M. Simpson, daughter of Nassau W. Senior, and author of *Many Memories of Many People* (1898) in which she was to write lovingly of Leslie Stephen's first wife, Minny Thackeray. A passage from Mrs Simpson's book is quoted in his *Mausoleum Book*, ed. A. Bell (Oxford, 1977), p. 18.

23 AVS's first cousin, Edmund (Jo) Fisher (1871-1918), architect, sixth of the eleven children of her mother's sister Mary (1841-1916) and Herbert W. Fisher (1825-1903), private secretary to the Prince of Wales, 1860-70, and in 1890 appointed Vice-Warden of the Stanneries. Edmund married Jane Freshfield.

24 Stella's philanthropic cottages were probably in Lisson Grove, Marylebone; see n. 92. AVS would write about this charitable work in 'Chapter Fifty-six' of *The Pargiters*, ed. Mitchell A. Leaska, 1977 (Kp A50); see also *Octavia Hill's 'Letters to Fellow-Workers' 1864 to 1911*, 1933.

25 Presumably for a holiday.

26 James Anthony Froude, *Life and Times of Thomas Carlyle*, 1882, 2 vols.

Friday 8 January

Rained all the morning. Thoby and Nessa were taught waltzing in the drawing room by Stella – Thoby dances in the most extraordinary way, galloping round the room as hard as he can go, and at last landing Nessa in the table.

Read most of the morning.

Aunt Mary[27] came after luncheon, and stayed for tea at 4. Herbert [Fisher] also came to tea. Nessa and I drove to Butts[28] in the carriage (which was hired for Aunt Marys benefit) and bought 3 shillings worth of tulips, also a bag of chestnuts for Adrian. He and Thoby roasted them after tea, with rather disastrous effects upon A who could not sleep last night, and had to be moved down to Stellas room, where he was all night. Jack doused Shag[29] with water – poor old beast, and made him choke and snuffle for a long time afterwards. Thobys match not to be played tomorrow.

O

Saturday 9 January

Rained in the morning. Nessa and Thoby danced in the drawing room. They are progressing satisfactorily, though Thoby is still rather scornful of the time. Hilary Holman Hunt[30] came to luncheon, and he and Thoby went afterwards to the Aquarium.[31] He has grown up in to a proper young gentleman, a little taller than Thoby, and very much older.

Nessa and Adrian and I went to the Polytechnic[32] after they had gone. We went to see the Animatographs,[33] but by some mistake were hustled

27 Mary Fisher, *née* Jackson; see n. 23.

28 John Butt & Son, fruiterers, Kensington High Street, W.

29 The Irish Terrier obtained in August 1892 by Gerald Duckworth, and the subject of AVS's essay 'On a Faithful Friend' published first in *The Guardian*, 18 January 1905 (Kp CO4), and reprinted in *VW Essays*, I.

30 Hilary Holman Hunt (1879-1949), son of the Pre-Raphaelite painter William Holman Hunt (1827-1910). Hilary and his sister Gladys, like the Stephen children, had spent summer holidays in St Ives, Cornwall.

31 The world's first aquarium, founded in 1853, was part of the Zoological Gardens, Regent's Park.

32 Young Men's Christian Institute between Cavendish Square and Regent Street which, since 1882, had occupied the old Polytechnic Institute.

33 The current name for cinematograph (or biograph) which in 1910 was shortened to 'cinema'.

in to the wrong room, and had a lecture on the Rontgen Rays[34] instead. We were shown photographs of normal hands and diseased hands, a baby, and a puppy – and a lady and gentleman from the audience had their hands photographed – the gent. declared that a piece of needle was in his hand, but the photograph did not discover it. Afterwards we went and had coffee and shortbread in an A.B.C.[35] in Regent St – and bussed home, getting back at 5. Read after tea and finished the 1st vol. of Carlyle – Adrian has gone back into his own room – Thoby is in Georgies.

0

Sunday 10 January
Read all the morning – got the 2nd vol. of Carlyle, which is to be read slowly; and then I am to reread all the books father has lent me –

After luncheon we thought we should like to go out for a walk but we found it to be raining hard. Then Gerald suggested that we might go to the Albert Hall.[36] We went to the gallery, for which you do not have to pay, and then A. treated us to threepenny reserved seats from which occasional glimpses of the piano and the organ could be had. Thoby left after 3 pieces, unable to stand it any longer, and we came away before the end. We met Will [Vaughan] on the way down the road, and Eustace[37] on the doorstep. Gerald dined with Herbert F[38] at the Savile.[39] It is a week today since I began this diary. How many more weeks has it to live – At any rate it must and shall survive Nessas Collins and [As] Renshaw.[40] It has a key, and beautiful boards, and is much superior.

0

---

34 X-rays, named after their discoverer Wilhelm Röntgen (1845-1923).
35 Aerated Bread Co., Ltd, bread and flour manufacturers, with numerous tea-rooms throughout London.
36 The concert programme for 10 January included Merkel's *Adagio* and Elgar's *Salut d'Amour*.
37 Eustace Hills (1868-1934), barrister, was Jack Hills' younger brother.
38 AVS's first cousin Herbert A. L. Fisher (1865-1940), first son of Mary and Herbert W. Fisher, historian and later Vice-Chancellor of Sheffield University; he married Lettice Ilbert.
39 The Savile Club, 107 Piccadilly, W.
40 Collins and Renshaw were and are printers and publishers of diaries.

Monday 11 January

Nessa began her drawing,[41] and Adrian bicycled down with her. Thoby and I started on a long walk at 10.30 – We went down to the Embankment, and walked down it city-ways, till we came to the Pensioners garden. Went in and saw a great monument erected to the soldiers who were killed in the Chilianwala(?)[42] Came out again by another gate, and walked along till we came to Ebury Street and thereabouts – Then by some wonderful process we found ourselves again in the Chelsea Gdns where we had been half an hour ago – By my great skill we traced our way through slums of the Southwark description, till we came to the South Kensington Station. Thoby pronounces "Cadogan" 'Cadōgan' with emphasis on the o –

Stella had spent the morning with Jack looking at her cottages-to-be – and lunched with him somewhere in that region – In the afternoon Thoby, A. and I went to the mechanical part of the S[outh]. K[ensington]. M[useum].[43] and then came home & Nessa being at her drawing. Thoby went with Gerald to dine at the Savile, where they met Mr Luxmoore and Graves[44] and afterwards to Under the Red Robe.[45]

O

Tuesday 12 January

Very foggy all the morning, and we did not go out. Stella went to

---

41 Since 1896 Vanessa had attended Arthur Cope's School of Art, Park Cottage, Pelham Street, South Kensington; her classes were on Monday, Wednesday and Friday each week.

42 The gardens are in the grounds of the Royal Hospital, Chelsea, founded by Charles II to house old and disabled soldiers. A tall granite obelisk by Charles Cockerell was erected in 1853 'To the memory of 255 officers, non-commissioned officers, and privates of the 24th regiment who fell in Chilianwala [the Punjab], 13 January 1849'. The question mark in parentheses is AVS's.

43 Founded in 1856 and now called The Science Museum; it housed a collection of working models of machinery and apparatus for every kind of scientific research and educational purpose.

44 Henry Elford Luxmoore (d. 1926), senior assistant Master at Eton College, 1864-1904, and George's tutor. Clarence Percy Rivers Graves (1871-1937), one of George and Gerald's contemporaries at Eton.

45 Adapted by Edward Rose from the novel by Stanley Weyman, playing at the Haymarket Theatre.

Laura,[46] and was away for luncheon and tea. We lunched at 1, and afterwards went to the Zoo, bussing to Park Lane, and then to Baker St. We saw nothing particular – except a Klippspringer [*sic*] – a little yellow and black spotted creature – Thoby says renowned for jumping – The Chimpanzee – Daisy – came out of her cage, and sat affectionately in Nessas arms, holding on to her neck tight. There was a beautiful Gibbon which sang most melodiously while we were there – It is supposed to say "Hoolock" – We undergrounded back home from St Johns Wood and got home about tea time.

Jo Fisher came to dinner, Will Vaughan came in afterwards, and so did Roland Vaughan-Williams.[47]

Nessa discovered an extra 10 shillings in our purse, which if Stella pays the 5ss. she owes, will make us have £2(almost) independently of the £2, kept back for Stella's present – We shall have to be very economical. What with photographs, birthdays etc – Toast[?] to tips.

O

Wednesday 13 January

Nessa went to drawing. Us three and Stella went to Hyams[48] to buy Thoby a suit and A. shoes. Went on top of bus to Piccadilly Circus – most icy – dismounted and went to A.B.C. at the corner and had coffee and cakes – Then bussed up to Oxford St. Came home in a fourwheeler, and got back in time for luncheon. After luncheon Nessa went back to her drawing; Stella to the work house,[49] and Father to Wimbledon. Thoby and Adrian took off the top of the old organ, and examined its inside, which was most curious, but were not able to do what they wanted – to take out the broken bit of the handle. Then they tried soldering on by a piece of lead the remains of the proper handle – But this failed also, and the organ in a most dilapidated condition. We went out after these performances into the gardens, and afterwards A. bought a 2lb. pair of dumbells, with which he is going to strengthen his arms! Had dinner at

---

46 Laura Makepeace Stephen (1870-1945), the only child of Leslie Stephen's marriage to Minny Thackeray, spent most of her life in institutions for the mentally disturbed.

47 A cousin of Ralph Vaughan Williams, who was to marry Adeline Fisher; see June 1897, n.15.

48 Hyam & Co., Ltd, clothiers, 134-40 Oxford Street, W.

49 Kensington Union Workhouse, St Mary Abbott's, Marloes Road, W. In England, workhouses were established by the parish and administered by Guardians of the Poor where paupers were lodged and the able-bodied set to work. *OED.*

7.15, and started for the Pr[ince]. of Wales Theatre. Jack, Stella and us four in the landau. The play[50] very amusing – or rather Arthur Roberts very amusing – the play, to me at least, inexplicable. Coming back the carriage window was broken by a loafer[?] – Home at 11.30. Play – the White Silk Dress –

0

Thursday 14 January

Stella was away all the morning and afternoon at Laura. We four went out to Black[51] about my medicine in the morning, and did nothing else. I was extremely irritable all day, and was perpetually fighting over something – At last, Nessa and I marched out in the afternoon by ourselves. Walked by Kensington Palace – most soothing – Tried to imagine ourselves in the middle of last century – Everything very quiet and old-fashioned – Miss Maria [Vanessa] much struck by the picturesqueness of the red bricks in the winters day. T. and A. had meanwhile walked to the Marble Arch, and had bought chestnuts, which they roasted in the dining room after tea. Gerald away, and Jack out for dinner, so Stella scrubbed A. and T. Finished the 2nd vol. of Carlyle – the first part of his life before he settled in London – Most extraordinary phenomenon – When I was dressing to go to the Play on Wednesday, Pauline declared that one of my shoes was missing. Has not been found or even traced since. Suspicion centres in Jerry – who has taken to paying us visits up here. A. says he must be held innocent till proved guilty.

0

Friday 15 January

Nessa went to drawing. Got 1st volume of the Carlyles Life in London. Thoby, A., Stella and I, went to the stores;[52] about a clothes basket as far as I could make out – Bussed back. While waiting for our bus at Hyde Park Corner, another one came past, in the corner of which I saw a grin-

---

50 *The White Silk Dress*, a musical in which Arthur Roberts sang and acted.
51 Probably James Watt Black, physician, 15 Clarges Street, Piccadilly, W.
52 Army & Navy Stores, Victoria Street, SW.

ning nodding face – Lisa Hoby – and also Constance.[53] Nothing more than grins and nods could be exchanged happily, and the busses soon carried us apart. In the afternoon Thoby Adrian father and I, went to the S[outh]. K[ensington]. M[useum]. Went in by a new door[54] – near where the Middletons[55] used to live, much shorter than going round to the Brompton Road entrance. Saw the pictures and the manuscripts. Dinner at 7. Went to the Gay Parisienne.[56] Very good indeed – especially the Frenchman and Ruth. Much the same kind of thing as the White Silk dress, only better. Home by 12, or a little before. My shoe miraculously turned up in time to go to the play. Were given little boxes of Cherry Blossom[57] at the play – To be given to Pauline and Lizzie – Terrible snow for the next week – Horrible wind, freezing. Altogether disgusting.

Saturday 16 January

Did not get up till 10.30. Miss Kay[58] came to see Stella. Stella and Nessa and I went to High St. When we got there S. found she had brought no money with her, and decided to go round to Margarets[59] to borrow some. Margaret was in her room. Stella got 6.6. out of her, and we bought buns for the monkeys and Zoo animals whom we were going to visit. After luncheon we – us four – started for the Zoo. Went to St John's Wood and walked down to the Zoo. Saw much the same creatures as on Tuesday. Almost all got nuts – Went away about 4, and got our trains safely. Adrian and Thoby insisted upon buying manuscript books at Youngs, which was just shutting, which took some time. Then A. bought a lb. of chestnuts at Butts as usual. Read after tea on my sofa in the other room. T. and A. began again on the unfortunate organ – May it never be restored to its old powers!

Florrie stakes her existence (which Lizzie thinks rather impious) on a

---

53 Elisa (b. *c.* 1879) and Constance Victoria (b.1883), the daughters of John Hoby (d.1902) of 29 South Street, Thurloe Square, South Kensington, a bookseller and stationer with a shop at 35 Chapel Street, Belgrave Square, SW.

54 The new door to the South Kensington Museum (later the Victoria & Albert Museum) was probably that in Exhibition Road.

55 Presumably a reference to Bella and John Henry Middleton; see n. 88.

56 By George Dance and Ivan Caryll, at the Duke of York's Theatre.

57 A famous brand of boot polish.

58 Angela Kay (b.1872), daughter of Sir Ughtred and Lady Kay-Shuttleworth of 28 Prince's Gardens, SW; see Feb. 1897, n. 20.

59 Margaret ('Marny') Vaughan in Young Street, W; see n. 62.

cold winter. As we came home from the Zoo it was snowing, and the wind most horrible, and cold – Gerald out to dinner. Father reading us Esmond.[60]

O

Sunday 17 January

Snow over everything. Stayed in all the morning and read most of it – Nessa and Thoby had wonderful games of chasing each other round the table – Gerald went to Oxford for the day. In the afternoon I persuaded the others to take a walk – which was most horrid – round the Serpentine; the wind ferocious and icy; everything slushy and cold and damp – It was not thawing, I think, but the roads managed to become a mass of dirty melting snow. Very glad to get back home and have tea, which was at half past four. Afterwards we sat in the drawing room, and heard General Beadle[61] discourse – till the Vaughans (Emma and Marny)[62] came.

Eustace Hills came to supper, and afterwards Father read poetry – The bath water lukewarm which was most disappointing. Found an old knife, which I have polished and sharpened, and which for the future shall be my knife. The organ again under Ts and As hands. Just as the handle was got well on, and they were going to turn it, everything smashed, and it is hoped that they will give it up.

Monday 18 January

Nessa went to her drawing in the morning. Stella and I meant to go to High St. but she insisted upon putting the books in the nursery tidy, so that it was too late to do anything, but bicycle once or twice up and down the road. Freezing hard – Slippery frozen snow all over the roads and pavements – No wind but horribly cold – Phil Burne-Jones[63] came and sat with us while we had luncheon and afterwards talked to father

---

60 William Makepeace Thackeray, *The History of Henry Esmond*, 1852.
61 Major General James Pattle Beadle (d.1902), living at 6 Queen's Gate Gardens, SW. ('the Prince of Talkers': QB, I, p.29); he was a distant cousin of Julia Stephen and father of James Prinsep Barnes Beadle (1863-1947), painter of military subjects and a pupil of G. F. Watts.
62 AVS's first cousins, Emma ('Toad') Vaughan (1874-1960), the youngest sister of Margaret ('Marny', 1862-1929), both living at 9 Kensington Square Mansions, Young Street, W. They were the daughters of Adeline and Henry Halford Vaughan.
63 Philip Burne-Jones (1861-1926), son of the artist, Sir Edward Burne-Jones.

about some mystery – probably Stellas wedding present – in the study – We four and Stella bussed to Regent St. and went to the Polytechnic to see the animatograph which was very good, and then had some coffee and buns at an A.B.C.

Afterwards A. and S. went to Liberty[64] to buy some stuff, and we three to the New Gallery where Mr Watts[65] is exhibiting his pictures – We got home at tea time. Thoby had a letter from Graves enclosing orders (or whatever they're called) for four seats – for the White Elephant[66] which Thoby has been to. Gerald is going to get another place, and we shall go tomorrow night – Gerald out at the Digbys[67] where Enid and Sylvia[68] are going. Nessa had a most dismal letter from Lisa Hoby. This diary today beats my 1896 diary[69] – Wonderful creature!

0

Tuesday 19 January
Thoby and I walked to the Marble Arch and back in the morning. Stella and Nessa and Adrian went out shopping in High Street – Thawing slowly – comparatively warm and comfortable. Stella made me have beef tea for luncheon – most disgusting stuff. After lunch we all (us four S. and father) went to the National Portrait Gallery. It was rather dull, and we spent our time in yawning. Father left us, and we went on to the National Gallery, which neither Thoby or A. has ever seen. But it was four as we got there, and just shutting up. So we paid a visit to our usual shops – corner of Piccadilly Circus, just where the bus starts, and had hot buttered toast. Paid a visit to Aunt Minna[70] on the way home. She

---

64 Liberty & Co. of Regent Street specialised in oriental and artistic fabrics and furnishings.

65 George Frederic Watts (1817-1904), painter. He lived for over 20 years at Little Holland House, Kensington, with Sara, *née* Pattle (1816-87), and Henry Thoby Prinsep (1793-1878), Julia Stephen's aunt and uncle; see QB, I, p.15. The Exhibition at the New Gallery, Regent Street, was in celebration of Watts's 80th birthday.

66 A farce in three acts, by R. E. Carson, playing at the Comedy Theatre.

67 Unidentified.

68 Enid and Sylvia (and Ida and Maud) were the Milman sisters and the granddaughters of Henry Hart Milman (1791-1868), the Dean of St Paul's; Sylvia studied painting with Vanessa.

69 Has not survived.

70 Sarah Emily Duckworth (1828-1918) and not, strictly speaking, an aunt to the Stephen children, being the sister of Herbert Duckworth, Julia Stephen's first husband; she lived at 9 Hyde Park Gate, SW.

mysteriously told Nessa and me that she had a spare "Oak Davenport" which she would give us. We accepted it gratefully, not in the least knowing what an Oak Davenport might be. Now Gerald tells us that it is a kind of writing desk – which will be very nice. Dinner at 7.40. Drove to the Comedy, and saw the White Elephant – which was not very good. Home at 11.30. Nessa wrote to ask Lisa Hoby to tea on Saturday.

Finished 1st vol. of Cs Life in London. Got next.

Oo

Wednesday 20 January
Nessa went to drawing. The "Oak Davenport" arrived, carried down the street by T. and Maurice.[71] Was put in the night nursery. It is a great writing desk, with drawers and cupboards everywhere. Rather too high to write at, but will do very well for papers and odds and ends. Dated 1690.

We three and Stella went to Gloucester Rd. Station to get A.s ticket[72] and then she went on to see Cousin Mia,[73] and Thoby went for a walk in the gardens, and A. and I home. Freezing, windy and horrible. Nessa did not go to her drawing in the afternoon. Went with S. to the Nat[ional]. Gall[ery]. and afterwards went to Oxford St, where S. had to change some razors. We went into an ABC as usual. When father was reading to us in the evening, Enid MacKenzie[74] in her night gown and Mr M's fur coat came in. Their servants room had caught fire – Gerald rushed over, and poured pails of water over the place – Then came roaring down the street a fire engine – shouting and halloaing. The men jumped off in a moment and found that the fire had succumbed to pails of water before their arrival. Leaving three of their men, they galloped off again – A crowd had followed them, and stood gaping in the street. Then came *four* more fire engines – the men swearing at finding nothing to do. Soon they mounted, the crowed yelled and the horses cantered away – So ends the fire –

---

71 Possibly Aunt Minna's manservant.

72 A season ticket to enable Adrian to travel on the Metropolitan Railway to Westminster School which he had been attending since September 1896.

73 Julia Stephen's first cousin, Maria MacNamara, *née* Bayley (d.1917), wife of the surgeon Nottridge Charles MacNamara, FRCS (d.1918), and mother of eight children; they lived in Grosvenor Street, Mayfair.

74 The Muir-Mackenzies were neighbours, living at 21 Hyde Park Gate, SW.

Thursday 21 January

Adrian went back to school. Thoby, Nessa & I walked to Gloucester Rd. station to see about As season ticket, and afterwards went out in to the gardens. The pond all frozen over, except a narrow place round the edge which the Park keepers break.

We had settled to go down to Westminster in the afternoon, to meet A. there and learn whether he would be allowed off early, in which case we were going to have gone together to Bensons[75] in Bond St. to buy Stella and Jack a lamp for their wedding present – but father said he would go with us, and after lunch came Will [Vaughan], who joined us also, so that we could not do it – moreover A. got out no earlier than usual – We walked about in Deans Yd, and Little Deans Yard, round which are built the school houses – Lost ourselves in the odd cloisters and squares, and finally came out by the Abbey door. We went in, and found a service just ending – After it was finished the Abbey was shut and we had to go – Walked back with Father and Will to Hyde Park Corner – met on the way the great Sir William Harcourt[76] – muffled up in a beautiful fur coat, very fat and comfortable – Father went on to tea with Mrs Humphry Ward,[77] and we took the bus home. Somehow Nessa and I escaped paying our fourpence – Met Justine[78] coming up the road. She is much better, and gave back the money Stella had lent her, and a glass of Californian Honey as a present!

O

---

75 W.A.S. Benson & Co., metal workers: lamps, candlesticks, &c., 82-3 New Bond Street, W.

76 Sir William Harcourt (1827-1904) was at the time leader of the opposition; at Cambridge, an Apostle (a member of the University's élite intellectual secret society), his chief sparring partner was James Fitzjames Stephen. In preparing his brother's biography, Leslie Stephen would have seen a good deal of Harcourt.

77 Mary Augusta (Mrs Humphry) Ward (1851-1920), niece of Matthew Arnold, popular novelist, and an opponent of woman suffrage.

78 Justine Nonon, a figure from AVS's childhood, 'was immensely old. . . . She was a hunchback; and walked like a spider. . . . I used to sit on her knee. . . . She was French; she had been with the Thackerays . . . and used to bring Adrian a glass jar of honey. I got the notion that she was extremely poor . . .' *MoB*, p.74.

Friday 22 January
Nessa went to her drawing. Stewart[79] arrived here at 11, and he and Thoby went to see Lord Leightons pictures.[80] Stella and I went to Soars[81] with a photograph, to Aldous'es[82] for some flowers for Lisas[83] tea party, and to the Gloucester Rd. Station about As season ticket, which is now finally disposed of. Outside the station we met Mr Gibbs,[84] and Stella taking the green bus to go to Cousin Mias, he walked all the way back home with me. It began to snow, and he made me hold his arm, and trot along under his umbrella. He promised to come round on Monday morning – Aunt Mary sent me, as a birthday present, a case of jams – 10 pots of jam – four of which I have kept, the rest, being nasty ones, were given to Thoby. It snowed all the afternoon, and Nessa and I did not go out – Thoby and Stewart went to the Animatograph at the Polytechnic, and came back here at 4. Tea for them was at 4.15, and at a quarter to 5, they started for Clifton. Nessa and I had a quiet tea alone, though not allowed to read – After tea, Nessa drew at the "Oak Davenport" which holds all our paper now and is very nice, and I wrote on a table beside her. Florence Maitland[85] came to tea, sobbing for her monkey, which Fred had made her sell – She wished to rebuy it on the way home, but Gerald, who went to the station with her, forbade this – Harry Stephen[86] for dinner. Jack had to go out on business.

$0+$

---

79 Charles Robert Stewart (1879-1944), Thoby's Clifton College friend, living at Hove, Sussex; he entered Selwyn College, Cambridge in October 1897, was ordained deacon, 1902, and priest, 1903.

80 At the Winter Exhibition in Burlington House.

81 Probably Soars, carver and gilder, 1 Sussex Villas, Kensington, W.

82 James Aldous, florist, 36-8 Gloucester Road, SW.

83 Probably Lisa Hoby; see 23 January.

84 Frederick Waymouth Gibbs (1821-98), barrister and long-time friend of Leslie Stephen; he came as a child to the home of Sir James Stephen (1789-1859) as a companion to Leslie's eldest brother, Herbert (1822-46).

85 AVS's first cousin, Florence Maitland, *née* Fisher (1863-1920), wife of F. W. Maitland; see Jan. 1905, n.12.

86 AVS's first cousin, Harry Lushington Stephen, 3rd Bt (1860-1945), third son of Leslie Stephen's eldest brother James Fitzjames, 1st Bt (1829-94); Judge of the Exchequer Division of the High Court and, from 1901 to 1914, a judge in the High Court of Calcutta.

Saturday 23 January

Nessa began lessons with father – It is not yet settled whether I am to do any or not this term – Eustace Hills came in the morning and he and Stella went out together – Snowing and blowing hard – Nessa and I went out in the gardens for a short walk, but it was so icy that we came quickly home again – Two or three degrees below freezing. Stella told us that Jack had been having an operation this morning, which will make him stay in bed for three weeks. Not at all a serious one however. Snowed all the afternoon, so that we did not go out. A. came home for lunch, as the snow has made football impossible. Lisa Hoby arrived here about 3, and was shut up talking confidences with Nessa till tea time. A. and I mooned about the house – Everything cold, and uncomfortable. Stella went to see Jack – Found him very well. After tea we told ghost stories, and at last, about 7 o'clock LH declared she must go – Went accordingly. Nessa and she are to go to Mr Watts's pictures next Saturday morning together – Began the Newcomes.[87] Letter from Georgie for Thoby – Florries cold winter prophesies look as if they were coming true – Stella has made me some beautiful red cuffs, which I have forgotten to put on or I should be writing more legibly.

O

Sunday 24 January

Stella and us three walked up to Lisa Stillmans[88] in the morning, to say that Jack could not sit to her. Saw her and Effie, and Peggy's new dog called Bruno. Very cold, but not blowing – Eustace Hills came to lunch. Afterwards he and Stella went to see Jack – Sylvia and Maud [Milman] came in the afternoon with a present for Stella from Mr Milman[89] –

---

87 William Makepeace Thackeray, *The Newcomes*, 1853.
88 Lisa, a portrait painter, and Effie, a sculptress, were the middle and eldest daughters, respectively, of Maria Stillman (1844-1927), a Pre-Raphaelite painter, and William James Stillman (1828-1901), American painter and special correspondent for *The Times*; Stillman's first wife, Laura Mack, had committed suicide in 1869. Peggy Middleton (b.1894) was the daughter of Bella, the youngest of the Stillman sisters and the widow of John Henry Middleton (1846-96), Slade Professor of Fine Art at Cambridge, 1886-95, and Art Director of the Victoria and Albert Museum, 1892-96, who commited suicide on 10 June. Bella and Peggy Middleton now lived with the Stillmans at 12 Campden Hill Gardens, W.
89 Arthur Milman, father of the four Milman sisters (see n.68), lived at 22 The Grove, Boltons, SW, now called Little Boltons.

Nessa and I resolved to light a fire in the night nursery – We had to make it three times before anything more than the paper would catch – At last a feeble piece of wood began to burn, and by judicious bits of paper and coal every now and then, a most respectable fire was made. This was triumphant, as Pauline had offered to do it for us, being scornful of our methods, and we had refused to allow her to touch it – this being accomplished Nessa sat down at the Davenport to write to Thoby, and I read on the table behind her. I finished the last volume of Carlyles Life in London before the tea bell rang –

After tea Nessa did her lessons, and I wrote, the fire having warmed the hands sufficiently –

After dinner father read Tennyson. A hot bath for the first time these three weeks. Adrian came up at night.

O

Monday 25 January
My birthday. No presents at breakfast and none til Mr Gibbs came, bearing a great parcel under his arms, which turned out to be a gorgeous Queen Elizabeth – by Dr Creighton.[90] I went out for a walk round the pond after breakfast with father, it being Nessas drawing day. Went out with Stella to Hatchards[91] about some book for Jack, and then to Regent St. for flowers and fruit for him; then to Wimpole St. to see how he had slept, and then to Miss Hill[92] in Marylebone Rd. Jo [Fisher] was there discussing the plans for Stellas new cottages with Miss Hill. All three learnedly argued over them for half an hour, I sitting on a stool by the fire and surveying Miss Hills legs –

Nessa went back to her drawing after lunch, and Stella and I went to Story's[93] to buy me an arm chair, which is to be Ss present to me – We got a very nice one, and I came straight home, while Stella went on to Wimpole St. Gerald gave me £1, and Adrian a holder for my stylograph

---

90 Mandell Creighton, *Queen Elizabeth*, 1896.
91 Hatchard's, booksellers, 187 Piccadilly, W.
92 Octavia Hill (1838-1912), philanthropist and founder of the Society of Women Housing Managers in England, lived with her sister, Miranda, at 190 Marylebone Road, NW. She was a pioneer of housing reform and of improving the dwellings of the poor; in 1884 she was appointed by the Ecclesiastical Commissioners to manage their Southwark property.
93 Story & Co., 49-53 Kensington High Street, W.

– Father is going to give me Lockharts Life of Scott[94] – Cousin Mia gave me a diary and another pocket book. Thoby writes to say that he has ordered films for me. Got Carlyles Reminiscences,[95] which I have read before. Reading four books at once – The Newcomes, Carlyle, Old Curiosity Shop,[96] and Queen Elizabeth –

O

Tuesday 26 January
Stella went to Jack in the morning, and Nessa and I sat over the fire and lounged. We went out into the gardens and met Mr Stapleton[97] and his daughter (or grand daughter?) who said they were going up to the Pond, and so we went with them. Mr Stapleton a chatty old gentleman, talked to Nessa of St Ives, and Haslemere and cricket – The pond is frozen over, but not yet ready for skating – it was only just freezing in the morning, with a strong wind blowing – from the West – but as cold as any East. After lunch Stella went again to Jack, and father, Nessa and I went for a walk in the gardens – Started by the Pond, and then round to the Serpentine and right down to the other end; across the road, and home by the barracks. The Duke of Devonshire[98] passed us father said. Finished my birthday cake for tea, so it has had a very short life, poor thing. Wrote to Thoby and Cousin Mia after tea – Father finished Esmond to us this evening – His present for me came – Ls Life of Scott – in a great brown paper parcel – I expected one huge closely printed book, but instead behold 10 beautiful little blue and brown gilt leathered backs, big print, and altogether luxurious. The nicest present I have had yet.

O

Wednesday 27 January
Father and I went for a walk after breakfast. Round the Pond, on which men were sliding and one or two skating, though notices were up to for-

94 J. G. Lockhart, *Memoirs of the Life of Sir Walter Scott, Bart.*, 1839, 10 vols.
95 Thomas Carlyle, *Reminiscences*, ed. J. A. Froude, 1881.
96 Charles Dickens, *The Old Curiosity Shop*, 1840.
97 Probably John Stapleton, living at 7 Pelham Place, South Kensington, SW; otherwise unidentified.
98 Spencer Compton Cavendish, 8th Duke of Devonshire (1833-1908), statesman and a member of the Government.

bid them – Afterwards I went out with Stella to Wimpole St., where we heard that Jack had had a very good night, and then to Grosvenor St. to see the house which was burnt on Monday night.[99] The windows were all broken, and we saw into black empty rooms; the roof was off, and everything was burnt and blackened. Icicles hung down where the water had been thrown – The house next door was black too, though not actually burnt. There was a crowd standing round, and looking at the house. We went on to Curzon St. to see Flora Baker,[100] and tell her about Jack, and then bussed to High St. to buy S a hat, and home again in time for lunch. N lunched with the Milmans with Marie[101] who was full of the fire; through which however she had slept. A came home about 3, there being no football, and we went to Gloucester Rd. station about an umbrella which he had left in the train. Were told to go to the Lost Property Office at Moorgate St[ation]. We went on up to the Pond, which we found guarded by 6 or 7 park keepers, to prevent the people from going on the ice. One park keeper said that there would be skating tomorrow. It was not freezing when we came away.

Father began the Antiquary[102] to us. Wrote to Marthe[103] who sent me a card. Finished 1st vol. of C[arlyle]s R[eminiscences]

Thursday 28 January
Stella went in the morning to Jack. Nessa and I looked up our skates and went to the Pond to see if there was any skating. It was just above freezing, but a good many people were on the ice, though notices were up forbidding them – After some time we gathered up courage, and slithered about near the edge. Then we joined hands, and got on fairly well – the ice was very bad in parts, and in parts good. My left leg (attributed to the left skate being crooked) was very weak and unhappy, but grew stronger after a time. Nessa most respectable, and able to go comfortably alone. In the afternoon S went to the work house, and father walked with Nessa and me up to the Pond – It was most dreadful ice

---

99 On 26 January, the town house of Constance, Countess De La Warr, at 60 Grosvenor Street, W, was destroyed by a fire which spread so quickly that the Dowager Lady De La Warr had to jump out of a window on to a mattress.

100 Probably the sister of Major George Duff Baker (1860-1938) of the Royal Artillery; they lived with their mother at 38 Curzon Street.

101 Probably Maria Milman, sister of Robert Milman (1816-79), Bishop of Calcutta, and the niece of Henry Hart Milman.

102 Sir Walter Scott, *The Antiquary*, 1816.

103 Unidentified.

now – the top thawed, and cracks and holes everywhere. More people were on it, and it was impossible to get a nice skate – It began to snow, and the wind (a west one) rose, so we took off our skates and went back home. I have decided that Jack is to give me skates for a birthday present, though the thaw is sure to set in directly – in fact it looks as though it had already. On Saturday we are to go to Wimbledon with Gerald if the ice will bear – Jack had a very good night. Going on alright –

O

Friday 29 January
Walked in the morning with father. Went round the Pond as usual. No one skating, and we heard that 40 of yesterday's crowd had fallen in – and been dosed with "immersion mixture" – It was just freezing. Nessa at her drawing – Stella and I went to Westerton,[104] about a book for Jack, and then bussed from Hyde Park Corner to Victoria St[reet]. We bought skates at the Stores – Jacks present to me. S also bought Nessa a pair. They are screwed on to your boots by 8 screws, and have nothing else – cost 17.6d. Took the Royal Blue from V. station and got out at Oxford St. Went to Wimpole St., and asked after Jack – Miss Daniel[105] said he was remarkably fit, and so we went away again. Bussed home. After Lunch father took me to see Carlyles house [106] in Chelsea – Walked there – Went over the house, with an intelligent old woman who knew father and everything about him – We saw the drawing room, and dining room, and Cs sound proof room, with double walls – His writing table, and his pens, and scraps of his manuscripts – Pictures of him and of her [Jane Welsh Carlyle] everywhere. Took a hansom home – Nessa and I asked the park keeper whether there was skating, were told no, and so came back. We are to go with our new skates to Wimbledon Park tomorrow if it freezes tonight – Thawed most of today –

O

Saturday 30 January
Woke up to find it thawing hard. Everything dripping, and skating out

104 Charles Westerton, librarian, 27 St George's Place, SW.
105 Probably the matron of the nursing home.
106 24 Cheyne Row, Chelsea.

of the question.[107] Our beautiful skates are put away in their boxes till next winter. Nessa met Lisa Hoby at Sloane St. as they had agreed, and went with her and Constance H. to Mr Watts's pictures.

Margaret [Marny] Vaughan came just as we (S and I) were going out, so that we had not time to go to Kittie's[108] as we had meant. Bussed to Bond St. and up to Oxford St. and asked after Jack at Wimpole St. – Stella went up and sat with him for a quarter of an hour. I waited downstairs with Miss Daniel, and several other odd people. When S came down, she said we must post off to Ebury St. to fetch the French Revolution[109] which Jack wanted and which Eustace had promised to send him, but had forgot – Took a hansom there, and sent it off by a messenger. Hansomed back home again. A in for lunch, because of the rain. Jack had said we could easily skate in the afternoon – the ice always safe 4 days after the thaw had set in but father would not hear of this – anyhow the rain made it impossible. Went with Stella to Bond St., she going on to have tea with Jack – She put us in to a four wheeler, the busses being full, and sent us home – Aunt Minna came up here after tea, and examined our rooms – and was satisfied.

Finished the 2nd vol. of C's Reminiscences – Tomorrow I shall begin my beautiful Lockhart.

Sunday 31 January
Got up very late indeed – about 10 o'clock – Went up to read with father, and then began my beloved Lockhart – which grows more and more beautiful every day – Read all the morning. In the afternoon we (Vanessa, A and I) went for a walk in the gardens – Round the Pond, which is thawing hard, and broken up all round the edges, and by Kensington Palace – Came home at 4.15. Jerry did not accompany us having been washed by Vanessa after luncheon. He later came down to us while

107 In a letter from Leslie Stephen to Thoby, dated 30 January 1897: 'It is a regular thaw, though Stella wants to take V[anessa] and V[irginia] to a skating place in the Botanical Gardens. I said that it was not safe as a lot of people fell into the round pond on Friday and the thaw will have made the ice worse. *She* said that Jack said it was safe. I said that Jack was a —— no, I did not say that because I have been told that she is to marry him on the 1st of April: a very proper day I think.' QB, I, p.52.

108 Katherine (Kitty) Maxse, *née* Lushington (1867-1922), whose parents and AVS's had been friends; in 1890 she married Leopold (Leo) Maxse (1864-1932), editor and owner of the *National Review* to which Leslie Stephen, and later AVS, contributed articles.

109 Thomas Carlyle, *The French Revolution*, 1837.

we were at tea, and caused great confusion – biscuits thrown under the table, where Nessa rescued them in a marvellous way with her feet – Stella came down and carried the little creature off. After tea Nessa did her lessons, and I wrote the History of Ms. and Js.[110] Grand Tour. Eustace Hills came to supper – and Jo stayed. Long bath room conference with Nessa. Water extremely hot – almost too much so – Have not yet given back Carlyles Reminiscences but I mean to tomorrow. Poor Queen Elizabeth gets on at the rate of 10 pages a day – Old Curiosity Shop always a fair day's battle[?] drawing to an end thank goodness. Newcomes a supper and odd moment book. Father read Peter Bell.[111]

O

110 Probably a reference to M[aria']s and J[an']s 'Grand Tour' – i.e. a literary work in progress which no longer survives.
111 William Wordsworth, *Peter Bell*, 1819.

Monday 1 February

Nessa went to her drawing. Father and I went out – up to Rotten Row, and back again. Afterwards Stella and I went to Dr Seton[1] – He gave me new medicines, but S. forgot to ask him about the cycling or lessons.[2] A terrible idea started that Stella and I should take lodgings at Eastbourne or some such place, where Jack is going next week – Impossible to be alone with those two creatures, yet if I do not go, Stella will not, and Jack particularly wishes her to – The question is, whether Nessa will be allowed to come too – If so it would be better – but goodness knows how we shall come out of this *quandary* as Vanessa calls it. Walked in the gardens with father in the afternoon – Very misty and quiet – Walked by Kensington Palace – Had a letter from Georgie this morning, offering me an enclosure as a birthday present; unluckily the enclosure was left out – I have been in a dreadful temper all day long, poor creature – and lead Stella and Vanessa a life – Can not protest *too* strongly against going (though I do) or else S will have to give it up, and her poor young man would be miserable – but think of going! If we go we should start next Monday, and stay away till Saturday. This is a dreadful fix – Poor Miss Jan is bewildered.

O

Tuesday 2 February

Raining hard. Stella went at 9.30 o'clock to Oxford, and Father at 10 to Cambridge. Nessa and I stayed in and did nothing in the morning. I finished the 1st vol. of Scott, and began the 2nd. Lunched alone together, which was very nice. Mrs Flower[3] had told Nessa that they would go to the Nat[ional]. Por[trait]. Gall[ery]. this afternoon at 2.15. A telegram came to say it was too dark, and so at 3, Nessa, Pauline and I started for

---

1   Dr David Elphinstone Seton (*c.*1827-1917) was treating AVS since her mental break-down in the summer of 1895; he remained the Stephens' family doctor until the death of Sir Leslie in 1904 (at the time he was also the Woolfs' family physician).

2   Lessons had ceased in the summer of 1895 and were not resumed until 15 February 1897.

3   Mrs E. Wickham Flower, a painter of flowers, active 1872-3, who gave Vanessa instruction in art history and took her to galleries. Her husband, Wickham Flower (*c.*1835-1904), was a Fellow of the Society of Antiquaries; they lived at Great Tangley Manor (decorated by William Morris in 1890) in Croydon, Surrey. Reference is made to her in the 14 January 1894 issue of *Hyde Park Gate News*: 'Mrs. Wickham Flower kindly gave Adrian 5 tickets for Santa Clause at the Lyceum.'

Wimpole St. Bussed to Bond St, then to Oxford St, by my skilful pilot-
ing reached 29 Wimpole St in safety – First we did a little business with a
dressmaker over the way. Jack is on the sofa, looks rather well than
otherwise – talked about dogs and the country next week. Told him with
great plainness that I *could not* go with him and St alone – Stayed with
him about half an hour, and had some tea; then took Poor Pauline, who
had waited patiently downstairs all this time, to an ABC – After a little
difficulty – the streets being rather mixed, I found Oxford St., and a bus
for Piccadilly again. Successfully got a Red bus, and home to a third tea
at 5.30 – Adeline[4] and Stella came back just before dinner, father not till
afterwards. Lady Emily Lytton[5] engaged to be married. Georgie sent
me his enclosure, which is a cheque for a pound. Makes our finances
very comfortable. Wrote to him and to Thoby for films he sent me yesterday.

O

Wednesday 3 February

Thick fog in the early part of the morning, so that father and I did not go
for our usual walk – It cleared up perfectly by 10 o'clock – Father and
Stella were shut up in the drawing room. Adeline and Marie[6] in the
dining room, so I was forced to stay up here and read – Stella and A[de-
line]. and I went to the Watts pictures. Stella left us and went on to
Wimpole St. Adeline and I came home soon in a bus. Adrian for luncheon, as he had to go on to Fairbanks[7] afterwards. I went with him and
Stella, and sat in the waiting room reading papers till he was ready. Mr F
had only filled his tooth with soft stuff as it has to be taken out. Mr F
gave S two tickets for As You Like It,[8] on Friday night – Stella and
A[drian] and I went to Hyams about As. boots, and then to an A.B.C. for
coffee and hot buttered scones, and then to Buszards[9] for Éclairs for
Jacks tea – A and I got into a hansom and went home – S. went on up to
Jacks. Eustace Hills came for dinner, and afterwards he and Stella and

---

4   AVS's first cousin, Adeline Fisher (1870-1951), third daughter of Mary and Herbert
    W. Fisher.
5   Emily Lytton (1874-1964), third daughter of the Earl of Lytton; she married the
    architect Edwin Lutyens in 1897.
6   Possibly Maria Milman (see Jan. 1897, n.101).
7   Dr Fairbanks, dentist, 18 George Street, Hanover Square, W.
8   See March 1897, n.8.
9   Buszard's Tea Rooms, 197-210 Oxford Street, W.

Adeline went on to the Speakers party.[10] Ida [Milman] has asked us to tea there tomorrow – No way out of it – Nessa has had to answer we are very pleased –

O

Thursday 4 February
In the morning Nessa Adeline Stella and I went to Walkers[11] the dress maker opposite Jack, about our jackets. Stood and had them tried on, by a horrible fuzzy female – Then Stella paid Jack a visit for a moment, it being 1.30, and we came home. Finished the 2nd vol of Scott, and began the third, also the Old Curiosity Shop – thank goodness. Now poor Queen Elizabeth must be despatched and then I shall be left to Scott and the Newcomes, which will last me some time. In the afternoon Stella and Adeline went to pictures, and Nessa and Father and I went for a walk in the gardens. Came home about 4, and father found a letter from Phil Burne Jones asking for Lisa's picture[12] – Nessa and I, after much consultation, decided to take it in a hansom to the Grange,[13] to ask there where P[hil]. B[urne]. J[ones]. lived, to take it to his studios, and then to go on to the Milmans. To begin with we did not find the Grange for some time, then we were sent on to 9 St Pauls Studios, which were found with difficulty, and then on to the Grove Boltons. Arrived just at 5, having had to pay the cabby 3s. instead of the 2.6. father had given us. Had a long dreary tea with the Milmans, dances were discussed afterwards, in which Miss Jan did not take much interest –

O

Friday 5 February
Raining hard, so that I did not go out with father – Adeline, Stella and I

---

10 William Court Gully (1835-1909), Speaker of the House of Commons, gave his first full-dress dinner party to members of Parliament and other distinguished guests that evening.
11 Probably Misses B. & M. Walker, Dressmakers, 8 Great Marylebone St (now part of New Cavendish St), which intersected Wimpole Street.
12 Presumably Lisa Stillman's portrait of Julia Stephen.
13 The Grange, 49 North End Road, West Kensington, was the home of Sir Edward Burne-Jones whose son, Philip, painted at 9 St Paul's Studios, Talgarth Road, West Kensington.

went over to look at Lady Laffans[14] house, which Adeline liked – We walked down to St Alban's Rd with her, as she was going to lunch and go to a concert with the Vaughans, and then come home again. Rained hard after luncheon, and as Stella was going to Wimpole St. and Nessa at her drawing, I stayed in and read – Had two games of billiards with father, both of which he won – Adeline sat with us part of the time at tea, and told us stories of the cabmen and the Vaughans – After tea wrote the Eternal Miss Jan,[15] which has not passed the first day yet, and Nessa did her lessons.

Jack Fisher[16] came here for dinner at 7.15, and they went on to As You Like It, afterwards, with Mr Fairbanks tickets. Kitty [Maxse] came as they were going and sat a little time with father. It is almost settled that we go on Monday to Bognor – Stella Jack Nessa and I, father perhaps coming down for two days from Tuesday to Thursday – Nothing I am afraid seems likely to stop us now – the whole thing most horrible.

O

Saturday 6 February
Stella Adeline Nessa and I went to Bond St. together in the morning – S. and A. left us there, and went on to Burlington House.[17] Nessa and I bussed to Oxford St. and went to Miss Walker the dressmaker about our jackets. Stood for about 20 minutes in her stuffy little room, while she clipped and stuck pins in to us – Afterwards bought two bath buns, and again 2 shortbreads at an ABC – eat the bath buns driving down Oxford St. on the top of the bus; when we got out in Piccadilly, we ran into S and A. They got out at Sloane St., and we finished our meal (the two short-breads) coming home. After luncheon Mr Studd[18] and Simon came – Mr

---

14 Emma, widow of Lt Gen. Sir Michael L. Laffan (d.1882), MP for St Ives, Cornwall, from 1852-7 and Governor of the Bermudas from 1857 until his death. Lady Laffan lived at 28 Hyde Park Gate, SW.

15 'The Eternal Miss Jan' was presumably a work of the imagination, no longer extant; see Jan. 1897, n.110.

16 AVS's first cousin, Arthur (Jack) Fisher (1868-1902), second son of Mary and Herbert W. Fisher.

17 In Piccadilly, which houses the Royal Academy.

18 See Jan. 1897, n.2; Simon appears to have been his dog. AVS would write of him on 11 October 1929: 'He went to Samoa, to paint Whistlers perhaps, & came back when Stella was dead & grieved for her I think. He loved her, in his fumbling ineffective way': *VW Diary*, III.

Studd is starting tomorrow for Samoa – He will probably be away a year. Stella had to go away and fetch Jack and so left Mr S and us together. Simon was photographed in a fur coat and hat and pipe; but at a second photograph we discovered that our Frend [camera] was broken. We went to South Kensington Museum with A[deline] and saw the pictures. A most drunken walk home up Queens Gate – Came home to find Jack comfortably seated in the drawing room, eating tea cake – Bognor almost settled upon – In a temper all the evening –

O

Sunday 7 February
Got up about half past 10. Adrian and Nessa and I went out into the gardens, and so did Stella and Jack, but separately – The ice on the pond all thawed, and boats sailing – The dogs have all got their muzzles off by this time – the muzzling order was taken off one day last week. Nessa therefore, lives in constant fear of a dog fight, and a wicked spotted creature followed us all the way down the street, for the pleasure of fighting Shag on the door step – Nessa waved her umbrella wildly and screamed at Shag and the spotted one, till they slunk away in dismay. Eustace Hills and Scamp[19] for luncheon. After lunch, Mrs. Kay[20] and two little Kays came, and the two little Kays examined the bugs, which they are going to collect. Finished the 3rd vol of Scott, and began the fourth, and finished at last Queen Elizabeth – Now the question is what shall become of her – She is far too beautiful to lie about the nursery at the mercy of the ink pot or of Pauline, and far too big to live in any of our bookshelves. Bognor settled on for tomorrow. Two vols. of Scott and the Newcomes shall go with me.

O

Monday 8 February
Started from Victoria at 10. Gerald came to the station with us, and we were well-supplied with papers. Came here (Bognor) at about 1, and

---

19 Probably Eustace Hills' dog.
20 Sir Ughtred and Lady Kay-Shuttleworth lived at 28 Prince's Gardens, SW, and had six children: two sons, Lawrence (b.1887) and Edward (b.1890) – both killed in the war – and four daughters, Angela (b.1872), Nina (b.1870), Rachel (b.1886), and Catherine (b.1894); the 'two little Kays' would have been Catherine and Edward.

found our lodgings. 4 Cottesmore Crescent. We are the end house of the Crescent, which has never been finished – It was very dismal and cold – looking out on to the sea which is a black and rather inferior sea. We had luncheon, and afterwards went for a walk up the High St., and bought various odds and ends. Jack has lodgings at an hotel near here, but comes always for meals. Bicycled with Nessa once up and down the "Esplanade", but it was too windy and cold for more. Then Jack and Stella sat in the dining room together, and Nessa and I in the drawing room reading. After tea this was repeated till dinner – of which I partook – and after dinner Stella read the guide book aloud to us, and we went to bed. If all the days are to pass like this, my 2 vols of Scott will have a very quick ending. How I wish at this moment that I could find myself in my comfortable arm chair in the nursery at home! Five more days!

O

Tuesday 9 February
Walked in the morning on the sands –

Very dull and grey and windy and cold. Came in soon and read. Nessa and Stella went to the station, and to shops. We wrote yesterday to ask Mr Studd whether we might have Simon here for a week – But he did not come by either of the trains. Father came by the 4 o'clock one – We – N and I – walked along the Esplanade as far as possible, and then came home to tea – After tea read again till dinner time – Began and finished "A Deplorable Affair" by W.E. Norris,[21] which S had got from the Library along with Peter Ibbetson[22] and another book – She also bought a pile of pink wool which I am to convert into a petticoat for Peggy [Middleton]. We may be going to Goodwood[23] and to Arundel,[24] both castles near here – It was too windy to bicycle, and altogether very dismal – We are the only people here, apparently; except 3 or four girls schools, which parade up and down outside in the rain – Two bath chairs have also been discovered. Stella slept in Nessas bed, Father being in her room – This diary is written under difficulties.

O

---

21 William E. Norris, *A Deplorable Affair*, 1892.
22 George du Maurier, *Peter Ibbetson*, 1890.
23 Built by James Wyatt between 1780-1800, the seat of the Duke of Richmond.
24 See April 1897, n.35.

Wednesday 10 February

Bicycled on the sands in the morning. They are very hard and level, and bicycling there for the first 20 minutes is very nice, but it is dull afterwards. We soon went in and read, leaving Stella and Jack to wander about arm in arm. It began by being fine but soon changed to drizzling and mist – I finished the 4th vol. of Scott and began the 5th. Stella Jack Nessa and I went out just before luncheon to change a pipe, and buy various things. After lunch we all walked along the Pier, which is very long, and very very dull. Two ladies fishing but otherwise no one else there at all. Stella and Jack made a pretense of walking on with us, but soon turned and went back alone. We – father Nessa and I – marched on solemnly to the very end of the path leading from the Parade, and then discovered that it only led to another muddy uninteresting road, so we resolved to go no farther. Came home over the fields, which are perfectly flat, and covered with thick clay into which you sink at every step. The drizzle developed into rain before we were half way home, and we splashed along in the mud and wet, umbrellaless, most dismally – "Never saw such an ugly country and such bad weather in my life" is fathers remark – to which I agree –

O

Thursday 11 February

Father went about 10 o'clock. It was raining very steadily, and a mist as usual over everything – Nevertheless, Jack declared that we must get out, so he and Stella went out for a walk, and Nessa and I, with great courage started forth on our adventures. We had no map, no watch, and no knowledge of the country – so that we felt ourselves justified in laying in a stock of biscuits and chocolate in case we were benighted – We found the roads muddier and worse than we have ever ridden on – we were forced to ride on the footpath which in this part of the world is usually a little higher, smoother, and dryer than the road – Soon however we penetrated so far into the country, that footpaths ceased to exist – and therefore we had to plough on as best we might in 6 inches of sticky clay – (Jack declares the country to be a sandy dry one). We had ridden about 3 miles out of Bognor, I suppose, and felt very desperate – The mist blew in our faces, the mud spirted all over us – and behold – here was a school of little boys marching towards us! Their remarks shall not be entered here, Miss Jan says; we pushed on as fast as possible, and at last found ourselves in the respectable High St. of this town. So ends our first bicycle ride. In the afternoon Stella read Mad[emoiselle] de Mersac[25] to us, as we refused to go out again –

O

Friday 12 February
Misting again, though not actually raining. Walked on the sands after breakfast – The Frend [camera] arrived from Becks,[26] in a new box, all rubbed up and beautiful, smelling strongly of Jargonel.[27] We tried shutting Nessa up in the cupboard to put in the films, but there were too many chinks. Then she suggested being covered by her quilt, and everything else that I could lay hands on – She was accordingly, buried in dresses and dressing gowns, till no light could penetrate. Soon she emerged almost stifled having forgotten how to put the film in. I hustled her back again into her burrow, however, and she contrived to manage it – We took 2 photographs of S and J on the sands, but the light was bad and I do not know whether they will come out – We settled to go to Arundel in the afternoon by the 2.25, to see the Castle. We just missed the train, and had to hire a fly – The fly was dragged by a most broken down old horse, all ribs and knock knees. It is 9 miles to Arundel, through very flat uninteresting country – great brown ploughed fields, and ditches and miserable wind blown trees – through this we were drawn first at a trot, which became slower and slower till the creature merely walked – Jack insisted upon something more spirited, but, after a spirt of two minutes, the horse stopped, and refused to move – We got out and walked – The castle shut up and being repaired – Saw a little of the park, only a herd of deer, then tea and home by train. A terrible idea started that S and I should stay here next week –

O

Saturday 13 February
Walked on the Esplanade in the morning – Drizzling and misty as usual

---

25 William E. Norris, *Mademoiselle de Mersac*, 1880, 3 vols, first published in 15 instalments from January 1879 to March 1880 in *The Cornhill Magazine*, which had been edited by Leslie Stephen from 1871 to 1882.

26 R. & J. Beck, Ltd, opticians and makers of telescopes, 68 Cornhill, EC.

27 Presumably the brand name for a chemical preparation using jargonel pear essence, i.e. amyl acetate.

– We came in very soon, and I finished 5th vol. of Scott. Stella read aloud Mad. de Mersac, which I have already read in the Cornhill. After lunch we returned the books to the Library, and bought wild ducks and sprats which Jack wishes to give away. Nessa and Stella packed. I absolutely refused to stay another week in Bognor with Stella, and she, not very much liking the idea either, consented that we should *all* of us go to London – Thank Goodness! Another week of drizzle in that muddy misty flat utterly stupid Bognor (the name suits it) would have driven me to the end of the pier and into the dirty yellow sea beneath – (Hear hear). So all our clothes were squeezed back into the boxes, we had tea at 4.30 – Maginnis carried away the luggage, and, after good byes to Miss Axford,[28] who protested that such weather had never before been seen, we marched away to the Station. We changed at Barnham, and then got a train right through to Victoria which we reached at 8. Gerald was in waiting, and he Nessa and I got in to a four wheeler, and drove home. Found father with his hair and beard cut, and several packages of linen from Mrs Hills.[29] My comfortable arm chair, paper and books – So good bye to that beloved Bognor!

Sunday 14 February

Quite sunshiny and fine. Went out in the morning to the gardens. Stella and Jack went over the bottom house[30] which they may be going to take for 6 months – Adrian found when we came home, that his watch was gone, so we went out again and discovered it and the chain lying in the road, a gentleman just about to pick it up – Gerald out for lunch. After lunch Simon and Augusta[31] appeared. We photographed Simon 6 times – on the chair with a coat and pipe, and lying on the ground – Mr Gibbs came, and wished to know all about Bognor – the great wave and the sea wall – After tea Nessa and I developed in the night nursery. One very good one of Stella and Jack on the sands,[32] the others all dim and under exposed. We took 10 altogether, one having slipped back without being

---

28 Presumably their landlady at Bognor, with Maginnis as one of her staff.

29 Jack's mother, Anna, daughter of the Rt Hon. Sir William R. Grove, and wife of Herbert Augustus Hills (1837-1907), Judge of the Court of Appeals, Cairo, who retired from judicial service in 1903; they lived at Corby Castle, Cumberland.

30 24 Hyde Park Gate, where Stella and Jack were to live after their marriage.

31 AVS evidently meant Augustus – Reginald Augustus (1873-1948) – Arthur Studd's brother, looking after Simon since Arthur's departure for Samoa.

32 This snapshot is probably in the earliest of Vanessa Bell's photograph albums now in the Tate Gallery.

exposed. The Catholic Church came out, but not well, and we thought it too uninteresting to keep. Harry Stephen in bed with influenza. Stella went twice to see him – The batch of films is 1515M.

O

Monday 15 February

Nessa went to her drawing. Jack was here till about 12, as he had to go and see his doctor – I did two Greek exercises by way of beginning lessons, and then Stella and I went out – We went to the Studio[33] to see Mr [J. Watson] Nichol but he was not there, and then we went on to Harry [Stephen] in a cab – Stella saw Herbert[34] who said he was quite well, and getting up, and so we came home. Nessa went back to her studio after lunch, and Stella and I went to Harvey Nichols[35] to buy stuff for Sophie's dress, then bussed up to Baker Street, and went to the Leafs.[36] We saw Lotta and the Baby, who is not yet out of his room, and as fat as ever. Came back by underground to High St. and Stella stopped at DeVere Gardens[37] and saw Harry, while I went back home – My old board has been restocked with blotting paper, and made to look youthful once more, and I use it with great joy after tea, so that Mr Gibbs [blotter] has been removed to the day nursery for scrappiness – whence it comes to pass that I am using him now – Adrian had to sit up late with father doing his sums which finally about 9.30 came right.

O

Tuesday 16 February

Millicent Isham[38] came to see Stella in the morning, stayed talking with

---

33 At Arthur Cope's art school in Pelham Street; J. Watson Nichol was a tutor at the school.

34 AVS's first cousin, Herbert Stephen, 2nd Bt (1857-1932), first son of Mary and James Fitzjames Stephen.

35 Harvey, Nichols & Co., linen drapers, 8-16 Lowndes Terrace, Knightsbridge, SW.

36 Charlotte (Lotta) Leaf (1867-1917), second daughter of John Addington Symonds (1840-93), historian and translator, and wife of Walter Leaf (1852-1927), classical scholar and banker; their son Charles was born in 1896; they lived at 6 Sussex Place, Regent's Park, W.

37 32 De Vere Gardens, W, was the London home of the James Fitzjames Stephen family.

38 AVS's first cousin, Millicent (1866-1961), next to the youngest of the Vaughan sisters; she married Vere Isham, 11th Bt, in 1895.

her till rather late. We got out at last, however, and went to Madame Walker the dressmaker near Wimpole St about our coats which she made very badly. Stella scolded her thoroughly, but Madame Walker said not a word, and looked so provoking that I would willingly have dug her own scissors into her – or at least cropped off a great part of her horrid fuzzy wig which she tickles your nose with – We had to stand and be tryed [*sic*] on all over again, so that when Nessa was finished it was so late that she had to go home alone in a hansom, to have her lunch, as Mrs Flower was going to take her to pictures at 2.15. I stayed and was done at great length and then we took a hansom and came home. In the afternoon Stella and I shopped steadily in High St – bought innumerable things with great business-likeness. We met Peggy and Bella[39] in one of the shops and walked with them to their blue bus. Bought among other things large ream of foolscap of which I mean to appropriate some.

O

Wednesday 17 February
Nessa went to her drawing. Marny turned up early in the morning, and sat with Stella so that I was driven in to the dining room to translate a Hans Andersen[40] story – that is to look out every other word. Afterwards Millicent came, and she and Stella and I went to the studio to see Mr Nichol about Nessa – He said she might come back there at any time to make up her three days[41] – Then Stella and I leaving Millicent and Emma [Vaughan] who had joined us at an Estate Agents, walked home again. When we got to the top of Queens Gate we could not see Shag and Jerry – We came home however, expecting that they would come back soon – Florry after a time was despatched to Queens Gate to search, and came back saying they were nowhere to be seen. So Nessa and I started out, Nessa on her bicycle down Queens Gate, and I in the gardens. Nessa discovered them playing half way down, and I took them home – Ellen[42] was in a dreadful state till her beloved Jerry was safe in her arms again. After this Stella, Father and I went for a walk in the gardens, and after father had gone in, Stella and I went on to shop in

39 See Jan. 1897, n.88.
40 AVS was probably translating one of his German editions, the language she was learning at the time; see QB, I, p.50.
41 For the three days Vanessa missed classes while at Bognor.
42 A servant.

High St. Adrian back for tea. Finished 6th vol. of Scott. Began 7th. Father gave me a book Mr Fabre[43] sent him. Justine [Nonon] came.

O

Thursday 18 February
Very fine and sunny, so we thought we would bicycle down to Cheyne Walk [44] and photograph Simon, the other ones not being good. Arrived at 97, with out any accidents, though once I was forced to dismount in the middle of the road, a van showing a disposition to run at me. We found that the Frend would not work, and were just going out of the garden, when Nessa wound the shutter, and mended it. So we took 8 of the beautiful creature, in a sunny patch at the end of the garden – After lunch Stella went to the workhouse and Nessa and I walked to the studio to get her two sheets of drawing paper, which she wanted to stretch. Home by way of Gloucester Rd. N bought a "sand paper block" from Soars and some note paper – two packets from Lords[45] for 6½ each – The consequence is that I have done nothing but scribble ever since – We developed Simon after tea, two of him are very good, the rest very fair – one has somehow moved, and the dog appears twice on the same plate – I have toned all the other photographs. Jack goes back to his lodging to night.

O

Friday 19 February
Raining in the morning so that I did not go out with father. Miss [Angela] Kay came, and I did some more Hans Andersen. After she had gone Stella and I started off for Victoria, where Stella wanted to get a character of a woman – However when we found out through what slums we must walk to get to this place, S. said it was impossible; so we turned and fled straight home again. In the afternoon S. and I shopped in High St. and afterwards walked up Campden Hill, to the Stillmans.

---

43 Possibly Jean Henri Fabre (1823-1915), French entomologist and professor of natural philosophy; the book has not been identified.

44 Where Arthur Studd lived and Simon was being looked after by his brother Augustus in his absence.

45 Stephen Watkins Lord, bookseller, stationer, and newsagent, 12 Gloucester Road, W.

Found Effie and Lisa in their studio, which is a comfortable little room at the top of a house opposite No. 12.[46] Sat and was talked to by Lisa, till another lady came in. Poor Miss Jan utterly lost her wits dropped her umbrella, answered at random talked nonsense, and grew as red as a turkey cock. Only rescued from this by S. proposing to go away. So we left, I with the conviction that what ever talents Miss Jan may have, she does not possess the one qualifying her to shine in good society – Adrian came home, saying he had left his bag in the train, and messengers were sent over London forthwith. Finally a Greek book was extracted.

φ

Saturday 20 February
Stella went to Oxford with Jack, having luncheon here at 12.30. We went out to post a parcel in Gloucester Rd. I carried it, and lost the letter which was tucked into the string. This was only discovered when we reached the post office, so I posted off home, in the greatest state of merriment, goodness knows why, and found it on the doorstep! Nessas hair came down and she refused to put it up again, saying that as she had looked in the glass before coming out her hair therefore must be allright – Went and sat in the gardens to recover ourselves – The crocuses there coming out – Mrs MacKenzie [neighbour] possesses a snow drop, and *my* box a squill – Nessa's box has a few green sprouts; she was so jealous of my flower that she routed the cocoanut fibre off her bulbs, and uncovered one poor little creature, which has not yet been coloured, and will most assuredly perish before its time – In the afternoon we bought some things in Gloucester Rd. and walked through the [South Kensington] Museum – Adrian back for tea – triumphant because of the match which Westminster has won – Oxford beat Cambridge by 2 goals to 1 –
Stella and Jack came back from Oxford in time for dinner.

O

Sunday 21 February
Very fine and sunny again – printed a great many photographs – The last ones of Simon which we took at Chelsea are most beautiful – Read

---

46 Effie and Lisa's studio was at 28 Campden Hill Gardens, W, opposite No. 12 where the Stillmans lived.

things with father, and went out for a walk in the gardens. Stella and Jack lunched with the Morpeths.[47] Gerald in for lunch. Afterwards we went out again in to the gardens and paid a visit to the little White House – Came home and read till tea time. Adrian developed some of his photographs after tea, but they are not very good – Eustace Hills came to supper, and brought Scamp. Father did not read after dinner. I managed to finish the 7th volume of Scott, to begin and finish the 8th volume and to begin the ninth volume. This is partly explained by the amount of Diary in the 8th, which I have just read, so that I skipped it, but it was a most wonderful feat nevertheless – Eustace has given Stella and Jack a picture of London by Herbert Marshall;[48] Westminster Abbey, I think, from the river, and Jack has bought another of the Thames in winter – a snow covered barge.

O

Monday 22 February
Nessa went to her drawing. I went out with father early – Afterwards did some history – (beginning Oman[49] again) and some German, and then went with Stella to Curzon St. to enquire after Mrs Baker[50] – who is ill. Stella sat with her and I waited in the dining room – then it was time to go home – After lunch Stella went to see Mariana,[51] a play in which Miss Robins[52] acts, and I went out to meet Peggie in the Park with Lisa. We walked up and down the Broad Walk for some time, and at last she appeared – then we had a game of ball by the Round Pond, and she went home. Lisa marched off round the Row, taking one enormous stride, to

47 Charles James Howard (1867-1912) and Rhoda Ankaret (1867-1912), daughter of Col. Paget L'Estrange, were Lord and Lady Morpeth of Naworth Castle, Carlisle, neighbours of the Herbert Hills of Corby Castle; Charles was the eldest son and heir of George James Howard, 9th Earl of Carlisle (1843-1911), whom he succeeded as 10th Earl in 1911.

48 Herbert Menzies Marshall (1841-1913), Trinity College, Cambridge. He obtained a Travelling Studentship for Architecture at the Royal Academy in 1868 and later published *The Scenery of London*, containing four pictures of Westminster Abbey: pp. 15, 58, 140 and 158; it is presumably the original of one of these that Eustace gave Stella and Jack.

49 Sir Charles W. C. Oman (1860-1946), historian; the exact title has not been traced.

50 Presumably the mother of Flora and Duff Baker.

51 By José Echegaray, opened at the Court Theatre on 22 February.

52 Elizabeth Robins (c.1865-1952), the American actress, feminist and writer.

my three very respectable ones. She told me stories of Mr Middleton[53] and the Royal Family. She left me at the door and pounded off up Campden Hill. Stella and Jack out to dinner with Mrs Gully[54] – she promised Stella and me tickets for the Ladies Gallery when the Education Bill[55] should become exciting – Nessa is not thought sufficiently intellectual, poor creature.

O

Tuesday 23 February

Nessa went again to her drawing; as this week she is going to make up for the three days she spent at Bognor. Stella and I took a bus and went to Gracechurch St. to see Georgie[56] in Talbot Court – At Hyde Park Corner we found a great crowd, which ran through the Green Park also; we supposed this to be waiting for the Queen [Victoria]; unluckily we just missed her Majesty – The bus took us all the way to nearly the top of Gracechurch St. and after a little bungling we discovered Talbot Court, and Charles Booth's[57] offices on the 2nd floor – Here was Georgie correcting proofs – We only saw him for a minute as it was late – Mr Booth and Mr Aves[58] were in the room – We undergrounded back from the Monument – In the afternoon Stella and I went out into High St. and bought a basin; afterwards we sat in the gardens for a time – Nessa had gone out with Mrs Flower [to see] pictures. Georgie came home about 5.30, and showed us all his presents – a medal for Jack, a gorgeous fan for Stella, a cigarette making machine for Gerald, chocs. for father, a fan for Nessa, and portfolio things for Adrian and me – Harry [Stephen] for dinner.

O

---

53 Probably Sir Frederick D. Middleton, KCMG, CB, (1825-98), Keeper of the Crown Jewels.

54 Elizabeth Anne Walford, daughter of Thomas Selby, and wife of William Court Gully (1835-1909), Speaker of the House of Commons and MP for Carlisle, 1892-1905.

55 The House of Commons was currently debating the controversial Voluntary Schools Bill, which proposed public financial assistance for parochial schools.

56 Who had returned from Paris; see 7 Jan. 1897.

57 From 1892-1902, George Duckworth had assisted in the preparation of *Life and Labour of the People of London*, 1901-3, by Charles Booth (1840-1916), shipowner, social scientist, and President of the Royal Statistical Society, 1892-4.

58 Ernest Aves (1857-1917), Trinity College, Cambridge, contributed several chapters to Vols IV, V and IX of Booth's *Life and Labour* etc.

Wednesday 24 February

Nessa went to her drawing. Father and I went out for our walk after breakfast. I finished Scott, and father has given me Essays in Ecclesiastical Biography,[59] which will do for me for some time – Stella and I did a little German, and then Kittie [Maxse] came, and we all went to her [philanthropical] houses together; she left us there and we went on to Mary Coxes[60] to dispose of two tickets for Mariana for this afternoon – But Mary was out – then we went to Margaret Newbolt[61] to offer them to her, but she was engaged, and finally Stella bethought herself of sending Sophia[62] and Elizabeth. Nessa lunched at the Milmans. Stella and I walked through the Park on the way to Curzon St. to see the Queen, but though there was a great crowd, she had not yet come – We took our bus at Sloane St. and went to Marshall and Snelgrove[63] about Ss linen. Then we went to Mrs Baker, and walked back to H[yde]. P[ark]. Corner. The crowd was larger than ever, and we boldly put ourselves in front of it. Suddenly behold the outriders and the crowd falling back on all sides – I caught a glimpse of H.Ms. bonnet bowing to this side and that, but the people surged up and more was impossible – We saw drawing room ladies and hansomed home.

O

Thursday 25 February

Nessa went to her drawing. Father and I walked round the pond; I was in great discomfort, as, having lost my garter, I had tied a piece of white tape round my stocking. This miserable thing came off as we walked up the street, and the rest of the journey was performed with my stocking right down on my shoe – Afterwards Stella and I went to Miss [Octavia] Hill about the cottages and hansomed from there to Mrs or Miss Garret

59 Sir Leslie's father, Sir James Stephen (1789-1859), *Essays in Ecclesiastical Biography*, 1849, 2 vols.

60 Unidentified.

61 *Née* Duckworth, wife of Sir Henry Newbolt (1862-1938), barrister, poet and naval historian; Margaret was the fourth daughter of the Rev. William Arthur Duckworth (1829-1917) of Orchardleigh, and a cousin of Stella's.

62 Sophia Farrell (*c.*1861-1942), cook for the Stephen and related families from the 1880s onwards.

63 A department store in Oxford Street, W.

(Garett?) Anderson[64] – She is a lady doctor, with a great house in Berkeley Street. Stella wanted to see her about Flora Baker, and also about her fidgets. Mrs G.A. kept her a long time, so that we had to take a hansom home. She told Stella to take some medicines, and a pill, and never to have strong tea – As we got out at the Park Gates on this side, the horse slipped, and fell flat down – Stella managed to get out, and I followed her soon – The animal after kicking and struggling for a time got on to his legs, and we went home on foot. In the afternoon, we went over No. 24, and afterwards I went with S to the workhouse, and bussed back alone – Stella and Jack, Georgie and Gerald all out.

O

Friday 26 February
Nessa went to her drawing. Father and I went out for a walk. Afterwards Stella and I went·down to Dr Seton, but he was too busy to see anyone. So we paid a visit to Susan Lushington[65] – She gave me a piece of the Pyramids – so I declare; but said by others to be only a bit of an old jar – at any rate it is 100,000 years old! It is a little green piece of plaster looking stuff, my pyramid, and shall for the future lie in the Davenport. In the afternoon Stella and I bussed to Hyde Park, and walked through the Green Park to the Stores[66] – There was a levee[67] today, and we saw several most beautiful scarlet gentlemen – Stella bought father some shirts, and we bussed home again. I began to do some shorthand[68] for father, and after dinner read a little with him. Arthur Fisher came for dinner, and Susan Lushington came afterwards. This is written just

64 Elizabeth Garrett Anderson (1836-1917), physician (MD, Paris), living at 4 Upper Berkeley Street, W. She was Senior Physician to the New Hospital for Women, 1866-90, Dean of the London School of Medicine for Women, 1876-98, and active in causes for improving the status of women; she was the first woman elected as mayor in England (Aldeburgh, 1906).

65 Daughter of Judge Vernon Lushington (1832-1912) and sister of Kitty Maxse and Margaret Massingberd. The Lushingtons lived at 36 Kensington Square, W, and the parents had been old friends of the Stephen family.

66 Probably the Army and Navy Stores, Victoria Street, SW.

67 Held in the afternoon at St James's Palace by the Prince of Wales at the command of Queen Victoria.

68 There is no evidence as to what AVS meant by 'shorthand'.

before father calls for me to go out, and I can think of no sentence to fill the blank.

O

Saturday 27 February
Nessa went to her drawing. Father and I went out for a walk. I spent most of the morning in cutting sticks to keep off the cats from our boxes – Nessa declares now that the sun (in some mysterious way) does not reach her box – at any rate her plants are greatly stunted – Stella and I went to Dr Seton – He says I may do some Latin with Nessa in the mornings, but as far as I can make out, nothing else. We came home in time for lunch. Jack was back early too. After lunch Nessa and I undergrounded to the Monument, where we met Georgie – We then tried to go on the River in a steamer, but none were running – So we took a bus-ride on the other side of the river, through slums, and odd places. We also visited Billingsgate [fish market] – the most smelly place I have ever been to. We had coffee at Hills[69] in Victoria St., and then went to the Abbey, but it was shut. Nessa and I came home on top of a bus – George stopping at the Club[70] – Jack Fisher came to us at tea with 2 tickets for the Geisha.[71] No one wanted to go so they were given to Sophia and Pauline. Adrian came back from Charterhouse about 9. W[estminster]. was beaten by 3 to 1. Imogen Booth[72] may have diptheria [*sic*]. Father at Oxford.

O

Sunday 28 February
Nessa and I bicycled up to Lisa – Nessa sat to her for some time; while I read Harpers in a corner – Peggy came in as the sitting was nearly finished, and we sat down on the floor and dabbled with chalks. We had meant to go for a bike ride with Lisa and Bella but they said it was too

---

69 Tea-rooms, 120 Victoria Street, SW.
70 Reform Club, 104 Pall Mall, SW.
71 *The Geisha: A Story of a Teahouse*, book by Owen Hall, lyrics by Henry Greenbank, and music by Sidney Jones, at Daly's Theatre.
72 Third daughter of Mary, *née* Macaulay (1848-1939), and Charles Booth (1840-1916); the Booths lived at 24 Great Cumberland Place, W, where Vanessa and AVS would stay in 1904 during their move from 22 Hyde Park Gate, SW, to 46 Gordon Square, Bloomsbury, WC.

late – We bicycled home again – Roland Vaughan Williams for lunch, Georgie was out. After lunch Cousin Mia and [illegible] child arrived; the child was brought up to see me – a small MacNamara very shy and uncomfortable – Stella despatched Cousin Mia, and she and Jack went to Rum[?] Beadles[73] to choose the picture which he is going to give them – He was out however, so they came back again – Roland V.W. and Gerald paid calls together; Adrian went for a bicycle ride, and Nessa and I sat in and read – The end of the Newcomes is in sight. We had a long talk with Stella after dinner, which was very nice – Imogen B has not got diptheria [*sic*].

O

---

73 Presumably a reference to James Prinsep Barnes Beadle, painter, 17B Eldon Road, Kensington, W; see Jan. 1897, n. 61.

Monday 1 March

Nessa went to her drawing. Stella and I walked across the gardens, and rambled through the greater part of Bayswater till we came to Kensington Park Gardens, where we enquired after Sylvia Davies[1] and her little boy. We came home by bus. Father came back in time for lunch from Oxford. Stella told me that poor Eustace is chasing Miss Kay[2] – Most interesting to watch – After lunch Stella and I bussed to the Marble Arch and asked after Imogen at Great Cumberland Place – She is quite well apparently – up in the schoolroom, so that the diptheria [*sic*] was all a scare – Bussed home again, and then Stella took a hansom to the Beadles to choose her picture. She has not settled between one of Billiards Lane with soldiers riding up and one of the island – Stella and Jack were out to dinner at the Bakers. It rained in the afternoon, so that Nessa came home in a hansom – Sylvia [Davies] is coming to lunch on Wednesday. The Ecclesiastical Biography gradually pulling through, poor thing.

O

Tuesday 2 March   *Shrove Tuesday*

Nessa at home at last – I did some Livy[3] with her and father for the first time since November. Afterwards I did a little German, and then we went to High St. and bought some stuff for the drawing room chairs at Story's, also a piece of stuff for Georgie's writing table which Nessa and I are to give him on Friday – We did not have pancakes for lunch though it is Shrove Tuesday – Adrian says there is to be a tossing of the pancake at Westminster – the boy who catches it gets a guinea. In the afternoon Nessa went to Ford Madox Browns[4] with Mrs Flower. They met Mr Hunt[5] there, and he showed them round, and talked to them, much to their delight. Stella and I only got out at 4.30, as Will [Vaughan] came to

---

1   Sylvia, *née* du Maurier (1864-c.1909), married Arthur Llewelyn Davies (1863-1907), barrister; they visited the Stephens at Talland House, St Ives, Cornwall during their honeymoon in September 1892. One of their five sons, Peter (b.1897), was the model for J. M. Barrie's *Peter Pan*; they lived at 31 Kensington Park Gardens, W.

2   This was Angela; see Feb. 1897, n.20. Eustace Hills married her sister Nina Kay-Shuttleworth, after the death of his first wife; see Aug. 1899, n.28.

3   Titus Livius (59 BC-17 AD), Roman historian.

4   Exhibition of the *The Works of Ford Madox Brown* (1821-93) at The Grafton Gallery, 1896-7.

5   William Holman Hunt (1827-1910), painter, who, with J. E. Millais and D. G. Rossetti, founded the Pre-Raphaelite Brotherhood in 1848.

talk to father – We walked to Rutland Gate where S. called on Miss Eliot,[6] who was out. Then S got into a bus to go to tea with Mrs Humphry Ward, and I walked home through the gardens. Finished Bracebridge Hall[7] (a hair doing book) and the Newcomes. We had dinner at 7.15 and went to As You Like It[8] – I thought it (Miss Julia Neilson especially) not so good as the other time we saw it – We got home about 12.

O

Wednesday 3 March

Nessa at her drawing. We got up about 10 o'clock. It rained and snowed and blew so much in the morning, that Stella and I stayed at home. Marny [Vaughan] came about 11, and stayed till 12.30. After she had gone I did some Greek, and then Nessa and Sylvia [Milman] came. Luncheon passed very peaceably and the art students departed soon after it.

Adrian came about 3, and we walked with Stella to Rutland Gate where she called on Mrs Galton[9] who was unfortunately in. Adrian and I walked back through the Park. Dinner was at 7.30 as father had to go to some ethical meeting – Georgie was out to dinner. Extremely irritable all the evening. Pauline becomes more like a cow than ever – She insisted upon trimming the lamps in the night Nursery which has smelt of parrafin [*sic*] ever since – Gerald gave Stella a wonderful opal and diamond necklace as a sort of first wedding present.

O

Thursday 4 March

We went to Larkes[10] about a window box for Georgie which we are to give him tomorrow. I did some Livy again this morning – In the afternoon Stella went to Mrs Flower, and Father to Sotherans[11] to buy a book for Georgie. Nessa and I walked up to Hyde Park Corner through the gardens, to see the drawing room ladies, and perhaps the Princess of

---

6 Unidentified.

7 Washington Irving, *Bracebridge Hall*, 1822.

8 At the St James's Theatre with Julia Neilson and George Alexander.

9 Louisa Jane Galton (d.1897), wife of Francis Galton (1822-1911), scientist, writer and promoter of the study of eugenics; he was a member of the Alpine Club and a friend of Leslie Stephen. The Galtons lived at 42 Rutland Gate, SW.

10 Arthur Larke, florist, 15 Lower Phillimore Place, Kensington Road, W.

11 Sotheran & Co., booksellers, 37 Piccadilly, W.

Wales[12] – It began to rain and blew so hard that we turned tail and scuttled home – We only saw two or three white satin ladies hurrying back. I began to read Felix Holt[13] to Nessa, while she sewed Jack's curtains, before the tea bell rang. Jack and Gerald out to dinner – After dinner we made cigarettes with Gerald's machine – Stella went to the Freshfields[14] with Georgie after dinner.

O ϕ

Friday 5 March
In the morning Stella and I went to Mrs Garret Anderson. She did not say anything new – We went on to Cousin Henry[15] in Mortimer St. about some photographs. Then we walked down Regent St. and looked into all the shop windows. Lady Stephen[16] and Katherine came to lunch. Lady Stephen very proper and talkative. Katherine, very massive and intellectual – Tried to talk to father but she was snubbed – She eat, however, an enormous luncheon, almost demolishing a pineapple. Lady Stephen was very full of Miss Walpoles[17] broken off engagement, which Georgie heard of yesterday. "They have ceased to understand each other" she said. After these creatures had gone Stella and I went for a walk in the gardens – the grass is covered with crocuses in some parts, and the Almonds are getting pink. Stella went on to tea with Lady

---

12 On 4 March, at the command of the Queen, a drawing room was held at Buckingham Palace by Her Royal Highness the Princess of Wales on behalf of Her Majesty; about 190 presentations were made. *The Times,* 5 March.

13 George Eliot, *Felix Holt, the Radical,* 1866.

14 Augusta Charlotte, *née* Ritchie (d.1911) and Douglas W. Freshfield (1845-1934), JP, writer, traveller and one of Leslie Stephen's Alpine Club fellows, later the President of the Royal Geographical Society.

15 Henry Herschel Cameron, the youngest son of AVS's great-aunt Julia Margaret Cameron (1815-79), the photographer.

16 AVS's aunt Mary, *née* Cunningham, widow of Sir James Fitzjames Stephen (1829-94) and mother of Katherine Stephen (1856-1924) who became Principal of Newnham College, Cambridge, 1911-20.

17 Probably Maud Catherine (1870-1949), daughter of Sir Spencer and Lady Walpole; on 9 November 1897, Maud Walpole married Francis Caldwell Holland (1865-1948), third son of the Rev. Francis J. Holland and the nephew of 2nd Viscount Knutsford.

Lyttelton,[18] and I came home – Sylvia [Milman] has lent me three books – Began John Halifax Gentleman.[19]

O

Saturday 6 March

Stella and Jack went off early in the morning to buy a print. It rained, so that Nessa and I did not go out. Mr and Mrs Watts[20] came about one o'clock – We had to start off for Adelphi Terrace,[21] where we were to meet Adrian and Georgie. We bussed to Adam Street, and made a wonderful crossing, and Nessa guided us down a terrace and to No 9. Here we found a little deaf man with a glass eye who took us into his office, seated us on chairs, and began to address envelopes. Soon we heard some one in the hall who turned out to be Adrian. Georgie came down soon, and we went and had luncheon at Romanos[22] – After that was finished (about 6 courses) we bussed to Victoria, and caught the train to Dulwich. We saw the gallery[23] which I did not think very beautiful – There are some nice pictures, and a Sir Josh[24] – Mrs Siddons. In the middle of the gallery there is a door leading to the Mausoleum of the founders.[25] We walked over and waited for our train – came back to V[ictoria]. and had coffee at an A.B.C.

---

18 Lady Susan Mary Lyttelton (d.1937), second daughter of William George Cavendish, 2nd Baron Chesham.
19 Dinah M. M. Craik, *John Halifax, Gentleman*, 1856.
20 While he was a resident of her household at Little Holland House, G. F. Watts had been encouraged by Mrs Prinsep to marry the young actress Ellen Terry, some thirty years his junior; they parted little over a year later (one theme of VW's family farce *Freshwater*, 1935). In 1886 he married Mary Tyler. Little Holland House having been demolished in the 1870s, Watts built himself a new house a short distance away in Melbury Road, and gave it the same name.
21 9 Adelphi Terrace was occupied by the Royal Statistical Society, the British Economic Association and the offices of Charles Booth.
22 Romano's Restaurant, 399 Strand, WC.
23 Dulwich Picture Gallery, Dulwich Village, SE, designed by John Soane, opened in 1817, contains a valuable collection of paintings originally collected for King Stanislaus of Poland, whose abdication aborted the project.
24 Sir Joshua Reynolds (1723-92), English portrait painter and first President of the Royal Academy; the reference is to his portrait of Mrs Siddons as the Tragic Muse (1789).
25 Noel Desenfans, the picture-dealer who formed the collection, his wife, and Sir Francis Bourgeois, the landscape painter to whom he bequeathed it.

Father gave me Mr Lowells[26] poems –

O

Sunday 7 March
In the morning Jack Stella Nessa Georgie Adrian and I went to Mr Watts
on a bus. Nessa and I went into the studio, and the others saw Mr Watts.
We walked back home – Gerald was out for luncheon – In the afternoon
Adrian went out for a bicycle ride, and Nessa and I sat indoors and read.
Stella told us this morning that the beauteous Pauline is going! Too hard
work for that cow – she wishes to be a ladies maid – So we shall get rid of
her – and the question is who shall succeed Pauline the 1st? Now there is
a dreadful idea that Stella ought to have bridesmaids, and that Nessa and
I ought to be among them – I hope this was squashed after dinner by
Eustace [Hills] – but there is still a possibility of half-brides maids. Aunt
Minna writes to ask us three to go with her to La Poupee[27] on Saturday
perhaps in the evening – Gerald and Georgie out after dinner –

O

Monday 8 March
Nessa went to the studio – Stella and I went out at 11, to get Stellas future
cooks character – We bussed to the West Cromwell Road where the
mistress lived, and found Mrs Howard Smith at No. 10 – She was a horrid little skinny lady – would not answer for the cook's honesty – would
not say she was dishonest, that would not be right, the old hag said, but
we agreed that under such a mistress our tempers and our honesty
would be very much tried – so Mary Smith will most likely – with her
dreadful temper and her suspicious honesty become cook at No. 24. We
came back, and just began our history when Mrs Baker came in, and I
was despatched to the Nursery to do some shorthand – Lisa and Bella
came to lunch, and went on afterwards to Madame Dubois[28] with Stella
to see about some dresses – Stella came back so late that it was im-

---

26 James Russell Lowell (1819-91), poet, critic, American Minister in London, and a
   close friend of Leslie Stephen since the 1860s. Because the Stephen children were not
   baptised, Leslie preferred to call Lowell AVS's 'sponsor' rather than her 'godfather'.
27 With music by Edmond Audran, at the Prince of Wales's Theatre.
28 Madame F. Dubois, court dressmaker, 3 Sussex Place, South Kensington, SW.

possible for us to go and enquire after Mr Payn[29] as we had meant –
Thoby has got a star for Latin verses. Everyone in.

O

Tuesday 9 March
In the morning Nessa and I went to Barkers[30] to buy Peggy [Middleton]
a pot of violets – but there being no violets we had to content ourselves
with daffodils – These we carried up to Campden Hill Gardens, and left
at the door – To day is Peggy's third birthday. Mrs Flower came for
Nessa at 2.15, and father went to look at Effies [Stillman] bust of Mr
Bayard.[31] Stella and I paid a visit to Aunt Minna with some anemones
which she wanted to paint. Then we took a hansom on to the Stores
where we took father's shirts to be done up. Stella bought herself
gloves, and we had the pleasure of seeing Mr Bayard – We came home
and found Mrs Hain[32] waiting in the drawing room. Adrian came back
with a headache – A chill Stella declares. There is a scare in the Studio of
diptheria [*sic*] – which Maeve[33] has done her best to swell, by reporting
gossip to Cousin M[ia]: so that it is doubtful whether Nessa will go back
there. Finished Essays in Ecclesiastical Biography.

O

Wednesday 10 March
Adrian did not go to Westminster, as his temperature was below normal
– Nessa went to her drawing. Father and I had our usual walk. We went
to Savages about a match box[34] of fathers, and to the Post Office. I told
father that the E[ssays]. in E[cclesiastical]. Bio[graphy]. were done with,
and most boldly suggest Mr Lowells essays – So I have got Among my

29 James Payn (1830-98), novelist and miscellaneous writer; a friend of Leslie Stephen,
     he succeeded him as editor of *The Cornhill Magazine*, 1883-96.
30 John Barker & Co., Ltd, department store, including fruits and flowers, 63-71, 75-83,
     87-97 Kensington High Street, W.
31 Probably Thomas F. Bayard (1828-98), First US Ambassador to Britain, 1893-7.
32 Catherine Seward, wife of Edward Hain (1851-1917), JP, six-times Mayor and from
     1900-6 MP for St Ives, thereby known to the Stephen family.
33 One of the six daughters of Maria (Mia) and Charles MacNamara; see Jan. 1897,
     n.73, and Nov. 1897, n.4.
34 To Dr Savage for a hearing-aid ('match box').

Books, which rejoice my heart after my grandpapa.[35] Walked in the gardens with Stella, in the most virtuous way. The Almond trees are just coming out, and there are crocusses (croci – Stella's young man calls them) all over the grass. A reverend gentleman has written to the Times to record the first hawthorn flower – the earliest that has appeared in the Parish since 1884 when, as will be remembered, there was an uncommonly mild winter, and favourable spring – still I think your readers will agree with me, when I say that it is not an unprecedented phenomenon, this early visitor, etc etc. *Hear hear*! In the afternoon we planted in the garden, and afterwards went to Regent St., with our watches – The man said that they were so cheap and bad that they could never be made to go properly, so we took them away – Finished John Halifax Gentleman.

O

Thursday 11 March
Adrian did not go to Westminster – We went to Blades[36] with a prescription for Stella in the morning – Adrian went back home, and Nessa and I took a walk in the gardens. After luncheon Marnie [Vaughan] came to take Nessa and me to the National Portrait Gallery. We went on the top of a bus to Trafalgar Square, and saw all the Watts and George Eliot and Mrs [Elizabeth Barrett] Browning – skilfully missing the proper portraits upstairs. We paid a visit to the Goupil Gallery[37] on our way home, and saw some water colour drawings by a Mr Holloway which Marnie did not like, but which Nessa, and two old art critics who gave their opinions at great length thought very clever – Lotta [Leaf] came to tea with Stella, and brought a shawl from Mrs Symonds,[38] which is not very interesting. Gerald out.

O O+

---

35 James Russell Lowell, *Among My Books*, 1870 – i.e. after finishing *Essays in Ecclesiastical Biography* by her grandfather, Sir James Stephen.
36 Foster Blades, chemist, 10 Gloucester Road, South Kensington, SW.
37 At Waterloo Place, 5 Regent Street, exhibiting a collection of drawings by C. E. Holloway (1838-97).
38 Janet Catherine (1837-1913), wife of J. A. Symonds (1840-93) and mother of Charlotte (Lotta, b.1867) Leaf, Margaret (Madge, later Vaughan, 1869-1925), and Katharine (later Furse, 1875-1952).

Friday 12 March
In the morning I went out after breakfast for a walk with father. Adrian did not go to school as the Exeat began at 12.30, and his cold was still rather bad. Nessa went to her drawing. Stella, Adrian and I went to Kittys to see whether she would go and choose a dress with Stella in the afternoon, but she was out – Then we went to Margaret [Marny] Vaughans to ask her, but *she* was out; then Stella took a cab to Campden Hill to secure Lisa, but it was their at home day. Finally Margaret Massingberd was found able to go. In the afternoon Adrian and I went to the Museum,[39] in search of a mythical underground collection of bugs, which Miss Kay declares she saw; instead we discovered a notice directing [us] to an insect room open to students from 10 to 4, which we suppose she meant, but as we did not feel sufficiently student like to enter, we came home – Bookless –

O

Saturday 13 March
I did Livy in the morning with Nessa. Adrians exeat so that the lazy creature spent his time lolling in the drawing room – We settled to meet Georgie at the Monument Station at a quarter to two – starting from here at one – Nessa and Stella went out in the morning to buy a hat for Nessa to wear if she goes to Geralds and Phil Burne J[ones]s tea at the New Gallery tomorrow. We started for Gloucester Road at one (marvellous to relate) and arrived at the Monument punctual to a minute – We lunched at a little place opposite Talbot Court,[40] and walked afterwards to St Saviour Southwark. The Church looks quite new – though there are a few old tombs – one of a gentleman famous for his pills,[41] another of a crusader. After that we bussed to St Pauls, and saw the mosaics, but a service was just beginning so that we left and paid a visit to Burlington House – as it is the last day of the Leighton exhibition. They were mostly very ugly – We had tea at an ABC and then came home. Madges wedding present arrived[42] – an old looking glass. Finished Among My Books.

O

---

39 The Natural History Museum, Cromwell Road, SW.
40 The Grasshopper Restaurant, 13 Gracechurch Street, EC.
41 St Saviour's Southwark, now Southwark Cathedral, contains the effigy and tomb of Lyonel Lockyer (d.1672), famous quack and pill merchant.
42 For Stella and Jack, whose wedding was to take place on 10 April; see n.38.

Sunday 14 March

Nothing happened all the morning, except that Adrian typewrote, Nessa drew, and I searched the house unsuccessfully for books to read. Stellas and Jacks banns were read for the first time but we did not go to hear them – Father had breakfast early and went to Mr Merediths.[43] It was after a long time decided that Nessa should go to the New Gallery and that I should not – Phil Burne Jones fetched Gerald after lunch – Adrian and I walked to the Marble Arch,[44] which was crowded with meetings. We came home about 5 o'clock. Nessa came back about 6, declaring that such a dull thing as a party was never before invented – However the others said it was a success so many pretty people had never been crowded in a room together – and there were celebrities too – Sir E[dward]. Burne Jones; Sir Ed. Poynter Mr Henry James (whom Aunt Minna stalked, Nessa says) and Mrs Beerbohm Tree[45] – Father came back at 7.

O

Monday 15 March

Nessa went to her drawing. Father and I walked to Savages about his match box which has come undone – I got "My Study Windows" by Mr Lowell,[46] and gave back "Among My Books". It began to rain, so that Adrian and I stayed indoors. Adeline Fisher appeared at about 12.30, and told us stories of their dog, and of Tom and Boo[47] till Stella came in. In the afternoon Adrian and I went to the Zoo. We undergrounded to Baker Street, and then with great skill, changed into the St John's Wood train. We found our way to the gardens, where we bought 6 penny buns

---

43 George Meredith (1828-1909), poet and novelist; he was a friend of Leslie Stephen.
44 By Speaker's Corner, Hyde Park, still the traditional arena for Sunday demonstrations of the English right of free speech.
45 At the tea party given by Gerald Duckworth and Philip Burne-Jones at the New Gallery, Regent Street, the 'celebrities' were Sir Edward J. Poynter (1836-1919), classical painter, President of the Royal Academy, 1896-1918, and Director of the National Gallery, 1894-1904; Henry James (1843-1916), novelist and friend of the Stephen family; Maud Beerbohm Tree, *née* Holt (1863-1937), actress and wife of the actor-manager, Herbert Beerbohm Tree (1852-1917).
46 James Russell Lowell, *My Study Windows*, 1871.
47 AVS's first cousins, Edwin (Tom, 1883-1947) and Cordelia (Boo, 1879-1970), the two youngest children of Mary and Herbert W. Fisher.

to distribute among the animals – There were no new creatures – we saw the lions fed, with difficulty as the house was crowded – We came home by a quarter past five – Stella Jack and Gerald went after dinner to a party to hear Susan Lushington play[48] – When the new woman comes, she is to sleep and live in the Night N. – Nessa will move to S's room and I to A's.[49]

Tuesday 16 March

Adrian went back to school today after nearly a week's holiday. Adeline and Stella went out to dressmaker (Stellas wedding dress) and Nessa and I walked to High St. and bought a fichu for Adeline – In the afternoon Nessa and I went to the South Kensington Museum, and went over for the 20th time the picture gallery – Stella was given a biscuit box by the servants, and the [Carlyle] French Revolution from Lady Cunningham,[50] and a buckle from my dear Contesa [illegible] – who starts for Florence tomorrow – After dinner Stella and Adeline went to the 5 shilling dance – Nessa and I paid them a visit as they were dressing at about 10.30, in our most dilapidated dressing gowns – Jack went with them – Gerald is one of the stewards, and gives a supper – They did not come back till 5 in the morning!

Wednesday 17 March

I went out for a walk with father in the morning. Stella had to go and see Mrs Hills.[51] At about one she, Adeline and I went in to the gardens and looked at the flowers – the almond trees out, the crocusses going over, squills at their best, the other trees just beginning to seed – I shall turn into a country clergyman,[52] and make notes of phenomena in Ken-

---

48 She played the piano and gave informal recitals at home for friends.

49 While Thoby was at Clifton, Adrian presumably had the day nursery all to himself and AVS and Vanessa shared the night nursery – both nurseries on the third floor; on the second floor were George, Gerald and Stella's separate rooms; and on the first floor was Leslie Stephen's bedroom. When Stella married, Vanessa took her room on the second floor and AVS converted the day nursery on the third floor into a combined bed-sitting room. See *MoB*, p. 118.

50 Lady Harriett Emily Cunningham (d.1918), married Sir Henry Stewart Cunningham (1832-1920), brother of Lady Mary Stephen; Sir Henry was a judge in the High Court in Bengal, 1877-87.

51 Mrs Edmund Hills, *née* Juliet Spencer-Bell, Jack's sister-in-law, wife of his elder brother (b.1864), an army officer; they lived at 32 Prince's Gardens, SW.

52 See 10 March 1897.

sington Gardens, which shall be sent as a challenge to other country clergymen – Adrian came home for lunch, having fainted at Westminster – from the pain in his knee, which he cut playing football yesterday – Stella, Nessa and Adeline went to some plays[53] at the Albert Hall, in which the Miss Gordons were going to act, and I stayed in and read the Cruise upon Wheels[54] to Adrian. Dr Seton came about 5, and said that Adrian was all right, but that his leg must be kept quiet for tomorrow – Adeline went back in the evening to Oxford.

Thursday 18 March
Ethel and Alice Clifford[55] came in the morning, so that we did not get out till late – Adrian did not go to school because of his leg. Stella and Nessa and I went out in the gardens, though it was a most diabolical day – blowing and raining – In the afternoon we went with Stella to the workhouse and were inspected by the old ladies – Most of them were blind, so that they had to feel us over to find out how much we had grown – We bussed back to High Street, and there took a hansom home, as Mrs Hills was to come for tea. Stella and Jack dined out with her. I finished My Study Windows in the evening. Tomorrow I shall get a new book – Read to Nessa The Lifted Veil[56] after tea for it is quite light now till about 6.30. I am reading Tales of Three Cities and Silas Marner[57] – A great arm chair arrived from Herbert [Stephen].

Friday 19 March
In the morning Stella and I went to Libertys to change a screen which Florence [Maitland] gave her as a wedding present – After a long time we decided to wait till another stock of screens should come in – Adrian did not go to school as his leg was still rather bad. We bought some silk to make night gowns, of all things in the world, for Stella. We came back in a hansom – In the afternoon Stella and Father went to Laura, and Adrian and I walked down to Aldous to buy some Italian tulips. It was

---

53 The plays have not been traced.
54 Charles A. Collins, *A Cruise Upon Wheels*, 1874.
55 The daughters of Lucy Clifford, *née* Lane (*c*.1855-1929), the prolific writer of novels, stories, and plays; she was the widow of William Kingdom Clifford (1845-79), mathematician and metaphysician, whose *Lectures and Essays* were edited by Leslie Stephen and Frederick Pollock in 1879.
56 George Eliot, *The Lifted Veil*, 1859.
57 Henry James, *Tales of Three Cities*, 1884. George Eliot, *Silas Marner, or the Weaver of Raveloe*, 1861.

decided that Adrian should not go to La Poupee in the evening, as he has to go to school tomorrow. Georgie came instead. He and Nessa dined with Aunt Minna at 7.30. The play was a musical one, and very amusing. We got home about a quarter to 12 – Father gave me Coleridges Life by Mr Dykes Campbell[58] to read – and I gave back My Study Windows.

Saturday 20 March   *The first day of Spring*
We did not go out in the morning. Nessa and I undergrounded to the Monument, and met Georgie there; we had luncheon with him at the "Old Grasshopper"[59] the same place at which we lunched last Saturday, and then went back to the Monument where we met Adrian. We settled to go to Hammersmith and see the crews practice.[60] There was a great crowd on the bridge – the river was full of rowing boats and steamers – After waiting some time – a steamer was seen coming up the river, and as it came nearer, we saw a boat alongside it – It was the Oxford Crew who docked under the bridge in fine style – the crowd cheering, and the merry go rounds screaming – Cambridge had already done its work – We were home for tea – The Calendar announces to day as the first day of spring and accordingly a leaf very small and green – has appeared on the chestnut at the top of the road.

O

Sunday 21 March
In the morning we went out into the gardens. We forgot again till it was too late to go to St Mary Abbotts to hear the Banns read – Next Sunday will be the last time so that we must go. In the afternoon Adrian went for a bicycle ride, and Nessa and I sat in the Night Nursery – I began Wives and Daughters[61] to her for the second time – Gerald gave me the Heart of Princess Osra a kind of going on of the Prisoner of Zenda[62] – Mr Gully came to tea, and were had up to see him – It is as hot and stuffy as

58 James Dykes Campbell, *Samuel Taylor Coleridge, A Narrative of the Events of his Life*, 1896.

59 See n.40.

60 The annual University boat race between Oxford (dark blue) and Cambridge (light blue) is held on a 4½-mile course on the Thames, from Putney to Mortlake, in March or April.

61 Mrs Gaskell, *Wives and Daughters*, 1864-6.

62 Anthony Hope, *The Heart of Princess Osra*, 1896. Anthony Hope, *The Prisoner of Zenda*, 1894.

a summers day – instead of the second day of Spring – Read Mr Dykes Campbell – tomorrow he shall be finished. Father recited after dinner.

Monday 22 March

Stella dissapeared [*sic*] early in the morning with Jack to choose some furniture which Flora Baker is going to give them for a wedding present. I went out with father. Afterwards Stella and I walked to Mary Coxes to tell her about a job – cook, and we saw Ella – In the afternoon Stella and I hansomed to the Reform Club, where we met Georgie. We then went together to Strong i' the arms,[63] which is close by, and chose a ring for Jack which is to have his three whiskered wolf on it. We walked with Georgie to Piccadilly Circus, and ordered Stella's invitations for the wedding. Georgie left us, and Stella and I walked up Regent St., and took a bus at Oxford St. to take us to Notting Hill, where we were to see a Mrs ——[64] who is to let us her house at Brighton. She lived in St Mark's Road which we could not find so that at last we took a hansom and had a squabble over the fare.

Finished Dykes. Jack out for dinner.

Tuesday 23 March

Nessa and I took a note to Mrs Green[65] after Lily-Marthe Perrière came to see Stella and we also inspected her. She is small and dark, an ugly nose, but on Stella's authority, pretty eyes – At any rate she talks real French, which is one very good point in her favour, after Pauline's German English mixture – She is intelligent and willing and talkative, S says, and will most likely come here on the 30th – on which day Pauline will dissapear [*sic*] – In the afternoon Nessa went to Mrs Flower. Miss Edwards[66] came to luncheon, and stayed till 4 o'clock. She is deafer than ever – one ear stone deaf, the other you must shout into as loud as you can, and perhaps part of what you say will reach her. She went over all the presents, and enjoyed herself. Father luckily, lunched with Mrs Green. When she had gone, Stella and I shopped in High St – We – Stella, Nessa, Jack and I, dined at a place in Sackville St, and went on to

---

63 Longman & Strong i' the Arm (E. C. Ball), engravers, jewellers, silversmiths, 1 Waterloo Place, SW.
64 Mrs MacAnally, wife of the late Roden Noel; see April 1897, n.22.
65 Charlotte Green, *née* Symonds (1842-1929), sister of J. A. Symonds and widow of Thomas Hill Green (1836-82), philosopher.
66 Probably the Miss Edwards living at 1 Kensington Gardens, W, and connected with Octavia Hill's work at Southwark.

St James Hall and heard Nansen[67] lecture – the great man is very like his pictures – talks broken English. It was very hot and rather long, but very good. Home at 10.30.

Wednesday 24 March
Nessa went to her drawing – Father and I walked in the gardens, and he gave me the Life of Sterling[68] to read – I gave back the Coleridge. Stella and I hansomed down to Madame Dubois and Stella was tryed [*sic*] on her going away dress at great length – After that we walked up to High St and bought various things there – The most fiendish March wind that ever blew. Poor Edith Beadle[69] we met in great discomfort – "the wind has torn my veil off," the little creature screamed into Stella's ear, "my hair is coming down, and that dog insists upon pulling the wrong way!" After luncheon I bussed with Stella to the workhouse and came back by myself – Nessa had to walk down to the studio, because of the wind. She brought me back North and South,[70] and a dreadful closely printed historical novel by Edna Lyall[71] – North and South I shall read out aloud to Nessa – I finished the Heart of Princess Osra, which is rather a good book methinks –

Thursday 25 March
In the morning I did Livy with Nessa – Afterwards we went up to Aunt Minna to fetch Stella to go out with us. But a Mrs Giles[72] had appeared down the road, and Stella had to follow and remained shut up with her all the morning. Nessa and I went for a walk down the Row of all places, which was rather crowded. Nothing very exciting happened – The almond trees are all most beautiful – so quoth the *Marmot* (i.e. Vanessa – Miss Maria). In the afternoon we had to pack off early to the Queens Hall to hear Miss Florence May give a pianoforte recital – She looked

---

67 Dr Fridtjof Nansen (1861-1930), Norwegian Arctic explorer and oceanographer; his lecture was called 'Across the Polar Regions'. St James's Hall, 28 Piccadilly, W, and 73 Regent Street, W, then opposite the Geological Museum, is now Le Méridien hotel.
68 Thomas Carlyle, *The Life of Sterling*, 1851.
69 Edith Margaret Beadle (1852-1944), eldest daughter of Major General James Beadle and sister of the artist James P. B. Beadle; she lived with her family at 6 Queen's Gate Gardens, South Kensington, SW.
70 Mrs Gaskell, *North and South*, 1855.
71 Probably *In the Golden Days*, 1892.
72 Unidentified.

like a poor green melancholy poll parrot – she waded through an immense amount of music[73] – We came late, and deserted when she went
out of the room in the middle – Bussed home – Marny [Vaughan] came
to tea with us, and asked about Stella's wedding present – to be a photograph or a picture.

Friday 26 March
In the morning I went for a walk with father. As we were coming home,
we saw a poor young lady byciclist [*sic*] run over by a cart – she was
coming up Gloucester Rd. with another lady – and tried to turn round to
the right, and ran straight into the cart – The cart was coming slowly,
and there was nothing else in the road, so I cannot understand how it
could have happened – Afterwards Marny and I went with S to Mrs
Young and had her going away dress tried on – Margaret M[assing-
berd]. was there. Marny stayed for luncheon – In the afternoon Nessa
and I went to tea with the Milmans. It was better than the other time,
though the tea itself was rather uncomfortable – They gave me two
books by Mr Lowell.[74] We walked home.

Saturday 27 March
Stella had to dissapear [*sic*] upon Mrs Giles business – in the morning
Adrian came home at 12 and Georgie took us to Addison Rd. Station.
We had settled to pick dafodils [*sic*] in the country – Georgie saying that
he knew of some field where they were to be found. We reached St
Albans at 1.30, and lunched at the Peahen – a sunny inn,[75] with great oak
beams and *horses*. We saw the cathedral which has all been re-done, but
there are still pieces of old work in it.[76] Afterwards we bicycled 5 miles,
and dismounted by a river, and picked marsh marigolds and wood anemones – No dafodils [*sic*] appeared. There was an old tall chimneyed red
brick house – nice strong box trees – birds singing – fish darting down
the stream – a rabbit hopping about in the wood – We stayed here a long

---

73 Florence May gave her first piano recital at Queen's Small Hall, performing works
    by Bach, Beethoven, Schubert, Mendelssohn, Schumann, Otto Goldschmidt,
    Novak, Leschetizky, Liszt and Rubinstein.
74 The titles have not been traced.
75 In the High Street.
76 The central part of the cathedral is the church built in 1077-88 by Paul Caen, the first
    Norman abbot; a restoration was begun in 1856 by Sir Gilbert Scott, continued by
    Sir Edmund Beckett and completed by Lord Grimthorpe.

time, and had only 30 minutes to ride 4 miles – on our way back – behold a field covered with ds. – Lost the train at Welwyn.

Sunday 28 March
In the morning we three went to Church at St Mary Abbots! This was the last Sunday on which the banns were to be read, so that we had re-solved to go – It began at 11.30, and finished at 1.15 – We had rummaged the house for prayer books and hymn books, our search produced two hymn books (tonic sol fa) and one prayer book. This last however was left behind. A little black gentleman showed us into seats at the top of the church. Soon music and singing began, the row in front of us rose, and behind a wheezy old lady began to follow the choristers in a tooth-less tuneless whistle – so on for the rest of the performance. At certain parts we stood, then sat, and finally knelt – this I refused to do – My neighbour looked so miserable and uncomfortable – In the middle the banns of John Waller Hills and Stella Duckworth along with several others were read, and no one pronounced any reasons why etc. etc. Our prayers and psalms were rather guess work – but the hymns were splen-did – We had a sermon from a new pastor – he said we shall never hear the beloved voice again, alluding to the departed vicar[77] – the old ladies snuffled and sobbed – Finished Sterling.

Monday 29 March
Stella and Charlie,[78] who has been here since Monday, went to Brighton early in the morning. I was meant to go, but with the stubbornness of a mule and the ardour of a marmoset (my new title) I *refused*. The con-sequence was that the powers had to do without me, to which after some wrangling they consented. I walked down to the Studio with Nessa – bicycling after Miss Shaw Lefevres[79] accident is forbidden – I fetched Nessa back again, and saw some of the Studio celebrities – a Miss

---

77 The Hon. Edward Carr Glyn (1843-1928), Vicar of Kensington since 1878 and from 1897-1916 Bishop of Peterborough.
78 AVS's first cousin, Charles (1877-1916), sixth son of Mary and Herbert W. Fisher.
79 Probably Madeleine Shaw-Lefevre (1835-1915), first Principal of Somerville Col-lege, Oxford, 1879-89.

Bowyer a Miss Vivian, and a Miss Davies[80] – In the afternoon father and I bussed to St James St. – We had several perilous crossings before we reached the London Library,[81] where father got some books. Then there were more crossings, and we arrived at fathers tailor in Bond St. where father ordered himself a whole new suit for the wedding. He bought some books at Sotherans and then we wandered down the middle of Piccadilly, till we came to a shelter. It is a miracle that I escape to write this. Gave back Sterling and got Pepys diary.[82]

Tuesday 30 March
In the morning Stella, Nessa and I went to Mrs Roberts in Westbourne Grove about our dresses for the wedding. Margaret Massingberd was there. After a great deal of discussion a gray dress was fixed upon – but farther than that I did not penetrate. Adrian came home early after lunch because the governor of the Fiji Islands[83] an old Westminster, had asked a half holiday for them. Nessa went to the Nat[ional]. Gall[ery]. with Mrs Flower. Stella and Adrian and I bussed to Hammersmith and walked on the bridge – which was very crowded, but there was no sign of the crews. Stella took a train to Putney to see Mrs Hunt and A and I bussed home. This morning the beauteous Pauline departed. On Thursday Marie Perrière arrives – for the mean time we have quiet. Stella and Jack out to dinner with Aunt Minna. Stella made a proposal that father should give Nessa an allowance of £40 a year – 25 of which I should have.[84] We should buy out of this all our clothes etc; think of the joy of making a pair of boots last a month longer and buying for ourselves books at a 2nd hand bookstall!
    Not yet proposed to father.

Wednesday 31 March
I did not go out with father in the morning because he had a cold. About

---

80 Miss Ellen Bowyer, London landscape painter, exhibited between 1888-93 at the Royal Academy, the National Gallery and the New Watercolour Society; Miss J. Vivian, landscape painter, exhibited six works at the Royal Society of British Artists; and Miss M. I. Davies, exhibited one painting of flowers at the Royal Society of British Artists in 1893.

81 In St James's Square, SW.

82 Samuel Pepys, *Diary*, 1660-9.

83 Sir George Thomas Michael O'Brien (1844-1906), Governor of Fiji and High Commissioner for the Western Pacific, 1898-1902.

84 No explanation has been found for the inequality of their allowances.

half past 12, I walked down Queens Gate with Stella. She took a cab on to Westminster to take Adrian to Fairbank to have his teeth out – Nessa bicycled down to the studio, and met with no accident. On Friday the studio comes to an end. After lunch Adrian Stella and I bussed to Hyams to buy Adrian clothes for the wedding. We met Mr [Henry] James in Oxford Street. "Most extraordinary coincidence, my dear Stella Duckworth! I was just this moment, this very moment, thinking of you – in fact I had stopped 10 doors back to get you something – now I meet you!" This was carried on at great length with great difficulty in the midst of the crowd. After tea I helped Georgie with the invitations for the presenters and the wedding. The presenters are coming on Saturday. Miss Edwards and a few Southwarkers[85] I think are coming here after the wedding. How delightful. Finished the Antiquary.

---

85 Volunteer workers connected with St Saviour's Union Workhouse, Mint Street, Southwark, SE.

Thursday 1 April   *April Fools day*

In the morning we went to Mrs Roberts in Westbourne Grove – Margaret was not there this time. We had our linings tried on – I was forced to
wear certain underclothing for the first time in my life – All the invitations were finished and sent off in the morning – so that theres an
end of that job – Only ten days now to the wedding – what will become
of us – In the afternoon we shopped in High St. – meaning afterwards to
go on to Moorgate St[ation]. about A's unfortunate umbrella which has
lain in the Lost Property office ever since January. But the shopping
took too long so that we did not try to go any farther. Stella went to the
Workhouse and Nessa and I came home – Marie arrived after tea – Very
talkative indeed, and unlike Pauline. She has already given me the
history of the Janins,[1] and is willing to tell us anything we like. She talks
real French, and we stumble along in our half forgotten language as best
we may – However she does not want very many questions to make her
talk herself – Harry [Stephen] came to dinner – Began Caesar.[2]

Friday 2 April

In the morning I went for a walk in the gardens with Father. Afterwards
Nessa came home and we went to Mrs Youngs in South Audley St, to
see her wedding dress tried on. When we got there we were told that
Mrs Young could not come for half an hour. Margaret Massingberd was
there, and Violet Dickinson,[3] and soon Cousin Mia galumphed into the
room with a parcel for my darling Stella from her loving cousin Sheila[4] –
which proved to be a horrid little red and gold Browning – Georgie
appeared after we had waited some time, and he took Nessa and me with
him to choose the wedding cake at Gunters[5] – We ordered a 60 lb. one –
to cost 6 or 7 guineas. Afterwards we went back to Mrs Young and
found the wedding dress on – Margaret came back to lunch with us, and
Nessa went on to have hers at an A.B.C. near the studio, so as to get in as

1   Possibly a reference to Noel Clement-Janin (b.1862), playwright and well-known
    amateur artist, husband of Blanche Coulon of the Opéra-Comique.
2   Presumably to read his *Commentaries*.
3   Violet Dickinson (1865-1948) whose family, like the Duckworths, came from
    Somerset, was a friend of Stella's; in 1902 she would become and remain for many
    years AVS's most intimate friend.
4   Sheila MacNamara (1877-1938), the fourth daughter of Maria (Mia) and Charles
    MacNamara, and Stella's cousin; in 1907 she would marry Admiral Sir Edward E.
    Bradford (1858-1935).
5   Gunter's, confectioners, 63 New Bond Street, W, or 7 Berkeley Square, W.

much drawing as possible – Stella and Margaret went to some shop to buy Stella a hat, and I walked to Kensington Square and then to the studio, to fetch Nessa back. Oxford won the sports by 1 thing. Finished 1st vol. of Pepys.

Saturday 3 April
The whole morning was spent in arranging the presents. Marny and Emma [Vaughan] came and helped us. The books and jewels were in the back drawing room, and everything else in the front. At last the presents 170 in number, were all placed somewhere or other, and the rooms made to look tolerably tidy, and decent. A rug from Geralds bedroom covered the deficiencies of the drawing room carpet – At last after 3 or four hours of labour the flowers all put in water, the presents labelled – our dresses changed and a thousand etcs – the company came in – First Helen Holland[6] then Jessie Allen,[7] Aunt Minna – various unknown people – How lovely & that *is* beautiful! What a wonderful necklace! – this went on unceasingly, and not very much else. There was however a most scrumptious Charbonnel tea[8] in the dining room – with iced coffee – Edith Beadle collared Nessa and told her stories of her own doings for a long time – She was followed by Mrs [Holman] Hunt – Emma sat with me on the sofa and laughed – At seven the whole pack had departed – We went down and had a tea – only about 3 came, while there was room enough and tea enough for 100. Extraordinary.

Sunday 4 April
In the morning we did nothing – Jack stayed away till luncheon, when he and Susan Lushington appeared. In the afternoon the Milmans came to see the presents, which are still left on view – Lady Loch[9] came too, and much the same remarks as yesterday were uttered – Jack had supper out somewhere – this is the last Sunday of Stella Duckworth – next week Mr and Mrs Hills will be at Dover waiting for Monday to cross to France – The drawing rooms are still topsy turvy and will not recover till everything is over – "the beginning of the end" Aunt Minna cheer-

6 Florence Helen Holland, *née* Duckworth, Stella's cousin, in 1895 married Bernard H. Holland (1856-1926).
7 Probably Jessie Allen of 74 Eaton Terrace, SW.
8 Charbonnel et Walker, confectioners, 173 New Bond Street, W.
9 Elizabeth, daughter of the Hon. Edward E. Villiers, and wife of Henry Brougham Loch (1827-1900), created 1st Baron in 1895; they lived at 23 Lowndes Square, SW.

fully calls this. Indeed it is in danger of becoming very dismal – After dinner father read the Ancient Mariner[10] which was rather a failure – almost ending in the middle furiously. My dear Pepys is the only calm thing in the house –

Monday 5 April

In the morning we went to Mrs Roberts for the 3rd time. Margaret Massingberd was there – Our dresses have developed into respectable grey paduasoys (I hope) – In the afternoon we went to Mrs Youngs to see Stellas wedding dress tried on for the last time. M.M. and Cousin Mia again there – the dress was in much the same state as last time; but after a little battle between Margaret and Cousin Mia about the lace, everything went smoothly and was finished – So we shall not see it again till Saturday – then we shall faint – this time next week – everything will be over once and for all – Good gracious what a week this unfortunate diary will have to contain! We (Nessa and I) have resolved to be calm and most proper behaved, as if Stellas marriage were nothing at all touching us – Cousin Mia shall be entrusted with the task of tear manufacturer for the family – oh dear, I wish it was over – Home by bus – Poor Helen Holland crowded out and had to walk.

Tuesday 6 April

At about 11 Thoby arrived – with out Stewart – He eat an enormous breakfast, and then we went out with Stella and Lizzy [servant] to Marshall & Snelgrove to buy Stella's dusters etc. for her new house. Then we ordered new bicycling skirts at another shop, and then came home very late for luncheon in a fourwheeler – Stellas presents pouring in very fast now – Today she had a great many silver things – In the afternoon Nessa and Thoby went out to buy the dogs wire muzzles. The muzzling order is on again for ever. £20 fine if they are discovered muzzleless. Thoby went on to fetch Adrian back from Westminster, and Nessa, Stella and I went to tea with Herbert, Harry and Rosamond – Dodo Booth, a Freshfield, Nora Pollock, Susan, Katherine were there.[11]

---

10 Samuel Taylor Coleridge, *The Rime of the Ancient Mariner*, 1798.
11 Herbert (1857-1932), Harry (1860-1945), Rosamond (1868-1951), and Katherine (1856-1924), the children of Mary and James Fitzjames Stephen; Antonia Mary (Dodo, b.1872), the eldest daughter of Charles Booth; Nora Pollock (1884-1969), daughter of the Rev. Herbert Charles Pollock (1852-1910), rector of West Hackney, London; Susan Lushington; 'a Freshfield' has not been identified.

Dear Ros. has become most prosperous and stout with her rest cure. She took a chair by me and talked. We came away soon – meeting Georgie and Thoby just at the door – Jack in for dinner.

Wednesday 7 April
We came down very late for breakfast, and Georgie had it with us. He and Thoby went to the bicycle shop in the morning to see whether they would allow Thoby anything off his old Premier – Stella had offered to give him a new one – We went out with Stella into High St. and she had her hair done as an experiment for next Saturday – Aunt Virginia[12] appeared, but would not stay for lunch – A. came home for lunch – T. had it with Georgie at the Reform. At 3.30, A., N. and I went to Bensons in Bond St. to choose a lamp for Stella and Jack's wedding present – We met Gerald there – When we had chosen it, I got faint, and came home in a cab – Finished North and South and the 2nd volume of Pepys.

Thursday 8 April
In the morning Nessa, Stella and I went to Mrs Roberts for the last time. Our dresses were tried on in their finished state, and M.M. thought them satisfactory – Afterwards we shopped in High St. – In the afternoon Thoby went for a bicycle ride on his new bicycle, and Nessa and I went with Stella to High St. and afterwards on to Earls Court – there we discovered that she had lost one of her opal rings – the one Jack gave her – So we came back and asked at all the shops whether they had found it – but there were no traces, and it is now given up for lost. After tea we four marched into the drawing room and presented Stella and Jack with the lamp – which they approved of, so they said – Jack was despatched – not to be allowed here till he is a married man – Dear Miss Pitman[13] wrote a most enthusiastic crazy letter to Stella – The presents pouring in –

Friday 9 April
We did nothing all day but arrange presents, and write cards etc – All the morning was spent like this. In the afternoon Stella and Father went to Highgate [cemetery][14] – At last about 11 o'clock at night things were more

---

12 AVS's maternal great-aunt, Virginia, Countess Somers, *née* Pattle (1827-1910), widow of 3rd Earl Somers (1819-83).
13 Possibly Rossella (1816-98), sister of Sir Isaac Pitman (1813-97), inventor of the shorthand system.
14 Presumably to visit Julia Stephen's grave.

or less finished. Mrs Jones[15] arrived with a supply of underclothing. We went to bed – but Stella and Georgie & Gerald stayed up till 2 packing in her room. Jack stayed away all day long – Too much to do to be dismal, though the last evening was in danger of ending unhappily. Remembered however (Nessa and I) our resolve to be calm and collected –

Saturday 10 April   *Stella & Jack's Wedding Day*
The morning was still rather a hurly burly – The finishing touches to everything had to be given – Eustace came often to arrange things with Stella – Huge boxes of flowers arrived throughout the morning and had to be arranged – orange flowers had to be mixed with all the Southwark and workhouse favours – great white satin cockades. Adrian did not go to school. At about 12 the Fishers came – and Stella went up to dress. M. Emile the hairdresser did her hair and also Nessa's – Goodness knows how we got through it all – Certainly it was half a dream, or a nightmare. Stella was almost dreaming I think; but probably hers was a happy one. We went to the church at 2. Jack was there looking quite well and happy. Then at about 2.15 or 30, Stella and father came in – Stella walking in her sleep – her eyes fixed straight in front of her – very white and beautiful – There was a long service – then it was all over – Stella and Jack were married – We went up and saw her change her dress – and said good bye to her. So they went – Mr and Mrs Hills! These are some sentimental tokens of the day. White rose leaves from S's bouquet and red tulips from ours that Jack gave us –

Sunday 11 April
In the morning we did nothing which was very nice after this last week of doing something. Adrian played with his microscope – a wonderful one which Stella gave him, and Georgie tried to summon up courage to prick himself and examine his blood – Yesterday there was no room to say that Stella and Jack gave Nessa and me two most superior bridesmaids presents – beautiful gold watches the best, Georgie says, that can be made, with our initials on the back, and "From Stella and Jack" inside. These arrived as Stella was dressing on Saturday, and she gave them to us just before we started for the church – Harry Stephen came for luncheon, and the wedding cake was eaten – Afterwards Georgie said we would go to Highgate, and take there some of Stellas white roses, and our carnations – Georgie, Gerald and Thoby bicycled & A.,

15 Unidentified.

N. and I drove in a victoria – our man raced the bicyclists all the way home which was rather alarming, but they just won – However I was thankful to get home safe at all – Trying hard to finish Pepys before Wednesday, so I may have a new book.[16]

Monday 12 April

In the morning we went to Larkes in High St. to order some flowers for No. 24 [HPG]. Adrian went back to school as usual this morning. After luncheon Thoby went for a bicycle ride to Wimbledon and thereabouts, and Nessa and I paid Kitty Maxse a very long visit. M.M. came in while we were there, and a most extraordinary time we had of it – Kitty begins – Margaret catches her up half way through, and they finish together – We sitting screaming with laughter – to sit and laugh was throughout our part: such a stream of talk and laughter never in my life have I heard – War[?] is silent and dull compared to it. At last at 4.15 we got away – We bought 2 pkts of paper at Lords for 1.3d. which will last me till the summer I should think. Unhappily they are rather smoother than my last 6½ lot – Georgie had the fire lighted in his room, and I sat there and read which was very nice. Finished 3rd vol. Pepys.

Tuesday 13 April

In the morning Nessa and I went to High St. to buy some stuff to trim a hat, and to give A's watch to have a glass put on – I wrote to Stella, sitting in Georgie's room which is most comfortable and quiet. In the afternoon Nessa and I bussed to Mrs Young's, and asked Julia to write a description of the wedding-dress for one of the papers, and we presented her with a piece of wedding cake – The roar of carriages and carts was so dreadful that I forced Nessa, much against her will, to walk into the gardens from Park Lane, and through them home – Thus we escaped the bus and the streets which were in a most fiendish state of uproar. Packing for Brighton began –

I got the 4th & last vol. of Pepys, which has to be finished by tomorrow – Father suggests Macaulay's History[17] as a good solid work for Brighton!

To bed very furious and tantrumical –

---

16 AVS appears to have set herself a rigorous reading schedule.
17 Thomas Babington Macaulay, *The History of England*, 1849-61, 5 vols.

Wednesday 14 April
The morning was spent indoors, finishing our packing. Kitty came and talked to father, and Cousin Mia and Aunt Minna were most affectionate. Adrian came home about 12, and said that he had got his remove – in to the lower fifth, and a silver penny for being top of his class in French – At a quarter to three we started for Victoria – Father, Marie and I in a cab with Jerry – the rest bicycling – The roads up to Victoria were all blocked, and about 200 yards out of the station we came to a standstill – Father was miserable: We had lost the train. It was no good going on – he tried to get out of the cab, but luckily was too much jammed in to move – However at last we got to the platform, and more wonderful still, secured a fairly empty carriage – for the crush was terrible – We got to Brighton at a quarter to 6, I think. Our house is 9. St Aubyns. After tea we walked to 2nd Avenue and saw the Fishers – Everything fairly comfortable. Plenty of books. Began Macaulay's History.

Thursday 15 April
In the morning we bicycled as far as Shoreham, but it was most dreadfully windy and dusty, and when we got so far, Nessa and I turned back, and left the others to go on – The rest of the morning we spent reading. I gradually plodding through the first volume of Macaulay. I have two vols. here – I shall not read the other; also Wives and Daughters, and Lambs essays[18] – so I manage to keep going – but a fortnight! What is to happen to us – I wish this moment I were sitting in my beloved arm chair, with a nice quiet morning of London in front of me – No such luck – In the afternoon the rest bicycled – Father and Herbert Fisher walked and drove together and N. and I went to Second Avenue and got Emmie[19] to come out with us to buy some cider. We walked on the parade with her and then brought her home to tea with us. After tea we – Georgie, Thoby, N & I walked back with her. G. saw Hervey & N & I sat in the drawing room. Then Emmie walked back to St Aubyns with us, and told us of a certain romance[20] which we knew already. Thoby dined with the Fishers.

---

18 Charles Lamb, *Elia*, 1823 and 1828 and *The Last Essays of Elia*, 1833.
19 AVS's first cousin, Emmeline (Emmie, 1868-1941), fourth of Mary and Herbert W. Fisher's children; her brother, Hervey (1873-1921), since childhood had suffered from crippling spinal tuberculosis.
20 Presumably a reference to Adeline and Ralph Vaughan Williams.

Friday 16 April   *Good Friday*

It was behaving in the most diabolical manner – pouring with rain at intervals, and a wind capable of disturbing Mr [James] Dykes Campbell[21] – nevertheless, Cor[delia]. and Tom [Fisher] came round in the morning, and we all walked back with them – The poor bank holidayers all penned up in their hotels, and nothing to be seen but crazy old shut up flys, and bedraggled four in hands – the top passengers holding on tight, and the poor little horses struggling desperately – We got a flower at the Fishers for Nessa to paint – In the afternoon Nessa and I stayed in – Nessa painting and I reading – Truly such a dismal place was never seen – All the books are poetry – except a few bad novels, which probably have found their way in since the Hon. Roden's demise;[22] and a sprinkling of terribly religious works – sermons and missionary reports, belonging to the Rev. [David] Macanally. The pictures are religious, or portraits of the Royal Family from the Queen. One or two works by the Princesses themselves. Everything rather gruesome.

Saturday 17 April

Still raining and blowing hard – This is a most disgraceful place – nothing else seems to happen – However Georgie and I and father went out in the morning to order a bed for Thoby, and in the afternoon we played a kind of cricket on a piece of waste ground near the house. But the wind was dreadful, and the game was cut short by a violent shower of drizzle – Herbert & Boo & Tom [Fisher] came back to tea – After tea they played knuckle bones – a game which is Thoby's chief solace now – Thoby & Georgie dined with Baxter[23] at his hotel, and Adrian & Father dined with the Fishers, so that Nessa & I had a most delicious high tea together – an ommelette [*sic*] etc.

This is written with one of the Rev Davids quill pens – the result is not beautiful – No – I shall not again desert my beloved Swan [pen].

---

21 See March 1897, n.58; no explanation has been found for this ambiguous phrase.

22 Roden Berkeley Wriothesley Noel (1843-94), poet and critic, son of the 1st Earl of Gainsborough. The Hon. Roden's widow, Alice, *née* de Broe (d.1919), in 1896 married the Rev. David MacAnally (d.1897), formerly Vicar of Penge; the house now belonged to the widowed Mrs MacAnally.

23 Probably Reginald Truscott Baxter (1871-1939), Clare College, Cambridge, and a contemporary of George and Gerald Duckworth; Baxter at this time was a solicitor in nearby Lewes, Sussex.

Sunday 18 April

Fine today for a wonder, after a Brighton fashion – strong sun & strong wind. In the morning we all went for a decorous walk on the sea wall – It was far more crammed than the Church Parade in London – a most disgusting spectacle, though rather amusing – all the third rate actresses turned out in gorgeous clothes – tremendous hats, powder and rouge; and dreadful young men to escort them – We met Gerald bicycling from the Station, and he went on [to] the house, and then came back and met us – In the afternoon he went to the Fishers, and Father went for a walk with Herbert & Will, who came over for the day. We four with Georgie bicycled to Shoreham, and came back through the country – Coming home it was hot and calm, but going the wind was as diabolical as usual – Georgie dined with the Fishers – We walked on the sands after tea.

Monday 19 April   *Easter Monday and Primrose Day*

In the morning Gerald took us and the Fishers – Emmie Boo Tom and Adeline, to the Pier. There we had the happiness of seeing the execution of Mrs Dyer[24] – unfortunately when about 3 of us had had the treat, the machinery refused to work, and the back of the platform had to be opened, and some thing done to the electricity – afterwards she was hung successfully. In the afternoon we settled with the Fishers – Adeline and Herbert, to train to the Dyke & to bicycle round somewhere & so home – The trains were crowded – but at last we got places with the bicycles in the van – After the train finally moved off for about 100 yds it came to a standstill, and backed us into the station again, where we waited till two trains came back again from the Dyke. When we got to the Dyke, we decided to come home by Bramber. We climbed down the Dyke over the grass, in a most perilous way – when we reached the bottom it began to pour – We arrived after many adventures, which unluckily there is no room here for, at Shoreham thoroughly drenched.

Tuesday 20 April

The rain had dissapeared [*sic*] by this morning, leaving the roads muddy and bad, it is true; but nevertheless the sky was as blue as Stella's renowned Italian ones,[25] and the wind which was cold and fresh, was at

---

24 Mrs Amelia Elizabeth Dyer, Reading baby-farmer and murderer, was hanged at Newgate on 10 June 1896. The penny-in-the-slot machine commemorating her execution must have been on the West Pier: the Palace Pier was not opened until 1898.

25 Stella and Jack were in Italy for their honeymoon.

our backs. We started from this house at 11 and rode through Brighton to the Lewes road – There was one long hill, and a bad piece of muddy ground to begin with, but when we had scaled the hill, which we did comfortably on our feet, behold a beautiful smooth descent of two miles & a ½ lay before us! Georgie, T. & A. flew down this with their feet up, but N. & I were more prudent – it was most exciting and splendid. If I was a poet (which Miss Jan does not claim to be) I should write something upon this way of travelling. This diary is too small to allow of very much prose, and that is quite inadequate – We had twenty minutes to ride three or four miles in if we were to catch the train at Lewes – We rushed through the town and down a very steep narrow road which led to the station; the train was in but we managed to seat ourselves and to see our bikes in the van – We got to Uckfield at 1, where Will [Vaughan] met us – Lunched with them all. After lunch at 3, started with them back to Lewes – Another most beautiful ride. We stopped on the way and picked primroses in a wood. Tea at Lewes. Train back to Brighton at 5.40.

Wednesday 21 April
It rained all the morning, to make up for yesterday. Adrian & Thoby went out on to the beach, but Nessa & I stayed in & read. Georgie had to go to London by an early train. In the afternoon Thoby & Adrian & the Fishers went to see the play on the pier. Father took Nessa and me for a walk along the Parade to the Steine or someplace of that kind – near the Pagoda at the other end of Brighton – I regret to say that various circumstances conspiring to irritate me, I broke my umbrella in half – Father went to tea with the Fishers, and Emmie Tom & Boo came to tea with us. Emmie told us stories of Florence [Maitland] and her animals, which, if we go to Gloucester[26] this summer, we shall have quite enough of – After tea Thoby, Adrian & the Fishers went off somewhere (we never fathom their motions) & Nessa, Emmie & I walked along the Kings Road, where Emmie had to buy some things. Everything however was shut for Wednesday. Letters from Stella; they start to come home on Friday. Finished 1st vol. of Macaulay –

N ⊕

---

26 Horsepools, Brookthorpe, was the Maitlands' Gloucestershire estate.

Thursday 22 April

In the morning at about 11, we went to the Fishers to get them to come with us on the Parade. Emmie had promised to come, but she said that business made it impossible. So Adeline came in her stead – nursing a poor half starved mouse of Toms all the time. We saw Joey,[27] who was inaudible, and the South African minstrels,[28] and the Scotch family, who play on violins and flutes and various instruments[29] – Adeline walked back with Nessa & me, and told us of Kittie's engagement[30] once upon a time to Lord Morpeth – A letter for Georgie from Stella, but nothing very much in it – In the afternoon we trained to the Dyke with father, Tom & Boo, & Charlie & Adeline; we examined the top of the Dyke, which is crowded with switch backs etc. and then started to bicycle home. All the winds that have had a place in this diary, must yield ignominiously to the wind which met us now – Several times was I blown into the hedges, and the bicycles behaved in a most drunk way – lurching from side to side – Home safely after a rather horrible expedition – Began 2nd vol. of Macaulay.

Friday 23 April

At 11 o'clock the riding master came for Nessa & Thoby. Georgie is giving them three 2 hour rides each, to have while they are here. They only rode for one hour today – Father and I went for a walk along the Parade. He told me stories of Macaulay, and various old gentlemen whom he had known – After luncheon Nessa Georgie Father and I went to see the race course. We took a bus to Castle Square, and then walked along the Lewes road – We went into the Churchyard and saw Grannie's grave[31] – Georgie gave us each a piece of sweet briar from it – Afterwards we walked on to the downs – The wind of yesterday as ferocious as ever – we were forced to take off our hats, and let the wind disport itself at its own free will among our hair. Father surprised us when we were at the bottom of the hill, by disdaining a bus, and hailing

27 'Joe', Dr Lynn (d.1899), the popular Victorian magician.
28 The South African Minstrels were probably the (blacked-up) Gates Band who played at 11.30 a.m. during the daily promenade.
29 There was no Scotch family: AVS was probably referring to the Meier family, Alpine singers performing on guitars, zithers, xylophones and Alpine violins.
30 See Sept. 1897, n.19.
31 AVS's maternal grandmother, Maria Jackson, *née* Pattle (b.1818), died on 2 April 1892 at 22 Hyde Park Gate, but was buried in Brighton, where she had lived her last years.

a sleeping fly by the sea-wall. This creature carried us back to St Aubyns, which was a long way off – Boo & Tom had tea with us. Letter from Stella for me –

Saturday 24 April
Nessa and Thoby went for a two hours ride at 11 – Adrian went to catch lice on the beach with Boo and Tom – a disgusting employment – for the benefit of Boo's sea anenomies [*sic*] – Emmie came round here about 12.30, & I walked to 2nd Avenue and back with her. After luncheon Adrian dissapeared [*sic*] again on some expedition with the Fishers, & Nessa & I sat on the beach – Nessa attempting a picture of the Pier, & I reading Barchester Towers[32] to myself. Father & Thoby went to the Bird Museum. Georgie did his work here. We came back soon, as it was very cold & windy, and the youthful population of Brighton insisted upon watching over Nessa's shoulder. Gerald came after tea. Adrian dined and had tea with the Fishers – We only saw him for a short time at luncheon. My hot water bottle streamed into my bed; we covered the wet sheets with a towel, fastened down with safety pins, which was rather a wonderful proceeding.

Sunday 25 April
Stayed in all the morning, and read. Adrian & Thoby went as usual to the Fishers, where they spent the morning. After luncheon we all started for a walk – Will Vaughan came round and went with us. At 2nd Avenue, Gerald Nessa Thoby & I separated from the rest & went in search of Uncle Herbert. Meanwhile the others marched on, and left us behind – Gerald stayed to tea with Aunt Mary, & Uncle Herbert. Boo and we three walked on the Parade. We ended by sitting in the Avenue Gardens; opposite the sea – where we met Emmie & Adeline & a Mr Robjohns – an Australian friend of Emmie's, who met with a bicycle accident outside their door, & was brought in and recovered in their hall – but one ending to such a story! Boo came back to tea – Adrian & Tom spent the afternoon fishing off the pier. They have captured one unfortunate dab and live in hopes of some thing more glorious – but nothing else has bit as yet – Adeline came to dinner & told us stories of her dear Miss Roden – & of her brother Conrad –[33]

---

32 Anthony Trollope, *Barchester Towers*, 1857.
33 Frances Noel (b.1864) and Conrad (b.1869), the children of Mrs MacAnally's first marriage to the Hon. Roden Noel.

Monday 26 April

We started on our famous Arundel expedition at 11.15 this morning. Adeline & Charlie went with us. It was very hot and dusty; for the first time this fortnight the wind was low and stuffy – What there was of it, kept at our backs – We rode most comfortably, dismounting at the hills, and allowing ourselves to look at primroses, and woods, regardless of so many miles an hour. At Worthing we had the pleasure of seeing the Duke of Cambridge[34] opening the water works in the distance, surrounded by a body of guards – We had luncheon at Angmering, at the Horse & Groom – of eggs and bread and butter. A quiet sleepy little place, a swan sitting on its nest – most peaceful after Brighton glare – We reached Arundel at about 3, and saw the castle[35] – We mounted the keep, & were shown Cromwell's cannon balls, and the Empress Mauds bedstead – together with some ancient stuffed owls. The castle is all being hideously rebuilt – but from the town in the valley the long line of black wall (the Castle) looks very solid & old – trained back from Ford[36] – 22 miles. A. M[ary]. talked to us after tea.

Tuesday 27 April

In the morning Nessa & Thoby rode for 2 hours, & Adrian went out shrimping with Tom. Father & I started for a walk along the sea wall. We met Adeline & Boo, who went the rest of the way with us. In the afternoon Emmie turned up, and sat with Nessa and me till 4 o'clock – Charlie carried father off to a Public House to play billiards, and Thoby and Adrian went out with Tom & Boo. Emmie told us wonderful stories – my dear Miss Roden was talked of a great deal – Emmie went at 4 to give Hervey his tea, & at 5 Nessa & I followed and had tea for the first and last time this Easter with the Fishers. After tea we turned[?] up letters with Emmie, in the hope of finding some from Granny – but there

---

34 William Frederick Charles George, 2nd Duke of Cambridge (1819-1904), a cousin of Queen Victoria.

35 Arundel Castle in West Sussex was the home of the Dukes of Norfolk for 500 years. The Empress Matilda or Maud (1102-67), only daughter of Henry I, was consort to the Holy Roman Emperor Henry V and claimant to the English throne; she was besieged in the Castle in 1139. In the 17th century Cromwell's Parliamentary forces bombarded the Castle and subsequently occupied it. It was almost completely rebuilt by C. A. Buckler, 1890-1903; the restored Keep was the only part open to the public at this time.

36 From Ford Junction, about 3 miles south of Arundel, there was a direct train service to Hove and Brighton.

were none, only two negatives which I have appropriated of her beautiful (*attractive rather*) head –

Wednesday 28 April

Nessa & Thoby rode for the last time in the morning. Adrian and I did
nothing. Adeline came to see if everything was finished in the morning,
which most wonderful to say, it was. Thoby, Father & Adrian lunched
with the Fishers. Nessa & I alone; after lunch at 2, came a final scramble
– the last boxes packed and we set off on bicycles to the station; – Aunt
Mary brought father there – we said goodbye & started. On the way I
virtuously finished the 2nd vol. of Macaulay. Met at Victoria which we
reached at 4.20 by Georgie. Stella in bed with a bad chill on her innards
like she had at Christmas. They have a nurse, Dr Seton three times a day
– they say she is getting better – but everyone getting miserable. Everything as dismal as it well can be. Oh dear – how is one to live in such a
world, which is a Miss Janism, but very much my mind at present. To
bed in my new room, which was lonely & dismal too. Dr S. declares her
to be much better & going on very well – Somehow things will get
straight again – but it is most depressing.

Thursday 29 April

Stella rather better this morning so they said. Nessa went and sat with
her all the morning as the Nurse was asleep after last night – I went out
with Thoby & Adrian to buy some beef tea in High St. Afterwards came
back and sat in the drawing room at No 24 – to be there if Nessa should
want anything – Nessa lunched there, and Georgie stayed at home for
lunch. Afterwards Thoby, A. & father went to the Zoo; Georgie & I
bought some things in High St., and then I went back & sat at 24. Stella
was worse in the afternoon – the pain was bad – After tea Nessa went
back again, & I sat again over those eternal old Graphics and my
Macaulay which is the only calm and un-anxious thing in this most agi-
tating time – Dr Seton came after dinner, and was rather frightening. It
is Peritonitis – she is to be kept quite quiet – There is to be another
nurse, & straw put down on the road.[37] Poor Jack very unhappy. This is
one of the most terrible nights so far. No getting rid of the thought – all
of these ghastly preparations add to it – the people jar at every possible

---

37 Straw used to be laid over city streets to deaden the noise from carts and carriages
   outside houses where there was serious illness.

occasion. I slept with Nessa, as I was unhappy. News that she is better at about 11 o'clock – What shall I write tomorrow?

Friday 30 April

Stella better this morning. Dr Seton came at 10, and was very cheerful. We stayed in and saw the people who came to enquire – Cousin Mia arrived & sat ponderously in the drawing room, telling long stories of Iona Carroll[38] etc. Gerald and Georgie stayed here most of the day, & were most cheering – Everyone seems to think her really better. Dr Seton came again at 2, and was pleased: said she is absolutely safe, & no complications. Nevertheless Jack decided to ask Sir W. Broadbent[39] to come, though it was unnecessary. In the afternoon suddenly Aunt Mary came creeping up to 24 – and sat in the kitchen. She had not had G[eorgie']s good telegram before she started & his letter had frightened her – She was very anxious that they should have another opinion – She went by the 5.40 – Thoby & Stewart also went – Thoby had been allowed to see Stella for a moment. Broadbent came at 7 – He was not quite so encouraging about her as Seton, but said it was satisfactory, which I suppose must be believed. He comes again tomorrow. Jack came after dinner & said Stella was decidedly better – quite different. Slept with N again.

---

38 Probably Jane de la Tour Carroll (*c.*1836-1907), artist and sculptor, daughter of the Reverend Theopholis Carroll, living at Kensington Gate.

39 Sir William Broadbent, 1st Bt (1835-1907), Physician Extraordinary to HM Queen Victoria and Physician in Ordinary to the Prince of Wales.

Saturday 1 May

Stella had a better night than she has had yet; Dr Seton came at 10, & was delighted with her. Nessa & I went for a little walk to Church St. and bought some nails and a postal order for Beck [photographic suppliers] – Came back & spent the rest of the morning at the front drawing room window which has become our chief resort nowadays on the look out for enquirers doctors cabs etc. Cousin Mia came here of course, & went away satisfied. After luncheon Hester[1] & Aunt Anny arrived – Hester went for a walk with us in the gardens; very stiff and exclamatory & proper. Broadbent came at 5, and was much more satisfactory than yesterday. Everything going on as well as possible. Poor Aunt Minna came down having just arrived from the country very much frightened by the straw etc. knowing nothing of Stella's illness. However the good reports cheered her up – For the first time since Wednesday, I read quietly and happily at my cherished Macaulay. After all books are the greatest help and comfort.[2] I slept in my own room tonight. Better news still late at night.

Sunday 2 May

Dr Seton came at 11, and was perfectly happy about Stella – She has had a good night, no pain – pulse & temperature normal. What more could one want? Georgie & I therefore went out contentedly to hear Father lecture at the Kensington Town Hall upon Pascal.[3] There was a fairly large audience composed of sensible ugly young teachers & middle aged ladies and very strong minded respectable tradespeople in black – The proceedings were enlivened at intervals by songs and music from the gallery. The lecture was very deep rather too deep for the audience; very logical & difficult for the ignorant (i.e. Miss Jan) to follow – Not quite as good as I have heard from him – however it went off comfortably.

In the afternoon Georgie & we three went for a walk in the gardens. Broadbent and Dr S. came at 4. Broadbent quite enthusiastic – Thoroughly good straight forward recovery – absolutely no danger –

---

1 Hester Ritchie (later Fuller, b.1878), daughter of 'Aunt Anny', Anne Isabella Ritchie, *née* Thackeray (1837-1919).

2 Cf. Cicero's *Pro Archia*, VII: 'Books are . . . a refuge and relief . . . they are with us by night, they are with us on long journeys, they are with us in the depths of the country.'

3 Delivered to the West London Ethical Society, published in *Studies of a Biographer*, vol.2, 1899.

Jack asked him to come on Tuesday. Jan most jubilant – & went comfortably to bed for the first time. Read Mr. [Henry] James to quiet me, and my beloved Macaulay.

Monday 3 May
Stella had a very good night & no pain – so everyone went happily to their work as usual. Thank goodness this seems to be the beginning of a quiet happy week – Dr Seton was expected at 11, but sent to say that he had caught a chill & could not come – If Jack wished for anyone, to have Broadbent, but it was not in the least necessary – Jack however did sent [*sic*] for Broadbent. Nessa & I went out in the morning to buy some flowers & grapes for Stella & Dr Seton, and two fresh eggs which S. may now have – In the afternoon we went out shopping in High St. and bought various uninteresting things. Adrian lunched with the Macnamaras, and went afterwards to a play at St James[4] – He also had tea, and I suppose made himself very agreeable as is his custom – declared that the Mac[Namara]s: down to Pat[5] possessed undeniable virtues and a most beautiful kitten – So much the better. Broadbent came at 5.40, and stayed a short time – thinking it I expect rather ridiculous for him to come at all – Everything as good as it could be – Will come again tomorrow if Dr S. is still unwell.

Tuesday 4 May
Nessa went in to see Stella this morning. She was struck by her looks: fatter decidedly than after the wedding & looking altogether better – This is most satisfactory – but I am unreasonable enough to be irritated –

We went out to Barkers on one of our usual uninteresting everyday errands – After luncheon at about 3.30 Broadbent came as Dr S. is still ill. He said she was getting on splendidly etc: So we went out for a walk in the gardens and, to reduce attacks of Peritonitis, had ices (the first of the season) in the white house in the Park. Afterwards we walked down by the Horse Guards and watched the ladies coming back from the drawing room. Such a hideous set of bedecked old frumps I never saw – At tea time a series of visitors came, so that poor Marmot [Vanessa] – had to sit and entertain in the drawing room – Father began Caleb

---

4   *The Princess and the Butterfly*, by Arthur Wing Pinero, starring George Alexander and Julia Neilson.
5   Patrick (1886-1957), youngest son of Maria (Mia) and Charles MacNamara.

Williams[6] to us by William Godwin. Read in bed as is my usual custom nowadays, and finished off Mr H[enry] J[ames].

Wednesday 5 May
The papers full of the fire at Paris, which happened yesterday afternoon.[7] A bazaar full of people was burned down – they think 200 were killed – Most ghastly details in the Daily Chronicle & the Times. Nessa went to her drawing for the first time this term. Walking as it was raining. Adrian went in and saw Stella who gave him some green sleeve links – We went round to ask after Doctor Seton who is much better. After luncheon I went in and saw Stella for the first time since the wedding. She looks better than I expected, and seemed altogether less ill & weak – She was thinner however than Nessa & Adrian had described her. We sat & talked for about half an hour, & then the nurse said it was time for Mrs Hills to go to sleep, so I went. Adrian & I went out to High St to buy some plates for his Kodac [*sic*].[8] When we came in I found a telegram for Georgie which I opened: it was from Vicompte [*sic*] de Luppe[9] to say that his mother was burnt yesterday in the fire. Also another telegram from M. Bourgain[10] to say that she is safe – Stella gave me a pencil from Paris which I have on my watch chain.

Thursday 6 May
The war[11] was hustled into the back columns of the papers to make room

---

6 *The Adventures of Caleb Williams*, 1794.
7 'Charity Bazaar in Rue Jean Goujon . . . destroyed in a few minutes. Dead and injured estimated at 200 . . . Cause: electric wiring set fire to the hangings': *The Times*, 5 May. 'The lamp of the cinematograph [beside the Bazaar] set the place on fire,' said the *Pall Mall Gazette*. *Severine*, a feminist periodical, reported that the French aristocracy had beaten down the women who stood in their way and left them there to roast.
8 Kodak was the proprietary name of the first popular portable camera, patented by George Eastman in 1888.
9 Actually Comte José-Louis de Luppé (1837-1912), Député in the Basses-Pyrénées; his wife, Comtesse Louise-Marie Aldegonde de Rivière, died in the fire and was later identified by the name in her wedding-ring.
10 Unidentified.
11 The Graeco-Turkish war of 1897.

for the fire. The duchesse d'Alencon[12] is dead, besides any amount of other grandees. The papers each with ghastly accounts, but they do not agree as to how the fire was started – In 12 minutes everything was finished – In the morning A. went back to Westminster & Nessa & I after a great fight were let off lessons till Monday. We went & saw Stella who seems fairly well & comfortable – We went out afterwards. We went to High St & bought some braid & something else which I cannot remember – a catalogue of the classes at King's College – that was it – which I may go to. After lunch I talked to father about it, and decided to begin next autumn if I begin at all. In the afternoon we went to the work-house – Met the Milmans on the way & walked in the gardens with them. Georgie insisted upon my putting out my light early or I should have finished the 3rd vol. of Macaulay.

Friday 7 May

Nessa went to her studio and Adrian to his lessons so that I was left alone. I went out to High St to buy a diary for Georgie, and then came back & saw Stella, who seemed pretty well. After lunch I went in again and sat with her – before this however, Mrs Green – that wicked old harpy – as for the future I shall call her – came to see Father. I was in my usual position behind the folding doors – nevertheless she saw me & shook hands with me. Then she proceeded to tell Father stories of the Symondses – among others that Catherine Symonds will eventually mark my words Mr Stephen (in a low voice) become a Roman Catholic! – This amused me so much that I repeated it to Stella. Afterwards it turns out that Mrs G. was telling this as a profound secret to father, and that she did not know I was there! I sat with S all the afternoon. At 4.30 I went out with Nessa to High St. Finished 3rd vol. of Macaulay & began 4th.

Saturday 8 May

In the morning Nessa & I and Georgie went to the Bank to get back Stella's & Jack's chest of silver. On the way there we saw a hansom overturned in Piccadilly – I saw it in mid air – the horse lifted from its

---

12 Sophie Charlotte of Bavaria (1847-97), youngest sister of Elizabeth, Empress of Austria, in 1866 married Ferdinand d'Orleans, Duc d'Alençon, son of Duc de Nemours, one of the seven children of Louis Philippe; the Duchesse d'Alençon's body was not immediately found, but was later identified by her maid from an inscribed wedding-band and a gold watch.

legs, and the driver jumping from the box. Luckily neither horse nor driver suffered though the hansom was broken – Then again, I managed to discover a man in the course of being squashed by an omnibus, but, as we were in the midst of Piccadilly Circus, the details of the accident could not be seen. We brought the chest back in a four wheeler, which, strange to say, carried us home safely. In the afternoon Adrian was carried off by Joe to Kew, & Nessa & Georgie went to the R[oyal] A[cademy]. & then to the Kays for tea. I perambulated less magnificent quarters – Gloucester Rd in fact – I bought some flowers & took them to Miss Totley[13] – Stella getting on well – eating roast chicken etc. Georgie & Joe went to a Bow Music Hall, & Georgie spent the night in the slums.[14]

Sunday 9 May

Georgie away in his slums. Gerald down about 11.30; the rest of us straggled out of bed at various hours – I indeed, was rather early – Nothing happened at all – We sat in the drawing room – Adrian & Gerald playing chess – I reading beloved Macaulay – a very tough 5th volume & Nessa sitting with Stella. This Sunday a most distinct improvement upon last. Then we were not out of the wood (as Broadbent said) Vaguely unhappy. – Cousin Mia a fixture – melancholy and large in the drawing room, and sympathetic enquirers dropping in every now & then – Now that old cow is most ridiculously well & cheerful – hopping about out of bed etc: Thank goodness, nevertheless – In the afternoon Jack kidnapped me, & carried me off to see Stella – where I was examined by Doctor Seton. No lessons – milk and some medicine which I forget. Otherwise exactly the same remarks – long anecdotes – Afterwards we went out into the Gdns and patronised the White house (Kensington Palace). Father recited Sohrab and Rustum[15] after dinner.

Monday 10 May

Nessa went to the drawing. Father & I began our morning pond walks. Afterwards I sat with Stella, & then went out to High St, & bought some grapes (I think – today is rather vague, as I most disgracefully forgot to write for two days). After luncheon [I went back to Stella & sat with her all the afternoon. She went to sleep when I was reading to her, & my

---

13 Probably Stella's nurse at 24 Hyde Park Gate, SW.
14 At his research for Charles Booth's *Life and Labour of the People of London*, 1901-3.
15 Matthew Arnold, *Sohrab and Rustum*, 1853.

creaky shoes made me sit still there till she woke up at 4.30.][16] (This is all mixed up with Thursday –) I cannot remember at all what happened in the afternoon; but I think I shopped in High St – A most dreadful failure – At any rate in the evening Mr Gibbs came round, & offered to take Nessa & me to Brooks[17] with him on the 22nd, where we could see the Procession[18] beautifully – However Gerald may have a window or a roof top already so we are not sure about it.

Tuesday 11 May

In the morning Nessa & I went round to 24 – found Stella most prosperous, & and sat with her for a little. Then we went back here, and mended Georgie's gloves – of all characteristic employments! Afterwards we went to Gloucester Rd with my prescription, & bought some gardening tools. Father has taken up Doctor Seton's notion that I should be healthfully employed out of doors – as a lover of nature – & the back garden is to be reclaimed – that will be a truly gigantic work of genius – nevertheless we will try. Accordingly a fork, a spade, a hoe & a rake were ordered for 7/6, & tomorrow I begin operations. We ought to have gone on to Mrs Pixleys,[19] but we were too exhausted. All the afternoon I spent with Stella; Nessa went out with Mrs Flower to the New Gallery.[20] Who should pay us a visit at tea, but dear Edith![21] She wished one of us to go with her to the Park to see the Queen pass by after the drawing room – She gave us a most animated description of At. M[inna]s. clothing in Spain – her appearance in her night gown etc –

Wednesday 12 May

In the morning Nessa went to the studio. I did not go out with father early. Sat with Stella for a little in the morning, & then went to the Pixleys, whom I neglected yesterday. After ringing three times I was let in,

---

16 The two sentences within brackets were deleted by AVS.

17 Brooks's Club (founded as a Whig club), 60 St James's Street, SW.

18 22 June would be the day of Queen Victoria's Diamond Jubilee.

19 Possibly Beatrice Ada, *née* Higson, who in 1891 married James A. Pixley (1863-1911), Trinity College, Cambridge, and a member of the firm of Pixley and Abell, bullion-brokers.

20 To see the Annual Summer Exhibition of works of Living Artists.

21 Edith Anna Duckworth (1866-1953), daughter of Russell Duckworth, JP, and niece of Herbert Duckworth.

asked after Mrs P's sister who has Peritonitis – Mrs P herself came to see me in her horrid little drawing room. Then I dissapeared[*sic*] and had the pleasure of seeing a cart horse fall down – In the afternoon I sat with Stella the whole time. She got up & walked down stairs and lay on the sofa, very comfortably. Dear Nurse Wyllie has gone, & only Nurse Peck remains. Dr Seton came & said if it was fine & warm she might go out tomorrow. Adrian did not come till 7.30, & he spent till 10 doing Algebra with Father – Georgie & Gerald both out.

Thursday 13 May

In the morning we went round as usual to Stella – Afterwards we went out to market in High St – one of our jobs took us to Herbert & Jones[22] to buy some sponge cakes for Stella's tea – While we were waiting for them – I heard a stampede in the street outside – shouting – as the stampede became more violent – & then a crash. Evidently the runaway had collided. A glimpse out of the door – to which the young ladies all crowded to get a better view – showed one horse on the ground and a second prancing madly above it – a carriage was smashed up & a wagon turned over on to its side. The young ladies were dispersed by the appearance of an infuriated steed at the door – pushing it with its nose; however he was captured in time. As soon as things were quieter we fled – without the sponge cakes – No one hurt. The afternoon spent in gardening.

Friday 14 May

Nessa went to her drawing. At 12.15, Stella went out for the first time (yesterday was too cold) in a bath chair. Just as we had started, we met Adeline and Emmie [Fisher] coming down the street. They are staying with Aunt Virginia. They went out with us into the gardens for a little walk, & then left us. We marched solemnly up & down the Flower walk and then went home. In the afternoon Father & I went out together. When we arrived at the Serpentine we lazily sat down in 2 arm chairs; and lolled there for half an hour, watching the river, & the peacocks on the other banks. These creatures occasionally screamed mournfully, and were answered from afar off by other peacocks – ducks kept up a perpetual quacking – This was most soothing however, after a week of

22 Herbert & Jones, cooks and confectioners, 48 Kensington High Street, W.

ferocious carriage wheels & accidents – Bought a diary for Nessa[23] from Father. Finished vol. 4 of Macaulay –

Saturday 15 May

In the morning we went to Stella & sat with her for a little, & then came back & gardened. Nessa was valiant, & created another flower bed by the garden wall, but I basely deserted her, when the worms & stones became too numerous, & the heat was too great. We had arranged to go to Westminster, & to see the Lords & Commons cricket match. Georgie was to meet us there – But at luncheon time A. arrived saying that there was only an ordinary match. We had to go to Vincent Sq^{re} nevertheless to meet Georgie at 3.30 – He came at about 4. & we stayed till 5 & watched a very dull game between the Masters & Boys. As a refreshment afterwards Georgie took us to Gunters in Sloane Sqre. – Where we had the most gorgeous strawberry ices – Gerald out to dinner. Stella & Jack went for a drive. Began 5th & last vol. of Macaulay.

Sunday 16 May

We went round in the morning & saw Stella. I was extremely gruff & unpleasant, which, however, is to be ascribed to the effect of the hot weather on my nerves – Nothing else! Stella walked up the street with Jack, & in the afternoon went for a drive. We – father G[eorge] H[erbert] D[uckworth] Nessa, A. & I, went out into the gardens & sat under the trees for some time – Georgie went fast asleep. Father went to lecture on Nansen[24] at 7. o'clock, so that dinner was put off till he came in – about a quarter to nine. Georgie, Nessa & I had a long talk in my room about various things – Lesage[25] came to tea – also General Beadle & Mr Gibbs. But I sat upstairs & read. Nessa poured forth Parisian French; & Mr Lesage is going to present her (if father allows) with a book!!

Monday 17 May

Nessa to the studio. I went over to Stella, & sat with her for some time. Then she told me to go down Gloucester Rd. & order a Bath Chair for

---

23 For her birthday, 30 May, which was also Stella's.

24 'Praising the Arctic explorer for his courage, he [Leslie Stephen] remarked that his scientific results – the mapping of an utterly useless region – were really a pretext for a fine display of manliness . . .' Noel Annan, *Leslie Stephen: The Godless Victorian*, 1984, p. 318.

25 Presumably a French friend of George Duckworth.

her that morning, which I did. Afterwards at 12.30 we went out in the gardens (Stella in her bath chair) & sat under the trees, where father joined us. In the afternoon we drove in a Hobbes[26] – terrible ordeal! The horse however proved stolid & as lazy as our Bognor steed: almost breaking down up hill – walking at a funereal pace – But I forgave it its sins, & only wished it could impart some portion of its contented disposition & complacent mind to its brethren. I sat with Stella till tea time. Adrian did not come home till past 8, which was rather alarming – Gerald came back from his party to see whether he had been run over, & everyone was much disturbed. Finished the 5th & last v. of my beloved Macaulay!

Tuesday 18 May

Nessa went out to market in High St. for various things connected with tonight's feast. Susan Lushington who was to be the lady, could not come. I spent the morning with Stella. Nurse Peck went away. Stella walked up & down the street a little. Aunt Virginia & Adeline appeared at luncheon time & we were interviewed in the drawing room. Afterwards Nessa went to meet Mrs Flower, & I went for my now usual much to be dreaded drive in the Park with Stella. I have now got Carlyle's French Revolution – the 5th volume of Macaulay being restored to its place. In this way I shall become surfeited with history. Already I am an expert upon William[27] (Hear Hear!) & when I have mastered C's 2 vols. I shall be eligible for the first B.A. degree – if the ladies succeed. Lesage to dinner. Adeline who was asked did not turn up.

Wednesday 19 May

Nessa went to her drawing. I went over to Stella, & found her still lying in bed. However she soon got up, & went down to the drawing room. Dear Edith Duckworth appeared, & talked till about 1 – then we all three marched up the road. Father met us, & he & Stella went out into the gardens together. After luncheon the inquisitive hour[28] – as our

---

26 Henry Hobbs, Job Master, Hyde Park Gate Mews, Kensington, W. 'Perhaps one house out of every six in Hyde Park Gate kept a carriage, or hired one from Hobbs whose livery stable opened its great yard in the middle.' *MoB*, p. 121.

27 William of Orange (1650-1702); see Vol. III of Macaulay's *The History of England*, 1860, 5 vols.

28 Living now at 24 Hyde Park Gate, Stella could no longer directly supervise the regimen Dr Seton had set for AVS and so quizzed her during their afternoon ride through the Park.

usual melancholy trot in the Park is called – took place. Afterwards I sat with Stella till tea time. After tea we again went in to Stella, & gossiped with her till late – Then we dressed for dinner with At. Minna & afterwards the play. Gerald came with us, the dinner was very odd – G & Edith making jokes against At. M. in whispers the whole time, & then we drove to Terrys Theatre & saw the French Maid.[29] A musical, rather vulgar play. Home at a quarter to 12.

Thursday 20 May

Went over to Stella in the morning, & sat with her till 1. Then of all people in the world, Mrs O'Brien[30] appeared – bringing with her photographs of the little O'Bs. (Conor, Harry etc) as hideous as ever, & which Stella found herself incapable of admiring. Then we walked up & down the street, & Stella had luncheon with us – for the first time since the day before her wedding – Afterwards we took the drive in the Park. I wish they would cease to exist! Brer Muddie[31] came to dinner & afterwards went over to Stella. I read in bed as usual, The Scarlet Letter,[32] & was stopped by Georgie & Nessa at 11 o'clock. Gerald out as usual to 2 dances only this time! Nessa bought 13s worth of flowers for the back garden.

Friday 21 May

I went over very late in the morning to Stella, & found At Minna permanently (so it seemed) seated by her side, pouring forth a stream of gossip – questions etc. which, I being in a very bad humour, made me so angry that I turned my back, & made myself generally unpleasant! Stella suffered more though, for she had a headache. We did not go out therefore, but she came round to luncheon. Adrian came back from Westminster

---

29 A musical comedy by Basil Hood, with music by Walter Slaughter.

30 Julia, *née* Marshall (d.1907), sister of James Marshall who was killed on a climbing trip at Courmayeur, the Alps. She made friends with Leslie Stephen when visiting Switzerland to see her brother's grave; she 'favoured' Leslie, who had just lost his first wife, and his friends hoped he would marry her.

31 The only clue to the identity of Brer Muddie is in the 31 October 1892 issue of *Hyde Park Gate News*, in an item for Adrian's birthday (probably written by Vanessa): 'The newly wedded couple Mr & Mrs Davis [Arthur and Sylvia Llewelyn Davies] made their appearance at the end of tea and "Brer Muddy" present [*sic*] Master Adrian Stephen with a beautiful little box of chocolates. The evening soon gone and so was Master Adrian Stephen's birthday.'

32 Nathaniel Hawthorne, *The Scarlet Letter*, 1850.

early, as he had a half holiday on account of the concert. He spent the afternoon in doing his prep: & in buying white gloves, black trousers & an evening tie (for the concert) with Nessa. I sat with Stella until Mrs Edmund Hills came, & then I came back here & read till teatime. None of us went to the concert; A. came back at 11.30 just as I finished the Scarlet Letter.

Saturday 22 May
The day of our great water party. We – Georgie, Nessa & I started for High St Station at 10. We changed at Reading, & got to Goring[33] at 11.15. We put our clothes, cherries etc. in the drawing room of the Miller of Mansfield (the Inn of the place.) & then we went down to the boat house to see about the boats. There we met Sir Condie Stephen[34] – of all people! We rowed out down the stream, & paddled industriously into the banks – N. & I rowing. At 1.30 we had lunch at the M. of M. – & at 3. we went down to meet the train. Gerald, A. & Lesage & Miss Booth[35] came by it. All the other people we had invited did not turn up – My space is gradually dissapearing [*sic*], & I cannot say in the shortest way all that we did – However, briefly – we splashed leisurely down the river to Tilehurst – picked buttercups on the way, & eating cherries. At Tilehurst we had tea, & once more rowed on to Reading. This we reached at 8.30, & caught the train earlier than the one we meant. Home about 10.30. Father at Cambridge.

Sunday 23 May
The morning we spent in the garden. This desert place is under our hands, becoming a quite beautiful spot – There is one large round bed, which you see from the drawing room window, & another long one behind it against the wall. Both these we planted liberally with half grown pansies, lobelia, & sweet peas. We are going to buy some grass seeds & cover the bare patch of earth which surrounds our beds. In the afternoon we saw Stella for a little, & then gardened again. Father away at Cambridge. Gerald went out after dinner on a bicycling party – with

---

33 A village on the River Thames about 8½ miles north-west of Reading.

34 Sir Alexander Condie Stephen (1860-1908), diplomat, living at Albert Gate, Knightsbridge, and no relation to Leslie Stephen.

35 Antonia Mary (Dodo) Booth (1872-1952), eldest daughter of Mary and Charles Booth; in 1899 she would marry the Hon. Malcolm MacNaghten (1869-1955), barrister.

the Lewises[36] & Grays[37] as usual to Bow to explore the Catholic Churches.[38]

I began Miss Mitford's Notes of a Literary Life,[39] as a night book – superseding The Scarlet Letter, by my dearly beloved Hawthorne.

Monday 24 May

In the morning Nessa went to her studio, & I round to Stella. We stayed talking there for some time, & then we went in to the gardens & sat down. She came back to luncheon with us. After lunch Stella & I gossiped till about 4, when we made up our minds to take a walk – at the top of the road we met Nessa coming back from her drawing so we all together went on to the Gardens, & sat on chairs. After tea Nessa & I delved a little in the garden – which grows more & more beautiful, & went round again to Stella. I determined to finish the 1st vol. of the F[rench]. R[evolution]. by night – but when bed time came there were still a good many pages left – in the middle of my nightly forbidden reading, I shut up, thinking G[eorge]. was coming. However it was a false alarm, & the 1st vol. was finished.

Tuesday 25 May

We began our marketings with Mrs [Edmund] Hills for the first time. We walked with her down Gloucester Rd. and bought various things – to be sent to Mrs J.W. Hills. She told us an extraordinary story of her husbands proceedings yesterday night. He came home quite deaf – having suddenly become so in the morning. After an hour or so of shouting at him, they agreed to send for Dr Coates.[40] He came & squirted warm water down one ear, & a piece of wax which had got over the hole dropped out. Now he hears like an ordinary being. He has also bought Stella a jay – a featherless jay. In the afternoon (I had lunch with Stella) we went & sat in the gardens. Nessa did some marketings in High Street. After tea I went in again to see S's cat – a stray half Persian

---

36 The children of Sir George Henry Lewis (1833-1911), the eminent solicitor; Alice (b. c.1863) was the child of his first wife, Victorine Kann (d.1865); the children of his second marriage (1867) to Elizabeth Eberstadt were George (1868-1927), Gertrude (b. c.1870), and Katherine (b.1878); the Lewises lived at 88 Portland Place, W.

37 Probably Gerald's ex-Eton friends.

38 Our Lady of Refuge and St Catherine of Siena.

39 Mary Russell Mitford, *Recollections of a Literary Life*, 1852.

40 George Coates, MA, MD, physician and surgeon, 30 Brechin Place, Gloucester Road, SW.

which comes every evening to have milk. Today its mother sat & watched over it in the garden. The jay arrives tomorrow in a new cage!

Wednesday 26 May

Nessa went to her drawing, though it had begun to drizzle. At 11, when it was comfortably pouring, I ran over to 24, & spent the morning with Stella in arranging her Venetian glass in the china cupboard, & afterwards in reading Punches. She had luncheon with us. After lunch it had cleared up a little. We went down to Childs[41] in a fourwheeler, & ordered a chain for Nessa's birthday. We were shown some wonderful things in the shop – a locket made out of a sovereign etc. After dinner – (Georgie & Gerald both out) Lisa Stillman came in to hear father recite – Love in a Valley[42] which she could not think beautiful – However she declared her mind changed when it was recited – & we had some others of Mr Merediths – Jacobi (my mouse) visited me at night as usual & eat some of my supper, dear creature!

Thursday 27 May

Showery, & rather cold. We went out into the gardens, & walked about a little, & then came home again. Stella did not lunch with us; as for the future she is only to come every other day. In the afternoon I was dragged to Cocoatina Smart[43] (so named by Kitty) & had my head washed by a beautiful young lady – This operation lasted about an hour, & then we went home again. Stella & Nessa spent the time shopping in High St. Georgie & Gerald in for dinner – but both out afterwards. Gerald told indecent stories,[44] & Father read aloud some ridiculous translations of French by a schoolboy in the P[all] M[all] G[azette],[45] so that we spent a most laughable evening – Thoby's paints arrived addressed to Miss V.S. so that Nessa opened them.

Friday 28 May

In the morning, I went out by myself – Nessa was at her most ———— (to be filled in as desired) studio, & Stella went to Libertys with Gerald to

---

41 Child & Child, jewellers, 35 Alfred Place, WC.
42 George Meredith, 'Love in the Valley', 1851, 1878.
43 Ciccognani Smart, hairdresser, 10 Lower Phillimore Place, W.
44 His stories were scatological.
45 The item's headline reads: 'The Patriotic Spirit – Some Reflections on the French Translations of Minor Smith and Others' – the others being third-form pupils.

choose an evening dress for G. to give Nessa on her birthday – However they found nothing, so that it had to be put off. I got some pills at Coopers[46] & then went to enquire after Marny, whom Emma thought had the flengs.[47] I saw Emma who said it was not flengs, but measles! They have a nurse, though it is a very slight attack because Emma, not having had flengs herself, cannot nurse Marny. In the afternoon at 3, who should arrive but At. Mary! She & Stella spent the afternoon talking together, & at 4.30, when Nessa came in, she & I went to High St. & bought our present for Stella – 2 glass water jugs – 2.11. each also some chocolate. Finished the first vol. of Miss Mitford – a most gossipy night book – just fulfills [*sic*] its part.

Saturday 29 May

It began by being fine, but at 12 the rain came on. We were out with Stella buying shoes flowers etc. & had to take a fourwheeler back – Gerald had settled to call for us at 4, & take us to Mrs Winkworth's[48] garden party. But the rain grew worse & worse, till at last the whole sky was black, & no gap anywhere. So at four no Gerald appeared. However, at 5, it began to look more cheerful; blue sky actually showed itself, & as we were going down to tea, Gerald came, expecting to find us ready dressed. We changed most speedily, jumped into a cab, & found ourselves at Holly Lodge by 5.30. Here was a band, a crowd of people – Booths, Lewises, Caves,[49] Brer Muddie, Susan [Lushington] etc etc etc. Eat ices (3) & came away.

Sunday 30 May   *Stella's and Nessa's birthday*

Today Stella (Mrs John Waller Hills) is 28, and Nessa (still *Miss* Stephen thank goodness – but who, I say, can tell what next year is to bring – change of names & otherwise!) is 18. We went over to 24 early, with our present for Stella & she gave Nessa her watch chain – gold with 12 beautiful bits of blue enamel – We lunched with them, & spent the greater part of the afternoon there – They had dinner here, & we had an uproarious evening together. Next for the greatest & most beautiful of

---

46 Cooper & Co., chemist, 80 Gloucester Road, South Kensington, SW.
47 No satisfactory description has been found for this 'ailment'.
48 Mrs Emma Winkworth lived at Holly Lodge, Campden Hill, W.
49 The Caves were probably the children of Edith, *née* Symonds (*c.*1836-1912), and Sir Charles Daniel Cave, Bt, sister and brother-in-law of J. A. Symonds, and thus cousins of Madge and Katharine Symonds and Lotta Leaf.

either of their presents! Behold! Georgie presents Nessa with a wonderful *opal necklace* – almost as splendid as Stella's wedding one. This is my
envy & my delight. No room on page for more description of it – Gerald
a 5 pound note; and a dress to come – Father books. A. – slippers. T.
paints. Jack book. At. M[inna]. blouse (in which N. looked very lovely)
but the opal necklace!!!!!!

Monday 31 May
After yesterday's thunder storm, it was fine; though still hot & uncomfortable, today. In the morning Stella & I went out to see Marny. Before
this was reached, Helen Holland came: sat with me alone for some time,
& then walked with us through the gardens, & to High St. We bought
some canary seed & some oats, which the young man declares will
cover our garden with beautiful grass. Then we went to St. Albans Rd:
& talked to Emma through a sheet window (for fear of infection). Marney going on all right, has her nurse still. This was rather a terrible walk
– horses behaving violently. In the afternoon Stella & I went out in to
the gardens, & sat under the trees; as we were going away Mr [Henry]
James came up, & walked with us part of the way home – Then we met
father & the two went into the gardens again together. Adrian came
back from school, feeling unwell, & did not eat any tea. His temp: normal however, though it is possible that he has pleurisy. Much better
after dinner & sleep – played whist, & was quite well. Georgie came
home. He & Gerald both out to dinner & then to dances.

Tuesday 1 June

It was very rainy & dark in the morning, & we had made up our minds that it was no good going to Miss Kay, as we had settled, to see the bugs. However it cleared up, though rather late, & we set off as fast as we could for Prince's Gdns. They – Miss Kay, & Rachel[1] (a small 9 year old Kay) were waiting for us. Rachel & I talked together the whole time, in the most affable way, & Miss Kay & Nessa. The bugs were downstairs at the Mu[seum]. Nothing very wonderful. Mrs Flower came for Nessa. Stella & I went into the gdns. & sat & talked to a very nice baby. Adrian came back after tea, having been rather giddy at school, but it is only his liver – Georgie says – I was woke this morning at 4.30, by a flash of lightning, which lit up my room, & was followed by a tremendous thunder storm, & wind & rain. Finished the French R.

Wednesday 2 June   *Derby Day*   *Galtee More won*

Nessa went to her drawing. I was to have gone out with Stella, but just as we started forth, Mrs Mitchell Ennis[2] & Aunt Minna came & walked S. off to 24. Then Miss [Octavia] Hill came about the cottages, & stayed till 12.30, & then Mrs MacKenzie,[3] about the jubilee & broken windows if not illuminated. So that we did not get out at all. I stayed over here, & began Cromwell,[4] which succeeds the French Revolution. Also Lady Burton's[5] 2nd volume which came this morning. In the afternoon Stella & I went into High St., & bought an evening cloak for Nessa to wear tonight. High St even more diabolical than usual – the horses in a most wicked & rampant condition. Nessa's birthday cake for tea. At 7, we (they) dined: little Lesage also – & then went to the opera at Covent Gdn – Gounod's Faust – to which Lesage treated us. It lasted till 11.30 – rather too long, but very nice. We meant to have supper afterwards but Lesage was so much shocked at the idea that we gave it up. Lesage goes to France tomorrow at 9 A.M. Home & to bed at 12.30.

---

1   Angela Kay-Shuttleworth and her sister Rachel; see Feb. 1897, n.20.
2   AVS is probably referring to the wife of Edward A. Mitchell-Innes (1863-1932), barrister, on the Executive Committee of the National League Opposing Woman Suffrage.
3   The neighbour living at 21 Hyde Park Gate, SW.
4   Thomas Carlyle, *Cromwell*, 1845.
5   *The Romance of Isabel, Lady Burton, the Story of Her Life*, told in part by herself and in part by W. H. Wilkins, 1897, 2 vols.

Thursday 3 June

In the morning we three[6] went down to enquire after Marny (who has the measles). We talked with Emma, through the dining room window, & learned that she was going on very well etc.

After luncheon we went out in to the gardens with father, & sat upon chairs near the Pond. After sitting there for some time, we got up & went for a little walk. Stella became suddenly giddy; though only for a moment, so that we went straight home again. Violet Dickinson came to tea with her. We dug in the garden & finished the place that we mean to sow.

The sweet peas are holding their heads up a little, but the pansies have perished rather in the rain. Read Cromwell: harder to get on with than the F[rench] R[evolution] but better than some other works that I have had to devour.

Friday 4 June

Nessa went to her ——— drawing. Stella & I sat indoors for some time; Stella doing her sheets with Polly. Then At. Minna came, & afterwards, Evelyn Duckworth,[7] a spectacled Orchard Leigh one, whom I have not seen before. At last however we set out into the gardens, & walked up & down the flower walk, & looked at the flowers, peonies especially. Stella had luncheon with us. Afterwards she, Father & I, went & sat out in the gdns. At 4, Nessa came out to us (Father left to go to the L[ondon]. L[ibrary].) & we walked to Campden Hill – Stella had said that today I would have tea with Peggy. I was shown in to the drawing room, where Bella sat talking to a friend. We had tea together in the drawing room, & afterwards played games, the knife ran away with the spoon, until Nessa came to fetch me. She had had tea with Stella in High St. – They bought some paper which I do not like.

Saturday 5 June

We were to have gone to Oxford – Georgie, Nessa & I, but Georgie came into me before breakfast & told me that Stella had been bad in the night – the pain had come back again. So their plan of going to Clearwater Farm till Wednesday had to be put off, & everything was upset.

---

6 AVS, Vanessa and Stella.

7 Frances Evelyn Duckworth (1865-1926), daughter of the Rev. William Arthur Duckworth of Orchardleigh, sister of Margaret Newbolt, and niece of Herbert Duckworth.

Dr Seton came at 10.30 & said she was better. Tem. 100, not much pain: He came again at 4, & said she was no worse – She eat 3 cherries which may have made her bad, but they do not quite know what it is. She was sick a great deal, & has 2 nurses. We went into the gdns in the afternoon, rowed on the Serpentine, & had tea in the park. Then we came home & found Adeline here. Dr Seton came after dinner, & said she was much better, & the attack will probably be prevented –

Sunday 6 June
Stella had a good night & no pain, which was a comfort. Dr Seton came at 10.30, & was pleased – says he thinks he has stopped it in time. We sent off some telegrams. It was dreadfully hot – a steam rising out of the ground, & everything hazy. Adeline, A. & I went out into the gdns – which were all misty & hot. In the afternoon father went out, & we planted seed in the back garden. This is to produce grass – but whether the sparrows will have left any is a question. As soon as we had left the garden, the horrid little creatures swooped down twittering & made off with the oats etc. – Dr Seton came at 8.30, & was still more satisfied. Says he hopes – he will not be positive, but still he very much hopes that the actual peritonitis has been avoided, & that soon she will be well.

I got up at about 12, seeing them all in the road, & rushed down in my dressing gown – barefooted – However they were only chasing cats!

Monday 7 June   *Whit Monday – Bank Holiday*
Stella had a good night, & was better in the morning. Dr Seton came at 10.30, & was very much pleased. Adeline, Nessa & I went out in to the gdns, & walked about for some time. Georgie – had a holiday today, because of Whit Monday, & the rest of the world were taking their holidays in the gdns & other places. In the afternoon we wanted to go to Miss [Irene] Noel, with At. M[inna]'s carriage – but her telegram said she was away till tomorrow. So instead we went to Lords[8] & saw a match between Somerset & Surrey (?)[9] – the first day – Nothing very exciting however. Came away at 6, & undergrounded home with a terrible bank holiday lot. Dr Seton came at 7.30, & was most cheerful. In a few days she will be well. But she will have to go away, & not eat cherries or chocs. for some time –

---

8   Lord's, England's premier cricket ground, St John's Wood, NW.
9   AVS's parentheses.

Tuesday 8 June

Stella had a very good night, though she was sick once. Dr Seton came at 10.30 & said she was getting on as well as possible Broadbent will not come till tomorrow or the day after. We went out with Adeline into High St. to buy Nessa an evening dress – or at least a skirt & silk for a body but there was nothing in High St. neither skirt nor stuff. This is to be her wonderful coming out dress to be worn at a party at Cousin Mia's on the 16th – In the afternoon we went to Harvey & Nicholls [*sic*] & bought stuff for the dress (silk). Then we took the bus to Notting Hill Gate – another, & another till at last we came to St Marks Rd. at the ends of the earth – touching Worm Wood Scrubbs! [*sic*] We found dear Frances[10] in, with an Indian uncle of hers – Most delightful – talked & laughed. Then we were shown Miss Baldwin[11] – an emaciated female who plays the piano loudly & badly – quite cosy. No room to say more of this wonderful pair.

Wednesday 9 June

Stella had a very good night, though she was sick once. Nessa went to her drawing. Adeline & I stayed in till about 12 – it was pouring: & then when it had stopped, we went out. Today was Georgie's great Eton Ramblers match against Westminster. We went to South Audley St. walking all the way there & back across the park, & asked whether At. Virginia was in London or abroad. Then home again, & watched the ducks in the Serpentine. After luncheon we (A[deline]. father & I) had settled to go to Vincents Square, but it was raining, so that we thought they would not play. Adeline & I went out together rather aimlessly, & half way down Queens Gate decided to call upon Mr Gibbs[12] – He was out however. Then we went to Rosie Marrable[13] & talked to her for some time – a dry disagreeable little creature: Then we went to Nessa at

---

10 Frances Gertrude Alice Noel (1864-1941), daughter of Mrs MacAnally from her first marriage to the Hon. Roden B. W. Noel; see April 1897, n.22.

11 Presumably daughter of the Baldwins listed as also living at 125 St Marks Road, Notting Hill, W.

12 F. W. Gibbs lived at 38 Cornwall Gardens, SW; see Jan. 1897, n.84.

13 Theresa Rose Marrable (1862-1936), artist, daughter of George Marrable (b.1820), living at 25 Onslow Square, SW, and niece of Madeleine Marrable, *née* Cockburn, who for many years was President of the Society of Women Artists.

the studio, & with her on to the Milmans: afterwards to the Vaughans,[14] & at last after all these extraordinary calls, home. Finished 1st vol. of Cromwell.

Thursday 10 June   *Adeline Fisher engaged to Ralph Vaughan Williams*
Stella had a very good night, though she was still sick. Nessa & Adeline were debating about the wonderful dratted never-to-be-finished evening dress – I was reading in the drawing room. Suddenly the front door bell rang, & Ellen announced Mr Vaughan Williams – I escaped by the little room door & went up to tell Adeline (he had asked for Miss Fisher). Adeline descended, & for a little time we heard no more. Then the door went, & we beheld A. & a strange gentlemans back walking up the st together. The back we thought we recognised as Roland VWs. We thought nothing particular about it, though as the morning wore on – they went out about 11 – it became suspicious. They did not come back for lunch – not until 3.30 – then – Adeline was engaged![15] Broadbent was with Stella – when he came out he was completely satisfied – amazed at having been sent for – etc. We went out shopping. Miss Noel came to tea – A most exciting afternoon – In the evening A[deline]. & Gerald went to the opera, so the day was finished – Good heavens – what a whirlpool – No room for more!

Friday 11 June
Adeline & I went out in the morning into the gardens, where we sat quietly for a little. Nessa went in to see Stella, whom she thought very well, & bright. At. Mary & Ralph V W came about 12 & sat in the drawing room talking together. A. & Ralph – so for the future he must be called, went out & had luncheon together. At. Mary with us. At. Mary saw Stella also – At. M & A went away – A. to Oxford, & At. M to Brighton at 3. Ralph is a tall stout solemn young gentleman – very stiff & proper at first sight – rather like Roland V.W. Afterwards sat with Stella for about an hour, & thought her looking very well really – only

14 The studio was in Pelham Street, SW; the Milmans lived at 61 Cadogan Square, SW; Marny and Emma Vaughan lived in Young Street, W.
15 Adeline Fisher (1870-1951) and Ralph Vaughan Williams (1872-1958), composer, were married on 10 October 1897; Roland was his cousin.

thin. We went in the evening to the Yeoman of the Guard[16] at the Savoy, & there saw a gent – exactly like R.V.W. Came home about 12, N & I alone, keyless. Threw stones gently at Ss window & then went to 24. However roused S at last.

Saturday 12 June
Stella had a good night, & we went in to see her after breakfast. She then irritated me extremely by saying that I should have to go with her when she goes away, which I with great vehemence, declared to be *impossible*. Georgie suddenly suggested that we should go off to Windsor, & boat to Datchet & look for houses for her there – which we accordingly did. We got to Windsor at about 1.30, & had lunch & strawberry squash at Laytons:[17] then we took a boat & rowed 1 mile or so down to Datchet. It was terribly hot, & so less nice than it might have been. We tramped over Datchet at the bidding of a telegraph boy, but unsuccessfully – no houses to be found. Then we took the boat back to Windsor – waiting by the bank a little to cool. Had ices at Laytons & then the train home. If only this horrible plan were not hanging over my head!

Sunday 13 June
Broiling again. Perfectly breezeless, & the sky blue & misty with the heat – Gerald sits in an arm chair by the open window in his shirt sleeves, Georgie gasps at intervals; Nessa sneezes with hay fever – A. *bicycle rides* & prints photographs, & I growl at every thing – the effect of nerves doubtless! We struggled out in to the gardens & sat upon chairs, hoping that this was cooler than the house. Then we came home again, & said it was very hot – This is awful – After luncheon father went to Kew – wanting to take us too, but we boldly refused. After tea we sat with Gerald in the gardens. No more heard of the going away plan but my fears are many. No book but Cromwell to read, & that requires a refrigerator. After dinner we planted geraniums in the boxes, lighted by a bedroom candle, & the policeman's lantern! To bed at 11.30 – hot, hot, hot.

Monday 14 June
In the morning I went over & sat with Stella for some time. She is very well, & gets up on to the sofa. Dr Seton even says she may travel on Fri-

---

16 Gilbert and Sullivan, *The Yeomen of the Guard*, a comic opera, 1888.
17 Layton Brothers, confectioners and dining-rooms, 1 Thames Street.

day, but as they have found no house, this is doubtful. I went out to Herbert & Jones for Stella, & bought sponge cakes. Nessa at her drawing. I cannot remember what happened to me in the afternoon – I think I went out somewhere but I forget any thing about it. At Minna sent round to ask Nessa to go & make the tea for various ancient females, At Annie amongst them – So she went, & I had tea alone. I began Cowper's[18] letters as a night book – Finished Miss Mitford some time ago. The grass in the back garden, so long despaired of is already sprouting! Very thin & weakly indeed, but it is a comfort to think that the wretched sparrows did not get it all.

Tuesday 15 June
We went over to Stella in the morning. Afterwards Nessa went to High St to buy odds & ends for her blessed dress (which has to be finished by tomorrow – & which Mrs Dickson is now working on).

I went to Gloucester Rd. with a telegram, & then came home. In the afternoon we went into High St again; Nessa having lost some whalebone, which she bought in the morning. Then we extravagantly had ices in the Park, & then home again at 4. Nessa had to try on the dress – At about 5, who should arrive but Adeline & Ralph V.W.! on their way through London to Brighton. Then on top of them came the Milmans, whom we had invited to tea. We insisted upon A & R having tea alone in the drawing room, which they did. We had tea together downstairs. The Ms. stayed till about 7. Planted flowers after dinner.

Wednesday 16 June
Finished 2nd vol. of Carlyle's Cromwell. Nessa went to the studio. I sat with Stella. I went out down Gloucester Rd. & bought Marmalade for Georgie's breakfast – & then came home again. In the afternoon, I walked part of the way down Queens Gate with Nessa – she had to walk to the studio because of the wind – & then bought a basket of strawberries at Aldouses new fruit shop, for Jack's dinner tonight. This is the 2nd & last day of his exam[19] – poor creature!

After tea Nessa & I went out with Aunt Minna & had ices – very bad – in the Park. Nessa went back early, & to dress for this blessed dinner party. Mrs Dickson & Marie [servant] had been hard at work at it all

---

18 William Cowper (1731-1800), poet.
19 Presumably his Law Society examination; he worked at Messrs Roper & Whateley, Solicitors.

day, & the last stitch was put, just as she was ready to put it on. She looked most beautiful, so all these fittings & bastings have been worth something after all – she went down with a Senior Wrangler.[20] Her first dinner party.

Thursday 17 June
We went over to Stella in the morning, & discussed the great dinner. It was very long, & rather heavy & dull. Nevertheless the Senior Wrangler a Mr Cowell, behaved decently – did not eat with his fingers, or talk once of Euclid, & as for Nessa's looks! Crikey!!! They got back about 12 – We went out with Emma Vaughan to try & get Jubilee Medals for the workhousers at Porters[21] but could not. After lunch we sat with Stella for some time & talked of Adeline's engagement. Jack told Stella of this the day before yesterday, but as she thought that one was not supposed to know she could not talk to us of it. Poor Ralph is a *calf* – according to her – & also, I am afraid, to us – However they are very much in love, & there is a chance that he has genius. In the afternoon we went down Gloucester Rd to get some oil for Stella, & then came home again. After dinner we planted the East end flowers in the garden – I have a beautiful new box for my bedroom – Began 3rd vol. of Cromwell.

Friday 18 June
Nessa went to the studio. I sat with Stella for some time, & then went out down Gloucester Rd. to get some things for Peggies tea this afternoon. Flying from the Gloucester road horses (a particularly vicious & ferocious race) I went to Queens Gate, & met Nessa coming back, & walked home with her. After luncheon we went over to Stella, who goes down stairs today, & then I stayed here at home, & Nessa bicycled off to her ———— studio. Bella & Peggy came about 4, & we had tea at half past. Bella very moral, & severe. Peggy rather naughty & amusing. Played games with her till about 6. Then they went which was rather a relief. A letter from Miss [Frances] Noel to ask us to go to tea there

20 Philip Herbert Cowell (b.1870), Fellow of Trinity College, Cambridge, Senior Wrangler, 1892, and Chief Assistant at the Royal Observatory, Greenwich, 1896-1910.
21 Probably Nathaniel Porter, stationer, 7 Sussex Place, South Kensington, W.

tomorrow, & a letter from Dorothea[22] (the 2nd) to say that she will come here on Wednesday – to stay till Friday or Saturday.

Saturday 19 June

We sat with Stella for some time. Then I went & gardened a little. Nessa put flowers into her boxes, & I read, so that we did not go out. In the afternoon at about 4, we started to get to dear Fanny [Frances Noel]. This was no easy proceeding, but wonderfully we managed it – though the green bus cost 3d. instead of the lawful 1d. We had tea with the delightful creature – a delicious cake, & a remarkable kettle (wh wd not boil). She talked to us, & screamed with laughter – exactly like Madge. We came home again (having had one short glimpse of old Baldwin in the hall). Poor Mrs B. scuttled away into the kitchen when she saw us. We lost our way rather coming back, but found it again. But it is a pilgrimage only to be occasionally undertaken!

Sunday 20 June

We did nothing all the morning. Very hot & thunderous. Gerald away at the Phippses[23] – at Knebworth, & Georgie lunching with the Humphry Wards – Harry Stephen came to lunch with us, which put the house keeping department rather to its wits end – but a leg of mutton was produced from the servants dinner, & things were tided over. Afterwards, at about 4, Georgie came home, & proposed that we should go to the Albert Hall & hear the concert[24] – So we went, & met Susan Lushington coming back – who had just been shouting God Save the Queen with thousands of others, & was, she said overflowing with Loyalty. We came in for the old Hundredth to which we stood up & hats were taken off – various men[?] also & others joining in the hymn. Most exciting – such a crowd of well dressed beings, I never saw. H[arry] went

---

22 AVS's first cousin, Dorothea (1871-1965), youngest daughter of Mary and James Fitzjames Stephen; a zealous Christian, she became a teacher of religion in India.
23 Unidentified.
24 Featured on the programme was the Royal Artillery String Band, conducted by Cavaliere L. Zavertal; the music included *Loyal Hearts* by L. Zavertal and a *Patriotic Overture on National Airs* composed for Queen Victoria's Diamond Jubilee; at the close of the concert, the audience was invited to unite in singing the 'Old Hundreth' – i.e. the 100th Psalm.

early in the morning to W[estminster]. A[bbey].[25] service with Edith D[uckworth].

Monday 21 June

Adrian's exeat began. Nessa went to her drawing. At about 11 A. & I went round to 24, & saw Stella. But she had had a slight attack of pain again in the morning, so that we did not stay more than a minute. I stayed in in case they wanted anything, & A. went to see the camps in the Park.[26] In the afternoon Dr Seton came & Nessa & I went over & talked for a long time to him. He says that she will be well soon; but that they will not be able to go away on Saturday. N. went to High St, & father A. & I sat in the gdns & then came home. Thoby arrived at about 5.30. We had dinner at 7, & at 8, the bus, a red Hammersmith, came round. We drove to the Stanleys in Harley St,[27] & then went through the streets with them. A most wonderful dreamlike sight – the streets as bright as day – crowded – with stands full of people. St James St – hung from side to side with electric lamps, & festoons of stuff. Home about 11.30. The night wd have been most red letter – if it were not for Stella –

Tuesday 22 June   Diamond Jubilee Day

Today was the great Diamond Jubilee Day, very cloudy & still early in the morning, looking almost showery if such a thing dared happen. We got up at 7.30, & had breakfast rather past 8, starting in the carriage Nessa Thoby & I, at 8.30. We got to St Thomas'es Hospital at 9.30, & watched the soldiers & the crowd for some time. There the crowd was not allowed on the [Westminster] bridge, & we had nothing but lazy volunteers to look at. So we strolled in the hospital gardens & had ices: then we waited again. The procession was to pass at 1.30, but – at 12.30 a Captain Ames,[28] & the sailors appeared & then followed troop after troop – one brilliant colour after another. Hussars, & Troopers & Lancers, & all manner of soldiers – then Indian Princes, & at last carriages

---

25 The 60th anniversary of the Queen's accession was celebrated by special services at Westminster Abbey, attended by the Lord Chancellor and members of the House of Lords.

26 Rest camps for soldiers from outside London, engaged in the Jubilee procession, who commuted daily.

27 Actually 18 Mansfield Street, one block to the east and parallel with Harley Street.

28 From the *Royal Jubilee Procession* (a souvenir programme): 'Capt. O. Ames of the 2nd Life Guards rode at the head of the Royal Jubilee Procession on 22 June 1897. He was the tallest officer in the British Army at that time.'

Saturday 21st June 97.

Adrian & I went up from Mama
went to the drawing- We about 11
R. & I went round to 24, &
saw Stella. But she had had a

...

Diamond Jubilee Thursday 22nd June 97.
Day. Sunday. Sunday 22nd June 97.

Today was the Great Diamond
Jubilee Day; very cloudy & still
foggy in the morning, looking almost—
...

with the little Princesses & the big ones – Finally the cream coloured ponies were sighted:[29] every one stood up & waved: shook their pocket handkerchiefs, & stamped their feet – the Queen was lying back in her carriage, & the Pss. of Wales had to tell her to look up & bow. Then she smiled & nodded her poor tired head, & the whole thing moved on – But there was a great deal more to come – & it was not over till almost 2.30. Then luncheon & then home at 4.30. So ends the Jubilee day.

Wednesday 23 June

Stella had a very good night, & was better in the morning. Georgie & Thoby & Nessa went in to see her. Thoby went away at 10. Nessa went to her drawing though it was hot enough to boil a lobster, & I had a succession of respectable dull visitors, & answered the invariable "How is Stella?" till I hated poor Stella & her diseases. The heat was really dreadful, & A. & I were too old & exhausted to go farther than the chicken walk.[30] In the afternoon A. & I went down & met Nessa at the studio, & went with her to Davies[31] where we had very delicious ices, & then to Thompsons[32] where we had more ices – finally home. I bought myself a most delightful blotting pad, which I am now using, on the way. Dorothea arrived at about 6.30, as fat as a grampus, & blowing like that animal – terrible in her heat, & perspiration; & general cowlike stout appearance. Father gave me Arnold's History of Rome.[33] Finished the 3rd & last vol. of Cromwell.

Thursday 24 June

Marie, coming in to call me at a quarter to 8 this morning, gasped for breath & rushed to the window, flung it open, & then apologised for her behaviour. But really your room was so hot, that I could scarcely breathe. So for the rest of the day it remained, relentless, thundery sunless heat –

Adrian took a parcel of 12 books to a 2nd hand bookstall in the

---

29 'The Queen's state carriage was drawn by cream-coloured horses . . . The Princess of Wales accompanied her, with them was the Princess Christian. Accompanying the carriage on horseback were the Prince of Wales in Field-Marshall's uniform and the Duke of Connaught, General Officer commanding the troops, and the Duke of Cambridge': *The Times*, 23 June.
30 A name the Stephen children probably gave to some path in Kensington Gardens.
31 Probably John Davies, coffee and dining-rooms, 3 Peel Place, Kensington, W.
32 Not traced.
33 Thomas Arnold, *The History of Rome*, 1840-3, 5 vols.

Brompton Rd. & got 3s. for them! Nessa & I tried to go for a walk, but paid a visit to At. Minna on our way up the street, & spent the rest of our time there. Seton came in the afternoon, & Nessa had a long & interesting talk with him. Stella going on flourishingly. Then we went out & had tea in the Park – in the midst of which, the heat suddenly burst into a thunder storm, with plentiful drenching rain – the most rejoiceful sight on earth. It sank into the ground almost audibly & the air immediately got cooler. We sat under the trees for a little & then went home – cool for the first time.

Friday 25 June

Nessa went to her drawing; & Adrian went back to school. So I was left alone. Dear Dorothea started off somewhere to buy herself a hat. I went for a solitary walk in the gardens, which were misty & quiet, & then came back again – After lunch Broadbent & Seton came to see Stella. Their report most satisfactory – every thing going on as well as possible. Nessa went to her drawing, & I for another solitary walk in the gardens.

I can hardly write this – that never to be mentioned without anger – Marie having thrown my beautiful pen *out* of the window on to Dorothea's balcony – consequently producing severe dislocation of the nibs, & general shock to the system, wh. it will probably never entirely get over. After tea read my Roman History, a terrible plough, & talked to Dear Dorothea. Nothing to fill up this blank with, & therefore out of consideration to the enfeebled powers of my beloved it shall be left empty –

Saturday 26 June

Nessa & father went off early in the morning to Clifton. Dorothea & I, after a virtuous morning spent in reading solid works, went to De Vere Gardens to look for a Spanish Dictionary for Rosamond.[34] We explored the house, which is huge, & deserted, & hideous. Then we went to buy D[orothea] some stays & gloves – This done in High St. we sat in the gardens & talked learnedly, & then came home & had lunch together. Gerald came for me at 2, & we got to Paddington at about 2.30. We got to Windsor at 3 – (impossible to write sense or any thing else with this pen) & saw the end of the Eton & Winchester match – Eton beaten by about 50 runs. Then we went into the Chapel, & had tea in Mr Vaugh-

---

34 The James Fitzjames Stephen family's old London house was at 32 De Vere Gardens, W; Rosamond (1868-1951) was Dorothea's elder sister.

an's[35] garden – near the river. Then walked up & saw the castle, &
looked down on the Thames winding beneath us – oh dear – before this
we had narrowly escaped death in a Canadian canoe, which threatened
to collapse us in to the water at every movement – After the castle we
had dinner at Laytons – then home at 9. This is a very bare record – but
no room for more.

 Nessa & father got back at 10.30.

Sunday 27 June

In the morning we stayed in & did nothing. It was very hot, & steamy,
& disagreeable, & the History of Rome did not prosper. After luncheon
we three went out in the gardens where we came across Lady Kay, &
Miss Nina Kay. We hurried on to another destination near Kensington
Palace! Then Nessa went home, & A. & I took a constitutional round
the Serpentine. Came home; Nessa & D discussed "religion & the gospels", while D. was undressing, & then went & had tea with Jack at 24.
After tea I read religiously; & A did his preparation & ran his new
engine – Nessa did hers also, & I was the lazy boy of the party. After
dinner Father recited as D asked him to – Maud, & the Spanish
Armada[36] – Georgie had to work at night,[37] & Gerald went to At. Min-
nas.

Monday 28 June

Dorothea & I went for a long tramp round the Serpentine – D. talking
loudly & vehemently all the way. We came in about 12.30. High St. &
the top of our road are all decorated most brilliantly with masts from
which hang lines of coloured flags – red *bunting* & flags & lamps of
every colour & description. The schoolchildren were already all
crammed into the gardens behind the railings, & a crowd was forming
all along the road. Nessa came back at 1, & we took kitchen chairs &
placed ourselves by At. Minna, at the top of the road. In a moment,
behold the life guards marching down High St – then came the Queen

---

35 'Toddy' Vaughan was an Eton classics master.
36 Alfred, Lord Tennyson, *Maud*, 1834-56, 1837-56. Thomas Babington Macaulay,
 'The Armada', 1832.
37 See May 1897, n.14.

herself passing directly in front of us; & the other Royal Princesses.[38] I have never seen her so close or so well in my life, & that without any fuss or trouble – only mounting a kitchen chair. In the afternoon D & I went to the R[oyal]. A[cademy]. together – terrible – then to an ABC & home in a dreadful crush. Nessa went out to the Lushingtons[39] after dinner. Home 12.30.

Tuesday 29 June
Nessa went with Georgie & Gerald to Mrs Young's where she is going to have 2 dresses made. D & I took our usual vigorous tramp in the gardens – discussing Ds. poetry which she gave me to read! Then we lost Jerry & had to walk back in the broiling sun to find him. After lunch we went out to buy things in High St, & at 4 the great Dorothea departed – Nessa & I promptly started forth to Thompsons to recover ourselves by eating ices. Nessa went to her first ball – or dance at the Freshfields[40] – They started at 11, & did not get back till 3 A.M. Nessa most triumphant, having danced all the night with George Booth, Fred [Maitland], Dermod [O'Brien] & various others[41] – Looked most beautiful – the envy of all the other fine ladies.

Wednesday 30 June
Nessa went to her drawing – but the rest of the morning is rather vague – I went in to Stella for the first time, & found her very well – then afterwards I may have bought strawberries, or I may have taken a solitary walk in the park, both of them the usual employments of mine nowadays – but this diary has been neglected (owing to the disablement of my pen) & I cannot remember – Anyhow in the afternoon I bought strawbs. at a shop in Church St. where I went with Father – Afterwards we sat in the gardens a little & then home. He lent me 12 vols. of

---

38 The Queen came to London from Windsor to attend a garden party at Buckingham Palace, part of the Diamond Jubilee celebration, and on her way passed through Kensington; several thousand school children were assembled in Kensington Gardens to greet her.

39 The Lushingtons lived at 36 Kensington Square, W.

40 The Freshfields lived at 179 Airlie Gardens, Campden Hill Road, W.

41 George Macaulay Booth (1877-1971), son of Charles Booth, was at Trinity College, Cambridge; he was later to join the family shipping business. For F. W. Maitland, see Jan. 1905, n.12. William Dermod O'Brien (1865-1945), a well-known amateur painter, educated at Trinity College, Cambridge; he later studied art on the Continent and kept a studio in Chelsea from 1893-1901.

Froude's History of England,[42] which he has not room for.[43] I am to read 'em some time – at present they have a whole new bookshelf for themselves – Finished 1st vol of Arnold's Rome.

42 J. A. Froude, *History of England from the Fall of Wolsey to the Defeat of the Spanish Armada*, 1856-70, 12 vols.

43 Presumably in his study at the top of the house.

Thursday 1 July

In the morning we went over to Stella – then we started forth on some of our – Nessa's – multitudinous shoppings. But Mr Gibbs kidnapped us half way up the road, & we had to go with him to Cornwall Gdns & to take his birthday present to Nessa The Three fates to be framed at Soars – At last however he let us go, & Nessa trundled off to High St, & I into the gardens. In the afternoon we took 3 large baskets of strawbs. & two packets of sugar to the old ladies at the workhouse – We ladled them all out into equal portions, & left them happily chewing. "The most delicious of fruits" one old creature informed us. My squirrel dear Jacobi is the most delightful creature that ever was. We pursue each other round the room!

Friday 2 July

Nessa to her studio as usual – I went round to Stella, who begins to get up now for luncheon, & then I took my solitary wanderings in the Park. After luncheon, when Nessa & I were sitting with Stella, the nurse was suddenly called away to see Gerald; who had gone to his office rheumatic in the morning, & came back still more so – not able to look up; & all hunched – The nurse rubbed him; & he went back to St James St. I went to Cooper's for some medicine for him; & to Dr Seton's. Dr Seton came at 6.30 & gave him more medicine, & said he was to be rubbed etc. Georgie away playing cricket. Reading Shirley[1] – We have taken to walking in the streets after our nightly game of whist – now that it is nice & light. At. Minna went to Scotland for the summer.

Saturday 3 July

In the morning we sat with Stella. Nessa went secretly to Mrs Young's[2] with Gerald; whose rheumatism was still rather bad. I sat the whole morning with Stella who was very flourishing. After lunch father went to see the match at Westminster, old Ws. v present Ws. Nessa & I went to Baker St. to see the little [Charles] Leaf. Lotta[3] away, so we played with the baby. He has grown very big, & very fat – with a large mouth – very like his papa, though with Lotta's eyes. Came back & had ices at H[erbert]. & J[ones]s. Adeline [Fisher] came about 7.30, with Adrian, old Ws – beaten. Charlie [Fisher] out first ball. Broadbent & Seton came

---

1 Charlotte Brontë, *Shirley*, 1849.
2 Possibly because Leslie Stephen objected to the expense of a new dress.
3 See Feb. 1897 n.36.

to Stella. Reported most satisfactory. Georgie back from playing cricket
– Gerald away with the Gordons.[4]

Sunday 4 July
We stayed in & did nothing all the morning. I type wrote Dorothea's
poems which arrived last night – very long, watery effusions, with
which she is going to invade the magazines. In the afternoon Adeline
asked me if I would like to go with her to Lambeth to hear her Ralph's
concert there. I dutifully said yes; & we started at 3, meaning to get
there at 4. We waited at Gloucester Rd station for 20 minutes, & no
trains came – then Adeline suddenly looked at the clock, & behold it was
3.30, so she said, we cannot go – It takes an hour to get there – where-
upon, she burst into tears on the platform, bewailing her fate, cursing
the trains, & altogether miserable. Now comes the wonderful part of
this history. I felt a practical rush of ideas enter my brain – Let us take a
hansom – Let us fly this station. We fled. A hansom to Victoria; another
to St Barnabas Church[5] – We arrived at 4 – exactly – Thank Heaven
gasped Adeline – but it did not begin until *4.30*! Heard the music – very
good. Home at 7.

Monday 5 July
Nessa went to her studio. Adeline & I went down to St Alban's Rd; to
see Emmie. Here I will tell a little story which properly belongs to last
night – Emmie behaved very badly to Adeline, made cutting little remarks to her face, & still cuttinger ones when her back was turned:
which made Georgie very wrathful – However the evening passed off
calmly enough – father reciting – till it was about 10.30. Then Emmie
said that she & Charlie must go home. Georgie tried to prevent her, but
she insisted – Then he lost his temper – 'I think you behave very badly
indeed to Adeline': he said; 'I cannot think how you can do it!' Upon
which Emmie burst into tears (a repetition of yesterday's platform
scene) says 'beast beast, I hate you!' etc. etc. etc – All the bawling &
squalling & tears & attempts at peace making, & Adeline's sneers, &
Charlies roars of laughter, cannot find room here – But even this morning, Emmie was very dismal, & tearful – I sat in & Ralph came to lunch

4 Probably H. S. C. M. Gordon (b.1871), a contemporary of Gerald's at Eton who became a publisher with Williams and Norgate.
5 In Guildford Road, South Lambeth; in 1949, or thereabouts, it merged with All
Saints, also in South Lambeth.

– Adeline terribly irritating. An unselfish martyr – oh for arrows &
stones to throw at her! I sat with Stella most of the afternoon, & had a
very nice long talk – Then Nessa & I went out & had ices – Finished 2nd
vol of Hist. of Rome.

Tuesday 6 July
Nessa & Adeline went to Mrs Youngs to try on the great dresses. I sat
with Stella, & then went into Gloucester Rd. & bought strawberries.

Goodness knows how the rest of the day was spent – I have got into
the bad practice of not writing my diary for two or three days, & then I
have forgotten what has happened.

So the afternoon must dissapear [*sic*] unaccounted for.

Began 3rd & last vol. of Rome.

Wednesday 7 July
In the morning Nessa went to the studio, & I went down Gloucester Rd.
with Stella's medicine – In the afternoon I sat with Stella for some time;
& talked to her about various things, & Adeline's anger "So bad for
Stella to have Ginia always with her!" & then Nessa & I went out & had
ices at Hills. We have tried all the ice selling shops now, & have come to
the conclusion that Herbert & Jones is the best. Came home & found
Ralph V.W. here. Adeline insisted upon bringing him down to have tea
with us, & made every one very uncomfortable. Fred [Maitland] came
to dinner. Finished & despatched Dorothea's poems.

Thursday 8 July
Nessa, Adeline & Georgie went to Mrs Young's about those terrible
dresses. How I wished they were finished once & for all, & never to be
mentioned or thought of again! I stayed in all the morning – I sat with
Stella for a little; & then came back here. Mia [MacNamara] appeared, &
embraced me affectionately three or four times. In the afternoon we
went down to Dr Coates with a note from Stella to come & look at
Jack's leg, which has an abscess – This diary has been woefully
neglected lately – what with one thing & another – Improvement must
be made! (hear hear).

Friday 9 July
Nessa went to her drawing. Adeline departed for Gloucester at 8.30 to
meet Ralph at Paddington & travel down with him. I went in to Stella,
but before I had been there 5 minutes that old shop keeper Mrs

[Edmund] Hills came & turned me out. Then Emmie came with her squirrel – a most unattractive stolid little beast compared to my Jacobi – who escaped, by the bye, last night, & was found on top of the curtains in the morning. In the afternoon Georgie, Nessa & I went to Vincents Square to see the W[estminster] & Charterhouse great match. Found Emmie there. We watched it a little, & then went back to High St. & had ices & bought things. Nessa & Georgie went to the Booths dance[6] – Nessa beautiful in her blessed Mrs Young ———. I read & wrote in bed till 1.30.

O

Saturday 10 July
Went to Lords for the Eton & Harrow.[7] Nessa in her Mrs Youngs dress. We went in to Stella & showed ourselves. Home about 6. Georgie went to stay with Cousin Addie.[8]

(This is where I left off writing my diary – I fill in these days from memory, this afternoon Tuesday July the 27th.)

Sunday 11 July
I was very miserable & achey with rheumatism? We sat out in the gardens in the morning. In the afternoon we did nothing. It was baking hot. I went in to see Stella; she & Jack were having tea together. She lying on the sofa & he in the big chair beside her. I sat at her feet & soon Jack went out of the room & we talked together.

Monday 12 July
I spent the whole day with Stella, as she would not let me go out because of my aches – I sat with her, & we talked of everything – The same in the afternoon – She was sitting up, & very well & happy. I can remember no more of the day.

Tuesday 13 July
In the morning Nessa & I went over to Stella. I was rather worse, & had

---

6 At 24 Great Cumberland Place, W.
7 The annual cricket match held at Lord's in early July.
8 Julia Stephen's cousin, Adeline, Duchess of Bedford (1852-1929), widow of George Russell, 10th Duke (1852-93), living at 26 Hertford St, Mayfair, W, and Chenies, Rickmansworth.

a little fever – We spent the morning with her. She was in her dressing room, writing letters – In the afternoon father wanted us to go out with him, & she wrote him a letter to say that I was not well enough. Nessa went out shopping & she lay on her bed; I sat in the big chair & tried to go to sleep. I got very hot; & Dr Seton came, & made me go to bed.[9] She sat with me for some time.

Wednesday 14 July

I hardly saw her all the morning; she did not want me to talk, & would not come in to me. But in the afternoon, after Dr Seton had been, she sat by me, & then Nessa came, in her Mrs Young dress she was going to Kittie's concert[10] – Stella gave me my tea & then she went to give father his. Nessa came back, & we all sat together in my room & talked.

At night I had the fidgets very badly, & she sat with me till 11.30 – stroking me till they went.

I slept in Jack's dressing room, just opposite their bedroom.

Thursday 15 July

She came into me before breakfast in her dressing gown to see how I was. She only stayed a moment; but then she was quite well. She left me, & I never saw her again.

She did not come to me all day long, & I guessed that she was ill. I asked Nessa & she told me that Stella had had a little pain – but they thought the worst was over; & she was already better.

Friday 16 July

Stella was better the nurse said. But it was not true – she was ill all day – Broadbent came & saw both of us, & said she was getting on very well.

She called out to me often through her open door, & asked how I was, & I shouted back.

---

9 AVS remained at 24 Hyde Park Gate, ill, from Tuesday 13 July to Saturday the 17th.

10 'Kitty Maxse was a gifted pianist which she expended unreservedly in the service of others. Only lately a friend had spoken with enthusiasm of the memory of years ago, of her golden head aureoled against the black of the pianoforte as she sat playing softly on by the hour in the drawing room of their house in Montpelier Square, a dwelling familiarly known as "Montpiel" to those favoured ones who had entree there': from her obituary in *The Times*, 10 October 1922.

Saturday 17 July
She was better they thought today. She had hardly any pain. Again she called out to me & said she was very comfortable.

Young Broadbent[11] came to see me – she wd. not let him see her, & said I might be carried across home. I had not been out of bed yet, but Georgie lifted me up, wrapped in Stella's fur cape. She called out "Goodbye" as I passed her door –

Sunday 18 July
I was put to bed in the spare room opposite Nessa's with Nurse Carr to look after me – a nurse they had got for Stella but whom she did not like. We heard that Stella had had some sleep.

Williams[12] & Broadbent came in the afternoon – & decided to operate – Dr Seton was ill with sciatica.

They operated on her at about 7 o'clock. At half past we heard that it was successful, & that everything was as satisfactory as possible.

Monday 19 July
At 3 this morning, Georgie & Nessa came to me, & told me that Stella was dead –

That is all we have thought of since; & it is impossible to write of.

Tuesday 20 July
[*This page is blank.*]

Wednesday 21 July
Stella was buried by mother's side in Highgate.

None of us went –[13]

Thoby & Adrian are both here, & will stay till we go to Painswick.

Thursday 22 July
I forget what happened. I came downstairs, & went out in to the gardens about this time.

---

11 Walter (b.1868), son of the physician Sir William Broadbent, who himself became an MD in 1897; see April 1897, n.39.

12 Not traced.

13 It is unlikely that Stella's burial was accompanied by any service; if there had been, moreover, the Stephen family, being agnostic, would not have participated.

Jack has gone back to his work; he comes every evening when they have gone down to dinner, & later at 10.

So we see a good deal of him. Madge [Symonds] telgraphed to ask if she should come, & we answered yes –

Friday 23 July
Forget what happened. Charlie & Adeline who have been staying at Aunt Minna's (she has come back from Scotland) went away to Brighton.

Saturday 24 July
Jack took Nessa & me to Highgate to see Stellas grave. We went by bus & tram. The grave is next mother's – near you as you go in. It was covered with dead flowers – We sat down & talked for a long time, & then came home & had tea with Jack on his balcony. Madge did not come as she might have done.

Sunday 25 July
Georgie found the telegram to Madge in his pocket, so she has heard nothing. We decided after a long time to write & ask her to come either in a week or in September or not at all. Will's [Vaughan] being at Painswick complicates matters. We looked at Stella's clothes & jewels, & Jack gave us some.

Monday 26 July
Various people keep on coming, & our time is well taken up in seeing them. Kitty especially has been here; & we find that we never knew her before. Cousin Mia has gallantly held aloof – Alas – others have not been so generous. Helen Holland discusses Religion for hours with Nessa – At. Minna & Mr Gibbs haunt the place – Sally Norton[14] & Flora Baker are here a great deal – It is all very strange.

Tuesday 27 July
Packing going forward in all earnestness. Lizzie almost frantic with

---

14   Sara (Sally) Norton, daughter of Susan (d.1872) and Charles Eliot Norton (1827-1908), American scholar and man of letters, professor of art history at Harvard, 1875-98, who had been a friend of Leslie Stephen since 1863. The Nortons regularly visited England, and had stayed with the Stephens at St Ives.

strapless boxes, & other nightmares. However at nightfall Sophie is despatched with the greater part of the boxes – Shag into the bargain.

I went for a walk (I insisted on the walk) with Gerald. Dr Seton came & saw me & Adrian & reported very flourishingly on us.

Wednesday 28 July

At last! At a quarter to three our huge omnibus piled inside & out with luggage of every description – Nessa, Father & I squeezed in in the corners, started for Paddington.

We arrived after the usual journey at Stroud[15] at 5.45, & drove in the Painswick Bus (a wonderful conveyance) to the Vicarage, about 3 miles from the station. A large very dear comfortable house, with a really nice flower garden, & lawn, & fountains, & green turf. Looks in to hills & woods.

Thursday 29 July

I woke up to find a hot what in London would be a stuffy sunless day – here there was scorching sun, & no breeze to carry it away & no houses to shelter us. Father proposed walking up to the Maitlands at the Horsepools,[16] so Nessa & I & Georgie went with him. Thoby & Adrian departed on their own private excursions. We started through the churchyard with its 99 yews,[17] then down a steep hill of some length, & up a still steeper & longer one. At the top was the horsepools. We sat with them, & a monkey & 2 dogs, for a time, & then came home again. It was broiling, & the hills were very severe exercise. We stayed at home all the afternoon. I attacked Froude again (I have the 12 vols here!) We played cricket after tea. Georgie & I had a very nice long talk in the garden after dinner.

Friday 30 July

Broiling hot again. Father, Thoby, Adrian & Georgie went for a walk – Nessa & I stayed at home, & I attempted to pick flowers in the gardens, but the sun was so violent that we had to go indoors. In the afternoon we

---

15 A market town in Gloucestershire, about 3 miles south-west of Painswick and its nearest railway station.

16 Horsepools, Brookthorpe, was the Maitlands' Gloucestershire estate; it was therefore presumably through Fred Maitland that the Stephen family rented the Painswick house, about 2 miles away.

17 The churchyard of St Mary's, Painswick, is famous for its 99 clipped yews, planted in 1792.

lounged about the place; I botanised with Father, & the rest played tennis. Two letters came for Nessa – one from Helen H[olland]. & Meg Booth[18] – Helen splendid – but I have no room to reproduce her choicest bits. After tea we went for a walk – up on to the top of a hill where there were moths & butterflies. Jane Breed[19] is here. Reading Alton Locke, Villette, Froude, & P[ot]. P[ourri]. from a Surrey Garden.[20]

Saturday 31 July
Another boiling day. Georgie & Thoby went out bugging in the morning, & Father & I went down into the valley, at the bottom of the garden, hunting for plants. Only a few common ones were found, so we came home. Father & Fred [Maitland] went out for a walk after luncheon, Thoby bugged, & at 4 the pony cart came round to take us to Stroud. I can not even attempt to do justice to the said pony cart in this short space – but it might have carried Miss Austen, when the roads were "dirty," & have excited no remark. We got to Stroud about a quarter to 5, & shopped. The train was an hour late arriving at 6.20 – We drove back again after tea at the George, Gerald & Jack biking. Home about 7.40.

---

18 Margaret (Meg, 1880-1961), daughter of Charles Booth. In 1905 she wrote two stories, *The Brown House, and Cordelia* which AVS would review for *The Guardian* on 6 December 1905 (Kp C2.12), and reprinted in *VW Essays*, I. In 1906 she was to marry William (Billy) Thackeray Denis (b.1880), son of 'Aunt Anny' and Sir Richmond Ritchie.

19 Unidentified.

20 Charles Kingsley, *Alton Locke, Tailor and Poet*, 1850. Charlotte Brontë, *Villette*, 1853. Maria Theresa Earle, *Pot-Pourri from a Surrey Garden*, 3rd ed., 1897.

Sunday 1 August

Read all the morning. Nessa painted a little down at the bottom of the garden, & Georgie & Gerald played tennis. Adrian mended – or attempted to – his eternal puncture, & Thoby set the Marbled Whites which he caught yesterday. In the afternoon Thoby & A. went out bugging, & the rest of us (except Gerald who went to the Horsepools) walked to Painswick Castle – a Roman camp,[1] on the downs about 2 miles away. Coming back we discovered Mr Bellows,[2] the Quaker – Father & Georgie stopped to talk to him – We came home & found Will [Vaughan] & Fred. Played cricket after tea –

Monday 2 August   *Bank Holiday*

In the morning Thoby Nessa Jack Georgie & I went to Painswick Castle, a roman camp on the down about 2 miles away to look for mythical Large Blues. Needless to say, they were not forthcoming. However we strolled about, with the bluest of skies above us, & the fir trees – scenting the air strongly. Down in the valley there are gipsies, & blue straight pillars of smoke – One ought to be a poet if one lives in the country – & one is ? what – In the afternoon we did nothing. The sun is overwhelming. Father & Fred went out for a walk. Will came & we played cricket after tea. Jack & Gerald went back at 6. We have had one or two nice long talks with Jack. Finished 1st of Froude.

Tuesday 3 August

Broiling again. Father pursued me up to my room – my refuge & hiding place, & took me out for a walk in the valley: where the sun's rays are concentrated to the utmost of their power. Oh for London & the shade of High St.! In the afternoon (I lost my temper terribly in the morning,) Nessa took me for a walk. We sat in an orchard & talked. Most calming. I can write no more. This pen is terribly infirm.

Wednesday 4 August

Read & lounged about all the morning, which was as usual terribly hot.

---

1 AVS is probably referring to the Lodge, which, according to H. Thomson, 'is higher up in the valley beyond Painswick . . . which belongs to the lords of the manor. . . . In 1868 Roman remains were found at Ifold farm, north of the town, and Mr. [Welbore] St. Clair Baddeley in 1903 unearthed a villa there . . .': *Highways & By-ways in Gloucestershire*, p. 213.

2 John Bellows (1831-1902), Quaker; a printer, lexicographer, and archaeologist; he is buried in the Painswick churchyard.

I began David Copperfield[3] to Nessa – despairing of the novels which this house produces. She is painting from the summer house. In the afternoon Father went to the Horsepools, & I read to Nessa. After tea Thoby & Georgie went to practise cricket, & Nessa & I bought some cotton & things in the town. Baking, baking baking. Madge wrote to say that she will come the first week in September.

Thursday 5 August

Read to Nessa & loafed about in the morning – In the afternoon we went out with Will to the wood on the hill opposite. After a dreadfully long hot walk we got back to find a telegram from Bean[4] to say that he arrives at Stroud at 6!

Thoby had tea quickly & went off to meet him. A red headed conceited youth; very Cliftonian & talkative.

Friday 6 August

Stayed in & read all the morning. It began to rain & was showery off & on all day. In the afternoon the males (we are the only females in the place) went for a walk; & we sat in & read, & then went into the village, where we bought *sundries*

This pen grows worse & worse – After we developed – The others practised cricket. I talked to father.

Saturday 7 August

I read to Nessa in the morning. In the afternoon we went with father to the cricket ground to see the match between Painswick & Cheltenham – Cheltenham were all out for 9 so that Painswick beat them in the innings. Georgie made nothing. Gerald came.

The Beck things arrived. Here is a list with their prices if we want them again.

Album 6.6. Negative Album 2.6. Byrds printing frames 1s each. Masks 6. box of Eastman's solid paper 144 pieces 1.10. The size of our Frend is 3½ x 2⅝.

---

3   Charles Dickens, *David Copperfield*, 1849-50.
4   Thoby's friend, C. E. W. Bean, was at Clifton from 1894-8; he was the son of the Rev. Edwin Bean, one of the founders of *The Cliftonian*.

Sunday 8 August
The number of Gerald's bank notes are –

K 33 61914
K 33 61913
K 33 61912
K 33 61911

This wondrous announcement is occasioned by the gift of £20 each which Aunt Minna has just made us. Georgie has to give us £40 more. These are £10 notes.
Rained all day.

Monday 9 August
Forgot what happened.
   This poor diary is in a very bad way, but, strange though it may seem, the time is always so filled up here, that I get very little time for diarising – even if I wished to, which I don't having taken a great dislike to the whole process. But the "great work"[5] goes on steadily, & has received Nessa's approval. I may read Vanity Fair & Jane Eyre.[6]

Tuesday 10 August
We stayed in all day expecting Florence [Maitland] who came with Will & Georgie at tea time. Thoby & Bean went to Cheltenham. It has been very stuffy, with occasional showers of thundery rain. Wrote four letters,[7] & printed photographs. Froude gradually proceeds. I am in the 3rd volume now.

Wednesday 11 August
Father went for a walk with Fred in the afternoon. We went out to catch a mythical Comma in the valley but no traces of the creature were to be seen, & Nessa & I came back & shopped in the village – After tea the young men (?)[8] went to practice, & Marney & Emma arrived to pay us a visit. We photographed them. We developed after they were gone. Some rather good ones of the bridge etc.

---

5   Presumably a reference to the 'Eternal Miss Jan'.
6   W. M. Thackeray, *Vanity Fair*, 1847-8. C. Brontë, *Jane Eyre*, 1847.
7   Have not survived.
8   AVS's question mark and parentheses.

Thursday 12 August

Father went out with Fred again. Georgie had broken his bicycle &
wanted to have it mended in Stroud. So Bean Adrian & Nessa & I drove
in the pony cart down to Stroud – a wonderful drive – the pony trotting
almost all the way: Bean viciously whipping him up. Came back at
about 6.

Played cricket after tea; against Thoby Adrian & Bean. They just beat
us.

Friday 13 August

It was fine in the morning but rained steadily after luncheon & till tea
time. After tea Georgie Nessa Thoby & I went for a bicycle ride – the
first since we have been here, along the Cheltenham Road.

Began Adam Bede.[9]

Saturday 14 August

We – Nessa Adrian & I, went down to Stroud in the afternoon in the
pony chaise. Thoby bicycled. Georgie & Bean had gone down before to
play a match at Stroud. We stopped, & then had a very good hurried tea
at a bakers, then met the 5.29 – fairly punctual. Brought Sally [Norton]
up in the trap – She is very nice very pretty – rather podgy. Jack came
also.

He bicycled from Swindon.[10]

Sunday 15 August

In the afternoon we went out for a walk after the rain had stopped to the
castle. After tea Jack Nessa & I drove down to Stroud, to get his bag
which he had left there.

Solomon [horse] woke up for the first time in his life.

Monday 16 August

In the morning Sally had a telegram to say that Dick[11] arrives in London
today – so in the aft. at 3, we drove her down to Stroud in a dogcart from
the Falcon. She will come back again.

Jack left early in the morning.

---

9 George Eliot, *Adam Bede*, 1859.

10 An important railway junction on the Great Western Railway, where travellers
from London to Stroud had to change trains.

11 Richard (Dick, b.1872), son of Charles Eliot Norton; see July 1897, n.14.

Tuesday 17 August

In the afternoon we went for a walk to an old house which Nessa painted, a house with lions on the gate posts, & a sun dial – Thoby jumped into the moat & floundered about there on the way home.

Adeline & Ralph came & were rather irritating – Such a couple never was seen!

Wednesday 18 August

Alas Alas alas; this diary has been entirely neglected – today, I must confess, is Tuesday the 24th & I utterly forget what has happened on all these days. It has been raining disgracefully & we are alone for a wonder.

Thursday 19 August

The same thing must do for today – Rain goes on raining; I read David Copperfield to Nessa & Froude to myself. I am in the 5th volume.

Friday 20 August

Rain –

Negotiations with Charlie & Cordelia [Fisher]. Finally a telegram to say that Charlie arrives tomorrow by the 2.30.

Saturday 21 August

Adrian went down to Stroud in the morning, & had lunch there, met Charlie & came back with him at about 3.30. We started for Stroud together (Nessa & I) to meet Jack. Had tea there together, & met him & drove up together. He looks better I think, though very thin. We had a long talk this evening, in the summer house; raining hard.

Sunday 22 August

We went out in the afternoon to the opposite hills –

Today is the day on which Stella & Jack were engaged a year ago –

Father stormed to Georgie; which was very unhappy – Things are all in a tangle – One can do nothing but sit & grin. Talked to Jack in the summer house – How different –

Monday 23 August

In the afternoon Charlie Nessa & I drove to Stroud to meet Boo [Cordelia Fisher].

She came by the 5.29.

We had tea in Stroud, & drove up afterwards –

Off with Adrian all the time. Rather mad. Began Father's life of Fawcett.[12]

Tuesday 24 August

Nessa & I bought 2 penny buns – They looked so beautiful & shiny in
the post office window that I could not resist them, & we sat in a large
long grassed field & talked –

Boo & Adrian went to Stroud about his bicycle – & did not come back
till 8.30.

Nessa & I walked round & round the tennis lawn after dinner (our
custom nowadays) & discussed every thing.

It is hopeless & strange.

Wednesday 25 August

The first really fine day we have had since our first week here. – Hot still,
& blue sky.

At 2.30 we started for Gloucester. We saw the cathedral[13] there (I
have quite forgotten how to write) – & came back about 7.30. Gerald
here after his Droitwich[14] – As fat as ever – Dissapointing [*sic*].

Finished Adam Bede.

Madge writes to say that she will not come as it would mean an extra
journey, & they are all coming to London at the end of October – She
has not been well also. So after all this letter writing[15] etc. nothing comes
of it!

Thursday 26 August

Rained most of the day. In the afternoon we went out for a most grizzly
walk. Cordelia discussed family politics at great length – Most perplexing.

Friday 27 August

Rained.

We went out somewhere I think; but I quite forget.

---

12 Leslie Stephen, *Life of Henry Fawcett*, 1885.
13 Gloucester Cathedral, formerly the church of the Benedictine Abbey of St Peter;
     Edward II is buried here.
14 Regimen at the famous springs and salt baths of Droitwich, Worcestershire.
15 None has survived.

Saturday 28 August
Thoby Georgie & Charlie went to play cricket at Chalford[16] & we meant to join them there. But when we arrived in Stroud it began to pour. We read in the library, had tea, & met Jack. Drove back with him. Rain Rain Rain.
    Began 6th vol of Froude.

Sunday 29 August
Forget what happened.
    Very rainy as usual.

Monday 30 August
Nessa & I drove down with Jack & Georgie to Stroud before breakfast. Gerald came down after us on his bicycle Georgie having left his bag behind.

Tuesday 31 August
In the afternoon we went down to Charlie Watkins – the bagman in the valley, & behaved disgracefully.

---

16 A village about 3½ miles south-east of Stroud.

Wednesday 1 September

August over at last thank goodness! Never was there such a long month. If only September too were.

Rained steadily all day long.

Thursday 2 September

The rain it raineth every day – there is no more to be said. Reading Nicholas Nickleby, Froude, the French Revolution, & Letters of Wm Cory.[1]

Charlie & Cordelia went.

Friday 3rd September

Thoby & Gerald went to Symonds Yat;[2] had a most disastrous day – missing trains etc. & finally caught nothing – Jacobi escaped last night. He was seen skipping in the trees this morning but refused to come down. And now he has quite dissapeared [*sic*].

The first fine day for weeks – showery & very cold, but there is sunshine & blue sky.

We went to the Horsepools with E[rmengard]. & F[redegond].[3]

Saturday 4 September

Blowing hard & icily cold.

Jack bicycled from Swindon & got here about 6.

Sunday 5 September

Rained all day, except for an hour in the afternoon when Nessa & I tramped forth for a long muddy walk.

Monday 6 September

Jack & Gerald went. In the afternoon we went for a long walk with father – We lost Shag & Thoby, & were altogether furious.

---

1 Charles Dickens, *Nicholas Nickleby*, 1838-9. *Extracts from the Letters and Journals of William Cory*, selected and arranged by Francis Warre-Cornish, 1897.
2 Near Monmouth on the Wye, a beauty spot and observation point of 740 feet.
3 Ermengard (1888-1966) and Fredegond (1889-1949), daughters of Florence and F. W. Maitland.

Tuesday 7 September

Thoby went to Circencester[4] to meet Harry [Fisher] & bicycle back with him. We drove down to Stroud to get Thoby a present[5] – a knife; & then came back – Harry & Thoby came about 6 – Began Jane Eyre.

Wednesday 8 September

Father & Harry went for a walk in the afternoon. We went to Charlie Watkins, but fell into the stream.

Thursday 9 September

We went with Mr Bellows to Birdlip[6] – had lunch there, & afterwards saw a Roman Villa.

Friday 10 September

Thoby went to Stroud with Harry.

    We lounged about.

    Georgie came.

    Harry went.

Saturday 11 September

Nessa & I drove to Stroud to meet Gerald – Bought pocket knifes –

    Cashed my first cheque for £1.

    I have 19s. left.

    Jack arrived at dinner time. The question is "Shall we go to Corby[7] or not?"

    A great question.

Sunday 12 September

In the afternoon we went to Painswick camp.

    Debated the Corby question, & father gave his consent – So that we must consent to [*sic*] – I told Jack, after tea, that we had made up our minds to go – He was pleased, I think, so that it was obviously the right thing to do. At any rate it is settled which is a great relief.

---

4   A market town in south-east Gloucestershire, on the Churn, some 12 miles to the east of Stroud.

5   For his birthday, 8 September.

6   A hamlet 5 miles north-east of Painswick, with mosaics preserved in the nearby Roman villa.

7   Corby Castle in Cumberland, the home of Jack Hills' parents.

But it will be rather a rush – clothes getting etc.

Monday 13 September
They went on the usual early train.

I forgot what happened the rest of the day. Great clothes discussions between Nessa & me – Much alack – What solitary females we be!

Tuesday 14 September
Again I forget – This poor diary is lingering on indeed, but death would be shorter & less painful – Never mind, we will follow the year to its end, & then fling diaries & diarising into the corner – to dust & mice & moths & all creeping crawling eating destroying creatures.

Wednesday 15 September
Nessa & I went to Stroud to get some stuff.

Old G.W.[8] had the pony cart so we had to tramp on our feet. Bought things there, then took the bus back to Painswick.

Thursday 16 September
Forget again what happened. It is fairly fine now, & we have taken a good many photographs.

Friday 17 September
[The Maitlands came to tea. Took photographs of them.][9]

Reading the 9th vol of Froude – Thackeray, Jane Eyre, Rob Roy.[10] We stayed in all day, & had a fire in Nessas room, over which we sat & toasted. Letter from Margaret M[assingberd]. Wrote a clothes letter.[11] Georgie came.

φ

Saturday 18 September
Nessa & I drove dear Solomon down to Stroud for the last time. The good beast has much improved since we came here – today he beat all records, & trotted with hardly a stop. We have broken him of several

---

8 Unidentified.
9 The two bracketed sentences were deleted by AVS.
10 Sir Walter Scott, *Rob Roy*, 1817.
11 Not extant.

walkings up hills, & he is far more sensitive to the whip & the voice. We got there in half an hour. We had tea at our usual shop, & then went & met Gerald & Jack. The William Darwins[12] came down by the same train. We drove back again in wonderful style. Jack looks very well – Gerald terribly fat.

Sunday 19 September

In the afternoon Fred came & went out with father. Georgie, Nessa & I took some photographs of the churchyard & ducks. We saw a king-fisher down on the stream, & a moorhen.

Father dined with the St Clair Baddeleys.[13]

Monday 20 September

They went back as usual. I forget what happened afterwards.

This is most disgracefully kept!

Tuesday 21 September

Thoby went in the afternoon. Nessa & I drove him down to the station – He forgot all his bags – his cheque book & his topper – We had tea in Stroud, & then came back – our last tea & drive with Solomon. The Darwins and Baddeleys came to tea afterwards.

Wednesday 22 September

Raining – drizzly & misty & cold. Packed all the morning – & put back books & rearranged the house generally – then at 2.15 we drove off to Stroud, & departed.

Goodbye to Painswick & all its glories – the beauteous Solomon, the villagers, the churchyard, & all the sights & sounds that we have become used to all this long long eight weeks. Got home about 6 – I think. G & G to meet us at Paddington –

Very strange & unhappy. My room all done up new.

Thursday 23 September

Nessa went to Mrs Young in the morning. Adrian & I bought a sty-

---

12 William (1839-1914) and Sara, *née* Sedgewick (1839-1902), Darwin, living in Basset; he was the eldest son of Charles Darwin (1809-82) and was a banker in Southampton; Sara was the sister-in-law of Charles Eliot Norton.

13 Welbore St Clair Baddeley (b.1856), the historical writer, living at Castle Hale, Painswick.

lograph for him in High St., & then walked in the gardens. Everything very hot & stuffy. "The air tastes" as A. says mournfully.

Afterwards when Nessa came in we went to Margaret Ms & she took us to various shops & we bought innumerable clothes. In the afternoon ditto, so that all our buying is finished in one day –

Friday 24 September
In the morning I dragged Nessa & Adrian (I am fearful of Aunt Mary – so I put it in this way to show my utter selfishness) to Regent St. & there with terrible agony & excitement chose a nib for my pen.

When we came home I found it was too fine – oh the despair of that moment! So after lunch Nessa & I planned to go & get another one. We went over to Jacks & he asked us to go with him to Kitty's to choose papers for 14 V[ictoria]. G[rove].[14] At 4.30 we got away, bussed to Meeks[15] in the Br[ompton]. Rd & got setting boards – then on to Regent St, where we boldly demanded another nib, & got this most exquisite & delightful one.

Saturday 25 September
We started from Euston at 11.30. Gerald came with us to the station, & saw us provided with papers etc. We had lunch in the train & also tea. We got to Carlisle at 5.30 – & then took the train on to Wetheral.[16] We arrived at Corby at about 6. Mrs Hills & Susan Lushington here.

Terrible long dinner. Everything grand & strange. Jack unhappy. Old Hills silly. Mrs Hills talkative & rather unpleasant, Susan talkative and very pleasant – V.S. and A.V.S. silent & miserable.

Sunday 26 September
We walked by the river, which is most beautiful – tearing over stones & splashing & leaping & thoroughly enjoying itself – with Jack in the morning. The rest went to church. Susan & Mrs Hills out for lunch. After lunch we went out again with Jack – everything is miserable & lonely. Why did we ever come – Jack does not very much want us. Susan played after dinner which was nice.

---

14 Where he would shortly be living.
15 Edward Henry Meek, naturalist, 56 Brompton Road, SW.
16 A village on the Eden River, 4 miles east of Carlisle.

Monday 27 September

We went to Lanercost church[17] in the morning. It is about 10 miles off. Mrs Hills took a wreath for Christopher Howards[18] grave. Why should she do such things? We have heard all about him from her, which S[usan]. does not at all like[19] Oh Mrs Hills Mrs Hills what are you made of? After tea we walked down the river to see Jack & Mr Hills fishing – But they caught nothing. Sugared after dinner & got a mouse & an M.D.[20]

Tuesday 28 September

Went to Gretna Green[21] in the train with Jack, & bicycled back to Corby.

Susan went.

Wednesday 29 September

Went to Carlisle with Mrs Hills.

Thursday 30 September

Went to Gilsland[22] to the Roman wall with Jack.

---

17 Lanercost Priory, in the Irthing Valley, founded for Austin Canons by Robert de Vauz about 1144.

18 Third of six sons of George, 9th Earl of Carlisle (1843-1911), and his wife, Rosalind, *née* Stanley (1845-1921); Christopher was Lieutenant in the 8th Hussars and died of pneumonia in September 1896, after a steeplechase accident.

19 Christopher Howard's eldest brother Charles (Lord Morpeth, see Feb. 1897, n.47) became engaged to Kitty Lushington (later Maxse) when he was not yet 20; the engagement had the Countess of Carlisle's approval. Kitty broke off the engagement, however, and in 1893 Charles proposed to Rhoda Ankaret L'Estrange. Lady Carlisle strongly objected to the marriage and permitted none of the family to attend the wedding; hence Susan Lushington's irritation at Mrs Hills' gossip.

20 Sugaring is applying a treacle mixture to tree trunks to attract insects (see the entry for 13 August 1899). 'M.D.' has not been identified.

21 Over the Scottish border, about 10 miles north-west of Carlisle, Gretna Green was long known for its runaway marriages.

22 A village in the Irthing Valley on the railway from Wetheral, about 5 miles north-east, near Amoglanna, a station on the Roman Wall.

Friday 1 October
Watched Jack fishing. Went to Tuddenham.[1] Took photos. Lord & Lady Morpeth to dinner. Rather awful.

Saturday 2 October
Came home – Thanks be to the Gods!
    This week has been most awful & oppressive. Mrs Hills is ———. Mr Hills ———. Jack shut up, everything grand & uncomfortable. I am thankful to be back.

Sunday 3 October
We went to see Mr Gibbs who is not well, with Gerald. But he was out.

Monday 4 October to Saturday 9 October
[*These pages are blank.*]

Sunday 10 October
Adeline & Ralph are being married as I write.

Monday 11 October to Friday 15 October
[*These pages are blank.*]

Saturday 16 October
Today is Saturday the 13th of November. What a skip! But one day is so like another that I never write about them. Grey cloudy cold days. Jack stays with us till 14 V[ictoria]. G[rove]. is ready.
    I go to King's College,[2] Nessa to her studio.
    Life is a hard business – one needs a rhinirocerous [*sic*] skin – & that one has not got.

Sunday 17 October to Tuesday 9 November
[*These pages are blank.*]

---

1   The Hills's keeper.
2   In November AVS began classes in Greek and history at King's College, Kensington; Dr G. C. W. Warr (1845-1901) was her teacher there.

Wednesday 10 November
Lamoureux[3]

Thursday 11 November
[*This page is blank.*]

Friday 12 November
Hamlet[4]

Saturday 13 November
[*This page is blank.*]

Sunday 14 November to Friday 27 November
[*No pages were made out for these dates.*]

Saturday 28 November
I see that my pages give out – wh. is just as well. But if anything worthy of writing down happens before 1898, it shall be entered in one of the remaining pages.

The Fishers are in France for the winter. Gerald is going, in January, to start a publishing firm of Duckworth & Co.[5]

Maeve M[acNamara].[6] is to be married in February – a thousand notes of exclamation.

Sunday 29 November to Saturday 11 December
[*No pages were made out for these dates.*]

Sunday 12 December
My studies have almost come to an end. That great carcase of a Dorothea has been here for a week – ended up with a long discourse upon our duty to our Aunts – ought to stay in Godmanchester[7] – Oh

---

3 M. Charles Lamoureux, conducting Henry Wood's permanent orchestra at the Queen's Hall.

4 The symphonic poem composed and conducted by Edward German.

5 For Duckworth & Co., see Gerald Duckworth, Appendix B.

6 Daughter of Maria (Mia) and Charles MacNamara, married Frederick Goodenough in February 1898.

7 Lady Stephen's home town, just outside Huntingdon; her house still stands in Post Street, but has been divided into two separate dwellings.

what a remarkable set of heavy pompous worthy & intelligent creatures.

Rains today. Poor Mr Gibbs dying –[8]

Monday 13 December to Friday 31 December
[*No pages were made out for these dates, although a note about 25 December was made at the end of the journal (see below).*]

Saturday 1 January 1898
I write this morning what would more fitly have been written last night. But my diary has ever been scornful of stated rules! Here then comes the "Finis" What a volume might not be written round that word – & it is even hard to resist the few sentences that naturally cling to it. But I will be stern. Here is a volume of fairly acute life (the first really *lived* year of my life) ended locked & put away. And another & another & another yet to come. Oh dear they are very long, & I seem cowardly throughout when I look at them. Still, courage & plod on – They must bring some-thing worth the having – & [illegible] they *shall*. Nessa preaches that our destinies lie in ourselves, & the sermon ought to be taken home by us. Here is life given us each alike, & we must do our best with it: your hand in the sword hilt – & an unuttered fervent vow!

The End of 1897.

Saturday 25 December   *Christmas day*
Madge came on the 31st December.[9]
Discussed the Universe!
Meeting of Entomological Society.
L[eslie]. S[tephen]. president
G[eorge]. H[erbert]. D[uckworth]. Librarian
J[ulian]. T[hoby]. S[tephen]. Larva Groom
A[deline]. V[irginia]. S[tephen]. Secretary Chairman & Treasurer.
A[drian]. L[eslie]. S[tephen]. not on the Committee.

---

8   F. W. Gibbs died in February 1898, leaving AVS and Vanessa £1,000 each, and £500 each for Thoby and Adrian.

9   When, for reasons of health, J. A. Symonds retired to Davos, the Symonds sisters visited England periodically; Madge stayed with the Stephens at 22 Hyde Park Gate during the winter of 1889-90. From Katharine Furse, *Hearts and Pomegranates*, 1940, p.56: 'It must have been a very nice stimulating life for her and she became much attached to the beautiful Mrs Leslie Stephen and also to her beautiful daughter Stella Duckworth.'

Warboys 1899

In 1898, Adrian was still a day boy at Westminster School, Thoby a boarder at Clifton College, Vanessa at Cope's School of Art, George at work for Charles Booth as private secretary, and Gerald at his newly founded publishing firm, Duckworth & Co. Virginia was pronounced well enough to continue her studies with Dr Warr at King's College, and to take long London walks with her father. In October, when the family returned from their summer holiday, Virginia began lessons in Greek with Clara Pater.

A regularity of sorts imposed itself in 1899 upon the daily life at 22 Hyde Park Gate, and the summer holiday at the Rectory, Warboys,[1] in Huntingdonshire was the best Virginia had had since the summer of 1894 in Cornwall. During this period she began to keep a journal, quite unlike that of 1897. Her writing now became more detached, more self-conscious in style and manner. She was practising the art of essay writing for the first time. Her piece 'A Chapter on Sunsets' is even dated and signed.

WARBOYS SUMMER HOLIDAYS 1899

Warboys. 4 August 1899. (our first night)
This being our first night, & such a night not occurring again, I must make some mark on paper to represent so auspicious an occasion, tho' my mark must be frail & somewhat disjointed. However we came here sober [?] & with not much bother of spirit – save that twice we had to change – It must be owned – let us hope that future pages will fully contradict the statement – that the country thro which our train passed was dull in the extreme. A flat expanse of field, cornfield – turnip field &c

---

1   A Fenland village in Huntingdonshire (now Cambridgeshire) about 6 miles northeast of Huntingdon, with a Victorian clock tower at its centre; the old Rectory is early 19th century and in its garden is a section of a large pier believed to be from nearby Ramsey Abbey. In a letter to Emma Vaughan, AVS quotes Dorothea Stephen: 'We shall be glad if you will spend the summer near us at Warboys – only we think that you will have to change the name to Peace Girls': *VW Letters*, I, No. 25.

stretched unbroken on either side, till we gave up looking out of the window. Then we came to Warboys Station, found our primitive Omnibus, & drove off the mile to the Rectory. It had been raining all the afternoon (the first rain I have seen for weeks) & the sky was all clouded & misted as for steady showers. However as we drove along the sun shot a shaft of light down; & we beheld a glorious expanse of sky – this golden gauze streamer lit everything in its light; & far away over the flat fields a spire caught the beam & glittered like a gem in the darkness & wetness of the surrounding countries. Let me remark that the village of Warboys runs along the street for a mile to the gates of the Rectory; there are few shops, but we passed 4 windmills (attractive shaped things) & *Nine Public Houses*. Room for Dorothea's band of Hope[2] here! The house & garden I cannot describe now; how we snorted the air with our soot sated nostrils, & revelled in the country damp, cool & quiet. Our sensations were so exquisite, so crowded & so jubilant that music alone could keep pace with them or express a tenth part of their vividness. Black marks on [*Text ends here. The following page is missing.*]

5 August   The Second day at Warboys.

If I go on at this rate methinks I shall soon have finished this book – but the fever will not last – I know the disease well. Today was blazing hot; & we[3] loafed in the garden all the morning; & glided about the Pond in the Punt. I, with the help of 2 string bags, carted my belongings from the red Butterfly box to my room, & there settled to try & read Greek. Ignominious failure! Three times N. interrupted me, & the last interrruption called me to drive to the Station in the Pony Cart.

P.M. A. & N. held a grand cleaning of the Punt. They lashed it to the bridge, overturned it; filled the bottom with tolerably clean water, scrubbed it round with a duster, & then bailed out the water. In the evening the bottoms were laid with rugs so that someone might lie at full length – others sitting at the ends to use the oars.

Oh dear – the style of this work ought to undergo a radical change. All these details will swamp me in time. I find I write with greater ease than I talk sense or nonsense; writing would stand me in good stead were I struck dumb but being gifted with a tolerably facile speech the gift or possession is hardly to be envied.

---

2   Dorothea Stephen (see June 1897, n.22); the Band of Hope, now called the UK Band of Hope Union, is a temperance society with headquarters in London.
3   The four Stephen children.

The London train at Ramsey Station was late – Bank Holiday on Monday, & it was 7.30 when we started back for Warboys. I shall care little for the tastes of this world if the skies are still so glorious.

Such expanse & majesty & illuminations I have never seen. Pure air for fathoms & fathoms & acres & acres; & then such lavish cloud conglomerations; there is a vast space of blue into which the gods are certainly blowing wondrous cloud bubbles. The God babies methinks are amusing themselves.

The air was cold, & the roads desolate as we patter along home. What a beautiful world we live in!

Sunday 6 August

Somewhere in one of his essays[4] – or letters – Mr. Lowell describes his triumph when his thermometer touched 98 in the shade; the heat was then but a delicious exaggeration of sunshine; but when he met his neighbour, &, mopping brows, he learnt that the rival thermometer had touched 100 – then the heat became disgusting & oppressive, & he returned home a broken man. If I lived in the country I should become a weather prophet or something of the same kind. This thermometer rivalry sounds so delightful when one reads the page in a London bedroom, the thermometer a good 96 in the shade. I often wonder whether, if I lived in the country all the year round, I could think as pleasantly as these country writers write. "I love the country best in books." I can never bring myself to believe in the felicity & simplicity of a country life. These speculations though belong to a cold brained critic in London. I am, at the present moment (the emotion is fleeting I know, so I must chronicle it) in love with a country life; I think that a year or two of such gardens & green fields would infallibly sweeten one & soothe one & simplify one into the kind of Gilbert White[5] old gentleman or Miss Matty[6] old lady that only grew till now for me inside the covers of books. I shd. be writing notes upon the weather, & I shd. turn to my diaries[7] of past years to compare their records – I shd. tell how I 'bedded out' certain plants, & record the condition of my rose trees. I shd. perhaps, have seen a swallow on the wing for other climates, or have dis-

---

4   'My Garden Acquaintance' in James Russell Lowell, *My Study Windows*, 1871.
5   Gilbert White (1720-93), English clergyman and naturalist, remembered for his *Natural History and Antiquities of Selbourne*, 1789.
6   The indomitable spinster in Mrs Gaskell's *Cranford*, 1853.
7   The 1897 journal alone survives.

covered a sleepy martin presumably preparing for his winter sleep. I shd. propound my theories as to migration & hybernation. Alas, tho', as a Cockney I have no sound country education to go upon. I must blurt out crude ecstasies upon sky & field; which may perchance retain for my eyes a little of their majesty in my awkward words.

7 August

Monotony, so methinks, dwells in these plains. Such melting gray of sky, land & water is the very spirit of monotony. I lay in the punt, which has been padded with rugs & cushions & read a sleepy preaching [?] book;[8] the diary of some ancient Bishop written in flowing ancient English that harmonised with this melancholy melodious monotony (what an awful sentence!) of bank & stream. Activity of mind, I think, is the only thing that keeps one's life going, unless one has a larger emotional activity of some other kind. Ones mind thats like a restless steamer paddle urging the ship along, tho' the wind is fallen & the sea is as still as glass. I must now expound another simile that has been rolling itself round in my mind for many days past. This is that I am a Norseman bound on some long voyage. The ship now is frozen in the drift ice; slowly we are drifting towards home. I have taken with me after anxious thought all the provisions for my mind that are necessary during the voyage. The seals & walruses that I shoot during my excursions on the ice (rummaging in the hold) are the books that I discover here & read. It amuses me to carry on the comparison, tho' I admit that written down it has something absurd about it. What a force a human being is! There are worse solitudes than drift ice, & yet this eternal throbbing heat & energy of ones mind thaws a pathway thro'; & open sea & land shall come in time. Think tho', what man is midst fields & woods. A solitary creature dependent on winds & tides, & yet somehow suppressing the might of a spark in his brain. What nonsense to write!

This is a melancholy country. I went this afternoon with A. into the church opposite our gates. It is the church of St Mary Magdalene,[9] & it was built in the 14th century. The churchyard is full of sombre tombstones, with queer carvings & angels heads sprawling over date & name & all. There are many graves that are nameless; & I was startled

---

8   Unidentified.
9   Built of brown cobbles with a 13th-century steeple and a broad spire; the chancel arch is Norman and the font, decorated with flowers and leaves on its bowl, also dates back to the 13th century.

to think that I was walking over some ancient dust forgotten & undistinguished from the hillocks of the field. The graves rise in swelling mounds side by side all along the bottom of the churchyard.

After dinner we sit on our little terrace raised so as to overlook the garden & pond. The Pole star bright over our heads, & long black clouds floating in the pale night sky. A bat swoops down, & circles over our heads. What attractive creatures they are! & a moth suddenly looms across the lamp lit drawing room windows. T. rages [?] & jumps for his net which, having been surreptitiously used by A. to drag the depths of the Pond is naturally not forthcoming.

My pen, I must add, is rather unwell at present, & the aspect of this book distresses me. I cannot write prettily when my pen scratches & all joy in the art is lost to me. I love writing for the sake of writing, but when my pen is enfeebled it becomes a task & bother to me. The domestic Mary "a nice girl, but very empty Miss" investigated the mechanics of my pen before we came away, & something of its divinity has fled since.

Let me supplement this – today the 2nd of September [1899] after many trials writing to London four times over this morning [*Text ends.*]

8 *August*

A curate[10] was leaning over the gate while Adrian rode Reshnel [?] around the field. So G[eorge]. ran & asked him to come in; which he did & shook hands all round. N. complained to him of the Huntingdonshire harvest which has robbed us of butter, milk, cream & an extra helping hand. All the women he explained refuse to do anything but work in the fields. They wont go out to service, or stay & mind the home. At 7 or 8 in the morning they start forth in armies, with their huge sun bonnets & cotton aprons; & toil in the corn fields till dusk. This harvest over, there is the autumn harvest of potatoes. All the land that was Fen is now cut up into innumerable cornfields. We beheld the harvesters this afternoon as we rode back from Ramsey.[11] On one side of the road was a corn cutting machine sweeping down the standing corn; & on the other a field where corn lay all cut; & here & there women & boys were all tramping thro' it heaping the corn into stooks. Even a little child not more than 4 years old was harvesting with its mother. It wore a bright scarlet frock, & trotted behind with a small armful of gleanings. One of the women

---

10 From 1898 the curate of St Mary Magdalene was J. Blake Milward.
11 A market town about 3½ miles north of Warboys.

harvesters was I should think almost 70 with white scanty locks, & a wrinkled sun burnt wind scourged face. There is some picturesque element in this country – harvesters, windmills, golden cornfields. Everything flat with blue haze in the distance, & a vast dome of sky all around. The Nortons[12] came in the afternoon, American to the backbone. Buckets full of talk & talk after dinner till I crept up here & stretched my limbs.

[Undated, 1899]
Ramsey (or Ram's Island) a market town on the borders of the Fens. Long Street call the *Great Whyte* runs north, & the other, the High St. runs East & West. The town became infected by the plague in the year 1666 by means of a piece of cloth sent from London to be made into a coat for Oliver Cromwells cousin Colonel Cromwell,[13] who, with the tailor & all his family, also 400 people, died of the plague.

There was once a Benedictine Abbey founded in 969 by Aelwin, Alderman [Ealdorman] of all England & Lord of the East Angles, & dedicated to S.S. Mary & Benedict.[14] The Abbey which had the distinction of being "mitred"[15] stood at the upper end of the town, & occupied a tract of solid ground, 2 miles in length, surrounded by the dense & melancholy marshes & being inaccessible save by water, the beautiful perpendicular gate house & Refectory remain. Queen Isabella was here a fortnight in 1309. At the Dissolution there were 9 monks, & revenues estimated at £1,315; the modern mansion, the seat of Lord de Ramsey D.C.L. Lord of the Manor & Principal Landowner.

Sexton: David Sanders

This interesting observation (the first sentence or two illegible because of the curious ink, which I think of adopting for my permanent ink) is taken from our only guide book to these parts – Kelly's Huntingdonshire Directory;[16] whose first object is to detail the shopkeepers; a little information however, such as I have written above, is intermixed.

---

12   Charles Eliot Norton and his children Sally and Dick; see July 1897, n.14.
13   Col. Henry Cromwell, husband of his cousin, the poet Anna Cromwell, a passionate Royalist.
14   Ramsey Abbey was reputedly founded by Duke Aethelwine in 969; there is a statue there of Aelwyn.
15   When certain abbots were invested by the Pope with the privilege of wearing a mitre, the abbey was called a 'mitred abbey'.
16   *Kelly's Directory of Bedfordshire, Huntingdonshire and Northamptonshire, etc.* Kelly & Co., London, 1885.

9 August

This afternoon the Curate appeared, & took us over his church. He was rather ignorant, & had to answer "I don't know" to a good many intelligent American[17] questions. The two things of beauty are the Norman Arch, & the Font; also a third almost hidden though by a modern erection – the ancient windows, whose long brass latches are picturesque though doubtless inefficient. The curate who is the first live specimen I have ever shaken hands with, turned out to be a good fairly lively human being. Evidently his life in this place year's end to year's end is not enlivening; he absorbed American stories & finally produced jokes of his own with a delight born of much Parish small beer. He told a few parish stories, which I reproduce because I have nothing else to say. How Arthur Beehive, a parishioner met the Holy Ghost in the churchyard. This he declared saved him; & he told the story afterwards over his beer in the Public House. 'But 'ow did 'e address you Arthur?' said one wit. 'Were it Bee'ive, or Sir, or Harthur?' Also the Curate said, rather wickedly considering his calling, that his place is strictly a Baptist community. Every Easter children & adults together take total immersion – in the pond near the Station!!

We are to go & see Mrs Noble the baker who is a "character."
This line ends a verse on a tombstone here –

"He sleeps & all *his* well – "

The H. partly obliterated by some more lettered clerk or stonemason.

10 or 11 August

We had the Curate to dinner last night, which deserves full mention because I have never sat down to a meal with a curate in my life, nor had one, to my knowledge in the house. My interest was awakened in him very easily; I had a dim idea of mythical curates, dwelling in the pages of novels, & receiving satire at the hands of all wielders of Pens – but the fact that a Black Coated gentleman could be a Human Being & not a Hypocrite (outwardly at least – I cannot answer for the condition of the Curate's morals on the strength of one dinner party) was quite strange to me. This young man seems to be largely a person of intelligence with a rather peculiar gift of humorous sarcasm. Occasionally his judgments & stories are bitter; but on the whole, he is merely good humoured & muscular. This would all be explicable; or not needing explanation; but

17 From the Nortons, probably.

the surprising thing is that he is a Clergyman. He is moreover a Ritual-ist,[18] which I take to be a strict creed; & yet the first 5 minutes of his talk with us he declared that the only thing that made life in the country bear-able was rabbit shooting. What a life he must have – here especially. He makes no secret of his dislike to Mrs Way,[19] which he conveys to one in cumbrous irony; this lady evidently rules her husband, & would like to dictate to the Curate; certainly thinks him a most inferior creature – she is a kind of small Mrs Proudie.[20] The young man however not having much in common with Mr Slope their hostility is open – expressed on his acerbic side, I expect, by sarcastic civility; & on Mrs Way's by nag-ging [?] pretensions; the young man (I know not how to spell his name) has been here 10 months – nine months too many he says. The people about here are a peculiar race. So imbedded are they in their own delv-ing pursuits, living lonely self contained lives, with a few strong re-ligious opinions that only serve to narrow their minds, that a stranger is in their eyes a most contemptible creature. They are solid conservatives, & resent a stranger or an innovation in their lives. The Schoolmaster,[21] who has been here 25 years, says he still feels out in the cold; they do not look upon him as one of themselves. The curate is a man of humour but humour has a hard battle of it in such surroundings. Nevertheless he told his Curates Recollections with great glee – jumping & jerking in a peculiar way he has when something amuses him.

Well, the state of mind of a man like this must be odd. Better lodging in a London slum than gossiping over here –

I write distractedly. Vanessa is wandering round the room looking for a pair of her most valuable scissors, which she declares were last seen in this room & now have apparently vanished altogether. She insinuates, with some pertinacity that I know where they are, & that I might rouse myself sufficiently from my eternal writing to tell her. I strive vainly to remember the points of the great scissor question & tell her with an

---

18 Mr Blake Milward would have been a High Anglican, advocating the observance of symbolic rites close to those of the Roman Catholic Church.

19 The wife of W. H. B. Way, the rector.

20 The domineering wife of the Bishop of Barchester in Anthony Trollope's *Barchester Towers*, 1857; she eventually triumphs over the hypocritical and sycophantic chaplain, Mr Slope, against whom she struggles for supremacy in the quiet cathedral town.

21 William Alderson (b.1845) was Headmaster at the Board Mixed School, Warboys, from 1876-1909.

assumed briskness & confidence that I placed them in a certain china pot only yesterday. An interval of quiet supervenes – then Oh – Goodness – no scissors forthcoming – *Where* on Earth can they be –

12 August

Adrian & I have a habit now when the days are so hot, of keeping our exercise till after tea, & then of going out on our bicycles for an hour's hard riding. Besides picturesque advantages, this country possesses the solid one that all its main roads are excellently made, well hammered, smooth & free from stray stones. This country, too, does not hamper the cyclist by any disturbing Hills; you may ride & ride & ride without ever being forced to dismount & push yr. bicycle up a hill, or without ever having the delight of raising yr. feet & spinning downhill. This evening we went along the road which crosses the railway at the station by a Bridge & then runs as straight as a yard measure for a good 4 miles. These roads have their beauties to the eye of a Fen lover, but a Bicyclist is a mechanical animal. Not until we dismounted did we appreciate the scenery. On both sides it was dead flat – the road was slightly raised in the middle & runs through the plain like a straight white thread. This is the midst of the old Fen country. This solid ground on which we stood was, not many years ago, all swamp & reed; now indeed there is a pathway, & on either side grow potatoes & corn, but the Fen character remains indelible. A broad ditch crosses the Fen, in which there is cold brown water even in this hot summer. Tall rushes & water plants grow from it; & small white moths, the inhabitants of the Fens, were fluttering among them in scores when we were there. I wish that once & for all I could put down in this wretched handwriting how this country impresses me – how great I feel the stony-hard flatness [?] & monotony of the plain. Every time I write in this book I find myself drifting into the attractive but impossible task of describing the Fens – till I grow heartily sick of so much feeble word painting; & long for one expressive quotation that should signify in its solitary compass all the glories of earth air & Heaven. Nevertheless I own it is a joy to me to be set down with such a vast never ending picture to reproduce – reproduction is out of the question – but to gaze at, nibble at & scratch at.

After all we are a world of imitations[;] all the Arts that is to say imitate as far as they can the one great truth that all can see. Such is the eternal instinct in the human beast, to try & reproduce something of that majesty in paint marble or ink. Somehow ink tonight seems to me the least effectual method of all – & music the nearest to truth.

13 August

Tonight & last night we began our Sugar[22] campaign – Thoby rather, the rest of us have rather departed from that profession. Sugaring must be explained; briefly, it means that the trees at intervals are smeared with a decoction which is known as sugar, but which contains other ingredients. Rum, & thick black treacle mixed is one prescription & that most often adopted as being independent of the cooks kindness & the kitchens fire; the other is a compound, beer, & treacle (black), boiled up in some obliging kettle that, preferably, has no other vocation. An innocent reader (I suppose a reader sometimes for the sake of variety when I write; it makes me put on my dress clothes such as they are) having got this far still remains in the dark as the use of such a preparation. This then, is the most scientific way of catching moths. Indeed there is no other, unless you are an eccentric entomologist, & possess lighthouses, & sliding windows & such extravagances. [ ]A flannel rag is soaked in this compound; & then pinned to the rough bark of a tree; cascades & waterfalls of the alluring sticky brown mixture pour down to the grass & emit to the nose of a moth a faint & seductive smell. The moth roaming melancholy thro' damp woods suddenly snuffs a strange & delicious odour; rum! he follows it & reaches the fountain head, where perhaps he finds a dozen of his cronies already seated. He promptly folds his wings & settles on one of the veins of precious liquid, his proboscis in a second is imbedded in a rich drop, & in a few minutes he is imbibing like an opium eater. This is from the moths point of view – man, the hunter, starts forth in the following procession. Firstly of course the leader of the expedition, the renowned J[ulian]. T[hoby]. S[tephen]. He wears a large felt hat, & muffled round him is a huge brown plaid, which makes his figure striding in the dark most picturesque & brigand like. In his hand he carries a glass jar – of which more anon. 2ndly appears a female form in evening dress, a shawl over her shoulders, & carrying a large stickless net. 3rdly the lantern bearer (none other than the present writer) who lights the paths fitfully with a Bicycle lamp of brilliant but uncertain powers of illumination. Twice this evening was the whole expedition confounded by the sudden extinction of the wick, which when extinct sends odours sufficient to attract or stupefy all the moths in the garden. This lamp when alight sheds an oval disk of light on to the backs of the van & occasionally

---

22 See Sept. 1897, n.20; AVS would give a more elaborate description of the process in an essay called 'Reading' in *The Captain's Death Bed and Other Essays*, 1950 (Kp A30).

slides like a will-o'-the wisp to explore the neighbourhood. 4thly Ad[rian]. L[eslie]. S[tephen]. a supernumerary amateur of no calling who takes little interest in the proceedings & is proficient in the art of obscuring the lamp at critical moments; 5thly Gurth the dog member, whose services are unrequired & unrewarded; being the first to investigate the sugar & having been convicted of attempts to catch moths for no entomological purpose whatever. This then, is the procession that starts forth in single file about 9 o'clock in the evening. About six trees have been sugared in a circle round the garden, fronting the "miniature lake" & ending on the tennis lawn. Each tree was examined carefully in this way. The leader, the net carrier & the supernumerary advance in the dark, the lanterns disk of light being for the moment cast on one side. Perhaps it illumines a group of sleepy hens, who feel baffled & perhaps rather silly at the sudden dignity cast upon them. Then the leader calls out – Advance slowly – & the lantern bearer brings the light to bear gradually on the tree to be examined. The lantern generally advances till the full light is brought to bear, & then every cranny in the bark – every blade of grass at the foot is searched for possible occupants. In almost every tree we find one or two moths, drowsy but constantly sucking, who flutter feebly to the ground if disturbed, uttering a slightly tipsy protest at the indignity. The commonest moths – such as Yellow Underwings & Dark Archers – will return night after night the whole season through; so have we perverted the morals of moth land. A temperance preacher would find the text for many sermons here then – the Devil in disguise – with his beer pot empty in one hand – his poison pot in t'other – but let such moralisings be reserved for the preacher's mouth. The leader, should one of his guests strike his fancy, uncorks his poison pot, gently taps the specimen on the nose – the cork is shut – & the moth, his brain dazed with the delicious fumes of liquor, sinks into an all embracing arm. Death might come more painfully. The other night, as the light cautiously advanced, it was abruptly told to halt by the leader, a Red underwing was on the tree. By the faint glow we could see the huge moth – his wings open, as though in ecstasy, so that the splendid crimson of the underwing could be seen – his eyes burning red, his proboscis plunged into a flowing stream of treacle. We gazed one moment on his splendour, & then uncorked the bottle. I think the whole procession felt some unprofessional regret when, with a last gleam of scarlet eye & scarlet wing, the grand old moth vanished.

[Undated 1899]

I was one day walking in some fields near Warboys when someone called across a hedge to me – 'Can you tell me the right way to Warboys?' It happened that the road ran at some little distance, & though of course I could point the direction, I found it somewhat difficult to describe accurately the exact path by which it could be reached.

So as I could well shorten my walk & do the wondering voice a good turn, I called back "if you will come over here, I will show you, as I myself am going that way." The voice seemed to hesitate, & then I heard a creaking of thorns & twigs, as though some body were being thrust relentlessly through a very fine specimen of the hawthorn hedge.

18 August   Warboys Distractions

Yesterday we attended a garden party at the de la Prymes,[23] which deserves a page to itself – so stupendous & remarkable an event was it. But I have no time for that; I can only give a short account of todays diversion – our visit to Godmanchester. This has been long planned; innumerable trains correct & incorrect have been delved from the depths of Bradshaw[24] for us by obliging persons; today the great event took place. Our visit was to be made for the purpose of going on a water party down the river with Hester Ritchie[25] & a terrible oppressive gathering of Stephens. The morning dawned cold cloudy & with sudden onslaughts of driving rain. Our first excitement was a narrow escape of a missed train at Warboys. Behold Nessa – whipping the pony frantically – one hand grasping her hat – the wind & the rain in our faces, only 6 minutes in which to cover the half mile to the station. Off blows my hat – halt is called but [*illegible*] eager to lose no time jumps off & is rolling on his back. However this diversion over soon, & we reached the station in time for the train which was late. We sank into our empty third with a sigh of relief & comfort. All around were gray flat fields with the rain swishing over them & the pollard trees sobbing in the wind. "I believe," said I "that it is quite impossible for us to miss a train even if we tried to." As I said this I almost qualified my statement in my uneasy desire to propitiate the Gods at the last moment; but I re-

---

23 Charles De la Pryme (1815-99), JP and barrister, living at Wistow Lodge, about 2 miles from Warboys; his sons were Alexander (b.1870), Charles (b.1873) and William (b.1880), all three of them Cambridge men.

24 *Bradshaw's Railway Guide*, published monthly.

25 See May 1897, n.1.

solved for once in my life to be bold; & flaunt my good luck in the Gods faces.

Our journey from Warboys to Huntingdon[26] is one of those not infrequent train journeys in this part of the world which are a splendid triumph for the bicycle. You can bicycle with comfort & pleasure into Huntingdon under an hour. It takes just the same to do the 8 miles in the train; & the fares moreover for the return journey of 3 people amount to 7s.6d. There are 2 changes at Somersham & at St Ives; & at the first of these stations we had to wait 10 minutes & at the 2nd 5. The first – Somersham train we waited for & caught comfortably. At St Ives we had to cross various platforms to reach the one which, the guard assured us, was the Huntingdon platform. We had only 5 minutes at this, so that we lost no time in running across & getting into position for our 3rd class carriage. We waited; no train or sign of a train; so we investigated the machinery of a sweet machine, which, proving defective in every branch, we retreated to the weighing machine. So 20 minutes passed; then we became uneasy & captured a paper boy – "When does the Huntingdon train come in?" "Oh at 2.15" said he – No, no, said Vanessa; I know there is a train at 12.43. The paper boy smiled somewhat grimly – The 12.43 has already been gone 20 minutes, Miss, said he – from the other platform." We then had been intent upon the eccentricities of the sweet machine & the weighing machine while the train came in on the other side of us, took up its passengers & went on its way. It was now about 20 minutes past one. We ought to have arrived at 5 minutes past one – & we should arrive – when? I must say that when our faculties are effectually though rudely aroused by some emergency like this we take a practical view of the case. We spoke little, but decided in a few moments that a horse & cart must be found in St Ives capable of taking us with no delay to our Uncle & cousins[27] at Godmanchester. We went to the County Arms; but this had long ago given up keeping traps we were told; then to the Robin Hood whose trap was just gone out; then to the Ramping Lion Inn, who did not possess a trap, & then to the Fountain – who did possess a trap – which trap could be at our service in 10 minutes. So we sat down in a little parlour which smelt of wine – the

26 The County Town of Huntingdonshire, 59 miles north of London; Godmanchester, the home of Lady Stephen, is on the south bank of the river Ouse opposite Huntingdon.
27 The uncle was presumably Sir Henry Stewart Cunningham (1823-1920), brother of Lady Stephen.

Inn keeper came & sat with us to beguile the time. He was a young man, overflowing with good nature & talk. Before long he told us, what I guessed as soon as I saw him, that he was a stranger in these parts, & finds them terribly dull. On Mondays he said, we have a market, & then there's something doing, but on other days nothing happens ever. There never was such a sleepy place. He asked if we came from London – & when we said we did, he asked us many questions about London weather. Evidently a little change such as this was all the excitement he ever got. (This young man & the chemist are both people who testify to the character of the Fens & the Fen people. They are looked upon as strangers; & they on their side find the country, the people & the life terribly monotonous.) However soon our pony came to the door, & we started hastily. It is 5 miles to Godmanchester & it was now 25 minutes to 2. St Ives as we saw it driving through must just have one exclamation of admiration. It is all built along one winding cobble paved street. The river lies on the left; & St Ives crosses the river over the lengthy & beautiful bridge which has carried the name of St Ives into countries & towns far distant from Huntingdon. The last picture that I saw of it was in the Phillimores drawing room at the wedding party just a week before we came here.[28] The bridge is an old stone bridge; its claim to distinction being that in the middle there is a square tower – for what purpose I do not know. (I will look up the History of St Ives & its bridge in Kelly, & write it on the opposite page.)

We drove our five miles through quaint old villages – such as I have never seen equalled. Everything is old – such antiquity grows depressing after a time; there is only one new house in Godmanchester, so we were told – a new house being a house that does not date back to the 17th century, & this house had to be new because the original old one was burnt down. We reached Godmanchester at 2.15 & found the party on the verge of lunch. To cut matters short we had lunch & then, in a sharp shower of rain, started for the boat.

R[osamund]. – who loves the rich, is anxious to imitate their charms & flyaway manners. This, at least, is the explanation we have devised to account for her startling departure from all probabilities laid down by the principles of Heredity & Physiognomy. She is remarkably square,

---

28 On Saturday, 29 July, Eustace Hills married Margaret Blanche, second daughter of Sir Walter Phillimore (1845-1924), 1st Baron, Judge, and Agnes, *née* Lushington, daughter of Charles Manners Lushington, MP. The Phillimores lived at 85 Eaton Place, SW. Margaret was killed in 1904 when her bicycle collided with a bus.

& short; her face is also square & short, with small vivacious eyes, & a nose which might without unkindness be described as ridiculous – so aggressive & impertinent in its squat littleness is it. She was once described by her father as a "winsome frolic." This is a character that she trys[*sic*] to deserve. She is, I think tinged strongly with the usual Stephen solidity & cumbersomeness; so that her attempts to be winsome & frolicsome are oddly & ludicrously out of harmony with her appearance. A long course of preaching to the rich & to the youth of Godmanchester has made her manner to those younger than herself dictatorial. As we went down to the river she lectured us on the various objects of interest. I fear I did not profit.

The others are all Stephens without attempting to conceal the fact. They are immensely broad, long & muscular; they move awkwardly, & as though they resented the conventionalities of modern life at every step. They all bring with them the atmosphere of the lecture room; they are severe, caustic & absolutely independent & immoveable [*sic*]. An ordinary character would be ground to a pulp after a weeks intercourse with them. They are distinct & have more character than most of the world, so for that we will bless them & thank them sincerely. After we had rowed for an hour, the two boats came alongside & it was agreed to land in 10 minutes time. So we duly landed; & some of us sat down to make the kettle boil, & the others went for a dreary walk along the river brink. One remarkable sign of character in this race is that they are able to sit speechless without feeling the slightest discomfort while the whole success of the party they have invited depends on them. They acknowledge that it is drizzling & grey, that their guests are depressed & think the whole party a bore; they can bear the knowledge of these facts & support the discovery without turning a hair. I admire this as I should admire a man who could stand on the line immoveable [*sic*] while an express train rushed towards him. This kind of heroism however, is not calculated to smooth a tea party.

Picture us uncomfortably seated on a towing path; half the party in a ditch, the other half in long grass – a cold wind blowing, with occasional drops of rain – no glow in east or west – but a grey melancholy vista of sky. Sir Herbert fought wasps & eat bread & jam – then we slowly packed our basket & started back for Godmanchester. I sat in one boat with Lady Stephen, & Adrian & Harry to row. We kept well ahead of the others. The rain fell now with a vengeance. We got back however in time to escape an absolute wet throughness.

So ended a somewhat grim day of pleasure. This has taken me considerably longer to write than the whole day itself: such a relation of details is extraordinarily difficult, dull & unprofitable to read. However there is no end to writing, & each time I hope that I may make better stuff of it.

St Ives was anciently called Slepe[29] & appears under that name in the Domesday book, but acquired its present name from Ivo a Persian bishop who, it is said, travelled thro' the land preaching & at last came here, where he died about the end of the 6th century.

St Ives has a market every Monday for cattle, sheep & pigs; it was granted by charter of King Edward 1st about the year 1290. A great part of the town was destroyed in 1680 by a fire which broke out at the end of White Hart Lane on the 30 April in that year; the wind being very high, it crossed to the Sheep Market consuming everything in its way down to the waterside & laid in ashes houses belonging to 122 families.

Over the river is a stone bridge of six arches said to have been erected by the Abbots of Ramsey; two of the arches were rebuilt in 1716 by the duke of Manchester; near the centre, over one of the piers is an ancient stone building, the lower part of which was anciently a chapel but which is now used as a dwelling-house. The church of All Saints is an edifice of stone, in the Norman & Perpendicular styles &c. The register of baptisms & marriages dates from 1561, & burials 1563; one of the parish account books contains under date 1634 the signature of Oliver Cromwell then a resident of St. Ives.[30]

Extract from the Huntingdonshire Gazette.
TERRIBLE TRAGEDY IN A DUCKPOND

A terrible tragedy[31] which had its scene in a duck pond has been reported from Warboys. Our special correspondent who was despatched to that village has had unrivaled [sic] opportunities of investigating the details as well as the main facts of the disaster, & these we have a melancholy pleasure in now presenting to the reader. It seems then that three young

---

29 All the following information is presumably taken from *Kelly's Directory*.

30 Oliver Cromwell, whose statue is in the market-place, lived in St Ives for five years, 1631-6, as a tenant farmer.

31 The 'tragedy' that follows presumably had its origin in some actual boating incident at Warboys.

persons – Miss Emma Vaughan, Miss Virginia Stephen & Mr. Adrian Leslie Stephen, niece, daughter & son respectively to the distinguished author Mr. Leslie Stephen were punting by moonlight on the night of the 23rd inst. The piece of water which has now such an evil reputation, is about a quarter of a mile long, broadening & narrowing considerably in its course. It is covered at all times by a carpet of duckweed – the green shroud alas of three young lives! Mr. Leslie Stephen & his family are staying at the Rectory for 7 weeks & one of the chief attractions of the Rectory garden is this sheet of water, which moreover possesses a Punt. On the evening of the ill fated 23rd of August the aforementioned young people – aged respectively 25, 17, & 15, planned to go for a moonlight punting excursion. That this excursion was undertaken solely for the purposes of pleasure is proved by the fact that 3 arm chairs have been discovered, in all probability the last seats on land or water of the young people so soon to meet their doom. Sounds of revelry & merrymaking are said to have reached the shore; the water was partially illuminated by the light of the moon, but in other places pitch black in the shade of the trees. The house lies at a short distance from the water, but the kitchen premises in which alone were those capable of hearing cries for help, or of answering them, are at the back of the house, so that no sound of revelry or of anguish told of the scene that was being enacted not half a mile away. But we must hasten our unwilling pen to enter in upon the details of the disaster. It is supposed then that the boat (or Punt) was rendered in nautical language, topheavy by the 3 chairs which we have already mentioned, & that an incautious movement on the part of one of the crew caused the whole thing to capsize with deadly swiftness & sureness.

How can we describe the scene that followed? The angry waters of the duck pond rose in their wrath to swallow their prey – & the green caverns of the depths opened – & closed – The cold moonlight silvered the path to death – & perhaps tinged the last thoughts of the unfortunate sufferers with something of its own majestic serenity. We know not if their end was promptly consummated, or if terrible shrieks & agonised struggles for air preceded the merciful rest that soon was theirs. Alone, untended, unsoothed, with no spectator but the silver moon, with no eye to weep, no hand to caress, three young souls were whelmed by the waters of the duck Pond. But why continue this harrowing tale? Let us resume our narration of well authenticated facts – no less harrowing than these indeed, but enacted in a more prosaic atmosphere. It chanced that 10 o'clock was the hour in which Miss Vanessa Stephen & Mr. Thoby

Stephen the eldest son & daughter of the house were to return from a country visit that they had been paying. The catastrophe which we have just described took place about 15 minutes before.

The travellers unwittingly entered the Hall; the house was slumbering with no traces of fear or disorder. Calm servants brought coffee – the ordinary facts of the day were discussed; till it entered some one's head to note the absence of a number of the family. A servant who was called, stated that she thought she had seen them last by the pond; doubtless they were about to embark on the punt.

Such an expedition would have been so ordinary that no further notice was taken for the time. As minute after minute passed & still no sign was made by the lost ones, the family became uneasy; they put on cloaks (for the night was now advanced to the hour of 11) & went into the garden. They shouted "Emma! Virginia!" "Adrian" addressing each by name several times in succession. Their voices echoed thro' the peaceful scented garden; bats chirped in the hedges; moths flew past them, the stillness was awful in its intensity. The searchers came to the edge of the pond; but the moon had now risen to the summit of the sky & the surface of the water was quite indistinguishable from the fields on the other side. [ ] In the blackness the eye could discern no floating body – no capsized punt. Perhaps the darkness was merciful. Let us hasten on our tale. No one can bear to dwell on such a story as this; but it is one of the most gruesome & heartrending that ever had to weigh down

(This harrowing tale stops abruptly here; but a fuller & improved version[32] will be found somewhere, which I have, with great labour, concocted for the benefit of Emma Vaughan.)

26 August

[We have just come back from an expedition to St Ives. T. N. & I drove there in the pony cart when the fury of the midday sun was over; & came back in the cool of the evening. Such an expedition always has charms for me, though I doubt that any other rational person would understand them could I – which alas is an impossibility – write them down faithfully.][33]

---

32 Now in the Sussex University Library: Monks House Papers (MHP/A10). It was published in *The Charleston Magazine*, Spring 1990.

33 The first paragraph within brackets was deleted by AVS; the brackets around the following paragraph are AVS's.

...ch an expedition would have been so enduring that no further notice...

[Terrible misfortunes with my pen have interfered severely with the progress of this work. I now am forced to resume, but I do so reluctantly; & the next pages (few I trust) will be written with a *steel nib*!]

3 September   A Chapter on Sunsets

A showery day with wind & watery clouds is excellent material for a sunset. A day of unclouded majesty, heat & serenity has a sunset of extraordinary magnificence of light so unapproachable by pen or paint that the author & artist prefer for the sake of their art the more attainable forms of cloud which can be likened by an imaginative person to castles & hills & rocky towns that have their counterpart on earth.

No one – save a poet – can express in words or paint the human significance & pathos of the suns unclouded rain of light – that makes the Heavens a delight & a difficulty to look upon. This land, as I have had occasion to remark before, is a land whose chief attraction is its sky. It is as if you were slung on a flat green board in mid air; with only sky sky sky around & above & beneath you. In this way alone I think that the Fen country deserves to be called one of the most beautiful countries in England. We have this moment come in from a sunset expedition – an account of which I must at once write down, or I shall never attempt it. Nothing methinks is so impossible as to describe a real sunset in pen & ink 3 days after that sunset has faded from the sky.

To begin then. Today has been windy stormy & raining – too great an abundance of water indeed to make a really grand sunset.

[Today][1] at 6.30 we started along the Huntingdon road, & the sun [was] then just entering the cloud belt on the Horizon. It sank so [slow]ly that we, who reproached G[eorge] for having brought us out [so] early, found ourselves in a minute in the midst of the performance. [So] quickly did the clouds catch the glory, glow, & fade, that our eyes & mind had ample work merely to register the change. The main features were three; a red ball of a sun, first; then a low lying bank of gray cloud, whose upper edges were already feathery & fixed to receive into its arms the impetuous descent of the sun god; thirdly, a group of trees which made our horizon; casting their arms against the sky; then fourthly, a cloud shaped like an angels wing, so – [*drawing*] The edge of this was [*two illegible words*] with fire – vivid & glowing in the east like some sword of judgment or vengeance – & yet the intensity of its light melted & faded as it touched the gray sky behind; so that there was no clearly defined outline. This is one observation that I have made from my observation of many sunsets – that no shape of cloud has one line in it in the least sharp or hard – nowhere can you draw a straight line with

---

1   The page is damaged; barely distinguishable words have been editorially restored and bracketed.

your pencil & say "This line goes so". Everything is done by different shades & degrees of light – melting & mixing infinitely – Well may an Artist despair!

This was the central point of the sunset – but when our eyes found an instant to leave it there was another glory, reflected indeed but no less glorious & perfect of its kind than the original, all round. The afternoon had scattered gray clouds pall mall about the sky. Some of these were now conglomerated into one vast cloud field in the east & south – others were sailing like solitary icebergs. All bore on their way the imprint: the dying kiss – of the sun. The icebergs shone glowing pale crimson; the ice fields were broken up into exquisite blocks of crimson lint – a crimson which looked all the more delicate & exquisite that it is besprinkled with soft cold gray.

This was all over in 10 minutes – when we got back home the east & west were rapidly taking on the darkness of night. No gleams of crimson lived to tell that the sun had sunk.

Sept. 3rd AVS

4 September
[*The first part of this essay is missing.*] richness of the soil. No one unconnected with the labour & cultivation of earth finds a place here. This land is 20 feet below the level of the sea; elaborate pumping machinery & innumerable dykes drain the waters off the fields; it is rumoured that one of these great machines is now going out of order, the landlord who possesses it being unwilling to spare money sufficient for its repair. Should it stop work one day the water would well up over the fields & drown the Fen men. We met a Fen funeral coming back from Warboys, where the dead had been buried. There were about 5 bakers carts & a cart which had been used in carrying the corn, all filled with men & women dressed in deep mourning. They came from the east along the absolutely straight white road. We saw them crawling towards us with the sky heaping clouds & the wind blowing blue spaces around them. As we passed them, a boy looked down at us very sullenly & with the peculiar sodden depressed look that Fen men & women have; they were absolutely silent; & the procession went on to the heart of the Fen. I dreamt most vividly of this last night; how I looked into the womens faces; & the carts passed on & on into the [night?] they were going back to some strange dark land, & they said the only time they saw the light of day was when they came to Warboys to bury their dead. There is a curious feeling in this land of infinite sky: so that you can become a

weather prophet lying on yr. back in the Fen, & observing the cloud batallions [*sic*] floating far away, & blue sky long before its warmth is felt.

Here I must turn round & retrace my steps on the other side of the page. Today is the 4th of September. I have already counted our days several times over, & we have hardly more than a fortnight left. We go back on Thursday the 21st of September.

An Old Curse   [?8 September]

Today, for the first time since we have been here we woke to a grey sky & steady downfall of rain. All the morning it rained with short intervals of cessation. Nothing is more melancholy than a day spent indoors in the country, without sun, & on the other hand a day spent out in the rain has charms, which, in a dry summer like this, appeals to one more than an orthodox fine weather outing. So after lunch we three[2] draped ourselves in our worst London clothes & cloaked ourselves to satisfy some mythical God who decreed that what [*sic*] feet are dangerous, & so set out on bicycles. The little children at the Lodge – terribly bored poor little creatures when their mother forbade them to take their great amusement of swinging on the gate, came to the front door of the cottage & looked at us with a mixture of awe & admiration. They thought we were defying some authority at home & that we should be made to repent afterwards. It was worth defying authorities had such existed, to feel the cool showers of rain trickling over our cheeks, & to smell the exquisite damp refreshed odours that arose from the road & fields. The Roads which are almost always deserted today showed not one single passenger. We had the County of Huntingdon to ourselves; beside an unknown acreage of air & sky. So we rode & rode & rode till the spires of St Ives were seen in the haze at the bottom of the hill. We had ridden over 5 miles in a little over half an hour, which, for such bicyclists as we are, encumbered too with heavy cloaks, & with the muddy road to hold back our wheels, we considered a creditable performance. The business which took us to St Ives was primarily to lay in a supply of an article of confectionery which is not attainable at [*page damaged*] [. . .] we rode we debated the great question [. . .]

[*Page damaged*] by a stroke of chance[?], proposed [. . .] would be sim-

---

2   AVS, Vanessa and Adrian.

plified if each of us bought what we had suggested (each having suggested some present for a joint present[3] which had been promptly scouted by the other parties into agreement.) N. was to buy a bicycle lamp. A. a lens, & I some old books.

I had remarked when we were last in St Ives an old curiosity shop, containing old silver, old china & old furniture, & in a dusty corner seemed tempting bundles of old books. I cannot say what acute pleasure it is to me to buy books; & I shall be more than satisfied if T. has half my delight in his present. We rode straight to the shop, & were asked to wait for the woman to come back by a young girl who was somewhat dumbfounded by my demand to be shown old books in good bindings. While we waited we explored the shop & its treasures. A collection such as this mounts to my head like the fumes of some delicious wine; I long frantically to buy everything I see, & the most ordinary object is possessed with strange fascination for me. There were old candles of Sheffield plate, & delicate old china cups, with a little blooming[?] flower on a white ground & [*paper damaged*] cracks testifying to their age & worth; there were solid tables of black oak; wonderful inlaid cabinets of the most mellow mahogany; writing tables with endless scrolls of inlaid yellow wood & innumerable drawers, pewter plates & mugs & dishes, & old books. The old books were all bundled away in the background, tied into stacks so that examining them was a work of difficulty. The shop woman when she did come proved to be a thin nervous woman who knew my likes about her wares, but had much belief in their beauty & value. She was very much pleased to find customers, & asked us to take our time in looking over her things. The books she said were worth very little – any of them you can have for twopence, save 4 well kept volumes of Captain Cooks Voyages[4] which attracted me, & which I finally bought as a present for Thoby.

Monday 18 September

Today we had our first fire. Such a statement, coming at the top of innumerable records of one hot moment following another needs some explanation. It must be found in the date that heads this page. Behold we are arrived at the 18th day of September, & in two days time we shall be back in London. This work has undergone so many changes since I last

---

3 8 September would be Thoby's 19th birthday.
4 *Captain Cook's Discovery of, and Other Early Voyages to, the Hawaiian Islands*, 1778-94, 4 vols.

wrote that before proceeding to expatiate upon the 18th of September I must explain briefly the state of the case. The work heretofore was contained in one modest paper book,[5] that fronted the world in a state of nature – naked but not ashamed. Boards it recked not of, now it boasts boards that amount to the dignity of a binding, being ancient tooled calf – the tooling resplendent today as a hundred years ago.

A sudden idea struck me, that it would be original useful & full of memories if I embedded the foregoing pages in the leaves of some worthy & ancient work, the like of which might I knew be bought at St Ives old Curiosity Shop for the sum of 3d. So one day a week or two ago, A. & I drove over there; & demanded old books; the womans husband scours the country for old books & old furniture of all kinds; & the result of his book finds – the modest libraries of country parsonages, sold by the widow to swell her slender purse – & chance outcasts of country gentlemens bookshelves are all bound rudely together like so many bales of wool, & stacked upon each other in dusty corners. This, methought, was favourable hunting ground for an acute bookworm; but our minds are not married to that pursuit; we were invited to explore & untie these bales which with some difficulty we did. Truly I think there was not much need of acuteness here![ ] They were almost all books of the last century & in that degree to be reverenced. But such an undesirable [?] [*illegible*] collection I have scarcely come across. A London Bookseller tries to redeem his eternal sermons in calf clothing all mildewed & ink stained by a few modern flashy novels.

A country book stall I find rakes in this class of work alone; not one book of the dozen I opened & turned down again could possess any interest for book lovers or any other human being. "—— On the World" – "Sermons on the Beauties of Nature translated" an old volume of Cowpers[6] poems, all bescrawled & underlined, otherwise I might have bought it. Montgomery's[7] poems – a French grammar – several remnants of family bibles – the title pages torn away from the discretion of a public book shop – &c &c &c. At last I gave up glancing at the title page & confined myself wholly to the outward aspect of the book. I selected one, & A. one also; his indeed was slightly above the average – a good old copy of Xenophon, possessed by three generations of Hoskings, who studied it from the year 1705 at University College, Oxford

---

5   See below, n.8.
6   William Cowper (1731-1800).
7   Probably James Montgomery (1771-1854).

father & son & grandson. My work – the present volume, attracted my attention firstly because of its size, which fitted my paper – & 2ndly because its back had a certain air of distinction among its brethren. I fear the additional information given on the title page that this is the Logic of the "Late Reverend & Learned Isaac Watts D. D." was not a third reason why I bought it.

Any other book almost, would have been too sacred to undergo the desecration that I planned; but no one methought could bewail the loss of these pages.[8]

LOGICK:
OR, THE
Right Use of REASON
WITH
A Variety of RULES to Guard Against
ERROR in the AFFAIRS of RELIGION and
HUMAN LIFE as well as in the Sciences

By Isaac Watts D.D.

LONDON

MDCCLXXXVI

Wednesday evening, 20 September
The day has come at last of which I have thought so much. It is my habit, on this the last page of the book, to sum up my judgment & deliver my verdict on the summer entire. But I feel that I have left unexpressed one

---

8 AVS used the Warboys journal for two purposes: for essay-writing during her holiday and for experimenting with various nibs; in many instances she used the same page for both purposes, and this gives the original journal its appearance of immense chaos. She seems to have taken the sheets upon which her essays were originally written and pasted them within the pages of Isaac Watts' *LOGICK: OR THE Right Use of REASON* etc., so that they might have a handsome leather binding; she then – probably in 1902 – tore the pages apart and used these sheets, or portions of them containing no writing, for further experimentation and penmanship exercise. Although the essay pagination is not consecutive in the original, the content of the essays themselves is continuous and logical, from beginning to end, except for some damaged or missing portions. All the exercises and experimentation fragments have been reproduced exactly and restored sequentially in Appendix E.

phase of the summer, the last autumnal phase which, before I reach London, I want to write down.

Briefly then a change has come over the country since I last wrote. Then it was summer; now it is autumn. I drove back alone from St Ives on Monday, & felt the change each step of the five miles. Where the corn stood yellow & luxuriant, there are now fields of brown clods, which leave a decided impression on ones eyes when one sees the country spread beneath one. The still days of haze & blue distance are over; a sharp wind comes racing over the plain, & brown coveys of partridges rise from the stubble that yet stands. The summer wealth of cultivation is over; & the earth is preparing for her time of sleep & slow reproduction. The hedges all along the roads are laden with scarlet berries, which if nature shows in this liberality her intention of inflicting on bird & man a hard winter foretell months of ice & snow. The little brown birds rise in a cloud & go twittering high up in the air over the brown fields. There is that mellow clearness in the air, which softens & matures the land & the mens faces who till it. There is a look & feeling of melancholy in everything – that melancholy which is the sweetest tongue of thought.

"The woods decay – the woods decay & fall –
The vapours weep their burden to the ground"[9]

This – if it be a legitimate quotation – expresses the next stage of autumn. At the present moment the change from summer is more exquisite; though as delicious as winter. Brown & ruddy colours have stolen across what was green & gold; a thousand delicate vivid hues have supplanted the prevailing luxuriant green in hedge & grass & leaf & plant. But for me the definite touch that has spelt autumn is the subtle difference in the air. It brings with it odours of burning wood & weeds; & delicious moisture from the shaven earth; it is cleaner & more virile; it is autumn in its youth, before decayed woods & weeping vapours have come to end its substance. We saw, what I always love to see when we bicycled to Ramsey (for the last time) on Saturday, weed burning on the hill. Look at the picture of Sir John Millais of children burning leaves[10] & my theories will be revealed. I cannot attempt to explain in

---

9 Opening lines of Tennyson's 'Tithonus', *c.* 1842, 1860.
10 Sir John Everett Millais (1829-96), artist, one of the founders of the Pre-Raphaelite Brotherhood; the picture referred to is 'Autumn Leaves', 1855-6, in the City of Manchester Art Galleries.

words the charm & melancholy, the colour & the interest, of the picture.
We thought the hedge was burning; the wind blew the flames so high &
such a distance. At moments there was only a smouldering white
smoke, & then of a sudden the flames leapt out & lashed their tongues.

Well, the time has come to have done with Autumn & with everything else. I have spent the evening packing our Red box for its return
journey; & now my room is swept bare of books & everything save
what I carry in my own bag.

Tomorrow at this hour I shall be in my room in London! The roar of
the city will be booming in my ear, which 7 weeks of Warboys will have
made as sensitive as any country cousins. I write this down to see if it
looks any more credible in pen & ink; but I cannot bring my mind to
bear upon the change. I know that we are going on a journey tomorrow,
but I cannot realise, though I repeat it to myself all day long, that the
journey will end in London –

I add this last of last words in a moment which I have stolen before con-
signing this work to my bag. I am packing my own precious Goods
which are the last to be packed & the first to be unpacked.

Well then farewell Warboys. The summer ranks among our happiest
I think; & this land of plain & sky will remain a distinct & lovely picture
in my mind were I never to see it again.

Goodbye to Fens & flat fields & windmills & sky domes.

> Farewell Manchester
> Noble Town, Farewell.
> Thursday Morning
> September 21st   a swans song

———————

Now we have returned to London.

This is written on the 23rd of September [1899]. This was written
after spending a whole summer at Warboys.

1903

Early in 1902 Virginia was taking lessons in Greek, now with Janet Case, who was to become a lifelong friend. At about this time, George Duckworth took it upon himself to introduce his half-sisters into society, where they felt themselves painfully out of place. Virginia, especially, simply could not shine there. 'I don't know how its done,' she wrote. 'We aint popular – we sit in corners & look like mutes who are longing for a funeral.'

Violet Dickinson, who had been a friend of Stella's and had probably already met Virginia, now became one of the most intimate people in her life. Virginia responded to her with eagerness and affection, and wrote a prose piece called 'Friendship's Gallery' at Fritham House, Lyndhurst, sometime in August-September of 1902. Thirteen years her senior, Violet became the person to whom Virginia turned for reassurance. Sir Leslie learned of his abdominal cancer in the spring of 1902, was operated on at the end of the year, and in the autumn of 1903 it was to Violet that Virginia wrote daily bulletins of his declining health. Although she was powerless over the fact of her father's approaching death, with pen and ink at hand, Virginia discovered herself mistress over a world of her own making, and was learning too that, whatever discord life offered, with words she could restore a certain measure of order.

DIARY
HYDE PARK GATE
1903?[1]

---

[1] The label was apparently attached considerably later, when AVS was no longer certain of the year, hence the '?'.

INDEX[2]

A DANCE IN QUEENS GATE[3]

About two hours ago, when I went to bed, I heard what I took to be signs of merry making in the mews. A violin squeaked, there was a noise of loud voices & laughter. It reminded me how once, as a child, I woke at dead of night: it seemed to me – 8 or 9 I suppose really & heard strange & horrible music as of a midnight barrel organ, & was so frightened that I had to crawl to the cot next mine for sympathy. But I am too old for that kind of blind terror; my critical mind when awake enough to think at all about it, decided that the fiddle squeaking &c. was token of a ball – not in our street – but in Queens Gate – the tall row of houses that makes a background to the mews. The music grew so loud, so rhythmic – as the night drew on & the London roar lessened, that I threw up my window, leant out into the cool air, & saw the illuminations which told surely from what house the music came.

Now I have been listening for an hour. The music stops – I hear the chatter, the light laughter of womens voices – the deeper notes of festive males. I can almost see the couples wandering out from the ball rooms to the balconies which are starred with small lamps. They look straight

---

2   The page numbers are AVS's.

3   This essay would have its fictional counterpart in the 1907 section of *The Years*, 1937 (Kp A22): London, pp. 141-6; New York, pp. 132-7.

across the mews to me. The music has begun again – oh dear – the swing & the lilt of that waltz makes me almost feel as though I could jump from my bed & dance it too. That is the quality which dance music has – no other: it stirs some barbaric instinct – lulled asleep in our sober lives – you forget centuries of civilisation in a second, & yield to that strange passion which sends you madly whirling round the room – oblivious of everything save that you must keep swaying with the music – in & out, round & round – in the eddies & swirls of the violins. It is as though some swift current of water swept you along with it. It is magic music. Here the bars run low, passionate, regretful, but always in the same pulse. We dance as though we knew the vanity of dancing. We dance to drown our sorrows – but dance, dance – If you stop you are lost. This one night we will be mad – dance lightly – raise our hearts as the beat strengthens, grows buoyant – careless, defiant. What matters anything so long as ones step is in time – so long as one's whole body & mind are dancing too – what shall end it?

Then comes in the very height of the rhythm, some strange, solitary sound – that does not belong to the tune – no violin wails with that voice – nor is it the speech of triumphant trumpet – no – it falls not discordantly – but as though dropped from another world & time – the solitary stroke *one*.

A church is tolling. It says just this single thing – very deliberately, not raising its voice above the music, but nevertheless it stands out pure, quite distinct. The whirling valse has not drowned it, has no power over it. The dance quickens – towards the end – winds up with a flourish – the dancers are left reeling about – gasping, laughing – all pressing to get out into the cool. I hear their voices clamouring again – some one laughs very loud – the voices reach me quite distinct though I cannot hear the words. Well! – I am sitting out my dances – & I enjoy it.

Behold, I am tired of the noise & the chatter – I lie back on my pillows – turn out my light; I lie in the cool & look out through my open window. In a moment if I choose, I need think no more of the dancers – I am looking into the awful night sky – It is so thick tonight that not a star shows – The same sky stretches round the world, I think – But the music again! Brave little mortals fiddling & dancing beneath it! Besides lying here I see something that pleases me.

There is a great glass skylight under which I suppose the dancers are drinking champagne & devouring quails – At any rate there is a brilliant light behind it – It is like some transparent yellow globe in the night air. And from my bed I see the leaves of a tree outlined against it. I dont know why it is but this incongruity – the artificial lights, the music – the talk – & then the quiet tree standing out there, is fantastic & attracts me considerably.

But the music again! I am getting tired I confess. I can no longer dance in spirit – nor I fancy do the fiddlers fiddle with that gaiety with which they started. After all they are not inspired Gods, calling men to a more joyous & passionate existence, a dance which shall last through life & into eternity – they are pale, perhaps corpulent men, who fiddle thus every night of the week – fiddle till 3 o'clock every morning, & long for their glass of beer & the last dance on the programme. They fiddle every night, & it is part of their business to strike up thus – so courageously & freely – to lash their bows across their strings, as though the God himself were in their veins. The waltz drags a little – the pulse wants vigour – & listen – the church tolls again – one – two –

The clock is in no hurry – it can wait its time – no waltzer will out waltz *it* – But those fiddlers – my thoughts go back to them. There is something grim in the notion; they fiddle every night – the same tunes probably, but only once for the same dancers. They dont believe much in their fiddling & its wonderful properties. It earns them very little in hard cash, I daresay – & yet night after night they sit in their corner, & set couples dancing in mazes all round them. Send hot thoughts coursing through their brains – make men & women dream of love & freedom & life moving in rhythm & waltz music.

But these fiddlers dont believe a word of it. They look out with weary disillusioned eyes – no need to look at their music – they know *that* by heart, & the dancers too. Still they must stick to it. As long as people will dance, they must play. They are the only people, save a weary dowager with rheumatism in her back – who are really content when the final note of the dance is sounded, & the whole party falls back from the ecstasies of the waltz into more or less commonplace life. I can see them leaning back in their chairs, & hiding their yawns, which they know to be quite out of keeping with Gods & fumbling with their watches.

The music again! I begin to think someone has wound up this weary waltz & it will go on at intervals all thro' the night. Nobody is dancing in time to it now I am sure – or they dance as pale phantoms because so long as the music sounds they *must* dance – no help for them. Surely the music that seemed to ebb before, has gathered strength – it sounds louder & louder – it swings faster & faster – no one can stop dancing now. They are sucked in by the music. And how weary they look – pale men – fainting women – crumpled silks & trampled flowers. They are no longer masters of the dance – it has taken possession of them. And all joy & life has left it, & it is diabolical, a twisting livid serpent, writhing in cold sweat & agony, & crushing the frail dancers in its contortions. What has brought about the change? It is the dawn.

At last I stop writing, & look again at the sky. It is now a quarter to three. I said it was dark & tragic before – now it is more terrible. For the sky is deathly pale – but alive: it is very chaste, & very pure, & the breeze is ice cold, as though it blew off fields the sun has never warmed. The dawn is folding the world in its pure morning kiss of salutation. No lamplight can burn in the radiance of that whiteness – no music can sound in the pause of that awful silence. The Dance is over.

THOUGHTS UPON SOCIAL SUCCESS[4]   15 July

The 'season' dies hard. I calculate that for every one party that we go to, the average young lady goes to five: she has been out every night then both this week & last.

Our parties are rather miscellaneous: it seems to me that I generally dont know my hostess. One night she is an obscure lady in Addison Road – another she lives in Bruton Street, & has a name to correspond. In either case I feel rather strange, & inclined to be absent minded. I look round the room, see nobody there I know, & forget what one says next. Tonight was a very typical entertainment. I can only comfort myself when I think of our social peculiarities by reflecting that we have this in common with the women of the world – we are equally at home every-where – (not at all, that is to say) & we are confined to no one set in par-ticular. This explains why it is usual for us to come into a room, & after shaking hands with our hostess, sit silent all the rest of the evening. We always seem to be outsiders where everybody else is intimate. This is not really so of course: the truth is that we have not, or have not culti-vated, what one calls the 'social gift'. Now most young women of our way of life have specialised in this branch of learning. Their evenings are more important to them than their mornings – indeed I find it hard to conceive of them in the morning. Do they in truth exist before the clock strikes eight? My private belief is that the dinner bell calls them into existence – they spring up all over the drawing room like hyacinths in

---

4   This essay, and the following five, are out of sequence; one probable explanation is that AVS wrote them initially on separate sheets and sent them to Violet Dickinson for criticism, only copying them into her journal, heedless of chronology, when they were later returned; see *VW Letters*, I, No. 88.

June. By daybreak they are faded – a little crumpled perhaps – never mind – they fold themselves in sleep – to wake once more when the sun is set. Now I find this very beautiful & attractive but always a little puzzling. Has she a stalk or a body – is she clothed in silk or gauze or are they flower petals that shine on her? Above all, what does she talk about? I see her lips move – honey drops from between them apparently, but I know that I shall never hear what she says. If I come by she is silent – she folds all her petals closely round her; she might indeed be some flower one brushes past by night. Not a word of this do I write with any but an entirely admiring purpose. [ ] I protest that I do most honestly admire such scraps of society as I have seen – even though I myself take no part in it. Tonight for instance, it is literal truth that our hostess & one gentleman we were introduced to as we left, were the only people we spoke to while we stayed. That seems proof that we are not 'successful'. I do not know that that success is beyond our reach, if we ever take the trouble to work for it, but at this moment it is certainly very far from us. All the same I can sit by & watch with pure delight those who are adepts at the game. Success is always able to move my admiration; & really no success seems so rounded & complete as that which is won in the drawing room. The game requires infinitely delicate skill, and the prize is of the subtlest possible. [ ] All achievement is coarse beside it. [ ]

To be socially great, I believe, is a really noble ambition – for consider what it means. You have, for a certain space of time to realise as nearly as can be, an ideal. You must consciously try to carry out in your conduct what is implied by your clothes; they are silken – of the very best make – only to be worn with the greatest care, on occasions such as these. They are meant to please the eyes of others – to make you something more brilliant than you are by day. This seems to me a good ideal. You come to a party meaning to give pleasure; therefore you leave your sorrows & worries at home – for the moment, remember, we are all dressed in silk – without sorrow or bother that is – more than that, you must be prepared to be actively happy: if you talk it must be at least to express pleasure at something; better still if you can, say something amusing: seriousness is just as much out of place here as an old serge skirt. For two or three hours a number of people have resolved to show only their silken side to one another: Heaven knows the other may be anything but silk, but tonight it is ignored. Men & women living ordinary lives surely have their share of woes; to look at them though you would never guess it. They bow & touch hands gracefully; their faces all look pleased & animated. The talk is very swift & skimming: it is not part of the game to go deep: that might be dangerous. All this a moralist might say, is very artificial. Major So & So laughs as though he hadn't a care in the world; *we* know very well that he cant pay his butchers bill. Mrs Thingemajig is more amusing than ever tonight – didn't she lose an only son in the war? – & so on – it is easy to conclude that society is hollow – that the men & women who make it are heartless; but I believe there is another side to the picture. It strikes me that that mythical major is a brave man to stand there & laugh at other peoples jokes with his bills (most immorally) all unpaid. He deserves that a grateful country should pay them for him. And the Lady – you may call her heartless, but surely she does more good making the world laugh than by sitting at home & weeping over her own sorrows. The truth is, to be successful socially one wants the courage of a hero – [ ] There is nothing really so desperately difficult, I am sure, as laughter. The whole pressure of the world is to make you take things seriously.

Most of us think ourselves very virtuous for falling in obediently with its scheme. We go to church, to funerals, to sickbeds &c. &c. far more willingly than to marriages & festivals – It is a luxury to most people to express their emotions. Society is the most bracing antidote for this kind of thing; to be successful I think one must be a Stoic with a heart.

A GARDEN DANCE   30 June

Last night, I leant out of my window & took part in a dance which was being carried on with great vigour in Queens Gate. I have just come back from a real dance[5] – in which I joined in the orthodox fashion. Honestly, I enjoyed my window dance the most. To begin with, for this dance one had to be properly dressed – & that is a penance – while last night I could lie with my nightgown open & my hair tumbled over my forehead as it is at this moment. I often think of that famous painter[6] who would only work in his court dress – or kept different dresses for different occasions. Though I hate putting on my fine clothes, I know that when they are on I shall have invested myself at the same time with a certain social demeanour – I shall be ready to talk about the floor & the weather & other frivolities, which I consider platitudes in my nightgown. A fine dress makes you artificial – ready for lights & music –

---

5 Given at the new home of Sir Walter Phillimore in Campden Hill, Kensington, W; see Aug. 1899, n.28.
6 Unidentified.

ready to accept that artificial view of life which is presented to one in a ballroom – life seen by electric light & washed down by champagne.

The Phillimores who gave the dance, have lately moved into a very spacious house on the top of the Campden Hill. It has one of the largest gardens in London I believe. It is a white roomy house, easily made beautiful or picturesque had one a taste that way. But the Phillimores have aimed rather at comfortable solidity. Their walls are ornate crimson – they are fond of painting over large flat surfaces in distemper of a worthy green. In two of the bedrooms, where we took our cloaks off, I noticed a crucifix nailed at the head of the bed. That is characteristic. But it is of dancing that I am going to write. We had the usual struggle to force ourselves through the doorway; we squeezed a stout ladies [*sic*] hand. She bade us welcome with a smile which had already spent itself on fifty others & would have to do duty for an hour more to come, & we found ourselves shoved well into a thick knot of human beings. They were all pressing hard against each others backs & fronts – trying to say how d'y do – trying to introduce each other – finally trying to seize arms & waists & hurl each other thus united into the waltzing centre of the room. A small centre only was in a state of circular motion; from a little distance the dancers looked painfully like flies struggling in a dish of sticky liquid. We crossed the room slowly, because we had to move, & reached the windows. Here we stopped & looked about us, with the cynical coolness of youth just a little excited, & determined not to show its agitation. But indeed there was little to agitate the most youthful. No sight in the whole world is so ugly & depressing as a room full of people none of whom you know. You at once conclude that they are remarkably ugly or remarkably dull – or remarkably ill dressed. At any rate you lump them together under some common head. This is just what I did tonight, feeling pleasantly detached, & able to criticise the antics of my fellows from a cool distance.

Well, this didnt last long. Soon a middle aged gentleman, a little stout with an elderly sensible air came up to us. I remembered him with difficulty – & then he suggested as a sensible thing to do that we should walk round the garden. There was no wish on either side to dance, had it been possible. So I followed him out on to the grass. He was a companion who let one take in deliberate impressions without disturbing one to talk or listen. He sauntered along by my side, not, I think, altogether silent, but evidently without exerting himself to think of anything to say. I looked about & talked if something happened to strike me. If it had been a shade warmer, it would have been perfect – but the garden was just too chilly – the grass a little too damp. The graceful ladies held up their dresses rather nervously instead of letting them sweep like peacocks tails. All the same it was a very vague & graceful scene. Chinese lanterns hung in globes of different colours from all the bushes – dotted about promiscuously over the ground. These gave a little light; floods of light, laughter, & dance music of course, poured out of the house. Again I noticed that strange blending of the two lights – the pale light of the sky & the yellow light of lamps & candles both together illuminating green leaves & grass. It makes a curious unreal effect. We strolled sedately all round the garden, then turned back & found ourselves seats near the house. It was characteristic of our tête à tête that we confessedly chose seats from which we could watch the rest of the party. We had so very little to say to each other: what we did say was mostly of an external nature, prompted by the sights & sounds going on round us. I was thoroughly content to lie in an arm chair & watch the Ladies in their light dresses pass and repass – come flowing out of the windows & falling in cascades of lace & silk down the slope. It was like some French painting. All the time there went on a light ripple of talk & voices. Nobody came near enough to bother us with actual words. My companion was a straight forward plain spoken man; exactly what he seemed to be (really Director of the Bank of England[7] I discover) cool silent satisfactory – excellent garden company. At last he said with half a yawn, entirely polite though not in the least courteous, that he must go. He left me safe in the drawing room again. I found myself with Gerald [Duckworth], whose appetite for dancing is no longer keen; he prefers to act the part of benevolent Uncle to the company – which he does not unsuccessfully, & such a character is always popular.

The dancing space was smaller than ever, the contortions of the dancers more laborious. If half the people who had come had chosen to dance, the room would have been a solid block. But the garden received the overflow – the refreshment tables there were already full. Gerald, I discovered, takes a very serious interest still in the supper part of a dance. He became quite energetic when this grand question needed to be settled – where we were to sup, & what we were to eat. He secured two excellent seats & sent waiters flying for quails & champagne, just as

---

7   The Governor was Sir Augustus Prevost and the Deputy Governor, Samuel Hope
    Morley; there were 23 directors.

though he sat in his usual corner of the Savoy[8] & had his own private waiter to attend to him.

I had fixed one as the limit of our stay – enforcing it all the way in the cab with desperation but not much hope. But to my surprise we had no difficulty in leaving. There was really no inducement to stay.

Our fourwheeler was soon drawn up at the door, & we still left coolly appreciative but nothing more. Now I open my book of astronomy, dream of the stars a little, & so to sleep –

AN EXPEDITION TO HAMPTON COURT[9]   5 July

Most Londoners have travelled in Italy – Turkey or Greece – they run to Paris or Scotland almost for the week end – but, judging from my experience, the immediate neighbourhood of London itself is an unexplored land. On their map it might be marked blank like certain districts of Africa. It is sober truth that though I have lived my life in London I have only once visited Hampton Court. Kew,[10] Richmond, Hampstead, I know a trifle more familiarly perhaps – Various causes make it easier to go anywhere almost than to the suburbs of London. You have to make a days expedition; no one that I am aware ever sleeps at Kew or Hampton Court. They are essentially places which you visit between trains. You find yourself with a summer afternoon to spare – bethink you that you really ought to know these places a little better, & thus once in a dozen years you find yourself much to your surprise walking in the Orangery at Kew or treading the maze at Hampton Court. I am always surprised – pleasantly surprised to find myself here. Nevertheless I let years slide, & bear me to all quarters of England, before I go there again. The summer afternoon never comes – anyhow you spend it in the Gardens which lie at your gates. This occurs to me because today we have actually achieved the task: we have been to Hampton Court. It is true we planned the journey for a year – twelve perhaps will pass before we set

8 Savoy Hotel and Restaurant, The Strand, WC.
9 Royal Palace on the Thames, 15 miles south-west of London, begun in 1514 by Cardinal Wolsey; in 1526 he was obliged to surrender it to Henry VIII who partly rebuilt it. Sir Christopher Wren was the architect for the east and south wings, employed by William III who had the gardens laid out in Dutch style, with two orangeries, a wilderness and the famous maze. No longer a royal residence, its rooms were now largely occupied by aristocratic pensioners.
10 The Royal Botanic Gardens (of 9 acres) at Kew were established in 1759 by Princess Augusta; Kew House and Richmond Lodge were the residences of Princess Augusta and her son King George III.

about to plan another – but I write today with absolutely first hand knowledge. My information is crammed from no guide book or travellers tales. I have seen what I describe with my own eyes.

We started, then, at 11. The journey to Hammersmith really presents no scene worthy of description; besides it is comparatively hackneyed ground. It is after one has left Hammersmith that one enters strange land. The street begins to look far more like a village street; the houses are of a far more individual character, & they have space in which to expand. But yet it has marks of belonging – of being a distant though poor connection of a great town. You get an impression that the more respectable classes of London have retired here to pass their old age with greater dignity & peace than they can afford inside London itself. Piety has retired here too; I counted a surprising number of Convents & Sisterhoods as we went along; once or twice to my pleasure I could look down into their cloistered grounds & see the sisters themselves walking there – Once I spied into the garden of an orphanage for Roman Catholic little girls. The children were all ranked in two & two, following a dark sister in some kind of procession, & they all, for what reason I do not know, wore wreaths of white flowers round their heads – an innocent sight truly, as one passes. Then one began to catch glimpses of the river through steep little alleys which opened out of the main road, & once we came upon a whole fleet of barges moored together for the Sunday rest as we past [sic] over the bridge. The picturesque bargeman was removing a weeks cole [sic] grime on deck – his head buried in a basin, & white with lather. This was in Brentford I think, but to tell the truth I have no notion what villages we past [sic] through or in what order they came. They were not separated from each other, though originally as distinct as London from Birmingham. Nevertheless there were very few new buildings. Most must have been 60 or 70 years old I should think, & a common type was the pleasant square Georgian house. This must originally have stood in a space of its own, I am sure; Georgian houses were built for opulent people, who could afford light & air – At any rate the whole road to Hampton Court which it took us an hour & a half to travel, was well worth looking at. At half past one, at last, we reached our journeys end. In a moment we were walking the broad terrace of the Palace Garden. My one visit ten years ago, had not left in my mind any adequate picture of the beauty & space of this old garden. I had forgotten too the richness of the dark red palace itself. At first I felt simply inclined to pace slowly up & down the terrace & let my eye rest first on the smooth turf lit by brilliant flowers, then on the perfectly satisfying shape of the palace. But it was cold, & we were hungry, & somewhat to our surprise, half London apparently had had the same idea of visiting Hampton Court at the same day & hour as we had. The terraces & the turf which I felt ought only to have been peopled by ladies in brocade & gentlemen in kneebreeches & swords, swarmed with a very different class of person – perhaps more moral than their ancestors of Charles 2nds time, but in penalty for it far less ornamental. I could not help regretting the improvement in morality. I wished again & again – so did the whole crowd of us, I daresay, that I could have had those gardens to myself. They are meant for peace & luxurious medita-tion. We lunched – with our fellows – Everywhere we went it occurred to several dozen others to go too. I must retract what I said to begin with – that Cockneys dont go to Hampton Court. But doing our best to think ourselves alone, we strolled through the quadrangles after lunch. They are, I imagine, perfect of their kind: Oxford & Cambridge can show no better. Absolutely no alteration, no restoration, as far as one can see, has touched these old buildings since the careful hand of the Architect laid stone to stone. The difficulty was – not to imagine Charles & Nell Gwynn[11] idling there with voluptuous Court ladies lounging after them, but to remember that we who walked there were absurdly & mon-strously out of place. We paced the galleries. Here indeed the illusion so strong on one in the courts & gardens gave way almost entirely. These beautiful old cedar lined rooms which run all round the quadrangle have had their walls so papered with pictures that their domestic character has disappeared. Some of the paintings indeed are first rate – some bad – but good or bad they make the place into a public gallery where one goes prepared to take in instruction & pleasure, catalogue in hand. The rooms indeed have their old uses inscribed on them – Queens Bedroom – Queens private drawing room – Kings ante-chamber &c – but it is not possible to reconstruct them in your mind as they were then. Yet Henry the 8th walked here – & the little Edward the Sixth[12] was brought here to die, I think, & wits & beauties without end have past [*sic*] through these rooms, all of which one might have revived in ones mind, if the old chairs & tables had been left in their places.

After we had done our duty here, we spent an hour or so wandering through the gardens again, finding our way down to the lake side where

---

11 Charles II and his mistress, the actress Nell Gwynne.
12 Edward VI (1537-53) was in fact born at Hampton Court; his mother Jane Seymour died there 12 days later; Edward died at Greenwich.

we lay & watched an appropriate pair of anglers. They, like a sundial, are absolutely essential in a picture of this kind; the fish is never caught, the angler dreams away the whole length of the golden hours – that is a pursuit which like the registering of sunbeams, belongs to a less machine driven, & sunnier age than ours.

But we had overstayed our time already. It seemed absurd to be bound by ties made so far away – almost in such a different age, but long ago in London we had promised to come home for tea. That was impossible. If we strolled peacefully back, we should return in time for dinner. Most of our companions had exhausted their interest in Hampton Court. They had had an outing which they had enjoyed energetically, & were now eager to get home again. We had the darkening garden almost to ourselves as we walked across it, but in the dark we could see one or two dignified figures moving up & down the terrace as we passed. It was impossible to mistake them. They were no cockney trippers making the whole place hideous with their noise & Cockney faces; no, these Ladies are part of the palace. They belong to it. It is admirably appropriate I think [ ] that our aged aristocracy which finds no home in the bustling town, should retire to spend its last days in this old Palace full of tradition & ancient splendour – splendour even more beautiful I should think in its mellow age than in its prime. These old Ladies with their great names & bent old bodies stay in my mind as the very spirit of the place, which we surprised haunting the walks by dark. Here they dwindle out their old age, as in some royal almshouse. No retirement could be sweeter or more dignified than to this Palace by the Thames.

I myself anticipate my age in the delight with which I contemplate spending it thus!

AN ARTISTIC PARTY   1 July

Again we took [a] cab tonight & drove through the populous streets which look their gayest about this hour. We had four large cards for the Academy Soirée[13] – an entertainment unique, I should think, of its kind.

---

13 The Royal Academy's Annual Reception held at Burlington House; Sir Edward
    Poynter was its President from 1896 to 1918.

The courtyard in which Edward the Black Prince[14] stands was packed with carriages cabs & motor cars. so that it was almost difficult to get in & find one's way round the edge to the large door.

The Academy is a gloomy great place, even on its festive nights; you take off your cloak in a kind of catacomb, damp, with stone arches. The little urbane President, already looking a trifle bored, pressed our hands perfunctorily & we passed on into the great rooms. This crowd, I say, has a character of its own. Every other person you feel must be distinguished: the men wear a surprising number of decorations – Bath ribbons & stars & all kinds of humbler orders – so we decided when we saw their dress clothes (a rude test of merit!)

The women, as though to atone for their want of definite orders, dress up in the oddest ways. We found some queer specimens. Here was a stuffy black dress, somehow suggestive of high tea & bugles; here the artistic temperament had gone to the other extreme, & left bare a good deal of the person which is usually covered. But the most usual figure was the typical artist, or artists wife – clinging Liberty[15] silks – outlandish ornaments – a strange dusky type of face. Of course there were too others like ourselves, of no particular description. Still I could have been well content to take my evening's pleasure in observation merely. I was constantly starting at some face well known in photograph or caricature suddenly fronting me in the life. I was constantly wishing to point – with extended forefinger – at some delicious discovery, male or female, till they were too frequent to need remark –

It is not a party at which one talks. The conditions are somehow adverse. The great rooms indeed are full, but you never rid your mind of the public gallery feeling – & certainly the light & space are not becoming. The crowd as a whole looks badly dressed, & moves awkwardly. Its units never seem to dissolve & melt together. We drifted about, gazing at human pictures mostly, with snatches of desultory talk. We looked with admiration at those ladies, who are the high aristocrats of such gatherings as these – who know the President & all the more distinguished academicians. Their demeanour is beautiful. Exquisite in old lace & most refined evening gowns, they know well that they are the

---

14 According to one official catalogue, the 'Equestrian Statue of Edward the Black Prince', by Thomas Brock, was exhibited in the courtyard of Burlington House from May to August 1902 and then removed to Leeds for permanent exhibition; the statue of Sir Joshua Reynolds, by Alfred Dury, RA, in the courtyard today, dates from 1931.
15 See Jan. 1897, n.64.

Queens of the gathering. What they are, everyone else desires to be – at least this evening. They bear names as famous in the world of art as Russell & Cavendish[16] in the world of fashion. I am always impressed by the splendid superiority of these artist men & women over their Philistine brethren. They are so thoroughly convinced that mankind is divided into two classes, one of which wears amber beads & low evening collars – while the other follows the fashion. Each thanks God that it is not as the other – but the artist is the more intolerant. We must have past [*sic*] through all the rooms, & we began to get tired of human faces.

A cab home again! Down the brilliant charging Piccadilly, now thoroughly awake, as though it had slept all day. The wood pavement in the heat gets beaten to a shiny hard surface, which at night reflects the lamplight almost as though it were wet.

Home very sleepy, & to bed.

THE COUNTRY IN LONDON

I foresee that one day I shall write a book of maxims – like a Frenchwoman. I often think of things that sound to me remarkably like what in English we call 'Thoughts'. But mine have this drawback – they are very obvious – a little false – & after all where will one sentence lead you? All the thoughts, maxims &c. &c. &c. which we see so laboriously printed & translated from one language to another as though no one literature could be selfish enough to keep these treasures for itself – all, I say, have only one moment of legitimate life. I can imagine that they sound well at a dinner table – go off with an enlivening pop, as of dexterous little crackers. But they wont blow up anything or do much in the way of illumination. I am sorry that I began to write this page – I forget now where it was to lead me, or why I chose this circuitous path.

Well, I say, we are getting ready for Salisbury[17] – Heaven knows what that has to do with maxims! The pleasantest part of going anywhere almost is the thought of it beforehand. I am laying in books. That is what I mean by getting ready. I collect books on all conceivable subjects & sew together paper books like this I write in – thick enough to hold all the maxims in the world. I delight to plan what I shall read this

---

16 The Russells were the Earls and Dukes of Bedford, originating with John Russell, 1st Duke of Bedford (*c.*1486-1555); the Cavendish name reaches back to William Cavendish, 1st Duke of Devonshire (1641-1707).

17 The Stephens rented Netherhampton House, about 3 miles west of Salisbury, for their seven weeks' summer holiday; the Fishers took a house in the Close, Salisbury.

summer – I believe I begin putting aside books in my mind, to read in the summer, about October, Shakespeare for instance & the Bible – Then the time really comes, & I actually take a bit of paper & write Homer, Dante, Burkes Speeches[18] &c. &c. upon it. I feel already as though I had read some way in these books & profited greatly. I get the volumes together – lay them out on my table, & I think exultingly that all that thickness of paper will be passed through my mind. I wish I felt sure it would leave any impression there, but that is a doubt I put far from me, before I begin. It is quite true that I read more during these 8 weeks in the country than in six London months perhaps. Learning seems natural to the country. I think I could go on browsing & munching steadily through all kinds of books as long as I lived at Salisbury say. The London atmosphere is too hot – too fretful. I read – then I lay down the book & say – what right have I, a woman to read all these things that men have done? They would laugh if they saw me. But I am going to forget all that in the country. This summer holiday has always – almost – been a very happy time – I imagine that it is the nearest kind of thing to happiness that any of us get – not being a very cheerful race.

We settle into a very free out of door life. We are very full of talk & family jokes.

Family life, of a very independent kind, such as suits us four[19] self willed young animals only really flourishes in the country. But this is not what I meant to write.

I read a great deal, I say: all the big books I have read I have read in the country. Besides this I write – with greater ease, at times, than ever in London. But the books are the things that I enjoy – on the whole – most. I feel sometimes for hours together as though the physical stuff of my brain were expanding, larger & larger, throbbing quicker & quicker with new blood – & there is no more delicious sensation than this. I read some history: it is suddenly all alive, branching forwards & backwards & connected with every kind of thing that seemed entirely remote before. I seem to feel Napoleons influence on our quiet evening in the garden for instance – I think I see for a moment how our minds are all threaded together – how any live mind today is of the very same stuff as Plato's & Euripides. It is only a continuation & development of the same thing. It is this common mind that binds the whole world together;

18 Edmund Burke (1729-97), Irish-born statesman and political writer.
19 Vanessa, Thoby, Adrian and AVS.

& all the world is mind. Then I read a poem say – & the same thing is repeated. I feel as though I had grasped the central meaning of the world, & all these poets & historians & philosophers were only following out paths branching from that centre in which I stand. And then – some speck of dust gets into my machine I suppose, & the whole thing goes wrong again. I open my Greek book next morning, & feel worlds away from it all – worse than that – the writing is entirely indifferent to me. Then I go out into the country – plodding along as fast as I can go – not much thinking of what I see, or of anything, but the movement in the free air soothes & makes me sensitive at once. As long as one can feel anything – life may lead one where it likes. In London undoubtedly there are too many people – all different – all claiming something or losing something – & they must all be reconciled to the scheme of the universe before you can let yourself think what that scheme is. Of course, people too, if one read them rightly, might illuminate as much as if not more than books. It is probably best therefore in the long run to live in the midst of men & women – to get the light strong in your eyes as it were – not reflected through cool green leaves as it is in books.

But I think of my great box of books all littered about in the wide country room I am to have – with entire joy now – Nine months surely is enough to spend with ones kind!

EARLS COURT   22 July

We go once a year to Earls Court. I do not know that I want to go oftener – but I enjoy that one visit. This evening it was a little suddenly decided that the three[20] of us should go. It was a cool evening – again I cannot help thinking just too cold. We raked together the most miscellaneous garments, which had to be evening, & outdoor & waterproof at once. In the end we compromised: our shoes were indoor – our dress evening – now I come to think of it, only our hats could be rightly called out of doors. But it didn't matter. Earls Court is one of those places where you can wear exactly what you like. The first thing we made for was the Chute. The exhibition[21] is supposed to have something

---

20 Vanessa, Adrian and AVS.
21 Patterned on the Great Exhibition of 1851, the Annual Earls Court exhibitions focused on either international themes or special subjects in an effort to combine education, commerce and entertainment; their popularity depended, however, on the fairground sideshows and diversions such as the Upside Down House and the Water-Chute.

to do with fire engines; but really the name of the show is the only thing that changes; all else remains the same; without any stretch of the imagination one can think oneself in Venice (as given at Earls Court 3 years ago) or Constantinople which was last years name, I think. The chute, you will see, is equally appropriate to either. The Chute is unfailing: I tremble to think what my state of mind will be when I cease to appreciate the Chute. And yet last year I made six descents running without any hesitation, & this year I didn't mind stopping after the third – But this hardly bears thinking on: Each time we got a front seat – rushed down, with the usual shrieks & blowing hats, plunged into the water, reared up, & then wobbled back to shore – There was some difficulty in deciding what to do after this – but 'The River of Lava' written in twinkling lamps attracted Adrian & me so much that we paid our sixpences & took our seats in the boat. It was a horrid fraud; I travelled that river when it was the Styx; when it was a Venetian Canal – & under some other disguise. The point is that you are floated along a kind of drain which is worked by electricity so that the current floats you without oars. The way is variegated with grottos & sunsets & effects of light upon the water – but we all agreed it was a very bad show. "I would have paid a penny to see it" said Nessa deliberately. "On the whole I think it was worth threepence," said Adrian – but then he had been partly responsible –

And then – it is safe to conclude that we found seats at some little marble table & had ices. I can imagine no condition on which this would not be possible – tho' Earls Court ices must be almost the severest test of ice eating capacity that exists. Nessa had to leave us after this – with the deepest regret of course. Once more we toiled up to that crazy platform hanging over an underground railway – got our front seats & shouted as we went down.

But we were both of opinion that it would now be best to inspect the rest of the Exhibition. We wandered through a most perplexing number of courts all with bands in the centre & outlines of electric light, & crossed bridges & looked at any number of side shows, or their signs, which are perhaps more amusing. The showmen were expounding the merits of their marvels & mysteries in the spirit of the purest philanthropy. I had the greatest difficulty in restraining myself & Adrian from taking advantage of all their offers. We were terribly tempted by Spiders web[22] – which is the sensation of America – by the upside down House,

22 Probably the giant ferris wheel, first displayed in 1893 at the Chicago World Fair.

by various magicians & palmists. Adrian however was no longer to be restrained when we came to a tent in which for the paltry sum of sixpence you could enjoy a musical ride upon absolutely real live horses. The flap of the tent swung back artfully, so that you could look in & see the steeds waiting. He mounted: his piebald at the sound of a whistle & the tinkle of a musical box, started pacing round the circle – really no bigger than this room. Half a dozen other drugged looking ponies joined, ridden by a disagreeable shopkeeper & hairdresser who though they stuck to their saddles with some difficulty were always beating their beasts to go faster.

A woman dressed in a scarlet habit – if it can be called by so definite a name – circled round too. A lady in a short black skirt & a blouse jolted at the head of the melancholy procession, but, after cannoning several times with the rider behind, she thought she had had enough of it & dismounted. Meanwhile Adrian plodded steadily round – the most comic sight in the world. I thought the ponies would never have the strength to stop once they had begun – but a whistle sounded & they came to an end, more than anything else, in the middle of their stride. If it hadn't been so indescribably dingy, & degrading for any live creature, I could have laughed at the sight; I did laugh in fact – but nevertheless it was a depressing side show on the whole. As we left, a man came up & entreated us to laugh a hundred times for sixpence – All we had to do was to pay our sixpence & walk inside. It was such a generous offer that we accepted. Inside we found ourselves in a tent lined with looking glasses, of all conceivable curves & hollows: we grew long – & lop sided & gigantic & dwarfed. Our bodies were twisted every possible way till finally we were represented by a pair of legs only.[ ] When we felt we had secured as many of our 100 laughs as were forthcoming we left. The exhibition closes at ½ past 11 & till then we sat beneath a band & listened to popular tunes. We shall not go to Earls Court again for another year.

MISS CASE

Two days ago I had my Greek lesson from Miss Case.[23] I reflect that it may be my last, after a year & a half's learning from her – so wish, en-

---

23 Janet Case (1862-1937), classical scholar, taught AVS Greek from 1902, and became a close friend; she lived with her sister 'Emphie' and supported women's and pacifist causes. This would not be her 'last' lesson: AVS resumed her Greek in the autumn of 1903; see *VW Letters*, I, No. 105.

tirely presumptuously I know, to make a rough sketch, which is at any rate done from life.

When I first saw her one afternoon in the drawing room, she seemed to me exactly what I had expected – tall, classical looking, masterfull [*sic*]. But I was bored at being taught, & for some time, only did just what was asked from me, & hardly looked up from my book – that is at my teacher. But she was worth looking at. She had fine bright eyes – a curved nose, the teeth too prominent indeed – but her whole aspect was vigorous & wholesome. She taught well too. My varied experience of Greek teachers makes me a good judge of their merits I think. She was more professional than Miss Pater[24] though perhaps not so cultivated – she was more genial than Miss Clay & as good a scholar. [ ] But I am sorry to say – really now a little repentant – that she did not at first attract me. She was too cheerful & muscular. She made me feel 'contradictious' as the nurses used to say. After a time I found out her line of teaching, & rather set my back against it – at least I discovered certain opinions which she held very vigorously – & which when contradicted, were worth a good half hours discussion. I contradicted them; advanced life long opinions on the spur of the moment, & to my delight she took me quite seriously – or when I was in a lazy mood, drew her out; gave in at this point, led her on to another – & when she was fairly started on some theory of hers – let my mind stray. I began this system in pure idleness; it relieved the tedium of Greek grammar; & continued it from a genuine interest with a little malice mixed – I found out that she had theories of her own about the Furies; [ ] for six lessons I too had theories about the Furies: [ ] – & so with many other subjects. She was a person of ardent theories & she could expound them fluently. She used three adjectives where I could only lay hands on one – Aeschylus was strenuous, grand, impassioned & so on. But she was no sentimentalist: she had her grammar at her finger tips – she used to pull me up ruthlessly in the middle of some beautiful passage with "Mark the *ar*". I read a very

---

24 Clara Pater (1841-1910), the first Classics Tutor and eventually Vice-President of Somerville College, Oxford, living with her sister in Canning Place, Kensington, W. Walter Pater was her brother. She was probably the model for Miss Craye in 'Slater's Pins Have No Points', first published in *Forum*, January 1928 (Kp C295) and reprinted in *The Complete Shorter Fiction of Virginia Woolf*, ed. Susan Dick (London and New York, 1985).

lovely description of maidenhood in Euripides (?)[25] for instance [ ] –
how the maiden hangs like ripened fruit within the orchard – but the
gates ajar, the passer by spies in – & does not hesitate to pluck. That was
the sense of it, & at the end I paused with some literary delight in its
beauty. Not so Miss Case. "The use of the instrumental genitive in the
3rd line is extremely rare" her comment upon Love! But that is not a fair
example; & at any rate I think it really praiseworthy; aesthetic pleasure
is so much easier to attain than knowledge of his uses of the genitive – I
think it is true that she read with a less purely literary interest in the text
than I did; she was not by any means blind to the beauties of Aeschylus
and Euripides (her two favourite writers) but she was not happy till she
had woven some kind of moral into their plays.[ ]

She was always expounding their 'teaching' and their views upon life
& Fate, as they can be interpreted by an intelligent reader. I had never
attempted anything of this kind before, & though I protested that Miss
Case carried it too far, yet I was forced to think more than I had done
hitherto – & interested accordingly. It was upon these subjects that she
became really eloquent. She would spend a whole lesson in defining the
relation of Aeschylus towards Fate – or the religious peculiarities of
Euripides. This was the side of the thing that most interested her – & to
her great credit, she made me, at least, see her point of view. Then there
was our grammar. Many teachers have tried to break me in to that – but
with only a passing success. Miss Case went to the root of the evil; she
saw that my foundations were rotten – procured a Grammar, & bade me
start with the very first exercise – upon the proper use of the article –
which I had hitherto used with the greatest impropriety. She never
failed to point out, with perfect good humour that my exercises were
detestable – 'I haven't even attempted to correct this one' she said once –
with the cheerful laugh, which spoke of an undaunted courage. I never
once made her lose her temper, though I sometimes lost mine sufficiently to wish I could. Now that our lessons are over – for good perhaps
– I am amazed at the amount she stood from me –

But in all these ways she was an excellent teacher. I feel besides, that
she is a really valiant strong minded woman, in a private capacity. We

---

25 AVS's question mark; her reference is to lines 997-1001 (roughly) of Aeschylus's *The
Suppliant Maidens*: '. . . you who have/That bloom which draws men's eyes: there is
no simple/Guard for the fruit most delicate, that beasts/And men, both winged and
footed, ravage: . . .' (translated by Seth Benardete). There is no 'instrumental genitive' in the passage: AVS was just having her fun.

strayed enough from grammar to let me see this. She talked on many subjects; & on all she showed herself possessed of clear strong views, & more than this she had the rare gift of seeing the other side; she had too, I think, a fine human sympathy which I had reason, once or twice to test –

This, I know is most inadequate testimony to her – but under the circumstances of haste & discomfort, I can do no better.

I vaguely hope too, that our parting is not yet really final –

AN AFTERNOON WITH THE PAGANS

Matthew Arnold, I know, called them 'the Barbarians'[26] – but that implies a people without a religion; now they – that is the English aristocracy – are in my opinion very strong believers in the Gods – not the Gods of the Christian faith indeed – but of the very picturesque Pagan mythology. They believe in Bacchus, & in Pan, – & Zeus was an aristocrat. Artemis too – wasn't she a very finely built young Countess? In other words they believe enormously in leading a happy luxurious life – with the best of everything always at their command. They have no reason to doubt; haven't the Gods provided them excellently well? They shut their eyes & suck down their sugar plum. These at any rate are a few of the superficial impressions which I always receive from the aristocracy – & very pleasant they are too. I would be a pagan – if I could.

Yesterday we spent an afternoon at St Albans where Katie, that divine Giantess has taken a house. Beatrice was there & Lady Robert Cecil[27] We spent the whole afternoon under a tree in the garden. Katie lay stretched on a long couch, in the carelessness of perfect grace. She doesn't think how she looks – she just flings out her superb limbs – like a child resting after its play. Indeed the whole atmosphere of the place was one of careless ease. [ ] Beatrice flung herself back in her chair, hands behind her head – Lady Robert sat lightly upright glancing round her like some bright bird. Her eyes, poor thing, have to do double work;

---

26 Arnold's name for the British aristocracy in Chap. III, 'Barbarians, Philistines, Populace', of *Culture and Anarchy*, 2nd ed., 1875.

27 Countess of Cromer, *née* Katherine Thynne (1865-1933), married, as his second wife, to Evelyn Baring, 1st Earl Cromer (1841-1917). Lady Beatrice Thynne (1867-1941), Katie's sister; they were the daughters of the 4th Marquis of Bath. Lady Robert Cecil (1868-1956), third daughter of the 2nd Earl of Durham, married to Lord Robert Cecil (1864-1958), third son of the 3rd Marquess of Salisbury, would soon become 'Nelly' to AVS and a close friend. This visit to St Albans was made in June; see *VW Letters*, I, No. 86.

she is almost quite deaf – she heard nothing of what we said as we talked together, but her large eyes, seeing us laugh, laughed too. It was curiously pathetic. We talked hard. Marriage hasn't changed Katie; she was a great lady before: the change from the simplicity of her cottage garden at Chesham, to the splendours of the British Residency at Cairo[28] have only developed that side of her; the other is left untouched. She held forth as of old; declaiming her impossible theories in the same half laughing half serious way; pouring scorn upon us all – bantering her sister – laying her hands upon Lady Roberts shoulder to shout some intemperate remark into her ear; she was like a great benevolent goddess.

But all the time, one could feel, she was swaying the talk; even at such an informal party as this, she was leading – seeing what ought to be done next – what move would put everybody more at their ease. Nothing, one can well see, can be more perfect than her manner as a Hostess; she is perfectly dignified, but perfectly simple at the same time; one could no more suspect her of ill manners than the Venus of Milo. We talked on & on, always laughing I think – till Katie, after tea, suggested a walk round 'our domains' as she called them. She led the way; her step is perfectly stately & free. She took Lady Robert's arm every now & then in a caressing way – She sent for her chow dog; knelt on the lawn & played with it for ten minutes together; then, she saw a pump handle swinging; like the great child she is she must, despite Beatrice's chattering, begin to pull it; nothing happened – she pulled more & more vigorously – at last we heard water gushing. "Well Katie – you have had a brilliant idea" shrieked Beatrice, "its the drains". Katie was quite unconcerned though; gathered up her skirts with her delightful mocking smile, & swept on. Other people, Lady Roberts Husband, came in to tea; but our fly was at the door; Katie took our hands very kindly – "Good bye" she said, in a voice which sounded like a blessing – a half humourous blessing – & we went.

Well, that is a pleasant picture to think of – though we wont see it again for another twelvemonth –

RETROSPECT   30 July

Tonight is the last we shall spend in London for 8 weeks – a crisis to most people not worth talking about – but our family moves with the

---

28 The 1st Earl of Cromer was the British Administrator and Consul-General in Egypt until 1907.

unwieldiness & extreme deliberation of the 300 year old tortoise at the zoo. [ ] But that tortoise must in reality have anything but an easy time of it – if his weekly excursions in search of cabbage are preluded by any of the flurry & discomfort which are our lot at these seasons. But on this I will not dwell. My precious box is well crammed with books – the family boxes are corded & labelled down stairs – We shall have one final & supreme exertion tomorrow: & by this time tomorrow night we shall all be set down in, I hope, the most peaceful & mellow of country houses[29] some 70 miles or so by train from London – the distance though is not to be measured by miles. I ought now, therefore to write some kind of farewell to London – We close here our London Chapter with regret. Several circumstances, some I hope imaginary, make me feel perfectly callous at the thought of going. For 8 weeks, I shall not miss you, great City; in October we may meet on more friendly terms.

For some reason, partly weather I think, the 'season' has come to an end rather lamely: I like to leave London with a final blare of trumpets; sun burning, I mean, pavements heated slabs – trees burnt grass burnt – no shade anywhere. Then one has earned ones wages,[30] & may cool down in the country. Besides it is a little disappointing to miss that sun-roasting which is only to be had once a year –

When we were children the summers were always really hot. [ ] I can remember the smell of the gardens, all burnt up in the sun, the heat odour of the streets; it was all very good then – because it told of the end of the summer – & of St Ives.[31] But now there seems no reason, unless one looks at the calendar, why one should go away now more than at any other time. It isn't the end of the summer for the summer hasn't begun – March, April, May (as we understand it in England) have lasted so long, that here we are in August & the summer not yet come. Perhaps it will flame upon us in our flat meadows near Salisbury: that remains to be recorded – I wish for the sake of this book that I had anything more brightly coloured & picturesque to write here; it seems to me that all my events have been of the same temperate rather cold hued description; I haven't had to use many superlatives. I have sketched faint outlines with a pencil. But the only use of this book is that it shall serve for a sketch

29 Netherhampton House; see 'The Country in London', n.17.
30 Cf. 'Fear no more the heat o' the sun,/Nor the furious winter's rages;/Thou thy worldly task hast done,/Home art gone and ta'en thy wages:' *Cymbeline*, IV, ii, 258-61.
31 Cornwall, where the Stephen family went every summer from 1882 to 1894.

book; as an artist fills his pages with scraps & fragments, studies of drapery – legs, arms & noses – useful to him no doubt, but of no meaning to anyone else – so I [ ] take up my pen & trace here whatever shapes I happen to have in my head. [ ]

It is an exercise – training for eye & hand – roughness if it results from an honest desire to put down the truth with whatever materials one has to hand, is not disagreeable – though often I am afraid decidedly uncouth. I have gone on this plan for something over a month now, & propose, Ladies & Gentlemen, to continue it in the country.

There, with good luck, some live figures ought to cross my field of view – & I shall attempt to cast their shadow on the page. But of that, more anon. At present it only remains for me to say farewell to Hyde Park Gate.

Tomorrow I shall open at a new chapter.

NETHERHAMPTON HOUSE, SALISBURY.

August: 1903

NETHERHAMPTON HOUSE

We have wrenched ourselves free of London. Nessa & I after a titanic struggle in that station [Waterloo], which takes its name appropriately from a battle field, [ ] – accomplished the family transition to Salisbury. Already our boxes are unpacked & we have settled into some kind of order. The house is exactly what I expected – & hoped. The front view – we look on to the road – is of a little gray stone house, too humble to be itself ornate, but evidently dating from an ornate period – & in its humble way an imitation of a genuine great house. There is some kind of architectural device of urns at intervals on the gables; there is a hollowed recess in the wall, meant perhaps, were the thing on a larger scale, to stand a statue in. The garden gate, too, is uncommon – gracefully wrought in blue green iron, & surmounted by a coat of arms & a crest. This house, as a matter of fact, was built in Elizabeths time I think, as dower house to the Pembroke family; the coat of arms, besides various small statelinesses within & without, proclaim [ ] its aristocratic connections; various old countesses & dependent relatives have had their

lodging here, after the splendours of Wilton[32] – though at the present
time it is no longer used for this purpose. The Furses[33] who have it now
have done their decorating &c. in entire sympathy with the character of
the place – The wide rooms are furnished not too profusely with dignified old chairs, & solid tables: crimson & white is the scheme of the
whole place, with a touch of ruddy old wood. It is, I feel, a very characteristic English country house of the more modest sort; solid & unpre-
tentious, but with a certain quaint dignity of its own, greatly mellowed
by time. These little gray old houses are common all over England, but I
doubt whether you find them elsewhere – I have not had time to see
much of the garden – but it looks in keeping with the house – a walled
kitchen garden – broad grass walks – a sundial – all on a small useful
scale – kitchen garden teeming with fruit & vegetables – but of a comfortable airy kind. [*The next page has been cut out.*]

WILTON – FROM OUTSIDE THE WALLS

Yesterday, or the day before, we set off after breakfast to find out our
position in the world. Our garden is really only a bit of the meadow
shorn & cut off from the rest of the fields by a sunk fence. The house is
very long & low, but the front view gives really no idea of its size; it
turns round & makes a square court moreover, & only the face of the
house is gray. The rest – & older part – is built of red brick. We had
some curiosity to find the river, & the village of Wilton – our difficulty
was to decide which of the many streams we met was the river – in time
though we came to such a broad & vigorous stream that we decided to
name it the Wylye & count the smaller rivulets which cut up the
meadows as mere tributaries – trained to flow thus in order to water the
fields. Indeed a most elaborate system of canals, & hatches, & little
waterfalls is arranged all over the meadows, but the water is now for the
most part cut off, & the meadows are dry. We tramped along the road
finally, which is on one side walled off by a very high & neatly preserved brick wall. Inside lie the gardens of Wilton – miles & miles of
them, I should judge, by the time it took us to trudge this side of their
boundaries. At last we turned the corner, & came, very obviously, to the
Great Gate of Wilton. It is made in the shape of a Roman Arch – though

---

32 Wilton House, near Salisbury, seat of the Earls of Pembroke, was built in 1649 by
   Inigo Jones and John Webb.
33 Netherhampton House belonged to the sculptor J. H. M. Furse, eldest brother of
   Charles Wellington Furse, the portrait painter.

whether it is surmounted by the figure of a Roman Emperor, or whether one of the Earls of Pembroke has been clad in a toga for the occasion, I can not say.[34]

The other statue,[35] just outside the gates suggests that the modern military uniform at any rate is not the right stuff for bronze: The sculptor, moreoever, in respect for the nobility of his sitter has made him at least 3 feet taller than the most gigantic of ordinary mortals. As a work of art therefore, the statue is not convincing; but when one reads the inscription at the base one understands that a very heroic figure was needed. After this we walked through the town. There are moods when the little old South of England town, with its peace & quaintness are entirely refreshing: [ ] there are times when its eternal sameness – its somnolence as of one [ ] that has fallen asleep of a surfeit of roast beef & plum pudding – are depressing. I am craving, I think, for the bareness & warmth & brilliance of a foreign land. But Wilton is particularly apt to excite this kind of discontent; it is more smug & well pleased with itself than the majority of English villages like all those in small hamlets that sit in the shadow of a great house. It has the look of a very faithful old family retainer – as I have no doubt those that live in its cottages are – pensioned off by the great people & unswervingly loyal to them. Its whole world is circled by the 'Park'; its interest is concerned entirely with 'Her Ladyship' & the goings on at the Castle.[36] In almost every street you can trace the influence of the Herbert family. The three inns of course are loyally christened after the various titles of the Pembrokes; their arms, slightly battered by weather hang from all the sign posts: they, in their turn, have [ ] scattered fountains & almshouses all round them, & generally keep the village so tidy & sweet that it makes the most respectable setting for Wilton itself.

We – that is Adrian & I – commented upon all this – in no very friendly spirit. We professed to find the whole country side 'demoralised' & clinging to the great man of the place. This I suppose is an exaggeration; at any rate if we had been inside those high brick walls our

---

34 Designed by W. Chambers just before 1759, the gate is 'surmounted' by an equestrian statue of Marcus Aurelius.

35 The statue is of George Robert Charles, 13th Earl of Pembroke (1850-95); the inscription at its base is from 'Celestial Song' ('Bhagavad-Gita'), translated from the Sanskrit by Sir Edwin Arnold.

36 Sir William Herbert was created 1st Earl of Pembroke in 1551; the family were active patrons of the arts; the present 'ladyship' was Beatrix Louisa (d.1944), the eldest sister of Nelly Cecil.

point of view might have changed – but it is safe to say that the feudal spirit in England is not yet dead.

THE WATER MEADOWS

We are still exploring. Yesterday I took Nessa across the water meadows to a certain romantic looking church[37] – at least that was our intention. This church you see from our croquet lawn across an apparently flat & easily walked breadth of meadow. The church stands just higher among some trees. I had some vague notion that this was George Herberts church; at any rate it was an object to walk to. Nessa, too, was anxious to find the mythical railway, which is to supply the express train in her great Landscape. So we started gaily across the meadows. But before long we had to deviate; little streams just too broad & too deep to jump kept cutting us off; we had to walk sideways to find a bridge – often only a bare plank – sometimes a fence with but one sound rung left. It was a very tortuous & difficult path, but we kept our church in view, & steered for it as best we could. Our position got more serious though when we were both landed in mud up to our ancles [*sic*] – in which needless to say one of Nessa's shoes stuck bodily – & this leap only led to something worse – We tried to circumvent the stream – & coasted along it, flattening ourselves under barbed wire – (surely there can be no fear of trespassers here!) & scrambling through hedges. We were brought to a stop by hearing male rustic voices, alarming to pedestrians of the womanly sex – Men were making hay in the adjoining field & not only were they talking but they were talking of us – possibly to us. Seeing us stop, one of them advanced to the gate; we had to move up to hear what he said. He was evidently jocular – & we thought it best to anticipate any remarks he might have to make by asking boldly our way out? "Your fairly lost, you are" he said – [ ] which seemed to tickle him a good deal. 'Where d'you want to go?' It seemed idiotic to say nowhere – so I prompted Nessa – 'the Road' 'The Road?' 'You dont mean to say you've lost the road in broad daylight?' That was an excellent joke too – 'You wont find no road here – better go back the way you come' And so we turned & went – It was shouted after us that the sleek brown cows feeding at the other end of the field were dangerous – but we took no heed. We were far more troubled by the necessity of repeating all

---

37 George Herbert (1593-1633), the poet, was rector of the little church of Bemerton about a mile across the fields to the north-west of Netherhampton; here he spent the last three years of his life and was buried.

those muddy plunges & wriggles which had served to bring us here. We had immediately to cross the stream where Nessa had embedded her shoe; this experience had happily somewhat shaken her belief in shoes: & she agreed to my suggestion that for the rest of this walk we should be independant [*sic*] of bridges or lack of bridges – that we should bare our feet, & use them for the purpose – after all – for which they were created. The stream water was numbing cold at first, but the feel of the grass on the bare sole of ones foot is curiously pleasant. If you lay your palm on the grass, it feels very little; but ones foot, always gloved & cased as it is from contact with the earth is exquisitely sensitive to the coarseness of dry ground – the smoothness & coldness of grass – the warmth of those places where the sun beats. It was thus strangely charming to walk barefoot across two or three fields & streams. We found our road – & put on our shoes – only too soon.

Radcliffe[38] (the youngest & most omniscient) gives us this information about the water meadows. As you walk along the main river – the Wylye – you see that wooden shutters are let into its banks at intervals; these, technically called hatches, are at the mouth of a channel in the neighbouring field; they are made with two handles; if you raise a hatch you divert a stream from the main river into the channel behind; & thus the meadows for miles round are irrigated. The system is immensely complicated – worked out more than two hundred years ago, says the omniscient Radcliffe, & still in use: each main channel from the river feeds numbers of lesser channels, till the fields are threaded across & across. In September I think he said, the hatches are raised, but not all at once; each meadow owner is allowed to flow the water through his land for the space of five days. They each take a turn – Then when the land is thoroughly soaked, the water is cut off – the hay grows lusty – is mown – the cattle are turned on to graze off what remains – & this last is the stage that has now been reached.

THE DOWNS

We have the custom now every summer of hiring a pony to drive. Most years we have been grossly deceived; our stipulation, made in all simplicity, that the beast shall be 'quiet' has led the horse dealers to present us with every quality of broken down & antiquated steed – just capable of drawing an old Ladies garden chair. We are wiser now, & ask simply for a pony – The result is nothing very startling; our beast has

---

38 *Lancaster Radcliffe: The Official Guide*, E. J. Burrow & Co., Cheltenham, 1837.

the quality of quietness thrown in gratis, but on the whole he is a good willing animal – trotting like a slightly worn out machine till he comes to his stable door, when he stops. But our afternoon drive becomes a necessity. Here one has to keep to the road, which robs the drives of half their charm, and were not our eyes still sensitive to the beauty of grass & cornfields would make the process dreary enough. We had a note today to take to Broad Chalke, about six miles the other side of the race course. We started after tea – & it had turned to a beautiful evening. Somewhere I have read that the sky above the chalkland is of a peculiar pale blue – as though something of the whiteness of the chalk were reflected in it. It was true last night at any rate that the blue was pale – whatever the cause was.

Adrian, with his wonderful faculty for finding something wrong in his immediate circumstances – whatever they are – grumbled the whole time at the dulness [*sic*] of the country – in which I conceive he is wholly wrong. Such genuine country I conceive can never be dull; even though nature here hasn't taken much pains apparently with her material. She has kept a charm though which is entirely absent in more obviously interesting places. As we drove along through lanes deeply cut in the chalk, I kept likening the downs to the long curved waves of the sea. It is as though the land here, all molten once, & rolling in vast billows had solidified while the waves were still swollen & on the point of breaking. From a height it looks as though the whole land were flowing. Man, too, has done nothing to change the shape of these breakers. He has planted them to a certain extent, but has mostly left their grass untouched for his flocks. You see a thatched shed or so on the down side where the shepherd lives, but no other human house. The villages have all sunk into the hollows between the waves; & the result is a peculiar smoothness & bareness of outline. This is the bare bone of the earth –

SALISBURY CATHEDRAL

A restless devil lodges somewhere in this ancient gray house – this peaceful garden – even in my wide room. It is perhaps just a little overdone – the age & deep repose of it all. I felt this afternoon as though I must get into some brisker air. It is no fault of the house's that as I have said is so perfect that I should not know where to lift up my hand to alter, were it possible. But though it was hot, & cushions spread on the lawn, I felt a fretful desire to worry myself. I trudged off down the road, which is powdered with fine white dust, & very hard. I saw the spire of

Salisbury[39] in the distance, & made that my object. Three miles of dusty road, I knew lay between us – but that was just the thing I wanted. So I tramped – till my shoes were white too, & I was feeling stretched in the muscles of my legs.

Small red houses have marched out in the van & rear of Salisbury, as of every other town, combining, I imagine their architect to say, the advantages of a Cathedral city with pure country air. Any other combination would be preferable I think. I had made the spire my aim – now I grazed as close it as I could – invaded the sanctuaries of the Close indeed, where motor cars may not penetrate, or butchers carts, unless bearing clerical provisions. The close is the same as all Cathedral closes – very rich, very peaceful – with the air of a very comfortably cushioned Sanctuary from the sins & weariness of the outer world. The old ladies who let their dresses sweep its turf are infected by the atmosphere; they move with extreme leisure & dignity – as though earthly affairs had no longer any power to hurry them. Yet I can well imagine that their precincts cover as much scandal of an innocent sort as any similar space in Mayfair or Belgravia. It is a picturesque but relaxing little haven, I am sure, & the Bishop & Chapter would do much better turned out of their spacious Georgian houses, & made to share the common lot. I should suggest that the close, shut against Butcher carts & motor cars by all means, should remain open to people of a literary disposition – who lodged at their ease in Palace & Deanery, would certainly turn their luxury to account.

The neighbourhood of the Cathedral though is depressing. So much ancient stone however fairly piled, & however rich with the bodies of Saints & famous men, seems to suck the vitality of its humble neighbours. It is like a great forest oak; nothing can grow healthily beneath its shade.

All this is a form of heresy I know. A long walk in the sun, all along the valley too, leaves one little appetite to appreciate the value of the picture from an aesthetic point of view. A bare hilltop would have pleased me better than all the Closes & Cathedrals in England –

AN EVENING SERVICE

There is no denying – if you pretend to be a person of culture – that Salisbury Cathedral is beautiful – & culture or not, I honestly feel it to

---

39 The construction of Salisbury Cathedral was begun in 1220 and it was consecrated in 1258; the spire of 404 feet, added about 1320, is the tallest in England.

be so. It grows upon one; you find your eye wandering over the land-scape to look for it: & when you find it, you keep your eye there for some moments satisfied. We are on a level with Salisbury – & no hills lie between us. I have not yet in my walks passed beyond its range. Some-times I see the point of its spire – like an extinguisher – sitting on the side of the down. Oftenest I see it across the meadows – the whole church planted firm there – solid, & yet exquisitely light & graceful at once. It takes all kinds of tones – sometimes it is a pale gray – then almost white; today, for some reason it looked as though built of dark brown stone. George & I meant to spend a part of our Sunday appropriately in wor-ship within its walls – but decided that afternoon service, drawn out by sermon &c., was too great an expense of time. So we invented (as it turned out) an Evensong at 7 to suit our purpose, & drove over in time for that. But the first youth we stopped in the Close pointed out our mis-take – for some reason, Salisbury Cathedral provides no Evensong. Our only way of worship therefore – & a thoroughly happy one – was to drive slowly round the close. In certain moods I know, this kind of thing is intolerable; I would no more live here than lie myself down tomorrow in a venerable grave in the cloisters; but no place can be more amply satisfactory to spend an hour in – [ ] It is as though you shut thick ivy grown walls between yourself & the world; within them all is ancient loveliness & peace. English Cathedrals have certainly one inestimable advantage over the only foreign ones that I have seen; they stand in a perfect garden of their own, whereas the great French churches open on to the street. Here, for instance the Cathedral is circled by a rich layer of turf – & beyond that, like a zealous bodyguard, stand round all the houses of the close. These harmonise so perfectly with the prevailing spirit of the Cathedral that you hardly notice them individually till you stop especially to do so. They seem to me to act, I say, as a kind of body-guard: nothing vulgar shall taint the air of the cathedral; they treasure up & absorb the precious incense it gives out. And like the beefeaters, or some other ancient guard, they are eminently picturesque without rivalling the splendour of their monarch. [ ]

We had occasion as it happens to visit one of these very houses – a small one, on the outskirts of the close. Old Miss Fawcett[40] struck me as exactly the benevolent & mildly garrulous old lady one might expect to

---

40 Sarah Maria Fawcett (b.1830), sister of Henry Fawcett (1833-84), professor of politi-cal economy at Cambridge, born in Queen Street, Salisbury, as was her brother; see Leslie Stephen, *Life of Henry Fawcett*, 1885.

find in these surroundings. Indeed I should have been shocked had she turned out in any way different. But she was precisely the type I foretold – [ ] & we had no difficulty in carrying on a conversation. How should we – when we had met – in novels I suppose – so often before?

WILTON FROM INSIDE

There is one day – Wednesday – in every week when from the hour of 2 till 5 – the public can enter the great gates of Wilton as freely as any Herbert in the land. I have never been over one of our 'stately homes' in any capacity, so yesterday I thought I would earn that experience. I expected to find a crowd of wagonettes & bicycles – but as a matter of fact I had to enter modestly behind a solitary party of three – an elderly gentleman, who might be a banker in Salisbury, & his two nieces, who were young ladies from New York – & signed themselves thus in the visitors book. This at any rate was my guess at their relationship to each other; the gentleman was certainly English, for he took upon himself to do the honours of Wilton, & point out the qualities of English scenery, as though he were responsible for both, & had a lawful interest to any credit that might be laid to their account. A massive lodge keeper in livery admitted us, took our shilling, for the benefit of the Herbert Hospital,[41] & forwarded us across the courtyard to the care of a dignified house keeper within the doors. I felt unspeakably ignominious, as though I were admitted by favour of these gorgeous flunkeys, & had to hold myself in an attitude of servile attention to them. The good lady who took charge of us was a typical family servant. She was willing to gratify our awed curiosity as to the Herbert family & their belongings – & at the same time she clearly felt herself to be socially our superior. She did the honours with the condescending air of one to whom Greek statues & Vandykes[42] are a matter of course, but she expected our plebian respect. So we trooped behind her obediently, & were submissively awe-struck. When she [ ] thought I suppose that I was looking about me with too critical an air she enunciated in my ear some high

---

41 Magdalen, or Maudlin Hospital consists of a row of six four-room cottages, built in 1832 by the Rt Hon. Catherine Dowager of Pembroke and Montgomery; the inmates were selected from former employees on the Pembroke Estate at Wilton.

42 Those paintings by Sir Anthony Vandyke still adorning the walls of Wilton House include the portrait of Philip, Earl of Pembroke and his family, in the double cube room.

sounding title – as 'Portrait of Titian – by himself' which was to recall me from my impertinence.

There are undoubtedly a great many very good pictures – but a still greater number of worthless ones. I am a person of no discrimination in matters of art – I dont even know what I like – at once that is – & the conditions under which I saw the Wilton pictures were altogether unfavourable. Indeed it was difficult to appreciate the house itself even – ushered as we were from one museum like room to another, & bade admire the proper things as quickly as possible & pass on to the next.

Honestly, I was disappointed in my first view of a great house. I had imagined something more spacious & more harmonious. It was as though they had tried in parts to make an early Victorian style of decoration harmonise with the Vandykes – & had not succeeded. If they had resolved to keep the whole place in the style of one period – if the chairs & tables had been uniformly old instead of all styles & ages – the character of the rooms would have been distinct & beautiful. As it is your eye is distracted by a confusion of chintzes & leather chairs & handsome writing tables which are all out of character with the old chimney pieces & moulded walls. – But, having let a week almost, lapse between this sentence & the last, I can find nothing very profitable to say about the beauties of Wilton. The American young ladies I remember, showed a far more spontaneous interest in the photographs & armchairs of the Herbert family than in the famous Vandykes & Titians – though they did their duty manfully by these too. The Banker uncle produced for them the special privilege of holding the present Earls[43] portrait in their hands: & the housekeeper beamed a condescending approval.

She was so condescending indeed that as we stood in the hall, I was terribly un-easy in my mind what course to take with a certain half crown that lay in my hand. Half a crown was lavish payment I felt; but then it was the smallest coin I had; yet when I looked at the ladys face, the good breeding I saw there made my half crown seem paltry – not to say vulgar – I waited, like a coward, for the banker to decide. If he dared, I dared, & the half crown was doomed; but apparently he had no doubts in his mind. He bade her a hearty good day, & thank you – & left without putting his hand in his pocket.

I still have my doubts as to whether the glance that she cast on us as

43 Sidney Herbert, 14th Earl of Pembroke (1853-1913).

we left, had not appreciably increased in scorn – but I was soon out of range.

THE TALK OF SHEEP[44]

Since we came here, for various reasons, I have spent many of my afternoons in solitary walks. My solitude is genuine; I go quite alone – the dogs even refuse to risk a possible ride with Adrian for a certain ramble with me. I dont chase rabbits, & I sit down too much for any real dogs temper. But like Wordsworth – like many distinguished people (it is well to be in good company) I find solitude sufficient, strangely so. I walk generally straight out of the house & on to the downs. They are now stacking & carting the corn in some of the fields; corn I waded through up to my shoulder a fortnight ago. I remember it sighed in the wind like water. But the sheep are more interesting than corn or turnips. I like to get them penned together in dense ranks within a square of hurdles; it is my high ambition to learn to bleat some day so that the whole flock hearing me shall answer. One day, to continue this mild garrulity, Nessa & I stood for five minutes in deep laughter while the flock discoursed. There is a wonderful variety in the bleatings of sheep after all; one is clearly exhorting the rest to save their souls from damnation – another, if I mistake him not, denounced some ovine education bill – a third upholds the rights of the sheep to be considered the intellectual equal of the ram. But as they all talk at once, & pay no sort of attention to their neighbours, I see no reason to suppose that their grievances will ever be attended to. The universal tone of weariness – of hopeless regret which prevails in the babble makes me opine that the sheep themselves are aware why they still remain sheep.

The sheep becomes a picturesque animal only, I think, when collected into flocks & led by dog & man over the hillside. He is then pastoral & innocent instead of merely silly. The shepherd is admirable; scrutiny of his face shows that his whole mind is absorbed by his flocks, & is probably the unconscious recipient of a good many queer secrets of earth & air. He inherits his shepherdhood, handed down from father & son for generations, & probably is the nearest approach to a grazing human animal that we in England can produce. He has received the knowledge which Nature bestows on her children only – but as though in fear that they should blab it to the world, she takes away his power of transmitting it to others, or of understanding how it is unique.

---

44 The original (cancelled) title of this essay was 'Sheep as Conversationalists'.

A curious content, which I cannot put into words, comes over me when I reach the top of the down, & lay myself flat on the grass.

STONEHENGE

Providence has sent a very energetic visitor[45] – if not Providence, some power of benevolent intentions with regard to our education. Hospitality & the motive power of an enthusiastic young man have succeeded in driving us to Salisbury, & into every nook of the Cathedral – & yesterday again sent us as far as Stonehenge. Tomorrow we are to trudge to Romsey: the day before, I forgot to say, thanks to a telegram of permission from Lady Pembroke we explored Wilton House & grounds so thoroughly that our consciences are satisfied. Longford Castle[46] is now really the only 'Sight' that remains: Mr. Norman goes on Tuesday – or that, I have no doubt too, would be added to the list of the things we have 'done'. But Stonehenge was a rare accomplishment: a successful expedition – which is in its way a delightful & rememberable thing.

Nessa & I drove there, 12 miles, all winding beneath the crest of the downs, with the Avon at our feet. It was, to give a most important setting to the scene, a brilliantly clear day; hot in the sun, fresh in the shadow, & the trees & fields looked brisk & vigorous with the light on them, but by no means too hot. At midday therefore we could drive along with no discomfort, & it was a drive which needed open eyes.

I have come to the conclusion that England is a remarkably venerable place; from living in London all the year round one gets to think an old house the rarest of things; [ ] but in the country, the real country, it is just the opposite.

Where there is a large house it is almost certain to be two or three hundred years old – & it is exceptional to find a brand new farm or cottage. Country people, one forgets, have none of the reasons the towndwellers have for pulling down & rebuilding; so the old houses are allowed to stand as a matter of course, with a little patching & thatching, from one century to another. England therefore is now crusted all over with ancient dwellings; which have grown so much into the earth that

45 Ronald Collet Norman (1873-1963); he was to become Vice-Chairman of the BBC, 1933-5 and Chairman, 1935-9.

46 Three miles south-east of Salisbury, seat of the Earl of Radnor, an Elizabethan 'Prodigy house', built on an unusual triangular pattern for decorative rather than defensive purposes; it was taken by Sir Philip Sidney as a model for his castle in 'Arcadia'; see AVS's essay 'The Countess of Pembroke's Arcadia' in *The Common Reader: Second Series*, 1932 (Kp A18).

they seem part of its produce. Every little village we passed through had some house or cottage one wanted to look at; & every hamlet, I doubt not, has its tiny roots deep twisted in to the main root of the land – which would make an infinitely interesting study, I know.

We came at last – for I must pass here a great deal I pondered in my mind as I went – to the sign post, which points to Stonehenge. Our way had been by the river, & enclosed by downs. We now came out on the top of Salisbury plain, & the downs spread without check for miles round us. I suddenly looked ahead, & saw with the start with which one sees in real life what ones eye has always known in pictures, the famous circle of Stonehenge. Pictures give one no idea of size; & I had imagined something on a much larger scale. I had thought that the stones were scattered at intervals over a great space of the plain – so that when we settled to meet the riders at 'Stonehenge' I had privately judged the plan to be far too vague. But really it is a tiny compact little place – the stones might be arranged for instance as they are now – in the stalls of St James Hall[47] – But otherwise the pictures had prepared me fairly truthfully – as to shape & position that is; I had not realised though that the stones have such a look of purpose & arrangement; it is a recognisable temple, even now.

We promptly sat down with our backs to the sight we had come to see, & began to eat sandwiches: half an hour afterwards we were ready to make our inspection.

The singular, & intoxicating charm of Stonehenge to me, & to most I think, is that no one in the world can tell you anything about it. There are these great blocks of stone; [ ] & what more? Who piled them there & when, & for what purpose, no one in the world – I like to repeat my boast – can tell.

I felt as though I had run against the stark remains of an age I cannot otherwise conceive; [ ] a piece of wreckage washed up from Oblivion. There are theories I know – without end; & we, naturally, made a great many fresh, & indisputable discoveries of our own. The most attractive, & I suppose most likely, is that some forgotten people [ ] built here a Temple where they worshipped the sun; there is a rugged pillar someway out side the circle whose peak makes exactly that point on the rim of the earth where the sun rises in the summer solstice. And there is a fallen stone in the middle, longer & larger than the other hewn rocks it lies

---

47 Probably a reference to the circular arrangement of the seats round the pit or stage of
   St James's Hall.

among which may have been an altar – & the moment the sun rose the Priest of that savage people slaughtered his victim here in honour of the Sun God. We certainly saw the dent of his axe in the stone. Set up the pillars though in some other shape, & we have an entirely fresh picture; but the thing that remains in ones mind, whatever one does, is the stupendous mystery of it all. Man has done nothing to change Salisbury plain since these stones were set here; they have seen sunrise & moonrise over those identical swells & ridges for – I know not how many thousand years. I like to think of it; imagine those toiling pagans doing honour to the very sun now in the sky above me, & for some perverse reason I find this a more deeply impressive temple of Religion – block laid to block, & half of them tumbled in ruin so long that the earth almost hides them, than that perfect spire whence prayer & praise is at this very moment ascending.

It is matter for thought surely, if not for irony, that as one stands on the ruins of Stonehenge one can see the spire of Salisbury Cathedral.

THE WILTON CARPET FACTORY

I was up this morning at six – an autobiographical statement which needs, I feel, some explanation. We had over-night allowed ourselves to dwell long on the pleasures of otter hunting, a sport in which none of us had ever taken part – or have yet, for the matter of that. The hounds were to meet at Wilton at 7 – We agreed in all the fervour of the night before to rise at 6 this morning, & join them. At a quarter to six a dull thud against my door pulled me by the hair as it were out of all kinds of delicate & elusive dreams. We have no blinds in this house, & the brightness of my room, I suppose, helped to chase away all the doubts & mysteries which night spins over one's brains; I was awake, & in possession of the facts of the case almost at once. Soon I rose, dressed, & tumbled downstairs to breakfast. A breakfast which has been laid over night is never an exhilarating meal, but we each had a hot cup of tea, & started. Now every time I see what early morning is like I vow it is the rarest & fairest part of the day – in one sense it is certainly the rarest. One feels I suppose abnormally spiritual when one has vanquished ones fleshly longing for sleep, & thus the prize of your struggle – these extra hours of day light – wear a peculiar aetherial aspect which somehow makes you appear creditable in your own eyes. We stepped along the road, as light as stags; as though we had left our gross bodies in bed. [ ] Indeed the early morning is lovely, once in a way: I like to feel that I am in harmony with nature; going forth into the fields when her creatures are waking, & the strange life of the tillers of the ground has already begun. I saw for instance some harvesters working among the corn; they looked at us with the start of wild beasts surprised – they were so entirely one with the spirit of the fields.

But it is of carpet manufactories that I am going to write. The otter hounds, naturally, put off their meet; the first man we met told us the inevitable news: we had to enjoy the morning for 2 hours therefore before breakfast – which was sleepy work. After that we had to go to Wilton house – & having disposed of that, the notion of seeing the Wilton Carpet factory[48] crossed our minds. Providence, or again that power which takes our education to heart, arranged matters in a surprisingly convenient way – Wednesday it chanced was the one day in the week on which the factory is open to visitors. Wilton is the last place one thinks likely to hold a factory; its air tastes unpolluted by any smoke save that of snug domestic hearths, & its streets are surely the oldest in England. But nevertheless there is a factory – of a kind. It has little likeness I imagine to the factories of Birmingham & Manchester. We entered by a door which looked like the entrance to the stables of an inn, & found ourselves in a courtyard, which again looked very much like the courtyard of an old fashioned posting house. The buildings round it are low & ramshackle; there is no hum of machinery, no bustle of workpeople; I expected to be led on to some further, & more imposing buildings. But instead our guide – a wrinkled old countryman – opened a door on the left: we were in the factory. It was a long low room like one of the long rooms in a mill; down the middle there was suspended a wooden cylinder; round which were stretched the strings which make the foundation of a carpet. Girls were seated on one side of this, twisting coloured threads round the strings with most dexterous fingers; they then beat them down on top of the work already done with a metal comb. Above them was pinned the design of the carpet – but I remain quite unable to understand how they carried this out – as they did without hesitation – or how it resulted in the very elaborate pattern which was woven into the finished work. The benches were by no means crowded; but the girls that were there worked hard enough, & in silence. Their faces were not unhappy; but they had all of them – the youngest was twelve I suppose – the pale preoccupied look of people who sit long hours over hard work, from which their attention can never

---

48 The Wilton Royal Carpet Factory Ltd, in Warminster Road, one of the first manufacturers of carpets in England; the industry was encouraged by the Herbert family.

stray, though the depths of the mind are unstirred. We went through two or three rooms of this kind – all of them low & badly lighted, with no modern machinery or furniture. The look of the whole place indeed was dusty & ramshackle, & obsolete; our guide made it clear to us that this is indeed the case: Wilton no longer makes Wilton carpets. Axminster carpets[49] are its principal product – & these it is evident are slowly being superseded. All their work is done by hand – machines were started, but not enough work was demanded to make them pay, & the power room is now shut up.

We left then; nor will the Wilton carpet factories remain open to the public for many years to come.

ROMSEY ABBEY

The last of the sights within reach has been accomplished – Romsey Abbey,[50] that is.

It is a solid spacious place – only looking too thoroughly scrubbed & scoured to be entirely satisfactory. It is, our guide says, the finest Norman church extant, but it is a jumble of styles: restorers too have laid their cloven hoof upon it; it is a bewildering place to be let loose in, as I was, with an ignorant mind.

First I had an idea that Romsey Abbey was a disused ruin; an image partly painted from Tintern[51] I think, of ivied arches & mossy pillars standing un-roofed in the open air, like the ribs of a wrecked ship, was in my mind, & this perfectly preserved place put me to such confusion at first that I could not collect any other impressions. Then it has the look of a place but recently restored – after the original pattern no doubt; but the stone might have been quarried yesterday. Then, again, the atmosphere of the place is curiously profane. The side aisles have been turned into museums, where wooden models of the original Abbey are shown, & relics – such as a dead nuns hair & a scrap of the old altar cloth – are framed & glazed. There is moreover a singular heap of rubbish, against one of the walls – gargoyles & chippings off pillars & all kinds of frag-

---

49 Axminster Carpets, founded by Thomas Witty, who had studied Turkish methods of carpet production; the business merged in 1835 with the Wilton Royal Carpet Factory.

50 About 25 miles by rail south-east of Salisbury, the present structure of Romsey Abbey dates from about 1130, but remains of the earlier Saxon church (967) of the Benedictine nunnery were found beneath the flooring.

51 Tintern Abbey is the most romantic Cistercian ruin in England, on the river Wye, in Monmouth.

ments – piled there without attempt at arrangement. Nor do I know whence they come or to what use they are to be put. They strike one as somehow irreverent – a rubbish heap of Saints heads, & pious stone, which ought to be given decent burial or put to some proper use.

The church is very bare; there are but one or two monuments in the whole of it, & what stained glass there is is very new & thin in colour. Most of the windows though are plain glass – like those in Salisbury Cathedral – & it is partly this perhaps that gives the church its secular air. You dont want sober daylight in a church; it is too cynical & uncompromising; stained glass, as rich as you can make it, is essential to religion. But sacred or not, Romsey is a fine place; Milton might have written it, in stone.

LIFE IN THE FIELDS

For some time I have not had occasion it seems to me, to open this book. We have fallen in to the routine of country life, & the days are indistinct. It is in this kind of swoon, in which the body goes through its operations – the mouth takes in food, & the brain to some extent acts – that the country men & women pass their days – the Squire & his Lady I mean. I would fain believe that our lives are somehow regulated by the sun – that we rise near dawn; & sleep in the midday, & toil in the fields all through the light, till dark comes & closes our eyes – But this is a picturesque falsehood. The sun rises & makes all my room bright – but leaves me un-moved – the sun sets – & I am reading the newspaper by lamplight. The inventor of lamps freed us from the tyranny of the sun. But in another sense, we have become absorbed by the spirit of Nature, let us say – a vast quantity of it is distilled by these fields & downs; we inhale it peacefully. We become a great deal more dependent, I observe, upon the shades of heat & cold – of cloudlessness & rain. These accidents now decide our days for us. We spend so much of our time out of doors too, that we become sensitive to the various changes of temperature & aspect which mark the different hours of the day. If I lived here much longer I should get to understand the wonderful rise & swell & fall of the land. It is like some vast living thing, & all its insects & animals, save man, are exquisitely in time with it. If you lie on the earth somewhere you hear a sound like a vast breath, as though it were the very inspiration of earth herself, & all the living things on her.

STONEHENGE AGAIN

We have had singular good fortune in our expeditions; & our two visits to Stonehenge have impressed such pictures on my mind as I never wish to be obliterated.

We made a second expedition today – the 5th of September; but expedition is a hateful word; I would rather call it pilgrimage: because in truth we went in all reverence with a pure desire to enjoy ourselves. A day spent happily in the open air, counts, I am sure 'whatever Gods there be'[52] as worship; the air is a Temple in which one is purged of ones sins.

We drove over the Downs, instead of by the road – a straighter, & more interesting way. We saw nobody at all – it was a showery morning – which however, entirely justified the trust we put in it. We passed only those few men & women to whom the openness of the fields is as natural as the enclosure of my room is to me. On the plain itself the only people we passed were shepherds: they drift about in the wide space with their flocks, just as though they were in the Bible; they take advantage of this wet weather too; to add one bold stroke to their appearance which, I as an artist would hesitate to introduce; I should be half afraid of over picturesqueness: they wear long black cloaks reaching down to their heels, & flapping in capes round the shoulders; in one hand too they grasp a real shepherds staff. You may actually see one of these figures lying on his elbow, wrapped in his cloak, his dog lolling out his tongue beside him, & his flock grazing all round.

At the Farm where we put up, we had the rare experience of managing entirely for ourselves – & if you want to feel a fool try to do for yourself what you have always paid a servant to do for you. I have always thought that grooms were an uneducated race – but they might have truthfully laughed at me today. [ ] Everybody ought to know how to unharness a horse – lead him to his stable – fasten him there – & provide him with corn without a moments doubt. Otherwise not only the whole race of grooms but of horses likewise is for the time your superior.

But it was done – & we lunched – & we walked across to Stonehenge, & sat within the Circle. Our choice of a day gave us the whole place to ourselves. The solitary policeman whose strange lot in life it is to mount guard over Stonehenge had taken shelter behind one of his charges. The apoplectic sheep, who can imitate a standing motor car which is still pal-

---

52 'Out of the night that covers me,/Black as the Pit from pole to pole,/I thank whatever gods may be/For my unconquerable soul.' *Echoes*, iv, 'Invictus', 18-21, William Ernest Henley.

pitating to perfection, were grazing outside the Circle, & as far as we could see we had not only Stonehenge, but the whole ocean of plain entirely to ourselves. One can imagine why this spot was chosen by the Druids – or whoever they were – for their Temple to the Sun. It lies very naked to the sun. It is a kind of altar made of earth, on which the whole world might do sacrifice.

THE BEGINNING OF THE STORM

It is easier to write tonight than to sleep. A wind which has been playing about all day, suddenly goes to work in dead earnest. It is battering at my windows pressing them as tight against the frame as possible, & then swerving aside so that the pane released from pressure rattles loose. The wind has a wonderful compass of voices. You can hear it running up & down the scale as it swells in force & dies away. But this is a very full bodied tempestuous wind, not one of those that sing high & drearily without much change of key.

COUNTRY READING

It must be confessed that that boast of reading in the country has not been altogether fulfilled. I was not really happy in my choice of books – & I have brought some which no compulsion will drive me to open while we are here. I have read though, one or two that pleased me – Roderick Hudson[53] to begin with – That is a book which reminds me of an infinitely fine pencil drawing; it lacks colour, it lacks outline, but it is full of exquisite drawing, as an artist would say – & the slightest stroke, you see, has its meaning. You dont get any of that spontaneous & unreflecting pleasure out of it that you do out of the great books, [ ] but you get a marvellous amount of reasoned enjoyment. It is the enjoyment of the intellectual palate tickled by something fine & rare – you need be a little of an epicure to see how very fine & rare it is. [ ] But this isn't an altogether satisfactory style of art.

Next came Hardy – Tess of the D'Urbervilles,[54] which is of a very different type. He has taken a grim subject and stuck to it till the bitter end. It is [ ] written with the purpose of showing how a girl may be as pure as snow, & do things that women may not do – how in spite of her purity, the judgment of a brutal world descends upon her, ruins her life, & sends her to the gallows. All this is set forth with an almost savage in-

---

53 Henry James, *Roderick Hudson*, 1876.
54 Thomas Hardy, *Tess of the D'Urbervilles*, 1891.

sistence; the writer is so sternly determined that we shall see the brutality of certain social conventions that he tends to spoil his novel as a novel. Tess & Clare & D'Urberville have to represent types, & rather lose their individual features. But it is an impressive bit of work – & many things in it are purely admirable – Joan Durbeyfield for instance – the Dairy maids at the Farm, & Hardy is one of the few writers who can bring the fresh air into their books. His country is solid. [ ]

I read here too, Boswells Hebrides[55] – which has fired me to read all I can find of Johnson. What is the receipt I wonder for making such a book as this? Boswell apparently sat up at night – fuddled with wine as likely as not – & wrote down word for word the sayings that had dropped from Johnson's lips during the day. Many people could do this & have done it – but without success. The result is invariably a succession of bald & disconnected sentiments which might have been dropped by an eagle or a mummy. Boswell somehow manages to cut out a whole chunk of the earth & air & stick it all alive under a glass case for us to come & see.

THE STORM

I said something about the wind – the night afterwards it rose indeed, till we had the treat of watching a real gale at work. Much though we talk of our weather & its vicissitudes, we seldom get anything really out of the way in England. There are seldom great thunder storms, great deluges, or real gales. But the other night we went beyond our usual limits; it was a storm & no mistake about it. It rose so quickly that before we thought about it our shutters were banging, & in our little drawing room after dinner we felt in a state of siege. The walls were withstanding great pressure; & though we sat inside in still air the strain was perceptible. It was not a gusty wind, that blows & swerves aside; it was a high roaring wind all on the same key, & at the same pitch.

It never loosened its grasp – It would have been impossible for anyone to go out of doors – one thought of those who were on the roads tonight with honest pity. By midnight – we went to bed late knowing that sleep under such conditions would not be easy – one looked out of the window & saw the moon stationary; but all between it & the earth in a state of violent motion – clouds pelting along, & the trees writhing. [ ] The noise all the time was considerable – first the steady rush of the wind itself – then countless bangs & slams & creaks, as though all the

---

55 James Boswell, *Boswell's Journal of a Tour to the Hebrides with Samuel Johnson, 1773*, 1785.

doors & windows were being tested, & wrenched open & slammed shut again – & every now & again, there was another sound – a crack audible above the tumult, followed on one occasion by an alarming assault upon our window panes, as though something hard had stricken them. We saw that they were un-broken – fastened our shutters again – & went to bed. This went on through the night – when we woke the storm was passed, & it was bright daylight.

But it had done its work in the night. The whole place looked dishevelled; the front of our house was ripped of its creepers – the road was strewn with branches & leaves – the hedges & the flower beds were beaten flat. But it had done more than this. It had rooted out the very trees. A great sycamore, weighted with foliage had gone down before it & had fallen right across our lawn, crushing a wooden paling beneath it.

That was the first thing we saw – but when we went outside our gates we found that there was ruin everywhere. Fifteen trees nearly round our house were uprooted, & almost every tree had a great gash down its side where a branch had been torn off. The worse damage though was done in the Lombardy Poplar Avenue; this is one of the most beautiful things about here – the trees are very tall, & regular, & silver in stem & silver in leaf as they are, they make a kind of silver arch. Now there were gaps in the perfect succession of the avenue as five of the great trees lay flat bridging the river at their side. For such tall & stately trees they have extraordinarily little grip on the earth: their roots seemed only to be a few feet deep, so that they had fallen over with very little rending of the earth at their base.

All along the Wilton road there were fallen trees – fallen branches – & bricks from the wall. By afternoon men were at work sawing up the larger trees & putting them on carts, while the smaller branches were being plundered by children & old women with wheelbarrows to serve for winter firing –

The newspapers are now in, with a good many columns devoted to the 'Great Storm'.[56] In truth, it did a good nights work. It smashed Dover pier for instance, & blew away 70,000 pounds worth of good gold – every town almost woke to find some house or spire gone – & many men & women over England never saw the day after that night.

---

56 'An extremely violent south-westerly gale, accompanied by heavy rains, caused many shipping disasters, with considerable loss of life, and did immense damage to the Kentish hop gardens and to ungathered crops in many districts of England, Wales, and Ireland . . .' 10 September, *Annual Register*.

Never a storm comes – never do thunder & lightning wake me in the night, but some life, as unwitting as mine, is ended. There are many families today who will never forget – as I shall do so soon – the stormy night of September the tenth.

WILTON FAIR

Had I had time a full account, reaching to several pages of my best script should have preserved my memory of this our last entertainment. Nothing that I have seen since we came here has been so characteristic I feel of this part of the world. But I have let time slip, & must not for the sake of that truth which I make my aim here, attempt much in the way of description.

I remember though that our drive the day before, Friday [September] 11th, took us on to the Downs, & we observed an unusual commotion among the population of flocks. They were all attended by shepherds in their best Sunday clothes – & dogs too, who looked more than usually alert. Some were driven into their pens to feed, others were being hounded out – but the greater part of the flocks were marching along the road, all with their noses turned in the same direction. We met drove after drove, so closely packed in the lane that we wondered how on earth we were to pass. The shepherd whistled his dog, shouted something unintelligible to us, but at once understood by the dog, who clove a passage for us in an incredibly short time.

Every now & then we met a drove of calves – & the secret was out when a terrible puffing ahead, as of a goods train going at foots pace, proclaimed a traction engine. There were two of these monsters. Somebodys Steam Circus, it turned out – & these were followed by a whole caravan of gipsies. Next day was Wilton fair – These gipsies travel the country, from fair to fair, all through the summer. They are, we were told, the genuine breed, talkers of Romany & all the rest, who under pretence of earning a livelihood at fairs like the respectable world, live their own gipsy life, which is otherwise impossible. I never see a gipsy cart without longing to be inside it. A house that is rooted to no one spot but can travel as quickly as you change your mind, & is complete in itself is surely the most desirable of houses. Our modern house with its cumbersome walls & its foundations planted deep in the ground is nothing better than a prison; [ ] & more & more prison like does it become the longer we live there & wear fetters of association & sentiment, painful to wear – still more painful to break.

The fair itself is the greatest sheep fair[57] in this part of the Kingdom. It brings the shepherds from their downs – the farmers from their far away farms – & the country folk from all the villages within a days journey. It is thus a remarkable day in the calendar – a day of social meeting as well as of business. You could see here a very curious type of face – that of the shepherd who passes his life with his flocks on the down. He is far more interesting to observe than his sheep. His face is not coarsened; & yet is not the face of a man who has mixed with his fellow men; it is the face of a middle aged man but it has the freshness & simplicity of a childs. The eye is perfectly clear & shrewd; the face is tanned red & brown, & creased with a multitude of fine lines, but it is easy to see that they have come there when the eyes are screwed to observe the weather, or the brow is puckered against the wind – & have nothing whatever to do with any mental perplexity. His best coat is a relic of a more festive age, [ ] & is a rich chestnut, or plum colour, grown mellow with years; he wears corduroy breeches, a large felt hat, & he grasps a staff in his hand high up near the top. A more typically English figure I imagine it would be hard to find than this Wiltshire down shepherd.

OUT OF THE WINDOWS

The last night here has come – is almost fulfilled. I have but to put my head on the pillow – sleep & wake tomorrow within 3 hours of London. The journey is not to be measured by its miles; it is a very small journey, but one of great actual & traditional importance to us. Of old it meant still more; we ended the summer on that day, & opened the 9 months in London which were to be in some sort months of lessons & restraint. St. Ives was summer & holiday. It can be imagined that this was a very serious anniversary. Now it has lost much of its meaning – I find that time goes swifter as one gets older, & is less liable to fall into cycles according to the place you live in. But still I know that in some sense our summer is over. We leave the country till Easter – that is a really sad thought – for this country is beautiful as any country is, & has a [*Next page is missing.*]

LONDON

We are back – here I sit in my own room, where I have sat & slept since babyhood almost. It has a new red carpet – otherwise it remains the same, & I would not have it changed.

---

57 At the Wilton Great Fair held in September, over 100,000 sheep changed hands annually.

It is shameful to confess that two obstacles hindered any properly sentimental farewell this morning – one was our lunch, devoured in the train – the other the newspaper which we all read steadily as we eat. There are all manner of excitements – how deep they delve I do not know, but they agitate the surface considerably. Political statements I find are far the hardest to understand, partly I think because the politician as a rule has not studied the art of making his case plain in print. But anyhow there is no need to go into this. What is more to the point here, is that it was a perfect autumn morning – rich & warm & regretful, one of the few hot days this summer. When we got to London the heat which had room to expand in the country, was stuffy merely: the superficial impression of London was that it was in deshabille – sleeping off the fatigues of the season. The people in the street had a curious look of being only passing through: cabs with boxes were more numerous than cabs without. A London house feels undeniably small & stuffed after the country – but we shall shake down. Already Netherhampton fades, but I hope not beyond recall.

London (continued)[58]

London it must be confessed, is like a Lady whom one surprises in her dressing gown; she is not at her best. It is vexatious too, to find that the summer is in full swing; the only compensation for leaving the country at this time of year is the prospect of fires & long dark evenings spent within doors – evenings lightened perhaps by the visits of friends, & anyhow made pleasant in a thousand civilised ways which one misses in the country. But fires today would have been unbearable; in fact we wore our summer clothes. We walked in the gardens – where the trees have come down too. It is not to the credit of the storm to have knocked over these decayed old fogies – whose flesh has turned to a brown spongy substance, while their bark is a mere crust of soot. The earth which they dug up as they fell is barren & dusty looking – evidently not a nourishing soil.

But the worst of the Kensington Gardens are the people. There is a brood which comes out at these between seasons which is mercifully unknown at others. It is not indigenous; these are not cockneys – it is not upper lower or middle class. I can only imagine that September is the month when country people & foreigners choose to visit London. [ ] A small boy trotted up to us & began patting Schusters unresponsive

_____
58 AVS's annotation.

back; we asked if he had a dog? Yes, he answered at once, I have one to my home – "Where was his home?" "In America" – 'naturally' & he'd been in England 2 months & 14 months in Antwerp – & the astonishing child was prepared to give us his whole family history without hesitation. An English boy of the same age, if addressed by strangers, gazes at you for half a minute with a shy smile, & then trots away to his mother. But it doesn't seem to occur to him that an answer is expected – This American child, I make no doubt, would have been an appalling bore had one seen much of him – & he had a curiously unchildlike face already –

THE SERPENTINE

The evening paper is always prolific in tragedies & tonight's sheet was unusually so. Four young men all in the prime of life have fallen & killed themselves on Scafell[59] – the average number of husbands have murdered their wives while in drink or out of it, & love sick shop girls & maniacs have rushed to their knives & poison pots with unusual frequency. One might easily have sated one's horrid curiosity & passed without reading a certain insignificant little paragraph at the bottom of the column. 'A Suicides pathetic letter'[60] I think they headed it – & in my idleness I read. It was by no means an out of the way story & the Editor had judged his readers taste judiciously when he allotted his capitals to the Yarmouth murder.[61] This was printed I daresay for lack of something more blood curdling.

But I read it & it has stuck in my memory so that I can write it here. Yesterday morning then, the first Park Keepers saw something afloat in the Serpentine – *What* it needed little looking to tell. Bodies in the Serpentine are not uncommon in the early morning. They drew it ashore &

---

59 Four climbers fell to their death while ascending Scafell Pike in the Lake District on 21 September 1903.

60 From the *Evening News and Evening Mail*, p.3, col.2, 23 September 1903: 'PATHETIC LETTER. No evidence of identification was offered at the Westminster Coroner's-court this forenoon, in the case of the woman whose dead body was found floating in the Serpentine. The woman was poorly dressed, and her hat, shoes, and stockings were found hanging on the rails near the Serpentine. The only articles found on her were a small pencil and a piece of paper on which was written: "No father, no mother, no work. I do hope the Lord will help me. I do hope to be forgiven for what I have done." There were no marks of violence on the body, but, "Found dead" was the verdict of the jury. Mr. Troutbeck, the coroner, commented: "That is your verdict, gentlemen, but I do not agree with it." (The Serpentine is the curling artifical lake stretching diagonally across Hyde Park and Kensington Gardens.)

61 See Appendix C.

found that it was a woman who had been drowned, drowned herself presumably some hours before. She was quite dead, & there was nothing to be done but take her to the mortuary & leave her for her relations to identify. Her soaked clothes were taken off, & the pockets searched in case her name or address might be found there. Very few people go out of the world in silence; almost every dead man or woman who is picked up has written some word of apology or farewell or justification. The most friendless knows that some one – if only the coroner – will be curious to learn what drove him to this last step – & it was so in this case. A scrap of paper was found pinned to the inside of her dress as though she had meant to keep it from the water as long as possible. It was blurred but the writing was still legible. Her last message to the world – whatever its import, was short – so short that I can remember it. 'No father, no mother, no work' she had written 'May God forgive me for what I have done tonight'. This was her message & no more; name or dwelling place, friend or relation, she had none apparently. The inquest therefore could do nothing but declare that the body of an unknown woman age about 45 had been found drowned, & that as no relation claimed it it was to have burial at the hands of the parish. Here the newspaper ended – but I could not get the words out of my head. 'No father, no mother, no work,' & so she killed herself. Had this been the act & writing of a girl it would have been sad enough – but that a woman of 45 should have written this for testament struck me as infinitely sadder. She had had her trial in life, time enough in 45 years to make test of all human relationships – daughterhood, wifehood, motherhood. Whether she knew these two last we cannot say – happiest for her if she had never known them – for last night she counted them as nothing. It was for her father & mother that this middle aged woman yearned – a father & mother, maybe, who died when she was a child. Perhaps this was so & she grew to womanhood without them, & without needing them. She became a wife without thought of her parents, & a mother with hardly any memory of her own mother. But her husband leaves her for some other woman, & her children die, or desert her. Then of a sudden comes that pang – Without husband or children, I yet had parents. If they were alive now I should not be alone. Whatever my sin my father & mother would have given me protection & comfort. For the first time in her life perhaps she weeps for her parents & for the first time knows all that they were, & her loneliness without them. That sorrow I say is bitter enough in youth with the world before one & its promise; but in middle age one knows that the loss is one that nothing can heal & no fresh tie renew. Your husband may die & you can marry another – your children may die & others may be born to you, but if your father & mother die you have lost something that the longest life can never bring again.

It was something of this perhaps that the nameless woman thought before she made up her mind to kill herself. But there was one thing left which might make life endurable – without father or mother or other relation to care if she lived or died, & that was work. I do not believe that she coupled this word with the sacred names of father & mother in any merely material sense – by work she meant bread & butter, but she also meant something nobler. She had learnt perhaps the self respect & purity that come from work, & the blessed peace with which it deadens sorrow. Before she died then she would try to find work. I do not know where she went in her search; perhaps she came near this very street. But it is very easy to deny a strange woman work, who threatens to kill herself if you refuse. [ ] At any rate she found no work, as one may read in the bitter line which water cannot efface 'No father, no mother, no work' What then remained? There was still one scruple – one tie which kept her to life; though she had no home, no friends & no one would give her work, yet had she any right to lift the burden God had set upon her shoulders? She hesitated – but it was very heavy. She gave way, with a last appeal for mercy on her weakness. 'May God forgive me for what I have done tonight' Then slipping off the weight that had been too much for her, she sank in the waters. Whoever she is that sleeps tonight in a grave without a name, may she sleep well, as surely the tired have right to sleep.

Chance, who not infrequently decides our lives has decreed, there is no doubting it, that the end of my book shall coincide with our return to London. The first of October, wrote J.K.S.[62] is the natural birth of the year – whatever the calendar says; & so I take it. October begins work & pleasure lifts the curtain on that particular act of our drama which is played in London. Actors may change – their parts may be different but the sameness of scene gives a certain continuity to the whole, & does in fact influence our lives to no little extent.

---

62 AVS's first cousin, James Kenneth Stephen (1859-92), second son of Mary and James Fitzjames Stephen and a favourite nephew of Leslie Stephen; he was a gifted versifier and journalist who died in an asylum. Many years later AVS would write in *The Years*, 1937 (Kp A22), 'For it was October, the birth of the year' (London, p. 96; New York, p. 91).

Christmas 1904 to May 1905

When the family returned to London in September 1903, it was clear that Leslie Stephen's death was near. In November, when he had no longer the strength to write, he dictated to Virginia the last pages of his Mausoleum Book, *the autobiography begun shortly after Julia Stephen's death in May 1895. The final entry was a valediction to his children. He died at home on 22 February 1904. On 10 May, Virginia, now aged twenty-two, descended for a second time into the nightmare world of madness. At first she was under the care of Dr Savage and three nurses, and was later removed to Violet Dickinson's house, Burnham Wood, near Welwyn, where, for almost three months, she was cared for by Nurse Traill. It was here that she made her first suicide attempt.*

In October, after the summer holiday with her family in Teversal, Virginia went to Cambridge to convalesce with her aunt Caroline Emelia Stephen, and here the best possible restorative came to her from Frederic Maitland, who was working on the authorised Life and Letters of Leslie Stephen *(1906). Would Virginia read through her father and mother's letters and mark off passages he might quote? Would she also write a brief account of Sir Leslie's last years with his children to include in the biography? One has only to read through her letters of this period to see how Maitland's request made her once again feel useful and valued. As she helped to preserve the memory of her father, her own life became revitalised.*

During Virginia's convalescence in Cambridge, Vanessa and Thoby organised the move from 22 Hyde Park Gate to their new home at 46 Gordon Square, Bloomsbury. It was here in November that Violet Dickinson proposed that Virginia write for Mrs Margaret Lyttelton, editor of the Women's Supplement of The Guardian. *On 7 and 14 December, her first two book reviews were published, and on 21 December, an essay on the Brontë Parsonage at Haworth. At last Virginia was earning money by her pen. She had lost her mother. She had lost her father. But she had found work. In that sense, 1904 was the last of the 'seven unhappy years'. She went with her sister and brothers to the New Forest for Christmas a changed young woman, and when she returned in January Dr Savage pronounced her well enough to resume a normal life.*

New Forest   Christmas 1904[1]
Each blade of grass with a white line of frost on it.

The sunset makes all the air as though of melted amethyst; yellow flakes dissolve from the solid body of amethyst which is the west. Against this, standing as though in an ocean of fine air, the bare trees are deep black lines, as though drawn in Indian ink which has dried dull & indelible. The small branches & twigs make a fringe of infinitely delicate lines, each one distinctly cut against the sky. The highest tips of the branches are russet, & so is the top of the trunk, in the red sun light. The trees stand round in a circle, & in their midst is a kind of little stage of grass & heather-bog where it is greenest in which a pastoral play might be acted. Then the trees close together again, with pathways radiating at intervals to the open space – The trees have green velvet jackets of moss. This the brightest colour in the landscape. A peach bloom of silver & plum colour covers the trees at a little distance. Also a pale green lichen, seaweed like in its shape, covers the bark. The trees very often spread their branches into a symmetrical fan shape as though they had been clipped by a landscape gardener. A river in summer is as though made of plates of translucent glass, the top one of which slides. Mystery of sound reaching one through the trees; the distant music of hounds running. The note of the huntsmans horn, & far away voices of men shouting, all sound as in some distant romantic dream; as though falling through an ocean of waters.

The stone window frames at Kings[2] are iridescent like a butterfly's wing when the sun shines through the stained glass.

---

1 The four young Stephens stayed at Lane End, Bank, Lyndhurst, Hampshire, lent to them by Sarah Duckworth (Aunt Minna). AVS published an essay on Priory Church, Christchurch, at the edge of the New Forest, in *The Guardian*, 26 July 1905 (Kp C2.03) and reprinted in *VW Essays*, I.
2 King's House was the former residence of the Lord Warden of the New Forest.

This is at any rate a cheerful New Years day, as though we had turned over a new leaf & swept the sky clean of clouds. It was clear with frost at the turn of the night, when the New Year came in with the new day. T. & A. went out, with rum punch in their hands, to salute 1905; they shouted, & declare that innumerable owls answered them. This may be true, because on soft nights when I lie with my window open, I hear the mellow call of owls repeated again & again at no great distance, & the crude holloa of a baby owl, who has still to learn the call of an owl.

The afternoon was a beautiful specimen of winter light; the air as clear as though sheets of glass had been dissolved into atmosphere & all the colours were lively & delicate.

2 January
A cold silent day: Snow flakes dropping quietly, which by degrees turned to falling rain.

I went out into the forest in the afternoon; found it all still & dun coloured, rain pattering through the leaves, & the ponies[1] standing up against the trees for shelter. All the same, wonderful modulations of colour.

3 January
Bright morning: sad coloured afternoon, in which however we walked, & bogged ourselves, & cursed the mud, & could not look at the trees – which by the way, purple day by day. After screwing out fine-drawn theories about trees for 3 hours, I am not going to make more here. It may be my hopeful imagination – but I decidedly smell spring in the air. The dark doesn't fall like a knife in the early afternoon – & the spring is youthful & a time of hope & stir in the blood. I feel as though old man winter had a spark in him now.

Read, wrote, cursed, & walked – all as usual.

4 January
Home at 5.30 today. Not a bright day in the forest; so sunless in London, though clear at dusk when we reached Waterloo. Passed over the river, & saw the shores of either side spangled with the lights of London, like a Japanese print.

No letters of interest – nothing but a tune on the pianola, a Watts pic-

---

1   Indigenous New Forest wild ponies.

ture[2] to hang, & an air of great cleanliness & emptiness. J[ulian] T[hoby] S[tephen] walking via Winchester to Hindhead.[3]

5 January

A London day. That is to say only narrow strip of sky to be looked at, no bird noises, no sighings & moanings of trees & green growing things – no splash of water – only the interminable roar & rattle & confusion of wheels & voices. All this neighbourhood has asphalt, which does sensibly increase the noise. But ones mind "grows mouldy in the country" – Here at any rate one has no excuse for a speck of rust. Typewrote, read, & sent off several dull letters.

6 January

A rainy day, for the most part I think, but all the morning I spent making a large paper book[4] for the New Year. May its leaves bear fruit worth having! Then at 12 I dashed out to get a key for my clock, & to negotiate about a handle for my new black stick, bought at Christchurch. This will cost me 5s! Wilful extravagance! Home, to find the silver point press arrived – N. & A. already grimy & deep in mechanism.

Printed our first plates after lunch – & with success, though my book plate needs to be improved. Tea with Miss Sheepshanks,[5] a large kindly & rather able sort of woman. I am to start a girls club at Morley, & talk about books &c!

7 January

Morning rather vague; book plate printing I think, I achieved a passable

2 Probably the portrait of Julia Stephen, by G. F. Watts, referred to by Leslie Stephen in *The Mausoleum Book*, ed. A. Bell (Oxford, 1977), p. 32; it later hung at Charleston.

3 In a letter from Thoby to Leonard Woolf, dated 15 January 1905: 'I was in the New Forest at Christmas, where I got some hunting . . . From there I walked to Hindhead and stayed some days with Pollock. There were there J. Pollock . . . Waterlow . . . Meredith . . . and old [Clive] Bell': Leonard Woolf, *Sowing*, (Readers Union Edition), 1962, p. 106.

4 Presumably to write her book reviewing notes in; see B. Silver, *Virginia Woolf's Reading Notes*, 1983.

5 Mary Sheepshanks (*c.* 1870-1958), effective principal of Morley College, 1899-1913, an evening institute in South London for working people, where AVS taught a weekly class for about two years.

rose & bud[6] which now adorns my lovely new copy of [Edward] Fitz-gerald – Silverpoint is very kind to amateur drawing, & gives tone & depth where there aint any in the original. Today, I think N. & I went to the Academy Watts exhibition[7] which is weak & worthless – almost in-credibly so, considering his reputation. Not a single first rate picture there, & many 5th rate. His "ideas" here swamped his art. In the even-ing to Morley College soirée in the Waterloo Road: where I discussed a class with nice enthusiastic working women who say they love books. These people are refreshing after the educated. G[eorge]. Trevelyan[8] made a dull & raucous speech.

8 January
A white & gray day – the colour of Gurth[9] as we observed when we took him out in the afternoon – All the morning I worked at a death mask of Shakespeare, which is to make a book plate in his works – made something dimly like – elongated & cadaverous. Anyhow, I have stuck it in. A. away with B.R.[10] beagling. T. away at Hindhead; so N. & I im-proved our solitude by more or less heated arguments, about all kinds of things. Walked in Regents Park in the afternoon, a great gusty wind, tasting of country moors, set all our London petticoats flying. In the evening I worked at copy of a Greek Tanagra figure,[11] for a silver point book plate – a difficult job.

---

6 '. . . Nessa has bought a silver point press, and these are my first attempts; one is a rose . . . the other is a copy of Shakespeare's death mask! . . .': *VW Letters*, I, No. 209; see illustrations in Diane F. Gillespie, *The Sisters' Arts* (Syracuse, 1988), pp. 29, 30.
7 The Royal Academy of Art was exhibiting the works of G. F. Watts and Frederick Sandys.
8 George Macaulay Trevelyan (1876-1962), Fellow of Trinity College, Cambridge; probably the 'dull' speech he gave at Morley College as part of the Conference of London County Council of Teachers, 7 January 1905.
9 Gurth replaced Shag who had died in early December 1904; see AVS's essay 'On a Faithful Friend', published in *The Guardian*, 18 January 1905 (Kp C04) and reprinted in *VW Essays*, I.
10 Possibly William (Billy) Thackeray Denis Ritchie; see July 1897, n.18.
11 A small terracotta statuette, often representing a person of fashion; such figures were discovered in ancient tombs, principally in Tanagra, a hill town in Boeotia, and were prized by collectors.

9 January

Began, being Monday, work on the note for Fred M[aitland]:[12] which I mean to do as well as I can, & to which at present I shall give my mornings. Wrote a few pages: difficulties will come later. So far smooth, & delightful writing – It remains to be seen what stuff it is tomorrow morning.

Went down to the London Library this P.M. & consulted C.B. Clarke[13] about the sketches from Cambridge. They *do* possess a copy, wrongly catalogued. Question of its suppression not settled, but I think a most unlikely story. Windy, watery weather, all gray & turbulent – which I like. T. & A. back. Tea together. Now I dine with Violet [Dickinson].[14] Finished, thank God, with judicious skipping Mrs Grs. Town life in the 15th Cent.,[15] a learned but not masterly book; too many illustrations & not enough continuity to make good reading for any but specialists.

10 January

Found this morning on my plate my first instalment of wages – £2.7.6. for Guardian articles,[16] which gave me great pleasure. Also a book "Women in America"[17] for review, so that means more work, & cheques ultimately. Wrote at the Note for Fred all the morning, bringing it down to 1897: I shall finish sooner than I thought, as I know what I want to say, & have not much difficulty in saying it. I can only hope it

---

12 Frederic W. Maitland (1850-1906), Downing Professor of the Laws of England at Cambridge, and Sir Leslie Stephen's friend and biographer; he was married to Florence, the eldest of AVS's Fisher cousins.

13 Charles Baron Clarke (1832-1906), botanist and mathematician, settled in Kew upon retiring from work in India in 1877; a friend and contemporary of Leslie Stephen at Cambridge. AVS was presumably in search of 'Sketches from Cambridge – by a Don,' i.e. by Leslie Stephen, published first in *The Pall Mall Gazette* and reprinted in 1865 by Macmillan & Co.

14 See April 1897, n.3.

15 Alice Stopford Green, *Town Life in the Fifteenth Century*, 1894.

16 Reviews in *The Guardian*, 7 December 1904, of *Social England: a Record of the Progress of the People . . . By various writers*, ed. H. D. Traill and J. S. Mann, 6 vols., 1901-4; on 14 December 1904 (Kp C01) of *The Son of Royal Langbrith* by W. D. Howells; and an essay published on 21 December 1904 (Kp C02), 'Haworth, November, 1904', all three reprinted in *VW Essays*, I, where the first is listed under 'Apocrypha' in Appendix II.

17 *The Women of America* by Elizabeth McCracken, reviewed in *The Guardian* on 31 May 1905; see *VW Essays*, I.

will turn out well. Then took some prints from a new plate. Tea with Mrs Crum,[18] to whom I walked. Discussed the Morley College scheme, & settled to get Savages[19] advice first, as to my capabilities of work at present. Otherwise, to wait till October to begin. Mrs. H. Ward,[20] curiously, wrote to suggest Passmore Edwards work to N. & me, but I have a valid excuse!

Worked at Spanish,[21] which is really easy so far, & I expect easy to read, but talking is another matter.

11 January

N. to Cambridge for the day. The somewhat exacting demand of Nun.[22] Wrote at the Note all the morning, not altogether easy – & it expands under my hands, so it will be longer & take longer than I thought at first. No hurry however. Then dashed out into Oxford Street, to the old book shops, which fascinate me; lunch with A: out again to get glass cut for my autograph letters which I mean to frame myself. A poor old woman, blind, trustfully quavering out her song by the roadside in hope of coppers,[23] while the traffic went thundering by. Gerald to tea, brisk, & cheerful. N. in later. Chintz come to our excitement. Spanish &c. much as usual.

12 January

Wrote this morning, much as usual. At 12.30 a motor sent by Margaret[24]

18 Ella Crum, a daughter of Sir Edward Sieveking, and her husband Walter, living at 33 Manchester Street, W, were friends of Violet Dickinson; Mrs Crum held an unpaid administrative position at Morley College.

19 Dr George Savage (1842-1921), a prominent physician who specialised in the treatment of mental disorders; he was a friend of the Stephen family and treated AVS during her 1904 breakdown.

20 Mrs Humphry Ward was the moving force behind the foundation of the social and educational Settlement opened in Bloomsbury in 1897 and named after John Passmore Edwards (1823-1911), the radical philanthropist.

21 In preparation for her excursion, with Adrian, to Portugal and Spain from 29 March to 23 April 1905.

22 Leslie Stephen's sister, Caroline Emelia Stephen (1834-1909), at whose home, the Porch in Cambridge, AVS convalesced in the autumn of 1904.

23 Cf. passage in *Mrs Dalloway*, 1925 (Kp A9): '. . . this battered old woman with one hand exposed for her coppers, the other clutching her side, would still be there in ten million years . . .' (London, pp. 91-2; New York, pp. 123-4).

24 Lady Margaret Herbert (1870-1958), daughter of the 4th Earl of Carnarvon; she had married George Duckworth on 10 September 1904.

came to take us out, so we had to invent errands, & go whizzing through the streets, swinging under horses noses, & swerving round the corners, like a skater doing outside edge – pretty, doubtless, but perilous. A. out to lunch. I took Gurth to Regents Park for a walk; but Regents Park has none of the charm of Kensington Gardens – no good trees, or hidden places – flat open stretches of grass, where you never lose sight of houses. Read my review book, which might have been better. Finished the life of Morris[25] – a very interesting book, & a great man – so much superior as a genius to B. J.[26] but curiously inhuman.

Nessa dining with J[ack]. W[aller]. H[ills].

13 January

Wrote all the morning, rather laboriously. Went out for my usual tramp, which seems to resolve itself into a tramp down to the old book shops, where I look but dont buy anything. After lunch I made some frames for my letters: George Eliot, James Thomson[27] & Lowells verses are done now, & stand on my mantelpiece; rather successfully. Out to my walking stick shop, where I saw it with a lovely silver head, which moved even the old Jew lady to artistic emotions – not yet engraved however. I walked to the Library, asked for Fred's American books,[28] which aren't in – got a book about the relations of poetry & music, which may come in useful for my Morley lectures, if I give them. Then to Violets;[29] sat & talked for a time; found her full of ideas & news. Anthony Harte[30] is her own writing! Home: Will [Vaughan][31] & Gerald to tea. Will on his way through. Read at my review book which I hope to finish tonight.

---

25 John William Mackail, *The Life of William Morris*, 1899.

26 Edward Burne-Jones, see Jan. 1897, n.16 and Feb. 1897, n.13.

27 James Thomson (1700-48), poet.

28 Probably books by or about Leslie Stephen's friends and associates that Maitland needed in writing the *Life*.

29 Violet Dickinson lived in Manchester Street, W.

30 *These Thoughts Were Written by [Anthony] Hart* was inscribed: 'A Tract for the Sp[arrows] fr[om] V[iolet]. D[ickinson].'; see Holleyman & Treacher, *Catalogue of the Books from the Library of Leonard and Virginia Woolf* (Brighton, 1975), V/s, II, p. 6 and *VW Letters*, I, No. 210.

31 AVS's cousin, William Wyamar Vaughan (1865-1938) had married Margaret (Madge) Symonds (1869-1925) on 28 July 1898, and was now Headmaster of Giggleswick School, Settle, Yorkshire.

14 January

Wrote at my review, which is difficult because of the space allowed, only 600 words & many things to put into it. But at 11 to Savage, who was well satisfied, thinks me 'normal' & able to return to all my usual ways, going out, work, &c – so that horrible long illness which began in the 2nd week of April last year,[32] is now fairly put away, & I need think no more of it – for which the Lord be praised! I may do my working women once a week, so I must cudgel my brains for a lecture – finished my review. Nessa lunched with G[eorge]. & M[argaret].: Thoby & I went to the International,[33] which is full of cleverness, & affectation, then I went on to Miss Sheepshanks, to tell her I will come on Wednesday. Typewrote some things for Kitty to see,[34] & the evening much as usual. Began After London, by Jeffries [*sic*],[35] which seems an imaginative & interesting book so far –

15 January   *Sunday*

Finished typewriting some things to show Kitty this morning, which Nessa took to her. Then began to read Eugenie Grandet,[36] in the 1s. paper edition which I bought at Haworth Station,[37] when I wanted to buy Charlotte Brontë! The cover got so torn in my coat pocket that I decided to bind it before reading it: so I cut it up, & sewed it strongly, & gave it a good blue paper cover, & put it in the Press & it is now a nice looking & strongly bound book. Gerald & a youth called Burn Murdoch[38] to lunch: after which I left for the Queens Hall Concert: a stale programme, which did not much interest me.[39] Home; & wrote several

---

32 AVS was in Italy in April 1904; Dr Savage was called in on 10 May 1904, after her return.

33 At the New Gallery, 121 Regent Street, W; The International was an exhibition of art works from various countries, including Spain, Italy, France, Holland and England.

34 Probably the Note for Maitland as well as a draft of 'Street Music' for Kitty's husband Leo Maxse, editor and owner of the *National Review*, 1893-1932; they lived at 33 Cromwell Road, SW. Also see *VW Letters*, I, No. 216.

35 Richard Jefferies, *After London; or Wild England*, 1885.

36 Honoré de Balzac, *Eugénie Grandet*, 1833.

37 Haworth, the home of the Brontës, in Yorkshire, which AVS had visited while staying with the Vaughans in November 1904.

38 Probably Hector Burn-Murdoch (b.1881), Trinity College, Cambridge, admitted at the Inner Temple, 1904, and later lectured on English Law at Edinburgh University, 1912-14 and 1919-22.

39 Sunday Afternoon Concert; the Queen's Hall Orchestra conducted by Henry Wood performed works by Wagner, Grieg, Mendelssohn, Tchaikovsky and Berlioz.

dull letters, one long one to Fred, & paid bills, & sent Mrs L[yttelton]. my review, which is carefully done, but too long, as usual.[40] A north wind sweeping the streets, & frost –

16 January   *Monday*

Wrote all the morning on my "lecture" for the Working women, & chose Prose as my subject, which does not commit me to anything. It amuses me rather to write, as I can say what I like, without fear of criticism, and the subject interests me – but Heaven knows if it will interest them. This day was the coldest of the year, & colder in London, 20 something degrees of frost than elsewhere. The wind was dry & biting, & the streets slippery with sleet. However I went to the walking stick shop, which still hasn't done my job. A telegram from Kitty to ask me to dine, which I did, driving through white & gleaming streets. Kitty alone – asked me to write for the Nat[ional Review]: on the strength of the things shown her by Nessa – which I shall be very glad to do. Mr Chirol[41] of the Times is reading my things, with a possible view to asking me to write for the T[imes]. [Literary] Supplement. K. very charming.

17 January   *Tuesday*

Finished my Prose lecture, which must still be written out, as I cant trust myself to speak from memory – & with writing before me I cant go far wrong.

Nessa lunched with Violet. I was seized with a passion for rearranging my bedroom, so I turned the bed round &c: & hung pictures, & now it is fairly straight & to my liking – Madge, by the way, turned up before lunch, & I drove with her to the station, where Thank God, I did *not* get in to the train. I prowled round book shops in the Charing X road, all the afternoon & saw many things, which, were my purse obliging, I would get. Paston Letters,[42] Rabelais, & James Thomson. If I am taken on by the Times I shall think myself justified –, & I use my books. Adrian to

---

40 The review of *Women in America* turned out to be over 800 words rather than the 600 requested.

41 Sir Valentine Chirol (1852-1929), journalist, and head of the foreign department of *The Times*; AVS's first review for the *TLS* would appear on 10 March 1905 (see below).

42 *The Paston Letters*, 1422-1509, ed. J. Gairdner, 1904, 6 vols; see 'The Pastons and Chaucer', in *The Common Reader: First Series*, 1925, 1984 (Kp A8).

Cambridge: Invitation to dine with Crums to meet B. Richmond[43] of the Times!

18 January
Wrote all the morning at the [Maitland] Note which is within sight of the end. Heard that Mrs Lyttelton likes my review, which is as well. Snow[44] to sit to Nessa, to lunch & by the way to tea. Tisdall [Dentist] at 3 – Got books from the L[ondon]. [L[ibrary]. Then had a tooth sawn off in T's arm chair, preparatory to crowning – d —— it all! Then took Thoby's watch to Dent[45] – called for my walking stick, which is ready but wont be delivered till I produce the ready money – bother the old Jewess – who cant be an Artist after all, or she would take my cheques on trust. Home to tea – wrote & read after tea till dinner at 7.30 – after which drove – 10 minutes only it takes in a cab – to Morley, where I waited 15 minutes alone in a great dreary room with tables & chairs & flaring gas jets – meditating how on earth to discuss Sir T[homas]. Browne under these conditions & two women – nice & intelligent – came finally, but were readier to talk than listen.

19 January
Wrote all the morning at the Note – then changed & lunched with Elena Rathbone,[46] where we met a Miss White (artist)[47] & Mrs. Rathbone. We asked Elena to dine before the Booths dance[48] – then our motor (lent by George) came round & we executed a series of brilliantly successful calls – At. Anny – At. Mary. Palgraves, Hunts or Freshfields[49] – all, sans

43 Bruce Lyttelton Richmond (1871-1964), editor of the *TLS* from 1902-37.
44 Margery ('Snow') Snowden (1878-1966), artist, studied painting at the Royal Academy Schools with Vanessa and became a close friend.
45 Dent's, watchmakers, Pall Mall.
46 Elena Rathbone (1878-1964), the future wife of Bruce Richmond; Mrs Rathbone was her mother.
47 Probably Florence White, artist, of 9 Boltons Studios, Redcliffe Road, SW; she was a member of the Society of Women Artists and exhibited between 1881-1932 at the Royal Academy and other prominent galleries.
48 Mary and Charles Booth, living at 24 Great Cumberland Place, W.
49 Anne and Richmond Ritchie of 109 St George's Square, SW; Mary Fisher, 3 Onslow Square, SW; Francis Palgrave (1824-97), editor of the *Golden Treasury of Songs and Lyrics*, 1846; the Palgraves lived at 15 Cranley Place, SW; Edith and Holman Hunt, 18 Melbury Road, W; Augusta and Douglas Freshfield, 179 Airlie Gardens, Kensington, W.

Palgraves who were nice – out – so we force feed those dunning bills.[50]
Home, & Violet & Jack to tea. Jack to stand for Durham,[51] where A.
Elliott now is – that is if chosen as candidate, which he apparently will
be. Elena to dine; Adrian up from Cambridge – At Grosv[enor] Sq
having had my hair done by the family & Nessas being done by a hair
dresser. We all went on to the Booths, where were gathered the usual
representatives of a certain set, who are for the most part amiable but
dull. Danced till 2 & then home.

20 January

Up late, but wrote all the morning. I finished the Note, which fills 34
pages of hand writing: it is corrected for typing, which I must now do, &
then I shall be better able to judge – After lunch went to Tisdall, who
hurt me quite considerably by ramming a gold crown into my gum. To
my surprise, I found George in the waiting room – the 1st time I have
seen him since his marriage. Our meeting – under the circumstances
was difficult – & short. Got my stick & umbrella at last, the old Jewess
having the decency to speak civilly of a debt for 6d. that I had to incur
but which I have now paid. G. Booth, Radcliffe, Haynes[52] to tea – all –
well, men are not so amusing as women. Adrian back to Cambridge
after dinner.

21 January

Wrote a lecture – an odd kind of lecture! – upon our journey in Italy,[53]
for the working women. This is the kind of thing they really enjoy I
know – whether there were fleas in the beds at Venice. I shall have to invent some – &c &c. It is easy, though not instructive to write, & I rattled
off 12 pages. Nelly Cecil to be painted,[54] whom I did not see. Katherine
Stephen to lunch, very nice & large & sensible as usual, with a low

50 Conforming to insistent social conventions, i.e. returning calls.
51 Jack Hills was nominated as Unionist candidate unanimously to oppose Arthur
    Elliott, the Liberal Unionist MP for Durham City; he was elected in 1906.
52 George Macaulay Booth; Raymond Coxe Radcliffe (1852-1929), King's College,
    Cambridge, assistant master in mathematics and classics at Eton; Edmund Sidney
    Pollock Haynes (1877-1949), Balliol College, Oxford, the expert on matrimonial law
    and morals.
53 Following their father's death, the four Stephens, with Violet Dickinson, had visited
    Italy in April 1904.
54 By Vanessa; see 'An Afternoon with the Pagans' (1903), n.2.

gentle voice – just home from a week in India. Harry & Barbara[55] dont interest me, I am bound to say, but all Stephens must rejoice that one has achieved the feat of marriage. Motor & George in the afternoon, who drove us himself to Richmond, gave us tea at Star & Garter[56] & home.

A book from Mrs Lyttelton which is convenient.[57]

22 January

Up late, to do honour to the Sabbath, which I spend partly in bed, as there are no letters to make me come down to breakfast. Nessa for her Sunday jaunt to Kitty. I typewrote the Note for Fred, which I know to be beastly bad – all cobblestone sentences, brisk & matter of fact, without an atom of beauty or swing about them. And I write about prose! Anyhow they may be useful. Gerald & Marny to lunch. Poor Robert Brough, the painter, dead of the railway accident.[58] This carries out my theory that artists & people of gifts die earlier than the common herd. If he had been a Plumber he would have recovered – as it is – another tragedy, & we have had many lately. To Queen's Hall with Marny; fair concert:[59] Eroica disappointing – Nessa lunch Mrs. Prothero,[60] & dine Kitty who likes my writing!

23 January

Worked rather intermittently this morning, as Nessa was on the loose, but corrected half the Note which is typewritten. Oh – for some one to tell me whether it is well, very well, or indifferently done. Lunch at 1, as N. went to paint at Alexandra House.[61] At 3.30 I was in Tisdalls chair, & sat there an hour of acute discomfort & some pain having a tooth

---

55 AVS's first cousin, Harry Lushington Stephen (see Jan. 1897, n.86) in 1904 married Barbara Nightingale.

56 A hotel, at the top of Richmond Hill, a favourite resort of London society; it was pulled down in 1915 and replaced by the Star and Garter Home for Disabled Soldiers and Sailors in 1924.

57 See below, n.66.

58 Robert Brough (1872-1905), portrait painter who had studied at the Royal Scottish Academy. Between three and four in the morning of 19 January, a Scottish express collided with a mail train from Leeds to Sheffield on the Midland Railway; 6 people were killed and 14 injured.

59 Sunday Afternoon Concert; the Queen's Hall Orchestra, conducted by Henry Wood, performed the works of Beethoven, Brahms, Tchaikovsky and Elgar.

60 Mary Frances, *née* Butcher, wife of Sir George Prothero (1848-1922), Cambridge historian and editor of *The Quarterly Review*; they lived at 24 Bedford Square, WC.

61 At Kensington Gate, a residence for women students, to the west of the Albert Hall.

stopped & that infernal crown jammed into my jaw which was finally done – but it aches like [*illegible*] at this minute, & spoils my chance of a cheerful dance at the Freshfields tonight, where we are all going. Jack to tea – full of the Durham elections, whose candidate he is now. Russian massacres, & the poor timorous Czar in hiding.[62]

24 January

We were not home till 2.30 last night – this morning rather – as we knew many people, &, on the whole the dance was fun. A great gathering of Fishers, all amicable &c. So we stayed in bed late this morning. & I am ashamed to say that I did very little work; but I am rather at a loose end just now, as the Note is done, & I have not yet read my new Review book – So I cobbled my lecture a little. Tomorrow, q.v., with fresh brains, I shall try & write a pot boiler – as I have time. Nessa & Nelly Cecil & Nun to lunch, as vigorous & thoroughly cautious & in her sober wits as usual. Nessa chose a carpet with her after lunch, & went on a Bus to Hampstead & back, which is a lazy & pleasant way of spending an afternoon, which takes only one hour, there & back. At. Minna to tea. The vigour of these old ladies! Read my Review book after tea, & found it happily amusing.

25 January

Another lazy morning – read however the greater part of my review book, so that will be written tomorrow with luck – & then? – I must turn about for something fresh to do. My birthday,[63] by the way – the 25th but, as usual, it was somehow rather forgotten which one begins to expect at my age –! Violet to lunch, & she did bring a present – a huge china inkpot which holds almost a jar full of ink, & is rather too large to be practicable. I must cultivate a bold hand & a quill pen – Georges motor after lunch, in which we did various long distance jobs – then home, read my review book, & dinner at 7.30 as we went with Gerald to

---

62 On 22 January, 'Bloody Sunday', an army of striking textile and engineering workers, backed by a quarter of a million people, tried without violence to present a 'Workmen's Petition to the Czar'. The Semenovski regiment fired on the crowd in Nevski Prospect; much blood was shed and there were wholesale arrests. Outward peace was restored under General Trepoff, with plenary powers. The Czar was in hiding at Tsarskoe-Selo (*The Times*, 22-9 Jan. 1905).

63 AVS's 23rd.

Peter Pan,[64] Barries play – imaginative & witty like all of his, but just too sentimental – However it was a great treat.

26 January
Wrote my review all this morning – save for one very long & damaging interruption – without which I should have finished it. Aunt Anny & Hester, anxious to see over the house – which takes time. However they were enthusiastic, & finally I got a little bit of writing done. Nelly to lunch, so deaf, that to talk across a table is really hard work – but she has a charming alert mind – worth penetrating too. I then took Gurth, on a leash which I bought for him, to the London Library & back, as he must learn to be a street dog if I am to exercise him. I think the variety of street smells make up almost for the Gardens. Mrs Lyttelton to tea, large & healthy, & broad minded, a refreshing & inspiriting woman. Now to dine at the Crums –

27 January
Dinner last night at Crums amusing, ten people, among them M. Lyttelton, Bruce Richmond, & the Italian & English Villari[65] – Taken down by Mrs Crum – however Villari's Russian experiences had to be discussed; they were interesting; B. Richmond had my MSS in his pocket – but I got no chance to talk as he went off to the Times – However a letter from Kitty this morning to say that he & the great Mr Chirol approve, & I am to come & meet them to discuss – I dont quite know what, but I hope it means that I am to get more work, reviewing I suppose. Finished my Guardian Belle of 50 years ago book,[66] which I hope is sufficiently good – rather too long. A brute of a man spoilt my morning by mending the grate, however I did all I had to – Chintzes & new music came – the chintzes are delightful & make our drawing room bright & furnished looking. Motor this afternoon, did calls, & the French pictures;[67] some

64 The play in three acts by J. M. Barrie had opened at the Duke of York's Theatre on 27 December 1904.

65 Professor Pasquale Villari (1827-1917), Italian statesman and historian, attached to the Ministry of Public Instruction, Florence.

66 A review in *The Guardian*, 8 February 1905 (Kp Co5) of *A Belle of the Fifties: Memoirs of Mrs. Clay, of Alabama. Put into Narrative Form by Ada Sterling*, reprinted in *VW Essays*, I.

67 Possibly an exhibition at the Royal Drawing Society, Queen Anne's Gate.

of them lovely, one especially of a liquid & flowing sea. To tea with
M[ary]. Cone[68] by tube where I played with the children.

28 January

All the morning gone! These are the tribulations of friendship, I suppose, & so to be borne with a willing heart, but I grudge time, I must
say. [Nurse] Traill came at 10.15 – stayed talking all the morning, being
out of work, lunched here, went with me to the L[ondon]. L[ibrary].
after lunch, & then I left her & went on to Violets, where I found Mr.
Robinson[69] the gardener, & designer of grates – an interesting man,
whom I am to go & see on Wednesday morning. Tea with Violet, &
was blown up for my journalism. Promised to translate a bit of tough
Greek, as a penance – Home & Moorsom[70] to dine, a strange pompous
youth, who dissolved a little under the influence of bridge. I wonder
why young people – men especially – have the strange ambition to be
like the old. Nessa approves of the [Maitland] Note.

29 January

Soot fell in the night, so we had to breakfast in the study. I made a paper
book this morning for my translations. I think I shall begin with Thucydides. Gerald came to lunch, & afterwards Thoby & I went to the Zoo
which is beginning to treat its animals with greater attention.[71] A very
wombatty wombat, the most delightful creature there; it has a large
square head, with brown eyes, & the body is very fat & shapeless &
covered with brown fur, & it waddles on very short legs. In short it is all
that a wombat should be – The birds naturally attracted Thoby. To the
music of Everyman[72] with Nessa at Queens Hall, rather beautiful. T.
likes my Note.

30 January

Wrote all the morning at a paper which may, with luck do for Leo

---

68 Unidentified.

69 William Robinson, 63 Lincoln's Inn Fields, editor of several horticultural period-
icals, including *The Garden, Flora and Sylva* and *The Garden Annual*.

70 Kenneth James Calvert Moorsom (1878-1907), educated at King's College, Cambridge; clerk in the House of Commons, 1901-7.

71 In the early 1900s, alterations were made at the Zoological Gardens in Regent's Park
to make it possible to display the animals in a more natural setting, without cages.

72 Composed by Dr Walford Davies and performed by the Bach Choir, an amateur
society.

[Maxse]. It is about music![73] – naturally depends more upon the imagination than upon facts. Rather amuses me to write, since I have been ordered not to write for my brains health. Thoby's approval of the Note gives me great pleasure, as I think he meant it, & I am very glad to have made it good. Lunch with At. Minna, where I found Margaret [Duckworth]. She was very nice, & more get at-able than before. Sent me her motor to come home in, & first I went over [22] Hyde Park Gate – for the first time since last Easter – & saw all the empty rooms, & was glad to find that now the furniture & books are gone; they are not painfully like home. Saw my old room – so strange with the ink splashes & shelves as of old. I could write the history of every mark & scratch in that room, where I lived so long.

31 January

Finished my possible Nat. Review article – about which I am doubtful – Motor to fetch me to Margarets, where I lunched with Lady Burghclere,[74] a small vivacious woman, George & Theodore Davies.[75] Not exciting. To Traill afterwards, & with her to get Thoby's watch; home & Stebbing[76] to tea – also a telegram from Kitty asking me to dine, which I accepted. Stebbing much as usual; only dined with Kitty & Leo alone, & Kitty discussed the Note which I had sent her, & depressed me by insisting upon many alterations – chiefly omissions, to make it printable – only I dont want it to be printed. But I dont think she approved very highly, which depresses me – Home late –

---

73 'Street Music', a signed essay in the *National Review*, March 1905 (Kp C3), reprinted in *VW Essays*, I.

74 Winifred, *née* Herbert, wife of Herbert C. G. Burghclere, 1st Baron (1846-1921); Lady Burghclere was Lady Margaret Duckworth's sister.

75 Theodore Llewelyn Davies (1870-1905), Trinity College, Cambridge, Secretary to the Income Tax Commission, was to drown on 25 July.

76 Probably the son of William Stebbing (1832-1927) leader-writer for *The Times*, and brother of Selina Stebbing, living at 169 Gloucester Terrace, Hyde Park, W.

Wednesday 1 February

Worked at various small jobs this morning which came to an end at 12, as I had to meet Violet at Mr Robinsons in Lincolns Inn Fields, to see his grates. He owns 2 or 3 gardening papers which he edits in this enormous fire proof block of buildings, built by himself. He seems to have a genius for successful inventions. An iron grate is the best & I shall get one. Margaret Lyttelton to lunch, curiously like Angela Kay, only with a less pointed & delicately coloured face – the same difficulty in making easy talk – however we got on fairly. Then I went out to Nelly's new house,[1] in St John's Wood – where she has a long low room, with a great window with trees across it, which reminds one of the country. My Girls Club [Morley College] in the evening, 4 girls, talked about Venice & it was rather amusing.

Thursday 2 February

Started my translation of selections from Thucydides. I start with the beginning sketch of old Greece, which is interesting, & then I shall choose out good bits – speeches, I think. This is the first Greek I have done since my illness – since February, that is – almost a year ago. I remember the last morning's work at Thucydides, & how my brain felt sucked up. I am glad to find that I dont forget Greek & read Thucydides which is tough, as easily as I ever did. I am going to throw my Spanish grammar over board, I think, & start reading – & see how the plan works. I believe it is the only way, I at any rate can learn a language – Grammar is hopelessly dull, & infects the whole language. Snow to lunch: out for a tramp thro' the street with Gurth. Mary,[2] Jack, Gerald to tea.

Friday 3 February

Went through a whole file of notebooks this morning, & found out what Fred wanted, I hope, about serious books, & wrote him a long letter, which took some time. I then did a little bit of Thucydides till Traill came to lunch. After lunch I took her on the top of a Bus to Hampstead, where it was the clearest & loveliest of days, & from the top we saw blue hills which might have been Yorkshire moors, & heard early birds

---

1   The Cecils moved from 20 Manchester Square, W, to 25 Grove End Road, St John's Wood, NW.

2   Possibly Mandell Creighton's daughter, who studied painting with Vanessa at the Royal Academy.

giving their freshest songs – Spring is – oh well – a platitude! Anyhow Hampstead is a really good expedition. Home & Katherine Horner[3] to tea – a tall lithe goddess, with clear eyes & a pale skin –

Saturday 4 February
Worked at Thucydides all the morning, which does somehow amuse me, & I suppose is better than screwing articles out of my brain. I get nothing but criticism from Violet now – oh d—— it, & this makes me determine to invite no more than is absolutely necessary. I shall send things straight to the editors, whose criticism is important, in future. I should like more steady work at reviews, for the sake of my purse. How I hate criticism, & what waste it is, because I never take it really. Nessa to lunch with Mary Cone. Thoby in. I went out to the British Museum, & tried to get some plan of it into my head, but found nothing that I wanted to, except some painted bodys [*sic*] of Tanagra figures. It is a Mausoleum. Letter from Fred. Bothered some about the article for Leo, after Violets criticism.

Sunday 5 February
A lovely soft spring day with pillow like clouds, & warm blue spaces in between. Out into the Sunday streets, which always look dusty & dirty. Found out about a concert at Queen's Hall, to which I want to go. Home, & Gerald to lunch. Thoby out tramping. After lunch I read &c. till tea time when we had an odd succession of callers. First Henry Prinsep:[4] the Indian judge – a nice old boy with clear eyes, & a soft way of speaking like Granny.[5] Harry,[6] he says, is a very lazy judge. Then came Miss Millais,[7] a brisk little bird like creature as usual who never changes. Then came Ozzy Dickinson[8] who with great courage had to pretend to a

---

3   Katharine (1885-1976) was the younger daughter of Frances (1860-1940) and John Fortescue Horner (1842-1927) of Mells in Somerset and 9 Buckingham Gate, SW. Katharine had been one of Janet Case's pupils; in 1907 she would marry Raymond Asquith (1878-1916), son of the Prime Minister.

4   Sir Henry Thoby Prinsep (1836-1914), eldest son of AVS's great aunt and uncle, Sara, *née* Pattle (1816-87), and Henry Thoby Prinsep (1793-1878) of Little Holland House.

5   AVS's maternal grandmother, Maria Jackson, *née* Pattle (1818-92).

6   Harry Stephen, the Indian judge; see Jan. 1897, n.86.

7   Mary (1861-1944), the second daughter of the painter Sir John Everett Millais,RA.

8   Oswald (Ozzie/Ozzy) Eden Dickinson (1869-1954), Violet's youngest brother; he was a barrister and later Secretary to the Home Office Board of Control in Lunacy.

knowledge of a certain mythical "very charming" Mrs Allan. Then came Victor Marshall,[9] more like an old gray bear than ever – & so it was late when they went. Then we went to a most pompous & dull lecture at the Grafton Gallery: upon impressionism by a Mr. Rutter;[10] when the P.R.A. & other R.A's filed across the room.

Monday 6 February

Worked at Thucydides, who stimulates my perverse brain to write original melodrama. However I shall stick at him till I have finished the bit I meant to. Out before lunch to ask the price of a great hooded chair which I covet: but it costs £8.5. & moreover shuts out the light, so I shall look elsewhere. Nessa to draw at Alexandra House, & I went down to the L[ondon]. L[ibrary]. where I got some books about early Xtianity !! because I want to read about that – but these books, I see, dont give me in the least what I want. Then to Farr & Schar[11] with a whole regiment of maimed brooches. As I saw Clara Pater back walking up De Vere G[arden]: I called, found her out, & thus was a brilliant [*illegible*]. With Nessa to tea with Mrs. Prothero, where were many strange women, Imogen Booth[12] the only known one, who came back to tea, & stayed for some time – a straight fresh creature, like a very nice boy. V[iolet] D[ickinson] to dine.

Tuesday 7 February

Scribbled some pages about Florence for my working women, & did a little bit of Thucydides. Margaret [Duckworth] to lunch, which somehow fails to excite. Mrs L. sent round the Golden Bowl by Henry James, for review,[13] which comes in conveniently. Also it ought to be an interesting book – says she liked my last review.

After lunch I went to a Steinbach – MacCarthy[14] concert at the

---

9 Victor A. E. G. Marshall (1841-1928), brother of Julia Marshall and an old friend of Leslie Stephen; see May 1897, n.30.
10 Frank Vane Phipson Rutter (1876-1937), art critic, educated at Queen's College, Cambridge; his lecture was called 'Impressionism'; Mr J. Lavery presided.
11 Farr & Schar, jewellers and watchmakers, 13 Canning Place, Kensington, W.
12 See Feb. 1897, n.72.
13 A review in *The Guardian*, 22 February 1905 (Kp C06), of *The Golden Bowl* is reprinted in *VW Essays*, I.
14 Maud MacCarthy was a young Irish violinist; the London Symphony Orchestra, under the baton of Fritz Steinbach, performed works by Beethoven, Wagner, Weber and Brahms.

Queens Hall, which was one of the best concerts I have heard lately – a really good violinist & first rate orchestra & conductor, & they played Beethoven & Brahms. Needless to say, Queens Hall was practically empty, & I had a choice of excellent seats. Home & read my Review book; at 7.30 Gerald came, & I went out to dine at an Indian curry shop with him, which was strange & rather nasty, & then to the Talk of the Town[15] – a silly but amusing comedy.

Wednesday 8 February
Worked at Thucydides all the morning, & did a good bit. After lunch Nessa went on a wild goose chase to Alexandra House – At 4 I went out first to have my specs twisted straight as they are quite crooked & perpetually slipping from my nose; then on to Mrs. Crums, where I found a large tea party going on in various corners, of people I did not know, except Bruce Richmond, who very soon came to business. First told me about the Outlook,[16] which is just starting new, with the Nat. Review man, Garvin as Editor, & an enthusiastic literary man for the literary side. Would I write a review for them? So I said yes, with joy – Then he asked if *"we"*, The Times, that is, might send on books for review also – So I said yes – & thus my work gets established, & I suppose I shall soon have as much as I can do – which is certainly satisfactory. To my girls [Morley College]: 7 – so they increase rapidly.

Thursday 9 February
Finished my job at Thucydides – 13 foolscap pages, not an elegant, or very accurate translation naturally – but rather a healthy kind of work, which doesn't admit of literary refinements! Snow to lunch, rather depressed, in body & mind, like all these vagrant & mildly discontented young women – not enough enthusiasm to carry them through with a swing, & so their existence seems to drag, & lack point rather. Took Gurth out to the L. L. this afternoon – on a leash at first, but at so much risk & botheration, that I let him free on the way home, which was really more successful. The good Ida [Milman] to tea – somehow a trifle middle aged, always has been indeed, with her little characteristic nods & jerks – Then read my Henry James book after tea – which needs reading, & is very closely packed with words – 550 pages of small print.

---

15 A musical comedy by Seymour Hicks, playing at the Lyric Theatre.
16 *The Outlook*, a weekly publication, begun originally on 5 February 1898; J. L. Garvin (1868-1927) was editor from 1905-6 and later edited *The Observer*.

Henry James print too, wh. I am to boil into 7 or 800 words! Nessa dines with Crums, & she & T. to dance at Micholls.[17]

Friday 10 February

Read the whole blessed morning, & mornings are blessed – the long drawn out Henry James. I shall have earned the shillings I make by this review at any rate. Traill came & interrupted for 15 minutes, which is an interruption one has to suffer, though I grudge it. After lunch down to buy a pair of shoes with her at Kembers,[18] then to the magnificent Harrods,[19] & then home – Jack to tea, with me, as Nessa was listening to art criticism at the Slade.[20] Then read more Henry James, but my desire to finish today is not likely to be gratified I see – & after all if I can send it off on Monday, I shant be keeping it too late. But all this time given up to reviewing rather bothers me. I bought – I have earned the right to buy occasionally – a stand with 6 little shelves – & a flap on wh. to stand my lamp –

Saturday 11 February

I wrote an article on Essay writing,[21] which will do for the Outlook, or for Mrs L. but Heaven knows whether it is trash or not – anyhow it dont much matter. I want to make a little money to pay for the extravagant little table – which hasn't come – Jack to lunch, with Kong his rust coloured Chow – with a coat like the thickest of thick carpets. After lunch I went to the L. L. to return a book, stamping on the way innumerable little envelopes which invite people to our great evening party,[22] suddenly decided upon, for the 1st – That sentence strikes me as bearing the impress of Henry James – in which my mind is steeped! Theodore Davies to tea, cheerful & friendly, though Heaven knows

---

17 Edward Micholls (1852-1926), JP, living at 18 Airlie Gardens, Campden Hill, W.
18 Kembers & Co., bootmakers, Albert Gate Mansions, Knightsbridge, SW.
19 Harrods Ltd, 87-109 Brompton Road, SW.
20 Slade School of Art, University College, London.
21 Originally called 'A Plague of Essays', the essay was published in *Academy & Literature*, 25 February 1905 (Kp C07), under the title 'The Decay of Essay-writing' and reprinted in *VW Essays*, I. *The Academy* was a periodical founded in 1869 by a group of liberal Oxford scholars; in 1902 it absorbed *Literature* and was then called *The Academy & Literature*.
22 i.e. the formal housewarming party at 46 Gordon Square, set for 1 March.

why I find it difficult to talk to him. Then, now, to dress, dine early, & see Henry 5th,[23] a plan, actually of Thoby's.

Sunday 12 February

Play last night was good, & well acted, & of course gorgeously clothed. So we had a little excuse for being late this morning – Nessa & I that is – Thoby was off early to take his working men to look for birds in Surrey – which is somehow pathetic. A steady kind of day, bright & polished, & ice cold. All the morning I wrestled with Henry James, & wrote my usual semi-business letter to Fred, choc full of facts & dates – Nessa meanwhile upholstered a drawing room chair, with a view to our dinner tomorrow. After lunch I typewrote most of my Essay article; then, valiantly, as though plunging into a cold bath, N. & I went off, on top of a bus, to take the air. All the streets swept by the wind & gritty, & curiously empty of carts & full of walkers. Home to tea, & entertained Marny, & Mrs. O'Brien,[24] & a daughter Margaret, who plays hockey – a nice plain vigorous child, with bright eyes – Mrs O'B. as usual – Henry James I hope to finish tonight – the toughest job I have yet had.

Monday 13 February

Wrote my Henry James review all the morning – between, that is, incessant interruptions. Mrs. Prothero *wouldnt* dine then she would – meanwhile we had got Susan L[ushington]. so in the end I had to propose myself to Violet, as the table wont hold more than 8. However I did get my review done, rather a tough job, & I doubt whether she'll like it – but never was there such a book to review. Nessa to Alexandra House, where I fetched her, & we drove, or meant to drive to the Horners, but I thought the number was 49 – which it wasn't, & having tried many variations we gave it up, had tea in an ABC with Traill, & so home. I dined with Violet, where I found a dull cousin, & O[zzie]. [Dickinson]. After dinner I came home, & found the Ladies in the drawing room. The dinner a great success. G[eorge]. & M[argaret]; Mr. Tennyson;[25] Mr. & Mrs. Prothero & Susan.

---

23 *King Henry the Fifth*, with Lewis Waller, at the Imperial Theatre, Westminster.
24 Julia O'Brien, *née* Marshall (d.1907); see May 1897, n.30.
25 Probably Charles Bruce Tennyson (1879-1978), son of Lionel (1854-86) and grandson of Alfred, Lord Tennyson.

Tuesday 14 February

Wrote a lecture for my working women all the morning. It is about Benvenuto Cellini,[26] as I am at my wits end for a subject, & this has some relation to Florence, which I have been talking about, & there are a great many plums which it is no trouble to pick. But I doubt whether they will like it. Margery & Jill Parker[27] to lunch, very nice & lithe pretty young ladies, which I enjoy. After lunch the Freshfields came, & I bolted, out to my dear book shops, where I knew I could buy nothing, as I had no money with me. I found an interesting shop in a back street which keeps engravings – Some of Whistlers[28] – some of Legro's.[29] There I shall return with a purse. A note from Mrs L. to say the review is a 3rd too long:[30] oh d—— it all – So I must cut it down, spoil it, & waste I dont know how many hours work, all because the worthy Patronesses want to read about midwives. Dined with Nessa at [Dr] Savages; a large ponderous medical party. Talked to Warrington, Jean & Schuster.[31]

Wednesday 15 February

Worked all the morning at miscellaneous jobs – at my Cellini which I finished. Really I must find some way of doing these lecture jobs at other times – mornings are too precious. Then I tried to get some idea of a Spanish verb into my brain; then I finished my Essay article & typewrote it. Then, going down stairs happily, I found a letter from Mrs. L. enclosing that wretched review, & asking me to cut it down, & send it back as soon as possible. So I set to work with literal & metaphorical scissors & somehow patched it together, having cut out all the plot & a good deal else, so that it wont take more than 800 words & left it at Mrs. L's. house on my way to lunch with At. Anny [Ritchie] at the Sesame.[32] I know I have spoilt the review as a review, & wasted my work – but it

---

26 1500-71, Florentine goldsmith and sculptor; author of a celebrated autobiography.
27 Unidentified.
28 James McNeill Whistler (1843-1903), American painter and etcher.
29 Alphonse Legros (1837-1911), French-born painter and sculptor.
30 The published review was substantially cut; see *VW Essays*, I, p. 24n.
31 Miss Jean Thomas, proprietor of a nursing home for nervous and mental disorders at Cambridge Park, Twickenham, where AVS would be an inmate during July 1910 and later in 1913. Probably Edgar Schuster, first Galton Eugenics Research Fellow, 1905-6. Warrington is unidentified.
32 Sesame Club, 28-9 Dover Street, Piccadilly, W.

cant be helped. Lunch: Lady Gwendolen Cecil:[33] nice, shabby, & masculine; Lady Humphries,[34] – Hester [Ritchie]. Walked home, read 2 review books[35] sent by the Times – & to my girls club.

Thursday 16 February

Rather a lazy morning, as I didn't have to write. So I read a bit of Latin the Georgics,[36] instead – stately & melodious; but without the vitality of my dear old Greeks. However, there is a charm in Latin, which haunts one. Even that little bit of Virgil with T. in the summer,[37] when I was hardly able to use my brains, brought a sense of harmony into them, such as for many months they had not known; & therefore I dont forget it. Lunch early & Nessa to Alexandra House. I took Gurth out – he is a load on my conscience – for a walk in Regents Park. This is what he most enjoys. A languid spring day, so I was ready to sit & watch people more energetically walking; & even some little girls playing hockey in a corner. The number of men lounging out of work was astonishing – So I diagnosed them. Home & found Traill waiting who stayed to tea. A letter from Leo: delighted to accept my charming article[38] – which is a load off my mind – To be refused by a friend would have been most uncomfortable, & I had made up my mind to expect it.

Friday 17 February

Toiled away at the Georgics this morning; but it was full of technical words which I had to look out, & this rather spoilt my enjoyment. However Latin is worth a little work. Violet came to lunch, & stayed afterwards & worried me by insisting upon more fresh air – which means I must go back to the old habit which I hated of rushing out for half an hour before lunch. I dont think it a good plan, but I suppose I must

33 1860-1945, daughter of the 3rd Marquess of Salisbury and sister of Lord Robert Cecil.

34 Possibly Ellen Vincent (d.1934), wife of Sir Albert Humphries (d.1935), Chairman of the Executive Committee of the National Institute of Agricultural Botany.

35 Reviewed in the *TLS*, 10 March 1905 (Kp C1): *The Thackeray Country* by Lewis Melville and *The Dickens Country* by F. G. Kitton, reprinted in *VW Essays*, I.

36 Virgil's didactic poem in four books, celebrating peasant life and duty, composed 37-30 BC.

37 In a letter to Violet Dickinson, dated 17 September 1904: 'Traill and I and Thoby and Adrian begin the morning with an hours walk directly after breakfast. From 10.30 to 12.30 I do Latin with Thoby.' *VW Letters*, I, No. 180.

38 'Street Music'; see Jan. 1905, n.73.

agree, & isn't worth worrying over. To the LL. where I got two *Spanish* novels! I dont suppose I shall be able to read a word, but I want to try, as it is the only way of learning it. I cant learn out of a grammar. Then Nessa & I went to the Horners, which we found, & we had tea alone. Then came in Mrs. Horner, bright eyed & vivacious & fashionable. Then we went to Katharines room & Cicely[39] came in – an obvious beauty, without charm. K. has twice as much. Back through a lovely blue evening, found a letter from Literature & the Academy[40] asking me to write.

Saturday 18 February
As the Academy & Literature are so sensible as to wish me to write for them, I spent the morning in partly re-writing & polishing the "Plague of Essays" which will now do, I think. It takes me almost as long to re-write one page, as to write 4 fresh ones – & it is a job I hate – all niggly work, done with a cold brain. However I think I improved it in the end, & it is now ready. Out – as my orders are – & tramped along the Tottenham Court Rd. as usual, & bought a flame coloured azalea. Margery & Mrs. Snow[den] to lunch. Margery, I think, pleased & excited by my Easter scheme,[41] so I hope it will come to pass. Mrs Snow somehow like a homely old housekeeper, with nice manners, prim & "lady like", as one would say of something not quite the genuine thing. Out on top of a Bus with Nessa. Proofs of Street Music from Leo. So perhaps he means it for March. Thoby at Cambridge.

Sunday 19 February
Down late, as usual & legitimate on Sunday. Then it was a real Spring day, so after a little proof reading – & Leo prints badly – I took Gurth & walked to Violets. Nessa having gone to Kitty. Violet in bed, & I sat & talked, with egoism, I am afraid, of my writing which I had brought in my pouch. She sticks to it that Street Music isn't good, & that Plague of Essays is much better. This rather bothers me, as the Nat[ional Review].: will be read, & possibly signed. However it cant be helped, & Leo, according to Nessa says it's just what he wants. Jack to luncheon, after speaking to a large & enthusiastic meeting in the North. Politics in the rough dont much interest me, & seem mostly a waste of time &

39 Cicely Horner (b.1883), Katharine's elder sister; see n.3.
40 See n.21.
41 Her proposed journey with Adrian.

good English words. To St Pauls after lunch; all gilt & spangled with light & glittering mosaics, & very sweet boys voices. Clara [Pater] did not come; as it showered.

Monday 20 February
Wrote like the little Printers devil I am, all the morning at my Times Review. This has to contrive to review two books without saying a word about them – as indeed they are the productions of a pair of scissors, & I am not a critic of dress making of this kind. Indeed these two dreary manes of little facts & dates, all so carefully sifted & accumulated have cast a gloom into my soul. However I pegged away at my review; as I am allowed 1500 words; of course they wont come – so I had to beat my brains a little. However I finished it in the course of the day, & made it fairly good I hope. Lord knows! A very windy & snowy day – Talk of Spring! Nessa to lunch with Snow, & not back till late tea time. I sent my review off by 7 o'clock Post, to reach tonight if possible. Now I have no work in hand, & I want to read a little Greek. Thoby back from Cambridge.

Tuesday 21 February
I tried to make out a little Spanish this morning, but as I have to look out every other word, & then piece together the meaning of the whole laboriously it cannot be said to be amusing. Then I read a bit of Aristotle, the Poetics,[42] which will fit me for a reviewer! This book, I tried to read at Florence, I remember – & couldn't! Out for a dash before lunch. A very windy day; a regular March wind which blows, sunshine & then showers. In proof of this a black downy ball of feathers off my hat alighted on the pavement & I had to pocket it. A proof of the 'Plague of Essays' from the Academy came after lunch, so I am glad to say they will print it: it is better than the Music I'm afraid. Out to tea at Alexandra House, with Audrey Tolkas [?][43] – a nice fair plump & simple minded creature – but A. H. is a singularly dreary place – all these poor creatures struggling along to pass exams, on scanty meals. Nessa to dine with Nelly.

Wednesday 22 February
Read the Poetics all the morning – really excellent bit of literary criti-

42 Composed between 335-22 BC.
43 Unidentified.

cism! – laying down so simply & surely the rudiments both of literature & of criticism. I always feel surprised by subtlety in the ancients – but Aristotle said the first & the last words on this subject – in about 50 pages now. Katharine Horner to lunch, who begins to expand a little, & reveal her natural depths, beneath the surface of polite & shy young lady. Off we went after lunch on top of a yellow Bus all the way to Hampstead – my word the wind, it blew, & the sky grinned blue & brisk – & finally we got inside. But we had to wander on the blasted heath for ½ an hour before we dared go in to Cases – & then she was forbidding & fierce – not in the least glad to see us, & in a severely strenuous frame of mind. So our visit was not a success. Home, & found At. Stephen[44] & K[itty] to tea. Adrian up; N. & I to Morley where N. lectured – then they went to a dance at Hobhouses.[45]

Thursday 23 February
The family late & dissipated this morning after last night. They stayed to the end, & were not home till 2.30. Thoby's last words being that he, at any rate, should leave early. Adrian rushed back to Cambridge directly after breakfast, as he had a lunch party, & Nessa & I determined to have a holiday, & so off & see the Whistlers.[46] On the way, we looked in at my friend John Davis[47] & I bought that long coveted & resisted coal scuttle, all of beaten brass, & she bought a great looking glass, as tall as the Russian giant[48] for the Studio. This was extravagance – So I must write another article. Then to the Whistlers. He is a perfect artist – uses his gifts to the utmost & with the finest discretion, so that all his pictures are perfect in their way – & sometimes it is a very noble way. Oh Lord, the lucid colour – the harmony – the perfect scheme.

---

44 The widow of James Fitzjames Stephen.
45 Probably the family of the Rt Hon. Henry Hobhouse (1854-1937), MP for East Somerset, 1885-1906, living at 15 Bruton Street, W, and Hadspen House, Castle Carey, Somerset. There were four sons and two daughters: Stephen Henry (1881-1961), Arthur Lawrence (1886-1965), John Richard (1893-1961), Paul Edward (1894-1918), Rachel (b. c. 1882) and Eleanor (1884-1960).
46 The Whistler Memorial Exhibition, New Gallery, Regent Street, included the King's collection of 150 etchings from the Royal Library at Windsor; the exhibition was mounted by the International Society of Sculptors, Painters and Engravers.
47 Probably John Davis & Son, house furnishers, 203-4 Tottenham Court Road, W.
48 Probably the Russian giantess, Elizabeth Lyska, who in 1889, then aged 12 and 6 feet 8 inches tall, was being shown at the Royal Aquarium in London.

This is what matters in life. So cold we stayed in doors. At. Minna, E. Coltman,[49] Violet & Ly. Hylton[50] to tea – Ldy. H. a pretty aristocrat.

Friday 24 February

Worked at Aristotle all the morning, who remains singularly interesting & not at all abstruse, & yet going to the root of the matter as one feels, which somehow puzzles me. Nessa to Alexandra House, & if she wrote this diary, the first thing she would have noted would have been the black & damnable fog. I can vanquish all the fogs in London with a penny candle, & produce works of genius unhindered, whereas her day is at the mercy of the sun. Out & bought fire irons of wrought iron, to match my fender, which is a source of real joy to me. Also I bought that great looking glass, which will just fill the space over my writing table, & liven up the room. Out after lunch with Gurth & walked all the way to the L. L. & back – bought James Thomsons poems on the way – also a note book; & got some of Renan,[51] & so home. Gurth wears my life out. N. & T. out to Moorsoms. I put up my looking glass.

Saturday 25 February

Worked all the morning at Aristotle, which draws near an end. I must interrupt it though to write an article for Mrs L. as in view of certain rather heavy expenses, I must add to my quarterly cheque. A letter from Fred this morning which says that my Note is "really beautiful" & he could write a page in praise of it. This I quote, because his is an opinion I value, & it gives me pleasure worth having. Nessa to lunch – as usual with Snow. Late in the day I discovered a Symphony Concert[52] at the Queens Hall, & as my ear craved music I went & had to take a 5s. seat; & listened to a stiff, but on the whole interesting, programme. A long Domestic Symphony by R. Strauss, partly beautiful, partly unintelligible – at least to me on a first hearing. Boo [Cordelia Fisher] to tea, or

49 Possibly the niece or daughter of Anna, *née* Duckworth (d.1873), and Thomas Coltman (1798-1849).

50 Lady Alice Adeliza Hervey (d.1962), daughter of the 3rd Marquess of Bristol and wife of Lord George Hylton Jolliffe (1862-1945).

51 Joseph Ernest Renan (1823-92), French historian, Hebrew scholar, and critic; author of *Histoire des Origines du Christianisme*, whose first volume (*La Vie de Jésus*, 1863) is said to have made a deep impression on English intellectuals.

52 This was the first performance in England of Richard Strauss's *Symphonia Domestica*; Henry Wood conducted the Queen's Hall Orchestra.

rather to play the pianola. Pernel Strachey[53] on top of her – whom I was glad to see. She is appointed to Newnham, so our chances of meeting will be few in future.

Sunday 26 February
A Sunday morning; a fact which my unconscious body somehow realises, so that I sleep a good hour later, till all the good Irvingites[54] opposite are on their knees. Sunday is the most melancholy day of the week – because I dont work I suppose. All the morning I frittered away on odd jobs. I had to look through a great quantity of books, as Rosamond [Stephen] wants some – & is welcome to them! Gerald to lunch – very jovial & full of his "business" tells me my Plague of Essays Article is out in The Academy, with Virginia Stephen signed in full, which seems rather indecent publicity. We went with him to call on the Fishers. Saw Aunt Mary, Hervey, & Boo – somehow very much like Fishers. Home, & Marny to tea, valiantly through the rain. The streets are running with liquid & mud. Thoby back from his hunting tonight – which he has enjoyed.

Monday 27 February
Wrote an article on the Value of Laughter[55] for Mrs L., at least the greater part of it – I dont hurry, as I want to take a little more pains. Nessa to Alexandra House after lunch, & I took that extraordinarily ubiquitous dog for a walk. He never leaves me now, but follows me up stairs & down, sits by my desk as I write, all because I may take him out in the afternoon. I walked him right along Oxford Street. Streets I do enjoy more than the dreary Regents Park. I like looking at things. Home – & bought the Academy, with what purports to be my article in it; but my blood as an author boils; name is changed, half is cut out, words are put in & altered, & this hotch potch signed Virginia Stephen. They might have asked me. Dine early & out to A[lexandra]. H[ouse]. party, where they acted – a long entertainment.

---

53 Joan Pernel Strachey (1876-1951), later Principal of Newnham College, Cambridge, 1923-41; she was Lytton Strachey's elder sister.
54 The Irvingite Church stood on the opposite side of Gordon Square from No. 46.
55 An essay 'The Value of Laughter' was published in *The Guardian* on 16 August 1905 (Kp C2.2) and reprinted in *VW Essays*, I.

Tuesday 28 February

Wrote another page to my Value of Laughter which I finished; & then read some Aristotle, which has taken to the analysis of words, & therefore dont interest me so much. Out for a dash as usual; after lunch I typewrote my Laughter, & then N. & I set forth to work hard at the party, which is now imminent. We had to order cups & saucers; then to travel all the way to Kensington to borrow Marny's silver kettle, then to buy many small extras, then to Stewarts[56] & finally home for a late tea. Adrian, thank goodness, can come – So we shall meet the invasion four square. After dinner I got my proof from the Times, printed word for word, so I only hope they wont cut out at the last moment – also a cheque for £5 from Leo for my [Street] music, which seems ridiculous overpayment for barely two mornings work, & I wish it were better.

---

56 Francis Stewart & Co., bread and biscuit makers, 57 Piccadilly, W, and 46 Old Bond Street, W.

Wednesday 1 March

Worked all the morning – or meant to work all the morning – at Aristotle, but at 12 Kitty came, & stayed an hour – discussing the party. Indeed the party became an anxiety about this house; Adrian arrived & we went to lunch at the Austro Hungarian with him, as the servants must not be hurried. Then to Stewarts. Then back home, & tackled the work of arranging the rooms, putting flowers in water &c. This went on till 5 when we struck work & went out to get tea, – & more flowers. By 6.30 the preparations were made – the rooms as empty as a moonlit sky; & brilliant with light & sweet with flowers. We dined at the Hotel Russell with Jack & Gerald where Nessa upset her coffee over her dress, however it was washed out. Then home & the party began with Violets large collection of ladies, & did not stop till past 12. There were moments of difficulty, but on the whole it was garrulous & successful I think, & all went well.

Thursday 2 March

Finished my Aristotle Poetics this morning, rather lazy after last nights debauch. Adrian left, & I went out to meet Nessa at Nelly's & lunch there – Lunch over & Nelly drove us down in her motor car to Violets, where we fetched Gurth, & then on home. A terrible stamping & screaming going on in the Studio announced Rosamond, who was tumbling books out of the shelves, & choosing ecclesiastical history. This went on till tea time. She is singularly unattractive; & her manner does not liven her great stupid body. Violet & the clergyman's wife to tea – who was not – this is too indiscreet. Thoby out to dine; Sydney Turner[1] & Strachey[2] after dinner, & we talked till 12.

Friday 3 March

Began the Oedipus Tyrannus[3] this morning, as a sequel to Aristotle. No books to review, so I may as well grind at Greek for a bit. Nessa painting Nelly, who sits now in her own drawing room, by the window, with a green curtain & Troper [her dog] at her feet. Miserably cold days – &

---

1   Saxon Sydney-Turner (1880-1962), one of Thoby's contemporaries at Trinity College, Cambridge, and an opera lover, particularly of Wagner; in 1909 AVS and Adrian would accompany him to Bayreuth for the Wagner Festival.

2   Giles Lytton Strachey (1880-1932), future biographer, also one of Thoby's Cambridge friends; his *Eminent Victorians* (1918) brought him wide publicity.

3   By Sophocles (486-406 BC).

how I loathe the cold – it makes one feel servile. Out after lunch with Gurth to the L. L. where I had to look out the dates of various articles in the Fortnightly for Fred, & found what I wanted. I took a cab back with Gurth, & had a wrangle with the cabman who complained of Gurth's muddy paws. Wrote to Fred a long letter after tea, telling him not to print my Note. Dine with Thoby at Violets; Nessa at R. Cecils; then to St Loe Stracheys[4] where we met a good many people we know.

Saturday 4 March
Worked at Sophocles all the morning, & found it easier. Out as usual; my morning dash takes me down the Tottenham Court Rd. now, which is far more interesting than the same space of Kensington High Street. There are old furniture shops, & in Oxford Street old book shops. Altogether Bloomsbury is a more interesting quarter than Kensington. The Times sent me Barham of Beltana,[5] Norris's new novel to review. It will be a very easy job, & I am glad that the Times shows signs of keeping me on to do reviews. We – N[essa]. & I – met six working women on the steps of the National Gallery at 3, & took them laboriously through the Early Italians. What they think about – how far pictures are intelligible to them – I dont know. It is hard work. Marny to tea – Pernel dine.

Sunday 5 March
I ruined my chance of a Sunday sleep, which is the most delightful part of Sunday – by idiotically mistaking 9.30 for 10.30 & leaping from my bed, a good 30 minutes before I need. I had a long discourse at breakfast from T. who went down to Cambridge yesterday for the Greek voting,[6] & there he found that the world was talking of a grand practical joke played by Adrian & 2 others on the Mayor of Cambridge. They pretended to be the Sultan of Zanzibar & party, & were solemnly driven to the Guildhall, welcomed by the Mayor in his chain of office, & shown the sights of Cambridge – while porters & dons raised their hats. When

---

4 Amy and John St Loe Strachey (1860-1927), proprietor and editor of *The Spectator*; he was Lytton Strachey's cousin.

5 A review in the *TLS*, 17 March 1905 (Kp C1.1) of *Barham of Beltana* by W. E. Norris, reprinted in *VW Essays*, I.

6 'The Studies and Examination Syndicate at Cambridge had proposed to the Senate that Greek should no longer be obligatory for all students. Candidates for the Previous Examination (entrance) had been required to have a knowledge of Greek. After two days of voting, a considerable majority declined to make Greek optional.' *The Times,* 5 March 1905.

Sunday 5th March 64

I missed my chance of a Sunday sleep, which is the most delightful part of Sunday — by idiotically mistaking 9-30 for 10-30 & leaping from my bed, a good 30 minutes before I need. I had a long discourse at breakfast from J. who went down to Cambridge yesterday for the Greek voting, & there he found that the world was talking of a grand practical joke played by Adrian & 2 others on the Mayor of Cambridge. They pretended to be the Sultan of Zanzibar & party, & were solemnly driven to the Guild hall, welcomed by the Mayor in his chair of office, & shown the sights of Cambridge — While porters & dons raised their hats. When they were shown the Queen's native they all solemnly bowed, as loyal natives. Then to fill instead of taking the London train they leapt into hansoms, drove in to the country, & changes. The whole story is in the Daily Mail, without names, & other papers beg for photographs. Greek is still compulsory. Cut the afternoon — a dull & rainy day. finished my Norris novel.

they were shown the Queens statue they all solemnly bowed, as loyal natives. Then instead of taking the London train they leapt into hansoms, drove in to the country & changed. The whole story is in the Daily Mail,[7] without names, & other papers beg for photographs. Greek is still compulsory. Concert[8] this afternoon & a dull & rainy day. Finished my Norris novel.

Monday 6 March

Wrote my review for the Times, which as they only want 500 words it is easy to do. Nothing whatever to be said about the book; so I confined myself to generalities. Then read Sophocles. Nessa lunch with Nelly. I went afterwards to the L. L. where I was told I had 14 books out – What these are, I cant conceive. I couldn't get what I wanted, which was a book about Greek myths to make a lecture out of for my working women – so I tried to get something 2nd hand. I found a book by a man called St. Clair,[9] who tries to prove the dates of all the myths by astronomy. However I daresay I shall make out what I want. To tea with the Sidney Colvins;[10] a pathetic old pair, somehow. To Mildred Squash [?] after dinner, where people swarmed, & we talked till 12.

Tuesday 7 March

Worked at Sophocles all the morning, who is really not hard, & I have unearthed some gems. Miss Egerton[11] to lunch – who used to frighten

---

7 See Appendix C; Adrian would participate in another hoodwinking of the authorities on 10 February 1910, only this time with AVS in active attendance; this would become the equally well-publicised 'Dreadnought Hoax' – see QB, I, pp. 157-61 and Appendix E.

8 The Queen's Hall Orchestra, conducted by Henry Wood, performed The 'Tragic' Overture, by Brahms, Mozart's 'Non Temer' (*Idomeneo*), Schubert's Symphony No. 8 in B minor (The 'Unfinished'), Elgar's Variations for Orchestra, Humperdinck's Overture to *Hansel and Gretel*, and Wagner's *Huldigungsmarsch*.

9 Probably *Myths of Greece Explained and Dated: An Embalmed History from Uranus to Perseus, including the Eleusinian Mysteries and Olympic Games*, by George St Clair, 1901, 2 vols.

10 Mr and Mrs Sidney Colvin (1845-1927), Keeper of Prints and Drawings in the British Museum from 1883-1912; they lived in one of the official residences flanking the British Museum forecourt.

11 Blanche (b.1871), the eldest daughter of Lady Louisa, only daughter of the 7th Duke of Devonshire and widow of Admiral Francis Egerton.

me so at Hardwick,[12] a plain rather stiff, but nice creature, with a great under lip, & a cleft chin. Lady Louisa came in to fetch her & roamed about the drawing room. Out to Marshall & Snelgroves afterwards, & did what of all things I loathe. That is choose silk for an evening dress, & sit by while Nessa ordered a coat & skirt. However, clothes are necessary in this world – & at this moment comes a note from old Henry Prinsep to ask us all to go off to a dance there this very night. Somehow, I had rather stay at home, but we must at any rate look in.

Wednesday 8 March

Worked at my evening lecture, which is on Greek myths this time – a subject of which I know nothing. But they are really beautiful, & I should like to try & put them into English – not the dry bones which are preserved in the horrid little primer I bought. I made the experiment of only writing short notes, which I shall put into words on the spur of the moment. Directly I begin to read, their attention wanders. Nessa out to lunch – Nelly's portrait now nears a close. Margaret [Duckworth] sent round the new motor this afternoon, & we took Violet to pay a series of calls – we of course forgot our cards – To my women, & managed the speaking all right. It is certainly better than reading. Home & found Bell,[13] & we talked the nature of good till almost one!

Thursday 9 March

Read my Sophocles, who nears an end. At one, as I was getting ready to go out, the great Millicent[14] descended from a four wheeler, & settled in an arm chair, prepared for conversation. We waited till ¼ to 2, when a telegram to my dismay from Nessa said she would lunch with Nelly. So I had to make laborious excuses, & still more laborious small talk till 3 when we went together to the Aeolian Hall – a beautiful new Music Hall on Bond Street where Plunket Greene was singing Ralphs songs.[15] A great gathering of Fishers naturally, but I escaped afterwards, & walked home. Two novels to review for the Guardian, who will print my Essay on Laughter. Books always come upon me in a rush. Dined with Violet.

---

12 Hardwick Hall in Derbyshire was one of the seats of the Dukes of Devonshire; it is about 2 miles from Teversal, where the Stephens stayed in the summer of 1904 when AVS was recovering from her breakdown.
13 For Clive Bell see Appendix B.
14 AVS's cousin Millicent; see Feb. 1897, n.38.
15 Harry Plunket Greene (1865-1936), bass, sang works by Ralph Vaughan Williams and Arthur Somervell.

Friday 10 March

Finished my Oedipus Tyrannus which is a fine play. How I wish something would tear away the veil which still separates me from the Greeks – or is it inevitable? Margery [Snowden] to lunch, & she was painted by Nessa afterwards, & I went off with teeth set, to buy a new coat – as I have to lunch out &c. & my old one is shabby. It happened as always: I reviewed twenty coats at Marshall & Snelgroves & decided against them on score of price: went to Peter Robinsons[16] & took the first shown at a price quite ruinous, because I suddenly got bored. However it is a good coat. Nessa likes it, & if I work, I shall also spend. A letter from Richmond to offer me Miss Sichels Catherine de Medici[17] to review – column & a half. I told him I was not learned in Mediaeval French – which is strictly true! Sir Fred P[ollock].[18] & Meg Booth[19] to tea.

Saturday 11 March

Wrote a most bothering little review of 300 words only upon Miss Barlows book[20] – but the 300 words wouldn't come – or came wrong – & finally weren't very good. But a nondescript book like this which really suggests nothing good or bad, is d——d hard work, & I would rather write anything else – except indeed a dutiful letter. At one, in a storm of wind & rain, Nessa & I went out to lunch with Lady Alice Shaw Stewart,[21] really a delightful person, like a tame & combed out Beatrice, but very full of character, & even beauty. O[zzie]. Dickinson there – also Nicholls,[22] the art critic, & Sir Hugh. Not an alarming lunch, & we got on all right. Margaret [Duckworth] fetched us in a carriage & we drove to various places, ending with a grand musical tea party at Cousin Ade-

16 Peter Robinson's Ltd, clothiers, Oxford Circus, W.
17 The review of Edith Sichels' *Catherine de Medici and the French Revolution* was never published.
18 Sir Frederick Pollock (1845-1937), eminent jurist and Professor of Jurisprudence at Oxford, 1883-1903; he and Leslie Stephen were the founders of the 'Sunday Tramps', an informal organisation of Sunday walkers.
19 See July 1897, n.18.
20 A review in *The Guardian*, 22 March 1905, of *By Beach and Bogland* by Jane Barlow, reprinted in *VW Essays*, I.
21 Lady Alice Shaw-Stewart (1866-1942), sister of Lady Beatrice Thynne and (Katie) the Countess of Cromer, and wife of Sir (Michael) Hugh Shaw-Stewart; they lived at 20 Mansfield Street, W; see also 'An Afternoon with the Pagans' (1903), n.2.
22 John Bowyer Buchanan Nichol (1859-1939) of Lawford Hall, Essex, and 7 Bryanston Square, W; see *MoB* p.185.

line,[23] where half the splendid names in England passed before us – & some very queer figures. Home at last to our native Bloomsbury. Catherine de Medici here, & [*illegible*] wont work.

Sunday 12 March
Read all the morning, which on Sundays is not a very long one – at my novel – Nancy Stair,[24] which I finished before I had to dress & go out to lunch with the Protheros. It was wild with wind & rain &, – to sum up – I swore. The Bertram [*sic*] Russells,[25] Mary Spring Rice[26] &c to lunch – which was to some extent amusing. Home, & as the weather was beautifully rough, no one came to tea. I read a good bit of Miss Sichel, & tried to find out something about France of the Reformation from other histories. I find that she is not too learned: I shall be able to criticise on general grounds, & already some things occur to me to say. She is a clever woman, hunting for a style – but I cant correct her facts.

Monday 13 March
Wrote my review of Nancy Stair, which purports to be a true story with names, dates &c. Anyhow it dont read true – I hadn't much difficulty in writing a review – not that I over flowed my limit. I shant waste words again! Nessa out to lunch, so my day was rather solitary. Out to Hatchards to buy Stevenson[27] & Pater[28] – I want to study them – not to copy, I hope, but to see how the trick's done. Stevenson is a trick – but Pater something different & beyond. Eleanor Clough[29] & Jack to tea. Eleanor is a great big Freshfield-Ritchie, but the combination is more than usually successful in her case. After dinner to the Freshfields, where a

---

23 See July 1897, n.8.

24 A review in *The Guardian*, 10 May 1905, of *Nancy Stair. A Novel* by Elinor MacCartney Lane, reprinted in *VW Essays*, I.

25 Bertrand Arthur Russell (1872-1970), mathematician, philosopher and pacifist, in 1894 married Alys Pearsall Smith (1867-1951).

26 Mary Ellen Spring-Rice (1880-1924), daughter of Stephen Edward Spring-Rice, CB (1856-1902).

27 Robert Louis Stevenson (1850-94), Scottish novelist, poet and essayist; AVS was probably interested in his essays *Virginibus Puerisque*, 1881 and *Familiar Studies of Men and Books*, 1882.

28 Walter Horatio Pater (1839-94), essayist and critic, brother of Clara Pater.

29 Eleanor, *née* Freshfield, wife of Arthur H. Clough (1859-1943), son of the poet; she was the daughter of Douglas and Augusta Freshfield (see March 1897, n.14).

select company heard Tovey[30] play. V[aughan] W[illiams] &c. Tovey rather a fine lean head, with bright eyes.

Tuesday 14 March

Wrote this morning – *not* for any editor to see, which becomes a relief – I wanted to put down a few ideas about history,[31] as I shall have to generalise on that theme in my Sichel review. But Traill came in at 12 & sat & talked so my morning came to an end. She is between cases, & at a loose end. At 2 Elena Rathbone to lunch, alone with me, as Nessa out as usual. She is a straight beautiful creature, whom I always connect in my mind with some very beautiful Greek statues. Elena stayed late, & we messed about printing her dry points. Aunt Minna & Violet came on top & complicated matters. Out for a dash. Then read my Sichel & wrote a letter or two. Another book from the Times! – a fat novel, I'm sorry to say.[32] They pelt me now.

Wednesday 15 March

Wrote all the morning at an article on Greek – the Magic Greek, I think I shall call it & send it to the Academy.[33] I didn't finish it, but it amused me rather to do. Lunch early, & Nessa to Alexandra House. It was an impossible day: the sort of day that ought to be improved on. Altogether too barbaric for this eye. I struggled out against wind & rain, to a necessary tailor, & then home, & finished my Sichel book, & the problems of a review remaining to be solved – Dined with Cecils – took down long faced R. Smith,[34] & it was fairly amusing.

Thursday 16 March

Started my Sichel review for the Times, but it was heavy going. It is a satirical fact that when I am allowed ½ a column I can always fill 2, & when I am to have as much space as I like, I cant screw out words at any price. So I laboured – & did two pages, which isn't half what I must do.

30 Donald Francis Tovey (1875-1940), pianist, composer and musical essayist.

31 AVS's notes were probably on A. A. Tilley 'The Reformation in France', in *The Cambridge Modern History. Vol.II*, 1903; see B. Silver, *Virginia Woolf's Reading Notes*, 1983, XXXV, B.11.

32 A review in the *TLS*, 31 March 1905 (Kp C1.2) of *The Fortunes of Farthings* by A. J. Dawson, reprinted in *VW Essays*, I.

33 The essay was never published.

34 Reginald John Smith (1857-1916), son-in-law of the founder of *The Cornhill Magazine*, which Leslie Stephen had edited from 1860-82, and its editor from 1898.

It is hard work reviewing when you dont know the subject. At every step I tremble guiltily, & withdraw, to temper my expressions. So it will be dull. Out with N. in the afternoon, & succumbed at Waters[35] to a wedding present for Miss Power.[36] Miss Malone[37] to dine – a silent poor woman. Sydney Turner & Gerald after dinner – the first of our Thursday Evenings![38]

Friday 17 March

Worked at the beastly review all the morning – & finished it, I suppose – but it's bad, I suppose, & I expect to have it thrown back in my hands. Lunch early, & Nessa to Alexandra House. Another brutal mediaeval day; & again I had to go to my tailors, & there I stayed a long time, as the man has much the same feeling about his tailoring as I have about my reviewing, only he seems to be more successful. We promised to go to tea with Elena, right down the other side of London, & I fetched Nessa with that purpose, & our courage oozed & we came home to tea alone instead, & I got my review finished, & sent off, though I know I ought to rewrite it. Nessa & Thoby to the Sangers.[39]

Saturday 18 March

Very lazy all the morning, as the review was done, & my head too stupid to tackle fresh writing. So I read a bit of the fat novel, Fortunes of Farthings, which I must review for the Times, but novels dont take much brains. Unless they are Henry James, indeed. I had to stop early in order to travel all the way down to lunch with Aunt Minna – where was Evelyn Duckworth[40] – Somehow these Duckworths are not of a distinguished type – Afterwards I went round to Marnys whom I found at home, & we took a walk – singular to say – in Kensington Gardens, which seems to recall a very different age & called on Clara [Pater], who was out, & so home. All in to dine.

---

35 Henry John Waters, jeweller, 22 South Molton Street, W.

36 A bookbinder.

37 Unidentified.

38 The Stephens' 'At Home' on 'Thursday Evenings' was started by Thoby Stephen at 46 Gordon Square, according to AVS, on this date: 16 March 1905. Technically, the first 'Thursday Evening' was 16 Feb. 1905, with Saxon Sydney-Turner as the only guest; see QB, I, p. 97.

39 Anna Dorothea (Dora), *née* Pease (1865-1955), and Charles (Charlie) Percy Sanger (1871-1930), Chancery Barrister.

40 See June 1897, n.7.

Sunday 19 March

A day which would have done no discredit to June; & besides had all the freshness of spring. So to observe these things better I took Nessa on a yellow bus, branded with a red H, all the way to the top of the Steep Hampstead Rd. & then on to the edge of the Heath, from which we looked miles into a land of green fields, blue distance, & cloudy trees. This did refresh our eyes; & birds sang here as in the country, & it was pitiable to have to turn our backs on such beauty; & descend again into the black pit of London – but we had to. I went & heard Elgar conduct some of his music at the Queens Hall;[41] home & found W. Darwin,[42] Miss Pater & Marny at tea. Margaret Lyttelton had been & gone –

Monday 20 March

Worked at my Magic Greek article this morning, which wanted finishing, & finishing is what I hate. But I did it – typewrote it, & sent it to the Academy. It is a short column, I should think, so I trust they wont excise. Snow & Nessa very late for lunch; after which I went off to Hatchards to look vaguely for travelling books, but without success. Bought some strawberries 1s. a basket on the way home. I think this ought to be marked as a record! Violet to tea, & Nessa out to dine with the Booths. T. & I went out at 9.30 by the Gower St. underground to Gloucester Rd. & there we went to the Hilton Youngs[43] &c: evening, which was dress clothes & respectable, & I was very disreputable! Home by 12.

Tuesday 21 March

Worked all the morning at my rather long & lazy task of making notes for Wednesday evening. Greek history this time, for which I have to plough through Bury,[44] try to pick up a fact or two, not wholly dry. But

---

41 Sunday Afternoon Concert; Sir Edward Elgar conducted the London Symphony Orchestra in some of his own work, among which were the *Concert Overture, Pomp and Circumstance March No. 3* and *Sea Pictures*; also on the programme was Schumann's Symphony No. 2 in C.

42 See Sept. 1897, n.12; his wife, Sara, had died in 1902, and he was now living in London.

43 Edward Hilton Young (1879-1960), Trinity College, Cambridge, called to the Bar in 1904; his brother was the mountaineer, Geoffrey Winthrop Young (1876-1958), Trinity College, and Assistant Master at Eton from 1900-5. A regular visitor at the 'Thursday Evenings', Hilton was for a while much attracted to AVS and in 1909 proposed to her; see QB, I, pp. 131, 144.

44 J. B. Bury, *History of Greece to the Death of Alexander the Great*, 1900, 1902.

as I doubt whether they know if Greeks or Romans 'came first' as the Lady said, I dont expect to make much impression! Jack before lunch, as I was going out: so we walked out together, & J. most opportunely told me about passports, & he took me to Cook,[45] & managed to secure forms, & witness my signature &c; so that is done. Snow to lunch; at 3 the motor came – took us to get Nelly's picture. Then I went to the tailor, & on to Sylina Stebbing's[46] workshop, where I had tea. I then spent a long time in a bookshop. A quiet evening.

Wednesday 22 March
Worked again at that interminable Greek history. This will be a dry lecture & no mistake! I did as much as I could – that is brought the beastly thing down to the Peloponnesian War – & there I thought I might without discredit stop. After lunch – & Jack by the way, came to lunch – I went off to Heathers[47] to buy a hat for the voyage – which I did in my usual haphazard fashion. The woman persisting that I should need *shade* in South Africa! Then to Bumpuses,[48] where I found some really nice little books fit for the pocket, & yet good to read. Home, & finished the novel which I am reading for the Times. Out to my girls, who are in a new room tonight; & were, I think, rather bored by my history & dull maps. I said goodbye to them, & they beg me to lecture steadily at English History next term 'from the beginning'.

Thursday 23 March
Wrote my review of Fortunes of Farthings this morning, a dull long winded book, incredibly sentimental – all of which had to be watered down for the Times. Finished this, & typewrote it out; & then wrote a little for my own amusement. Adrian turned up for lunch, & we had the true history of the Sultan of Zanzibar from his own mouth. He is still apparently rather nervous, as the Mayor has set detectives to watch. Out to Tisdall in the afternoon, where I was kept waiting. Had my tooth stopped, out of sheer virtue, & it hurt rather. Then on to Violet, who is in bed – her cook just gone to the Hospital with appendicitis – altogether a lively state of things. Nine people came to our evening & stayed till 1.[49]

45 Thomas Cook, Tourist Offices, with numerous branches throughout London.
46 See Jan. 1905, n.76.
47 Presumably a misspelling for Henry Heath, hatmaker, 105-109 Oxford Street, W.
48 John & Edward Bumpus, Ltd, booksellers, 350 Oxford Street, W.
49 No record of this 'Thursday Evening' survives; but see QB, I, pp. 97, 100, 101.

Friday 24 March
A very lazy morning – but Adrian was up, & Nessa was in spite of great misery, awaiting Mr. Tonks.[50] So I sat in the Studio, & tried to comfort – & did not work whatever. At one Tonks came, a great raw boned man, with a cold bony face, prominent eyes, & a look of mingled severity & boredom. He trained for a doctor, & has more the look of a capable surgeon than of an artist. We talked valiantly, but it was not easy work. He then reviewed the pictures, with a good deal of criticism apparently, but also some praise. Out on various jobs which I must get done before we sail. N. & T. dined with Mrs. Flower.[51] At 10.30 I fetched them, & we went on to Susans [Lushington] evening party, where I talked to G. Lushington, Helen, Miss Malone &c.[52]

Saturday 25 March
Wrote at a kind of sketch of my Morley College proceedings,[53] to amuse myself – & possibly this may be of interest in future terms – so that I may see how I started, & which girls came. N. out to lunch with Snow; & T. & I lunched early as he had to get to Wimbledon as a volunteer.[54] I bought what is called an 'attaché' case – a light thin case, which will just hold my books & writing paper, & can lie on my knee in the carriage. To the L. L. where I met Mrs Lyttelton, who asked me to write her articles about my 'personal experiences' in Spain; which I suppose I must do. The Academy send back my Magic Greek, which entertained them very much but is "too uncompromisingly opposed to their point of view" to be printed. Rather a bore, but I am amused all the same.

Sunday 26 March
Made a paper book this morning for my Spanish Diary, by means of which I hope to pay some at least of my travelling expenses. It is a Grub St. point of view[55] – but all the same, rather a nice little bit of writing

---

50 Henry Tonks (1862-1937), painter and teacher, for 40 years, at the Slade School of Art which Vanessa had briefly attended in 1904; see F. Spalding, *Vanessa Bell*, 1983, p. 46.

51 See Feb. 1897, n. 3.

52 Probably Susan's uncle, Sir Godfrey Lushington (1832-1907), Permanent Under-Secretary in the Home Office, 1885-95. For Helen Holland, see April 1897, n. 6.

53 For the 'Sketch of Morley College proceedings' see QB, I, Appendix B.

54 Presumably as a member of some voluntary military service, such as the Officers' Training Corps, established in 1908 in the UK.

55 i.e. the point of view of a literary hack.

might be made out of the sea & land. Read some of my Spanish history which seems to be consistently disreputable – Snow & Gerald to lunch. Sending in day for the R.A. imminent,[56] & Tonks criticisms have to be carried out, an annual crisis, I suppose. Out to my weekly concert[57] – a singularly empty house, in spite of a good Beethoven – I suppose the fine day is better to many people than fine music. Marny & George to tea.

Monday 27 March

A wretched wet morning of course, as I had to spend it in the occupation of all others that I hate – shopping. But so it was, & I tramped through the mud & had to buy what are called blouses – &c. My room begins to assume the familiar aspect of a city in a state of siege, & I walk guardedly among corpses & all kinds of litter. Work, thus out of the question, so I suppose my Easter holiday has begun, & the plan which A. & I made one September day at Teversal is really to be carried out. Snow to lunch. I had Georges motor, & went to various places – got £25 among other things for the journey. Mary[58] to dine, & to a concert with her – which should have been Richter but wasnt.[59] N. & T. out.

Tuesday 28 March

To day, of course, wholly given over to making ready. The problem as usual, is that of books, what to take, & how to find room, – especially as my little case is to hold all, also writing material. One dress box is all my other luggage. I have taken: Borrows Bible in Spain: Borrows Gipsies of Spain – The House of the Seven Gables – The Scarlet Letter. Richard Feverel – Baedeker. Spanish grammar – 1st vol. Greens Conquest of England.[60] I shall try to find room for another book or two in my box, as

56 Works intended for the Summer Exhibition at the Royal Academy have to be delivered there on a specific day to enable the Hanging Committee to make their selection.

57 Sunday Afternoon Concert; the Queen's Hall Orchestra, conducted by Henry Wood, played works by Beethoven, Bach, Elgar and Mackenzie.

58 Probably Mary Creighton; see Feb. 1905, n.2.

59 At the Queen's Hall; in the absence of Hans Richter, the London Symphony Orchestra, conducted by Herr Franz Beidler, played a programme of Wagnerian music and Beethoven's 'Eroica' Symphony.

60 George Borrow, *The Bible in Spain*, 1843 and *The Zincali, or Account of the Gipsies in Spain*, 1841; Nathaniel Hawthorne, *The House of the Seven Gables*, 1851 and *The Scarlet Letter*, 1850; George Meredith, *The Ordeal of Richard Feverel*, 1859; John Richard Green, *The Conquest of England*, 1883.

I know these will come to an end. Having now ascertained that Maud[61] has room for an indefinite number of extra books, I am more happy in my mind. I went to the L. L. to try for books, but without success – then to tea with Violet. Goodbye to her, & home, to finish packing. And now this little book must find a corner, for it is to come too – & I wonder what I shall write next!

Wednesday 29 March
Our start was early, so we had to rush our last packings after breakfast – indeed we left before my last blouse came home, & only had about 5 minutes for train. Gerald met us at Euston – & thus we left at 10.45. Reached Liverpool about 2.30 & went in a Bus to the pier, where a great many people were walking up & down, saying good bye, & preparing to go. A huge steamer, the Oceanic, 2nd largest afloat was black with passengers, just leaving for America. The Anselm[62] came alongside in time, & we embarked. It is all white & clean & luxurious; we each have a cabin to ourself, in wh. I now write on my knees, & the sea is beginning to rise: We walked on the deck & saw all the lights along the Coast of Wales, steamers passing, & our own foam spread like white lace on the dark waters – a very lovely thing is a ship at sea.

Thursday 30 March
A singular day, among the days that I have so far recorded. Woke to find it a bright blue day, the sun glistening on the waters. We went on deck, got ourselves chairs, & settled down to watch the coast of England unrolling itself before us. We saw the Lands End near – & thought how strange it was to see it thus again, from the deck of a steamer. In the afternoon we passed the Lizard which is the last English land we shall see, & now we are standing away across the Channel, towards Havre, where we anchor tomorrow. I read a certain amount, & long to sleep, & then we take a turn, & the old gentlemen tell their old stories, & some one lends a glass & so on –

Friday 31 March
This morning again fine, & perhaps even calmer. Again we sat on deck –

---

61 The housemaid who packed AVS's clothes.
62 The *Anselm* was a Booth Line Steamship, equipped to accommodate 140 first-class passengers. This voyage would be fictionalised in the early chapters of *The Voyage Out* (Kp A1), 1915.

as though, A. said, we had died & were gone to live with the blessed. For the moment one can imagine no more blessed existence than this – stretched in the sun, passing slowly through the waters. Shovel board, however, interrupted our paradise, got up by a gentleman who strikes one full face, as a single nose. He is a typical Jew, & initiates everything, & is a friend with everyone. I read most of the day, & shall finish my Borrow. The Ships library, I find, is stored in a certain chest which stands in the dining room, & is useful as a kind of side board. The key to this is lost! Arrive at Havre where we anchored & went on shore.

Saturday 1 April
This morning we breakfasted just before 7, & caught the 8 train to Rouen. With us – or we with them – went the Lloyds & Mr. Booth,[1] & we reached Rouen at 9, I think. There we saw three great churches,[2] a funeral, & a burial ground. Perhaps, in a sentimental way, the most touching thing there is the little corner – of the meat market! – where Jeanne d'Arc was burnt. All the places where she suffered are marked & commemorated; but the statues of her are all worthless & insignificant. We lunched there, & came home at 5.30 – A great many new passengers have boarded, & we start tomorrow again, for which I shall be glad. Travelling fills me with restlessness. I want to see the next place.

Sunday 2 April
By nine this morning we were gliding out of the Havre docks, & were soon out to sea – but before long the engines slowly ceased beating, & the ship came to a dead stop. This lasted a good two hours, & all through the day the ships progress has been interrupted. Some part of the machinery gets too hot, apparently, & we have talked of nothing else all day. It is a bore, as a wait here means that we shant get to Oporto early. This partly makes us determine to take the train from Oporto to Lisbon, which will save two days perhaps. However this plan is not settled. In the evening a grand concert was given, when several new artists appeared; it is amusing to watch them, though hardly pleasant always to listen. A fine smooth day, & we pass on without movement.

Monday 3 April
We steamed a certain way this morning, & then our engines gave out again, & for four hours I suppose we rocked & drifted out of sight of land, & very much bored. There is a certain Professor Lee[3] on board, who is something like Sully[4] & C[live]. B[ell]. mixed, & diluted, & this don is inflicted on me, over & over again till I suffer from acute bore-

---

1 Constance, *née* Booth (b.1876), and Godfrey Isaac Lloyd, later a professor at the University of Toronto; Constance was the daughter of Alfred Booth (1834-1914), founder, with Charles Booth, of Booth Steamship Co., Liverpool, 1863.
2 Notre-Dame Cathedral, the Cathedral of St Ouen, and the Church of St Maclou.
3 Possibly Robert Warden Lee (1868-1958), Professor of Roman-Dutch Law, University College, London, 1906-15.
4 James Sully (1842-1923), Professor of Philosophy, University College, London, 1892-1903, and a writer on psychology; he was one of Leslie Stephen's original 'Sunday Tramps'.

dom. Books are no protection; he thinks his conversation must be preferable. At night now we sit on deck instead of absorbing the music of Jews. At night we passed Ushant, & saw many lights along the coast.

Tuesday 4 April
In the Bay of Biscay – through which we ploughed all day, out of sight of land. It was a little rough, but nothing to keep up its reputation. Really the dullest day so far, I think; as the people are maddening with their perpetual noise, & The Bore is loose. However we had a fine sunset in the evening, & saw a few porpoises in the distance, & a great many globes of Jelly Fish just beneath the water of all colours. Lay out till 10 on the roof of the engine house, in a large life belt.

Wednesday 5 April
We woke to see the coast of Spain – a very fine coast, romantic, heroic, like a very aquiline nose. We passed along it all day, quite close, so that we could see houses & streams. To our joy the Captain said he expected to reach Oporto in the afternoon, & being a man of his word, he did – & at once we were surrounded by boats & officials. Leshoenis (that is how you pronounce it) is a red roofed, Southern looking town, flashing in the evening sun, behind which there is a steep bank with feathery trees. But we could not land, so this impression is fragmentary. We began at once to take our cargo on board, which consists for the most part of paving stones for Monaco's harbour. They are going to work all night – & the noise is already sufficient. Our last night on board – & I must pack for an early start tomorrow.

Thursday 6 April
We landed this morning & went through the usual Custom house bothers. Women acted as porters – a touch of the East. Then we took the tram, a long ride to Porto (Oporto) in a broiling sun, an English August sun – & with great difficulty tramped the town & found the Booth Agent who could tell us nothing about our ship. Lunch at the Hotel, with a drove of Tourists. Then with Lloyds to see over the "Lodge" of one of the great port wine merchants,[5] which was a cool scented place. Then took train to Lisbon, A. & I alone for the first time, & reached it at 10.30. Finally got rooms at the Hotel Borges.[6]

---

5   Probably Silva and Cosens of Villa Nova de Gaia, a suburb of Oporto.
6   In the Rua Garrett 108.

Friday 7 April
A really delightful day – the town is spacious & brilliantly white & clean, every street almost with its swift electric tram, which makes sightseeing a delight. We found our way about easily, by this means, & soon got our bearings. We had to see Mr Dawson the Agent, & he promised us berths on the Madeirensa – so that is a mercy. In the afternoon we went up to the English Cemetery,[7] on a hill – by the gardens. This is a most lovely place, sweet with flowers, & so hot & shady & green that we stayed there a long time. We let loose a caged bird that was singing by Fieldings tomb – a pious act! Train by night to Seville.

Saturday 8 April
The night was more comfortable than I expected. We did not undress, but lay in a kind of sofa, with a pillow, which was quite soft. All day we travelled; arriving at Badajoz on the Spanish frontier at 8. And so through Estremadura, & Andalusia – splendid names! But the country is not beautiful; for the most part, flat, & treeless, & the sun was hot. The train stopped at every village on the way. In the afternoon we came to a wilder & more interesting country, & with very few roads & houses, & great views. At 8.30 we reached Seville, drove to Hotel Roma,[8] had a gloomy dinner & to bed.

Sunday 9 April
We began to explore Seville this morning. First to the Cathedral,[9] which looms everywhere. It is vast. That is the first impression. I dont very much care for such elephantine beauty – but it is fine. Service was going on – & so we could not see much. In the afternoon we took a carriage & drove for an hour in the gardens[10] which are lovely, though somewhat faded & out of repair, like everything else. The streets are very narrow, cobbled, with no pavement to walk on. Trams bad & not easy to get. It is

---

7 Cemiterio dos Inglezas is the first Protestant burial ground in Portugal (1717); Henry Fielding (1707-54), whose tomb was erected by the exertions of the British Chaplain in 1830, is buried here.

8 Hotel de Roma, in the Plaza del Duque de la Victoria.

9 Built on the site of the former great Muslim mosque, the Cathedral is the largest place of worship in Spain, and the third largest in Christendom.

10 Probably those of the Alcàzar; see n.12.

a difficult town to find ones way about in – We went to the great hospital[11] & saw the yellow city walls, which easily enclose the city.

Monday 10 April

Woke this morning under my mosquito curtains – which the beasts merely laugh at – to find, firstly the maid carrying on a long & emphatic speech in Spanish – & 2ndly a rain of pure English blood pouring outside. (That sentence by the way may be read 2 ways – but we do not live in the time of the Inquisition.) Out in a clear space to the Giralda, which is the Cathedral Tower, from which we gazed over Seville; a small town it looks from that height, soon dwindling off into fields. White houses with brown roofs for the most part. The rain was such that we sat a long time in the Cathedral – which is not really beautiful, though certainly impressive – in the same way that a steep cliff or a bottomless well is. In the afternoon we 'did' Alcázar,[12] a splendid gilt & mosaic Moorish building – a sight again which does not charm me.

Tuesday 11 April

A showery morning again, but not so bad, it turned out, as yesterday. We went out & bought photographs – our solitary extravagance, & then saw the Church of the Caridad, which was not very interesting. The most interesting part of Seville is its streets. After lunch we took a cab & drove to the Casa Pilatos,[13] as it was raining. There are court yards leading to court yards, all of white marble – simpler & more stately than the Alcázar. Also a great many dark long rooms, round the court yards, lined with beautiful tiles, cool & hushed. Then we bought a spirit lamp with great skill, & various necessaries for our 2 meals in the train tomorrow. I shant be sorry to move on, though I have enjoyed this.

Wednesday 12 April

At 7 happily I woke, & we dressed for 7.30 breakfast, & without much regret left the hotel at 8. We travelled all day long, & changed twice. We

---

11 The Hospital de la Caridad, founded by Don Miguel Mañara whose remains rest under the altar of the Church of the Caridad, which is structurally integrated with the hospital complex.

12 The fortress palace begun in 1181, of which only the Almohad wall and the Patio de Yeso remain; Moorish and Spanish architects later rebuilt the courts, apartments and gardens.

13 The 16th-century Mudejar palace, reputed to have been modelled on the house of Pontius Pilate in Jerusalem.

had to indulge in things called Berliner[14] – coupes for 2, as all the 1sts were crowded. But on the whole the journey was more comfortable than last time. We got finally to a wild hilly region – the Sierra Nevadas in the midst of which Granada is set. Here, at 8.15 we arrived & were driven by 4 mules to the top of the high hill on which the Washington Irving[15] stands. There we happily found rooms, dined & to bed.

Thursday 13 April
Out as usual this morning to explore. We find ourselves in the greenest shade, as of great English trees, filtering a Southern sun. We are right above the town, but the Alhambra & the gardens of the Generalife are across the road.[16]

Unhappily, owing to some red tape, we had to tramp all the way to the town to get cards of admission, which took some time. The gardens are worth a good deal. They are very hot & fragrant, all in little inlaid terraces like an Italian garden, with cool summer houses where one may rest & look over the city to the snow mountains beyond. In the afternoon we were taken over the Alhambra by the guide, a gorgeous Moorish palace & within battered yellow walls.

Friday 14 April
This morning we 'did' the town, which mainly consists of the Cathedral[17] – a dull florid building, very ornate, containing only one thing that interested me – the tomb of Ferdinand & Isabella. In the afternoon we meant to allow ourselves the luxury of bargaining 25 pesetas' worth of Granada ware. I bought 2 lace sleeves, & finally after long bargaining an old Spanish gilt frame for Nessa – Really it wasn't dear, & I like it. But Granada is not tempting in this way – at least we didn't find the right shops perhaps. After dinner A. & I with two people – father & daughter

---

14 An end compartment of a railway carriage, often with two seats facing each other.

15 Washington Irving Hotel, Paseo Generalife, just across the road from the Alhambra. Washington Irving, while Ambassador to Spain in 1826, wrote *The Legends of the Alhambra*, 1832, 1852.

16 The Alhambra, built on a plateau overlooking Granada, is the oldest Moorish palace in the world, begun in 1238 under the rule of Al Ahamar. The Generalife was the former summer pleasure retreat of the Kings of Granada; its name derives from *Gennat-Alarif:* 'garden of the architect'.

17 In its Royal Chapel is the tomb of the first Catholic monarchs of United Spain, Ferdinand and Isabella, together with Isabella's crown, sceptre and coffer, and Ferdinand's sword.

who have made friends with us – went up to a court of the Alhambra &
saw the gipseys [*sic*] dance –

Saturday 15 April
Rather a lazy morning, but we have paid our respects to most things
here, & can afford to be idle this last day. Indeed, you cant spend time
better than in idling in the Gardens here – leaning over the sunny old
wall, & looking down in to that strange large view beneath. After lunch
we went down the hill to the Post Office, where to my disappointment
there were no letters, so we must leave Granada without news, & now
shall hardly hear again. After dinner the usual accounts & bills, which is
not extravagant. Pack once more, which I loathe, & now to bed, as we
begin our return journey at 6 to morrow.

Sunday 16 April
At 6.30 this morning we breakfasted, & at 7 left in the Bus. We had a
long tiresome journey, as usual, changing &c; at 9 we arrived at a place
called Amonhon where we were to sleep. There being, we were told, a
'good second class hotel'. Making all allowances for Spanish hotels as
we did, we were not prepared for a little white cottage, a kind of public
house, by the side of a desert & a Moorish castle, where we had to spend
the night. There was one room, so we lay in our clothes on the bed, &
managed to sleep a little till 5.30 when we had to pay 3 pesetas, & our
train started at 6.

Monday 17 April
We travelled till 12.30, & then stopped at Badajoz – where we had to
wait 6 hours – a very dreary time, as we were sleepy, & miserable – the
town hot & dirty, & we had nothing to do. We tried to find something to
look at, & listened to a comic performance in the Cathedral,[18] which I
likened to the singing of old country songs by half tipsey [*sic*] farmers.
The Cathedral might perhaps be fine; but they have defaced it with
glass. At 7. or so we happily left Badajoz, got an empty first class, which
took us without change to Lisbon. We eat some hard boiled eggs &
slept fairly well stretched on the seats.

Tuesday 18 April
We were woken by porters at Lisbon, rather to our confusion – so we

---

18 The Catedral de San Juan in the Plaza de España, dating from the 13th century.

had to put on our shoes, & scramble out, it being then about 5.30, a cold drizzly morning too, & the usual wait & bother about luggage. We came to the Central Hotel,[19] where we had baths – which were badly wanted – tidied, & at 8 some breakfast. The [Constance and Godfrey] Lloyds came in, & the whole Anselm party are staying here. The Madeirensa is late, of course, & wont start till Thursday – which is a dreadful bore, & means that we shall just have too little money to get home with. I have written to Sophie[20] for some. Mr. Dawson & Miss Dawson came round, & took us sight seeing all the afternoon. In the evening we went to the play, & to bed at last.

Wednesday 19 April

A lazy day, as it had a right to be. The Lloyds were out sightseeing, & we had satisfied our consciences. A walk to the Post Office, unfruitful, was enough for the morning – & a lazy tram drive, which landed us at the top of the Avenida took up the afternoon.

It was rather a wet day, as Mr. Dawson said was likely in Lisbon – two hot days, & then rain.

A dull evening, & to bed.

Thursday 20 April

A morning spent indoors. We packed & made ready for the boat; & felt quite prepared to leave Lisbon, & ready for England again. At 4 the whole party collected in the Black Horse Square,[21] which is the finest square in Lisbon, vast, empty, save for an old statue on horseback, which time has stained green. A boat took us a mile up the river to the Madeirensa, which we found to be a decidedly small boat: I had a room to myself – A. had to share. We started at once, & the sea was rough, & the boat rolled, & we were slightly ill!

Friday 21 April

A monotonous sea day, a little spoilt by our now haunting fear of sea sickness, which however did not return. We are not to stop anywhere, but make straight for Liverpool, which we reach late on Sunday – too

---

19 The Grand Hotel Central, Caes de Sodre.

20 Sophia Farrell (*c*. 1861-1942), cook to the Stephen and related families from the 1880s onwards, who had moved with them from Hyde Park Gate to Gordon Square.

21 Set on the bank of the Tagus River and dominated by a bronze equestrian statue of King Jose I.

late to land – another delay. The party on board is very sea sick, & depressed. The weather cold, & the quarters not over comfortable, & especially infested with smells. We passed through the Bay of Biscay, or at least began to pass & lost sight of Spanish land. I think my dates are wrong.[22]

Saturday 22 April
Sailed all day rather more cheerfully in the Bay, which was calm again however, & we did not suffer.

The voyage is monotonous, when you have once gone through it; however there is no reason to complain:

The party more vigorous, & a grand concert at night.

Sunday 23 April
Our last day. Woke somewhere near Pembrokeshire, & saw a light house, & then a long reach of land.

All day we were in sight of the Welsh Coast, which was familiar looking, & interesting. Towards evening we passed many light houses, & much discussion as usual, as to our where abouts. Took on a pilot at 8 who is to take us to Liverpool.

Some where about 10.30 or 11 we entered dock & anchored.

Monday 24 April
Break fast at 8, & every one eager to get on land & catch trains home. No letter with money. So I had to borrow £1.10 from the Lloyds, which just saw us through. We got the 9.40 train, crowded, & terribly late; however we reached Euston at 3 & went home in a few minutes, which was as usual, a thing worth travelling for. Nessa there – a good lunch – letters &c. & much talk. Thoby at camp at Dover[23] – a cold rather rainy day.

So our journey is over, but it was a good journey.

Tuesday 25 April
A delicious night in a spacious & clean & stationary bed, & comfortable dressing – not to speak of a bath – all of which one appreciates after Spain. A letter by the way, to return as I must do with a vengeance, to journalese from Bruce Richmond, with the unfortunate Sichel review

---

22 Actually her dates were correct.
23 See March 1905, n.54.

which has been hanging like a stone round my neck, & haunting my nights. It is not "academic" enough – sorry he misled me – an excellent article, but a professed historian is needed – to which I cordially agree, & Sichel goes to the waste paper basket!

Wednesday 26 April
Began work of a kind – an effort to fix some kind of sketch of our journey for Mrs. L.: but as usual the thing wont come – & after struggling 2 hours, I produced one scored page which has nothing to do with the subject. I can only hope for better luck next time. In the afternoon I changed a few pesetas & francs for still fewer silver shillings, wandered aimlessly with N., home at 4.30 for Fred who had much of great interest to say. He is to send his MS.[24] & I am to type write it. Pass book, & my balance better than I expected, so I paid some bills!

Thursday 27 April
A morning devoted to art! – happily successfully. I went off after breakfast to the New Gallery which might or might not have hung the Nelly picture[25] – & to my great relief found it in The Catalogue, & saw it hang fairly in the gallery, which is quite a cheerful beginning. Dashed home, & general rejoicing of a mild description. Went in the afternoon with A. & N. (most unwillingly) to the show again – a Sargent &c: but not a striking lot. Bruce Richmond sends me 3 books about Spain to review! – as I said I had come back from Spain. A general article wanted, wh. means I suppose that I can be as silly & amateurish as I like – but I earn money anyhow.[26]

Friday 28 April
Worked again at my Spanish Sketch[27] – which wont resolve itself into

---

24 Of *Life and Letters of Leslie Stephen*, 1906.

25 The Portrait of Lady Robert Cecil at the 18th Summer Exhibition of Works by Living Artists at the New Gallery was Vanessa's first painting to be exhibited. The exhibition included paintings by John Singer Sargent, Sir George Reid and George Henry, among others.

26 A review in *TLS*, 26 May 1905, called 'Journeys in Spain' (Kp C2), of *Letters from Catalonia and Other Parts of Spain*, 2 vols, by Rowland Thirlmere and *The Land of the Blessed Virgin: Sketches and Impressions in Andalusia* by W. Somerset Maugham, reprinted in *VW Essays*, I.

27 Part of this 'Spanish Sketch' was probably published as 'An Andulusian Inn' (Kp C2.02) in *The Guardian*, 19 July 1905, and reprinted in *VW Essays*, I.

words – however I did a page or two, & I suppose that will make one article – & I try to take pains & be sincere, & typewrite paragraph by paragraph so as to get the hang of the thing. After lunch N. & I to Beatrice [Thynne] at Manchester Sq: we saw her for an hour & a half – unchanged, save that Egypt dyes her more tawny, & she is a little more dishevelled than ever, it seems. We smoked cigarettes! – Home – Both Thoby & Adrian left after dinner – Adrian for Cambridge & Thoby for St Ives! – a journey which makes one jump.

Saturday 29 April
Wrote again at the Spanish Sketch – a fresh one this time, which goes a little better. Jack to lunch, & after that I at last got down to the L. L. & changed some books. I must now solidly drudge through the beginnings of English history, & with this purpose I have got Freeman & more Green,[28] but Green for some reason runs off my mind like water.

C[live]. B[ell]. to tea – a nice garrulous old man, with his odd information oozing out – rather pouring buckets full, so that we sit & are pumped into. Nessa's first commission from a Mrs. Seton to paint one or both of her children came after tea.

Sunday 30 April
April has a real title to its name[29] – a cryptic sentence, which I am too lazy to unknot. Anyhow it rained, & then was fine – & N. & I sat in the drawing room for 3 hours & discussed the ethics of suicide! a cheerful theme which the thought of [Nurse] Fardell[30] naturally suggests to my mind. Gerald to lunch, & afterwards I went to my familiar concert where we had the Pathetic,[31] a little threadbare now, & ones emotions less volatile. Home, & Fardell to tea, whom I escaped. Jack to dinner.

---

28 Edward A. Freeman, *History of the Norman Conquest of England*, 1876, 6 vols, and probably John Richard Green *The Conquest of England*, 1883 or *History of the English People*, 1877-80, 4 vols.

29 Probably reference to the children's verse: 'March winds and April showers/Bringeth vo'th May flowers . . .'

30 Presumably one of the nurses who looked after AVS during her 1904 illness and who nursed Vanessa and Thoby after the Greece expedition in 1906; see *VW Letters*, I, Nos. 287, 288 and 290.

31 Sunday Afternoon Concert; the Queen's Hall Orchestra, conducted by Henry Wood, played Beethoven, Handel, Verdi and Tchaikovsky.

Monday 1 May

Wrote again very laboriously at my Spanish job. Snow to lunch & to paint out half her Academy pictures.

Out with Gurth to get various things. Gurth disgraced me by barking in the shop, which sounded like a Lion roaring in a Cave.

Read a bit of my history, & some more of the Spanish twaddle – How I wish I could be brave & frank in my reviews, instead of having to spin them out elaborately.

Dine with Beatrice [Thynne].[1]

Tuesday 2 May

Worked again at Spain; Granada this time, but they are dry bones to preserve.

To the R. A. with Nessa after lunch, which is an Exhibition – that is true. The only pictures, Sargents & the one Furse, & the Furse is better than the Sargents to my thinking.[2]

History & typewriting as usual.

Wednesday 3 May

Worked at my Spanish stuff, & finished Granada, & so the three dry little sketches are done, but whether they have any conceivable use, even as wage earners, remains to be seen.

After lunch Violet appeared, & we went with her to the New Gallery where we again confronted the portrait in the balcony. Then to the R. A. – that painted desert, where again the only thing that shone out was the Furse. Sargent gets blasé. Home, & Nelly to tea, & she & Violet left in her motor car.

History & dull review books.[3] Thoby back from St Ives at 8 – & much delighted.

Thursday 4 May

Wrote at a fourth & final sketch, Granada this time.

Out after lunch with Gurth to get tickets for the Joachim concert at

---

1 At 15 Manchester Square, W.

2 The annual Royal Academy Exhibition; the picture by Charles Furse, who had died the previous year, was the Chantrey Bequest purchase of his large equestrian group entitled 'The Return from the Ride', portraying Mr and Mrs Aubrey Waterfield, now in the Tate Gallery.

3 The 'dull review' book was *Arrows of Fortune: a tale* by Algernon Gissing, reviewed in *The Guardian*, 17 May 1905, and reprinted in *VW Essays*, I.

the Bechstein Hall,[4] where Gurth accompanied a Lalo's song with a voluntary bass of his own composition & I had to remove him in haste.

Sylvia Milman[5] to lunch, by the way.

No one yet to our Thursdays, which have not really begun.

Friday 5 May

Wrote a thing possibly for the Academy about the Protestant Cemetery at Lisbon – my last bit of 'copy' – after which I shall settle to sober reviewing, & English history.[6]

Nessa off for the day to a cottage near Reading which Kitty & Leo have taken for a fortnight, & missed her trains both ways, & only got back for a late dinner. I went to the Fishers, dutifully, & had a long solitary talk with Aunty Mary.

Saturday 6 May

Finished my Fielding,[7] & put finishing touches to the other wretched things, which are very bad, & I am doubtful whether to send them. Out to Tonks' show[8] with N. but found it had not begun, so to the L. L. where we sat & read Magazines for some time.

Home – & no one to tea. So I all but finished the 3rd of my Spanish review books, which is a mercy. So next week I shall write that.

Sunday 7 May

A holiday morning expedition to Hampstead, which, like the Cockney I am, still manages to delight me – There is something fantastic – I mean phantom like – about this little vision of country in the heart of London.

To a dull, & empty concert after lunch.[9]

[Clive] Bell to dinner.

---

4   A series of six private subscription concerts by the Joachim Quartet at the Bechstein Hall (now the Wigmore Hall), Wigmore Street, W, was to take place between Monday 8 May and Friday 19 May.
5   See Jan. 1897, n.68.
6   The Protestant Cemetery essay has not been traced.
7   Reference to the Protestant Cemetery essay.
8   An exhibition of works by Henry Tonks, at Carfax and Co., 24 Bury Street, SW.
9   Queen's Hall Sunday Afternoon Concert; Sir Alexander Mackenzie and Mr Arthur Payne conducted the London Symphony Orchestra in works by Beethoven, Brahms, Mackenzie, Wagner and Berlioz.

Monday 8 May

Worked all the morning at the review of the Spanish books for the Times; over which as usual I groan & struggle. But I can write without an evil conscience this time.

After lunch all the way down to the Milmans, where we renewed acquaintance with Maud, after many years, in which she has grown into a proper young Lady.

To dine with Adrian at the Robert Cecils & then to the play with L. Robert [Cecil] & Beatrice [Thynne].

Tuesday 9 May

Finished after a fashion my Spanish book review this morning, which is dull reading, I think, though virtuous.

Adrian & Snow to lunch.

After lunch Violet came, & I sat with her in the Square Garden,[10] for some time.

At. Minna to tea –

Adrian back to Cambridge after dinner, having eaten 2 dinners.[11]

Mrs. Lyttelton sends me Miss Robin's new book to review.[12]

Wednesday 10 May

Began work on my English History lectures for my working women. I have read Green, & Freeman's first volume, with copious notes;[13] & now boil these down, into something as readable as I can make it. It amuses me, as English History always does, & Freeman is a good manly writer with no nonsense about him.

P.M. – Something dull – a walk.

Meg Booth dines & to a concert for which I had bought the wrong tickets. To my working women – 3 this time.

Thursday 11 May

Worked at History again.

P.M: Out with Gurth & met George in a carriage & pair, who asked me to call on Margaret, but she was asleep.

---

10 i.e. the Gordon Square gardens.
11 A required part of the English legal apprenticeship at the Inns of Court.
12 A review in *The Guardian*, 24 May 1905 (Kp C1.3), of *A Dark Lantern* by Elizabeth Robins, reprinted in *VW Essays*, I.
13 See below pp. 278-80.

Home.

Our 'Evening' – Gay,[14] Bell, D. MacCarthy[15] & Gerald – who shocked the cultured.

Friday 12 May
As it must be confessed that I write this on 27th May, it is useless to pretend that I can record what happened on the 12th. I suppose I may safely say that I wrote something, probably touching upon Spanish Sketches in the morning – & went out in the afternoon.

Saturday 13 May
So ominous a silence means – what I recognised before, that my Diary sinks into a premature grave. It is a hopeless attempt: writing an extra page every day, when I write so many of necessity bores me, & the story is dull.

Sunday 14 May [to] Tuesday 30 May
[*These pages are blank.*]

Wednesday 31 May
We will solemnly renounce this diary, now that we come to an end of the month, & find, happily that the book provides no more pages – for they would assuredly be left blank.

Such an exercise can only be fulfilled when it is voluntary, & words come spontaneously. Directly writing is a task – why, one asks, should one inflict oneself thus? The good is nullified. But there is no need of such reflections. All but six months find some sort of mirror of themselves here; the sight is one that profits or pleases.

Thursday
[*This page was undated and blank.*]

---

14 Probably Russell Kerr Gaye (1877-1909), Trinity College, Cambridge, and a Fellow from 1900; he committed suicide on 11 April 1909.
15 (Charles Otto) Desmond MacCarthy (1877-1952), Trinity College, Cambridge, literary journalist and drama critic.

AVS's Notes to the 1904-5 Journal

[*The following notes by AVS begin at the end of the volume and move forward. Page numbers within brackets have been editorially supplied.*]

[*Page 1*]

$$30) \; 170 \; (5$$
$$\underline{150}$$
$$20$$

[*Page 2*]

BOOKS 1905

Jan:

√ Life of William Morris[1]
√ Paters Renaissance[2]
√ Layards Nineveh[3]
  Thorpes Northern Mythology[4]
√ Traills Social England[5]
  Galtons Heredity[6]
√ Greens Townlife in 15th Cent:[7]
√ Oxford History of Music[8]
  Dixons (Canon) works.[9]

---

1 John William Mackail, *The Life of William Morris*, 1899.
2 Walter Horatio Pater, *Studies in the History of the Renaissance*, 1878.
3 Austen Henry Layard, *Nineveh and its Remains: With an Account of a Visit to the Chaldaean Christians of Kurdistan, and the Yezidis, or Devil-Worshippers; and an Inquiry into the Manners and Arts of the Ancient Assyrians*, 2 vols, 1848-9.
4 Benjamin Thorpe, *Northern Mythology, Comprising the Principal Popular Traditions and Superstitions of Scandinavia, North Germany, and the Netherlands, etc.*, 3 vols, 1851.
5 *Social England: A Record of the Progress of the People . . . By Various Writers.* ed. Henry Duff Traill and James Saumarez Mann, 6 vols, 1901-4; reviewed in *The Guardian*, 7 Dec. 1904, reprinted in *VW Essays*, I.
6 Francis Galton, *Hereditary Genius: An Enquiry into its Laws and Consequences*, 1869.
7 Alice Stopford Green, *Town Life in the Fifteenth Century*, 1894.
8 *The Oxford History of Music*, ed. W. H. Hadow, 6 vols, 1901-5; Vol. V, *The Viennese Period*, reviewed in *The Guardian*, 14 June 1905, reprinted in *VW Essays*, I.
9 Richard Watson Dixon (1833-1900), historian, poet and divine, was author of many works; possibly AVS was referring to *History of the Church of England . . .*, 1885, but more probably to *The Last Poems of Richard Watson Dixon . . .*, ed. Robert Bridges, 1905.

√ W. Morris'es Early works[10]
√ Defence of Guenevere.[11]
√ Freemans works. on Towns. Architecture[12]
Mackails *Latin Literature*[13]
√ History of Indian Mutiny[14]
√ Jeffries "After London"[15]
√ Life of Stone Wall Jackson. Henderson.[16]
Feb.

[*Page 3*]
√ Barham of Beltana W.E. Norris.[17]
~~Catherine de Medici Edith Sichel~~[18]
√ Fortunes of Farthings.[19]
Magic Greek.[20]

[*Page 4*]

WORK DONE

Before Xmas 1904
Haworth[21]

---

10 Probably William Morris's *The Earthly Paradise*, 3 vols, 1866-70, and *The Life and Death of Jason*, 1867.

11 William Morris, *The Defence of Guenevere*, 1858.

12 Edward A. Freeman, *The History of the Norman Conquest of England*, [Towns:] Vol. IV, p. 327-Vol. V, p. 472; [Architecture:] Vol. V, p. 599-646, 6 vols, 1876.

13 John William Mackail, *Latin Literature*, 1895.

14 George William Forrest, *A History of the Indian Mutiny, Reviewed and Illustrated from the Original Documents* . . ., 3 vols, 1904-12; AVS reviewed Vols I and II in *The Guardian*, 22 Feb. 1905, reprinted in *VW Essays*, I.

15 Richard Jefferies, *After London; or Wild England*, 1885.

16 George Francis Robert Henderson, *Stonewall Jackson and the American Civil War etc.*, 2 vols, 1898.

17 W. E. Norris, *Barham of Beltana*, 1905, reviewed in *TLS*, 17 March 1905, (Kp C1.1), reprinted in *VW Essays*, I.

18 Edith Sichel, *Catherine de Medici and the French Revolution*, 1905; AVS's review was not published.

19 A. J. Dawson, *The Fortunes of Farthings*, 1905, reviewed in *TLS*, 31 March 1905 (Kp C1.2), reprinted in *VW Essays*, I.

20 'Magic Greek', an unpublished essay by AVS.

21 'Haworth, November, 1904', published in *The Guardian*, 21 Dec. 1904, (Kp C02), reprinted in *VW Essays*, I.

Review:

√ Royal Langbrith[22]

   Arrows of Fortune[23]

√ Next Door Neighbours[24]

√ Feminine Fiction[25]   } Guardian

√ On a Faithful Friend[26]

   ~~Boswell as Letter Writer~~[27]

1905

   Note for Fred[28]

   Christchurch[29]

   Review: New Forest[30]

√ Women in America (800)[31]

√ A Belle of the Fifties (1000 words)[32]

√ The Golden Bowl. Henry James. (800)[33]

---

22 W. D. Howells, *The Son of Royal Langbrith*, 1904, reviewed in *The Guardian*, 14 Dec. 1904, (Kp C01), reprinted in *VW Essays*, I.

23 Algernon Gissing, *Arrows of Fortune: a tale*, 1904, reviewed in *The Guardian*, 17 May 1905 and reprinted in *VW Essays*, I.

24 W. Pett Ridge, *Next-Door Neighbours*, 1904, reviewed in *The Guardian*, 4 Jan. 1905 (Kp C03), reprinted in *VW Essays*, I.

25 William Leonard Courtney, *The Feminine Note in Fiction*, 1904, reviewed in *The Guardian*, 25 Jan. 1905, reprinted in *VW Essays*, I.

26 'On a Faithful Friend', published in *The Guardian*, 18 Jan. 1905 (Kp C04), reprinted in *VW Essays*, I.

27 'Boswell as Letter Writer', an unsolicited essay sent to Reginald Smith of *The Cornhill Magazine*, and rejected; see *VW Letters*, I, No. 206, to Violet Dickinson, early Jan. 1905.

28 AVS's note on her father Maitland printed in his *Life and Letters of Leslie Stephen*, 1906, pp. 474-7.

29 An essay on Priory Church, Christchurch, in the New Forest; it was published under the title 'A Priory Church' in *The Guardian*, 26 July 1905 (Kp C2.03), reprinted in *VW Essays*, I.

30 See *VW Letters*, I, No. 206 (2nd paragraph) to Violet Dickinson, early Jan. 1905; the New Forest essay has not been traced.

31 Elizabeth McCracken, *The Women of America*, 1904, reviewed in *The Guardian*, 31 May 1905, reprinted *VW Essays*, I.

32 *A Belle of the Fifties: Memoirs of Mrs Clay, of Alabama, Put into Narrative Form by Ada Sterling*, 1905, reviewed in *The Guardian*, 8 Feb. 1905 (Kp C05), reprinted in *VW Essays*, I.

33 Henry James, *The Golden Bowl*, 1905; the review, entitled 'Mr Henry James's Latest Novel', was published in *The Guardian*, 22 Feb. 1905 (Kp C06), reprinted in *VW Essays*, I.

√ Street Music (National Review)[34]
√ The Plague of Essays (Academy)[35]
√ Dickens Country   ⎫
√ Thackeray Country   ⎬   Times[36]
√ Value of Laughter[37]   ⎭
√ By Beach & Bogland[38]
√ Nancy Stair[39]

[*Page 5*]
Number of words in a foolscap typewriter @ 450
[Number of words] " " page of my MS. book 400
~~325~~

5. Clarendon Terrace
Kempton
       Brighton[40]
The Academy
      5-7 Southampton Street[41]
      Strand W.C.
               2 columns   column[42]
                        10S
                    1
                     10
                    1
                     1.10

---

34 'Street Music', published in the *National Review*, March 1905 (Kp C3), reprinted in *VW Essays*, I.
35 'A Plague of Essays' published under the title 'The Decay of Essay-writing' in *Academy & Literature*, 25 Feb. 1905 (Kp Co7), reprinted in *VW Essays*, I.
36 F. G. Kitton, *The Dickens Country*, 1905 and Lewis Melville, *The Thackeray Country*, 1905; the review was called 'Literary Geography' and published in *TLS*, 10 March 1905 (Kp C1), reprinted in *VW Essays*, I.
37 'The Value of Laughter' was published in *The Guardian*, 16 Aug. 1905 (Kp C2.2), reprinted in *VW Essays*, I.
38 Jane Barlow, *By Beach and Bogland*, 1905, reviewed in *The Guardian*, 22 March 1905, reprinted in *VW Essays*, I.
39 Elinor MacCartney, *Nancy Stair, A Novel*, 1905, reviewed in *The Guardian*, 10 May 1905, reprinted in *VW Essays*, I.
40 The Brighton address has not been traced.
41 Address of *Academy & Literature*.
42 Probably a calculation of article or review lengths to estimate the fees AVS would earn.

10

10

15

1.10

<u>10</u>

[*Page 6*]

NOTES

Hotels in Madrid

1. Hotel de Rome. Messrs Votti & Co. 9/ to 12 a day
2. Hotel de la Paix. J. Capdevielle 9/ to 14
3. English Pension Hotel. Miss Briggs
                              Calle Major 92.

Train from Lisbon to Madrid leaves the Railroad Station, Lisbon 11-5 a.m. arrives Madrid 8.30 next morning.

    fares. first class single   £2.11
                    return   3.8
           second single   1.18
                    return   2.7.

Passports advisable though not strictly necessary.

[*Page 7*]
[*Here the notebook is turned upside down. AVS begins her notes, in pencil.*]
    [Edward A.] Freemans History of the Norman Conquest

Vol. 5 [Chapter XXII]

England alone has a Chronicle for 700 years. This & Domesday book the great authorities for Early Eng. Hist. One great object of D[omesday]: was to see that the Danegeld was paid – laid on in the Danish invasion 2 years before. Also W[illiam]. wished to know exactly how he had portioned out land among N[ormans]. & [*illegible*] D[omesday]: 1st statistical document of modern Europe. Cf. [Charles] Booths Life & Labour 'a map & picture of England' a word of Ws. confiscations.

[*Page 8*]

Chap. 22. F[reeman, Vol. 5]. 653 [*sic*/ p.65]

We owe our national unity to Norman Conquest. Only bad result the mixture of tongues. Character of W. Rufus [p.] 72. Affection for his father. Doesnt plunder his fathers churches. W. gladly accepted [p.] 75. revolt of the Normans in favour of Robert – disadvantages of being

278

separated fr. Normandy. Odd leader. Rebellion suppressed by English.
W. a great fighter, was ambitious Schemes of foreign conquest. Wishes
to have Normandy, [*illegible*] Roberts weakness. W. brother Norman
leaders. [p.] 79. By the help of Eng. W. was safe upon his Throne. 1088
last struggle between 2 races. Ws. oppression.

[*Page 9*]

Dicey Law & opinion[43] Vol. 1. 56 –	Legal status of women in 18th cent. The married womans property act not yet passed. This the result of Mills' 'The Subjection of Women' – also much impetus given by the Princess, appeared in 1856 – quoted by Lord Lifford in the House of Lords. Tenigrove [?] suggestion of womens Colleges – put into practice by Miss Clough along with others at Newnham, 1860. Began in Cambridge – Girton? – Spread to Oxford, Lady Margarets. Somerville &c.

[*Page 10*]

Freeman [Vol.] 5. [p.] 81

Death of Lanfranc

1090   Beginning of foreign wars.

Ws dreams of continental conquest.

Normandy under Robert in a state of anarchy. Western part made over to Henry. To the interest of Ns to have one King.

[p.] 86   R craves help from Philip K. of France. beginning of French English wars.

1091   William goes to Normandy; assigned lands wh. hemmed in N. to N[orth]. & S[outh]. to help R. to recover lost provinces. Either prince without child to succeed to the lands of both on the death of one.

W. & R leagued against Henry.

Hereditary kingship: Kingship to be bartered to his next of kin by the King. Further disputes between W. & R.

1096   Beginning of Crusades.

R. went on pilgrimage.

Redemption of the Holy Land from its infidel oppressors. R.

---

43 Albert Venn Dicey, *Lectures on the Relations Between Law and Public Opinion During the Nineteenth Century*, 1905; AVS's notes are unrelated to Dicey and have not been traced.

pledges the Duchy of N[ormandy]. to W. for 10,000 marks. English taxed to produce it.

[p.] 95   Possessions of N. marks beginning of E[nglish]. & F[rench]. wars. W. supposed to covet crown of France.

[*Page 11*]

F[reeman]. [Vol.] 5. [p.] 102

1097   war with France.

1098   peace with France.

W. wins Maine.

Wars in Wales & Scotland.

Vassalage of Scotland renewed. Wales more effectually subdued than usual.

Conquest of South Wales.

Speech in South Wales – Castles.

Cornwall 1905

*During the summer months, Virginia paid visits to relatives in the country, went to
the Trinity College Ball at Cambridge and continued reviewing books for* The
Guardian. *In the early months of the year she had also begun writing for* The
Times Literary Supplement. *So she was in high spirits when she set off in
August with her sister and brothers to Carbis Bay, near St Ives, for their summer
holiday. Here in Cornwall, Virginia found the twelve years of her childhood preserved, and this August of 1905, in twenty years' time, would be recollected and
reimagined in the third part of* To the Lighthouse.

DIARY
CORNWALL
1905

Carbis Bay[1]   *11 August*
It was with some feeling of enchantment that we took our places yesterday in the Great Western train. This was the wizard who was to trans-
port us into another world, almost into another age. We would fain have
believed that this little corner of England had slept under some en-
chanters spell since we last set eyes on it ten [eleven] years[2] ago, & that
no breath of change had stirred its leaves, or troubled its waters. There
too, we should find our past preserved, as though through all this time it
had been guarded & treasured for us to come back to one day – it mattered not how far distant. Many were the summers we had spent in St
Ives;[3] was it not reasonable to believe that as far away we cherished the
memory of them, so here on the spot where we left them we should be
able to recover something tangible of their substance?
    Ah, how strange it was, then, to watch the familiar shapes of land &

---

1   The four Stephens lodged at Trevose View, Carbis Bay, Cornwall.
2   The last visit of the family was in fact in 1894: Julia Stephen died in May 1895.
3   In 1882 Leslie Stephen took a lease on Talland House, St Ives, where the family went
    every summer.

sea unroll themselves once more, as though a magicians hand had raised the curtain that hung between us, & to see once more the silent but palpable forms, which for more than ten years we had seen only in dreams, or in the visions of waking hours.

It was dusk when we came, so that there still seemed to be a film between us & the reality. We could fancy that we were but coming home along the high road after some long day's outing, & that when we reached the gate at Talland House, we should thrust it open, & find ourselves among the familiar sights again. In the dark, indeed, we made bold to humour this fancy of ours further than we had a right to; we passed through the gate, groped stealthily but with sure feet up the carriage drive, mounted the little flight of rough steps, & peered through a chink in the escalonia hedge. There was the house, with its two lighted windows; there on the terrace were the stone urns, against the bank of tall flowers; all, so far as we could see was as though we had but left it in the morning. But yet, as we knew well, we could go no further; if we advanced the spell was broken. The lights were not our lights; the voices were the voices of strangers. [ ] We hung there like ghosts in the shade of the hedge, & at the sound of footsteps we turned away.

From the raised platform of the high road we beheld the curve wh. seemed to enclose a great sweep of bay full tonight of liquid mist, set with silver stars & we traced the promontory of the island, & saw the cluster of lights which nestle in its warm hollow.

The dawn however rose upon that dim twilight & showed us a country of bright hill sides, of cliffs tumbling in a cascade of brown rocks into the sea, &, alas, we saw also not a few solid white mansions where the heather used to spring. They have cut a broad public road too, where we stumbled along a foot path on the side of the moor, & there are signs, as [A.] said, that the whole place has been tidied up since our day. There are differences though, which only strike a very fresh eye, & in two days time we see only the permanent outlines of the moor & island, & the place is in substance & detail unchanged.

Yesterday, for instance, we followed foot paths to Trencrom,[4] which was, 11 years ago, our punctual Sunday walk. The brambles still stretch across it, & the granite blocks in the earth still bring you to your nose. At the corner we came to the Peacock farm, where the dunghill was as large as ever though there was no successor to the proud bird of old days. So, at every turn of the road, we could anticipate some little

---

4   Trencrom Hill, about 3 miles south of St Ives, with a hill fort.

characteristic – a water trough – or a plank over the stream – which had impressed itself minutely upon our childish minds, & great was our joy when we discovered that our memory was right. To find these details unchanged, indeed, gave us a keener pleasure than to find the big hills in their places.

These trifles testified to the scrupulous exactitude of our observation, & proved how accurately we had known our mistress.

Also it was clear that where such details were untouched we should find no larger change. Indeed every step of our walk might have been taken eleven years ago, & we should have found nothing to surprise our eyes. On the top of Tren Crom indeed, I was considerably surprised to see how large a view of the surrounding country was unfolded; moreover I had no notion that from this point you can see both sides of the coast at once; Hayle Harbour[5] on the North, St Michael's Mount[6] on the South, & all the long stretch of bay which ends in the Lizard point.[7] But as these features of the landscape have not changed in eleven years, or in eleven hundred, the change must be in my point of view & not in the outlines of the earth.

Monday 14 August

Today we did what we have long promised ourselves to do on the first opportunity, that is we hired a fishing boat & went for a sail in the bay. But the sea was so calm that great stretches of it had a dull surface, & our sail made no attempt to lift the boat. Our boatman, had to take his oars, & for amusement we lay back & watched the tawny sail flapping against the sky, & tried to make the man discourse of the sea. He was induced to tell us how, last winter, he had been capsized in his herring boat; how he had been rescued as by a miracle, as he clung to the keel; how he would be off on the same toil next month, & how he would make one of the crew of the seine boats which lie waiting for pilchards in the bay. At this moment the monotony of our slow progress was relieved by a sudden exclamation of porpoises; & not far distant we saw a shiny black fin performing what looked like a series of marine cartwheels.

We sailed into the midst of a whole school of these gymnasts who

---

5 A small port on the estuary at the head of St Ives Bay, directly across from Lelant.

6 A steep mass of granite and slate, connected to the shore by a causeway.

7 The southernmost peninsula in England, a bold promontory rising 186 feet above the sea, with a lighthouse built in 1752.

came so near that we could hear their gulp for breath before they dived again. Porpoises remarked the boatman, are a sign of pilchards in the bay.

This evening we observed two or three long black boats rowing out beyond the point; later we saw the dotted circle of a net lying on the water between them. This was surprising because the seine boats seldom take up their places before September, & there is rarely any likelihood of a haul before October.

However as circumstances were favourable to an after dinner walk – to tell the truth our water supply has failed, & we had to dine at the Hotel, we strolled up to the little white house on the crest of the hill, where the hewer sits with his eyes on the water below ready to discover the floating cloud of pilchards. The boats lay directly beneath this point, & a little group of people was clustered round the hewers seats talking the delightful vernacular of Cornish fisher folk. They talked of "tucking" & "shooting the seine" & interpreted the shouts of the men in the boats, who were trying it seemed, to drag their nets clear of the rocks. Then we looked towards the island, a vague shape, of neutral tint, & saw a light burn suddenly from the point. This was some signal to the boatmen apparently, which was answered by fresh cries, which had a wild sound in the falling dusk. The good people chatted of last years haul, & the mens wages, & who owned this boat, & who that; & meanwhile exquisite scents of warm escalonia hedges were blown from the wood behind. St Ives from this point & in the dark is divested of detail; you see only the promontory of the island running out in to sea, & the exquisite curve of the bay. The land has lost its opacity, & seems a vague mist like substance starred with lights, & circled by pale & luminous waters which still mirror the light of the west.

The other day as it rained A. & I turned from the main street into the shelter of the Church.[8] We looked for little more, but we found ourselves in a quaint but really beautiful old building, shaped something like a ship, it seemed, with a dark ceiling of oak, & strange old carvings wrought in the black pews & rafters. The sound of the sea might be heard by the congregation & there was something touching in the thought that generations of fisher folk had knelt here within the hearing

---

8   In the old part of St Ives, the 15th- century parish church, dedicated to the Irish St Ia, believed to have suffered martyrdom in 450 at the mouth of the Hayle River; St Ives is named after her.

of its voice & prayed for safety on its waters, & prosperity in their fishing. There is more of quaintness, perhaps, than of beauty; as though the worshippers were poor people who could not afford much more ornament than a slab of graven slate when they died.

As we passed out, we were stopped by some piece of information volunteered by the caretaker; an elderly woman in black who sat near the door. Suddenly she dropped her professional voice, & asked us if we had ever had friends who lived here? We answered naturally, that we had lived here ourselves for some 13 summers; "Ah" she cried & there was what is rare, the thrill of real emotion in her voice, "You are Mr. Stephen. Let me shake you by your hand my dear. Sit down a moment & talk to me."

We sat & for some half hour or so, she poured forth her memories, her constant remembrance & gratitude, & her joy to see some of the old family at least, once more. 'It sets the heart beating in my body' she cried, & wiped away a tear which wept for many sorrows. She had heard of our coming, & had asked every visitor to the church for news of us; even as we came in she was speaking our name to a couple of strange sight seers. She was not, I should guess, a woman of any special refinement but it would be hypercritical not to see that in this instance she was genuinely & deeply touched. To have left so deep an impression on a mind not naturally sensitive to receive it, so that after eleven years tears will start at the thought of all the beauty & charity that are recalled by a name [Julia Stephen] seems to me perhaps the purest tribute which can be paid to the nobility of a life which did not seek for any other fame.[ ]

And as I heard those humble words of the love that one woman felt for another I thought that no acclamation of praise throughout the whole world could sound so sweet, or could mean so much.

It has become the habit for me to spend my afternoons in solitary tramping. A great distance of the surrounding country have I now traversed thus, & the map of the land becomes solid in my brain. Twice these walks were taken in the teeth of heavy rain storms. I walked, it seemed, toward the very front of the torrent, up among grey hills. Both times it swept like driving smoke across the sea, & all the cheerful shapes & colours evaporated. One could just see the hazy outlines of the hills which lifted themselves out of the mist, but the sweep of the bay filled almost instantly with dense vapours.

At Knills monument[9] I had to take my bearings, & repeated "A blinding mist came down & hid the land!" & reflected how easily I might share Lucy's[10] fate. The delight of the country is that all moods of the air & the earth are natural, & therefore fit & beautiful. There is nothing incongruous about a wet day among the hills, as there is when decent streets & brick houses are exposed to the shock of an uncivilised storm. One may fancy even, a storm rejoicing among these granite hills when the wind & rain beat upon them as though they loved the conflict. But the sunny days give one, after all, a more spontaneous pleasure, the scents of the earth & the budding gorse are sucked out of them by the heat, & all the land glows with a mellow August radiance. The air becomes of a richly luminous quality; you see all things through an amber coloured medium.

Up on the hill today the only sound we heard was the tap tap of the stone breakers as they chipped the granite blocks, & we noticed the curious creamy richness of the stone pit in which they stood; the sun every now & then, making it gleam silver.

Today we set apart as a day of pilgrimage to certain old St Ives people, who in spite of the passage of eleven years, still cherish some faithful memory of us. So at least we were told, though I think we delayed the expedition a little from fear we might find that this statement had been exaggerated. The farmers daughter who used to bring us our chickens & help in the house, the woman who took in our washing, the old man who kept the bathing tents & his wife; these were the people we proposed to visit in their cottages in St Ives.

There was no doubt, at any rate that Jinny Berryman, as she was, did cordially remember & welcome us. It was a pleasure to see the blank respectful face of the woman behind the counter in the eating shop glow with sudden recognition when we spoke our name. We were made to sit down, & hear how we had changed, or had remained the same; whom

---

9 Just west of Carbis Bay, the monument erected in 1782 to commemorate St Ives's Mayor, John Knill, a smuggler turned lawyer; AVS wrote of St Ives's history: '. . . every twelve [five] years or so, old men and women over seventy danced round Knill's Monument – a granite steeple in a clearing – and the couple who danced longest were given a shilling? half a crown? – by the Mayor . . .' *MoB*, p. 132.

10 Lucy Ashton, the eponymous tragic heroine of Sir Walter Scott's *The Bride of Lammermoor*, 1819. In love with the son of Lord Ravenswood, whom her father has ruined, Lucy is forced to marry the dissolute Frank Hayston; mad with grief she stabs her bridegroom and on the following day dies in convulsions.

we were like & whom we in no way resembled, how we climbed the tree in the garden, & how in short, we were much as other children are, but to this woman at least, remarkable in all we did & said.

At Mrs Daniels the same story was repeated, & if possible our greeting was more hearty. She too, must grip our hands fast, & look close in our faces by the light – If one had changed she would have known the other "any where". We were like, we were unlike, we were, at any rate, the old family come back again, & that seemed a joy that could hardly be put into words.

All kinds of trivial half forgotten memories revived & we did our share of question, & anecdote; we asserted that there was no place like St Ives, & that we had never forgotten its washer woman. Indeed, we were not guilty of insincerity; her portrait had been lying unexposed in some dim recess of our brains, & at the first sight of her face the old picture became clear again, & with it a multitude of slighter impressions which seem to cluster round it. I could see her once more tramping up the drive with her basket of clean clothes, leaning away from her burden, & ready to put it down & talk good humouredly if we stopped her.

She married the squint eyed carpenter, who might be seen on the glass roof of the grape house, filling the crannies with putty.[ ] His temper had grown no sweeter though he came in & shook us by the hand at his wife's bidding. "John," she remarked, "is as old fashioned as ever." We left, luckily, before I had divulged the fact that I took him for her brother; the doubt whether he might not, after all, be her son, kept me silent.

Eleven years have had the effect in St Ives as in other places, of deepening wrinkles, & bleaching the brown hair white, but they have also had the stranger property of uniting the people whom we thought old even then, in marriage.

It seems to be a deliberate action among the poor here, as though it were a step that recommended itself as a precaution against old age. Jinny Berryman, however, was too hasty it seems, even in her long deferred marriage, for after a wedded life of nine days she left her husband, & though they meet in the road they have never spoken to each other since. The man was married before to a woman who on her death bed required of her husband that he should take Jinny as his second wife. There is a curious little plot, or rather psychological study for a novelist.

We went on next to the Pascoes,[11] who still live in one of those delightful cottages beneath the apple trees on the steep hill leading from the beach.

We walked along the narrow cobble stoned passage which leads to their door, & in the shade of their creepers the old people within did not immediately recognise us. We had the usual moment of uncomfortable hesitation, & then the hearty explosion, which by this time was not unexpected.

The old couple had sensibly diminished in size during these eleven years; they were sitting over their tea, a fire in the grate, & a good loaf of bread before them. All the chairs were put at our disposal, & while one received the torrent of Mrs. Pascoes greeting, two others went through the old story with Mr. Pascoe. The men, for the most part, have a less lively recollection of us than the women; they, probably, came more seldom into direct speech with us.

Mr. Pasco however had taken a lively interest in our bathing; he was anxious to tell us the melancholy decline of St Ives bathing since our day; how the tents are run on wheels, & owned by one man "a very selfish fellow"; how the working classes bathe, where only people of good family were wont to use that privilege; this, complicated with some mysterious story of ladies who wished him to help them on with their bathing dresses; (it sounds unlikely I know) had made it necessary for him to retire; which as we made haste to add, must have further hastened the melancholy state of things which we had observed on the beach.

Mr. Pasco, further, had had influenza two years ago; & wore his thumb bound up in a red rag. It is not necessary here to give the details; I will only say in his words that "caustic is poison for tumours".

He had moreover, like others whom we visited, read his papers for eleven years with an eye for the name of Stephens [*sic*]; & was thus well versed in the facts of our history, though the papers must have lied in some particulars, or his eyes cannot be as good as they were once. Thus he knew that G[eorge] was married, but insisted that he was still living in Chadwick; he was also of opinion that since his appointment as private Secretary he had gone to China. China, I remember, was one of the places which Mr. Pascoe had seen himself, when he was in the Navy.

Mrs. Pascoe was, I may confess it here, chiefly memorable for some

---

11 Albeit in name only, Mrs Pascoe and her husband (both also living in St Ives) appear briefly in *Jacob's Room*, 1922 (Kp A6): London, pp. 51-4; New York, pp. 52-6.

trouble in her 'pipes'; about which we used to enquire. She is now a little shrivelled woman, with a white fretful face, & very bright eyes. She had talked of us a hundred times in the last week, she assured us; & her intense interest at seeing us was really a little embarrassing. She was mistress of so many forgotten details that her reckoning of the number of thoughts she had spent on us in a weeks time, was probably no over statement. One can imagine that mewed up in the corner of the dark little room, without book or work, her thoughts must feed on slight food. "I cant believe that I see you there before me in the flesh" was a phrase that recurred, as though some persistent phantom had at last taken shape. At the news that G[eorge]. was coming here next week, she gave up her attempt to wrestle with the English language, & covered her face with her hands. A calmer mood followed this excitement, & she enquired into every circumstance of our lives minutely.

She had followed our fortunes without dropping the least link in the chain of evidence available to her; but our attention to the vicissitudes of the Pasco family was by no means of so fine a quality. We cheerfully remembered a daughter, when she was named, but our imagination refused to supply us with any record of Mrs. Pascoes nieces husband; who was responsible for the black dress to which our attention was directed. Nor did we acquit ourselves very creditably when the family history of the Whiteheads was recounted for our benefit. Miss Whitehead, I can at least remember, is now on the continent, recovering from a severe chill in her legs.

As Mrs. Pasco drew a melancholy sigh of self importance, & began to enumerate the many troubles which had visited her of late, we hastily remembered that we had already stayed too long. The catalogue threatened to be exhaustive. The good Pasco presented us each with little bouquets which he had picked from his garden, & offered to "pilot" us, "if I may have my joke" to his daughters house.

The outline of these Bays suggests that nature has a certain meditated felicity on occasion, & she appeals to one with a peculiar force when she thus appears to fashion her materials consciously.

The impetuous sweep of the large bay, curving round so that it half completes the circle, gives one an impression of beautifully curbed vitality; again in hollowing the three smaller bays in the flank of the large one she must, one would think, have had an eye to the fair proportion of the whole. They do not interfere with the single large impression; but they add something original; & unexpected. She seems to have perfect

facility in describing these spirited & graceful lines. The third of the
bays, Lelant Bay, is in some respects the loveliest of the three. It makes
the rounded corner of the large Bay; but the sweep of white sands is
intersected by the Hayle river, which draws a blue line down to the sea.
At low tide the course of the stream is marked by certain stakes, driven
in at irregular intervals. They look curiously bare & desolate for some
reason, a perch for white sea birds, & strike the distinct note, it seems, of
Lelant bay. At ebb tide in the evening the stretch of the sands here is vast
& melancholy; the waves spread themselves one over lapping the other
in thin fan shaped layers of water; so shallow that the break of the wave
is hardly more than a ripple. The slope of the beach gleams as though
laid with a film of mother o' pearl where the sea has been, & a row of sea
gulls sits on the skirts of the repeating wave. The pallor of the sandhills
makes the scene yet more ghostly, but the beautiful sights are often
melancholy & very lonely.

I thought today on my solitary walk on the scarcity of good roads in
Cornwall. In the South you find it difficult to escape from the road;
broad & smoothly hammered they drive across the country at all angles.
Even the lesser paths are workmanlike & strike directly to their destination. We have here our High Road, which however bears such marks of
rusticity that it would be accounted a lane elsewhere. Once you step
aside you must trust innumerable little footpaths, as thin as though trodden by rabbits, which lead over hills & through fields in all directions.
The Cornish substitute for a gate is simple; in building a wall of granite
blocks they let two or three jut out at convenient intervals so as to form
steps; you often find these arranged beside a gate which is heavily
padlocked, as though the farmer winked one eye at the trespasser. The
system of course has its advantages for the native, or for one well
acquainted with the lie of the country; it keeps the land fluid, as it were,
so that the feet may trace new paths in it at their will; but the stranger
must often prefer the cut & dry system of regular high roads.

The secondary roads, moreover, are not only badly preserved, but
sometimes after starting out bravely enough they dwindle off into a
track across the heather. The pedestrian then should sketch his path
with a free hand,& trust that he will find some little trodden line to guide
him; for in the course of an afternoon's tramp he need not strike the
road.

There are very few villages in this country, & the little clusters of
gray farms which gather among the hills connect themselves with the

main road by some roughly worked roadway of their own, leading directly into the farm yard. A traveller who follows the track finds herself at the end of half a mile or so confronted by a lean sheep dog, & a sour looking farmer's wife who is scouring the milk pails & resents the intrusion. But for the walker who prefers the variety & incident of the open fields to the orthodox precision of the high road, there is no such ground for walking as this.

It was more, perhaps, to fulfil a tradition than for the sake of any actual pleasure that we took the train into St Ives this afternoon, the day of the Regatta.[12] I, it must be confessed, secretly expected some present & not merely retrospective enjoyment from the crowd, the gay flags, & the fitful trumpets of the band. This was the scene I remembered; vaguely joyful & festive, without reference to the swimming or the sailing which we pretended to watch. I remembered the crowd of little boats, the floating flags along the course, & the Committee boat, dressed with lines of bunting, from which naked figures plunged, & guns were fired. A certain distant roll of drums & blare of trumpets, we confessed to each other, never fails where ever we hear it to suggest St Ives Regatta day on such [a] bright afternoon as this. We listen from the beach, safe in a Nurses hand again. The band was playing on the Malakoff, now as then; on close inspection we saw that a venerable clergyman waved the conductor's staff, although the music that issued from his beat was certainly secular in type. Two or three little booths for the sale of sweets & cakes lined the terrace, & the whole population of St Ives paraded up & down in their reds & greens.

There was the Committee boat, & the little rowing boats, the flags on the water, & the swimmers poised for a moment before the gun sent them shooting into the sea, & the general stir of talk & movement. Reduce it all to a French impressionist picture & the St Ives Regatta is not a sight to be despised.

These are rough notes to serve as land marks. At nine this morning, we

---

12 'Every year, in August, the Regatta took place in the bay ... A crowd of St Ives people gathered to watch in the Malakoff, that octagonal space at the end of the terrace which had been built, presumably, in the Crimean War and was the only attempt that the town made at ornament. St Ives had no pleasure pier, no parade, only this angular gravelly patch of ground, set with a few stone seats upon which retired fishermen in their blue jerseys smoked and gossiped.' *MoB*, pp. 131-2.

sat over our breakfast despondently, the mist deciding us to give up our expedition to Mullion.[13] Suddenly T. threw up the window & shouted "pilchards in the bay".

We leapt as though we were in the seine boat ourselves, & before half past nine we were out by the Hewers house[14] on the point. It was at once obvious that the news was more than true. Not only were there pilchards but two nets were already out, lying like dark scars in the water in the bay. The gathering of the Hewers was not large as yet, but it was eminently professional. A line of watchers stood on the wall all the way along: some with megaphones, others with globes tied up in white bags. Great was the excitement for the schools of fish were still passing through the bay & all the pilchard boats were in motion like long black insects with rows of legs. Our friend Mr. Hain[15] called us to him & showed us a certain faint purple shadow, passing slowly outside the rocks. That was a shoal he said – the boats were coming round to shoot their seines over it. As they neared the place the megaphones brayed unintelligibly & the white globes were waved emphatically. Answering shouts came from the boats. Finally we saw that two boats had stopped & the rowers were picking up handfuls of net & dropping them over board; as they did this they slowly separated, & made the dotted line of the net spread out in a circle between them; all the time the shouts went on, for the men at the hewers were guiding every movement; they alone could tell the exact position of the fish. The net was then joined & the boat went through various manoeuvres with the low ropes. It was just possible for us now that it was thus circumscribed to see the faint spin of deeper purple within the circle; it looked like one of those sudden ruffles of shade which pass across the sea like blushes.

The crowd was now gathering, & we walked from one point to another vainly trying to interpret the hoarse commands of the megaphone which might, for all we understood of them, have been in Cornish. Mr. Hain came running down again, after a time with the news that another school was sighted round the head land; the boats were not yet on the spot. At the Hewers house an intense excitement prevailed.

13 A fishing village on the south Cornish coast.
14 A small stone look-out post situated on Porthminster Point, the headland between St Ives and Carbis Bay; his job was to alert fishermen to incoming shoals of pilchards.
15 Edward Hain (1851-1917), shipowner, six times Mayor of St Ives and its MP from 1900-6; his wife had initiated a fund for a nurse at St Ives in memory of Julia Stephen; a sum of £500 was raised of which £200 was contributed by Leslie Stephen.

The shoal having rounded the point was the property apparently of the Carbis Bay boats, which had hitherto remained at anchor. They were now underway, & the Hewer who directed them had clambered on to the roof of the Hewers house to make directions more forcible. The boats came slowly towards the floating shadow which we thought we could detect beyond the Carrack[16] rocks. As they neared it, the megaphones roared like foghorns. A certain dwarf in particular had leapt to the roof & was brandishing the white globes as though they were dumb-bells. The boats began to drop the seine; they had half completed the circle when a storm of abuse broke from the hewers house. Language such as I will not try to reproduce swore at them for a boatload of incompetent monkeys; the school was further to the westward & not a fish would enter the nets. "To the west, west, west," roared the megaphones & the naked voices took up the word in the agony of excitement. But pilchard boats are unwieldy things, & their motion was slow. The Hewers could actually see the fish slipping past the point & the net cast in empty water. A thousand pounds as we afterwards learnt, was floating out of their reach. No wonder that the excitement was painful. The net finally enclosed a small portion of the school, & the rest fell a prey to the rival boats. Four seines were now shot & we thought it time to take a boat to the first of them which had been slowly drawn close in to shore. We therefore walked round to the harbour & were rowed out to the spot. When we came near we saw that the enclosed school was of a deep & unmistakable purple; little spurts of water were flickering over the surface, & a silver flash leapt into the air for a second. We took up our places by the row of corks & waited; after a time the empty pilchard boats with their baskets drew up & let down a smaller net, called the tucking net, in the centre of the larger one, so that all the fish were gathered in a small compass. Now all the boats made a circle round the inner net, & the two boats who held the net gradually drew it up. The water within seethed with fish. It was packed with iridescent fish, gleaming silver & purple, leaping in the air; lashing their tails, sending up showers of scales.

Then the baskets were lowered & the silver was scooped up & flung into the boats; it was a sight unlike any one has seen elsewhere, hardly to be described or believed. The fishermen shouted & the fish splashed. The baskets were filled, emptied & plunged into the bubbling mass again, again & again. Nothing seemed to lessen the quantities. The little

---

16 To the eastern end of Carbis Bay.

boats took their fill of fish as they liked; the fishermen stopped to pelt the onlookers with fish; the wealth was inexhaustible.

Three seines lie out in the Bay tonight full of fish which cannot be taken in till Monday. The owners watch anxiously, & the wind is high.

The Lands End

We make expeditions, it seems to me, more for the sake of the going & the coming & the delicious meal in the open air, than because there is any special sight of beauty to be found in the spot where we pitch our resting place. I have found, on my walks here a dozen places as I think to which one might fitly go on pilgrimages, but they are sudden, unexpected, secret; no one, perhaps, will step that way for weeks, or will see precisely what I saw for months, or even years. Those are the sights which surprise the solitary walker & linger in the memory. So, as these little visions are not to be evoked at will by any combination of steam & horse, it is safer to fix upon certain recognised spots & to make them the goal of any expedition you choose to undertake.

Such a goal is the Lands End, where the imagination at any rate is infallibly impressed, & one is tolerably sure to find more substantial beauties for the eye. Unfortunately, the pitch of green turf, with the craggy rocks on it, the cliffs, & the romantic line of coast are the property nowadays of a hundred eyes; every ten minutes or so a lumbering brake or a dusty motor car deposits its load of sight seers upon this [ ] little stretch of land.

But though the spot itself is thus made hideous, the land all round is still lonely & very beautiful. On the rim of the horizon the eye may see some rock shaped shadow to which, as the sun sank & made it golden, we gave the name of the Fortunate Isles. When Cornwall was chill in the shade, there was bright daylight over there – perhaps perpetual afternoon.

St Buryans[17] is the landmark for miles, a perfectly unornamented square church tower rising with some suddenness from a stretch of singularly bare country. There was a Cornish cross, somewhat mutilated in the graveyard, but when we tried to enter the church we found the door locked, & no one to give us the key; the only creature about the place was a stone mason, who could be heard chipping a fresh name at the base of an old tombstone.

---

17 St Buryan church at Land's End, a 15th-century granite structure with a massive 90-foot tower; the Cornish cross is a 700-year-old carved gravestone.

Today, Sept 14th, we were forced to take our lunch on our backs, & set off at midday to Castle Dinas[18] some five or six miles distant. Lovely are these autumn days on the heath; the gorse is still as smooth as silk, & the air fragrant. I had almost said, regretful, as though there were some tinge of melancholy in its sweetness. All the months are crude experiments out of which the perfect September is made.

It is not unpleasant to leave the sea, & strike inland. The eye tires of the unstable waters. There is a certain austere dignity among these hills although they are not actually beautiful. We were almost at the top of the Castle hill when we bethought us that we needed water. We knocked at a farm door; it was locked, the windows were shut; we could hear no one. The next farm was deserted too, save that some kittens were playing on the flags.

There was nothing for it but to descend the hill once more to a distant farm where a man was working on a corn stack. We entered the little cobble paved garden & found the farmer washing potatoes in a saucepan; a large boned benevolent man, more kindly than shrewd. He would gladly give us water; & his wife came out of the farmhouse on hearing speech. She was the dour one of the two, pale, with dark eyes, which looked at us doubtfully at first. We were invited to sit in the house while water was fetched from the well.

These little visits to the country people in their lonely farms are always a pleasant part of our expedition. I like to get into talk with the old people, & to see the surroundings which they have made for themselves. The kitchen, in these farms, is always a large low room, dark with its thick rafters, & all the family possessions are displayed on the mantel-piece or on the walls. Above the great fire place hung 'my grandfathers sword', it was a hundred years old & an old curiosity dealer had offered to buy it some days before. A. took it down and flourished it, like the dragoon who had wielded it once, & the farmer stood in the door and chuckled. An old blue pot was brought out from its safe recess for our inspection; which was called a "puzzle jar" because though full of holes, there was yet a tube up the handle which would carry the water to your lips safely. Meanwhile the woman stood watching us, not unfriendly, but still with some doubtful hesitation in her gaze. And yet nothing could be more hospitable & courteous than their treatment of these four strangers; they brought the water, lifted down cups from the shelf & packed them in a basket, & let us go out as though they had but

---

18 Castle-an-Dinas is a Celtic hill fort, roughly midway between St Ives and Penzance.

fulfilled the simplest of duties. So perhaps they had; but it is refreshing to find people who are still sensitive to such commands. That is the great charm of the country people here; perhaps from their contact with wholesome earth or air these natural instincts toward their kind are perfectly frank & trustful; all they say & do seems marked with a certain sincerity.

Castle Dinas itself, though our best castle, is but a fragment; a ruined gateway, perhaps, which has served as a stall for cattle. The hill on which it stands is scarred in the usual way with ditches & ramparts, upon which the turf is smoother & greener than elsewhere.

There are the usual blocks of stone tumbled & half buried in the earth, which once stood high in the air; & from the ruins you behold the same sea & the same hills which this vanished castle tower once looked down upon & which maybe it once held in sway. Far away we could see the glittering line of the Atlantic as it nears the Lands End.

It is a great thing in this little lodging house that we look on the sea from all the large windows. When I wake in the morning I discover first what new ships have come in to the bay, all day long these silent voyagers are coming & going, alighting like some travelling birds for a moment & then shaking out their sails again & passing on to new waters. Where do they come from, & whither are they bound? A ship moves in mysterious ways. In the morning we see the luggers starting for their fishing grounds; late in the afternoon they come racing back on the wind, like so many birds swooping on their prey. Most beautiful of all are the great sailing ships, which ply up & down the Channel.

At the sea, especially perhaps this distant Cornish sea, people seem to strip themselves of some of the integuments in which they wrap themselves where the criticism of eyes is to be dreaded. We seem to have come to a common agreement here not to look surprised at bare heads & hands; to accept hair flying in the wind, & bathing towels wrapped round the neck, as the simple & natural things. This unconventionality of dress is reflected in the tanned faces & the free stride of the legs. We are all consciously taking holiday & running wild in the open air. The results are sometimes a little crude, perhaps; ladies, stout & middle aged, conceive themselves under this fresh stimulant in their first youth again; shorten their skirts, throw aside their bonnets, & caper as they walk, consciously, almost defiantly as though they asserted a right which your mild glance of inquiry would deny them.

But the high tide of the summer holidays is over, & the blatant holiday maker has already lost his sunburnt skin in some City office. The remnant are more sedate; they detect an autumnal flavour in the breeze, & huddle in thick cloaks & fur jackets.

August has a certain fiery & sultry quality of her own, which fades before her last days of the month are over. September has mellowed whatever there was of roughness in her heat: the days are more perfect, but less vigorous. The summer in fact is on the wane; peacefully fading like some brilliant spot of light. The colours of the sunset are every-where.

When the sun sets you may see from this window little sparks of light scattered among the sandhills where no houses themselves are visible; the windows are thus emblazoned by the sun.

It is a mistake to keep rigidly to the coast; strike inland & cross the hills, & then you will sight a broad ribbon of sea beneath you, & ships set like toys about it. The land has been draped in all kinds of strange folds at the edge, so that instead of a sheer cliff you find beautiful little valleys with triangular beaches at the bottom of them. Here we spread our tea, & that finished, walk home again in the dark. Last night it was dusk when we started, but we had to take a long look at the Gurnard's Head[19] & the misty shapes beyond, through which suddenly there flashed the fitful glare of the St Just lighthouse.[20] It was late then when we turned back, & we resolved to keep safe upon the road. Before that could be reached we had to fight our way through a forest of ferns which bound ones legs to-gether & brought one to ones knees. The road when we reached it was of a vague white mist upon which our feet struck hard, even to our sur-prise. As. figure stalking ahead was blurred & without outline, & at a hundred yards distance we had to send our voices out after him to make sure that we had not lost him. In this mystification we left the road, & stepped into a vast trackless country, without mark or boundary. Before us dozens of lights were scattered, floating in soft depths of darkness without anchorage on the firm ground. A. trod on unswervingly, clear-ing aside the mists as though the road lay bright before him. Once in this strange pilgrimage we groped our way through a farm-yard, where the shapes of dim cattle loomed large, & a great lantern swung an unsteady disk of light across our faces. The voice of the farmer bidding us good night recalled us for a moment to the cheerful land of substance, but our

---

19 A bold promontory just west of Zennor, with a headland fortification.
20 At St Just-in-Penwith.

path lay on into the darkness again. We stumbled across fields which swam in dusky vapours; we struck the road, & suddenly a great light shone in front of us, & a cart wheel crunched the ground just beyond us as though the sound of its approach had been muffled in the night. Now we had come to the lights in the valley, & we passed lighted windows, scarcely able to irradiate a yard of the blackness that pressed on them, & could just discover long black figures leaning against the walls quiescent. Night was weighing heavily on this little village; all was silent though not asleep. Then we went on, up to the top of a hill, & again beneath us we saw those great swarms of lights which spring up in the dark where by day there is nothing. And so once more we found the road again, & the familiar lamps of homes. But how narrow were those walls, & how intense that light after the vague immensity of the air; we were like creatures lately winged that have been caught & caged.[21]

For three days, it must be confessed, we have fallen under the tyranny of cards. No one can resist the neat packs waiting there on the round table, with the chairs drawn up invitingly. At first we hesitate & trifle with our desire; shuffle the cards meditatively as though the action were some merely idle movement of the fingers, for which the brain was not responsible. Then perhaps we deal out one – two – three; glance at the numbers displayed, comment audibly; how strange, what luck were one playing. Chance sends an audience. [ ] The second pack must be broached, [ ] in case it too will yield a surprise; then some one in the next room detects us, & shouts derision; "Cards after breakfast!" "Cards!" echo several, springing suddenly into life at the sound of this magic word; & all further pretence is dropped. The chairs are drawn close with alacrity; the room is noisy at once; all talk together; the cards fall in dropping showers; at length it is ready & the order to start is given. All heads are bent close to the work; eyes circle feverishly; hands deal out the pack, three by three, turn, & begin again.[22] Aces fall out into space in the middle; then the fury quickens. You must dab your two on to the ace before your neighbour has done scratching the table polish, & then back again in an instant & on with the next. Collisions occur at this point, three two's fight over the prostrate ace, & all, strange though it may

21 This paragraph appears to be an early version of an essay AVS published under the title 'A Walk by Night' in *The Guardian*, 28 December 1905, reprinted in *VW Essays*, I.
22 The game described is Racing Demon.

seem, got their first. Meanwhile the swift dab dab dab in the corner warns the disputants that some one is running his cards off by the score – We all fly back to our packs, paralysed at the thought that we are missing chances. Suddenly, on the verge of a 'run' which will dispose of at least four more cards, with luck, a yell of "Stop" puts an end to all our schemes. The cards must be counted, & it is lucky if the ten minutes work has not left you some six or seven points less than you were at starting. Hope revives with the freshly shuffled thirteen, although the strange fact is that each new pack is without exception the worst that the player has ever seen. Kings, Queens, & Knaves, the whole royal family, sit absolutely at the top; only the most supreme skill will be able to do something with a thirteen like this. When each player has delivered himself of these the necessary groans & objurgations the signal is given again, & the old process is repeated. I shall not trouble myself to describe it again; although I will willingly act the whole thing a score of times.

Certain circumstances have made me write here less frequently than I meant, so that it comes to pass that I write these words upon the eve of our return.[23] The lights of London will be round me at this time of evening tomorrow, as the lighthouse gleams now. That is a thought which comes with real melancholy, for, besides the actual beauty of this country, to part with it is to part with something which we knew long ago, & may not see again for years. I wish that I had seen more of it while I might. There is in truth, as I thought once in fancy something of our own preserved here from which it is painful to part. Or is it possible that one has come to that age when partings are more serious & meetings less pleasurable? On the whole I prefer to think that there is good reason to regret this departure more than others.

---

23 i.e. 4 Oct. 1905.

Giggleswick 1906

At 46 Gordon Square, Virginia continued to write reviews and teach at Morley College. Thoby's 'Thursday Evenings', started in March 1905, resumed, and in October Vanessa launched the 'Friday Club', a group formed to discuss the fine arts. There was much overlapping in the membership of both groups, the most regular attendants being Clive Bell (who had proposed to Vanessa and been refused), Desmond MacCarthy, Walter Lamb, Lytton Strachey and Saxon Sydney-Turner. At first Virginia felt a little uncomfortable in the company of these young Cambridge men. 'They sit silent, absolutely silent, all the time; occasionally they escape to a corner & chuckle over a Latin joke.'

These gatherings formed the nucleus of what would later be called the 'Bloomsbury Group', though, of course, they never called or even thought of themselves as that. But with these new friendships under way, both Virginia and Vanessa now felt free of the particular social world that George Duckworth had tried for several years to urge upon them.

By the spring of 1906, Virginia, aged twenty-four, could call herself a professional writer. And although she often chose to be alone, rarely did she feel lonely. The first pages of the journal at Giggleswick reflect her state of solitary calm.

Itinerary.

Giggleswick. April. 1906.
Blo Norton Hall. Norfolk. August 1906.[1]
New Forest. Xmas. 1906.
The Steps. Playden Sussex. Aug. Sept. 1907.
The Close. Wells. Somerset. Aug: 1908.
Manorbier: Wales. Aug: 1908.

---

1   The journal for Greece 1906 has been moved from its original position in notebook VII and inserted directly after the Blo' Norton section to establish proper chronology. Inserted among the 77 unnumbered pages of these journals (Notebook VI) is a torn sheet upon which AVS has written: 'Harry Richmond [see Italy 1908, n. 13] La Cousine Bette [Honoré de Balzac, 1846] Wuthering Heights [Emily Brontë, 1847]. [*And in pencil on the verso:*] when he wrote this. There was probably a great deal more scandal than there is now – at least I should think that very probable.' [*The source has not been identified.*]

In a placid & matter of fact frame of mind the solitary traveller starts on his journey. If you are one you have so strangely little to think about; your wants are so easily satisfied. So, then, smoothly & unlaboriously I travelled from one end of England to the other today, asked but little information, found trains & carriages, directed my luggage, & deposited everything at Mrs. Turners, in Giggleswick, delightfully late – because it mattered to no one.[2]

It is just that scrupulously clean, prosaic lodging I wished; & so far my solitude has been exquisite, & delightfully amusing. When will I dine? When will I breakfast? I settle precisely according to my own taste, & then the door is shut on me, & I may read for two hours peacefully if I like. The only sound that distracts me is the Northern Express shooting to Edinburgh.

For this is no smug suburban lodging, beneath a park door; the moors rise in waves all round; great crags of rock make a back ground, dimly seen in the April twilight & wild scents of the moor are driven in at the open window.

It [Giggleswick] is a discreet little Northern town, swept clean & simplified, out of all pettiness & vulgarity by the nobility of the country in which it lies.

But Mrs. Turner is locking her door, & jingling the candles outside, & really, as one may gather, nothing profitable is to be looked for in the scratching of a pen tonight.

The second day [13 April] of my solitude opened propitiously with sun & sky. I celebrated the day with a bun, my only sacrifice to the gods, if it could in any way deserve such a name.

With curious reserve not a bell rang to tell the world it was a feast

---

2   AVS was at Giggleswick, Settle, in Yorkshire (the location of Giggleswick School, of which her cousin W. W. Vaughan was headmaster) from Thursday 12 to Wednesday 26 April, lodging with Mrs Turner; Vanessa joined her there on 21 April, after painting Lord Robert Cecil's portrait at Chelwood Gate, Sussex. The lodging house was about 10 minutes' walk from the Vaughans, and proved to be an ideal base from which to explore the surrounding country; in a letter to Madge, AVS had written: 'I am bringing a great box of books, and I shall shut myself in my room and read.' And to Violet Dickinson: 'There is a discreet elderly person called Mrs James who waits on me, and provides meals whenever I want them; I had sausages for dinner last night. . . . There is a Greek austerity about my life . . .' *VW Letters*, I, Nos 265 and 266, respectively.

day;[3] holiday was kept vigorously however in the roads. I walked out along one which I christen the Sacred Way, because it leads beneath such tremendous hills, pale with shivered sheets of stone, & met bicycles & motor cars flashing along till walking was hardly pleasant. But I could trace various routes over the hills, to be carried out I hope, if all goes well – that is to say if Gurth is willing. In explanation of this singular clause, I must explain that Gurth ran from me, swiftly & stealthily this afternoon, as though bent on some sudden & criminal errand. He fled back here, cowered in the doorway, & trembled & shrank away when I tried to coax & then to coerce him to rise. What strange wave of fear or boredom came over him I cannot explain to my own satisfaction at all.

So it came about that I walked over High Rigg[4] – (a guess) with W[ill]. & M[adge]. & saw the largest view in the countryside. The moors rise & roll away, for miles on either side, tossing themselves into great promontories like Ingleborough,[5] or in to strange sugar loaf blocks, & then surging on their way again till they reach the Lake. But the mist covered them.

The moors are given up entirely to sheep, & are intersected by stone walls, no tree or hedge grows on them. Here and there you see a bleak stone house on the hill side, in which the shepherd lives. In many ways this land is like Cornwall; but I have not time to determine the differences.

All the sheep had their lambs, & were therefore bold & even defiant.

You find strange fortifications on the moors, fosses & ramparts, so smoothly built & carpeted that either nature was the architect, or some primeval man.

A book of the place becomes necessary.

Again I have accomplished a day of partial solitude; except that I begin to make conversation with Mrs. Turner when she brings me my meal. But she is polite rather than communicative.

The unhappy spell of holiday [Easter] is still upon us: the roads are almost impassable. So, dragging Gurth on a chain, I crossed the road, & took the pathway shown me at the back of the wood, & so on to that high moor, with its pale side of ash gray rock. It was a curious walk. I

---

3   13 April was Good Friday.
4   The area between Giggleswick and Lawkland.
5   With an elevation of 2373 feet, one of the highest of the Yorkshire hills.

followed a narrow pathway, on the ridge of the moor, protected by a stone wall, from a sheer drop of I don't know how many feet. The road wound directly beneath, so that a motor car even might be followed for some distance, squirming back on the white road.

Then I found a less precipitous place, where I might descend from these rather bleak altitudes. But it was not easy walking. The side of the hill, which is sufficiently steep to need an almost sitting posture, is strewn with a thick layer of loose gray stones; some of considerable size. As you walk they slip beneath you & rattle down, in a miniature avalanche, to the bottom. And if one looked down, the sight was a little giddy: so I clambered somehow, unseen happily & caught at trees & bushes till the descent was over. And after that I found me a grass seat beneath a rock, & lay in the sun, looking at that skeleton like hill before me, & others rising grand & tragic behind it & far away into the distance. A walk here, I find, tends to be rather an heroic undertaking. I amused myself with planning the countryside into Bloomsbury & Piccadilly, & setting St James Streets & Marble Arches on all the hills & valleys. Thus my domestic life passes like some very placid hours on a lake without a wave.

All the trees here are red & purple, but not green yet. It is not a country that is very sensitive to changes of the season I imagine. In winter it looked much the same.[6] Two thousand years ago it looked as it did this afternoon; in that continuity lies its singular grandeur & stability perhaps. Two thousand years again may leave it equally unchanged.

A monotonous song has been sung by the wind all day. At night it rises. But the sun was brilliant, & made a fair Easter morning [15 April]. At eleven the Sabbath peace of Giggleswick was broken by military music; the dogmatic tune of Christian soldiers thumped out of brass & drum, & the volunteers marched to church, protesting as it seemed the righteousness of their proceeding at every step. Then there came a procession of clergy & choir; & I had half a mind to see the service, which promised to be instructive; but on the whole decided the other way.

In the afternoon I made the ascent of the Attermaier [Attermire][7] (how you spell the strange foreign sounding name I know not) – the

6   AVS had stayed with the Vaughans in Giggleswick from 18 to 29 November 1904.
7   One of the several prehistoric limestone caves discovered during the mid 19th century in the Settle cave country.

moor which makes a high background for Settle. It screens all view of the country on the other side. I persevered though the way was steep & deceptive, & gained such a view of all the country round as rested my eyes completely. But it is a strange country. You get into a desolate sea of moors, gray as bone, with but a sprinkling of green on them. These merge into each other, sink & swell again, till one can reach no further. No road or house seems to adventure out there; & the likeness to a barren sea scape is unavoidable. On the other side however, the country is more cultivated; & the plain is set with houses, & threaded by the Ribble [River]. All through Settle there were groups converging, waiting the 'abatement of the Sabbath.' Tomorrow, all the furies will be let loose once more, & then, perhaps, peace.

One might almost keep silence over today [Monday, 16 April], for it has been tacit in its quality, uttering nothing memorable in its course.

I walked, & was stopped on the road by an elderly gentleman who had laid a match a minute ago to a train of gunpowder, & was waiting for it to blow a crack in the rock, when "pieces might be flying." So I waited with him under shelter, & heard a pop, like a toy gun, which was satisfactory & innocent, & went on my way.

It was difficult to beat against the wind, but I made a laborious circuit without much delight in it, & struck the road on the top of Giggleswick hill, & dropped down into the valley.

I saw a hare, & several trains & climbed walls made exactly as walls ought not to be made; high & loose, without any foothold. I generally made a hole, carrying several lumps down in my petticoat. And Gurth has to be pulled by his collar.

After tea we visited a certain master & his wife,[8] nameless even here, for decency's sake. The wife is fresh from Newnham, & has brought all her crudities to air in this congenial atmosphere. The cottage on a Yorkshire moor is strenuous soil for theories; I imagine the letters she writes home, & her delight in herself as a suitable person in the right place.

It was an ordinary cottage; but ungainly tables, green carpets, & rush chairs have made it self conscious, a cottage with a purpose. The crudity of these young people may be gauged by the fact that they write their creed, in red ink on a strip of brown paper over the hearth – It is a quotation I am told from William Morris; & they have Christened their son after a hero in George Meredith. All wrong – all wrong, I cry with

---

8 Unidentified.

emphatic but ambiguous voice; because I can't say exactly where the confusion arises, or what it is that makes the combination of literature & life, drawing room & kitchen so disastrous.

Today [Tuesday, 17 April] was memorable at least for a really successful walk, to a place called Feizor[9] – a wizard like name, to be set beside others like Attameier [*sic*], as something singular, & belonging to no regular system.

We got into a strange vale between two moors; all turf, with flocks & herds feeding there, but no house or human creature. It stretched a long way, sequestered from wind or any blast from the outside world, a dreamlike hollow between gray moors; & finally we looked down upon Feizor, a little village of farm houses, a centre, I suppose for this pasturage land.

I thought what an odd fate it was to live in an old stone house all the days of one's life in the village of Feizor when the whole of the world lies open to one. The road which joins it to the main line is grown with grass; & as we walked along it, we came upon tinkers of some kind, making a shelter out of the hood of a cart; & ranging their household goods in the ditch – They sprang up & asked us for matches, had I been alone it would have been unpleasant. You could see the elemental look of demand in the mans face; as though it were his natural instinct to ask other people to supply him. The great melancholy moors, sweeping all round us, like some tragic audience, or chorus, mutely attendant, grew black, & veiled with mist. Rain came down, & the country seemed well pleased at this change of mood. Storm & rough weather suit it better than bland & innocent skies. But words! words! You will find nothing to match the picture.

Today the singular & rather pleasant phenomenon was seen of great white flakes of snow falling across a deep blue sky. But they were merely tentative, or decorative, & ceased by midday. In the afternoon however, walking to Lawkland,[10] there was a bright line of white on the top of Ingleborough; which indeed is majestic enough to veil his crown in the clouds occasionally. It was a lovely walk, along the valley. We met a shepherd digging mournfully at a drain which cuts across the road. One of the lambs, apparently, had run into the funnel of this thing,

---

9 A hamlet about 3 miles north of Giggleswick.
10 A hamlet 3 miles north-west of Giggleswick.

which stretched into the fields; & had gone probably too far to be dug out alive: A tuft of wool on the briar showed where he was lost. The minute & anxious care with which every separate lamb in the flock is watched surprises the stranger; the lambs seem so innumerable, & their destinies so unimportant. But every field, did one know it, is full of these details which are important facts to an experienced eye.

Lawkland is an old Manor House;[11] too small to be restored, & thus a beautiful specimen of simple domestic building, standing just off the road where every one may see it. All its graceful gables, & worn traceries are there untouched; & it is flanked by rough farm houses, of an earlier date still perhaps. You see how neatly self sufficient the old house was – & still, perhaps, remote in the Yorkshire moors as it is, needs all its resources.

The Matrons of Giggleswick sat in conclave this afternoon upon the scheme for boarding out poor children. Substantial squiresses, ruling their broad acres with capable thumb, parsons' wives, village gossips, &c. &c.; but the Yorkshire type of gentry is distinguished, & decided. They had come driving in from distant Halls & Parsonages, & rattled off again, in dog carts & high gigs.

When one makes a perfectly successful undertaking of any kind, some sort of offering to the Gods seems fitting. And of all undertakings, these short expeditions, which last no more than an hour or so, are those which are most easily finished & made perfect in their round sum of good or ill. If I had any Gods then, or any tribute to lay at their feet, I should make some offering for the gift of three – no two & a half – sweet hours of accomplished happiness, which were bestowed on me this afternoon. With a purpose I make use of words implying some thing handed down to me, as it were, from on high; because the hours seemed so complete in themselves, so little the result of what had gone before or the prelude to that which was to be that one might figure them simply thus – as a gift set down in the course of an ordinary day. But this preface is more than sufficient. I delay in truth, because I shall get no nearer the words by making a direct search for them than by thus dallying upon the outskirts.

In the face of those great moors, even perhaps in their midst, is to be found a country very different from them, united only by its rare beauty.

---

11 Presumably Lawkland Hall, with its large central tower, the property of the Ingleby family since about 1572.

The contrast is part of the charm. You walk upon very gentle downs, which fold themselves into steep hollows, & are fringed with slender groves of trees. It is an undulating, & suave country, lacking the abrupt majesty of the moors, but excelling them in a certain charm; a kind of pathos from its more immediate connection with low human kind. One gray farm, with its walled garden, will do much to humanise a whole sweep of field & down. And by that one means here, perhaps, something by no means cheerful & domestic, but melancholy & appealing rather; for the land remains a half tame thing; with all & wild creatures fearing for freedom in its eyes.

For 2 hours I met no single person; but listened to the queer cries & laments of plovers & curlews, wheeling close above my head, for the afternoon was almost cloudless, & singularly warm.

"A very dark morning Miss" said Mrs Turner; but I confess that I am no judge of the morning's complexion at 6. am – from lack of material. Indeed, now I think of it, I was surprised to see how much light contrives to shed itself while I am asleep; I thought that the day blossomed as my eyes opened. I will not attempt here the most dreary catalogue that exists: that of a day's expedition. I shall say only that we found ourselves at the Manchester Zoo[12] at 11.30: or thereabouts: & if that fact does not write its own history in more pertinent figures than I can come by, imagination is a broken winded jade. The Manchester Zoo! How grotesque are these strange little side shows in to which life eddies one on occasion. Had anyone predicted that I should visit Calcutta in the course of the year I should have agreed more readily than to the suggestion that this should be an expedition. You can imagine Cremorne after Pendennis had spent a night there, in the daylight, with the fireworks gone out.[13] You can imagine the ghastly pale grottoes, & exhausted lamps, the gimcrack temples & Pagodas, in which one might still buy a bun; though one passed with horror. And occasionally, more grotesque still, one came on a cage of real lions, & a live Zebra; & a great house full of melancholy monkeys, sick & peevish after their nights debauch. It was almost unkind to visit them at this hour of deshabille; But perhaps the most ghastly touch of all was when a man fired a rocket from the edge of a chilly pond, & the light shot into a pale April morning which seemed

---

12 Part of a large entertainment park at Bellevue Gardens.
13 W. M. Thackeray, *The History of Pendennis*, 1849-50; the fireworks were at Vauxhall Gardens, not Cremorne – see Chapter XLVI, 'Monseigneur S'Amuse'.

to extinguish it instantly by the force of cold common sense. A rocket at 12 midday in the Manchester Zoo! No wonder the hyenas howled; & the hippopotamus [*sic*] wondered if he had sufficient energy to yawn.

Blo' Norton 1906

Between 20 and 23 June Virginia wrote 'Phyllis and Rosamond' and probably at about this time too 'The Mysterious Case of Miss V', neither of which was published. Also in June 1906, she wrote a two-column piece for The Times Literary Supplement *called 'Wordsworth and the Lakes', for which she received £9. 7s. 'This is the largest sum I have ever made at one blow,' she announced proudly to Violet Dickinson. It was during August 1906 that Virginia also wrote 'The Journal of Mistress Joan Martyn', first published in* Twentieth Century Literature, *25: 3/4, Fall-Winter 1979, and reprinted (together with the two pieces above, published now for the first time) in* The Complete Shorter Fiction of Virginia Woolf, *ed. Susan Dick, 1985.*

Blo Norton Hall   4 August

It is a theory that the newer you are the better you like old things. No one but an American young woman, conscious of crudity as of some scourge of the flesh, would have plunged into such depths of age as we find here. The house is Elizabethan;[1] & it has been too inconsiderable to restore – beyond what is needed to make it a living house; it is too remote & solitary & ancestral for anyone to wish to live here, except Americans who find all these qualities, I suppose, medicinal. Still, it is rather comfortable even for English people, to find that such houses go on unheeded & untended, accumulating quaintness & beauties with every year, all over England; despite the great towns & villas.

And age has a great charm.

Nothing of our own day could reproduce the harmony & exquisite peace of this little old house, as it struck our eyes, yesterday evening. It is so modest, & sound, & solid all through; as tho' the centuries had

---

1   From 3 to 31 August, the Stephens rented Blo' Norton Hall, a moated Elizabethan manor house in Norfolk on the Little Ouse river, about 7 miles west of Diss. Thoby and Adrian stayed for only two days before returning to London, and setting out for Trieste on 10 August. AVS and Vanessa's guests during this holiday were George Duckworth, Hester Ritchie and Emma Vaughan.

only confirmed its original virtues. As you were made honestly, they seem to say, so all time to come shall but prove & establish your virtue.

And such domestic beauty, all small & quaint & even humble as it is, appeals to ones sympathies. It is so good to find that humdrum people should live so respectably; beauty & splendour were then not for the surface alone, but they sank down & down, till all layers of the state were well steeped in them. A self respecting decorous place England must have been then! The American, I began to say, needs a deep bath of antiquity; & few English people, I think, could endure such a dose as Blo' Norton Hall is prepared to give them, without being drowned in it. We are to begin with 7 miles from a railway; & every mile seems to draw a thicker curtain than the last between you & the world. So that finally, when you are set down at the Hall, no sound what ever reaches your ear; the very light seems to filter through deep layers; & the air circulates slowly, as though it had but to make the circuit of the Hall, & its duties were complete.

Nor have such investigations as we could make today pierced behind the curtain. We seem to be in the middle of what in geography is called an 'undulating plain' well cultivated, but, apparently, almost deserted. The corn brims the fields; but no one is there to cut it; the churches hold up broad gray fingers all over the landscape, but no one, save perhaps the dead at their feet, attend to their commands; the windmills sail round & round, but no one trims their sails; it is very characteristic that the only sign of life in the land should be that produced by the wind of Heaven. How sleepy & ancient a people must be, who rely on the free gifts of Heaven still. But the wind seems fairly competent; the sails turn slowly, all day long. This, need I say it, is the kind of rash note an impetuous traveller makes; & it is only made because after all, such notes are the things one thinks before one begins to reason or to know. And like the images of childhood, they stay bright.

A second day [5 August] reveals the fact, as facts go, that the country has possibilities. This morning for instance, we wandered into a lush fen, humming with dragonflies, & scented with meadow sweet. A pale windmill guarded it, stationary today I observe; for though the wind is God's wind, & will blow in spite of the Sabbath, one must not require it to work for human profit on a Sunday. Or how do the orthodox interpret these symbols? Again in the afternoon, we stepped some four miles out his way with Thoby. We had prudently to keep to the high road, which was flat, but umbrageous & lined with broad strips of green on either side. We passed the temples of three different sects, so that, reckoning by the number we met on the road there must be 10 orthodox Christians, 6 Methodists & 2½ Anabaptists in Hopton.[2] Children count only as halves, because when they grow up they may think for themselves, & swell the number of the hostile sect, or, presumably build a fresh chapel for themselves. The Churches, I tell myself, & this is only a whisper after all – date from that era before the Black death, when sheep farming prospered, & piety throve: but now that the sheep are gone, & Americans live in the Halls of the landowners, how does piety thrive at all? And yet look at the great solid chapels! So thinking, arguing, & expounding we tramped along till we reached a crossroads, where the sign post waved in three different directions. Here was the appropriate place to part; one road led straight to Dalmatia & the wilds of Thessaly; the other back here to this profound seat of solitude, dug, I think, somewhere very near the heart of England. Dont I feel the steady beat of the great Creator as I write; & doesn't the Church there record its pulse this evening, & for six hundred years of evenings such as these?

The fens almost surround this house. And all the land is very flat, so that the landmarks resolve themselves into churches & windmills. The river, the Little Ouse deserves its diminutive; you may leap it – fall in as I did this afternoon – but all the same it is not a hazardous jump. You are sure of the mud at any rate. And there radiate various minor tributaries, ditches I should call them, did not I know of their relationship with the river, & these are sometimes fenced with barbed wire. Altogether, though a walk in the fen has a singular charm, it is not to be undertaken as a way of getting to places. Windmills have a way of staying absolutely still, or receding, to one who approaches them thus.

However, after leaping & circumnavigating, & brushing through reeds, & scrambling beneath barbed wire, it is pleasant to lie on the turf & try steering by windmills & towers to indicate on the map where you are precisely. Today I found the twin sources of the Waveney & the Little Ouse.[3]

In a very short time unfortunately, it becomes clear how shortsighted was that opinion of mine that Norfolk had no inhabitants. It is not neces-

---

2   A village in West Suffolk, a mile west of Blo' Norton.
3   The twin sources of the Waveney and the Little Ouse rivers are about 2 miles west of Blo' Norton.

sary here to go into details, which would be impolite; so I will only make the innocent remark that directly you begin to study the habits of creatures they become astonishingly frequent & well ordered. Here, it seems, one needs only but very little trouble in order to discover a whole net work of society – Squires & Parsons & detached ladies living in cottages, who are all entertaining & paying calls, far more punctually & assiduously than in London.

But it is more to the point to remark that I found the real heath, not a mile from our door. It is a wild place, all sand & bracken, with innumerable rabbits, & great woods running alongside, in to which I plunge; down green drives as shady as any in the New Forest. It is a strange lonely kind of country; a carriage comes bowling over the hill, & you watch it pass & disappear & wonder where it comes from & whither it goes, & who is the lady inside.

Shall I confess, without meaning any kind of confession, that it is possible for one day to be much like another here, & not in the least dull?

I go for my usual walk; which has for me the interest of a discovery, because I go, armed with maps into a strange land. Windmills are my landmarks; & one must not mistake the river for a ditch. The heath attracts me most; because there are no fields. The fen plays you false at every step – I walked through a jungle of reeds & fell up to my nose in mud. And if one foundered here, the weeds would wave & the plover call, & no robin redbreast would bury one![4]

If this were the time or the place to uphold a paradox, I am half inclined to state that Norfolk is one of the most beautiful of counties. Indeed, let the artifice stand; for so there will be no need to expound it. And truly, it would need a careful & skilful brush to give a picture of this strange, grey green, undulating, dreaming, philosophising & remembering land; where one may walk 10 miles & meet no one; where soft grass paths strike gently over the land; where the roads are many & lonely, & the churches are innumerable, & deserted. There is no use in a closer gaze at present. But it is worth saying that the more you walk here, & become initiated into the domesticities of the place – it is full of them – the more you love it, & know it. And that says as much for a place as for a person.

---

4   Cf. 'Call for the robin redbreast and the wren,/Since o'er shady groves they hover,/And with leaves and flowers do cover/The friendless bodies of unburied men.' John Webster, *The White Devil*, V, iv, 100.

It is so soft, so melancholy, so wild, & yet so willing to be gentle: like some noble untamed woman conscious that she has no beauty to vaunt, that nobody very much wants her. [*Page torn out of notebook here.*]

It is one of the wilful habits of the brain, let me generalise for the sake of comfort, that it will only work at its own terms.

You bring it directly opposite an object, & bid it discourse; it merely shuts its eye, & turns away. But in one month, or three or seven, suddenly without any bidding, it pours out the whole picture, gratuitously. Some such surprise may be in store for me still; on the heights of the Acropolis the Norfolk fens may swim before me; & I know I shall have to wait many months before I can see Athens. Like the light that reaches you from the stars, it will only shine when some time after it has been shed.

So then, to come to the heart of the discourse, there is no use in presenting here a picture of Norfolk; when the place is directly beneath my eyes. I see at this moment a wall, coloured like an apricot in the sun; with touches of red upon it. The outline & angles of the roof & the tall chimney are completely filled with pure blue sky, as though some gigantic brush had laid a smooth wash of paint across the background. It is the kind of blue for a reason which I can hardly explain, that makes me understand why it should be said to 'drip' from the wings of a flying bird.

A certain look of dishevelment in the creepers & shrubs that climb the wall is token that there was a great gale the other morning; which is further borne out by the recumbent posture of an apple tree in the middle of the lawn. It has spilt all its apples in the downfall. And a very keen eye or nose, or both, may detect a look & scent in the trees & the air which, in spite of the sun, hints at September. Without refining & matching words, no one could mistake the day for a summer's day. Yesterday, I took a bicycle ride to a place called Kenninghall.[5] We will not talk about the bicycle; or there would be no time to deal with the church & the village, & some aesthetic outrage also would be committed upon our senses. Now Kenninghall is famous in the Ordnance map for a Saxon burial ground:[6] & readers of Jefferies[7] will take their chance of a

5   About 5 miles north of Blo' Norton.
6   The Saxon burial ground probably refers to the inhumation cemetery, about half a mile west of Kenninghall Church, discovered in 1869.
7   Richard Jefferies (1848-87), English novelist and nature writer.

bask upon such smooth turf. But at Kenninghall the Christian church alone was obvious; the curiously moulded tower, with its gilt clock, showed itself most decorously gray against the soft plumage of the trees. Moreover there were gravestones with home made elegies. As for instance the inscription upon Mrs Susan Batt (shall we say) of whom it is written.

> She nothing took that plainness could not get
> And most abhored [*sic*] the running into debt

which, I think, has the virtue of drawing a picture of the righteous old lady, albeit the lines are angular. Parenthetically, we may write down another fragment, retrieved from Market Weston:[8]

> His superior intellectual attainments
> Could only be appreciated by
> the Superior Few.
> This they did:
> But his moral worth
> &c &c

This is broken up duly into long lines & short, set with capital letters, & cut deep black into a square sheet of marble. It is an eddy of the eighteenth century formalism; when the superior few were not ashamed to call themselves so.

A very curious & interesting & entertaining article, I observe here (I blush I swear it) might be written upon Epitaphs; because when you have exhausted the surface oddity, there is really a solid lump of truth to be dug out beneath. I mean the attitude is perfectly honest; & so, very characteristic of the age & the people.

However, Mrs Susan Batt was no Saxon; & we must contrast the graves.

So on the authority of the map, we asked a small native for his Saxon burial ground, & were directed by him to the Christian Churchyard; Saxons they may have been to him; &, to the shame of Kenninghall be it spoken, no one there not even the photographer, knew where the Saxons were buried; or indeed had ever heard that there were Saxons. So taking the map's word for it, we decided to consecrate a mound in some gentleman's Park; certainly I could see no reason why Saxons should not have been buried there.

---

8   About 2 miles from Blo' Norton, on the Suffolk side of the Little Ouse.

But as one had to climb a gate, & walk half a mile, we decided to do our conjectural meditations from a distance; the charm, I own, was not very potent, whether one must blame the distance or the doubt.

The advantages of a bicycle, almost I would say the advantage, is that it gets you to places. Our grandparents never saw Thetford or Diss, unless it was upon the wedding tour, in a high gig; or upon the Christening of the first born, or some other solemn feast, demanding the sanction of the market town.

But I can ride there in an afternoon; to buy postcards or grapes, or merely to look at certain curious old houses.

A very hot August day, a bare road across a moor, fields of corn & stubble – a haze as of wood fire smoke – innumerable pheasants & partridges – white stones – thatched cottages – sign posts – tiny villages – great waggons heaped with corn – sagacious dogs, farmers carts. Compose these all somehow into a picture; I am too lazy to do it.

At any rate after an hour's riding I dropped down into Thetford, which seemed to me with its girdle of wall & river, & the smooth turf slope outside something like an Italian town. Perhaps the knowledge extracted from the guide book that there was a nunnery[9] here in the Middle Ages helped my imagination. Certainly I saw with my own eyes a Roman Catholic Padre step out of his monastery door, with a biretta on his head, & examine with long ecclesiastical nose the Dahlias in his neighbours garden. The rivers Thet & Ouse (I think) circle Thetford; & which ever way I went, seemed to take me across low stone bridges where anglers lounged, with their rods across the broad stream. Nursemaids were sitting on the rivers banks, leaning on the elbow over a paper novel, while their charges dabbled in the water. No one was ever able to say exactly what does go on in these medieval towns set in the heart of England at about this hour on a Summers afternoon. It is all so picturesque & accidental that to the traveller it seems a pleasant show got up for some benevolent purpose. For when you come upon stalwart men leaning their elbows on a parapet & dreaming of the stream beneath, while the sun is still high in the air, you reconsider what you mean by life. Often in London shall I think of Thetford, & wonder if it is still alive; or whether it has really ceased, peaceably, to exist any longer. No one would notice if the whole town forgot to wake up one morning.

9   A Saxon nunnery, founded by Uvius, Abbot of Bury, to commemorate the battles of
the Saxons and Danes.

But coming home in the evening through great open spaces of field it was born [*sic*] in upon the mind that something was alive enough. Call it what you will. For the whole air was rich with energy, & brilliant with colour.

Greece 1906

On 8 September – Thoby's twenty-sixth birthday – Virginia, Vanessa and Violet Dickinson left London, travelled through France and Italy, and sailed to Patras. Thoby and Adrian, who had ridden on horseback through Albania to Greece, joined them in Olympia on 13 September.

[*The autograph calendar and timetable below head the volume.*]

1906

September

Sun.		2	9	16	23	30	→ Athens
Mon.		3	10	17	24		→ Euboea / Nauplia
Tue.		4	11	18	25		
Wed.		5	12	19	26		
Thr.		6	13	20	27		→ Corinth / Patras
Fri.		7	14	21	28		→ Olympia
Sat:	1	8	15	22	29		→ Corinth

October

Sun		7	14	21	28	
Mon	1	8	15	22	29	→ Constantinople.
Tue	2	9	16	23	30	
Wed.	3	10	17	24	31	
Thr	4	11	18	25		
Athens Fri	5	12	19	26		
Sat.	6	13	20	27		

sailed
~~Constantinople~~

November.

Sun		4	11	18	25
Mon		5	12	19	26
Tue		6	13	20	27
Wed		7	14	21	28
Thr.	1	8	15	22	29
Fri.	2	9	16	23	30
Sat	3	10	17	24	

Olympia. September 14th!

It is not worth while wasting ink here upon the journey through Italy. It was hot, it was cold – we missed trains – found Hotels – & passed meanwhile from one end of Italy to the other. The central heat was lodged in Greece; as we drew near, the whole of this little bridge from country to country crumpled up & disappeared. I write bad English I know; but I must state merely that we reached Patras[1] at 6.30 on Thursday morning, & some day I will find the dates. You get a little blasé with much travelling; & after a day spent in looking at soaring hills & remote valleys from the steamer the mind will throb but little faster for the name of Greece. That indeed must sink in legitimately, as it surely does by its own authentic fire.

Patras like most sea ports is cosmopolitan, & very garrulous. We saw men in skirts & gaiters however. Turks, Albanians & Montenegrins scattered about among a humdrum crowd. But in the evening, having heard meanwhile a plaintive Greek song we interpreted the words generously – We left for Olympia in a great first class carriage which we had naturally to ourselves. Now it was evening, & the bloom on the hills shone purple, & the sea turned its innermost heart to the light; it was a heart of the deepest blue. On the other side of us was a screen of hills, sudden & steep & incessant, as though the earth had nothing better to do than throw up impatient little mounds. The look of the place thus is fiery & somewhat fragile, for the lines are all very spare & emphatic. No fat pastures & woods cushion the surface: but on the plain the earth was thick with dwarf vines, stooping with pyramids of fruit. You saw baskets heaped with grapes at the stations: Stafeelé stafeelé – I cried – & brought great bunches to the door.

The stations were many; we stopped that is at sheds where, by the light of a lantern, men were drinking wine, with their horses tied to a stake; as the railway curved the whistle shrieked a continual warning, for the line is like a modest little road, & in truth the train would do no great damage to a flock of goats.

Olympia

So then, at 9 o'clock we jumped out at Olympia, found Thoby & Adrian, heard our own tongue once more, & drove up to the Hotel.

But of Olympia[2] it is difficult to write.

---

1   A port in the north-west of the Peloponnese, on the Gulf of Patras.
2   The sacred precinct excavated by the Germans from 1874 to 1881.

Baedecker [*sic*] will count the statues; a dozen archaeologists will arrange them in a dozen different ways; but the final work must be done by each fresh mind that sees them. The pediments of the temple line the two sides of the museum; [ ] but we wont write guide book – There is the Apollo.[3] He looks over his shoulder – seems to look across & above the centuries. He is straight & serene but there he has a human mouth & chin, ready to quiver or to smile. So might a Greek boy have looked, stripped, in the sun. And there are other noble fragments, somewhat broadly chiselled, because they stood on a height; the hair is a smooth band of stone; the drapery graved in rigid lines. Ah but the beauty!

Then you come to the separate temple, where the Hermes[4] stands still, so lightly & with such a spring in his step that you expect him to turn & go. There, I think, you have the God; for he looks out & away, as though some serene vistas in the far Heaven drew his gaze.[ ]

So we pile words; but it is a pretence. You must see him, & let the eye spring like a creature set free along those curves & hollows; for it has secretly craved such beauty! You dont know, till you satisfy it, how much it has craved. And the stone – if you call it stone – seems also acquiescent to the sculptors hand: it is almost liquid, of the colour of alabaster, & of the solidity of marble. There is a beautiful polished foot which you may stroke with your own soft flesh. The Germans have supplied plaster legs. Let us note it. If only it had been possible to stand the statue in the air! Cold stone needs that background. The theatre[5] is – once more we might quote the Guidebook: for our purposes it is simply a flat circle of grass, scattered with innumerable fragments of stone. There are broken pillars of all sizes, & tiles, stones, lion heads, inscriptions; it is like, perhaps, a very disorderly pagan graveyard. But you may trace certain temples, & the course of the race ground. Still this is not what the vagrant mind dwells on most; there was thyme growing by the pillars, & fine grass. And there were little hills tufted with delicate green trees all round; & the Alpheus [river] passing on one side.

---

3   From the west pediment of the Temple of Zeus at Olympia; he is watching over the legendary battle of the Thassalian Lapiths, whom he is supporting against the neighbouring centaurs.

4   The Hermes of Praxiteles from the Temple of Hera, holding in his left arm the infant Dionysius, discovered in 1877.

5   AVS means the Stadium, below the Kronion hill, the original 600-foot Olympic running track; south of the Stadium bank runs the Alpheus River.

Olympia and Corinth –

But it was all very clear & orderly & Greek; you trace a certain austerity in the landscape, for all its grace. I cannot lay my hands on any words but those that come uppermost to night, & it is peculiarly purposeless to belabour such a perfect image with ill fitting adjectives. This, I may say, is written at Corinth,[6] & a band of wailing women are singing beneath my window. Do they lament the nations fall,[7] or some private woe, or are they merely celebrating the new restaurant which was opened with fireworks this evening?

Such was the prelude to a night spent in no kind of philosophic or aesthetic meditation. When you rise at 1 at 2 at 3 & at 4 to investigate your bed & find certain round black bodies traversing the sheet, & squash them, & shudder & tie yourself in a silk bag & swathe your head in a net; when you repeat this, I say, hourly till the morning breaks, White-chapel[8] is the image impressed upon your mind; dirtiness is the only quality the Greeks possess. The Greek world is limited to your bed stead. So I spent the early morning sitting in the drawing room, reading the Christian Herald.

However, in a short time I was ascending the Acro Corinth[9] on a grey pony; you climb a precipice, & bask on the top beneath a Turkish fortification. You see Salamis[10] & some of the most famous lands of the world beneath you. The colour of the country seen thus in great spaces from a height is that of tawny sand; it might be a desert, save for some squares of thin green. And you see Corinth lying by the edge of the gulf. But it was not a day for seeing far, & it was very hot, & I had spent the night in pursuits of another kind.[11] So we drove back again, & I confess that the pleasantest part of the expedition was due to the fact that our coachman was also a vine owner; & as we drove through his land, hospitality & a desire to see how his crop was doing, made him beg us to dismount & taste his produce. And so we had the experience for the first time of sitting on the ground & eating grapes from the tree in the open air. The skins were warmed through, & that made the globe of juice within all

---

6 The ancient city is about 3½ miles south-east of the modern town.

7 Probably a reference to the fall of Greece to the Turks.

8 A notorious district in London which harboured thieves, beggars, prostitutes, etc; see AVS's description of the area in *Flush*, 1933, (Kp A19), Chap. IV.

9 Corinth's acropolis from antiquity to medieval times; the hill is 2,000 feet high, and a jumble of the remains of fortifications of Christian, Venetian and Turkish origins.

10 The largest island in the Saronic Gulf, opposite the Bay of Eleusis.

11 i.e. pursuing bed bugs.

the sweeter & more cool. Grapes for nothing! ponderous bunches of blue & white & purple grapes, hanging so close that you must hesitate, like the donkey,[12] before you chose which to eat. Here you realise that nature can be benevolent; & so man becomes generous too.

Athens

There is so much to grasp in Athens that there is no need to attempt any single description. By proceeding quietly looking here & there at leisure, a solid picture slowly composes itself. I will not try to reproduce here the whole of it; but like a free English woman I will deal deliberately with the days adventures, whether they are significant or irrelevant. And after all, every step is on sacred ground.

You come to Athens along the brink of the sea, so that from the train window you look down into little bays where clear waves are breaking; & this peaceful curve of the sea is Salamis, & there, on that height of cliff opposite, Xerxes[13] sat (so we say) two thousand years ago, on a September afternoon like this. It might have been a stretch of the Cornish coast: for the water was as lucid & brilliant as the Atlantic at midsummer; but the hills were mountains, & the whole place seemed chiselled like a statue.

It was too dark when we came to see anything not directly illuminated by electric light; but it was just possible to distinguish a dark ridge above the lamps.

Acropolis

When day broke we all went to our separate windows, & saw that a great crag of rock surged out of the darkness, tawny & cleft with shadows, upon which two groups of columns, one tawny as the rock itself, the other white & fragile, were established. Indeed on the edge of the rock there were more columns, but the dark columns we knew were the Crown & Queen of the place, the Parthenon[14] herself.

When you are close up to them, you see that the Parthenon is far the largest of the temples; & you see also how the surface of the pillars is

---

12 Buridan's Ass was placed between two equally tempting bundles of hay and starved to death because it couldn't choose between them.

13 King of Persia (*c.* 519-465 BC), in order to repair the military prestige of Persia and avenge the defeat of his father at the hands of the Greeks, assembled the greatest army of ancient times and in 481 BC marched it against the Greeks.

14 Erected between 447 and 432 BC and dedicated to the virgin goddess Athena.

chipped & scarred. The ravages are terrible, but in spite of them, the Parthenon is still radiant & young. Its columns spring up like fair round limbs, flushed with health. When we saw it first however the light was so fierce that we could hardly raise our eyes to the frieze: & for all the marble scattered at ones feet – slabs of marble, drums of marble, splinters of marble seemed to flash light at us from beneath. So with a numb feeling as though our minds had been struck inarticulate by something too great for them to grasp we cooled ourselves in the museum which lies at the base of the hill. Here there is perhaps the most beautiful thing we have yet seen. The head of the boy,[15] with braided hair which guide books call slightly archaic. But the mouth seemed freshly carved in its soft & sensitive lines only that morning. Stay though: for the stone was also immortal.

Beautiful statues have a look not seen on living faces, or but rarely, as of serene immutability, here is a type that is enduring as the earth, nay will outlast all tangible things, for such beauty is of an essence that is immortal. And this expression on a face that is otherwise young & supple makes you breathe a higher air. It is like the kiss of dawn.

Street of Tombs

In the evening, as the sun was going down & painting all the air in ruddy colour, we drove to the Street of Tombs.[16] It is an untidy little plot of ground, separated from the road by high railings, & the grass grows high, & at every step you stumble on some fragment of pottery or marble. There are not many tombs here, & those that there are have been rudely enclosed in wire cages. There is a child parting from her parents, while her pet dog leaps on its hind legs;[17] there is a woman handling her jewels before she leaves them.[18] These were the tombs that were cut, probably by humble masons, in scores, for all Athenians who could afford them. The richness of Greek earth was shown us here, visibly. The ground was rough & unkempt, as I have said; suddenly we realised that we were stepping on the top of drifts of dust, & that beneath, if you dig, the earth was packed with treasures. Three workmen were hacking

---

15 No. 698 in Room VII, Ephebos.

16 Branching off the Sacred Way in the direction of Piraeus, just outside the Sacred Gate; the burials are mostly 4th-century BC.

17 The Tomb of Eucoline: the principal figure is of a little girl and her dog, with members of the family grouped around her.

18 The Tomb of Hegeso, daughter of the Proxenos, examining the jewels of a casket held by a female slave.

at the ground at the far end of the enclosure – & had already laid bare a foundation of stone, the plan of house or street perhaps; an archaeologist was measuring with his rule, & entering statements in a note book. Since that, you feel that all lumps in the earth are but so much ugly dust heaped negligently over some well ordered temple or statue beneath.

Acropolis

We also visited the Acropolis at sunset. And when you speak of 'the colour' of the Parthenon you are simply conforming to the exigencies of language; a painter using his craft to speak by, confesses the same limitations. The Temple glows red; the whole west pediment seems kindled, as if for the first time, in the sunset opposite: it rays light & heat, while the other temples burn with a white radiance. No place seems more lusty & alive than this platform of ancient dead stone. The fat Maidens who bear the weight of the Erechtheum[19] on their heads, stand smiling tranquil ease, for their burden is just meet for their strength. They glory in it; one foot just advanced, their hands, one conceives, loosely curled at their sides. And the warm blue sky flows into all the crevices of the marble; yet they detach themselves, & spring in to the air, with crisp edges, unblunted, & still virile & young.

But it is the Parthenon that over comes you; it is so large, & so strong, & so triumphant. You feel warmed through & through, as though you walked by some genial hearth. But perhaps the most lovely picture in it – at least it is the most detachable – is that which you receive when you stand where the great Statue[20] used to stand. She looked straight through the long doorway, made by the curved lines of the columns, & saw a long slice of Attic mountain & sky & plain, & a shining strip of the sea. It is like a panel, let in to the Parthenon to complete its beauty. It is soft, & soon grows dark, though the water still gleams; then you see that the white columns are ashy pale, & the warmth of the parthenon ebbs from her.

A bell rings down below, & once more the Acropolis is left quite alone. We walked home through the clamorous streets.

---

19 Built between 421 and 395 BC, its portico is supported by six caryatids – i.e. figures of 'fat Maidens' in place of columns.
20 The Athena Parthenos. The nave of the Parthenon forms a kind of chapel which is illuminated through the great doorway; the gold and ivory Athena figure was made by Phidias and consecrated in 438 BC in the presence of Pericles.

Eleusis

We drove fourteen miles to Eleusis, following it may be supposed the sacred way.[21] On such days, we know, the people of Athens formed together, garlanded in fine draperies, & marched in procession to their mystic rites which none might know.

Once again, the Ancient Greek had the best of it: we were very belated wayfarers: the shrines are fallen, & the oracles are dumb. You have the feeling very often in Greece – that the pageant has passed long ago, & you are come too late, & it matters very little what you think or feel. The modern Greece is so flimsy & fragile, that it goes to pieces entirely when it is confronted with the roughest fragment of the old. But then there is very little of it; & if you choose you may see exactly what the Greeks of the 5ᵗʰ Century saw. Here are the olive groves, the hills spotted with green on the gray, the white road, the sweep of the Bay, looking to Salamis, the ancient fishponds where the priests caught trout. And at last, after a very hot drive in the trail of that decorous procession – they chanted, & one danced – & before them a stone image was born – at last, I say, we reached Eleusis – some two thousand years after our time.

There is a great deal to tantalise you in these Greek ruins; innumerable fragments & scarcely one whole piece anywhere. The museum, if one may so abuse the clean & simple shed where the more delicate fragments are placed, holds some exquisite things. There is for example a noble victory,[22] headless, wingless & armless: still her draperies & her fair body are enough to stamp once more that supreme Greek image on ones mind. And you find hints & reflections of this in a dozen smaller pieces. Indeed you can never collect a roomful of splinters without including some that are priceless – a fold of drapery, or a foot, or a hand. It sounds, like a true note struck high above the tumult.

Germans and modern Athens

A horde of Teutons invaded us, needless to say; & had the audacity to

---

21 The Sacred Way leaves Athens by way of the Sacred Gate and leads to Eleusis where annual secret fertility rites associated with the goddess Demeter (the 'Cult of the Mysteries') were performed in the Telesterion.
22 In the room with the colossal Roman caryatids from the lesser Propylea is a headless Nike.

pose themselves in the midst of the Temple of Pluto;[23] it was a photographers shop to them. Now near by, watching with quick & merry eyes, stood a group of small children, barefoot, carrying babes in their arms. They had asked for pence & had received none, but a gruff refusal; nevertheless they attached themselves to the party & attended the sitting not without a spice of malice, I conceive, in their interest. You can imagine the spurious motives, of sentiment & a kind of jocose arrogance which drove the Germans to this disposition of themselves: "The Past and the Future" – they will call it: it is a joke in thoroughly bad taste. The little Greeks, slender & vivacious who watched the performance, might be read as comment. Indeed it is curious to trace nationality in this cosmopolitan crowd, & one is never, or seldom, out in ones guesses. And you see in the German type but a lump of crude earth, as yet unchiselled by the finger of time. We English come out of the trial tolerably well; the Greeks are spent & attenuated; but the fire when there is any, burns pure.

The modern town of Athens is like most foreign towns, so a British traveller may summarily conclude, for the roofs are of fluted brown tiles, the walls are white, & there are shutters to the windows. And so it follows that the modern town is rather fragile & gimcracky, built to flash in the sun, to bask & to bake. Then there are certain great squares where the people crowd; there are trams & there are official buildings. People chatter & shout a great deal, & jostle each other on the pavement. At noon there is a lull; everybody snores; at 4 we wake again, & begin to chatter. The liveliest scene perhaps is that of the streets at evening, when the sun has just sunk & the boats in the Piraeus have fired their guns.

Acropolis
To say that the scene from the Acropolis is beautiful is an easy way out of the difficulty; all the land is bloomy as a peach, with feathery purple shadows; far off the sea gleams like dull silver; up, in the sky the clouds are trembling across the dome in crimson & gold. Meanwhile the moon is just sharp enough to cleave the blue with its thin silver edge; & one star, hangs near it. The pillars on the height are rosy as dawn; then they turn creamy white & then fade altogether. In the narrow streets which

---

23 At the end of the Sacred Way just within the Sanctuary at Eleusis is the shrine of Pluto, the Plutonion, a triangular area on which a temple once stood and an adjacent grotto reputed to be the entrance to Hades.

climb almost to the top the lights are flaring, & you walk in a curious soft air, blue with daylight still, though the lamps are pouring yellow into it. It is still quite warm, & the atmosphere has a curiously tangible quality to it; the streets are crowded & people come swarming down them, happy & garrulous, in crowds.

Pentelicus

Athens, as every schoolboy knows, lies in a plain; & the famous mountains stand round her – Hymettus, Lycabettus, Pentelicus[24] – & others I daresay, whose names I have forgotten. They are grey green for the most part; but Pentelicus wears a white scar on her side, where the Greeks used to quarry marble. We started early to climb the height, for although the ascent was to be made by carriage & mule, Pentelicus is after all higher than any English mountain, & thus claimed our respect. An Athenian carriage is a most respectable vehicle, savouring somehow of the undertaker, & not at all of Greece; it is black & shabby, & is drawn by two thin horses. It looks most incongruous upon a country road stuffed with picturesque peasants, & their bags & boxes, & turkeys & goats. Yet you meet it often in this guise "moving house" for some rustic family. It travels slowly, & it was midday when we had bargained for our horses – who were transformed to donkeys – & had dismounted at the monastery, of – I dont know what – at the foot of Pentelicus. The country is for the most part so bare & dry that these little spots, where the firs grow, & great planes, & water gushes, are exquisite – as an idyll by Theocritus.[25] We eat our lunch in the shade of a great tree, while our donkeys grazed, & our guides lay on their elbows watching us. An aged monk came down from the hill side burdened with brushwood; another, tall & melancholy, stood at the monastery door. Then the ascent began, four of us[26] perched on high wooden saddles, in single file, each attended by a boy or man to guide & belabour. We climbed what Murray[27] calls a chimney (I think): that is a little hill in the

---

24 Hymettus is in the south-east, near Athens, with an elevation of 3,370 feet; Lycabettus, a mountain of 900 feet, is in the north-easterly direction; the Attic plain at the north-east is separated from the Plain of Marathon by Mount Pentelicus, on whose slope is a monastery founded in 1578.

25 Greek poet, (320-250 BC), author of the *Idylls*.

26 Vanessa had become ill at about this time and presumably did not join the others in the expedition.

27 Richard Ford's *Murray's Hand-Book for Travellers in Greece*, a popular guidebook that ran into many editions.

mountain, which was paved with loose blocks of marble. Soon we had to dismount; the agony of our guides – they curst like lost souls – failed to move our steeds. It was hot & steep, & one had to leap from stone to stone, without the agility of a goat. Then we found that we were directed to a great cave,[28] which was cool as a temple, & had some claim to fame. I forget what. And then it appeared that the guides wished to descend; pretended that they had done their duty – swore they could go no further without food, & turned our donkeys downward. This could be conveyed sufficiently by signs; our expostulations though couched in pure English – cut the air. They answered with a gabble of Greek: so it was not the least of their sins that they would talk Greek.

So English oath and Greek oath beat the air fruitlessly; for the Greek could not understand the Epithet "squint eyed monkey" nor could we interpret the vigour of his language; Greek we reflected is devoid of meaning. Action won the day: we turned our donkeys up the hill, & the Greeks gave in with more of laughter than anger. The Greek boys, in spite of the heat, ran & rolled, & chanted the odd wavering songs of the nation. Meanwhile we climbed, & touched the hill top after 5 hours or so. The view was worth much: directly beneath was Marathon,[29] & Euboea;[30] we could see Salamis, & the outlines of many promontories. The sea flowed everywhere. It was too late to stay, so we stumbled down again, by a path this time, leading through a valley sprinkled with black goats. The goatherd sat in his cloak by the wayside – demanded matches. The valley was sweet with thyme.

Marathon is as flat as a table, brown, with a perfect curve cut out of it by the bay. Small islands white as sand floated in the sea. Euboea is long & prominent, with bays scooped in the side. But there was little space for reflection!

Acropolis
Almost every evening we climb the Acropolis & come in this desultory

---

28 Presumably a reference to the Quarry of Spilia, one of the ancient marble quarries of Mount Pentelicus; at the north-east angle of the quarry is a natural cave, the Stalactite Grotto, where rock-cut inscriptions and carvings indicate that it was an early Christian place of worship. For AVS's (or VW's) undated story, 'A Dialogue upon Mount Pentelicus', see *The Complete Shorter Fiction of Virginia Woolf*, ed. Susan Dick, revised ed. (London, 1989).

29 A plain near the ancient Greek village on the eastern coast of Attica, and the site of the Athenian defeat of the Persians in 490 BC.

30 A Greek island in the Aegean, the second largest after Crete.

way, to know its corners sufficiently well. As I foretold, in thought &
speech, it is a place that overpowers you like a wave; in time you can
'take it in', or rather be borne consciously to its heights, where you
breathe & expand. White & blue & tawny red; it is such a picture as you
cannot love sufficiently. It is a matter of proportion, we tell each other;
at any rate, when you have gazed at the patterned colours of the Parthenon an image of such life is left there that all other buildings seem mean
& frigid as tho' cut out by brainless machines 'in comparison'. It was
worth while glancing down into the streets, at the Palace[31] or the Exhibition[32] just to have that sight instantly corrected - or rather erased
altogether – by one look at the Temple. And this medicine will never be
at hand again. But the amusement did seem significant because it was so
spontaneous; the eye was acted upon unconsciously, as though it had to
choose between red & green. This is beauty – that nothing at all. It is the
same with the statues.

Modern Greeks

The poorer people of Athens – & all the people seem poor – have a pleasant habit of lounging up here in the evening, when their work is done;
just as we stroll in our parks. They sit about on classic marble, chatting
& knitting; but they do not vulgarise the place as we Tourists must do;
but rather make it human & familiar.

The people of Athens are, of course, no more Athenians than I am.
They do not understand Greek of the age of Pericles[33] – when I speak it.
Nor are their features more classic than their speech: the Turk & the
Albanian & the French – it seems – have produced a common type
enough. It is dark & dusky, small of stature, & not well grown. It is true
that the streets are dignified by the presence of many rustics, in their
Albanian dress; the men wear thick white coats, kilts, much pleated, &
long gaiters. But this you may see written in a dozen guide books. I have
seen no native women who could be distinguished from an Italian
woman; & indeed, you see very few women. The streets are crowded
with men drinking & smoking in the open air, even, in the country,
sleeping beneath the wall; but the women keep within. You generally

31 The New Palace, now the Presidential Palace, on the north side of the National Gar-
    dens, built by Ernest Ziller, 1890-8, for the then Crown Prince Constantine.
32 The Zappion, an exhibition hall in Zappion Park adjacent to the National Gardens,
    built by Ziller for the Zappas brothers.
33 The Age of Pericles is thought to range from 450 to 401 BC.

see them leading children, or looking from an upper window, where, presumably, they work. But the mind has no difficulty in making brigands.

Nauplia

We travelled down to Nauplia[34] by steamer. And if this steamer had not smelt, & if it had not had the cruel consequences of smelling ships, no voyage could have been more pleasant. The sea was only broken by the leap of the Dolphins; we passed so near the shore that we could see the little villages folded among the hills; now & then we stopped in the harbour of some more important place. The towns built pyramids up the hills; & altogether you had as fair & various a view of the Greek coast as you could wish. There are not many towns,& the land is very bleak & stony. You could not imagine a walk in such country; nor, with the level sun upon it, was it really a beautiful land. It was too fierce, too precipitous; &, in that light, too much of the colour of bare bone. We had a small company on deck who, like most of the poor people who are not inn keepers, seemed courteous & cheerful. There was a small boy for instance who gave us a lemon in return for our egg, & kissed our hands when we left. It was a long journey, for we crossed the gulf, & the dents on the map became deep bays, & we slackened steam, & went slowly on our way till 9.30 when we anchored

Nauplia Tiryns

[in Nauplia. It was dark, & lanterns swung on shore; it was clear from the lights round us that we were lying in the curve of a bay; twisted poles of light lay upon the water. Next morning indeed we found ourselves looking across a smooth bay to a circle of hills; & there were hills behind us, & on every side save one. The water lapped in front of the door, & there were many fishing boats at anchor. Tiryns is the first sight to be done, for it lies only a mile or so along the road. It is simply a pile of old stones, till you come to look closely. But then it has meaning & even beauty. The Greeks chose their sites well; here the palace was built on a flat table land, gazing up into the hills.

With a plan in your hand you can enter by the main gate, trace the servants quarters, & the Lords Castle above; & you can even assert that this was the mens hall, & this the bathroom; here, among the columns,

---

34 On the Gulf of Argoli, about 23 miles south of Corinth, and according to legend, founded by Nauplios, son of the sea-god Poseidon.

still stands the domestic altar. I looked for an alabaster lining in vain. But there was an arch of huge stones where treasure was stored, & there was hoarded shadow for us still. The Homeric palace hummed with heat. It was enough to impress one more than all guide books; but a foundation, solid, like an English Castle, only 'pre-historic'.]³⁵

Epidauros

We are now in the land of ruins & prehistoric remains; there are no statues, & no temples so that a different kind of interest is required. We drove for 20 miles today for instance (& I write, stupidly, with a street in its evening clamour beneath me) to Epidauros.³⁶ The country when you penetrate within the bare line of the coast, is strange & beautiful. There are long red roads, that pass through red fields rough with stones, & planted with twisted olive trees, or with dwarf vines; there are incessant hills, but inland they are covered with little green bushes, & the high folds among which we drove today reminded us again of Cornwall. Oddly enough the narrow streets of Athens reminded us of St Ives. Three sad jades drew our carriage the 20 miles; We passed many flocks of goats, many sumpter mules, many carts laden with wine skins. But there were only two small villages, & there was no sign of our snug English civilisation. [Epidauros, or rather the Haeron lies again, on flat land beneath a circle of hills.

There is the great theatre, so perfect that we could sit in its upper seats & look down upon the stage & hear the voice of one speaking there as in the best of halls. And the grey seats scooped out of the hillside, with wide air & country all round are as noble a theatre as could be had. Ruins of Roman Houses, Temples of Asclepios – Tholos – are scattered innumerable. It needs learning to see anything but chips of stone. And in the museum chaos is still more chaotic: they are fitting temples together, hammering the old stone into the right shape.

The place is very lovely; although you must leave the ruins for bed. It is so wide & harmonious, & the country is all grouped round decorously.

And there was the drive home – but to write is impossible. This is the

---

35 Matter in brackets cancelled by AVS.
36 Ancient Epidauros was prosperous as a health centre and is the site of the shrine of Asclepios, the Greek god of healing.

worst inn we have struck hitherto; & sleep – if possible – is the best way of cutting it short.][37]

Mycenae

Such words as I have hastily & barbarously applied to Epidauros are singularly inadequate; & when I consider Mycenae,[38] my next attempt, I might well leave a blank page. Where does the place begin – where stop – what does it not gather on its way? There never was a sight, I think less manageable; it travels through all the chambers of the brain, wakes odd memories & imaginations; forecasts a remote future; retells a remote past. And all the while it is – let me write it down – but a great congeries of ruined houses, on a hill side. So you may see the outline of a wall in an English farmyard, tenanted 60 years ago by a serf; these were built let us say one thousand years before Christ; they have certainly lain in ruins since the year – was it four hundred & sixty? But among these houses, you come across something far more definite; an αγορα,[39] a tomb, a palace with a flight of steps. The whole hill top is crowded with dead stones; & yet they are not dead. The tracery is too emphatic: the mark is too deeply scored.

The imagination does assert again & again, as you walk, that the place is crowded & compact; it is true there is little to see & nothing to hear. But the tremendous stones are not to be ignored, & the two lions, which guard the gate, do still consciously admit you to something august which is beyond.[40] I tremble to write of the classics, because that might savour of the perfunctory impulse of the guide book; but the taste of Homer was in my mouth.[41] Indeed, this is the pearl of seeing things here; the words of the poets begin to sing & embody themselves. This is no pretence, moreover, as it may so easily be at home, in a London room; it needs no effort; but if statues & marble are solid to the touch, so, simply, are words resonant to the ear.

As far as I could tell – Baedecker [sic] makes short work of archaeol-

---

37 Matter in brackets cancelled by AVS.

38 One of the most historic sites in Greece; from here Agamemnon set out to conquer Troy.

39 An agora, market-place of Mycenae, the centre of public life.

40 The acropolis of Mycenae is entered through the Lion Gate, its opening roughly 10 feet high by 10 feet wide, surmounted by two erect confronted lions, their front paws resting on joined altars.

41 During this holiday, AVS read the first four books of the *Odyssey*; see B. Silver, *Virginia Woolf's Reading Notes*, 1983, XXXIV, B.4-5.

ogy – there was a place of assembly, ringed with upright slabs of stone, in double rows, so as to make a passage, when properly roofed.[42] Then there was a tomb, which they call the tomb of Agamemnon:[43] & here, when the earth was first disturbed, gold gleamed, & amethysts, & beautiful ornaments, which still held the light. Higher, but at a very small distance, was the King's palace;[44] with his rooms, properly distinguished doubtless, by their separate uses. Then there were more graves on the side; & terraces circled the whole summit, leading to Gates,[45] which presumably admitted & rejected the outer world. As I stumbled I picked up an earthenware handle with its little pattern still brightly stamped on it; & once more it was easy to believe that the whole crest was packed with unbroken litter, of the prehistoric city. The circumference of the town is not large; but then every foots pace of it is set with stone, & it must have been a populous town; so closely occupied because the outer world was vast and lonely. How far history, or mythology, warrants me, I do not know; but I conceived that here was a single spot of intense, & brilliantly painted life, girt in by great wastes of desert land. The people had not come yet. And I conceived that the Kings & people of Mycenae lived a decorous life, strictly ordered, as the town itself is graven in distinct divisions. They were simple & austere, as tho' conscious that they lived with a great eye upon them, an isolated people, adventuring alone; but in the limits of their town they lived with much ornament & decoration: the king wore purple robes, & his limbs shone with beaten gold. They had many festivals, & when it was summer they marched down the hill side in ceremonial procession, glittering in dyed clothing & ornament & gold, with offerings outstretched in their hands. The valley was kindled by the sun, & they threaded it like bright summer flies. And the thyme smelt sweet as ambrosia. And in the

---

42　AVS is presumably referring to the Royal Grave Circle A, to the immediate right after entering the Lion Gate; 88 feet in diameter, the circle consists of a double ring of standing stone slabs which encloses six shaft graves.

43　About half a mile south-east of the Mycenean Citadel is the Tomb of Agamemnon, the so-called Treasury of Atreus, the most impressive of all the *tholos* or beehive tombs.

44　The Palace of Agamemnon is reached by the Royal Road, a ramp leading from the inner court of the Lion Gate; the Palace rises in tiers to the highest point of the walled Citadel which is reserved for the court and its retainers.

45　The Postern Gate on the north wall and the Sally Port on the south wall, close to the Great Cistern.

evening they were all gathered in order in their courts, & perhaps a great beacon burnt; in case man or God beheld it.

And yet after all, they may have thought many of our thoughts, & felt many of our passions. Certainly they beheld the same hillside, grey with rock; ominous & melancholy I thought it, in the September light. There is no Spring any more was what I read in it, overlooking Greece, & thinking of her people. Or did I think of the whole world? – but that, really, is a doubtful argument. These lines hint, at least, that Mycenae leaves a great body of confused meaning in the mind; nor will it be possible to spin a coherent tale till I have made sure of the earth & the sky. And then guide books will do the rest. These things were dug up in the year 1885? by Dr Schliemann;[46] that statement will content a mind safely housed in London; with compasses & maps hung upon the walls. We dont realise these things except just for seconds, on the spot; & then it is hopeless to say what you see. There is a force of gravity in the mind which keeps it always safely tied to the earth; or, with Mycenae to waft it, it might circle in vague air for ever.

But I did see, for a second, as through a chink, down, down, for miles beneath my feet.[ ]

When you remember the English countryside there is much to surprise you in the Greek. We should call the hills here 'sights' & travel miles to view the picturesque; for while we have our beauties we also have our long level lapses. Now Greece is always in a state of ferment & effervescence; every journey you take seems to lead through beautiful, or majestic or romantic country places. There is no rest; but a perpetual curve & flow, as if the land ran fluid & exuberant as the sea. Take, for instance, the little journey from Corinth to Athens; I say 'take' & then stop. For there never was a scene less easy to fit with words, though it is also true that, like all Greek things – poems & temples & statues - there is a certain form & finish even in the landscape that makes separate views of it detach themselves like pictures. I think particularly of the bay of Salamis as we saw it this evening from the train windows. Now the line runs on a ledge along the cliff, so that you look down upon a road which skirts the bay, & so directly in to the water. And this evening the moon was rising before the sun had set; so you had a curious marriage of two lights; the soft silver of the moon, & the ruddiness of the sun; &

---

46 Heinrich Schliemann (1822-90), German archaeologist known for his excavations of Homeric sites, his first made in 1874-6.

while the moon lay softly white across the sea, those waters did actually sparkle, blue, pure & tender, & alive beneath it. So that the whole bay was luminous, & warm;[ ] as though filled to the brim with some live fluid at the same time that it became a phantom.

And there were dusky green olive trees standing against the water; & blue islands rising like icebergs on the horizon.

But perhaps the most exquisite thing was the white road "pearl white", someone would have said, which went so abruptly along the cliff that it needed a parapet by the edge. Here you saw small figures walking, & carts driving: nor could you help believing that they were on their way from Athens & that the road, in spite of the railway, was still the great thoroughfare. It had the look – which is very rare – of a real road; & that will outlast all railways, so long as man has two legs. So the hills grew black & sharp of outline, & the water became paler and paler, till the transition was complete. But there was a wonderful pause.

Certain accidents which are to be attributed – certainly not to us – to clocks to hotel keepers – to streets – in fact to the whole Greek nation – certain accidents, at any rate made us miss our train to Calchis;[47] we had to spend the morning in Athens. Now Athens can be seen the wrong side out; you can walk round & round her without catching sight of the Parthenon, & you may then fairly call her a flashy modern town, deserving of abuse.

At five this morning we[48] stood before the Inn at Calchis waiting for our carriage, while the rain poured. Even so we could see the boats, drifting down the current, & the great steamers gliding among them. In the sun it would have been beautiful; in the mud it was vague & comfortless as a dream. At last our horses came, & we mounted to drive 32 miles to Achmetaga.[49] Now you have to travel along a plain, & to climb a mountain, & to curl like a langorous serpent round the front of the precipice; & then you must descend, as tortuously into the valley, & drive among steep hill sides covered with trees, & the trees cluster thick in the valley, over the dry bed of the stream. We proposed last night to go straight on, driving all night, to reach Achmetaga this morning, but

47 The capital of the island of Euboea.
48 AVS, Thoby, and Adrian.
49 In northern Euboea; the estate bought originally by a cousin of Lady Byron and now owned by the grandson, Frank Noel, father of the Stephens' friend, Irene Noel (1869-1956).

the driver said no: it was dangerous. So we amused ourselves by count-
ing the number of times we should have fallen over the broken parapet,
or stepped right in to the great hole in the road, or fallen headlong down
the precipice; for surely as we narrowly escaped these dangers by day,
we should have been snared for a certainty by night. A Scotch mist was
quite dark enough. We baited our horses at an inn on the way, which we
might then examine curiously. It was a barn, with a wall separating it
into two rooms. One was stable, the other bedroom dining room living
room &c. for husband & wife & children. We looked in through the
iron grating, & saw the woman in a corner, working her distaff; she sat
on a mat. The children played round her; there was a hole in the chimney, & a heap of ashes on the floor, & bread & onions stood on planks.
Here was England in the 14th Century; it was dark & probably smelly:
tins & plates gleamed in corners. A man like a serf brought us bread &
water.

But we pressed on, & at 2 o'clock found ourselves entering a village –
almost the first we had passed. There were hovels heaped up in a valley,
& a square white house raised among them. Shutters & terraces showed
that we had come to our goal; & so we dismounted & found ourselves in
an English drawing room. English drawing rooms it is true are
generally more richly furnished; There are carpets on the floors, &
many chairs. This room suggested that its windows were perpetually
open, & as its owners lived out of doors there was not much need for
any decoration but what was cool & simple. Still, however open & rick-
etty, the place had the effect of making you feel that you had come to the
genuine living place at last, after skimming a factitious exterior for a
long time. Here people lived, not merely stayed. And this impression remains; indeed for the first time Greece becomes an articulate human
place, homely & familiar, instead of a splendid surface. We walked out
down a lane that might have been in England – for it had a hedge, & was
muddy, to see an encampment of Wallachian shepherds.[50] Murray has
his paragraph; they are a nomad people, tending sheep, who roam in the
mountains all the summer, & pitch their tents, or rather their huts, in the
winter. These had just come down; & we were asked – & how good it
was to ask & answer easily as in English! – to go inside their huts. They
are made of boughs, & the dead leaves serve for lining to the roof. A
family of twelve children lived here; brown & sallow, gentle & com-

---

50 Wallachia was formerly a principality in south-eastern Europe, now a part of Roma-
nia.

municative. They shook hands – the women were weaving cloth, in an outer court; & inside was the sleeping place of the family. They live, presumably, in the open air; we peered round, & tried, not very success-fully, to imagine the whole life, built on such a foundation. But this needs more imagination than any other feat of archaeology; for mud huts belong to the dark ages. The people did not look robust or fierce; one or two women had notably fine faces, aquiline & expressive. Then we tramped some way over the estate; & this would be a dull record,[ ] but all the time, somehow – I can't define it – you felt the place arrange itself in its natural order, & this was something beautiful. Here were the olive groves - here they dug a trench – here come all the village people, trooping home from work with their salutations, prompt & respectful. Miss Noel knew each by name; each spoke to her. Now this seemed to give what was wanting to Greece before; & it is a very essential part of it. The people use the same plough that they did in the days of Homer, says Mrs Noel, & though the races have changed, their lives cannot be much different; the earth changes but little.

Achmetaga stands on a flight of steps, with its garden in terraces; & a view far & wide to distant mountains, framed by tall trees. The garden like the house, is somehow rather ramshackle & bare; a group of women sat this morning picking walnuts from their shells on the lawn. Meanwhile all the government of the village it seemed was transacted in the house. The nurse came for her medicines, the servants for their orders, strange figures kept walking in at the door to ask for treatment or advice. No one seemed to have any precise calling, & yet everyone seemed able & willing to do something. The groom wanted to know what soup we would have for dinner; & also he would lend a hand in the farm. Or that was my impression; the place was full of simple garrulous creatures, eager as children to be directed to their tasks, eager as chil-dren to stay & chatter with their mistress.

In the afternoon we set off to dig on a hill which had already yielded an arm or a leg or a pillar of hewn marble. Indeed it did not need an archaeological eye to see that the hill boded something; for it was shaped & buttressed, & might be divided into halls & palaces by an eye that remembered Mycenae. So after a little debate, a trench was cut across the summit; till the pick axes grated on the rock. Many fragments of Greek pottery were thrown up – indeed they lay thick on the surface, but neither statue nor temple. We laid bare the foundation of a wall, further on, also; (I did strike three blows for the glory of Greece) but our excavations were ended by the sunset: soft earth still lay packed above the rock & its treasures.

That there are treasures no one who has seen the place can possibly deny; but the native Greek who wielded a spade, professed a very cynical interest in our activities. Why, he mused, dig up stones when you might be digging up potatoes? & as most landowners agree with him, the chances are that the Temple & town of [*blank space*] will lie beneath the earth [ ] forever. And it does seem a curious mania, when you are in the heart of the same country & its life to start disturbing all that it keeps buried. This is the healthy influence of real country life for such are not the opinions of a tourist.

When we[51] came down to breakfast this morning we were told that a man had been murdered in the fields near by. That was the first time I ever heard the word used, gravely. We eat our breakfast in melancholy; but if it was sad it was still more strange. He had been at work in his field, when a man came up to him; he was an old enemy, for they had quarrelled last year over a bean field, & there had been threats. "If you move I shoot you," he cried; the other swung round, & was shot twice in the body. And then the murderer ran, & the peasants working in the field pretended that it was a hare only that had been shot, for they were of the family of the criminal. Then an old woman came by – saw the man groaning, & had him carried up to the village here. Mrs. Noel went for a doctor, but it was some hours before he came, & then he was little better than a peasant, put into coat & trousers. At lunch they said that the man had to die; & as we sat in the wood beyond the village one man after another came past us, striding down from the mountain to see their kinsman before he died. All the peasants are related. Meanwhile telegrams were sent to the ports to stop the runaway; & the gendarmes arrived, a small body of lazy looking little soldiers - 'who come to eat only' says Mrs. Noel. The murderer has become a fugitive; he will hide in the mountains all day, & come down at night to see his relations who will give him food. Or perhaps he will try to leave the country.

We left all this – but I am wrong if I suggest excitement or tumult – no one seemed much surprised or horrified; & drove to the coast, some five

---

51 AVS, Thoby and Adrian stayed with the Noels in Achmetaga from 1-5 Oct.; Vanessa remained with Violet Dickinson in Athens, where for the next two weeks she was ill; see QB, I, p. 195.

miles distance. The peasants were peacefully working in the fields, & bade us good day as we passed.

The coast is very steep, & gray; like Cornish cliffs; gray rocks stained with yellow lichen stand out in perfectly clear water. And on the horizon there are the delicate outlines of islands. The top of the cliff, was scattered with gray stones; & we did once more & still more undoubtedly, construct a whole village here; courts & doorways, even an altar. No one has ever dug here, nor is there any rumour of a town. That is the charm of this place; the life has gone on naturally for hundreds of years; covering what it chose to cover; & the most enthusiastic must acquiesce. Still, if I had a spade I should like to try my hand up here, for here was the hill top, & the wide sea. And it was all the more beautiful because it was so unknown; such temples there must have been all over Greece; the spirit was not a thing of the surface or as beautiful as those of Athens & Olympia. Here flourished the unknown artists of the soil, working for the delight of their own peasants.

Then the sea shone with that strange luminous glow as though the water were lit from within – & the sun sank & we drove home. It was quite dark by the time we reached the house, & Omar[52] rose & fell with the horses hoofs. There we heard that the wounded man had died, not an hour after we had left, in the middle of the afternoon.

Whether it was arranged by providence or, as seems more likely, by another power, it is certain that we have been seeing a new side of Greek life. And is it not to study sides of all things that we travel? & shall we forfeit our claim to the honourable title of tourist?

Not while there is a pen – a very old one, & a drop of ink – a very dry one. For these as we will explain one day are the philosophers stone. You make a pass in the air with a dirty stump of goose flesh, having first spread a white sheet on your knee. Soon a procession begins to cross it; there is no doubt whatever; here are the bores & the dullards, the cheats & the liars, but their only purpose now is to amuse a leisure hour. So I thank the Lady who has just finished stamping a walz [sic] on the piano, & I forgive the bundle of flesh who takes her nourishment at regular hours next my table. After all they let me draw the following reflections upon Greek domestic life – & that is very valuable.

For this hotel is patronised solely by natives, although I cannot diagnose them further. I conceive that the mother & the daughter who plays

52 Presumably their driver.

are here to buy clothes for the coming season; they may be little officials in Sparta or Nauplia. But in the capital they are ladies – after 11.30 P.M. that is. It is not necessary to speak gently, & smile sweetly in the early morning, any more than it is necessary to lace oneself into silk, & tie bows in ones hair. But sometimes nature rushes out like a pent river. The mother had to lean against the door the other day to support her stout frame while she shrieked Greek like a fish wife. But her face grew white, & her dull grey eyes gleamed like an adders. Now the daughter has still good reason to conciliate the world; so she not only bows & smiles with some graciousness, but directly her meal is finished, she hastens to the drawing room, & there alone – for doesn't she love music for itself, its own sake – she belabours the small sharp piano with merciless fists. It is to do her bidding, you hear at every stroke; & if it is disobedient, a good blow will teach it to know better next time. Mean while she smiles unperturbed; & gradually the room fills, & she hesitates & yields & has her little triumph.

Perhaps the mother wishes that she had been taught to play Valzs [*sic*] in her youth; she squints in the glass, draws her boa closer to hide the folds of her neck, & enlarges to the young man from Patras upon the education which is thought necessary for girls nowadays. But the education I should sum up thus: there is no doubt that she can play Valzs: there is no doubt that she can do her hair; but there is no reason to suppose that she can read, write or talk. And although much can be done without those accomplishments, still, if you meet her, sitting by herself in the drawing room, dull, vacant, pallid, & infinitely bored, you can even pity her. Perhaps she can't read literary Greek; for she never touches a newspaper; perhaps she cant marry into the circle above her own; the young man from Patras may represent the ambition of her life; certainly he makes her smile. So they wait on day after day; punctual at meals, elaborate in dress, silent when they are together, & condescending when they can find some one respectable to talk to them.

There were many stories told us by the Noels which might be copied here. How for instance it is necessary to bribe the best doctor in Athens with the present of a pig before he will sign your nurses certificate – how, in short all classes have their price; how all Greeks lie, how all Greeks are dirty, ignorant, & unstable as water.

And considering that Mr. Noel has lived among them – as he was born among them – for some fifty years not only do his words carry weight, but it is the kind of weight that is absolute. It would have been so easy, in such a length of time with such associations, to have grown to love the people, so that a stranger hinting at their faults would have been driven back "Not a bit of it – I know the people". But as it is, he does know the people & this is his knowledge.

Like a shifting layer of sand these loosely composed tribes of many different peoples lie across Greece; calling themselves Greek indeed, but bearing the same kind of relation to the old Greek that their tongue does to his. For the language they talk is divided from the language that some few of them can write as widely as that again is divided from the speech of Plato. The spoken language because it has not been fixed by grammar or spelling, twists itself afresh on each tongue. The peasants drop syllables, & slur vowels so that as proficient a speaker as Miss Noel could not undertake to write down the words that ran so swiftly fr. her tongue. Nor could she either read or write the Greek of the newspapers; & still less could she read the Greek of the Classics. So you must look upon Modern Greek as the impure dialect of a nation of peasants, just as you must look upon the modern Greeks as a nation of mongrel element & a rustic beside the classic speech of pure bred races. These are the thoughts that force themselves upon you when you are out of sight of the Parthenon; & I have discovered that you may spend ten days in Athens without once seeing that temple. Early in the morning sometimes I fling open my window & see pillars standing on a great rock which surprise me.

After all, we are in Athens; but Athens means many more things than the Acropolis, & the sanest plan is to separate the quick from the dead, the old from the new, so that the two images shall not vex each other. It is amusing to be able to abuse entirely, just as it is far better to praise enthusiastically.

So I take some pains to put old Greece on my right hand and new Greece on my left & nothing that I say of the one shall apply to the other. The justice of that division has been proved etymologically, & ethnologically, – *indeed* & I daresay I could go on proving it through all the arts & sciences, but these shall be sufficient.

The reading that you do in a sick room[53] is really not to be called reading any more than the exercise gone through on a railway journey. The book is the anodyne, which will last you till the station is reached or the hour comes for giving the patient her food. You measure such a space

---

53 Presumably sharing the sick-room duties with Violet in looking after Vanessa.

on your watch against so many Chapters of print; & so you plod on, grateful for the opiate, that can but blunt the hour of its pang. Yet even so, some books drone in a different key from others; some do even send an occasional thrill of oblivion down your spine, & let you dream that you are free to follow them whither they call.

Now a book I have been reading in this spirit for some days – the Letters of Merimée to an unknown woman[54] – has pierced the dull hide that surrounds the nursing woman more frequently than any of the novels. They were too far & visionary; but Merimée was dealing with a real world in which people were ill & angry, where the rain was wet & the sun was hot, & it was rather agreeable to be told that such things went on outside the bedroom door just as usual.

And then there began to be a mystery, or rather a puzzle which one might piece together idly when the book was shut, & refashion again, with surprising ingenuity, when the book was open. Now the nature of the puzzle was & is – for I have not solved it – something like this: Merimée writes to a young woman who is conceivably half an English-woman, as often & as intimately as though he were her lover, & a clan-destine lover at that. For they have to contrive meetings unknown to her family. But now the puzzle begins, for instead of writing as a lover, he writes as a caustic, candid & often indifferent friend, whose interest is of the intellect, or at any rate of the morals, & whose heart is rather re-pelled than softened. She is called selfish, insincere, vain, & a score of other unpleasant things, in almost every letter; still he writes, some-times daily, never at any long intervals. To this the reader must make his own reply, for the unknown Lady is engulfed in her title; you do not hear her voice once, throughout the two volumes. When she travels, her destination is marked with an initial only; her friend Lady M is curtailed in the same way. So then she outlived her friend, & ordered the letters to be printed, but wished for certain reasons that her name should be un-known. One reason & a good one was perhaps that she did not care to

---

54 Prosper Mérimée, *Lettres à une inconnue*, 1873; Mérimée's *inconnue* was Jeanne-Françoise Dacquin (1811-95), known to her family as Jenny. 'She was well-educated, intelligent, independent, and determined, and had already published prose and verse pieces under a pen-name . . . A woman of principle, she had no intention of entering into any relationship with Mérimée other than platonic friendship or marriage; he, on the other hand, was impressed by her personality, amused by her wit, attracted by her beauty and irritated by her adamance. Thus there grew up between them a curious mixture of love, comradeship and exasperation which lasted literally until Mérimée's dying day.' A. W. Raitt, *Prosper Mérimée*, 1970, p. 110.

own her faults in public, & yet with a candour like that of Merimée himself, she desired that the letters should be printed in full. And again, it may be that after two printed volumes of letters, covering some twenty years, had passed between them, after he had died even – the correspondence was still secret. There is no hint that her friendship was shared by brother or sister; for all we know, save for a line dropped early that it was best to meet by stealth – these two knew each other face to face, alone, isolated from their kind. They do not seem to have met often, but they wrote always, till one of them – the man – brought the correspondence to an end two hours before he died.

And what did they write about?

It is here that the natural ingenuity of the reader is taxed or inspired, as the case may be. To read the letters intelligently you must construct a reply; they demand it as imperiously as certain notes struck on the piano demand, & seem to imply their harmonies. So the letter read alone sounds querulous as though reaching after their fellow notes, when all shall be concord.

And your curiosity is the more whet because it must have been such an odd kind of concord; if you could hear these two voices speaking together it would not be a dulcet sound, or a loving sound, or a passionate sound that they would make in unison; but it would be something sharp & curious, something that would ring a new note in the ear, not to be forgotten. This indeed is the puzzle that amuses my vigil; what kind of harmony was there when Merimée & the veiled Lady spoke together?

Before you can make sure of or even guess at the nature of the concord you must draw forth her notes from his, & if you can, induce her to speak some phrase in her proper person. From him you know that she is difficult, not above the arts of the coquette, & except that she uses them to veil a rare mind, & perhaps, a rare nature. About the mind indeed there can be no mistake, for Merimée would not have scrupled to call her a fool had she been ordinarily intelligent; & if he does not often compliment her, he writes to her as easily of all that interests him – literature & archaeology & politics – as though there is no question of a step down between their minds. It is her character that vexes him, particularly that part of it which is concerned in their relationship. She was unstable, & cruel & insincere; sometimes she did not write, or they went for a walk, & she left him in a temper. From such symptoms at the beginning an observer might predict love, only different from vulgar love in that the man held a pen in his hand. His jealousy, & his sensitiveness to trifles, written out clearly in faultless French, are no more than the usual passion, eager & fretful, which in most foams inarticulate. But then it leaves the natural channels; it broadens & becomes slowly both clear & smooth of surface; & the natural channel surely led to the meeting of the streams. But for thirty years these two currents run side by side, so equably that - to continue the metaphor – the same body of water seems to pass always, neither less nor more; & the only change is that the stream runs smoother, & you seem to see to the depths.

The experiment has often been tried, but it has failed so often that this long drawn out success has an interest on that account alone. A man & a woman, then, may come so near, & stay so near, & keep always just so much distance between them, & draw nothing but profit, apparently from the alliance.

Still, whatever the reason, you cannot help feeling that each was a lonely person all the days of his life; & some cowardice entered into the arrangement. Merimée becomes terribly interested in his health by degrees, & we read that he adopted two old Englishwomen, to whom he seldom spoke, in the same way perhaps that he adopted a lizard & a cat. There was some pleasure in tending the lonely creatures, in seeing the warmth come back to their limbs from his own hands, & he could be sure that it would never return in robust measure.

The unknown lady it is clear did not rouse him from these sad & valetudinarian ways. She was even more fastidious than he was. He is always glad to tell her of ridiculous Englishwomen he has seen, because it will make her laugh; & he likes to hint in writing at some broad story because he can imagine the disgust or the blush which he would have seen on her face opposite him.

So, as she was more fastidious, she was also more cynical; for sad as he is often his distrust has much depth in it; whereas the lady we conceive, was repelled too easily to dislike or distrust much more than the surface.

But it is dangerous to draw features within the veil; for you are always baffled by her silence. And when you consider that for thirty years a man was constantly addressing this phantom, you must endow her beyond question with some peculiar power. She was neither a mere coquette, nor a mere blue stocking, although she was vain of her dark eyes, & could read Greek.

Still less was she a commanding woman, of great spiritual height, to lead & inspire. Again, she was not famous, or rich, or aristocratic, the one thing that we know of her for certain is that she suited Prosper Merimée; & so we are led to ask, what was it that Prosper Merimée wanted? To begin with it seems, he needed a correspondent, he needed some one to whom he might write rather than talk, who would receive the deliberate utterances of his mind, & understand them. Then this person must be as incapable of inspiring a false word as of uttering one, meaning by false a defect of taste or judgment. She must be able even to advise upon questions of literature.

But it is more difficult to describe the nature of the personal qualities that were necessary; because these were very subtle, & upon one side they were suppressed, so far as we are concerned. If we are certain that Merimée did not want passion we are confident too that he needed some thing more warm than reasonable agreement to flavour the correspondence.

They were scarcely affectionate, very often; the great bond lay perhaps – outside those many intellectual sympathies – in their common boredom & in their common candour. Some affinity had drawn these two together; they continued the intimacy as much because they agreed in finding others dull as because they found each other amusing; finally they brought it to an end, or submitted to its ending, in a condition as nearly approaching the serenity of love as was possible to the temperament of either. The letters, as I have said, tend always to become simpler & more gentle; as though doubts & plainings ceased altogether.

Whether we rate their affection high or low, we cannot question its integrity. And there lies the singular charm of the letters & of the two characters which they reveal. You feel perfect faith in a man who tells a woman her motives & her faults; who despises democracy, & who predicts, in a low monotonous voice, that his country will go to war.

The unknown, on her side, was also clear sighted; although she did not like improprieties & believed in the Pope. The Roman Catholic Church & the conventions were, however, just the reservations which were necessary to draw all other scales from her eyes.

Conformity in such large matters allows considerable latitude in all else; certain it is that she travelled considerably, like Merimée himself, that she lived somewhere in the Provinces, that she read widely, & that she saw her correspondent Merimée whenever she stayed in Paris.

Naturally, they have much to write about that demands no closer scrutiny than the last letter from Mr. Balfour to Mr. Chamberlain.[55] Merimée knew everyone; & she was an excellent listener.

Still, few letters passed between them that do not suggest some addition to the mystery, or some solution of it.

It is so calm & clear now, you think; they are proved friends & no more.

But the last line of the last letter adds a final shock:

Je vous embrasse.

He had never said that before; & certainly he was never to say it again. For in two hours he was dead.

It is no wonder, were I to write down all the circumstances of the case. Certainly it is not the fault of Greece – that we all cry O to be in England!

It is almost strange how the longing grows & what it desires; it will feed on names, so that the simple word Devon is better than a poem; it will make pictures better than any in Greece out of a wet London street, with lamplight twisted on the pavement. And six lines of description – It was a winter's night & the stars rose above bare fields – will raise tears, I swear it.

But yet we are not patriotic; indeed it is amusing to read the newspapers & find how little interest it is possible to take in all the frizzling & bubbling that goes on still in our island. George Wyndham[56] does not call anti Imperialists traitors; & so he tells the world, & the world listens gravely. Out here it seems to matter very little what George Wyndham calls anybody; & traitors & imperialists are nothing more than names. The Times loses its stately proportions: it is the private sheet of a small colony of islanders, whose noise is effectually shut up in their prison.

But it is not for the people we crave; it is for the place. That keeps its magic; so strong that it seems to send shocks across the water.

On a flippant afternoon, here in Athens – for the street cut out in clear colours & washed in bright air – has a certain levity – you think of stern Yorkshire moors; cool smells blowing off the heath, stone houses, a light or two in the hollow.

---

55 Arthur James Balfour (1848-1930), British statesman and philosopher, Conservative Prime Minster, 1902-5; Joseph Austen Chamberlain (1863-1937), British Liberal statesman, responsible for bringing down Balfour's government.

56 The Rt Hon. George Wyndham (1863-1913), chief Secretary for Ireland, 1900-5, with a seat in Mr Balfour's cabinet since 1902.

Or you think of a great London square, where the lamps are just lit, & all the windows stand out red for the virtuous evening.

Or you think of clear autumn mornings, with the trail of burnt leaves in the wind, a crisp page on the desk, & a brisk fire in the hearth.

There are many pictures; they come up, one after another, till you must stop thinking for there are many leagues of the inhospitable east to travel first.

England has a sound of everything that is clean & sane, & serious; besides, it is a modest place, full of fresh beauties. Ah yes, we will go home & discover them all; there is no such beauty to be found elsewhere.

When there is a choice of nationality in steamers – French Italian German or Greek – an unprejudiced English mind will incline towards the German; cousins we are, at heart; we have the same ideas of cleanliness, that is. Blood really amounts to that; for beautiful as the French language is, I will not trust my body – no, nor my soul, to a people who know not the tub. Now this is a really valuable confession; had I red ink on board with me, I would underline it, to catch a vagrant eye in future.

We did well, then, to trust to our old congenital instinct; for the Dalmatia, of the Austrian Lloyd service, upon which we embarked yesterday, has shown just those solid sensible virtues which one esteems in an individual & admires beyond all others in a ship. She is only half full; she is clean; she is well served, & her table is sound & sober. So we left the Piraeus, & trod for the last time upon Greek soil. Circumstances again, at which a discreet diary can only hint, gloomily, made it impossible to think one appropriate thought; but then has any one ever thought the thing he had suggested to him?

But I can answer in some sort for belated effort on the part of my own brain. At about 5 o'clock we had our last view of Athens, & its plain, & the famous hills. I have had reason to think of Athens only as a modern town, speaking a barbarous language, peopled by liars & cheats; as though to cancel that impression – to win back a faltering lover, albeit an insignificant one – the place seemed to glow once more in its beautiful old guise; the lights came trembling across the hills, & only the Acropolis was visible, standing high beyond the town. Stalwart & red & significant – alone & apart from all the modern world. To that then & the delicate impetuous hills, I could say farewell; for they are Greece, & so I have known them, & shall always know them. Silence, awful & unbroken, washes over them for ever now, & no human cry shall stir them any more. After all the tumult that frets their base is but ephemeral; & a wise man will hear it no more than the Greeks hear it, who have been dead two thousand years. The sun sank, & single lights opened here & there, upon the mainland of Greece. We doubled Cape Sunium[57] in the night, & all day we have been steaming along the coast of Asia Minor, with an island springing now & then on our left. In the evening we stopped, in a neck of sea, commanded by great guns, where lies the famous town of the Dardanelles.[58] A little further & we came to Abydos[59] in Sestos, with the mound where Xerxes sat; his ghost might watch many strange passengers crossing from shore to shore. Shall we say that the coast of Asia Minor is like many another coast – a faint dark streak, that swells & sinks, & is sprinkled here & there with white houses in clusters? And then you must add, to propitiate somebody or other, that we also passed the plain of Troy.[60] But all that is too finely embedded in my mind to be extracted tonight. The good trustworthy ship plods on her way down the sea of Marmara & lets me write a neat hand, as though I bestrode a soft pacing nag.

When we wake at 5.30 we shall be exposed instantly to all the splendour of Constantinople. But I think of Greece.

And so we were, exposed, almost before our eyes were open. For waking at half past five I saw the land streaming past us, sharp black, with the pale lights of dawn upon the sea. At six I was on deck, & suddenly we found ourselves confronted with the whole of Constantinople; there was St Sophia,[61] like a treble globe of bubbles frozen solid, floating out to meet us. For it is fashioned in the shape of some fine substance, thin as glass, blown in plump curves; save that it is also as substantial as a pyramid. Perhaps that may be its beauty. But then beautiful & eva-

---

57 Cape Sounion is at the south-east tip of Attica, on the highest point of which is the Temple of Poseidon.

58 The 40-mile strait between Europe and Turkey, connecting the Sea of Marmara to the Aegean; also called the Hellespont.

59 An ancient town in Asia Minor on the Hellespont; it was here that Xerxes crossed the strait on his bridge of boats when he invaded Greece. Sestos is the narrowest point of the strait opposite Abydos; see n.13.

60 Site of the 10-year Trojan War, the Plain of Troy stretches from the foot of the sloping ridge surmounted by the ruins of ancient Troy (Ilium).

61 The Cathedral of St Sophia, originally built by Constantine, was burned during the Nike Revolts of 532 and rebuilt by Justinian; it was turned into a mosque after the Ottoman conquest.

nescent & enduring, to pluck adjectives like black berries – as it is, it is but the fruit of a great garden of flowers. The sun was rising swiftly, opposite the town, & the whole sweep of grey houses piled high & curved freely was picked out lavishly & fantastically with golden windows. And so the colour was of gray houses, & pale golden panels, & dark tufts of green, for all the buildings were spaced with a soft fringe of trees. We passed rapidly before this wonderful sight, which seemed to renew itself afresh before our eyes, each instant, & so came to the crowded pool of the river, where the Golden Horn[62] branches off from the Bosphorus[*sic*]. But here my point of view was certainly eclipsed; nor do I remember any more, as novelists say, & they have all the best devices – until – well, it would be convenient to say until about 6 o'clock in the evening, when I sat before an open window, & saw the sun set behind the town which had reflected its uprise.

From this position you see over the town, or as much of it as a square window will compass, & that is enough to give you some idea that Constantinople is to begin with a very large town. Remembering Athens, you felt yourself in a metropolis; a place where life was being lived successfully. And that did seem strange, & – if I have time to say so – a little uncomfortable. For you also realised that life was not lived after the European pattern, that it was not even a debased copy of Paris or Berlin or London, & that, you thought was the ambition of towns which could not actually be Paris or any of those inner capitals. As the lights came out in clusters all over the land, & the water was busy with lamps, you knew yourself to be the spectator of a vigorous drama, acting itself out with no thought or need of certain great countries yonder to the west. And in all this opulence there was something ominous, & something ignominious – for an English lady at her bedroom window. At any rate, it was a stirring sight to look upon; & if I may use the shorthand of a hack writer, a most beautiful one into the bargain.

The Golden Horn drives a broad blue wedge between two high banks of houses; so that, as some one says, a battle ship rides at anchor in the street before your door. Then the sunset in long bars of flame & scarlet with a border of chimneys & mosques drawn black upon their lowest margin; the blue waters were lit up & golden lights were sprinkled upon them. Up in the air, & deep down in the earth the lamps burnt; & then the moon, a crescent, swung slowly up the sky, & a pure drop of light, the evening star, turned the innumerable lamps to gold.

---

62 An arm of the Bosporus forming the harbour of Constantinople.

There are few experiences more exhilarating than the first dive into a new town – Even when your plunge is impeded – as ours was this morning – by a sleek Turkish dragoman.[63] Still, when the driver cracked his whip, & the horses started down the hill, all our obstacles were forgotten. Innumerable pages have been turned in the history of Constantinople, but this, the last, was turned fresh for us. And yet, apart from the chafing of strange sights upon our senses, there was really nothing very memorable in our descent upon Stamboul.[64] A view does not by any means promise beauty of detail; & the streets were insignificant, & the national dress – a fez & a frock coat – is a disappointing compromise. We reached a battered doorway, upon which there was some florid heraldry. 'The Sublime Porte'[65] commented our guide, staying the carriage that we might do our homage. Beyond the gates the grass grew in the cobbles & a soldier lounged in a sentry box; imagination had done the work better already. Then at length we reached S. Sophia, by a narrow passage of paving stones, as though we approached by a back door. That little ceremony on the doorstep, when we cased our heretic leather in slippers, had a certain childlike pride in it. Travellers have made so much of the virtues of the change, considered aesthetically, that there is no longer any genuine interest in it. Perhaps it is a little game, kept alive for the amusement of the stranger & the profit of the native. At any rate we paid our tribute to the oriental superstition graciously, & shuffled in through the doors with lively satisfaction in our toes; But then I left half my tribute at an early stage, & defiled the carpet with stout English boots.

Perhaps this digression is artfully intended to reproduce here something of the hesitation which made my mind also waver from the business in hand at this point. Here was St. Sophia; & here was I, with one brain 2 eyes, legs & arms in proportion, set down to appreciate it. Now what ever impression it made was certainly fragmentary & inconsequent; as thus – strange rays of light, octagonal & colourless; windows without stained glass; no screen across the church; & was it a church? No; it was a great hall of business, or learning or law; for it was empty & circular, & the flagged pavement was covered with carpets.

---

63 An interpreter or professional guide for tourists.
64 The modern name for the old section of Constantinople.
65 Originally the official name of the Ottoman Court at Constantinople, and later used as the synonym for the Turkish government; justice, in earlier days, was administered from the gate of the Sultan's palace, hence the name.

There were men in turbans squatting together at one end; they rose &
went away, talking loudly, when their conclave was finished. There
were many single figures wandering up & down the great open space,
reflectively; there were one or two who, seated at the side, rocked their
bodies rhythmically to the tune of the Koran spread open upon their
knees. Here was a group with white turbans from Bokhara;[66] the guide
did not scruple to elbow his way through their devotions, nor did they
mind the interruption. Such were the worshippers in the mosque of S.
Sophia; nor did their worship seem inappropriate to the place. It is so
large, & so secular, so little the precinct of an awful religion that this
miscellaneous worship did not offend it. Nor did the great place strike
one as 'beautiful'; for though there are patches of mosaic left upon the
arches, the zeal of the Turks has stripped the temple bare of ornament. A
Turk may not see the sign of the Cross at his prayer or that prayer fades
into mist said our guide, with a wave of his hand; & rather than nullify
his devotions the decoration of the whole building had been corrected &
erased altogether till it has no virtue or vice left in it. Crosses have
become safe patterns without meaning; sacred heads have been obliterated from the wall, & shields of wood proclaim the true faith where
Christian angels used to spread their wings. There is a niggardly temper
in all this that makes the great mosque not very sympathetic to the
stranger; although to qualify my blame, there is much that cannot avoid
being uttered in honest admiration.

If it is not a temple of religion as we understand the word it is surely a
temple of something; so much you may read in the fanatic nodding of so
many turbans, & the earnest drone of so many voices.

Still what exactly it is all about, what is fine in it, & what is puerile –
that is a puzzle that I entrust to the consideration of some three more
days.

And as I have not yet said anything of the 'yellow dogs of Constantinople' I will quickly add that there are many dogs, mostly yellow,
that they have neither master nor occupation; that they seem content &
respectable, & that they choose to inhabit the centre of the street, with
the consent of the population. But a long life of perpetual meditation is
bad for the health, & the dogs seem to have little vigour of body or of
mind. And they are probably ignorant of the domestic affections. At this

---

66 A part of Uzbekistan, USSR, formerly a state of western Asia, with many mosques
and once second only to Mecca as a holy place of Islam.

moment they see fit to protest against some breach of the immemorial tradition of the road.

The Turks have undoubtedly one valuable gift, which is the gift of names. 'The Golden Horn' has whispered sweetly in ears that never left London; & to wake the imagination is half the battle, where places are concerned. Certainly, the actual waters are a little disappointing as the real thing must always be, bends the figure of the thing, for it is almost blasphemous to test any place as crudely as we tested the Golden Horn today. We paid our fare & took a penny steamboat upon its very waters. It is not much different in beauty from other rivers that pass through other towns; certainly the houses on the bank are less regular, & the traffic on the stream is more various & vivacious. Also you have shaven green down for background, which comes running to the waters edge here & there, & the prospect – half closing ones eyes – is perhaps as gay & happy as such sights can be. But on the whole the most splendid thing in Constantinople – this is the verdict of a three day old tourist[67] – is the prospect of the roofs of the town, seen from the high ground of Pera.[68] For in the morning a mist lies like a veil that muffles treasures across all the houses & all the mosques; then as the sun rises, you catch hints of the heaped mass within; then a pinnacle of gold pierces the soft mesh, & you see shapes of precious stuff lumped together. And slowly the mist withdraws, & all the wealth of gleaming houses & rounded mosques lies clear on the solid earth, & the broad waters run bright as daylight through their midst. It is such a sight as you can watch at all hours, for it is so large & simple that the eye has always much to speculate upon; & there is no need to compose it with careful forefinger. Nature & art & the air of Heaven are all equably mixed, in vast quantities, with a generous hand. But this is worse than S. Sophia!

As for those observations upon manners or politics with which all travellers should ballast their impressions, I confess I find myself somewhat out of pocket today. The truth is that travellers deal far too much in such commodities, & my efforts to rid myself of certain preconceptions have taken my attention from the actual facts. Were we not told for instance, that the female sex was held of such small account in Con-

---

67 Thus making the date 24 or 25 Oct.
68 The hills of Pera are across the Golden Horn; its Galata Tower is the most conspicuous structure in the quarter.

stantinople – or rather it was so strictly guarded – that a European lady walking unveiled might have her boldness rudely chastised? But the streets are full of single European ladies, who pass unmarked; & that veil which we heard so much of – because it was typical of a different stage of civilisation & so on – is a very frail symbol. Many native women walk bare faced; & the veil when worn is worn casually, & cast aside if the wearer happens to be curious. But it does have so much virtue in it as to suggest that it hides something rare & spotless, so that you gaze all the more at a forbidden face. And then the passionate creature raises her shield for a moment – & you see – a benevolent old spinster, with gold rims to spectacles, trotting out to buy a fowl for dinner. What danger has she got to hide from? Whom would a sight of her face seduce?

The men save for their red caps & an occasional nose like a scimitar, might be citizens of London, save that the breezes of the Bosporus[*sic*] have tanned their skin & expanded their chests. But their faces are reserved; & that is the real mark of a civilised people. They have something to think about, & you can pass the time without the help of speech. And more over they are courteous to strangers, & will offer you fragments of many different languages in order that you may choose your own.

But when we come to consider the question of the West & the East – then indeed – we lay down the pen, & write no more.

Today more by chance than by design we stumbled – or more strictly shuffled, into the most beautiful mosque in Constantinople.[69] And as the only other mosque that I know is S. Sophia, the audacity of this remark needs all the excuses that I can give it. You raise a great leather curtain, & so admit yourself to a sight that is as strange as it is beautiful. The mosque is none other than a vast empty drawing room; you might dance in silk here, or drink afternoon tea, or merely live a gentle life. For there are great windows of white glass, shedding all the light of a brisk October morning upon rich Turkey carpets, & pillars gay with tiles. The place invites you to come in & sit on the floor at your ease; you will think cheerful thoughts, & they will be thoughts of high wholesome things. For while there is a beautiful glow of colour from window & from floor there is nothing to distract the mind; it is as though you walked inside a great painted bubble. The strong voices of men praying

---

69 Presumably a reference to the Suleiman Mosque, completed in 1557.

were not unlike the voices of those same men in the market place; & a child ran in fearlessly, clapping his hands & crying aloud, as though he pursued some outdoor game within the temple, & found it as good a playground as any & saw no reason to cease his joy. The round pillars are laid with white tiles upon which are painted rich patterns in blue, & there are panels of green & other colours, so that the whole place, based upon glowing carpets of many hues gives forth a radiant tide of light.

Worship then seemed but little dissevered from real life, & the crowd of recumbent figures testified that the mosque called with authoritative voice even amid the clamour of the street. Friends dropped in, saluted each other, & turned as naturally to their devotions as, a few hours before perhaps, they had turned to their ledger.

And the devotion seemed none the less sincere that it could stand the light of the day & the brilliance of silk & mosaic; nor did it seem in any way strange that men should say their prayer to rare carpets & painted tiles, without the figure of a saint or the symbol of a cross to inspire them.

On the third or the fourth day it is well to leave all duties undone, in order that you may lose your way in the unrecorded slums. Here even a stranger & a tourist may stumble upon something that is quite without self consciousness; & then the town for the first time will become a real town of flesh & blood.

That part of the prescription which consists in losing yourself we followed very carefully; & we had the delight of walking streets that led nowhere just because we chanced to find ourselves in their path. Now in the purlieus of Constantinople a great deal of the Gorgeous East still runs warm; a vine was laced across the road, & a various torrent of red fezes, turbans, yashmaks, & European respectability came pouring down it, like a turbulent Highland water. But no one stopped to look at us, & the eccentricities of all our dresses seemed but part of the ordinary composition.

We had to find a Bazaar, the Grand Bazaar[70] indeed, & in time, after mingling with all this busy & happy life, we took refuge in a great honeycomb of little shops, built beneath a single roof & divided into streets & alleys like the ways of a city of dwelling houses. To buy, it is necessary to be possessed of infinite time, & infinite duplicity. The silks

---

70 A vast rambling structure with several thousand shops, thought to be the largest of its kind in the world.

were ruinous, they were hideous; in England you might buy them for half the price; still the fact remained explain it how you would that we wished to buy, & were extravagantly prepared to pay the sum of 4 piastres a pique – the English are a great and generous race.

Did he hear aright? Could anyone make such an offer seriously? No, it was an insult to our intelligence to suppose that we could so misjudge the excellence of Broussa[71] silk – An American might be thus ignorant – but in England taste & knowledge surely forbids. And did Monsieur on his part, so grievously misunderstand his own interests as to charge the English more than it was right to pay? There were ladies willing to buy in the hotel; but such a price would amaze them. Something of this kind did get itself translated into French, & interpreted into Turkish, & at intervals of 15 minutes a piastre was dropped from the price; till the process of squeezing could be carried no further without encroaching on that halfpenny worth of profit which alone remained, & without making us still more late for our tea. But I have little doubt that the shop keeper had a right to smile over his plump cigarette.

After two minutes thought it does not seem to me that any law of hospitality binds you either to speak well of your hotel, or keep silence. For though there is something a little callous in the notion of abusing a man beneath his own roof, yet when you are paying liberally for every minute of that shelter, your purse has a right to the first claim on your charity.

This hotel then, to be brutal & candid, is not to be recommended, although it would be scarcely fair to abuse it.

It has a strange likeness to a shabby English public house, of the early days of the nineteenth century. Prince Albert & a fat deer might hang above the side board, & there is the mahogany table all ready for the keepsakes & the bibles. Mild respectable people who wish for a quiet dinner come here & breathe congenial air in the long dismal dining room. There is a great table, spread with cold silver baskets, & laid with accurate covers for the guests who never come. We dine in furtive corners, as though our needs were too modest to require a dinner table, & certainly all our cheer such as it is, is not sufficient to kindle the vaporous room.

The servants of this dusky old place are of a piece with the decorous oak chairs, which have been patched together in the back. They are old,

---

71 A city in north-west Turkey noted for its carpets and silk stuffs.

& slow, & full of antiquated gentilities, picked up in the days when they served in private families.

There is a sombre old woman, who crawls about the place like a spasmodic fly; she buzzes into a room, & cannot find her way out again without crawling over your hands & face so to speak, with her unnecessary questions.

She must needs pull all the chairs straight & fold the towels a dozen times because she hopes to convince you that she was once a 'med' [maid] & is competent to become one again. In this proud capacity she went to Manchester, where she learnt to spoil English; & her conversation therefore, must be carried on in a tongue that is intelligible to no one. She tells you a story however, from which you may make any tale you choose, sad or gay; today it was about a Greek who had died, & gone down a dark passage opposite the dining room window, & two young ladies who wished to become actresses & a gentleman who had left a bag in the hotel, so that he must certainly be a friend of ours.

She muddles her wits with a contemporary, who squints; & cannot bear to see trouser pockets full of coins. It is a dirty habit he remarks, bowing profoundly; So Sir, I have cleared them all out.

The poor old man honestly lost two gold coins in the process.

So they lean over the stairs together, meddle with innumerable towels, – discuss the great days when they lived with Lords & Ladies in the noble City of Manchester. Can they read English? Let this [page] dry in the open.

[Waking at night – & the dogs are good watchmen, you hear a soft funereal sound, like that which mourns over the graves of soldiers. It is the beat of a muffled drum, rhythmical & regular, which neither sinks nor rises nor passes on its way. Yet it is three o'clock in the morning. Soon a chant rises in the lull between the beats, a priest, you fancy, chanting the dirge over the body that is thus lamented. Again some metallic instrument chimes against the soft thud of the drum.][72]

The last thing, as it is generally the first, that such superficial travellers as I am should enter in their note books is the state of a people's religion. Indeed the only remark I can make with any confidence is that no Christian, or even European, can hope to understand the Turkish point of view; you are born Christians or Mahommedans[*sic*] as surely as you

---

72 Matter in brackets cancelled by AVS.

are born black or white. The difference is in the blood that beats in the pulse. And that difference was stated explicitly when we took our seats this evening in the gallery of S. Sophia. We gazed as we might have gazed at creatures behind a cage; only the truth was that these creatures were neither our captives nor our inferiors; they suffered us to watch them, but they would not suffer us to pray with them.

We climbed the long slant that leads to the top of the church, & half way up we heard shrill cries echoing in a great space, like the cries of many children, let out of school. And when we looked down into the church there were troops of children, who played hide & seek among the august pillars, & chattered like monkeys as they ran.

Their voices sounded thin & even plaintive as they floated up through vast depths of yellow air. But no cry could disturb the serenity of that great hall. Rings of hanging light made little islands in the immense gloom; & gradually, as the lamps were lit all round the arches, a soft golden glow shone forth from ceiling & column, till the air seemed warmed to the core. The hall began to fill with dark figures, & the children were hushed, though they flitted in & out like soft bats. And all the while the light grew slowly brighter, till the line of all the stately arches filled in the picture. Meanwhile the people took their places in rows along the mats, & you heard a voice rising & falling, with sacred words. The air was crowded, & yet you could hardly distinguish separate figures; only you had the feeling that at the bottom of this vague amber coloured air multitudes were gathered together, slumped like shadows.

The voice seemed but a thin thread to unite so many bodies; but at certain moments all the long lines rose & fell simultaneously, kissed the floor, & stood upright again, the puppets of an unseen power.

The circles of light were dim, & the whole of this punctual action was carried on in the twilight, silently with only one voice sounding plaintively alone. But simple & melancholy as the ceremony seemed to us, it was also wonderfully beautiful. The subtle lights, which were all woven of burnished golds & soft blacks, poured over all & revealed nothing thin or harsh; [ ] they revealed nothing but suggested more than can be drawn forth. So we watched, a scene which we shall never understand; & heard the true gospels expounded in an unknown tongue.

The mystery of the sight, & the strangeness of the voice, made you feel yourself like one wrapped in a soft curtain; & the worshippers within are quite determined that you shall remain outside.

Of all ceremonies this of saying good bye is the most trying to the

spirits; nor is the task any the easier when you bid fare well to a town &
not to a person. You should be able to say something that fits the occasion; & if I had a subtler tongue I think I could say a great deal at any
rate, whether it hits or misses. Now for instance there is the puzzle of S.
Sophia; why is she the most cryptic church in Europe? Why does she
grow more beautiful & more mysterious the better you know her – or
the shell of her?

You must begin at the beginning & confess that the Turk himself is
the riddle; a tough, labyrinthine riddle, by which wise heads – the Times
newspaper even – are still constantly confounded. For the first impression is also the last at the end of a week; & if it is superficial it is also
vivid. Constantinople is a place of live nerves, & taut muscles; so we
read directly we saw the town laid at our feet; but continuing the metaphor we also said that the eyes of this great giantess were veiled.

The streets & bridges are crowded with men & women, horses &
carriages; here is an English diplomat & here a lean native, who pro-
poses to start a pilgrimage in a fortnights time for Mecca. A sleek
merchant hustles him on his way to his office; but nevertheless he
understands; the two may meet on the same praying rug at sundown.

There is faith enough; & business enough; & life enough to keep
both eddying swiftly along the stream. No one who has visited the
Mosques & the bazaars can doubt the force of the current. But at the
same time, no one knows exactly where it tends; a dozen stories of the
place show that it can take a subterranean channel, & it was not ten
years ago that the Turks & Armenians massacred each other in the
streets.[73] So perhaps if it were your lot to spend your life here you might
think your station one of some risk – as a resting place beneath a vol-
cano. Happily a traveller need not trouble himself with the intricate
roots of all these strange separate flowers that we look at above ground.
The strangeness is attractive; & then the town upon which the drama is
played is fair enough for any tragedy.

But can we make this plain on a white sheet of paper? You must remember not only the morning veil of mist, & the stately domes that
shine through, & all the gold & white & blue of the town at midday, but

73 In August 1896, the succession of massacres of Armenian Christians by Turks and
    Kurdish tribesmen throughout the Asiatic part of modern Turkey culminated in
    Constantinople itself. For days the streets ran with blood as crowds raged through
    the Armenian quarter of the capital; by the time order was restored, 6,000 corpses
    were strewn throughout the city.

you must also think of the little streets crowded with live people, you must remember the turbans & the veiled women, the arab horses & the yellow dogs; & finally you must return to the great mosques, & see them filled once more with a dark crowd that kneels & rises & cries its faith aloud.

In the daytime you must see all this, & hear the clamour of the street & the bazaar; in the night when the dogs even are silent, you must hear the muffled beat of a drum, & listen to a voice that neither falls nor rises, but pleads always, in earnest & in confidence, for something that is given to the faithful who spend the night in prayer.

[*The following accounts appear at the end of the notebook. Page numbers have been editorially supplied.*]

[*Page 1*]

	drachmas.
Hotel bill	70
"	71.
"	57.25
deck ticket	15.
veils	3.
	231.25

Drs. bill. Christomanos.	20.
Champagne.	36.
Chemist & champagne.	50.
Nurses present cabs.	9.80.
Nurse.	55.
Maccas.	100.
~~French money for boat~~	~~30.~~
Extra on deck tickets	15.
Tips	12.
Chair	60
Turkish money	24.80
Nurse for basket & eggs	5.
Tips	18.
Tips	5.
Roussos	100.
Champagne	30.40

Cabs to Piraeus	10.
Tips	1.20
Tips	2.
Tips on boat landing cabs	30.
other tips.	9.

$$4)593:/=148.25$$

[*Page 2*]

	drachmas	
brought forward.		
private expenses.	~~231.25~~	8.4
share of common exs.	148.25	3.4
Violet expenses	35	11.8

$$27/414.50 / 16$$

$$\frac{16}{162}\ \frac{27}{144}$$

$$\frac{27}{432}$$

11.8

$$\frac{1.7.}{12.15}$$

$$\frac{22.}{34:15}$$

231.25

27

$$\frac{15}{135}$$

$$\frac{27}{405.}$$

added to 144:

  rug.

  jacket.

  under vest.   27/86:

$$\frac{81}{}$$

27g

AVS.	rug	20.		
		18.		
		38		

VS.	rug	30.		
	for self	18.	AVS	3.80

vest &		77.50
drawers		9
		86.50

& stockings	29.50
	77.50
	38.
	115.50

[*Facing page 3*]
1.20
7.60

owed V. 9.80

[*Page 3*]

Expenses at bazaar.

V.S.	£	s.	d.
cloaks	1.	5.	
silk		4.	2.
Turkish delight		1.	4
		2.	6
	1.	13.	0
	1̶.	1̶5̶.	6
£5. L	3.	4.	6
	1.	15.	6
	5.	0.	0

A.V.S.			
cloaks	1.	5.	
silk		10.	
		4.	6.
scissors		2.	6.?
Turkish delight			.8
cabs		2.	6.
Lanterns		2.	6.?
	2.	13.	2

28	2. 13. 2.	6.	
	1. 15. 6.		
	4. 8. 8.	20	120

$$\frac{4}{80} \qquad \frac{88}{-32}$$

Owed to Nessa   £3:7.-

[*Facing page 4*]

4)38(9:6.

$$\frac{36}{2} \quad \frac{4}{.2}$$

	drachmas
Roussos.	100.
Hotel VD. & VS.	144.55
Champagne.	30.40.
Cabs to Piraeus	10.
Tips	1.20
	2.

1
27⟋288⟋10   4⟋288.   15⟋15
27   27⟋72
18   71
                1

27	144	27
10	43	3
270	187	71

£ 3.10.

$$\frac{3.10}{4}$$
$$12.0$$

[*Page 4*]

Expenses in Constantinople
paid by A.L.S.

for Nessa common stock		£.	s.	d
	tips chemist	1.	1.	5
	Champagne		12.	5½
	Smelling bottle		2.	6.
	Medicine		1.	8.
		1.	18.	½.

Private between A.L.S. & A.V.S. £. s. d.
 3rd part of guide &c.   ~~8.~~ ~~2.~~
 choc: 15. 1
 cabs. steamers. mosques.   1. 6.
 tea.   ~~10.?~~

                7
            £~~1.~~ ~~6.~~ ~~7~~
            1. 3. 7
AVS payed to ALS ½ napoleon.= 8. 4.
owed from Athens. ~~£3.10~~ 12. 2½
  from Constant: 1. 3. 7
            8. 4
            12. 2.

[*Page 5*]

 Violet owed by common stock

           £ s. d.
 dr. at Con.   1. 10.
 ALS   1. 18.
            3. x8

4.15
3. 8
8. 3   £ 1. 10

             7
        £ 1. 17

[*Upside down and written presumably at a later date:*]
But many of the accounts in this book had afterwards to be corrected.
We found that only a very few pieces of our money could be [*Unfinished.*]

New Forest 1906

Thoby returned to London from Greece on 21 October. The rest of the party went on to Constantinople. During the second part of the journey Vanessa fell ill once more, and when she, Virginia, Adrian, and Violet Dickinson returned to England on the Orient Express, reaching London on 1 November, they found Thoby in bed with fever. His illness was diagnosed as malaria or pneumonia, and it was only after ten days that typhoid was identified. Virginia cared for her brother and sister at Gordon Square. Vanessa recovered. Thoby died on the morning of 20 November. Two days later Vanessa agreed to marry Clive Bell.

To Violet, also stricken with typhoid, Virginia wrote daily bulletins, but withheld the fact of Thoby's death for almost a month. Her brother was dead in fact, but he remained alive in Virginia's imagination. Sixteen years later, she would resurrect him in Jacob's Room, *and in 1931 commemorate him through Percival in* The Waves.

In the grief and confusion that followed, a second name was added to the death list: Fred Maitland – 'whom I love' wrote Virginia – died of pneumonia on 19 December. On 21 December, Vanessa went to the Bells at Cleeve House, Seend, Wiltshire for Christmas. Virginia and Adrian went to the New Forest. They took with them a copy of Maitland's Life and Letters of Leslie Stephen.

The New Forest   Christmas[1]

Just now as I wrote these words & saw them dry in juxtaposition it struck me that perhaps their alliance was natural & not accidental; & that I had by chance laid my finger on a clue to an old puzzle. For why does the forest always disappoint me? & why does Christmas disappoint me too? Is it not that they both promise something glittering & ruddy & cheerful, & when you have it you find it not quite as good as you expected? The forest is too benign & complaisant; it gives you all that you can ask; but it hints at no more. There are the long green drives, & the tracery of the branches against the sky; there are wild open spaces when you are tired of symmetry, with their single elm & thorn trees, &

---

1   AVS and Adrian stayed at Lane End, Bank, Lyndhurst, the home of Sarah Duckworth (Aunt Minna), in Hampshire from 21-31 December.

their brambles & their bogs. "So wild – so free – so stately – so mediae-val:"[2] Such is the praise that you must give, & give willingly, but there is no residue that remains unexpressed for lack of the fitting word. To be candid the forest is a little sleek & a little tame; it is Saxon without any Celtic mysticism; it is flaxen & florid, stately & ornamental. We have no use for forests now, & yet this one is preserved reverently, when the old spirit has died out of it. So it comes about that there is always something artificial about the place, & its lovers. You will not find the real country man or woman here, anymore than you will find arduous fields that are still turned assiduously. No; the country labourers are wont to pose as characters learned in forest lore; & it is a lore that is consciously pictu-resque. Much of this attitude is probably inevitable, for the forest is dif-ferent from any other piece of England, & imposes different customs of necessity. It is easy, for example, or so I have found it, to feel yourself withdrawn from the outer world, & enclosed in a thick girdle of trees. The rolling land is fenced off, & you are forced through narrow ways between trees where ever you turn. Then there is all the peculiar lan-guage of the place to be learnt if you stay, & exalted beyond all others. You hunt, the deer & the fox: there is the old colonel of course who never misses a meet & knows his way through the forest better than any of the tufters;[3] such old gentlemen are not unusual, but in other countries surely they have fewer grooves in which to run so smoothly. The forest is an ideal place for the old & conservative; there are so many proprieties to be observed, & they are so decorous & easy of approach. So this is why Christmas is kept so appropriately here. You can almost fancy that the woods have been arranged for the festival, & hung with holly, & sprinkled with snow. Christmas day & the forest seemed to mix & melt indistinguishably; you left the dinner table & its turkey & its crackers, its cake with a jaunty sprig of holly in it – you stepped into a world where these emotions were continued unbrokenly. We walked along a crisp white road, & then beneath dark leaved ever greens. Here were berries glowing red; & all the twigs were iced with snow. Then it grew late & the jolly evening sky lit up – flame coloured, & clear & healthy – with the black trees sharp against it. But O for the dusky roll of some Northern moor, or the melancholy cliffs of Cornwall. There you hear the wind & the sea.

---

2 Untraced.
3 Hounds trained to drive the stag out of cover.

Golders Green 1907

Vanessa and Clive Bell were married on 7 February 1907 at St Pancras Registry Office, and it was agreed that they would occupy 46 Gordon Square. Virginia accordingly began looking for another house for herself and Adrian, and settled on 29 Fitzroy Square, just a short walk from Gordon Square. It was clear from the start that Virginia had reservations about Clive's being a worthy husband for her sister, but time would change that. On 10 April, Virginia and Adrian returned to London from Paris, where they had accompanied the Bells at Easter, and on 12 April they took up residence in their new home, where Virginia settled down once more to writing and book reviewing.

Golders Green & Hampstead   July
Last Sunday, the 6th, to be precise I made an expedition which seems to me to deserve commemoration. The Twopenny Tube[1] has now burrowed as far as Golders Green; so that sinking into an earth laid with pavement & houses at one end, you rise to soft green fields at the other; the ashen dark & the chill & the cold glitter of electricity is replaced by the more benignant illumination of daylight. Indeed on Sunday there was a sky & a sun; & the exuberant holiday making of the crowd had some excuse. Well, we all of us got out at Golders Green; which term I take to apply to a dusky triangle between cross roads, which was now occupied by a cluster of idle people sucking like bees at some gaudy & profuse flower. Their little island was a refuge from motor cars which shot past constantly almost shaving slices from the edge, & added a high blast or a low blast, not inappropriately to the tune. Some of us, for I must associate myself with my fellows, saw this too much in the light of melodrama; & chose one of the four roads as our way into the country. But no real country road, as I could not but remember, is raked

---

1   The Central London Railway was so called because for many years after its opening (1900) the fare between any two stations was 2d. With the development of the Northern Line in 1905, a tunnel was driven under Hampstead Heath which emerged 1½ miles away in the undeveloped fields of Golders Green; the result was a burst of speculative building and an increase of population in the area.

so persistently by huge barrelled motor cars; nor do strings & knots & couples of brightly dressed people fill all the way, so that you must steer to get past them. But there were fields on either side though one had to violate some instinct which held them forbidden before one crept under the paling. It seems so natural that all open spaces should be hedged off, or only available on payment; & half the people I think kept to the road in obedience to this traditional belief.

My way was across a field of long grass towards a slight mound – O if I could but use the real country names! – & there were occasional tracks, like those a ship leaves on the sea, to show that bold travellers had gone before me. But while I heard the throb of brass I could not count myself free. Now it is hard to describe the view, for it was indeed of a most singular kind. Golders Green is all red brick; huge factories or railway buildings are specially prominent; then to the North (perhaps) there was another separate hamlet, grouped as real villages are up a hill which was pointed by a Church spire.[2] And between them there was this soft land, undulating with long grass & curving into little mounds, & into one sufficiently steep screen just before me. Old lichen crusted palings, & streamlets & fields with cows in them, all seemed ready to prove that they were part of the neglected world, & then the tail of your eye was caught by a line of villas, like a block of childrens bricks set on end. A line of moving heads at a little distance showed me that there was, as I expected, a regular channel up to Hampstead, along which one might legitimately walk. I sat myself down in a corner, where the bushes shut out all sights except the fields, & there eat my luncheon. The walk which I took afterwards through the fields lacked somehow the stimulus of walks through real fields. I fancied dust & fatigue & a thousand annoyances; & found myself gravitating, half sulkily, towards that cut in the land where I should find a real road, & people. What motive it was, I will not determine. It had been but a short time before, a foot path; & the glamour of the afternoon to me was caused by the fact that it led us past a real country farm, with a yard & a dog; I looked in at the window & saw the family at dinner, & there was a stuffed jay in a case.[3]

---

2   Probably that of Temple Fortune.

3   The event was reported to Violet Dickinson: 'But this morning I knew I must see Life; so I went in the Tube to Golders Green, and walked through some dusty fields to Hampstead; and sat down in one, where there was a corner empty, and eat my sandwiches . . . Then I found a farm [probably Heath Farm], with a stuffed jay in the window, where the people were having Sunday dinner; then I climbed the top of the hill, and saw St Pauls on one side and Harrow on the other.' *VW Letters*, I, No. 369.

Playden 1907

Before leaving for Sussex, Virginia sent Violet Dickinson the comic 'Life' of her she had just 'very hastily polished off'. The piece was published as 'Friendship's Gallery' in Twentieth Century Literature *(1979). On 8 August 1907 Virginia and Adrian moved into The Steps, a cottage in Playden, a village about one mile north of Rye, for their summer holiday. The Bells joined them on 26 August and stayed at Curfew Cottage, Watchbell Street, in the middle of Rye itself.*

THE STEPS
PLAYDEN
SUSSEX

Aug. 8th
Sept } 1907.

Playden

It would need a great deal of time to begin with – then knowledge – then insight – then language to write here of Rye[1] in such a way as to do it justice. When you have lived five hundred years & filled them with the experiences of shall we say five million men & women, you are as complex as a chambered nautilus – as profuse of tentacles as one of those monster sea anemonies [*sic*] which must live on the food their sweeping arms bring in to them. Besides I have a theory that, better than all insight & knowledge, final & supreme fruit of it, is one single sentence, six words long maybe; & that if you have not this forming at the top of your pen you had better write sedately of other things; accumulating touches. And at present I have neither knowledge nor inspiration; only, I confess, a little weariness of all brick & mortar, that is steeped in history.

It requires more imagination though, not to read history into the land than to see a blank sheet of hill & valley. For Sussex soil has been turned

---

[1] An ancient Sussex town standing on an isolated hill and looking across the salt marshes; Playden is a hamlet just north of Rye.

infinitely often, has been smoothed like a coverlet, over graves, over seeds, has been rolled & raked & baked finally into those ripe old houses which are so lavish of their information. And yet we did not come to the country to listen to venerable gossip over tea cups; no; we came to hear certain melancholy birds who have learnt only the one cry, who have only the one comment to utter. We came to see the land that [ ] has kept its own counsel, obeyed its own will, since the day it carved itself thus, before any gave it name or likeness.

Tonight we speculated upon the stars; fancied ourselves moored, one of an innumerable fleet; & saw the earth shrink to the size of a button, its rim just over there where the lighthouse marks the sea. This shrinkage was the result of seeing the moon close at the end of a telescope, like a globe of frosted silver; with strange wrinkles & corrugations on the surface of the metal; & it was, for the first time, a visible token, shining in dead of night, that the sun was still blazing somewhere, in an August sky. You could fancy hard blue & white, on the other side of the world; all the palms flashing, & the drone of heat; people sleeping under umbrellas; great melons, & donkeys with water skins, men lounging within the limits of hard black shadows – while here we walked in the vast darkness, & the tobacco plants gleamed pale & their fine perfume powdered the air with sweetness. A true moon flower. But through the telescope it is no longer moonlight; but the hot sun, striking a frosty shield.

22 August August 1907

Perhaps some day it may be amusing to read here the name Peasmarsh:[2] it may be then so familiar that the surface shell of it will have no existence; or again, it may have broken & gone, like other names that I can now hardly remember.

We came upon the place the other day, as we looked casually for a cottage: the orchard suggests spring evenings, with Apple blossom. But whether the dark dry little house could be made habitable for a summer seems doubtful; when I look at those thick walls, & robust floors. It is a little snails shell of a place, just off the road; in a smooth reach of country, in no way remarkable. Still it would be pleasant – how pleasant I can still imagine – to think of it in certain London days, when all the world seems made of brick; to know that it lies moored there, ready for us to embark upon. I think especially of walking up at night, from Rye,

---

2 Peasmarsh is a village 3 miles north-west of Rye.

all the vague scents & coolnesses of a country evening washing over one's body, though things can scarcely be seen in that light: how it will slowly go out; and only lamps will be seen: at last 'our lamp'; & I shall tramp up the flagged path; and see my chair ready, the table spread, some garrulous old woman, carpenters wife or such like, will attend & tell me the news of the village – how there has been a sale, & someone has had a baby; & the postman is dead. She will apologise for her cooking, but hope I have everything I want; & leave me, lighting her lantern "O I can find my way Miss, & the Moon's getting up." Such are the contrasts that one must make, in this world, to strike a balance. But I will not continue this hasty & inadequate writing since the question demands sober treatment.

Last night, as it was fine as gauze, we speculated a little from our terrace, & heard the faint blare of drums & trumpet. A fair? we asked; & set off, for the sake of the walk, & perhaps some happy accident of light & rustic comedy, to follow the sound. We went down to Rye by the road; & met a number of silent passengers, driving or walking, though it was close upon eleven; which gave one an odd notion of the populousness of the country, & all the odd businesses that these people must be following. In Rye itself there was much pale light of street lamps, some lounging figures, but no fair to be seen, band to be heard. We walked back then, by way of the road skirting the marsh, which leads beneath our cliff. The flats glistened beneath the moon, & there were odd smooth barns by the wayside, all dark, like colour shapes in some 18th century water colour. Sportsmen might shoot snipe here in daylight, in long coats; by night there would be the poacher or the highwayman, or the great London coach, baiting its horses at the turn, or paying toll. When we stood silent, a little harmony of noises crowded upon our ears. The dogs bark of course, then the cough of certain sheep, out in the fields, then the cry of some bird. At last a great luminous train, semi transparent, came rattling before us; with a body like some phosphorescent caterpillar, & a curled plume of smoke, all opal & white, issuing from the front of it. Then there was a very dark land with bright bars of moon light across it, so white that our shadows were cut in them. And then our frail little house, which we manage to think so substantial, with its eye of light, like many others; no, we don't include the world here. We are dotted about on the surface & exclude an infinite number of things.

I have almost I think determined that two things lie outside my province

– cant be covered by any skilful casting of words; & the first is the details of an expedition; & the second is the appearance of a great space of English country. So that though there is every temptation tonight to say something of a whole day spent in the open air, of an expedition to Fairlight[3] & back, I don't see how to attempt it, nor does my conscience goad me to try. I should have to begin by saying when we started, what road we took, the nature of the vehicle, the adventures of the way, & all the time I should have to be painting a scene for this progress, running before with a brush in my hand, hastily filling in the fields & the sky. Something would then have to be written of Fairlight, its history & prospect; & again I must descend to the particular, & drag the cart up that weary hill. And there would be the picnic next – stay though, I leave the pony un-stabled – & a phrase or two of conversation, while the view is somehow introduced, made perhaps the text of the discourse. Then the Church would toll – & it would be time to go: we should stay a little, remembering, in mellow mood, other such expeditions; the shadows would lengthen, & that broad sunlight which befits all return journeys – a skilful pen might hint the parable without spelling it – would be observed now to lie across the land. And so on, & so on; till the beast was in his stable, & we at our tea. A conscientious annalist would not leave till the shoes were taken off, & the hair tidied, & no trace of this long drawn out misery was to be seen.

This is as it should be, if I were younger,[4] or more daring. But no: the things I really choose to remember are these, I think.

When we got to the top of the hill we saw the sea, far below, very flat; so much like blue vapour that the solution into sky was hardly visible. There were rounded green cliffs also; & corn fields which might be laid directly against the blue. Also there was a gigantic stone fabric, planted in the valley; an incongruous & painful sight, as of some brittle excrescence, which had managed to endure, against the natural laws. There was a graveyard; of no antiquity; indeed the church[5] was new, suggesting somehow a place of practical use, rather than of any spiritual significance. It was as weather & water proof as it seemed proof against any of the passions of mankind. Also there was a small boy who carried beer in a rough brown cloth, to the harvesters. He could not measure

---

3 About 3 miles south of Winchelsea, Fairlight Down looks towards the coast of France.
4 AVS was then 25.
5 Possibly St Andrew's, built in 1845 by T. Little, in the Early English style.

distances, nor did his mind seem able to get beyond the shadow of the hall. This year he will not pick hops, which is sleepy work; he will, so soon as the harvest is in, undertake a job in Bexhill; since he has left school.

The nut trees promise to bear well; as do the blackberries. "Look at them filberts." He was agile in mind & body; swift to see all things in hedges, reading signs all the way, invisible to us; brown quick little animal; & you shall become an airdrugged old labourer, with a crick in your back, living to be 80, & picking up in that time only a few habits of birds in this part of Sussex, some knowledge of the signs of the weather, & an animal kinship with the people in your village; perhaps at moments you will have a queer sense that this isn't all, & that you have had scarcely your rights here. But there will always be beer, & the knowledge that your fathers lived this life for centuries, & found it good enough. After all, one might fare worse; Uncle Bill, for example, went to sea, & never came back again. Ah they do say that there's fine things overseas; but I guess a man may bide here. 'Tidy bit' was his word;

Then there were great horses, stamping up the hill with a waggon of brushwood; where did they cut it – what will be its use – ? O the wish to know & to understand [ ] how this toil is organised, how the whole land yields its fruits punctually in the right places. A great imaginative feat it would be to understand the point of view of a Sussex labourer: There is too much of the 'pathetic fallacy' in all our novels; tears in a dogs eyes, joy in an old horse.

3 September

The wish to write down some picture of what is now going on here, in the county of Sussex, in the month of September, really vexes me, when ever I take a walk. Yesterday for example we all[6] started along the road to Winchelsea,[7] in a colourless eventide which soon became of a drifting grey tint as the clouds trailed along the wind & sprayed our faces. Winchelsea on its sombre mound grew almost ink black, with those deep liquid shadows (as though composed of many different grades of blackness): there was light towards Rye, but the highest point was the barrel of the windmill, which was gray. The clouds shift, drag apart, & go in

---

6 Clive and Vanessa had arrived on 26 August and were staying at Curfew Cottage in Rye.
7 The ancient companion town to Rye, situated on a hill rising over the marshes and the River Brede.

tattered sheets hanging down with frayed edges right across the landscape; filling all the air with different lights & glooms, populating it, giving it variety & romance. Our best view is that we take from the hill top here; you see Rye pointed with lights, sombrely massed upon its hill; dark tonight as though the rain had drowned some of those fine points so star clear on other nights. And the land all round was black & turbulent as the sea; while we could still see the clouds changing & travelling in the air; only it seemed as though the air itself was all broken & confused, a shattered medium, no longer a tranquil void for clouds to sail in. The river lay quite pale at the base of the hill; the clearest & most peaceful thing in the landscape.

There is a certain evening hour, when the tides meet I think it is, when walking is the finest treat; even on a chill day such as this. The road is but a blurred grey vapour – & people & things come towards you all distorted & unfamiliar; walking too at a strange quick pace, upon you & past you before you expect it. The light of a carriage lamp cast on the hedge has the effect of some spectral shrouded figure, just about to taper into a point & disappear. Happy ecstasies float the mind out into the vague; spur it & seek not to recall it.

It is beautiful at evening to walk out along the bed of the sea – now all slippery hay coloured grass, with curving dykes, to Camber Castle,[8] the grey trefoil which lies midway between Rye & Winchelsea. The grey of this old stone fuses the landscape, if, writing in haste & in private, I may so outrage – is it sense or sound? – All the view that is has a lovely pallor – whites & silver greens – pale straw colour; the pearl white sheep make the highest light in the landscape; & always on either side there are the two shaded bones of Rye & Winchelsea; Rye; it is true, still bristling with red roofs & chimneys, but Winchelsea all sunk into the dark layers of its foliage. In the background – if we walk upon a stage as it seems, with our faces to the audience of the sea, there are the softly flowing hills, & there behind Winchelsea a high screen of down, with an oblong church[9] on the top of it. It is a view full of charm of a certain transparent lucidity; a little shallow, as though you could see through the tints if the light were just a trifle stronger; but at sunset the depth is exactly right, & luminous.

---

8 The castle was built as one of Henry VIII's coastal defences.
9 Probably the early 14th-century church of St Thomas.

This morning the sound of a scythe sharpened proclaimed that it was the gardeners day. He comes only twice a week; Mr Gabriel is his name;[10] he stands six foot, but his prodigious stoop must waste at least ten inches. All day long he has been swinging his scythe across the lawn, so regularly that you might fancy him a figure moved by clockwork. Nor did he pause. But when I went to pick roses, & complimented him on the fineness of the crop, he bent willingly, all tremulous & bedewed with his toil. His eyes had pale rings round the pupils as you have seen in the eye of some vague old dog: He settled the degree of heat, 'the hottest day in the year,' & answered my remark that Mrs. D[ew]. S[mith].[11] was a fine gardener with a contemptuous "She studies a bit. Ah, I dessay she knows something about roses – But look at the terrace there – one would have thought it nice to keep it neat. Borders is borders – terraces is terraces – What are the beds for, I ask her – but she will have flowers right there, in among the stone work – untidy it seems to me. But then its her fancy. *We* made the garden, Miss; made the steps & the beds; ah, it was hard work."

Let me note the effect at Camber Castle tonight of the grey stone walls against a sky of scarlet plumes. The stones seemed as though blurred, with a rough surface, & the colour was more muffled than usual; with a suffusion of violet tint in it. The ring of castle wall holds in the heat, like a cup brimming with soft vapours.

The grass also within the circle is far softer, & richer, more of the nature of garden turf than the coarse sea-salt grass marsh land outside.

The chimneys of the town, rising in steps, make the outline, at a distance, of the little pyramid, bristle. All might still compress itself as though for safety, within the girdle of one wall; you see, from the East, tall lodging houses leaning back, their sides all ablaze with sheets of glass.

There is a little angle, in the town wall, a ledge with a seat running along it – a railing to save one from the precipice, where the natives of Rye

10 John Gabriel of Military Road, Playden. For further characteristation of the inimitable gardener, see E. F. Benson, *Final Edition*, 1940, pp. 188-91.

11 Alice Mary, widow of Albert G. Dew-Smith (1848-1903), who, with Horace Darwin, established the Cambridge Scientific Instrument Co. According to the East Sussex County Record Office, she leased The Steps in Playden (where AVS and Adrian were staying) in 1907 and remained there until about 1920. The Dew-Smiths had been friends of the Darwin family: see Gwen Raverat, *Period Piece*, 1952.

nightly observe the sunset. The sun sets just behind Winchelsea, staining all that steep space of air & chequering the marsh land with liquid yellows, & mellow shadows, before blotting it out once again for another night. The mounds, or cliffs, – you cant call them hills, so sudden & unexpected are they, solidify as evening draws on, & make great soft blots on the landscape, otherwise so wide & simple. And then the sea is still there to the South, hoarding the last blue, & still going about its business, carrying ruddy fishing boats, & all the busy craft of steamers. Now there is a pale yellow light, opening & shutting as some single eye, & a breeze drives the old creatures who are drinking their last dose of sunlight, to shelter. Will they have a lamp, & read some pious gross old book? or the letter from some daughter in service? You meet the same people night after night.

19 September
Here I shall make a short note of an effect last night. I had been half asleep over a wood fire, which with its dry brittle heat & its light clouds of smoke always induces a curious drugged sleep, almost intolerably heavy. Well, drifting about in this for hours as I thought, I got up at last, like a diver rising from depths of water, & went out upon the terrace, where A. was looking at the moon. Then dreadful weariness came over me that we should still be the same people, in the same bodies; wandering not quite alive, nor yet suffered to die, in this pale light. Sleep & night, I thought, should blot us out, for some time; but here we are as circumscribed as ever. This is the effect though of a night which is not night; the process seems continued indefinitely, & infinitely drearily.

September here means that the poles are stripped naked of the garlands of hops. Indeed a hop field is a graceful place, sweetly planted with alleys, & laced across with tender green ribbons; the earth is all flecked yellow & green & you walk beneath shade. Now I say, this has gone, as though beneath the blast of a storm; & the shadows, as it is September, are perceptibly thinner, nor is the coolness they offer grateful after the tempered though cheerful heat of the sun. Often I have observed this to change; the substance, the lushness, is gone out of things; hedges & fields, the sky & the trees – all are fresh & shrivelled a little, before the winter frosts. And yet, on a generous day, no light is lovelier, warmer, more melancholy; as of some perpetual afternoon.

Wells and Manorbier   August 1908

In the autumn of 1907, Virginia resumed what would be her last year of teaching at Morley College and began her first long work of fiction, eventually to be published as The Voyage Out. *She and Adrian organised their own 'Thursday Evenings' at Fitzroy Square, and the Play Reading Society, meeting alternately at Gordon and Fitzroy Square, was launched in December and continued until May of the following year.*

At Gordon Square on 4 February 1908, Julian Bell was born. Feeling deprived of the now maternal Vanessa's attention, Virginia and Clive turned to each other for affection and companionship. The result of this alliance, which appeared on the surface as mere flirtation, was Clive's becoming for the time Virginia's most valued literary confidant. 'I count immensely on your encouragement,' she wrote to him that autumn. He was indeed 'the first person who thought I'd write well.'

With her dogs, Hans and Gurth, Virginia went on holiday to Wells, Somerset, on 1 August, spending two weeks there and another two weeks in Manorbier, Wales. During this interval, she appears to have completed about 100 pages of her novel. With Clive's continued faith in her, Virginia's dependence on Violet Dickinson now began to dwindle.

Wells   1 to 14 August
When I read this book, which I do sometimes on a hot Sunday evening in London, I am struck by the wildness of its statements – the carelessness of its descriptions – the repetition of its adjectives – & in short I pronounce it a very hasty work, but excuse myself by remembering in what circumstances it was written. After a days outing, or when half an hour is vacant, or as a relief from some Greek tragedy – at different times, & in different moods it is written, & I am certain that if I imposed any other conditions upon myself it would never be written at all. Did I not take it to Cornwall at Easter,[1] & determine to note something serviceable – & did I even write my address?

---

1   AVS had gone to St Ives on 17 April, lodging at Trevose House, Draycott Terrace, and had been joined there by Adrian on 23 April and by the Bells on 24 April.

So once more I return to the old method; & protesting merely, that I am conscious of its faults – the protest of vanity.

I live in these lodgings[2] about as near the sacred precincts as possible. Bells toll, & people shuffle down the Close to prayers. It is exactly the place in which some grey superstition should linger; what breath can ever blow down these crooked alleys, all crusted with medieval stone; a print of Wells in the 17th Century is precisely the same as a photograph of Wells in the 19th. But if Christianity is ever tolerable, it is tolerable in these old sanctuaries; partly because age has robbed it of its power, & you can fondle a senile old creature, when you must strike with all your force at [a] young & lusty parson. [ ] Nevertheless the young minister to the old; there are theological students everywhere, young men lately come from college, who give up their days to studying its laws, & will give up their lives to expounding them. As a matter of fact they will hunt, & fish, & live much the same lives as the smaller country gentry. The Cathedral of course dominates the whole place, & Wells without it is no more than a pleasant country town, with the usual number of antiquities: I believe I wrong it though. Certain night walks have shown me battlements & a moat; & there is a stately square, which, when I first saw it, was crowded with farmers, listening in a circle, to the vociferations of a little old man in a cap & gown; he walked round & round his compound, in the middle of which a boy held his standard – a flaring gas jet. He bade the rustics not envy the rich – He had supple lips, & an infinite succession of phrases, though why he used them, I could not tell. Perhaps the peroration was to celebrate some brand of pills, for he did not look a disinterested servant of truth.

When I came here first, in the evening, I was delighted by the little wave like hills which seemed to form all round me; to culminate in one high mound, upon which stood the oblong of Glastonbury Tor.[3] Daylight shows that the country is full of curves & on one side they rise & continue very high – &, a mile or two outside the town become the Mendips. Somerset farm houses are built of grey stone, are of great age, have a way of backing into some recess at the base of a down, as though

2   The Vicars' Close in Wells, built in the mid 14th century, consists of two rows of 21 houses originally for the College of Vicars Choral, but gradually converted into lodgings for theological students.

3   550 feet high and crowned with the ruined tower of all that remains of St Michael's Chapel, destroyed by a landslip in 1271; it is about 5½ miles south-west of Wells.

to make room for the flat lawn, protected by a wall, which generally lies before them. They are sheltered places.

Mrs. Wall[4] was heard to night holding one of her long gossips with her 'gentlemen.' "The Church, she was saying, is like a tree." And then the metaphor blossomed; & I think 'Chaplers'[5] were a blight, & Atheists a canker – She is a Conservative, & distrusts working men who rule – would show them their weaknesses if she were consulted – for she is the staunchest believer in the Church, & the Superior powers of the Gentry, who treat her so kindly. Of course she gets more consideration from them than from her own class, with a glamour over it all.

But she deserves a little closer attention. When I first saw her, wavering about in the passage with clasped hands & bent shoulders, ready to welcome me, but keeping her distance, I said This is exactly what I had imagined of Mrs. Wall. She does not change, but is a subtler study than I expected. She has had this house for 30 years, & the number of students she has had in her charge must be some hundreds. She speaks of them as 'my gentlemen' or, when she warms, 'my boys.' 'It hurts me when they go, as though I lost a child.' She has been intimate with many, not a landlady, but a comfortable old gossip & confidante. It begins with care for their teas & dinners, & she keeps an eye on their punctuality, & would perhaps say something if they missed a lecture, or stayed too late in bed. She knows more than they do – who stay a year & pass on – of rules & characters, & must often put them up to useful information. They in their turn, ask after her rheumatics, & spoil her cat. So far as I know her, she is a woman of patient, deft & indefatigable industry – whose garrulity is checked by the fact that she must be sewing or cleaning; but she begins, I suspect, to allow herself liberties; & the middle aged daughter, who has a kindly pride in the multifarious memories of her mother, eggs her on to waste a little time. But the mother is not to be hoodwinked, & believes that she does her work still better than any younger woman. I can imagine that she is jealous of all the insignia of her office – the keys – & gold – & ordering of provisions, & will not entrust them to any one else.

Indeed, a woman of 75, who has had ten children, placed them & lost them, a widow, who for 30 years has paid her rent, & kept her house going, must have come by a certain insight & tact besides what we call

---

4 Mrs Wall, who kept AVS's lodging, was the widow of a railway guard and evidently knew Violet Dickinson's family; see *VW Letters*, I, No. 430.

5 AVS probably just means 'chapel-goers'.

commonly 'knowledge of the world'. I can imagine shrewd wisdom issuing from her lips, in no weak shape; & a distinct course taken deliberately, through difficult matters.

But in spite of this sharpness, she is not one of the rulers, & dwells with the mildest optimism upon her past & the present round her. Small things occupy her, & her tongue is always ready to tell you a story about the greatness of the Tudway family,[6] or the weather, or the cat, or, of course, she will dwell indefinitely upon her gentlemen. She has a sitting room, where every visitor, I suspect, has to do homage; there are lines of little photographs of young mens heads; there are pictures of Wells, & pictures of Bishops; she has a story for each of them, &, generally, a word of praise & gratitude for his kindness.

Never was there a more amiable, useful old creature than Mrs Wall; & I expect that if we knew all her life we should judge it one of the happiest. She begins to talk, not of retirement, but of death; 'I tell 'em I shant be here next time' – the time she means being the commemoration, which takes place once in four years.[7] 'Still, she adds, with a contented little smile, I said that last time – & here I am still!"

The Close has filled itself with theological students, & I am not sorry to leave. For they live a healthy life, in & out all day, much conversation, meetings on the stairs, greetings at the gate – till the cheery male voice is as the drone of bluebottles in my ear.

I have moved to a dusky old house in the Green;[8] one of those spacious houses, which are rather shabby & threadbare now, but were built for prosperity. A candle has to burn perpetually in a corner, to illumine the steep stairs; which have bannisters of carved oak & great oaken balls at the landing. A tree, all draped with foliage stands directly in front of the windows, & increases the dimness of the atmosphere within. The Cathedral Green is rather spent by the time it reaches this far corner, & the grass, upon which you may not walk, elsewhere,

---

6 Alice Constance and Charles Clement Tudway (1846-1926), JP, living at the Cedars, Wells, Somerset. Violet Dickinson, whose grandfather had been Bishop of Bath and Wells, 1854-69, was a friend of the Tudway family and apparently solicited Mr Tudway's help in arranging for AVS's lodging at the Vicars' Close.

7 AVS was probably thinking of the Triannual Festival of Wells Theological College, when former students returned for processions, celebrations and a service at the Cathedral.

8 The new address was 5 Cathedral Green, Wells, situated on the north side of the Cathedral; the lodging was run by Mrs Dorothy Oram, wife of a verger.

seems here to lose its sacred character & to become a playground of the children of the neighbouring houses. My house has two children attached to it, & I [am] led to think a good deal about the nature of children. They play all day in front of me. Did I ever play all day when I was a child? I cant remember it. They have no regular games, or hours; but merely tumble about, hit at balls, upset chairs, run into the house & out again, fall & hurt themselves, fly into passions, & talk incessantly. At a certain hour, the smallest child, aged 3, gets tired & runs off to her mother, who puts her to bed; she wakes, & comes out to join the sport again. Now, if they could think on waking, that today was to be like other days, & they would do no more than kick a ball, would they enjoy it? I believe not. The truth is, that each kick is an adventure, that may be entirely unlike anything else; each time they come trolling into the green, they really see something not seen before, or feel some new sensation. To wear a new hat is an immense pleasure, so Audrey, the 3 year old, told me. Or perhaps, it would be more accurate to say that these hours are so full of disconnected incidents that they really never perceive that they do the same things again & again. They never have a theory or could tell you how they spend their time.

This county has to my mind one fatal fault – no sea. Hills really exist solely that you may have a wide view from them of the sea, the horizon, & one or two ships between. Then you get a kind of flow of life round you; you return content to the same fields again. But when you see nothing but land, stationary on all sides, you are conscious of being trapped, on a flat board. Yesterday however, did its best to shroud this fact; all the air was hung with tattered clouds – or watery drifts of air, not rounded into a form; the most beautiful sky there is, perhaps; it is always moving, always letting through different lights & shades on to the land below. It is a wide land, uneasy, like the sea, full of mounds, & high lines into the horizon. When the sun gleamed, great bones of green & brown earth showed in the middle of this scene, which was coloured like some drawing in brown ink. The kingdoms of the world lay before me, a rich domain, teeming in the folds with apples, & meadows, with gray villages snug in hollows, & little steeples. Far away the sea, into which the land may spill its treasure. In Cornwall, I never think of the kingdom, or the population – this view, stands for many I suppose, as a symbol of their mother England –

[August 1908]

Manorbier[9] is as different a place from Wells as I could have chosen. It is a lean country, scarcely inhabited, & the one church[10] which does duty for many miles, is a threadbare place, a grey barn some 5 centuries old, to which a tower has been added at one end. The little bay however, is guarded by an immense mass of ruin, the Castle;[11] it is still foursquare, &, it is dark – you see a red glow in some of the slits & openings, which tells that some one finds it still stout enough to live in. Why anyone found it necessary to build such a fortress here, I cannot remember; & at present the character of the land seems markedly worn & poverty stricken, as though it could not support such a monster; or perhaps lay cowed beneath its feet. However this may be, I like my view of it. I have lodgings in a perfectly genuine cottage, inhabited by a stone mason & his wife. I sit in a room that corresponds to their kitchen, & observe the road. In the evening I walk down to the beach, which I have to myself, & pace a turn or two beside the sea. I like to turn back from looking out along the uneasy & melancholy gray surface, to find a beautiful reflection of it in the gray ruin, & the green & gray sand hills, sprinkled with sheep, which is just colonised by a dozen sky gray cottages. No one will ever make this a watering place, I prophesy; it wants somehow the boldness & self confidence to be a success. I have not walked far, but my investigations tend to show that there is something a little weak in the coast. It is just too low, or too sharp to be impressive. The land within swells into long breakers. I walked through a little village the other day, which seemed to me as deserted as any I had seen. There were cottages splashed with cream coloured wash, out of which came bent old women, of tremendous age; their faces were all white ridges, without any spirit left. Ah, the loneliness of these little distant places! I saw that the pillar

9 AVS had rented one room in a cottage called Sea View, in Manorbier, Pembroke-shire, South Wales, a small coastal village between Tenby and Pembroke, and home of the 12th-century historian Giraldus Cambrensis, son of the Norman noble, William de Barri. The Stephens and George Duckworth had stayed in Manorbier for about a month in March 1904, following Sir Leslie's death; and Vanessa and Clive Bell had gone there for their honeymoon.

10 The church, with its tall military tower, contains the tomb of a member of the de Barri family, the founders of Manorbier Castle.

11 According to Cambrensis, the Castle 'is excellently well defended by turrets and bulwarks, and is situated on the summit of a hill extending on the western side towards the sea-port, having on the northern and southern sides a fine fish-pond under its walls . . . and a beautiful orchard . . .' *The Itinerary and Description of Wales*, trans. Sir Richard Hoare, 1908, p. 85.

box was all discoloured; & there was only one house that tried to be a house – to wear the distinct dress. It had some odd ornament of piled stones in the gateways.

I come down from my room in Mr Barclays house at about half past nine, blowing out my lamp, & leaving my books. Sometimes it is quite calm, & gray outside; but tonight I was fairly whirled round by the wind & the rain. The only guide I had was the crunch of gravel beneath my feet – I could neither see nor hear. Suppose a cart advanced I should embrace the horse before I saw him. However I had but 200 yards to walk, & by moving my legs automatically, I became aware of a shape like the keel of a large boat on one side of me, & the faint refulgence of window. Still other people are on the roads, leading their horses, or driven to turn in at wayside cottages – The wind is really high; it is sensible peace to sit as I do, behind a pane of glass, with a glaring lamp beside me; even so, gusts get at my candle. I can't read at ease, for the wind is always leaping on to its own back. I hear water too, & the fluttering of a little bush beside my window. Think of the earth given up to this power tonight!

Italy 1908

Virginia returned to London from Wales at the end of August and set off for Italy with Clive and Vanessa on 3 September. Apparently at the beginning of the journey, Virginia wrote a sketch of Clive Bell.

ITALY.
September. 1908.

MILAN.
SIENA.
PERUGIA.

[*In the original volume the autograph calendar and timetable below face p. 317.*)

1908.

Sept.

Siena

Perugia

Milan

Sun		6	13	20	27
Mon		7	14	21	28
Tue	1	8	15	22	29
Wed	2	9	16	23	30
Thr.	3	10	17	24	
Fri	4	11	18	25	
Sat.	5	12	19	26	

Birth.
up bringing.
sensitive
precocious.
honest.
too kind.
college.
Paris.
Separates himself too emphatically.
Considers himself a thing to be polished separately.
Considers his gifts.
Affections.
knows the worth of all his endowments.
Cultivates friendship
Cynicism. self consciousness.
likes his own good manners.

It is important to remember Clive's birth & education when you consider his character. He is the son of a substantial country family, who are without culture or pretension, but spend their lives in the most sensible occupations, & are perfectly sure of their object. Not one of the arts, even in its baser forms, is suffered to disturb them, so that their views & conduct are of the most direct kind, & have probably a great deal of virtue in them.

When Clive went to public school, he realised that he differed from his relations in certain ways; first, I suppose, he was only conscious that the furniture in their house was oppressive; & he wondered, vaguely, why people should say such solemn things. He began, perhaps, to give himself little airs when he came back for the holidays, & was surprised to find that his rash statements were combated, as though the order of life, which he disliked, were not impregnable. Besides, his boldness, though it was laughed at, came to be expected of him; & he found himself with a reputation for originality. This reception made him precocious; he took to reading; he saw literature first as a long series of triumphs. When you had despatched Hamlet you were ready to attack Browning, & he had the sense in reading every book that he was providing himself with talismans to be used against the cheerful flattering people who teased him & admired him in the holidays. He was puzzled to discover how his knowledge was to be brought into play; & for the most part walked about stuffed up with it, or produced it with the most

violent distortions which even his self love could not approve of altogether.

He quoted Shakespeare in a shrill triumphant voice, when there was
no occasion for it, & scorned the young lady who asked him for the
name of the author. Unfortunately, no one at the family table could
carry on the discussion & Clive in a year or two tired of these public
triumphs, & wanted some one who would talk to him about history.

When he was about sixteen, & had been carrying on this random intellectual strife for a year or so, it suddenly came over him that he
belonged to the select race of people who are called clever. In his case,
the discovery led to considerable changes in his point of view; for he
determined to specialise. He saw, in a moment, what he had been aiming
at, in those crude attempts to impress his sisters, & convert his uncle; &
he saw also that the attempt was futile. For his schoolmasters who
began to take notice of him, opened up such a view of the intellectual
life, impressed him so indelibly with the brilliance of it, & the unlikeness
which it had to anything he had ever seen before, that he cherished no
more illusions about his home. At the same time he was convinced that
he was destined to be a scholar. He made great advances in his work, &
was confirmed in his opinion of himself by the distinctions which came
to him.

He might have been pardoned if, at this stage in his career he had been
more selfish & conceited than boys usually are; but it is much to his
credit that he was always gentle at home, & ready to talk, had there been
anyone to talk to. Some of his efforts to find sympathy had grotesque results. The first young lady he danced with, at his first ball, had to hear a
strange rhapsody – about art, & learning, & the only life worth living.
He got into correspondence with the most encouraging of these ladies,
who was something over thirty, & sent her the poems which, much to
his surprise, he found that he could write quite easily. [*Text ends here.*]

There are many ways of writing such diaries as these. I begin to distrust
description, & even such humorous arrangement as makes a days
adventure into a narrative; I should like to write not only with the eye,
but with the mind; & discover real things beneath the show. In default of
this – & I shall neither have time nor perseverance for much thought, I
know, I shall try to be an honest servant, gathering such matter as may
serve a more skilled hand later – or suggest finished pictures to the eye.

The fact is, that in these private books, I use a kind of shorthand, &

make little confessions, as though I wished to propitiate my own eye, reading later.

Besides I feel (at the moment) great distrust of my own words. Is it worth while to write? As I have had some amusement from reading about Greece,[1] I may as well do what I can with Italy.

There is not much to be said of Milan; unless it be that we entered here into Italian life. We walked out in the busy noisy streets, & felt irresponsible; tramped in the roadway; looked about a great deal without thinking much – understood vaguely that the populace were of the same mood.

There are great flat houses painted some clear colour, & decorated with bright green squares, at intervals. Flower pots make a graceful festoon of leaves on some of the ledges. It is all a little dusty, very dramatic – yellow walls defined against green plumage of parks. You exclaim Oh – & Ah – at the corners – so different from an English town in the provinces. I liken it to a sketch in water colour, by some spirited though not quite excellent master hand. It is much more sincere & sure of itself than we are, in our Brightons & Oxfords, as though done after some design, which the nature of colour & climate suggested.

Coming to Siena late at night, there was a charming landscape, like of course, backgrounds in Early Italian pictures – sharp blue hills, trees in profile against it – the Arno with a grey blue colour in its waters.

Siena itself is on the top of a hill, & all the streets go plunging down, or up, to the Cathedral on the summit.

They are paved with flat sheets of stone & are kept very clean; no raised pavement separates the street. People walk incessantly, burst into song now & again; there are cries, cracking of whips, clatter of hoofs. We visited the Cathedral,[2] on the occasion of some festival. It is striped black & white, with rose colour & blue in the arches; golden knobs; a ceiling of azure; fruits, faces, beasts, carved on every pinnacle or angle. In the chapels there were glittering images, & candles; & the high altar had all its tiers of wax alight. There were gorgeous priests, ministering here, with their backs to us, from which yellow satins gold embroidered, hung in stiff squares. One had a white hat, like the petal of a cyclamen, on his head.

---

1   This journal for Italy 1908 was written in the same notebook as that for Greece 1906.
2   In the Piazza del Duomo; its slender Romanesque campanile has alternating bands of white and black marble at its base.

It was the feast of the Virgin,[3] & a large crowd, in their Sunday dress, had come to worship. A strange worship compared with ours! Instead of rank of seats, movements all in order, & a service like a military performance, no single worshipper here knew what his neighbour did or seemed to attend to the clerical commands. The priests themselves were passing & repassing, forming into lines, changing vestments, & rapidly carrying on the ceremonials all the time, as though they were doing a mystic rite, not understood by the people. The people looked, wandered about, sank on their knees, & rose again; their faith seemed warm & private, not to be regulated by any common need. I fancied, however, that this very decorative performance did represent to them the sacred body of their religion; sealed within these yellow & inlaid casks – I supposed that all the glories of the Heavens had this tangible form for them – the more impressive because of all these mysterious weavings & symbols.

They smell the flowers that grew in the holy fields; imagine the Cross risen, & the body upon it; it is all yellow stained, splendid, & remote. Are these priests – or are they not rather people who were present at the scene themselves? The Bishop[4] sat on his carved throne, with his buckled shoes pompously displayed, his hands hid beneath his satin apron, & his face composed into a mask of rosy wax, smooth, & not a little contemptuous of earthly strife.

One little flat case holds all my travelling library. But happily you get the classics now, pressed & light, with decent print, though it lies thinly upon the page, & the paper shines, with only a faint leaden gloss, if you get it in the light. Is Thomas Hardy among the Classics?[5]

I have been reading Two on a Tower,[6] & asking myself that question. Let me see if I can discover an impression of the book & give reasons for it. In the first place, his conceptions are almost always bold, as though he despised mere form. It struck him to contrast the stars with minute human loves. Well, then – he must construct a star to express his mean-

---

3   i.e. 8 September.
4   Archbishop Paolo Maria Barone (1844-1909) presided over the services of the Feast of the Nativity of the Virgin.
5   See VW's 'Thomas Hardy's Novels' in *TLS*, 19 January 1928 (Kp C294), reprinted in *The Common Reader: Second Series*, 1932 (Kp A18), and 'Half of Thomas Hardy' in *Nation & Athenaeum*, 24 November 1928 (Kp C306), reprinted in *The Captain's Death Bed and Other Essays*, 1950 (Kp A30) and in *VW Essays*, IV.
6   Thomas Hardy, *Two on a Tower*, 1882.

ing. There is a certain gaunt honesty in his way of setting to work. He constructs a tower, puts an astronomer on top of it, & sends a country lady exploring there. At first you see it is the idea of the sky that is uppermost in his mind; he tries to render that – & does, I think, succeed excellently. He can always impress an idea upon your mind because he is perfectly sincere, & reflects certain aspects unflinchingly. They are grim or grotesque for the most part, but true as daylight. So, in his sturdy way, he shoots your mind up among the stars; explains different forms of wonder; notes, grimly enough, the immensity of the sky. His descent is not so successful I think. The loves of the mortals are angular for the most part. Still there are little scenes, like that of the choristers met in Mrs. Martins cottage,[7] which are evidently literal copies, touched with humour. Lady Constantine is the difficulty – the block that wont fuse, & yet must always come into play. The story is too fantastic; she has a husband, absent in Africa, who enjoins her to live in solitude. Hardy, moreover, distrusts ladies who live in drawing rooms; his boots creak & he does not know where to put his hat. They remind me always of Keene[8] drawings, of English women in the 70ties, bunched skirts, straight lines beneath the petticoat, & fingers like tallow candles. The objection however is very much smoothed away, in the course of the story; mainly I think, because Swithin, the astronomer, is understood. His relationship to her – the relationship of a very young, austere boy, with a students arrogance alight in him, making him a simple & perfectly logical figure, shows us what Lady Constantine felt – how she was older, soft, maternal; loved the temper that hurt her. But having established this position, Hardy goes on to complicate the story by means of the most arbitrary conventions. He forces his warm human beings against a wire frame work of plot, as though they could not stand up by themselves. There are all kinds of surprises, & deceptions; & instead of thinking of the stars or human love you think of letters & dates, hidden names & so forth. This, I conceive, is a pity, & hinders Hardy from being among the classics. You almost put him there for the sake of his intense original stare at things; he sees the country with unveiled eyes & sees angles & colours, that have been there from dawn, unnoticed by others. It is natural to him to see things always with a sort of rude honesty upon them, as though, at last, they had a chance to protest against the embellishments of the poets.

---

7 In Chap. II.
8 Charles Keene (1823-91), draughtsman who worked for *Punch*, 1851-90.

We are very leisurely travellers. We dip into one church or gallery in the morning, sit in our shaded rooms till it is time for tea, & the whole of our exercise consists of a gentle walk in the sunset upon the platform of the Fortezza.[9] This lies at the end of the gardens, & meditative pedestrians & peramulators [*sic*], old ladies with knitting & old gentlemen with newspapers, are the regular occupants. The fashion keeps to the carriage road, & the beggars have the ingenuity to choose their pitch by the wayside. The fortress upon which we walk is a high angular piece of ground, railed on all sides by a parapet; for the wall is a hundred feet or so in depth. If you lean over the edge you see steep vineyards beneath you, sharp ridges of bare earth rise everywhere, sprinkled, but never clothed with vines & olive trees. The earth, in Italian landscape, is always coming through the sparse vegetation. Beyond, there are hills encircling us, which soon grow blue, though they rarely carry much weight of clouds upon them. The trees on our eminence glow, as though some yellow painters-medium were brushed over them. It is infinitely pleasant to sit & let the heat of the day recede, till a breeze springs, & it is time for dinner. There are flowers with voluminous yellow petals, in the gardens, & trees decorated as with red rosettes. They have few leaves to bear such splendour.

This view which I speak of across the vineyards makes no offer of a walk. The earth affords no shelter, no soft places, but every foots space of it is laid bare to the eye. There are single roads, one suspects, leading from village to village. On every eminence a large white or brown villa has perched itself, so that the land, though so wild, is not lonely. No park, or clump of trees hide these naked places. At night as we sit on our terrace we see them lighted at either end; the lights go out very early. You get the impression of an immensely old civilisation; for the land everywhere is under the eyes of the cultivator, & no stretch of it is left alone.

We take our meals in company. A kind of conversation is started by these seasoned guests which has little likeness to any other form of talk. It seems to assert always that it is never going to become intimate; & yet it is kindly, humorous, & incessant. Travel, naturally plays a large part. 'Have you seen' & so on. To discuss ideas is hardly legitimate; nor should one ask for a name or profession. Two at least of the guests have

9   The Fortezza Medicea, adjacent to which is a triangular terrace called 'La Lizza', surrounded by a public walk with a panoramic view of the hills.

the peculiar stamp of the veteran lodger; they look up when a new guest arrives & are ready to place him in the catalogue of lodgers; they have faint pleasure in novelty, for their stories run dry. One old lady in particular, seems to have been sitting there since the early fifties of the last century.[10] She has spent her life, so far as she will reveal it, in travelling & testing the merits of different pensions. She pronounces the table here the best in Italy. At the same time she shows no enthusiasm; the life of a lodger is one of perpetual hostility.

Poor, a spinster, who begins to grow old, to travel is really her most agreeable life. I figure her the Aunt of large families of little country gentry; she has a certain distinction because she can talk of her travels. She professes to find English life lacking in colour, & sets off on these long rambling peregrinations, from one cheap pension to another, never leaving the hackneyed towns, or seeing much in them. She sits all day in a corner of the dining room, knitting, or writing in a fretful hand long letters to old friends; she waits for meals & watches the dish on its way round the table. Certain old gentilities forbid her to gobble openly, & in the pauses between the plates she discharges a vast amount of faded learning, savouring of the 6oties, when she drove over the Apennines in a great sun bonnet. She knows nothing accurately, but arrogates to herself a certain authority because she first saw pictures fifty years ago. She was taught French in Bath by an old gentleman who was page to Marie Antoinette – hints that her education was that of a lady.

Catch her though when she is silent & it is difficult to detect any life in her. You seek it in the eye; it is dull & fitful; her skin is like folds of old leather; creases are in the very flesh. But though the task seems so unnecessary, she will fill this torpid case with food & wine; what purpose they serve, let philanthropists declare.

Now & then, excited by an eddy of life, she ventures out into the full current of general talk – & volunteers some correction or theory of her own – at which we can only be silent, or perhaps, trusting her infirmities, smile in secret; she flounders deep, suspects some hostility, flushes, becomes emphatic – & tries to overawe us with a tremulous flourish, of venerable authorities. Poor old Lady! This venture was unsuccessful, & she retires to mumble peevishly, but her brain sinks into torpor once more. Food consoles her.

---

10 This elderly spinster appears to have been fictionalised as Mrs Paley in VW's *The Voyage Out*, 1915 (Kp A1) (London, pp. 441-2; New York, p. 362).

We have come on here to Perugia, & exchange the simplicities & familiar meals of Siena for all the comfort of a Grand Hotel.[11] The person of an English clergyman in evening dress dilutes the Italian atmosphere at once, you see it all as a cultivated show, somehow regulated so as to suit the taste of respectable English clerics, & satisfy their aesthetic needs. The scene after dinner is as like that wh. takes place in an English drawing room as possible; here on one sofa the thin, clean old lady reads about the Catholic conference,[12] with her plain daughter by her side, industriously; the pretty one, with great curves of red & white flesh on her bones, leans back to look up into the parsons face, & laugh friendlily when he speaks. Her mood is invariable; she is as simple in her heart as on her lips; The deepest of her plots is to be mistress of a good mans home, & bear him children.

She would blush that you should guess it, but everyone can see that the cheerfulness & sweet temper, which compose her charms & wiles, proceed directly from such ambition; no one could blame them, & there is something so perpetual about them, that it seems as tho' generation[s] of mothers had found them effective & bequeathed them as sufficient armour to their daughters. Viewed in this light, there is cause for alarm, & even for disgust. Old mother nature is not a skinflint; human beings might soar very high so long as such tools are adequate.

Perugia is circled by two or three roads, one above the other; & our hotel is perched with a few streets & squares, upon the very summit. When I look out of my window I see heads only in motion, & all the secret places on a crowd of roofs; here I see a hole, where the water will come through, unknown to the occupant; there is a servants window ledge with her cracked pots of green plants; here a tile sticks out, & a blue frock is hung to dry from it; the attic, where washing hangs out of the window to dry. But these brown roofs are very closely held in; & the country springs cut free directly beyond them. There are definite hills, ribbed with lines of olive & shaded here & there with trees, which have dark knobs for heads. A single road, laid upon them like an angular piece of tape, can be traced to the summit; in the sun the prospect is too bare to enchant me. In the evening however, when we take our walk along one of these circular roads, the fine blue mist has transformed them, the dis-

11 The Brufani Palace Hotel, near the Piazza Italia, in the centre of Perugia; see *VW Diary*, IV, 15 May 1935.
12 The 19th Roman Catholic International Eucharistic Congress took place in London from 9-13 September.

tant sky has lines upon it, as though faint layers of water colour had been left to dry; & had receded, leaving one distinct edge. The blue is entirely with out vapour.

A strange effect is produced when a whole tableful of live English people review the pictures of the old masters. Their 'art' seems a thing called forth from the mists & bade stand out in a continuous line, until it reaches us here in the 20th century. We seem to think each verdict we pass has power to change it; these good people rest cheeks against it, distinguish its virtues, flatter themselves that they have some power over it. When we look at it in another way though, it is more humiliating; for it is the unchanging thing, & shows us up as shadows against it. It bids us reveal ourselves. All the pleasure we take in a picture does not put us in possession of it; our mouthings before it, rearrangements & so on, will be smoothed out in a year or so. The picture has undergone these modulations from a dozen generations without change. It seems strange that painting should still be upholding such insignificant old women as the lady we met at Siena, giving them permission as it seems, to crawl over them for a space, & pretend dominion, representing something in them. She had a thing in her mind which she called her love of art; & assumed that her mind was the point where, for the moment, the arts of all ages met together. By the light in her brain centuries were illuminated. Perugino, Michael Angelo, Mantegna were dark without it.

I read Harry Richmond[13] at Siena. I complain that Meredith fails to satisfy me, at the same time that I recognise a remarkable brain. Instead of supporting his fabric, as Hardy does, with an intricate wire netting, Meredith contents himself, as I think, with flimsy vapour, shot with all the colours of the sunset, but without substance where there should be substance. His mind seems to be so stuffed with conceits that he never allows himself to dispense with them, to look quite frankly, or perhaps, is conscious that his power is not for seeing into things, but for covering them with a light of his own. So, at those times when sharp emotion requires that peoples characters should be distinct, that you may understand their action & feel its force, a fiery rhapsody obscures them completely. Has he really made so sure of his subjects that he can exhibit them in crisis? The temptation is great I imagine to cover them with brilliant generalities; explorers [?] of poetry – epigrams – aphorisms; birth-

13 George Meredith, *The Adventures of Harry Richmond*, 1870.

day book compilers will find such pages in Meredith full of treasure. I doubt though that the patient reader takes away one complete character, consistently developed. This failure is due to the intense centralisation of Merediths mind; all its power seems pent up within his own forehead, & turned upon the singular objects to be found there. In his novels, then, we get the shadow of something magnificent, & without likeness; red silhouettes of men, extravagant grotesques, an earth & sky all on fire as in perpetual sunset. It is a world of his own, as one says of the great writers; & so far, he too is a great writer. But now & again, as in Harry & Ottilia's love scene by the lake, in the adventures of the Priscilla, & the final catastrophe,[14] there is something surely not of Merediths world, or of our world; cardboard mountains have been lifted from the stage, light is made of time; I suppose that supreme cleverness, long underrated, tempts him to such imposition. The public he thinks is too stupid to find out, & by degrees he deceives himself.

A hot afternoon! – the sun strikes straight at me; masons are tapping perpetually at the roofs – however, let me try to grasp some ideas about painting.

I looked at a fresco by Perugino.[15] I conceive that he saw things grouped, contained in certain & invisible forms; expression in faces, action – &c. did not exist; all beauty was contained in the momentary appearance of human beings. He saw it sealed as it were; all its worth in it; not a hint of past or future. His fresco seems to me infinitely silent; as though beauty had swum up to the top, stayed there, above everything else, speech, paths leading on, relation of brain to brain, dont exist.

Each part has a dependence upon the others; they compose one idea in his mind. That idea has nothing to do with anything to be put into words. A group stands without relation to the figure of God. They have come together then because their lines & colours are related, & express some view of beauty in his brain.

As for writing – I want to express beauty too – but beauty (symmetry?) of life & the world, in action. Conflict? – is that it?

---

14 Harry and Ottilia's love scene by the lake, Chap. XXX; the adventures of the Priscilla, Chap. XIII; the final catastrophe, Chap. LVI.
15 Pietro Vanucci (Perugino, 1446-1523); his major decorative work was the frescoes in the Collegio del Cambio, Perugia, executed *c.* 1500 on an elaborate allegorical theme.

If there is action in painting it is only to exhibit lines; but with the end of beauty in view. Isn't there a different kind of beauty? No conflict.

I attain a different kind of beauty, achieve a symmetry by means of infinite discords, showing all the traces of the minds passage through the world; & achieve in the end, some kind of whole made of shivering fragments; to me this seems the natural process; the flight of the mind. Do they really reach the same thing?

Perugia

When you walk out of the front door here you find yourself apparently upon a parade, with the sea beneath. A blue vapour fills in the spaces between the white columns of the parapet; & the people are leaning & looking over, as they do at the sea side. But in truth it is dry land beneath, dropped down some distance; there are curved vineyards, groves of olives, & the hills which rise against the sky seem about on the level of our heads. At sunset, of course, there is a tremendous display; clouds of flamingo scarlet, & of the shape of curled feathers; spaces of crimson, with bars upon them; hills laid against the furnace so that their little fringe of trees is visible; but I like the foreground best with its soft green & brown, & its highest light the dull white enamel of the road.

After tea, instead of rummaging the streets after the fashion of our compatriots, we choose one of the roads which we can follow from our windows, & descend into the valley. Small paths branch at intervals, & lead between the vineyards. They are stony; lead past little square farms, washed salmon pink. Italian peasants are driving their ploughs through earth which has the appearance of extreme antiquity; it is so brown & dry that all the oil which holds the clods together must have been baked out of it. A pair of oxen, who are unwieldy & much given to contemplation, carry out this clumsy labour, & are of great value, for the sake of their creamy white colour, in the brown & grey landscape.

It is perhaps because I compare Umbrian vineyards with English fields that I am slow to come at any picture of this place. The divisions at first seemed to me perplexing: I found no solitude & no wildness; there were no deep clumps of shade, no fields with long grasses. The ground is singularly bare, & stony; brittle looking granaries of old pink brick, are dotted here & there, & perhaps there is an archway where women sit, handling maize. The snug circle of our farmyard does not exist. But the place is beautiful; the twisted little trees, now green, now black against the sky, are full of lines; lovely are the peaks in the distance, like a great encampment of tents of all sizes; here before us is Perugia on its hill, with all its long towers & square blocks massed in out line; there is no softness, nothing indistinct, but I begin to see that there is a character in this land, with its gnarled little trees, & its sharp outlines, which would soon make all other scenery insipid.

We spent the day at Assisi. It fronts us, on its hill top, some sixteen miles away, & between lies a perfectly flat space, lined with rows of trees, bearing the Tiber upon it. Assisi is another of these pyramid-shaped towns, which ascend with tier upon tier of whitish brown houses, till they culminate in a dome, or a long gallery of arches. Immense bare hills lie behind the town. When we had inspected the church[16] we strolled through the streets. As usual, the houses are very high, & the streets narrow, so that if you laid a strip of roof across the top you would make a deep tunnel. In this instance the houses were rather splendid, with great windows & balconies, door ways fortified with stone, but all the shutters were up, or swung open idly, so that you could fancy great empty rooms within. The streets were deserted, save for a donkey cart, or an old woman squatted against the wall. The hills & the wide stretch of country visible beneath you at the end of every street seem to make these cities a little incongruous. They seem to cling peacefully to their hill top – to offer lodgment for besieged men & women, who no longer require it.

---

16 Presumably the Basilica of St Francis.

Florence 1909

As a journalist, Virginia had a productive year in 1908. The Times Literary Supplement *published more than a dozen of her reviews and* The Cornhill Magazine *brought out six essays. Her sense of financial independence was steadily increasing. And by February 1909 she had completed the first seven chapters of the novel that would become* The Voyage Out. *Clive Bell read them and remarked on her extraordinary fictional method. 'How on earth', he asked, 'by telling us what it is like at noon, do you show us what it was like at five, at sunset, and at night?'*

Also in February – Virginia had just turned twenty-seven – Lytton Strachey, in an expansive moment, made her a proposal of marriage which she accepted. It was quickly withdrawn, by mutual consent. On 7 April, Caroline Emelia Stephen died, leaving Virginia a legacy of £2,500. She set off for Florence and Milan with the Bells on 23 April and returned, alone, on 9 May.

Despite her productivity and increased financial security, however, Virginia was not happy. Something was bothering her, causing a pervasive mood of discontent. Whatever in reality was behind this mood, although not apparent in this journal, did find its way into her novel, where an ambiguous oppression makes itself felt in Rachel Vinrace's isolation. Rachel could find no answer to her trouble. Neither could Virginia.

FLORENCE
April 1909

25 April

It is with great timidity that I write, remembering strictures upon empty & ladylike writing. Browning,[1] by attending to such criticism, mystified all generations. As for me – I write. The instinct wells like sap in a tree. The fault of most of my descriptive writing is that it tends to be too definite.

---

1   Robert Browning (1812-89), English poet; see *Flush: A Biography*, 1933 (Kp A19), Chapter 5: 'Italy'.

Florence

Descriptive writing is dangerous & tempting. It is easy, with little expense of brain power, to make something. One seizes some broad aspect, as of water or colour, & makes a note of it. This single quality gives the tone of the piece. As a matter of fact, the subject is probably infinitely subtle, no more amenable to impressionist treatment than the human character. What one records is really the state of ones own mind.

Looking at Florence the other evening I was much impressed by the subtlety of the colour. Of course the roofs are speckled brown – there are white walls, with ledges sticking out from them, & green shutters. The houses vary in size, & have projecting roofs. But the water – the sunset – the pale luminous stream – all rough where it falls over the decline – & the houses on the bank, with the red in their windows – to tell of this would need immense concentration. To make a good passage requires an heroic grinding of the mind – & here am I, half asleep.

Florence seems to me a very happy place. The poorest mother might let her children play among long grass, & wisteria blossoms. There are no dull streets. The smoke is like the trail of burnt leaves. Perfectly pure mud, with a fringe of grass, runs along the Arno. It is spacious, all wind blown, & sun baked, if clamorous, & pungent in smells.

The wisterias are in bloom – strange pale garlands, hanging against green leaves & blue sky. The little villas are set on all the ledges of the hills – gay little places, white & pink or yellow, suggestions of much happiness somehow. Today, as the wind blew, the hills were dusted with a cloud.

I do not think the hills themselves beautiful. The little valleys, up by San Miniato,[2] which shelter nightingales, are beautiful; but these great mounds suggest a stage to my mind. However, the city is lovely – I compare it always to a great basket of white & brown eggs. Even the Duomo has something homely in its appearance. One thinks much of the astonishing beauty of the place – its effect on life – how once, this shell was all aglow. Think of the palaces lit by night, the villas with the lovers in the garden – the streets full of banners & men with striped legs walking in procession.

The discomfort of writing here is intense – constrains my style to be tense, in the form of lapidary inscriptions.

Walking on San Miniato the other evening, it occurred to me that the

---

2   The Church of San Miniato, on the hill overlooking Florence, south of the River Arno.

thing was running into classic prose before my eyes. I positively saw the long smooth sentence running like a ribbon along the road – casting graceful loops round the beggar woman & the dusky child – & curving freely over the bare slopes of the hills. London!

We lunched with Rezia[3] today, met there the Countess & Joseph. The Countess is an Anglo Italian celebrity – a stout, decisive woman, broad, almost squat featured; her cheek dark red, & scarred by a dogs bite; her eye prominent – altogether her appearance is vigorous, imperious, & subtle too at the same time. She watches & springs, but calculations go on forever within the brain.

Look at the conflict of lines on the brow – She is much like a peasant woman; & is a woman of cultivation & race at the same time. Her talk was bold & free, also tentative. I suppose her reputation for learning is not based on the most solid foundations. On the other hand, her judgments of people are perfectly shrewd & unhesitating. A woman one guesses of many passions; with a great fervour for life. How many springs & autumns have found her intent on her game. She has not given an eye to the shapes & colours, perhaps – but in this I wrong her. She fingered Nessa's jewels like a child.

The Count[4] held me in the window. Agriculture was his topic. A dry elderly man with the skin round his eyes creased & indented, gone yellow in a circle – he talked of irrigation & crops, fitting together laborious sentences in French – a man infinitely bored, colourless, respectable, accustomed to wait patiently while his wife talks, & very glad to find someone to listen to him.

Today we had another experience of society. We had lunch with the art critic & his wife;[5] & tea with Mrs. Ross.[6] In case space should fail me

---

3   Principessa Lucrezia (Rezia) Rasponi (1879-1971) was the daughter of Contessa Angelica (1854-1919) and Conte Giuseppe (Joseph) Rasponi (1852-1941); in 1901 she had married Principe Filippo Corsini and they stayed with the Stephens at Fritham during their honeymoon. Rezia and Nerino Rasponi and their cousin Guido Pasolini were friends of George Duckworth. The Rasponis lived at the Villa Fontellerta.

4   Conte Piero Pasolini (1844-1920) was the Contessa Angelica's brother, who in 1874 had married Maria Ponti (d.1919).

5   Bernard Berenson (1865-1959), the authority on Italian painting, and his wife Mary, *née* Pearsall Smith, formerly Costelloe (1864-1945), sister of Alys (Mrs Bertrand Russell); the Berensons lived at *I Tatti*, at Settignano, near Florence.

6   Janet Anne Ross (1842-1927), daughter of Sir Alexander and Lady Duff-Gordon; she married Henry James Ross, a banker, of Alexandria, and from 1867 lived at Settignano, near Florence, in her villa Poggio Gherardo. The London home of her parents had been a rendezvous for English and foreign celebrities.

(the candle gutters intolerably, & the ink oozes) I will describe the tea party. The worst of distinguished old ladies, who have known everyone & lived an independent life, is that they become brusque & imperious without sufficient wits to alleviate the manner. Mrs Ross lives in a great villa, is the daughter of distinguished parents; the friend of writers, & the character of the country side. She sells things off her walls. She is emphatic, forcible, fixes you with her straight grey eye as though it were an honour to occupy, even for a moment, its attention. The head is massive, it is held high; the mouth is coarse & the upper lip haired. Such old women like men, & have a number of unreasonable traditions. Pride of birth, I thought I detected; certainly she has that other pride, the pride which comes to those who have lived among the chosen spirits of the time. A word of family, & her wits were at work at once.

I know not why, but this type, which the Countess represents somewhat too, does not much attract me. Only one position is possible if you are a young woman: you must let them adopt queenly airs, with a touch of the maternal. She summons you to sit beside her, lays her hand for a moment on yours – dismisses you the next – to make room for some weakly young man. She has them to stay with her for months – likes them best when they are big & strong but will tolerate weakness for the sake of the sex. She has led a bold life, managing for herself, & an Englishwoman who dictates to peasants is apt to become domineering. However, there can be no question of her spirit – many portraits showed the intent indomitable face, in youth & middle age, it is still the same, beneath white hair. It proved her power that her drawing room filled with guests. She seemed to enjoy sweeping them about, without much ceremony. Parties were bidden to admire the garden; young men were commanded to hand cake. Among the guests was a lean, attenuated woman, who had a face like that of a transfixed hare – the lower part was drawn out in anguish – while the eyes appealed piteously. This was Mrs. Meynell, the writer;[7] who somehow, made one dislike the notion of women who write. She clasped the arm of a chair, & seemed uncomfortably out of place.

This was no atmosphere for chaste expression – there was nothing to lay hold of. She walked with a curious forward spring, which, seeing that the body was spare & bony, encased too in black velvet, had an incongruous air. Once, no doubt, she was a poetess, & trod the fields of

---

7   Alice Meynell (1847-1922), poet and essayist, and wife of Wilfred Meynell, the journalist and editor; they had eight children.

Parnassus. It is melancholy to trace even such words as Mrs. Meynells to a lank slightly absurd & altogether insignificant little body, dressed with some attempt at the fashion. Did Mrs Browning look like that too? And yet, poor woman, had the fire of Sappho burnt in her what else could she have done? These gatherings are brutal things. Or is my theory proved – a writer should be the furnace from which his words come – & tepid people, timid & decorous, never coin true words. The poor thing looked furtive, as though found out – run to earth. She had a plain asthmatic daughter.[8] The wine further watered.

Laziness, or some feeling, akin to laziness perhaps, that the task was hard enough to require more thought than I could give it, prevented me from writing any thing more about Florence. Also, I became familiar with the marked aspects; & was on the search for something subtler. The scene is very emphatic in Italy, but I forbear to write of something hidden on the other side of the Alps. It is strange how one begins to hold a globe in ones head; I can travel from Florence to Fitzroy Square on solid land all the time. It would be possible, though, to note something about the people we met. There was for example that morbid young woman, Miss Murray.[9] She was a dark, angular woman, aged perhaps 35. The only notable thing about her was the fixity with which she looked at you. It seemed to show an intense, & perhaps limited spirit. She asked me to have tea with her one night. There was a strange lack of what one may call atmosphere about her. Although I was a stranger, she made no attempt to entertain me. We were soon on the rocks. She told me her history of course; & what feelings ruled her. She has to live in pensions because she has an invalid mother. She would like to teach physical culture in a school. To console herself she has recourse to Indian philosophies, which preach mystic doctrine, as I gathered. She had intuitions, & thought herself very morbid. She could fix her mind, for example, upon a stone, until it included the whole world of flesh & spirit. She was indifferent to death. Her morbidity consisted in the fact that she knew that she was singular, & made efforts to approach other people, always conscious of her unlikeness to them. If she had really believed in her stones, I suppose, she would have understood people by the light of them. Poor young woman! It seemed to me infinitely arid, &

---

8 This was probably Olivia (b. *c.* 1890); see Viola Meynell, *Alice Meynell: A Memoir*, 1929, p. 239.
9 Probably Margaret Alice Murray (1863-1963), Egyptologist and prolific writer on the occult; see her autobiography, *My First Hundred Years*, 1963.

out of tune. She was without humour, strained, & slightly elderly, & what imagination she had took this mystic form, which is imagination disembodied. And yet I think she was honest, unselfish, & clever above the average. I am never comfortable with these acute analytical minds. They seem to me to miss the point, & yet light on something which one cant deny.

Then there was Mrs. Campbell. A glance at her told one much, in a second. She is a tall old lady, aged over seventy, with white hair & a cap. She has a delicate face, with a clear cut nose, & expressive wrinkles. Her eyes are dim & kindly. She is clearly refined, cultivated, & by birth & tradition habitually polite. The thing that distinguishes her from other dignified old ladies is that she has a genuine flicker of humour, which lightens her good qualities – gives them point. She gave me the impression of a wavering flame, pale & thin of course, but still undoubtedly alive. I had reason to know, because I sat next her, & we had a charming relationship. It was charming because it was sincere, as far as might be. We played our parts of young woman & old woman. She answered my questions; which I made in as true a spirit as I could, pressing to the verge of impertinence. She saw that I was genuine in my interest, & this flattered her; in return she was playful, tender & affectionate, as one who knows much because she has lived, & can presume upon her knowledge without much acquaintance with individuals. Age gives her the right; besides the attitude which it produces is the most intimate possible between the different ages. When you have brought two daughters into the world, it is possible to take many things for granted in talking to younger women. It amused me to trace her natural conventions & prejudices; to mark how gently but firmly she insisted that she had lived most of her life in Mayfair, & married one daughter to a Member of Parliament who lives in Chesterfield Street, & the other to a soldier in the Lancers. Little facts produced at intervals showed how she wished to build up the figure of a well born Irish woman, educated by all the best masters, most carefully brought up in Belgravia; & she wished me to know these facts because she thought them something to be proud of; because she admired the dignity, kindliness & charity of the type they produce. She was no snob, though doubtless some of her content with her own advantages was not quite rational. She was Irish, & had therefore a faintly mystic turn, showing itself in a love of art & scenery in preference to people, & in a charming piety. She wrote devout books, – had done the life of Father Damien[10] into rhyme. I expect that her writing is graceful, & fresh, with no originality or much power.

---

10 Joseph Damien de Veuster, better known as Father Damien (1840-89), the Belgian Roman Catholic missionary who worked with lepers on one of the Hawaiian Islands, where he contracted leprosy and died. Mrs Campbell has not been identified, nor has her rhymed life of Father Damien been traced; both, nevertheless, found their way into VW's novels – see *The Voyage Out*, 1915 (Kp A1): '"I have an aunt called Rachel, who put the life of Father Damien into verse. She is a religious fanatic . . ."' (London, p. 165; New York, p. 141). See also *Jacob's Room*, 1922 (Kp A6): 'Sandra Wentworth Williams certainly woke to find a copy of Donne's poems upon her dressing-table. And the book would be stood on the shelf in the English country house where Sally Duggan's *Life of Father Damien* in verse would join it one of these days' (London, p. 160; New York, p. 161).

Postscript

With the above entry of May 1909, Virginia's journals come to an end. Before the publication of her first novel, The Voyage Out *in March 1915, she would survive a second suicide attempt and live through two more bouts of madness. And on 10 August 1912, Virginia Stephen would become Virginia Woolf.*

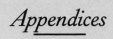

Appendices

Appendix A
Description of the Early Journals

Virginia Stephen wrote seven journals between the years 1897 and 1909. The first six of these are located in the Berg Collection of The New York Public Library; the seventh is in the British Library. A brief description of each follows; all other details of each journal, except pagination and lineation, are reproduced exactly in the text.

I 1897   Catalogued as '[Diary] Notebook 1897' 277 pp.; holograph entries in black ink on white unruled paper, one entry per page, *recto* or *verso*, each entry dated; hard cover diary with lock, measures 8 x 13 cm; Berg.

II 1899   Catalogued as '[Diary] Holograph notebook. Unsigned. Aug. 4-Sept. 23, 1899. No. 1'. Hard cover volume with label pasted on to front cover: 'Warboys Summer Holidays 1899'. 51 pp.; entries on 28 numbered (2 to 33) and 23 unnumbered sheets, unruled, written in black ink; volume measures 13 x 21.5 cm; Berg.

III 1903   Catalogued as '[Diary] Holograph notebook. Unsigned. June 3-Oct. 1, 1903? No. 2.' Soft cover, with label pasted on front (presumably at a later date): 'Diary/Hyde Park Gate/1903?' 156 pp.; entries on white unruled paper, *recto* page, in black ink; volume measures 15.2 x 22.3 cm; Berg.

IV 1904-5   Catalogued as '[Diary] Holograph notebook. Unsigned. Christmas, 1904-May 31, 1905. No. 3.' Soft cover, 136 pp.; entries on *recto* page in black ink on white unruled paper, each entry dated (dates from 1 to 31 January and 1 March to 31 May entered in red ink); volume measures 11 x 14 cm; Berg.

V 1905   Catalogued as '[Diary] Holograph notebook. Unsigned. Aug. 11, 1905-Sept. 14, [1905]. No. 4.' Soft cover volume with label pasted on to front cover: 'Diary/Cornwall/1905'; 56 pp.; entries on *recto* page in black ink on white unruled paper; volume measures 13.6 x 22.5 cm; Berg.

VI   1906-8   Catalogued as '[Diary] Holograph notebook. Unsigned. April, 1906-Aug. 1-14, 1908. No. 5.' Soft cover; 77 pp.; entries on *recto* page in black ink on white unruled paper, written during visits to Giggleswick; Blo' Norton Hall; New Forest; Golders Green and Hampstead; Playden, Sussex; Wells, Somerset; Manorbier, Wales; volume measures 13.3 x 21.4 cm; Berg.

VII   1906-9   Catalogued as 'Additional Manuscript 61837. Autograph note-book of Virginia Woolf describing a visit to Greece and Turkey September-October 1906 with comments on Mérimée's *Lettres à une inconnue* followed by an account of her visit to north Italy September 1908 with comments on Hardy's *Two on a Tower* and Meredith's *Harry Richmond* and on her visit to Florence April 1909. Reversing the volume lists of expenses in Greece and Turkey and an unfinished draft of a biographical description of Clive Bell.' 113 pp.; entries on numbered *recto* page in black ink on pale cream unruled paper; volume measures 13.6 x 18.6 cm; British Library.

In order to establish chronology in the published text, the journal for Greece (September-October 1906) has been removed from notebook VII and inserted in notebook VI, between the entries for Blo' Norton (August 1906) and New Forest (December 1906).

Appendix B
Biographical Sketches

BELL, Clive (1881-1964), art critic, married Vanessa Stephen in 1907, and from about that time became AVS's most valued literary confidant and critic, until her marriage to Leonard Woolf in 1912. He came from a wealthy Wiltshire family whose fortune was made in coal. At Trinity College, Cambridge, he was a close friend of Thoby Stephen, who, like Clive, was as interested in field sports as in intellectual pursuits. He met Vanessa in 1902, and in 1904-5 twice proposed to her and was twice refused. After Thoby's death in November 1906, she accepted him and they were married in St Pancras Registry Office the following February.

DUCKWORTH, Gerald de l'Etang (1870-1937), AVS's younger half-brother. Gerald, George and Stella (see below) were the children of Julia Jackson's marriage to Herbert Duckworth. Gerald was educated at Eton and Clare College, Cambridge. In 1898, with A. R. Walker, he established the publishing firm of Duckworth and Company which published AVS's first two novels *The Voyage Out* (1915) and *Night and Day* (1919). In 1921 he married Cecil Alice, the only daughter of Charles Scott-Chad of Pynkney Hall, near King's Lynn. For a number of years he was honorary secretary of the Savile Club.

DUCKWORTH, George Herbert (1868-1934), AVS's elder half-brother, educated at Eton and Trinity College, Cambridge. He was private secretary (unpaid) to Charles Booth, 1892-1902, and from 1902 to 1905 to Austen Chamberlain, when Postmaster-General and Chancellor of the Exchequer. In 1904 he married Lady Margaret Herbert (1870-1958), daughter of the 4th Earl of Carnarvon, and in 1908 was appointed secretary to the Royal Commission on Historical Monuments, but during the war he transferred to the Ministry of Munitions. He was made CB in 1919 and knighted in 1927.

DUCKWORTH, Stella (1869-97), AVS's half-sister. After her mother's death in May 1895, she took charge of the Stephen household and continued some of Julia Stephen's charitable works. She married John (Jack) Waller Hills on 10 April 1897 and died of peritonitis on 19 July, while expecting a baby.

HILLS, John (Jack) Waller (1867-1938), educated at Eton and Balliol College, Oxford, later solicitor at Messrs Roper and Whateley. In 1897 he married AVS's half-sister, Stella Duckworth, who died in July of that year. From 1906 to 1922, he was Conservative Unionist MP for Durham City, and he was re-elected in 1925; a supporter of social reform, especially in connection with housing. He was the second son of Anna, *née* Grove, and Herbert Augustus Hills (1837-1907) of Corby Castle, Judge of the Court of Appeal, Cairo. His brothers were Edmond and Eustace Gilbert Hills. In 1931 he married Mary Grace, daughter of Leon Dominic Ashton.

STEPHEN, Adrian Leslie (1883-1949), AVS's younger brother. After Evelyn's Preparatory School, Hillingdon, he entered Westminster (1896) and from there went up to Trinity College, Cambridge, 1902-5. When Sir Leslie died in 1904, the four Stephen children moved from 22 Hyde Park Gate to 46 Gordon Square. After Vanessa's marriage to Clive Bell in 1907, Adrian and AVS left Gordon Square to the Bells and set up house at 29 Fitzroy Square. Following Cambridge, he studied law briefly but did not settle on a profession until five years after his marriage in 1914 to Karin Costelloe (1889-1953), when both studied medicine and psychology in preparation for becoming psychoanalysts.

STEPHEN, Julia Prinsep (*née* Jackson, later Duckworth) (1846-95), AVS's mother and the youngest daughter of Dr John (1804-87) and Maria (*née* Pattle, 1818-92) Jackson, formerly of Calcutta. George, Stella and Gerald were the children of her marriage to Herbert (1833-70), son of William Duckworth of Orchardleigh. After seven years of widowhood, she married in 1878 Leslie Stephen and bore him Vanessa, Thoby, AVS and Adrian. She died on 5 May at 22 Hyde Park Gate.

STEPHEN, Julian Thoby (1880-1906), AVS's elder brother. After Evelyn's Preparatory School, he went to Clifton College, 1894-9, and from there to Trinity College, Cambridge, where his friends included Clive Bell, Saxon Sydney-Turner, Lytton Strachey and Leonard Woolf. In the autumn of 1904, he began to read for the Bar. His Cambridge friends began to call at 46 Gordon Square in March 1905 and the Thursday Evening 'at homes' he initiated at this time played a significant part in the formation of the Bloomsbury Group. On holiday in Greece in 1906 with his brother, sisters and Violet Dickinson, he contracted typhoid fever, and he died at Gordon Square on 20 November.

STEPHEN, Leslie (1832-1904), son of Jane Catherine (d. 1875), daughter of the Rev. John Venn, and Sir James Stephen (1789-1859), Permanent Under-Secretary for the Colonies, 1835-47, and later Regius Professor of History at Cambridge; and brother of Sir James Fitzjames Stephen (1829-94), the distinguished Judge. A man of letters, educated at Eton, 1842-8, Trinity Hall, Cambridge, 1850-4, and ordained a deacon in 1855. In 1856 he became junior tutor of Trinity Hall, as well as a noted cross-country runner. (He organised in 1881 and assumed leadership of an informal group of Sunday walkers called 'Sunday Tramps'.) A serious mountain climber by 1859, he was elected to the Alpine Club in that same year, becoming editor for the *Alpine Journal,* 1868-72. Harriet Marian (Minny, 1840-75), daughter of William Makepeace Thackeray, became his wife in 1867 and bore him a daughter, Laura (1870-1945). Minny died, as did his mother, in 1875. Julia Duckworth, the widow of Herbert Duckworth, with three children of her own, consoled him in his grief, became his second wife in 1878, and between 1879 and 1883 bore him four children. He resigned in 1882 from *The Cornhill Magazine,* whose editor he had been since 1871, to become the first editor of the *Dictionary of National Biography*. His health began to fail from the strain of the *DNB,* however, necessitating his resignation in 1890. As early as 1862 he realised his lack of belief in Christian dogma, and his *Essays on Free-thinking and Plainspeaking* (1873) defined his agnosticism. A more moderate statement of his Godless position appeared in *An Agnostic's Apology and Other Essays* (1893). The death of Julia in 1895 left him shattered, and his progressive deafness cut him off increasingly from his family and few surviving friends. He was knighted in 1902 and died of abdominal cancer at 22 Hyde Park Gate on 22 February. See Frederic W. Maitland, *Life and Letters of Leslie Stephen,* 1906, and Noel Annan, *Leslie Stephen: The Godless Victorian,* 2nd ed., London, 1984.

STEPHEN, Vanessa (Nessa) (1879-1961), painter, AVS's elder sister. She began her first drawing lessons with Ebenezer Wake Cook (1843-1926) and from 1896 attended classes three days a week at Arthur Cope's art school at Park Cottage, Pelham Street in South Kensington. In 1901 she entered the Painting School of the Royal Academy and studied life-drawing there with John Singer Sargent. Through her friendship with Margaret Symonds (Madge Vaughan), she met one of the leading contemporary artists, Charles Furse (1868-1904), who had married Madge's sister Katharine Symonds. She became interested in portraiture, and her painting of Lady Robert Cecil was her first to be exhibited, in April 1905 at the New Gallery. In 1907 she married Clive Bell, whom she had known through Thoby since 1902. Their first son, Julian Heward, was born in 1908. See Frances Spalding, *Vanessa Bell,* London, 1983.

Appendix C
Newspaper Reports

The Yarmouth 'Murder'
From the *Evening News and Evening Mail,* 21 September 1903:

DISCOVERED ON THE BEACH.

In patrolling the beach at Yarmouth yesterday morning a coastguardsman found in the wash of the sea a body, afterwards identified as that of W. Bradfield, aged 45, of 130 Cundy-road, Custom House, Victoria Docks.

He had come to Yarmouth with some friends, whom he left at ten o'clock on Saturday night to take a stroll on the beach. He did not return to his lodgings, and was not seen alive again.

The Zanzibar Hoax
From the *Daily Mail,* Saturday, 4 March 1905:

MAYOR HOAXED. CAMBRIDGE UNDERGRADUATES DARING TRICK. SUPPOSED ROYAL VISIT. IMPOSTERS RECEIVED WITH CIVIC HONOURS.

"Reply paid. Strand, Southampton-street. To the Mayor of Cambridge. The Sultan of Zanzibar will arrive today at Cambridge, 4.27, for a short visit. Could you arrange to show him buildings of interest and send carriage? Henry Lucas, Hotel Cecil, London." The above telegram, which reached the Mayor soon after one o'clock on Thursday marks the opening scene in one of the most audacious and carefully-planned practical jokes ever perpetrated by undergraduates. . . .

The Mayor and the Town Clerk, Mr. J. E. L. Whitehead, accordingly prepared to meet their distinguished guests, when a second wire came: "Telegram received with thanks. Unable to arrive till 5.43. No time for dinner. Henry Lucas."

An hour or two later, passengers on the Liverpool-street Station saw four gentlemen with dark complexions arrayed in gorgeous flowing garments and brilliant turbans on their heads drive up to the station. They were accompanied by a gentleman in ordinary clothes, the interpreter, "Mr. Henry Lucas." The four dark gentlemen were "Prince Mukasa Ali" and three members of his suite. Mr. Lucas took tickets for Cambridge and the party on arriving in due course drove to the Guildhall, where they were received by the Mayor and the Town Clerk, the former wearing his chain of office.

Here it was explained that the Sultan himself was unfortunately unable to come, and so his place had been taken at the last minute by his uncle, Prince Mukasa Ali. Refreshments were offered and declined, and, as the Prince announced that he must go back by the 7.5 train to Liverpool-street, the party went into the main room of the Guildhall, where a bazaar was being held, at which, however, the Prince made no purchases. . . .

King's College Chapel was, naturally, the first sight to be seen, but, perhaps for religious reasons, it was thought, the Prince declined to go inside. From King's his Royal Highness went for a few moments into Clare and then, passing Trinity Hall, went into Trinity College. As they passed into the great court the visitors stopped, struck with admiration, and lifting up their hands, expressed their wonder. The visitors, indeed, except upon this one occasion, spoke very little . . . and addressed each other by signs on their hands. . . .

Time, however, was now short, and after a walk up Trinity-street, the Prince and his suite took leave of their kind hosts and drove off to the station. . . .

From the *Daily Mail,* Monday, 6 March 1905:

THE UNDERGRADUATE JOKE. HOW THE 'PRINCE' AND HIS SUITE ESCAPED . . . .

The "Cambridge Daily News" gives further details of the conclusion of the practical joke. Hurriedly scampering out of the railway station, the quartette hired two cabs, which were told to drive "straight up" Station-road. At various points the drivers were instructed which turnings to take. At the level crossing on the Long-road the cabs were stopped in order to allow a train to pass. The occupants, still dressed in their fantastic garb, said nothing, and the cabmen, regarding them closely, wisely refrained from asking further instructions. Apparently they seemed to realise that some joke was or had been on foot.

Opposite the plantation between the Long-road and Willers' Nurseries the drivers were told to stop. Then followed some haggling, conducted on the part of the pretended foreigners in broken English and by the cabmen in their own expressive dialect.

"Who is going to pay me?" indignantly inquired one.

"I have got no money," piteously replied the Eastern potentate.

"Well," persisted the cabmen, "I want my money."

Trouble seemed to be brewing, but it was averted by one of the fares, who, standing in the middle of the road in a white robe and turban, declared, "Me pay you. Will give you the same as the other cab."

Then the "Prince" stepped in and solved the difficulty by giving both drivers a fairly substantial sum. After this both cabs drove away, leaving the practical jokers standing at the edge of the plantation.

Appendix D
Preserved Deletions

Although the text for these journals has been presented as a final reading, a number of deletions, judged substantive, have been preserved in this appendix. Their position has been indicated by [ ] in the main text, and the four words in the text which precede each deletion are given here. The deletion itself is enclosed within [square brackets]. The pagination beside each listing conforms with that of the printed text. No deletions have been entered for 1897, Christmas 1904 to May 1905, Giggleswick April 1906, Blo' Norton August 1906, New Forest Christmas 1906, Golders Green July 1907, Italy 1908 or Florence 1909.

Warboys 1899
p. 144 windows & such extravagances. [But this compound, laid on with a large brush in alluring cascades is – [*Unfinished.*]]
p. 152 on the other side. [The trees on the island cast so dense a shade that no object floating [*Unfinished.*]]
p. 159 need of acuteness here! [These second hand book shops collect in an extraordinary way all the old sermons & religious works of the last century; I think I could stock a clergymans library.]
1903
p. 168 an entirely admiring purpose. [And dropping all imagery, a drawing room full of people, all practically unknown to one, does give one a very queer feeling.]
p.168 of the subtlest possible. [I cannot altogether defend myself, but I feel that to play the social game really well demands great qualities; it is very rarely played well.]
p. 168 is coarse beside it: [You may be able to build a bridge or make a poem – but all the same you can fail when [*Unfinished.*]]
p. 169 courage of a hero – [or a heroine –]
p. 175 admirably appropriate I think [to set apart this old palace as background for our aged aristocracy.]
p. 181 pair of legs only. [which moreover could walk different ways;]
p. 182 as good a scholar – [of course dear old Professor Warr with his courtesy & deliberation would soon have [*Unfinished.*]]
p. 182 own about the Furies; [for six lessons I was determined to know all I could about the Furies.]

p. 182 theories about the Furies: [we argued them up & down & on any subsequent occasion, if I wished for a little diversion, I had only to [*Unfinished.*]]

p. 183 in Euripides (?) for instance – [which in my vanity I thought I had translated well –]

p. 183 moral into their plays. [I soon found that I was expected to understand all kinds of teachings & to interpret all kinds of views upon life where I had merely looked for enjoyment.]

p. 184 one of careless ease – [careless, but not negligent.]

p. 186 tortoise at the zoo. [He extends his head, once every two or three weeks, to take in a fresh supply of cabbages; & by these means will prolong his life]

p. 186 were always really hot. [We went about in cotton dresses; were out before lessons & after tea]

p. 187 anyone else – so I [having a few minutes to myself]

p. 187 have in my head. [I have no time or wish to polish & [*Unfinished.*]]

p. 187 from a battle field, [got our 8 large boxes hauled into a van]

p. 187 within & without, proclaim [it to be the property of a well born tho’ no longer prosperous family now living in retirement.]

p. 189 quaintness are entirely refreshing: [but again, sometimes one’s spirit rises against it – craves for something more original & independent – for bright colours instead of this eternal deep green & gray.]

p. 189 somnolence as of one [entirely satisfied with itself]

p. 189 in their turn, have [commemorated their birthdays & marriages]

p. 190 you are” he said – [A near sight of us apparently struck him as more comic than ever]

p. 194 spend an hour in – [let it be an evening hour, on the Sabbath.]

p. 194 splendour of their monarch. [They are homely, though dignified;]

p. 195 the type I foretold – [I felt at home with her at once.]

p. 195 awe-struck. When she [saw my attention wandering – as it did not infrequently [*Unfinished.*]]

p. 198 the rarest of things; [we prize our Kensington Square, our Cowley Street – old houses in Holborn –]

p. 199 great blocks of stone; [they are clearly set in some order –]

p. 199 I cannot otherwise conceive; [what it means, Heaven knows: they have been left over to serve as token of a sufficiently grim reminder of the [*Unfinished.*]]

p. 199 that some forgotten people [– one can hardly call them by any name we know now,]

p. 200 gross bodies in bed. [& were altogether of a more spiritual nature than the night before.]

p. 204 laughed at me today. [I never feel so helpless as when unable to make material facts go the way I want;]

p. 205 of the great books, [the books that create something like life,]

p. 205 & rare it is. [It would make no impression on nine people out of ten]

p. 205 bitter end. It is [you feel, a novel written with almost savage determination;]

p. 206 His country is solid. [But again the Clare family is a mistake.]

p. 206 & the trees writhing. [One felt like riding a ship in a storm.]

p. 208 better than a prison; [Wilton for instance is an oppressive inheritance]

p. 209 a more festive age, [when men were not ashamed]

p. 210 choose to visit London; [they are evidently wearing their best clothes & have done their best to hide the pleasant country simplicity which was [*Unfinished.*]]

p. 213 herself if you refuse. [You shut the door in her face, & are relieved when she has hailed off round the corner.]

Cornwall 1905

p. 282 the voices of strangers. [No, we were but ghosts; so long as we stood there in the shade of the hedge, we might believe that it was within our power to enter;]

p. 285 for any other fame. [The finest book in the world could not, I think, have achieved more for that poor dingy old woman.]

p. 287 the crannies with putty. [Luckily I did not insist that he was her son or her brother;]

p. 294 sight seers upon this [last little promontory of English land.]

p. 298 Chance sends an audience; [a private game between the two is agreed upon. stealthily,]

p. 298 pack must be broached, [not that we are going to play;]

Greece 1906

p. 319 sides of the museum; [It is a cheerful hall with a wooden ceiling. There is the Apollo, looking over his shoulder, with his straight face & the full round chin; There is the Lapith & [*Unfinished.*]]

p. 319 Heaven drew his gaze. [He is very merry still, but always tranquil]

p. 333 miles beneath my feet. [The air was warm & luminous; the next moment I trod on firm ground.]

p. 334 was luminous, & warm; [seething in the mellowest colours, with all the trouble of the west, & the quiet of the east,]

p. 336 be a dull record, [unless I could convey the same curious feeling]

p. 337 lie beneath the earth. [Greece must be full of underground palaces. Meanwhile all the hills grew mellow & a great flight of rooks came sailing down the sky.]

p. 356 nothing thin or harsh; [all was bathed in the rich grace of a tender autumn day.]

Playden 1907

p. 368 see the land that [since it hardened, has been perhaps meditating its own secret:]

p. 371 know & to understand [what an organised toil it is.]

Wells 1908

p. 376 young & lusty parson [who professes the same view.]

Appendix E
Experiments and Exercises: Warboys 1899

The writing exercises and penmanship fragments described in September 1899
note 8 are here given in the relative positions in which they appear on the page.
The lineation of the material has been preserved, and editorial explanations
have been supplied when deemed necessary. All bracketed page numbers refer
to AVS's original pagination. ('Verso' has, of course, been editorially supplied.)
Altogether there are in the Warboys journal, holograph entries on 28 numbered pages (2 to 33) and 23 unnumbered sides.

[*Verso 2*]
This book has now
This book has now got to be a kind of testing ground,
where I come to try my new pens. I have made the most
heroic resolution to change my ideas of calligraphy
in conformance with those of my family, which are more
generally accepted by the world as the correct ones.
[*Ink squiggle*]
dear but somewhat too romantic pen
This This is written with my dear, but somewhat too
romantic pen.

[*Verso 4*]
Time disentombs a certain number of things, & among
them this sheet of paper which has had a printed sheet
glued over it for the last 3 years. [*Written presumably in 1902.*]

[*Page 5*]
Sat. Aug. 5th [1899] As for the book & still
the glory grows & still we
[*Upside down:*]
The church is within two yards of our gate
The church is within two
The church is
The church is within two yards of our Gate, &
I am not sure that
Passing away saith the Lord

that this was not what she

This was one of those things that are never known
except when some one has left especial orders that they
are to be told to the world. I do not think that any
people but the Scotch would have fought so well, for
a cause of which they knew nor cared anything, save
that they were led by the Duke of Argyle.

[*Page 9*]
[*Upside down*]
Happy those who are
I think she had a much greater gift as a Parliamentary
speaker than anyone else I have ever known

[*Verso 9*]
[*Upside down:*]
Long life was not what she wished for. She was
only glad that there should be some reason for not writing.
She was very happy, & when the long dark winter was
at an end she said that she was glad to find that the
day was over in which she had to

Length of life never looked
Length

[*Page 11*]
[*Repeated in the text:*]
This line ends a verse on a tombstone here –

"He sleeps and all *his* well –"

The H. partly obliterated by some more lettered clerk
or stonemason.

[*Verso 11*]
[*Upside down:*]
This sheet of paper if it had followed the fate
which providence seems to have reserved for it would
never have seen the light of day at all, but would have
lain entombed under a literary tombstone no other than
a printed page from the celebrated Dr. Watts book of
Logic, or the right use of reason. When however I made
the disinterment, & lifted the Heavy Slab of logic
which completely covered it, I was delighted to find

that Time & the mouldering process of the Grave had
not in the least despoiled the virgin whiteness of the
sheet – though another hand has now done so. [*Written presumably in 1902.*]

[*Page 12 is missing.*]

[*Verso 13*]
This book in days to come will contain one of the very
rare records of Warboys before the fire – a landmark
for ever in the history of Warboys.[1] [*Written presumably in 1902.*]
Long ago she had known that there was no longer hope
for her, but she lived on but she
Long ago   hope which is said
Long ago she had known

    Happy her
    Whose
    Happy her
[*Upside down:*]
    There is something that I dare not think of.
The utmost politeness is
I am almost certain that the end
This was not possible of the past
                  the past
                  they smell sweet

[*Page 14*]
Blood running
As for Blood running   VS

[*Verso 14*]
Fritham house is about 11 miles from the nearest town,
which is a street of small cottages, & nothing more.
It is to be found marked in the County map as Lyndhurst,
& that is one of the things that most delight us,
though I do not think that there is really any great
reason why her name and address should not be known.

---

1   In a letter to Emma Vaughan, dated 27 September, 1900: 'By the way, do you see that
    Warboys has been almost burnt to the ground? 16 cottages, a brewery and a cycle
    manufactory . . . I only fear that poor old Miss Noble has not been burnt too . . .' *VW*
    Letters, I, No. 33.

[*Upside down:*]
   Lyndhurst is some six miles away. There are straight
steep roads leading down to it, along which our little
pony stumbles & jogs. He is a stupid old beast, with
a blunt brown nose and small pink eyes. He snorts with
scorn at the other horses we meet, though I confess
that it is difficult for me to see the reason of his
scorn. However he is a good beast, & once out of
doors he spends his time peacefully.

[*Verso 15*]

                                     Length of

When the wicked man turneth
                 when
away from his wickedness
then comes the day of judgment.

When the wicked man
   Turneth away from his
   wrath then comes the
      day of judgment.

When the wicked man
   Turneth away from his
   wrath then comes the
      day of judgment.
This was hardly to be expected, seeing that neither
she nor her husband were to blame in the matter. But
the whole thing was rather a question of the extraordinary
good which came from the greatness of Empire.

Length of

[*Verso 16*]
[*Upside down:*]
This at last
Warboys was then a very pretty rather deserted old village,
old as all those Fen villages are – with beautiful
houses of the 16th century to make its dignity in times
gone by. This had been the seat of one old Lords

who had hunting boxes as we call them now in the
Fens, & destroyed alas so many of the Fen inhabitants

This had been the seat of one of those old Lords who
had found the days too long.
I am very sorry that I cannot find anyone
to agree in this matter with me. This at last.

This   This was one of the last things that
T.
This was almost the end.
This was one of the last things that she ever said.
Home they brought
[*Rightside up:*]
This was

[*Page 16*]
    Long Life
This was I suppose a description of one of the Warboys
sunsets which were the most remarkable features of that
otherwise rather flat and melancholy
[*Upside down:*]
This is one of those [*Written presumably in 1902.*]

[*Verso 17*]
[*Upside down:*]
The woods decay, the woods decay &
fall; the vapours weep their burden to the ground
Man only comes & tills the earth & lies beneath
& after many a summer dies the swan.
This I
This I write in the year of a

But there was more in this than met the
there was more in this than met the eye

The only one great immortality consumes.
Like life, like death.
[*Rightside up:*]
for although
I am not ever now
This was almost

few that understood; none.

reading long tales of other days & people, which
seem to have taken everyone
[*In the left margin:*]
This was almost the

[*Verso 18*]
Happily this was the last time that such
a thing was possible. Afterwards
[*Upside down:*]
I will treat it with the utmost consideration.
This has the quality
This has the quality

[*Verso 19*]
[*Upside down:*]
The woods decay, the woods decay & fall
The vapours weep their burden to the ground
Man comes & tills the earth & lies beneath.
And after many a summer dies the swan.
The woods decay, the woods decay & fall
The vapours weep their burden to the ground,
Man comes & tills the earth & lies beneath,
And after many a summer dies the swan.
The only cruel immortality consumes
Home they brought
Home they brought the warrior
The woods decay, the woods decay & fall
The vapours weep their burden to the ground.
Man comes, & tills the earth, & lies beneath
And after many a summer dies the swan.
The only – the cruel immortality consumes.

The woods decay, the woods decay & fall, the vapours

Long afterwards there was some talk of writing a book
about this
[*Rightside up:*]
This paper is absolutely supreme. Never before, &
never since have I found one so delicious to write on,

& now the stock is exhausted. This was however one
of the things which no one heard who did [*Written in 1902?*]

Life was one of the odd
[*In the right margin:*]
This was not

[*Page 20*]
[*In the right margin:*]
Long ago she had known him, before he or she
was famous. The great question was – is this
right to be asked or not

[*Verso 21*]
   Over the river is a stone bridge.
   Over the river is a stone bridge.
   Over the river is a stone bridge.
   Over the river is a stone bridge.
[*Upside down:*]
   Length of days was never looked for or desired
by her. She was almost worn out but she said that the
work which she had undergone was gradually wearing her
life out. She was much exhausted.

[*Verso 22*]
   when he describes a fine day he at once
gives it the epithet
[*Upside down:*]
   Works of Lord
[*Rightside up:*]
One of the most remarkable of his characteristics is
this curiously sensual love of all that is beautiful.
When he describes a fine day, he gives it the epithet
"firm" which at once conveys to the mind an idea of
solidity & almost flesh. In the same way he uses
always what one may call language of the body in speaking
of things of the soul. His style
[*Upside down:*]
A very odd creature, said Mr. Gibbs with a smile. You

are almost too old to wear clothes, said the great Panjandrum[2]
with a little button on the top of his head. He had
grown much better looking.

[*Verso: unpaginated sheet:*]
indeed hard
indeed hardly spoke truth in the sense that
we mean truth at
                  Life was
[*Upside down:*]
This was one of the beings
a loofa was then given

                  Works of Lord Byron
This was one of the beings that she
22 Hyde Park Gate   Long they sought her through
  London   the villages in the empty
    SW   houses of the
This was almost the last time

Of every sort which in that meadow grew,
They gathered some; the violet pallid blue,
The little dasie that at evening closes
The virgin lilie & the primrose true, this
With store of vermeil roses
To deck their bridegroom poses
Against the bridal day, which was not long;
Swete Thammes, runne softly till I end my song.
  I have   I have never found
  Sweet Thames run softly till I end my song.

However there was one great consolation, & that was
that nowhere on heaven or earth was there

[*Verso 26*]
[*Repeated in the text:*]
The scene that was being enacted not half a mile away.

---

2 '. . . the grand Panjandrum himself, with the little round button at the top, and they
    all fell to playing the game of catch as catch can . . .': Maria Edgeworth, *Harry and
    Lucy Concluded*, by Samuel Foote (1720-77); see *Oxford Dictionary of Quotations*, 2nd
    ed., 1953.

We must hasten our unwilling pen to enter upon the details
of the disaster. It is supposed then, that the boat,
or punt was rendered in nautical language topheavy
by the amount of baggage &c. that was put upon it; &
when the
22 Hyde Park Gate

[*Verso 27*]
[*In the right margin:*]
This if it be a legitimate

[*Page 28*]
[*Repeated in the text:*]
   (This harrowing tale stops abruptly here; but a
fuller and improved version will be found somewhere
which I have with great labour concocted for the benefit
of Emma Vaughan) [*Aug. 1899, n.32.*]

[*Verso 28*]
William Gregory may guard against error in Religion,
Human Life & the Sciences by the help of Doctor Watts
if he will; but methinks, has the future the Right sort
of Reason met her guard [?] outside the covers of this particular
copy of Logick

   Long went the days

[*Page 29 is missing.*]

[*Page 31*]
[*Upside down:*]
Long ago there

[*The original 32 has been removed and replaced by "32".*]
   The Devil & all his works are hardly more terrible
to me when he lies among Christians.
   Long ago there was some question which I do not
now remember very accurately as to whether

   Long ago there was some question which I do not now

remember very accurately as to whether there could be
anyone
[*Upside down:*]
Tranquil & vast by the lights of
   Tranquil & vast by the lights of Fire. But
there was, as there always must be on these occasions
&c even the actions of the just
   This was almost the very end of the day. No more
work was there to be, no more play. She was worn out
& sleep which was the only thing she asked for or
wished for was denied her.
   She had slept
                as justice
           all that she ever said

[*Verso "32"*]
I do not think very highly – that is certainly not as
highly as I used of this brand of the manufacture. There
was at all times a very remarkable lack of dignity about
him, which one felt very strongly when one saw him either
for the first or for the last time. I do not think that
anything worse can be said than was once said
                        time

[*Facing page 33*]
   It is the rarest of all possible combinations –
first that N. & I should be quite alone for two days –
& alone in a country cottage.
   Thank God that through all these years of pain
& penance I have never said, or heard said in my presence
one word which could either sound to her irreligious

[*Following page 33 and unpaginated: both sentences cancelled.*]
   These second hand book shops collect in an extraordinary
way all the old sermons and religious works of the last
century; I think I could stock a clergyman's library.

Index

*Books by Virginia Woolf available from
Harcourt Brace Jovanovich, Publishers,
in Harvest/HBJ paperback editions*

Between the Acts
Books and Portraits
The Captain's Death Bed and Other Essays
The Common Reader: *First Series Annotated Edition*
The Common Reader: *Second Series Annotated Edition*
The Complete Shorter Fiction of Virginia Woolf
Congenial Spirits: *The Selected Letters of Virginia Woolf*
Contemporary Writers
The Death of the Moth and Other Essays
The Diary of Virginia Woolf *(five volumes)*
Essays of Virginia Woolf, Vol. One (1904–1912)
Essays of Virginia Woolf, Vol. Three (1918–1924)
Essays of Virginia Woolf, Vol. Two (1912–1918)
Flush
Freshwater
Granite and Rainbow
The Haunted House and Other Short Stories
Jacob's Room
The Letters of Virginia Woolf *(six volumes)*
The Moment and Other Essays
A Moment's Liberty: *The Shorter Diary of Virginia Woolf*
Moments of Being
Mrs. Dalloway
Mrs. Dalloway's Party
Night and Day
Orlando: A Biography
The Pargiters: *The Novel-Essay Portion of* The Years
A Passionate Apprentice: *The Early Journals, 1897–1909*
Roger Fry: *A Biography*
A Room of One's Own
The Three Guineas
To the Lighthouse
The Virginia Woolf Reader
The Voyage Out
The Waves
Women and Writing
A Writer's Diary
The Years